W9-ATB-143

CINEMA OF OUTSIDERS

OTHER BOOKS BY THE AUTHOR

The Habima—Israel's National Theater: A Study of Cultural Nationalism, 1979

And the Winner Is: The History and Politics of the Oscar Award, 1990

John Wayne: Prophet of the American Way of Life, 1998
Preface by Andrew Sarris.

Small-Town America in Film: The Decline and Fall of Community, 1991

George Cukor: Master of Elegance, 1994

Andrew Sarris, American Film Critic, in press

EMANUEL LEVY

CINEMA OF OUTSIDERS

The Rise of American Independent Film

New York University Press • *New York and London*

NEW YORK UNIVERSITY PRESS
New York and London

© 1999 by New York University
All rights reserved

Library of Congress Cataloging-in-Publication Data
Levy, Emanuel, 1947–
Cinema of outsiders : the rise of American independent film /
Emanuel Levy.
p.   cm.
Includes bibliographical references (p.   ) and index.
ISBN 0-8147-5123-7 (alk. paper)
1. Experimental films—United States—History and criticism.
2. Low budget motion pictures—United States. 3. Independent
filmmakers—United States—Biography.   I. Title.
PN1995.9.E96 L43 1999
791.43'3—dc21   99-6746
                         CIP

New York University Press books are printed on acid-free paper,
and their binding materials are chosen for strength and durability.

Manufactured in the United States of America

10   9   8   7   6   5   4   3   2

In memory of my mother, Matilda Levy,
who instilled in me a passion for film

Contents

All illustrations appear in two groups following p. 154 and p. 378.

Foreword

It's usually impossible to remember the specific date at which an idea for a book originates. However, *Cinema of Outsiders* may be the exception, for I got the first inkling to write a book about the new American independent film in September 1992, at the Toronto Film Festival, a glorious forum that has been much more selective in its choice of indies than most American festivals. Working for my second year as a *Variety* film critic, I was astounded by the range and quality of indies showcased that year. I saw *Reservoir Dogs* (for the second time), *Bad Lieutenant, Laws of Gravity, My New Gun, Equinox, Simple Men,* and *Swoon,* almost back to back! Little did I know that 1992 would turn out to be the best year in indies' history (see Appendix 2).

Throughout the 1990s, I immersed myself wholeheartedly in covering the burgeoning indie cinema. With the encouragement of *Variety*'s film critic Todd McCarthy, I indefatigably traveled from one festival to another, usually as a *Variety* critic and sometimes as a panelist or jury member.

My interest in independent film dates back to my graduate studies at Columbia in the 1970s. The first midnight movie I ever saw upon arriving in New York was John Waters's *Pink Flamingos.* This experience was followed by other midnight movies, such as David Lynch's *Eraserhead, The Rocky Horror Picture Show,* and *Liquid Sky,* all of which I saw in Downtown New York, a major center for producing and exhibiting indies.

Like many books, *Cinema of Outsiders* is personal: The need to understand my development as a critic-observer of the independent film world. Several of my books, *And the Winner Is: The History and Politics of the Oscar Award, John Wayne: Prophet of the American Way of Life,* and *Small-Town America in Film,* deal with uniquely American symbols. *Cinema of Outsiders* adds another significant panel to what has emerged as a rather logical and coherent research agenda, representing twenty-five years of teaching and writing about film.

I began to collect systematic data about independent filmmakers and films in 1994, not realizing the amount of work involved. Aiming to be comprehensive, I decided to begin my study at a crucial time, in the late 1970s. During the process, the research expanded and what was meant to be a reasonably manageable project became a huge book—in range and scope. Rather than providing a strictly chronological history of the new American indies, *Cinema of Outsiders* focuses on the link between indies and the social and political contexts within which they are made and viewed (See Introduction).

This book owes an intellectual debt to Andrew Sarris, who has shaped my thinking and writing quite profoundly. One of the first film books I read was Sarris's *The American Cinema*, the "Bible" of auteurism, which changed the nature of American film criticism and scholarship. In his book, films were no longer evaluated in terms of their plots, but as art works whose visual form, personal style, and mise-en-scène were more important than their contents.

Most of the directors discussed in *Cinema of Outsiders* are not auteurs in the way that the French critics and Sarris have used this concept. However, like Sarris, I use individual filmmakers and directorial careers as the central organizing principles of the rich material amassed. Hence, when John Sayles or Jim Jarmusch are discussed, I examine their films from the beginning of their careers up to the present. As I explain in the Introduction, this approach serves well my book since many independent directors are also the screenwriters of their movies.

Early on, Pauline Kael and her view of movies as an integral part of American pop culture influenced my work. Though her approach was more familiar to me than Sarris's from my studies in sociology, Kael's lack of prejudice against American movies that had broad commercial appeal, and her lack of guilt in enjoying and writing about "trashy" movies, registered strongly on my emerging film sensibility.

At present, no single film critic dominates the field as Sarris or Kael did in the 1960s and 1970s, but arguably the overall quality of American film criticism has never been better. I would like to acknowledge the contribution of J. Hoberman, who covered the indie cinema (American and foreign) in the *Village Voice* (and later *Premiere*) long before it became trendy among journalists. Other critics of the 1990s, with whom I have carried a "dialogue," include David Denby of *New York* (and now *New Yorker*), Todd McCarthy of *Variety*, Ella Taylor and Manohla Dargis of the *Los Angeles Weekly*, John Powers of *Vogue*, Kenneth Turan of the

Los Angeles Times, and David Ansen of *Newsweek.* The "interaction" with these critics has mostly been in my head, though I have enjoyed immensely our chats at meetings of the Los Angeles Film Critics Association, in press screenings in town, and while standing on line for screenings at Sundance and Cannes. Over the past decade, I have enjoyed the hospitality of festival directors across the country who have invited me to their forums in various capacities. My gratitude goes to Darryl Macdonald of the Seattle festival (and formerly Palm Springs and the Hamptons), Piers Handling and Michelle Maheux of Toronto, Serge Losique of Montreal, Tom Luddy and Bill Pence of Telluride, Mark Diamond of Boston and Palm Beach, Peter Scarlet of San Francisco, Alan Franey of Vancouver, Nancy Schafer of Austin's SXSW, Gregory von Hausch of Fort Lauderdale, Alonso Duralde of Dallas's USA Film Festival, Mark Fishkin of Mill Valley, and others.

Many of the films discussed in the book were first reviewed by me in *Variety.* I would like to thank Peter Bart, *Variety*'s editor-in-chief, for the opportunity to write for this magazine. A *Variety* critic occupies a special position in festivals like Cannes and Sundance. The pleasures—and responsibilities—of giving the first review ever for movies at their world premieres are truly unique. Since the magazine is distributed in these festivals, a *Variety* critic is inevitably subjected to the immediate reaction of his reviews—positive or negative.

Of the hundreds of indies I have reviewed for *Variety,* I am particularly fond of those "small" and "unheralded" films, such as *Go Fish, Cold Comfort Farm, Welcome to the Dollhouse, In the Company of Men, The Butcher Boy, Afterglow, Slam, High Art,* and *Trick.* Under pressure, some of these reviews were written very quickly, but it makes me proud to know that the combination of a rave review and *Variety*'s clout have enhanced the visibility and theatrical prospects of these movies.

Several friends and colleagues have read and commented on earlier drafts of this book or on articles presented in festivals and conferences. I would like to thank Rob Remley, Edward Johnson, Pamela J. Riley, Bill Shepard, and Andrea Walsh for their helpful comments. Over the years, I have benefited immensely from my movie conversations with my colleagues at Columbia University, Wellesley College, the New School for Social Research, and most recently Arizona State University.

Space doesn't allow me to mention all the individuals who have helped me research and write the book. Special thanks go to Quentin Tarantino and Miramax for permission to use photographs from

Reservoir Dogs, Pulp Fiction, and *Clerks,* and to Zeitgeist for pictures from *Poison.* While at Strand, Mike Thomas and his co-presidents, Marcus Hu and John Gruen, provided rare videocassettes for films I could not see theatrically or wanted to see again.

I am grateful to the following independent distributors and their staffs for supplying information about their films: Aries, Artisan, Fine Line and New Line, Fox Searchlight, Good Machine, Gramercy, Lions Gate (formerly CFP), Miramax, October, Orion, Savoy, Sony Classics, Strand, Stratosphere, Trimark, Triton, and Zeitgeist. The Sundance's press office under the leadership of Saundra Saperstein deserves a special recognition. Year after year, Saundra and her terrific staff have provided invaluable materials about all the indies shown in the festival.

The collection of data took place in many libraries across the country. I would like to thank the personnel of the Margaret Herrick Library of the Academy of Motion Picture Arts and Sciences, the Lincoln Center Library for the Performing Arts, the Museum of Modern Art (MoMA), American Film Institute (AFI), University of California at Los Angeles (UCLA), University of Southern California (USC), and Arizona State University (ASU).

I spent a most productive sabbatical from ASU in Los Angeles, where I worked on the first and second drafts of the manuscript. I am grateful to Dr. Joseph Comprone, former dean of Arts and Sciences, and to my chair, Dr. Andrew Kirby, for providing financial support for research assistants. Over the past five years, Lisa L. Plinski and John Catapano helped in gathering huge amounts of information, Laura Miller and Tamara Blaich in meticulous library work, and Dustin Stokes in typing the appendices of the book.

During the past two decades, I have shown numerous American independent films to my students at Columbia, Wellesley, and ASU, where I began teaching an annual course on the American Independent Cinema in 1994. My students have contributed to this book by incessantly challenging my ideas about film and popular culture. Their sincere, spontaneous remarks have continued to make teaching a most stimulating and rewarding enterprise.

It gives me a great pleasure to thank Niko Pfund, Despina Papazoglou Gimbel, and their enthusiastic team at NYU Press. Niko showed continuous interest in the progression of my study, offering useful comments in each and every phase of the process and improving the quality of the final manuscript. I have no doubts that without Despina's efficient management, the publication of my book would have taken much longer.

Finally, this book could not have been written without the continuous support of my friend Rob Remley. No writer could hope for a more inspirational and blissful encouragement. Rob's meticulous criticism has contributed immeasurably to the depth, clarity, and quality of my writing.

Although I am trained as an academic, for *Cinema of Outsiders* I consciously opted for a popular style that reduced scholarly jargon to a minimum. This book aims to reach educated people who go regularly to the movies and are interested in knowing more about their directors, production, meaning, and impact. It is my hope that *Cinema of Outsiders* will increase the understanding and appreciation of the new American independent cinema and will serve as a valuable tool for filmmakers, teachers, students, and moviegoers.

Introduction

Independent film contains a populist rhetoric, against the system, against the grain.

—James Mangold, director of *Heavy*

Independent film is really a way of thinking. I used to think it was where the money comes from, but now it's clearly about having a vision and a point of view when you want to tell a story.

—Nancy Savoca, director of *True Love*

What defines independent film is the question: Can this movie ever be made in a studio? If you say no, then that's an independent film. *Mallrats* notwithstanding, we've been responsible for some flicks that would never in a million years be made in a studio.

—Kevin Smith, director of *Clerks*

If you don't have a distributor, you're independent. If you have a distributor, none of us are independent.

—Chris Eyre, director of *Smoke Signals*

If it's personal to a director, then it's an independent.

—Ted Demme, director of *Monument Avenue*

Independent is a misnomer. By definition, it's an oxymoron. If you're truly independent, then no one can really categorize you and your film can't be pigeonholed. If you're against the system, you're part of the system by definition. I don't think independent means against the system, but you're always dependent on the money.

—Alan Rudolph, director of *Afterglow*

WHAT IS AN INDEPENDENT FILM?

A story has been circulating around Hollywood for decades about an alleged meeting between the independent producer Samuel Goldwyn and the Soviet director Sergei Eisenstein. Goldwyn is reported to have said, "I have seen Mr. Eisenstein's film *Battleship Potemkin* and admire it very much. We would like for him to do something of the same kind, but rather cheaper, for Ronald Colman." A second story, equally revealing, is set during a panel of the Independent Feature Project (IFP), when David Lynch was asked how dare he call himself an independent filmmaker when he had the Italian producer Dino De Laurentiis eating out of the palm of his hand. "To begin with," Lynch said, "Mr. De Laurentiis uses a plate."

These two stories show the unclarity and confusion that exist over the definition of "independent," as well as the problematic relationship between the independents and Hollywood. Over the years, the definition has blurred as a result of the increasing consolidation of power among Hollywood's majors and mini-majors. In today's Hollywood, Chris Hanley's Muse Productions and James Robinson's Morgan Creek are both considered independents. Hanley has never made a picture for more than $5 million, but has tried to make all his pictures edgy and controversial. Morgan Creek makes genre pictures—action, thriller, comedy—with large budgets, big stars, and massive marketing.

"Independent has become a label that makes it easy for people to analyze things that are a lot more complicated," says the director Alan Rudolph. "The independent spirit is trying to rely on as few outside controls as possible. But you can make an exploitation film without anybody bothering you. Does that make you an independent filmmaker?"[1] "There's an enormous confusion as to what the term independent means," notes Tony Safford, who programmed Sundance in the 1980s. "It's a word used to describe everyone from Gregg Araki, who makes features on a budget of $5,000 a piece, to Sydney Pollack." For Safford, Sundance is at the center of that confusion. Through its workshops and festival, Sundance almost makes it seem as if Araki and Pollack have something in common. "The context for independent is fraught with questions—contradictions that represent different modes and strategies of filmmaking."[2]

For many, the term "independent" conjures up visions of ambitious directors working with little money and no commercial compromises. Ideally, an indie is a fresh, low-budget movie with a gritty style and offbeat subject matter that express the filmmaker's personal vision. The expectation is for an idiosyncratic mindset, the stamp of truly independent filmmakers like Steven Soderbergh, John Sayles, Hal Hartley, and Todd Haynes, who stubbornly stick to their eccentric sensibilities.

The independent label evokes audacious movies that require a leap of imagination on the part of viewers.

In the past, the tag "independent" was applied to low-budget pictures that played for a week in the local art house. Referring to nonstudio, low-budget movies, distributed by a maverick company, the label had clearer meaning. In the 1990s, however, things have changed. Companies like Disney, Warners, and Universal have taken over independents such as Miramax, New Line, and October, and indies' budgets have increased to as much as $50 million.

Asked to define an independent film, the film critic Roger Ebert once said, "It's a film made outside the traditional Hollywood studio system, often with unconventional financing, and it's made because it expresses the director's personal vision rather than someone's notion of box-office success."[3] According to this definition, a single, passionate individual, rather than a committee, has creative control over the film. Not surprisingly, an anti-Hollywood bias still characterizes most definitions. *Heavy*'s director, James Mangold, found in New York's independent world "a good, healthy, anti-Hollywood sentiment, working outside the system, generating your own financing, trying to make movies free of a certain Hollywood aesthetic."[4]

Two different conceptions of independent film can be found. One is based on the way indies are financed, the other focuses on their spirit or vision. According to the first view, any film financed outside Hollywood is independent. But the second suggests that it is the fresh perspective, innovative spirit, and personal vision that are the determining factor. In his review of *Smooth Talk*, David Denby wrote, "Everything in the movie is a bit off. Like many independent directors, Joyce Chopra dislikes the Hollywood convention of tight storytelling. She just lets things play, and with an actress like Laura Dern, that strategy can lead to revelations."[5]

The producer Brad Krevoy holds that "the studios, with their hordes of executives going through every page of the script and telling a director what to do, are the antithesis of a pure independent, who basically executes his particular vision." Similarly, Fox Searchlight's Lindsay Law, claims that "the most important thing when a filmmaker says he is an independent, is that somebody cannot beat him into a pulp and force him to make a movie that the financier wants. It is more iconoclastic filmmaking, without the burden of attempting to make $100 million at the box-office."[6]

Strictly speaking, Spike Lee has made only two indies: *She's Gotta Have It* (1986), distributed by Island, and *Girl 6* (1996), released by Fox Searchlight. But where does *Get on the Bus* (1996) fit in? It was independently financed by black patrons, then picked for distribution by a major studio, Columbia. To complicate matters further, some of Lee's studio movies—*Do the Right Thing* (Columbia) and *Clockers* (Universal)—are more independent in spirit than *Girl 6*. The Coen brothers' movies have been financed and released by major studios, such as Fox (*Miller's Crossing*) and Warners (*The Hudsucker Proxy*), yet critics regard their work as quintessentially independent.

For New Line's Bob Shaye, "Independent is just a word that the eight established companies decided to apply to their competition when they designated themselves as majors. But it's now possible for an organization that's not a member of the fraternity to generate the talent and infrastructure to compete for the same customers."[7] Underscoring that point, in 1994 New Line outbid the majors in making the biggest script purchase in Hollywood's history when it paid $4 million for Shane Black's *The Long Kiss Goodnight*.

"It's getting increasingly difficult to really say what an independent is," said Russell Schwartz, president of Gramercy, the hybrid organization formed by Universal and PolyGram to distribute art films. "Unless you go back to the definition of total independence, everybody else is a hybrid."[8] Krevoy also emphasizes the distribution issue: "If there is distribution attached to a film before it's made, I am not sure how independent it really is." For John Ptak, of Creative Artists Agency (CAA), independence has to do with the producer's being responsible and operating under a completion guarantee: "Is he no longer independent, because he went into a production with a well-funded structure that had proper distribution around the world?"

The budget's size is a criterion too. In the past, IFP/West, which confers the Spirit Awards, limited award consideration to films with low budgets. In 1994 a Spirit nomination for the Columbia-funded picture *I Like It Like That*, which was budgeted at $5 million, and in 1998 several nominations for *Rushmore* (produced for $15 million by Touchstone) stretched the definition of "independent" past the breaking point. At the Sundance Film Festival, the criteria for inclusion in the Dramatic Competition are rather simple: Films have to be independently produced and their budgets must have at least 50 percent American financing.

Those who care about the quality of indies are concerned with the current lack of radically political and avant-garde visions, which had characterized the earlier American independent cinema. Indies have become more and more conventional, more mainstream. To what extent do indies form an alternative that's truly different? To what extent do indies challenge the status quo? How far can indies go if they are produced and distributed within a profit-oriented system?

In a recent issue of *Filmmaker*, Jim Moran and Holly Willis have offered a perceptive critique of the current notions of independent filmmaking.[9] *Filmmaker*, the indie magazine, has been charged with adopting the standard rags-to-riches tales of first-time filmmakers without noting how these tales sustain particular agendas. The magazine's wide coverage spotlights filmmakers as diverse as Quentin Tarantino and Nina Menkes, exhibiting no qualms about the artistic and political differences between them. *Filmmaker*'s annual Sundance issue is seen by some as proof of the magazine's complicity with the Sundance Film Festival, arguably the indies' most powerful institution.

The media curator Bill Horrigan distinguishes between two notions of indies: those that are acceptable to Sundance and those whose contents and styles render them virtually unshowable. Horrigan's point of reference is the work of a particular strand of independent filmmakers, from the 1940s through the early 1970s, that includes Maya Deren, Jonas Mekas, Stan Brakhage, Kenneth Anger, and Andy Warhol. For these filmmakers, "independent" meant opposition to the dominant media on several fronts: technological (amateur 8mm and 16mm instead of professional 35mm formats); institutional (interpersonal and communal versus corporate production); aesthetic (original and avant-garde against the conventional and generic); economic (love of film rather than love of money was the prime motivation); and political (exploring marginal and disenfranchised cultures instead of focusing on the culturally dominant). Though it was never a formal movement, what unified the early American independent cinema was its commitment to alternative points of view, democratic representation, and countercultural transformation.

At present, critics are disenchanted with the flattening out of the political implications of independent cinema, its reduction to a marketing tool. The discovery of *sex, lies, and videotape* at Sundance in 1989 was the event that turned the concept of independence into a tool. "When a film like *The English Patient* is called "independent," said the director

Jay Rosenblatt, "the term becomes ludicrous." *The English Patient* cost millions of dollars and was made completely within the classical Hollywood paradigms. Yet there's no denying that the film's achievements—Best Picture Oscar and global box-office—depended on a savvy marketing campaign that highlighted its underdog, against-the-odds origins.

The critic Peter Lunenfeld does not fault young directors for their desire to make large-budget productions—Hollywood has always relied on careerism for its vitality. But, for him, to do so at the expense of the history of independent cinema degrades the entire indie practice. Postmodernism has collapsed the dialectic between high and mass culture, but who would have thought that American audiences would end up settling for an easily digestible synthesis, middlebrow culture—although no indie would admit to being middlebrow.

Given the decline of radical film practice, the question of what should be celebrated in independent cinema remains a potent one. Historical, technological, and market conditions have always dictated the agenda of independent film. At the very least, one can suggest what American independent cinema is not: It's not avant-garde, it's not experimental, and it's not underground. With few exceptions, there is not much edge, formal experimentation, or serious challenge to dominant culture. A shift has taken place since the underground and avant-garde work of Cassavetes, Andy Warhol, and Paul Morrissey.

There is a wish for the old independent to be recognized on the same terms as the much-hyped current independent continues, along with the wish that indies would be written about in ways that did not necessarily involve success stories. However, simply revisiting an earlier era and proclaiming it the only true independent would be a mistake, as would viewing the history of independents as unified and located in a specific aesthetic practice. There never was a single type of independent film—it's the multitude of distinctive voices that makes indie cinema the rich collective phenomenon it is. Variously labeled "visionary," "personal," and "specialized," in the new American cinema "independent" is a sufficiently flexible term to embrace a variety of artistic expressions. Neither ideologically nor stylistically unified, indies have elevated eclectic aestheticism into a principle.

In this book, I adopt a loose, flexible definition of "independent film," one that combines the two aforementioned criteria. Although my definition doesn't depend on the budget size, most of the films discussed here are low-budget efforts.

WHEN DO I BEGIN?

While gathering information for this book, I had to decide when to begin my study, during what particular historical era. Some observers think of Jim Jarmusch's *Stranger Than Paradise* (1984) as a convenient beginning of the new indie cinema. But this is neither accurate nor fair to a filmmaker like David Lynch, whose *Eraserhead* was released in 1977. It is also unfair to the three Johns: John Sayles, whose 1980 debut, *Return of the Secaucus Seven*, signifies a beginning, and the iconoclastic director Jon Jost and the *enfant terrible* John Waters, both of whom began making movies in the early 1970s.

I decided to begin my chronicle of indies in 1977. As it turns out, 1977 and 1978 were important years for indies, artistically and organizationally. The Independent Feature Project (IFP) began as a sidebar to the New York Film Festival in 1978, when Sandra Schulberg programmed twenty films from the 100 submitted for showings at Lincoln Center. A number of quintessentially independent directors began their work in 1977–1978, including David Lynch, Charles Burnett, Victor Nunez, and Alan Rudolph.

Occasionally, I violate my own chronology and discuss films made before 1977 in order to include John Waters's *Pink Flamingos* (1972) or Joan Micklin Silver's *Hester Street* (1975). But, for the most part, my examination includes American indies made between 1977 and the beginning of 1999, the time of this writing. This historical scope of two decades permits me to explore trends and patterns of change in the indie film movement.

THEORETICAL PERSPECTIVE

In this book I use elements of various theoretical orientations: sociology, structuralism, semiotics, and the biographical approach. Despite points of divergence, these approaches complement rather than contradict each other, as they focus on different aspects of filmmaking and on different dimensions of film as a cultural product. The key concepts are social context and ideology in sociology, text and subtext in structuralism and semiotics, and social background and career in biographical perspective. My discussion contrasts the formal-aesthetic approach, which depicts films in terms of their intrinsic artistic merits, and the more extrinsic sociological perspective, which focuses on how films reflect—and are influenced by—broader social and political forces.

The independent cinema, like Hollywood, does not operate in a social or political void. Rather, it is interrelated with the historical, cultural, and political settings in which it operates. Using structuralism and semiotics, indies are analyzed as cultural texts and narrative structures imbued with meanings that are conveyed in specifically cinematic ways. Independent films, like all cultural products, are interwoven in a network of relationships with other institutions (economy, technology, politics), and they are subject to organizational, industrial, and ideological constraints that shape their themes and styles. Yet in its simple formulation, the reflection theory—that indies reflect their cultural setting—is not adequate or precise enough to explain the complex nature of indies. Critics need to be more specific in their inquiry, asking what particular aspects of indies (narrative, thematic conventions, visual style) reflect what aspects of the social structure. Indies may express cultural norms and trends, but they also express the personal vision (and politics) of their filmmakers, which may deviate from those norms.

Jim Jarmusch's movies can be grounded specifically in the socioideological contexts of downtown New York in the 1980s, and Hartley's deconstructive satires of working-class Long Island are as much a product of his background and upbringing as of his aesthetics. Indies should be analyzed in all their many facets: as narrative, ideological, artistic, and, yes, commercial, products. This book attempts to understand American indies in relation to the filmmakers who made them and to the audiences who view them.

Analyzing indies in terms of dominant themes and values reveals important information about the society in which they are produced and the filmmakers who have created them. Compared to most Hollywood products, which are tailored to appeal to the largest potential audiences, indies can enjoy greater freedom in expressing their creators' idiosyncratic vision because indies don't depend on large audiences. Unlike mainstream movies, which steer clear of controversial issues and employ stories based on the lowest common denominators, indies can handle, if they so choose, more difficult and challenging material.

Social geography also features prominently in my book. There are differences between indie film production on the East Coast (mostly New York) and on the West Coast (mostly Los Angeles), not to mention regional cinema outside urban centers. Indie directors are inspired and conditioned by their specific regions, whether they are urban New York, suburban New Jersey, or rural Minnesota. Amid the demographic trend of growing suburbanization, as a lifestyle, suburbanism continues to be a major stimulus—mostly object of satire—for filmmakers as diverse as Todd Haynes, Todd Solondz, Stacy Cochran, and Kevin Smith.

In conclusion, this book takes an interdisciplinary approach to American independent filmmaking over the past two decades. *Cinema of Outsiders* contextualizes American indies with regard to contemporary Hollywood on the one hand and the New American Cinema of the 1970s on the other. Indies of the 1990s occupy a particular place between mainstream Hollywood and the more specialized and esoteric art films. In the United States, cinema is first and foremost a commercial enterprise, but in this book I view films as personal works of art rather than products for entertainment.

DECONSTRUCTING INDIES

Indies are perceived as complex systems of verbal, thematic, and visual motifs, which can be articulated (or not) to form coherent (or less coherent) structured wholes. Five different codes are used:

1. *Cultural Codes:* These are culturally shared norms that prevail outside the film domain, in the society at large, and are used by all artists to convey ideas. Filmmakers borrow conventions from their broader cultures for their individual narratives.
2. *Artistic Codes:* Shared by other arts and media (e.g., theater and dance), these codes are not uniquely cinematic. The use of lighting and music prevail in many arts, although they are employed in vastly different ways.
3. *Narrative Codes:* These are textual conventions that determine the manner in which stories are told. Despite claims to originality, indies share recognizable conventions, typical conflicts,

and a gallery of familiar characters. In other words, indies tend to appear in cycles that follow trends and fashions.

4. *Cinematic Codes:* Stylistic conventions that are uniquely cinematic. These are devices used by filmmakers in telling a story visually: Camera set-ups and movements; long shots, middle-range shots, and close-ups; tracking and panning; cutting and editing; montage and mise-en-scène. Stylistic conventions include all the formal attributes that determine the film's texture, tone, and mood.

5. *Intertextual Codes:* Each indie exists within a larger system of films to which it refers by being either similar or different. As the body of films continues to grow, it becomes more challenging for filmmakers to distinguish their individual works from other movies. It is impossible to understand neo-noir films without comparing them to classic noir films of the 1940s. Similarly, the cycle of violent indies that deal with male camaraderie refer to—and quote from—seminal films such as Scorsese's *Mean Streets*. Indie comedies described in this book as "walking and talking" draw heavily on classic "hanging out" movies like *American Graffiti* and *Diner*.

Since intertextuality is a central concept in this book, it calls for a more detailed examination. Jonathan Culler has observed: "Works are not autonomous systems, organic wholes, but intertextual constructs, with sequences which have meaning in relation to the other texts which they take up, cite, parody, refute, or transform."[10] For some scholars, the term involves a celebration of the medium, an indication of the existence of an identifiable cinematic community.[11] Cinema, to follow these theories, is an institution in its own right with its own internal laws. Viewers bring to a specific film a set of expectations, based on previous experiences, which that film may satisfy or violate. This experiential aspect of films depends to a large extent on the "tacit contract" between filmmakers and viewers.[12]

"Intertextuality" suggests that the meaning of a particular work derives from its relation to a larger set of works. Allusions to other works can enrich a particular film by opening it out, by showing its responsiveness to other works. Intertextuality implies self-consciousness on the part of the filmmaker and is a matter of degree. References to earlier works may take different forms: There can be a conscious borrowing of a character or plot element, but a film can also comment or revise or correct established conventions (most of Robert Altman's work). Structuralists and sociologists approach intertextuality differently. Structuralists underplay the contextual aspects, following Oscar Wilde's dictum that "art never expresses anything but itself. It has an independent life and develops purely on its own lines."[13] In contrast, sociologists point out the sociohistorical contexts of intertextuality.

Umberto Eco has noted that it's not true that works are created by their authors, they are created by other works, because they speak to one another independently of their authors' intentions. Moreover, Harold Bloom regards literary creation as a quasi-oedipal struggle of writers against their precursors.[14] Burdened by the anxiety of following, writers are consciously or subconsciously influenced by their famous predecessors. In this book, I attempt to apply Bloom's "anxiety of influence," to the indie domain, particularly in Chapter 3, "Fathers and Sons," in which I discuss two seminal filmmakers, John Cassavetes and Martin Scorsese, examining their impact on the new indie cinema. The work of John Turturro, Sean Penn, Alexander Rockwell, and Nick Cassavetes is subsumed under the category "Cassavetes's legacy," and the oeuvre of Abel Ferrara, Nick Gomez, and Quentin Tarantino under "Scorsese's heritage." Similarly, in Chapter 7, I show Robert Altman's influence on Alan Rudolph and Tim Robbins, among others.

ORGANIZATION OF THE BOOK

Over the past five years, I have watched more than a thousand indies for this book. Obviously, some criteria of selection were necessary to narrow down the number of films to a more manageable size, around three hundred, to be examined in detail.

1. Indies were selected according to historical eras to reflect thematic and stylistic changes in indie film production. Indies of the late 1970s or early 1980s differ sharply from those made in the mid- or late 1990s.

2. Filmmakers with durability and track record, such as John Sayles, Spike Lee, John Waters, and Jim Jarmusch, receive lengthier discussions than filmmakers who have made one or two indies.

3. Following Leslie Fiedler's typology of American literature, this book includes indies from different geographical regions. Films about

the Midwest differ from those set in the Deep South. Thematically, films set in New York or Los Angeles are concerned with urban and racial issues, whereas films set in the Midwest typically deal with coming of age and family life.

4. I selected indies that were acclaimed by critics for their artistic merits, such as *Stranger Than Paradise, sex, lies, and videotape,* and *Poison.* However, I also discuss films that neglected to get their due recognition at their initial release or that received only limited (or no) theatrical distribution, such as *Rhythm Thief, River of Grass,* and *Bloody Child.*

5. The 300 indies chosen for this book by no means represent a statistical sample of American indie production over the past two decades. This book analyzes both exemplary (typical) and seminal (innovative) indies based on the theory that great film art can be typical (representative) as well as atypical (idiosyncratic).[15] The essence of film art may be located in the relationships between the routine and the surprising—the leap viewers are asked to make from familiar expectations to unfamiliar transformations.

6. Not included in my discussion are B-movies, straight-to-video, and genre films, such as broad comedies (*Dumb and Dumber*) and horror flicks, even if they are made by such masters as George Romero and Wes Craven. Also excluded are TV-like movies (e.g., *The Trip to Bountiful*), and costume and historical films (e.g., *Emma* and *Shakespeare in Love*).

Since the past two decades have been extremely fertile for American indies, foreign-language indies are also omitted. The material is organized thematically in terms of cycles or waves (the New African American or New Queer Cinema) rather than chronologically. The organizing principle is the individual filmmaker, who in the indie milieu is often also the writer. Some directors, like Hal Hartley, who is in the New York chapter, could easily be included in the comedy chapter. Similarly, in order to show the operation—or lack—of distinctly female or feminist sensibility, I have placed women directors in one lengthy chapter, rather than categorizing them by genre or region of their work.

1

The New American Independent Cinema

IT'S OFFICIAL: The American independent cinema has arrived! The *New York Times* puts indie films on its front page and devotes a special issue of its Sunday magazine to the independents. *Time* magazine singles out Miramax's Harvey Weinstein as one of the most accomplished Americans of 1997 and runs a major article on the Weinstein brothers. *Entertainment Weekly* commits a special issue to the independents, as do the stalwart industry trades *Variety* and *Hollywood Reporter*. The development of a viable alternative cinema, with its own institutional structure, may be one of the most exciting developments in American culture during the past two decades.

The success of independent films in the 1990s has prompted some critics to herald the renaissance of a vibrantly innovative cinema. Correspondingly, filmmaking has become one of the most desirable professions in the United States and a film degree one of the most sought-after diplomas in the academic world. Novelists are no longer our cultural heroes; filmmakers are. In the past, young, ambitious Americans dreamed of writing the great American novel. Today, their aspiration is to make the great American movie. With the entire globe looking to the United States for its supply of movies, the possibilities for young American filmmakers are seemingly endless.

Increased economic opportunities are certainly a factor, but passion and commitment are still the primary motivating forces. "It's a wonderful time for independent filmmakers right now—if you have an original story, if you don't second-guess yourself and make a Tarantino rip-off," said Miguel Arteta, whose feature debut, *Star Maps*, premiered in 1997.[1] "You have to make a story you're passionate about, because when you make one of these movies, it's nearly gonna kill you. You'd better like it at the end of the day."

THE GROWING PRESTIGE OF INDIES

Indie films have gained much respectability in the 1990s. One measure of their new cachet is the willingness of established actors to work for practically nothing if the role is right. A growing number of key players in Hollywood's creative community, such as the directors Spike Lee and Steven Soderbergh and movie stars like John Travolta, Bruce Willis, and Tim Robbins, now commute regularly between studio and indie films.

It wasn't always that way. Despite his stature in the indie world, John Sayles could not always get the actors he wanted for his films. For years, agents would not even show his scripts to their top actors. "It never used to be hip the way that it is now to be in little independent movies," Sayles recalled. "It was a signal that your career was in trouble."[2]

Mainstream Hollywood product dominates both domestic and foreign box-office charts, but it is independent movies that are creating waves and winning awards at major festivals around the world, including that most prestigious forum, the Cannes Film Festival. In 1994, for the fourth time in six years, Cannes conferred its top award, the Palme d'Or, on an American picture, Quentin Tarantino's *Pulp Fiction*. The picture was described by French critics as a "typically American lowlife serenade," a flashy salute to Los Angeles's cool, marginal world, but American critics stressed that, if anything, Tarantino was atypical of Hollywood, that his work was a parody of America, and owed a lot to European directors.

Tarantino's victory recalled the unexpected crowning of Soderbergh's *sex, lies, and videotape* in 1989, David Lynch's *Wild at Heart* in 1990, and Joel Coen's *Barton Fink* in 1991, all independent movies. American indies have also grabbed the limelight outside of the main competition. In the past twenty years, the Caméra d'Or, Cannes's prize for best first film, has been given to several American indies, including Robert Young's *Alambrista!* (1978), John Hanson and Robert Nilsson's *Northern Lights* (1979), Jim Jarmusch's *Stranger Than Paradise* (1984), Mira Nair's *Salaam Bombay!* (1988), John Torturro's *Mac* (1992), and, most recently, Marc Levin's *Slam* (1998).

European prestige is one thing, but what really counts in Hollywood is domestic visibility and box-office clout. What better measures of these indicators than the Academy Award, the most influential award in the film world. The flowering of independents first became visible at the 1986 Academy Awards ceremony, when William Hurt won the Best Actor Oscar for *Kiss of the Spider Woman* and Geraldine Page took Best Actress honors for *The Trip to Bountiful*. Both pictures were produced by Island, a small independent company.

In 1987, all five nominees for the Best Picture Oscar were made outside the Hollywood establishment: Oliver Stone's *Platoon*, James Ivory's *A Room With a View*, Roland Joffe's *The Mission*, Woody Allen's *Hannah and Her Sisters*, and Randa Haines's *Children of a Lesser God*. Announcing a major change, these pictures showed that Hollywood was opening up to offbeat, unusual work. The message was loud and clear: The independents were marching into the mainstream.

Howards End, *The Crying Game*, and *The Player* not only were box-office smashes in 1992 but also garnered more Oscar nominations than big-studio releases. This, of course, led Hollywood to seek further inroads into the independent community. Hollywood understands that indies are the soul of American film in a way that the potboilers of Roland Emmerich (*Independence Day*, *Godzilla*) or Michael Bay (*The Rock*, *Armageddon*) never can be.

Four of the five nominees for the 1996 Best Picture Oscar—*The English Patient*, *Fargo*, *Secrets & Lies*, and *Shine*—were independents, financed and made outside the studio system. In the same year, Hollywood spent its time, energy, and big bucks churning out and marketing big-budget, overproduced, special-effects, star-studded formulas like *Twister* and *Independence Day*.

Indie films have a particularly impressive record in the writing and acting categories. Recent winners of the Best Original Screenplay Oscar have included *Pulp Fiction* in 1994, *The Usual Suspects* in 1995, *Sling Blade* in 1996, *Good Will Hunting* in 1997, and *Gods and Monsters* in 1998. Half of the twenty nominated actors in 1997 were singled out for a performance in indies, including Robert Duvall in *The Apostle*, Julie Christie in *Afterglow*, and Burt Reynolds and Julianne Moore in *Boogie Nights*.

HEROES OF THE NEW INDIE CINEMA

In 1992, the hottest ticket at the Sundance Film Festival was *Reservoir Dogs*, made by a then unknown director named Quentin Tarantino. Tarantino became inspired by the success of Jim Jarmusch and the Coen brothers in the mid-1980s. Unlike Jarmusch, the 1980s indie leader who

has shown contempt for catering to the mass public, Tarantino is a natural-born entertainer whose work is more dazzling than consequential.
For inspiration, *Reservoir Dogs* drew more on old movies than on real
life, but as self-conscious as the film was, it still boasted a clever script
and superlative performances by an all-star cast.

In a few years, Tarantino has evolved from an unemployed actor-
writer working in a video store to the hottest American filmmaker. He
has become a crucial figure, replacing Martin Scorsese as a role model
for young indie directors. Like Scorsese, Tarantino is a cineaste who
knows movies inside out and is deeply committed to the medium. Unlike Scorsese, though, Tarantino didn't go to film school, instead getting
his education in a video store.[3]

Tarantino planned to use the money he received for his first writing
job—the screenplay for Rutger Hauer's thriller *Past Midnight*—combined with what money his friend-producer Lawrence Bender had on
his credit cards to make *Reservoir Dogs* guerrilla-style for $30,000. But,
after reading the script, Bender felt it had potential. "I told him I could
raise real money for this," Bender recalled. "But he said, 'No way
man.'"[4] Eventually, Tarantino relented and gave Bender a two-month
option on his script to find a backer. Fantasizing about the dream cast
for their yet-to-be-made movie, both immediately thought of Harvey
Keitel.

Bender's acting teacher, who knew Keitel, agreed to deliver the
screenplay to him. The strategy worked. Keitel fell in love with the
script, and his involvement changed everything. "Suddenly," Bender
recalled, "we weren't two guys peddling a script around town, now we
had Harvey Keitel."[5] With Keitel in the cast, Live Entertainment, a division of Carolco, committed a budget of $1.5 million. Things came easily
after that. Keitel put up his own money to fly Tarantino and Bender to
New York, where they assembled a top-notch cast that included Tim
Roth, Michael Madsen, Lawrence Tierney, and Steve Buscemi. With no
further financial worries, they finished *Reservoir Dogs* in time for Sundance, where it began its conquest of the festival circuit.

Reservoir Dogs swept through Sundance, Cannes, and Toronto like a
brushfire. Distributors who saw the film at Sundance were worried that
it would end up with an NC-17 rating for its graphic violence, which
drove many viewers out of the theater. That particular fear didn't materialize, although eventually the violence worked against the film's
broader acceptance. *Reservoir Dogs* left Sundance without winning any

awards, but it became the festival's most talked-about movie, and Miramax decided to distribute it. Over the course of that year, Tarantino turned up at festival after festival, receiving lavish praise from intellectual critics for making the hottest indie of the year.

Tarantino and Miramax milked the festival circuit before going public. When the movie finally opened, it played for only a few weeks despite critical support, confirming initial fears that it was too violent. Miramax's sparse marketing resulted in a modest box-office gross of $1 million. The movie was rereleased after the success of Tarantino's second feature, *Pulp Fiction*, but even then it failed to generate box-office excitement.

Lack of commercial appeal didn't stop *Reservoir Dogs* from attaining cult status within the industry. Most of the press focused not on the movie or its issues but on Tarantino as a self-taught auteur. In the end, Tarantino didn't promote *Reservoir Dogs; Reservoir Dogs* promoted him. Tarantino quickly rose from obscurity, and the fact that the film didn't do well didn't matter. It created enough of a stir to give Tarantino the clout to make his next film, *Pulp Fiction*, with a larger budget ($8 million) and a high-caliber cast.

Nihilistically cool and vastly diverting, *Pulp Fiction* won the Cannes Palme d'Or and went on to become one of the most commercially successful indies ever. Naysayers and skeptics rushed to label Tarantino as flavor of the year, although he proved them wrong and sustained the brilliance of his two instant classics with a third one, *Jackie Brown* (1997), which garnered decent reviews and respectable box-office takes.

Was Tarantino just lucky, the right director at the right time? Was he too talented not to be noticed? Tarantino was fortunate in one respect—his first film was embraced by cerebral critics as well as a national publicity machine starved for new heroes. Many indie directors resent the enormous publicity Tarantino continues to receive, as they resented Miramax's aggressive marketing campaign, which helped *Pulp Fiction* garner box-office grosses of more than $100 million along with seven Oscar nominations, including one for Best Picture. But Tarantino's artistic accomplishments shouldn't be underestimated because of the hype he generates as a media-created celeb.

Tarantino is the most loudly sung but certainly not the only hero in the new milieu. Richard Linklater raised the money for his charming feature, *Slacker* (1990), from friends and relatives and by drawing on credit cards and savings. A sale to German television and deferred fees for cast and crew made it possible to complete the movie for a meager $23,000. Most of the actors were nonprofessionals, either the director's friends or people he met on the street and hired on the basis of their off-beat looks. *Slacker* was shown for a whole year on the festival circuit before opening at the Dobie theater in Austin, Texas. Its regional success motivated Orion Classics to distribute the movie nationally.

The tale behind the making of Robert Rodriguez's *El Mariachi* (1992) has also become legendary. A young movie-struck director takes $7,000, earned as a medical research subject, and makes a picture he thinks might sell in the Spanish-language video market. Instead, the movie captivates agents and executives, gets a major release by Columbia, and earns Rodriguez the chance to work with better actors and a bigger budget on his next film, *Desperado*.

The most recent example of a director to hit it big—and quickly—is Edward Burns. In 1994, Burns was working as a messenger for a television show in New York. Living in a grungy West Village apartment, he was becoming nervous about his prospects as a filmmaker. "I was writing screenplays for six years, I just wasn't getting my foot in the door," he told the *New York Times*.[6] Burns attended the State University of New York at Albany before switching to Hunter College in New York City, where he majored in film. Taking a job as a driver and messenger for *Entertainment Tonight*, he wrote *The Brothers McMullen*, a semi-autobiographical comedy about three Irish-American brothers, in his spare time. The film was shot at his parents' home in Valley Stream, Long Island, for the incredibly low cost of $25,000, raised from family and friends.

Early cuts of the film were rejected by most film festivals, including New York, Toronto, and Telluride, but when Geoffrey Gilmore of the Sundance Festival saw the comedy, he immediately accepted it as a competition entry. At the same time, Tom Rothman, then president of Fox Searchlight, saw the movie and gave Burns the funds to complete it. The final cost of *The Brothers McMullen*, including revised editing and a new score, was less than $500,000.

The Brothers McMullen changed Burns's life overnight, as he recalled: "I quit my old job, I've got a career now, I have a little money in my pocket, and I have a new apartment." When Fox Searchlight decided to produce his next film, *She's the One*, for $3 million, Burns knew it was going to be "a world of difference" from his debut: "I won't have to do makeup myself; I won't have to do people's hair; I won't have to

block traffic, and I won't have to call the actors the night before to remind them to be on the set."

Young filmmakers know that a fearless producer can make all the
difference, particularly in the early phases of their careers. Along with
"hot" directors, a new breed, the gutsy indie producer, emerged. Over-
seeing fourteen features, including *I Shot Andy Warhol*, *Kiss Me Guido*,
and Todd Haynes's three features (*Poison*, *Safe*, and *Velvet Goldmine*),
Christine Vachon has made a career out of producing distinctive features without making the kind of compromises that afflict other well-
intentioned indie outfits. In the early days of her career, she was associated with the new wave of queer cinema, represented by Tom Kalin and
Haynes, among others. Vachon then coproduced Larry Clark's controversial *Kids* and executive-produced the breakthrough lesbian comedy
Go Fish.

A founder of the nonprofit film foundation Apparatus, for three
years Vachon co-ran the unit with Haynes and Barry Elsworth, producing shorts. "It was an exciting time," she recalled. "I was able to play at
being a producer." She then formed Killer Films with a partner, Pam
Koffer, and produced *Velvet Goldmine* and Todd Solondz's *Happiness*
(with Good Machine's Ted Hope), both of which premiered in Cannes,
and Bruce Wagner's debut feature, *I'm Losing You*, which played at Telluride. In a prolific, sustained career, Vachon has specialized in making
films that do not seem to be marketable.[7] Though Vachon can't do the
under-$2-million dollar movies any more, she readily admits that low-
budget movies are truly exhilarating, "because people are really making the things they are the most passionate about."

Along with "hot" directors and producers, a new force in indie cinema emerged, the producer representative, of whom the most successful and famous is John Pierson. For young directors, wishing to make
movies but lacking connections or cash, Pierson is a guru.[8] In 1985, a
producer of what would become the first AIDS film, *Parting Glances*,
asked for Pierson's help. Pierson sold the movie to Cinecom, and word
got out among producers and directors about his power. For more than
a decade, Pierson has been launching new careers by helping young directors finish their films and sell them to distributors. His impressive
record in features and documentaries is described in his book, *Spike,
Mike, Slackers, and Dykes*.

Pierson is highly sought after at annual forums, such as the Independent Feature Film Market (IFFM), where his suggestions for

improvements are taken seriously by directors. "Whatever you think is important," a Texas director was overheard to say.[9] "Every young person wants to make a movie now," Pierson recently complained.

> In my generation, we had a lot of people who weren't just saying "Me, me, me—my films. . . . If you're Jim Jarmusch in the early 1980s and you're watching Godard, Fellini, the Japanese masters, and you aspire to make great films like theirs, that's very different from somebody who is completely up to the minute in everything that's coming out now and is realizing what a pile of crap it is and saying, "I can do a better film than that." When that's your jumping off point, it's a totally different attitude. There are just going to be more bad movies.

Among his chores, Pierson has to listen to filmmakers recounting the "fabulous" story behind their films, each one of them envisioning a glorious profile in *Premiere* magazine. A prime example is Rob Weiss, who made the crime drama *Amongst Friends*, which Pierson helped to finance and then sell to Fine Line. Although Weiss spent months cultivating an aura of danger and celebrity around himself, *Amongst Friends* opened in 1993 and quickly died. The arrogant Weiss has yet to make another film.

FORCES SHAPING THE NEW INDIE CINEMA

Individual heroes—directors, producers, agents—continue to feed the media frenzy. But the new independent cinema doesn't exist in a social or economic void. As a social institution, it has benefited from the operation of artistic, economic, technological, organizational, and demographic forces. Several conditions have facilitated the emergence of the new American independent cinema as an alternative system to Hollywood:

1. The need for self-expression.
2. Hollywood's move away from serious, middle-range films.
3. Increased opportunities and capital in financing indies.
4. Greater demand for visual media, driven by an increase in the number of theaters and the adoption of home video as a dominant form of entertainment in the United States.

5. Supportive audiences: the Baby-Boom generation.
6. The decline of foreign-language films in the American market.
7. The proliferation of film schools across the country.
8. The emergence of the Sundance Film Festival as the primary showcase for indies and the rise of regional festivals.
9. The development of new organizational networks.
10. Commercial success—the realization that there's money to be made in indies.

THE NEED FOR SELF-EXPRESSION

The first and most important force driving independent cinema is the need of young filmmakers, many of whom are outsiders, to express themselves artistically. These young artists create alternative films that are different, challenging the status quo with visions that have been suppressed or ignored by the more conservative mainstream. This artistic condition, which is discussed in Chapter 2, benefits from the increased structural opportunities and the greater supply of talent coming out of the newly popular film schools.

HOLLYWOOD AND THE INDIE MILIEU

The emergence of a new cinematic force is not a coincidence: Promising directors come and go in cycles, and Hollywood sets the context in which those cycles occur.[10] Indies' recent prominence is directly related to Hollywood's abandonment of serious, issue-oriented, provocative films. Despite their big budgets, in terms of artistic quality and originality, the films the studios release are mostly minor. Committed primarily to the production of big "event" movies, the studios leave room for small, mid-range indies. The best indies serve as a reminder of why, by turning its back on the real world, most Hollywood fare seems tired and tiresome. While Hollywood focuses its attention on churning out profitable but forgettable fodder, an interesting thing is happening on the fringe: Independent filmmakers are enjoying exhilarating years marked by receptive audiences and critical encouragement.

After the success of *Bonnie and Clyde* (1967) and *Easy Rider* (1969), the studios' penchant for risk taking helped nourish an astonishing group of directors that included Scorsese, Robert Altman, Woody Allen, Francis Ford Coppola, Steven Spielberg, and George Lucas, all of whom revitalized the mainstream. These filmmakers established their reputations by making innovative films *within* the studio system. It's premature to judge whether the 1990s wave is on a par with that of the 1970s, but there's no doubt that its visibility and impact go beyond the indie world.

There has always been conflict between cinema as an industry and cinema as an art form, cinema as routine and cinema as experiment, but that conflict never precluded the making of personal films within the mainstream.[11] However, at present, the balance has tipped decisively in favor of cinema as an industry, with the great Hollywood cinema of the 1960s and 1970s repudiated. Hollywood economics affects the quality of films in several ways. First, big-budget productions divert resources from other films (how many indies could be made for the $80 million budget of *Meet Joe Black* or for the $90 million spent on *Starship Troopers*?). Second, the bigger the budget, the more a picture must hedge its bets by catering to broad audiences, which necessitates compromise, homogeneity, and standardization—in short, less distinctive vision.

The rise in production costs has resulted in the making of products on a coercive global scale, films that are meant to please audiences all over the world. Soaring budgets also mean that films must generate a lot of money in the first week of their release to prove profitable, a trend favoring blockbusters and cutting the theatrical release time of movies that are not potential blockbusters. With rare exceptions, current mainstream movies are not afforded enough play time to build word-of-mouth.

The prevalent climate in Hollywood encourages the production of routine films for innocuous, often mindless entertainment. Mainstream cinema has settled for a derivative fare that hopes to reproduce past successes (the remake and sequel syndromes). The reduction of Hollywood films to images and sounds that are attention grabbing but meaningless has resulted in a lightweight cinema that neither challenges the mind nor appeals to the heart.

Indies take the kinds of risk that are out of the question in mainstream Hollywood. "Commerce has overwhelmed art, which is why Hollywood movies aren't as good as they used to be," observed former Disney chair Jeffrey Katzenberg.[12] "The process has been corrupted. It is too much about money and not enough about good entertainment."

Katzenberg perceived a huge gap between filmmaking as "guerrilla warfare, meaning three guys with a camera strapped on their back" and "megablockbuster Hollywood."

Indie films are "the opposite of Hollywood, where they try and make pictures that fit a pre-existing audience," noted the filmmaker L. M. Kit Carson. "Indie films are from the gut."[13] Another notable difference concerns the budget. When an indie executive lies about a budget, he always inflates the figure, whereas studio executives invariably claim their films cost less than what they actually spent.

Arguably, the best cycle of indies in the past decade appeared in 1991–92, years that saw the release of the provocative *Poison*, the intimately touching *The Waterdance*, the emotionally satisfying neo-noir *One False Move*, the pleasingly feminist *Gas Food Lodging*, the politically incorrect *The Living End*, the revisionist *Swoon*, the hyper-violently droll *Reservoir Dogs*, the sharply satirical *Bob Roberts*, and the poetically evocative *Daughters of the Dust*. Singly and jointly, these films gave Hollywood pause. Made uncompromisingly, often on shoestring budgets, they were as well acted and as entertaining as studio fare. They dispensed, as Janet Maslin noted, with the "something-for-everyone" blandness of big-studio efforts and succeeded in reaching specific (niche) audiences, defined by race, gender, and sexual orientation, to whom they introduced new themes and characters on the American screen.[14]

The way for the 1990s directors had been paved by a group of now established filmmakers whose 1980s work was truly independent: John Sayles, Susan Seidelman, Jim Jarmusch, and Spike Lee. Critically and often commercially, these directors have attained the kind of stature that forces the studios to take notice. A forceful parallel evolution of nonfiction fare has had similar effect, focusing attention on the growing commercial viability of such documentaries as *Roger and Me, Paris Is Burning, Hoop Dreams*, and *Crumb*.

When Carl Franklin's *One False Move* appeared out of nowhere, attracting viewers and impressing critics, "nowhere" picked up added cachet. Film festivals, dominated by such unanticipated hits as *The Waterdance* (which premiered at Telluride), *Welcome to the Dollhouse* (Toronto), *Go Fish* (Sundance), and *Bob Roberts* (Cannes), have made viewers more willing to take risks. For those repelled by formulaic fare, expecting the unexpected has become a driving force that encourages the production of free-spirited, try-anything films.[15]

The corporate, market-driven thinking that has drained the art from Hollywood has had a similarly dulling effect on some foreign industries. When high-gloss violent thrillers, such as Luc Besson's *La Femme Nikita* and *The Fifth Element*, become the most prominent French films of the decade, the appeal of small, quirky but substantial movies only grows.

Karen Cooper, programmer of New York's Film Forum, which has consistently shown indies, stresses audiences's sophistication, a term once applied primarily to foreign-film audiences. She attributes the popularity of indies to the "particularization of experience," which is harder to find in Hollywood product.[16] "There are food stores that sell just pasta and clothing stores that sell just black. Films can do that, too, when they aren't just looking for the lowest common denominator."

When Film Forum showed Julie Dash's *Daughters of the Dust*, a powerful response greeted her ruminative evocation of a Gullah family in the Carolina Sea Islands. Hollywood produced Alice Walker's *The Color Purple*, which took the guts out of the novel by making a clean, neat picture, but it could never have produced an idiosyncratic or visionary film like *Daughters of the Dust*. Hollywood couldn't be bothered by box-office receipts of $1 million (which is what Dash's film grossed).

INCREASED OPPORTUNITIES FOR INDIES

It's easier to secure financing for indies in the 1990s than ever before. Increased capital from investors, both domestic and foreign, has been available, and there have been more opportunities for films to be seen, not necessarily in theaters but in ancillary markets (via television, video), on cable channels, and in the growing number of film festivals.

Young filmmakers, however, are still challenged to use their creative faculties to come up with ingenious strategies for funding. Joel and Ethan Coen made a three-minute trailer for *Blood Simple* to convince potential investors that they were competent to make a feature-length movie. It took the ambitious siblings a whole year to raise the $750,000 budget, which came from private investors, family, and friends. The film's commercial success (it earned a solid $5 million) enabled the Coens to strike a deal with Circle Releasing, which put up $4 million for their second feature, *Raising Arizona*.

The writer-director Neal Jimenez originally developed the script for *The Waterdance*, a candid drama about paraplegics, at Warners, but predictably the studio let it go. It was then rescued by the independent producer Gail Anne Hurd (*Aliens*), who brought it to the attention of RCA/Columbia Home Video (now Columbia-TriStar). RCA/Columbia's production support provided a training ground for many indie directors, including Steven Soderbergh, Carl Franklin and Allison Anders. Another home-video outfit, Carolco's affiliate Live Entertainment, backed Paul Schrader's *Light Sleeper* ($6 million) and *Reservoir Dogs*.

The greater demand for visual media, driven by the new video market, also played an important role. In the mid-1980s, when videocassette recorders penetrated the market, the rapidly expanding home video industry became so eager for product that many unconventional independent projects got funding. This boom, which lasted half a decade, eventually ended, forcing many video companies out of business.

Recently, indie filmmakers have shifted their focus to the European market and have become more dependent on foreign pre-sales to finance their projects. Jarmusch's two most recent pictures were backed by the Japanese electronics giant JVC. Other European companies, such as the Paris-based UGC, have financed Gregg Araki's two movies, *The Doom Generation* and *Nowhere*.

Given the nature of Boaz Yakin's debut film, *Fresh*, the producer Lawrence Bender encouraged the tyro director to look to Europe for backing, thinking that "Americans wouldn't get the point of this auteur film until it was made."[17] Bender's earlier success with *Reservoir Dogs* led to a meeting with the Paris-based company Lumière, which provided full funding. As Bender had anticipated, American distributors showed interest after *Fresh* began shooting. Ultimately, Miramax distributed the film and scored a success: *Fresh* grossed over $8 million in the United States alone.

Indies are now riding high in foreign markets. Overseas sales from licensing deals (in all media) for independent films peaked at $1.65 billion in 1996, according to a survey taken by the American Film Marketing Association (AFMA). The boom, fueled by the expanding overseas TV market, represented a 21 percent gain in revenues over 1995 figures. The biggest gains came in the licensing of films for theatrical distribution, which racked up a 37 percent increase, to $501 million in total sales.[18] "In an era when the competition around the world is becoming more intense, it's gratifying to see that the independents are continuing to be a vital force in the global marketplace," said Jonas Rosenfield, the AFMA president.[19] As expected, Europe dominates the world market for English-speaking, independently licensed fare, with a 56 percent share of global revenues in all media.

It often takes a resourceful and aggressive producer to get the necessary funding. Alexander Rockwell's In the Soup, budgeted at $800,000, was backed by the New York producer Jim Stark, who had earlier worked on Jarmusch's films. "Most producers aren't willing to do what is necessary to finance an offbeat, unpackaged movie," said Stark, which includes "everything from middle-of-the-night faxing to Japan to mortgaging your house."

Not to be underestimated is the importance of networking and personal connections. Christopher Guest's friendship with Castle Rock's Rob Reiner (who directed This Is Spinal Tap, with Guest as a star) saved the director from having to shop around for the $2 million budget of Waiting for Guffman. Spike Lee's Get on the Bus, made for $2.4 million, was entirely financed by private black patrons before it was picked up for distribution by Columbia.

Scott McGehee and David Siegel, who bypassed film school, learning their craft by making shorts on the streets of San Francisco, needed completion funds for Suture. Struggling to get their first film made under most challenging conditions became their schooling.[20] Thanks to the skills they learned scrambling to make shorts, McGehee and Siegel were "as scrappy as you can get when it comes to fund-raising." Eventually, they raised the $800,000 for Suture with the help of Soderbergh, who lent his name as executive producer.

New, revolutionary video and digital technologies have also proved a major factor. To offset production costs, Mark Rappaport resorted to a hybrid of film and video, which enabled him to make the inexpensive but highly interesting film-essays Rock Hudson's Home Movies and From the Journals of Jean Seberg.

A feisty guerrilla approach is as much a state of mind as a practical modus operandi. The New York–based Katy Bolger, who served as associate producer on Naked in New York and This World, Then the Fireworks, embraces her guerrilla status: "If you have taste or style or a sense of art, why work in Hollywood?" Hard work and tenacity continue to define the guerrilla style. The reputation of The Shooting Gallery (run by Larry Meistrich and Bob Gosse) is still largely based on its $38,000 success, Nick Gomez's *Laws of Gravity*, and on its continuing dedication to small pictures such as Whitney Ransick's *Handgun*. Stubbornly clinging to the fringe independent route and its lower costs has given the company a much coveted creative freedom.

One out-of-the-trenches director, Abel Ferrara, a mentor for guerrillas, advises struggling filmmakers "to play every card, every person and keep doing it."[21] Despite some success with *King of New York* and *Bad Lieutenant*, it's still a hustle for Ferrara to sell his vision. Ferrara holds that guerrillas shouldn't succumb to any "false time frames" in order to get their projects done.

There always seem to be new funding opportunities. John Sayles's *Men with Guns* was financed by a new production company formed the Independent Film Channel (IFC) and Microsoft cofounder Paul Allen, in his first foray into indie film. IFC Productions, a venture headed by Jonathan Sehring, is committed to coproduce a number of features each year. Allen formed Clear Blue Sky Productions to develop and finance independent films.[22]

Next Wave Films, a finishing fund aimed exclusively at no- budget indies, began its operation in 1997 and is committed to films of exceptional quality made by filmmakers of potentially major talent. Funded by the IFC, the program supplies up to $100,000 to four films a year. The films must have budgets of $200,000 or less, and principal photography must be finished. For Next Wave president Peter Broderick, the cash factor is less significant than the help he can offer in securing deals with postproduction houses and labs.

GREATER DEMAND FOR VISUAL MEDIA

For two decades, American filmgoers have been buying roughly a billion tickets each year. In 1989, the film industry was a $5 billion business (1.1 billion tickets sold), the highest gross since 1984, and, in 1993, as a result of summer hits and record-breaking holiday season, a new peak of 1.2 billion tickets sold was reached. Then, in 1998, the film industry boasted an all-time record business of $6.88 billion in sales, with an estimated 1.4 billion tickets sold.

In 1984, the studios' cumulative revenues from domestic ticket and videos sales was $2.4 billion, of which a third came from videos. In 1985, the cumulative take was $3 billion, with half coming from videos. Video distributors became an important source of production money in 1987, when for the first time more (1,040,000) video cassettes were rented than theater tickets (1,030,000) sold.[23] In the 1990s, studios' domestic revenues from rentals of home videos amount to about 23 percent.

Initially, industry executives feared that video would become Hollywood's enemy, a dreaded competitor for viewers. Quite the contrary, the VCR revolution shored up the Hollywood industry, and many VCR owners became more avid moviegoers *after* purchasing their VCRs. Renting videos apparently exposed them to movie culture, encouraging them to read and know more about movies.[24]

Simultaneously, entertainment news coverage became more visibly aggressive in all the media, evidenced by the popularity of film magazines like *Premiere*, the showbiz publication *Entertainment Weekly*, and the consistently high ratings for *Entertainment Tonight* (*E.T.*) and *Access Hollywood*, not to mention popular shows on network E!

The fact that nonconventional movies, such as Billy Bob Thornton's *Sling Blade*, Kevin Smith's *Chasing Amy*, and Robert Duvall's *The Apostle* have played on hundreds of screens at multiplexes all over the country is most encouraging. The increase in the number of screens nationally has itself been a positive factor for the new indies. In 1975, there were 16,000 screens, in 1985, 22,000, and in 1998, more than 28,000. Multiplexes now program at least one or two high-profile indies on their screens.

SUPPORTIVE AUDIENCES

Arguably the most important factor in the evolution of independent cinema has been supportive audiences. The maturation of the baby-boom generation, which possesses more sophisticated taste, more disposable time, and more money to spend on movies, has provided indispensable backing for indies. The core audience for indie films is small—about 5 to 10 percent of the market—but it's a loyal and appreciative one.

Indies are directed at specific sectors—niche audiences—of the fragmented market. The typical indie public is composed of:

1. College students and college graduates.
2. Singles and childless couples.

3. Discriminating viewers seeking provocative entertainment.
4. Informed viewers with sharper sensibility and greater awareness of new film releases and new directors.
5. Frequent moviegoers who go to the movies at least once a month.

About a third of moviegoers choose a film because of a favorable review, according to some studies. Of those who cited reviews, 20 percent were influenced by newspaper reviews and 18 percent by television ones. Television ads stirred 20 percent of those questioned to see a movie, but newspaper ads were less effective, motivating only 10 percent.[25] Although positive reviews may increase a movie's run, TV advertising is the backbone of marketing campaigns. "Advertising completely opens the movie," said Chris Pula, New Line's president of theatrical marketing.[26] "One of the challenges is to create brand awareness very quickly. If we don't hit after the first weekend, we're like spaghetti sauce on the shelf." Other influences include word-of-mouth and big-name stars. In one survey, about 20 percent of moviegoers said they choose movies on the basis of a friend's suggestion; a famous actor stirred interest in 10 percent; trailers motivated 5 percent; and convenience of show times brought in just 1 percent of respondents.

Since the late 1970s, teenagers have been the most reliable moviegoers. Constituting a large share of opening week audiences, they can make or break a movie. In the 1970s, 89 percent of moviegoers in the United States were under age 40, and teenagers made up 42 percent of this group.[27] It was not always this way. In 1976, before the "teenage epidemic," the two leading movies at the box office were *One Flew over the Cuckoo's Nest*, Milos Forman's drama about a mental hospital, and *All the President's Men*, about the Watergate scandal—serious movies that appealed to mature audiences. It's inconceivable that these two movies would be made by the studios today, let alone score major success.

For nearly a decade, in the years between *Star Wars* in 1977 and *Top Gun* in 1986, Hollywood spurned adults. In the 1980s, the studios aimed at moviegoers between the ages of twelve and twenty with sex comedies and action-adventures.[28] But, in the 1990s, teens are outnumbered by middle-aged baby boomers who don't want to see gore or youth fare. In 1990, when *Driving Miss Daisy* topped $100 million, it underscored a new trend: Teenagers no longer were the prime audience; aging boomers were making up an increasing part of first-run movie audiences. And attendance by forty- to forty-nine-year-olds has steadily increased. In the 1990s, the new parents in the audience are the teenagers of the 1960s, who have remained consistent moviegoers: In 1990, 23 percent of ticket buyers were over age 40.

While the studios continue to target the teen market, the real growth audiences for indies have been relatively older viewers, for whom selling movies requires a fresh, subtle approach. These adults are attracted to a wider range of movies dealing with more mature themes. Viewers with college educations want more sophisticated fare than what's shown on television, and they respond to critical acclaim and word of mouth.

The aging and graying of America has affected the kinds of movies made. "Adults are quality driven, review driven, subject-matter driven," said Thomas Pollock, former head of Universal. "The critics are speaking to that adult audience. If a critic praises a teen-age movie, it doesn't mean much, because the teen-age audience doesn't read. It's very easy to motivate the twelve- to fifteen-year-old market with TV advertisements. You cannot advertise adults into going." This factor works in favor of indies, which are much more review-driven than Hollywood movies.

Independents have always catered to older audiences. The producer Ismail Merchant, the director James Ivory, and the screenwriter Ruth Prawer Jhabvala had made many movies before they hit the box-office jackpot with *A Room With a View* and *Howards End*. Other adult films that thrived, such as *Henry V*, *My Left Foot*, *The Trip to Bountiful*, *Kiss of the Spider Woman*, were also not premade for an existing audience. The return of older moviegoers has been more than a temporary aberration. As the baby-boom generation ages, it continues to go to the movies, instead of staying at home watching television. Efforts to attract older viewers include an increased output of niche pictures aimed at specific demographics. The improved quality of the filmgoing experience—large screens, good projection, comfortable seats, versatile concession stands—are key factors in providing an inviting environment for older viewers.

In the 1990s, audiences for indies come from the new foreign markets, which means distributors have their eyes on overseas audiences in China, India, Russia, and other countries where American movies have not played regularly. American movies, both studio and independent, have made strong inroads internationally. Strategic releasing in Eastern

Europe and Asia, where privatization of the economy continues to accelerate, has increased revenues for all American media, including movies.[29]

The size of the over-forty audience has doubled in the past decade and now represents 30 percent of ticket sales. Conversely, the percentage of the population that seldom goes to movies has shrunk from a high of 45 percent to less than 30 percent. The studios have zeroed in on the largest segments of the population that does go to movies, neglecting the niche segments. Teens comprise close to half of "frequent" moviegoers, but they are not the prime watchers of movies on cable or the majority of video renters.

In the 1980s, all the studios made forays into indie fare, resulting in a raft of specialized divisions. With few exceptions, these divisions lasted only a few years. A similar cycle seems to be operating in the 1990s, with the studios again aggressively pursuing specialty divisions. Disney acquired Miramax, Sony bought the former Orion Classics team, now called Sony Pictures Classic, Universal co-ventured with Polygram in Gramercy Pictures, Universal purchased October Films, Twentieth Century-Fox established Fox Searchlight, and Paramount built its own classic unit.

The key to indie survival is developing niche audiences. New Line has been very successful with horror (the *Nightmare on Elm Street* series) and black-themed pictures (the *House Party* series, *Friday*, *Set It Off*). Miramax has been inventive in marketing art-house films (both foreign-language and English-speaking) to the masses. Sony Classics has been effective with nontraditional foreign (*Farinelli*, *La Vie en Rose*), American indies (*Welcome to the Dollhouse*, *In the Company of Men*) and even documentaries (*Crumb*). Strand Releasing and Jour de Fête have built a name for themselves with gay-themed and other specialty fare.

THE DECLINE OF FOREIGN-LANGUAGE FILMS

The decline in the popularity of foreign-language films has contributed to the increased success of American indies. "Independents are taking up the space a Fellini or a Truffaut film used to occupy," said Philip Garfinkle of Entertainment Data. "Though an *Il Postino [The Postman]* occasionally breaks through, only American-style product travels well."[30] This Italian film was indeed the exception, first winning an

Oscar nomination for Best Picture, then, with Miramax's help, running for months to a cumulative gross of $22 million.

Which came first, the decline of foreign cinemas or the shrinking market for foreign films in the United States? No matter; indie filmmakers have captured the art-house audiences, appealing to viewers who two decades ago embraced the work of Bergman, Fellini, Truffaut, Godard, and Kurosawa. The death of Kieslowski (*Red*), the last of the breed of European art directors, may have signaled the end of an important era of international cinema.

During the European film renaissance that took place after World War II, Americans regularly saw a variety of foreign-language films in first-run theaters.[31] Art theaters in big cities and campus colleges screened subtitled films with actors little known to most Americans. There were a few exceptions: Films starring Marcello Mastroianni, Sophia Loren, Jeanne Moreau, Catherine Deneuve, and Gérard Depardieu, to mention a few international stars, always played better.

But ever since that renaissance ended in the 1980s, art houses have become a rare commodity in the United States. Cinema Studio, one of a handful of New York theaters that regularly showed foreign films, closed its doors in 1990, following upon the closing of the Thalia, the Regency, and other houses. Foreign-language films are increasingly difficult to find in first-run theaters; the only place to see a plethora of foreign films is in specialized venues, such as the New York Film Forum, Los Angeles Nuart, and in major festivals.

In the 1990s, foreign-language films in the United States amount to no more than 2 percent of the entire market. For foreign movies, the major stumbling block to crack the American market remains language. About fifty foreign-language films are released in the United States every year, yet few gross more than $1 million. The top end has been about $20 million for the Italian sentimental melodrama *Il Postino* and the Mexican erotic movie *Like Water for Chocolate*. In today's market, the Japanese *Shall We Dance*, with its $10 million grosses, and the Italian *Life Is Beautiful*, with its Oscar for Best Foreign-Language Picture, rank as blockbuster.[32]

The aversion toward English dubbing is new. In the 1960s, *La Dolce Vita*, *A Man and a Woman*, and *Z* grossed more than $10 million each by opening with subtitles, then moving into dubbed versions in urban centers. Released in 1960, *La Dolce Vita* still ranks as the fourth biggest foreign grosser; at today's admission prices, its box-office would translate into about $70 million. The last time the dubbed strategy worked was in 1977, when *La Cage aux Folles* attained more than $17 million (over $30 million by 1998 standard).

For a foreign-language movie to "play" in the 1990s, it needs to be framed as an event, like the Oscar-winning or Oscar-nominated films that Miramax has succeeded in promoting: the Italian *Mediterraneo*, the Mexican *Like Water for Chocolate*, the French *Ridicule*, the Czech *Kolya*. Even the rare foreign film that wins recognition at Cannes or Venice often has trouble securing release, let alone finding success, in the United States. Foreign-film aficionados must turn to videocassette—but, again, foreign films on video appeal primarily to those with an already developed interest in foreign cultures.

Distributors claim that American audiences are reluctant to read subtitles, are uncomfortable with the lack of sync in dubbed films, are bored by foreign films' slow pacing, and are unhappy with a technical quality that falls short of Hollywood standards. Acknowledging the complaints about subtitles from young viewers, Miramax's Harvey Weinstein speculated: "American independents may be more appealing to a generation that listens to radio and watches TV, where reading may be eighth on the list."[33] What makes the situation worse is that foreign cinemas are experiencing a decline in productivity as a result of Hollywood's growing dominance.

In a 1997 essay, Susan Sontag lamented the death of cinephilia, the special love inspired by film. Cinephilia was born out of the conviction that cinema was a unique art: modern, accessible, poetic, mysterious, erotic, and moral—all at the same time. Cinema had apostles. It was like religion, a crusade. For cinephiles, cinema was both the book of art and the book of life. Going to movies, thinking about movies, talking about movies became a passion among students of the 1960s. The temples were the cinematheques, which specialized in exhibiting films from the past and directors' retrospectives. The 1960s and 1970s represented a feverish age of moviegoing, with new masterpieces released almost every week.

According to Sontag, in the present climate, one is hard pressed to find remnants of cinephilia—not just love for movies, but a certain taste in films, a desire to see and resee cinema's past. Playing no role in the era of hyperindustrial films, cinephilia has come under attack as quaint and outmoded. And yet cinephilia does exist, albeit in an altered form and on a smaller scale. It doesn't revolve around foreign films; 1990s cinephilia is defined mostly by exciting American directors—Scorsese, David Lynch, Tarantino, Paul Thomas Anderson, and a few others with a loyal following.

The lowered expectations for quality and the inflated expectations for profit have made it impossible for ambitious American directors like Scorsese or Coppola to work at their best level or on material that suits their talents. Abroad, some of the greatest maverick directors have stopped making films altogether. Godard now makes films on video about the history of film that are shown in festivals. Global financing, international casts, and coproductions have had disastrous effects on the work of Bergman and Tarkovsky.

THE PROLIFERATION OF FILM SCHOOLS

The film schools that have sprung up all over the country produce a large number of ambitious filmmakers eager to take advantage of the new opportunitiess. Driven by a desire to communicate with images, most graduates insist that money is not the prime motivation for choosing a film career. Perceiving movies as the medium of their generation, young directors are encouraged by the prestige of indies, which has made it easier for them to catch the industry's eye.

After decades of struggles to establish their validity and identity, the nation's top film schools are enjoying an unprecedented boom. Currently, hundreds of film programs in the United States offer a wide range of production courses as well as critical studies. Schools in New York and Los Angeles have the added advantage of proximity to the film and television industries. As more graduates are landing jobs, more applicants are clamoring for admission to schools.[34]

Two ways into the film industry exist: film school or on the job training, working your way up through the ranks. Given the intense competition for jobs, aspiring filmmakers hope that a degree will give them the edge. Many aspirants would rather go to school than invest the years it takes to work their way up. Schools offer a short cut into the industry, and prestigious ones are preferred because of their link to Hollywood. In 1992, 72 percent of first-time directors were graduates of film schools, compared with 35 percent in 1980. By 2000, more than 80 percent of all new directors will have gone to film school.[35] Not surprisingly, a survey posing the question "Should you go to film school if you want to get into Hollywood?" found that those who went to school think filmmakers should go, and those who didn't, think it unnecessary.

Radical changes in the entertainment industry were reflected in film schools during the 1970s. When the studio system, previously the de facto academy for filmmakers, was disintegrating, schools began to fill the void, gearing themselves more and more toward feature films. A generation ago, before names like Spielberg or Scorsese had made their mark, formal schooling was seen as a liability. The old guard, who had risen through the system, perceived film students as wise know-it-alls with weird ideas about art. But today, a school pedigree is not only respectable but a legitimate way into a film career.[36]

In 1996, U.S. News and World Report ranked the top five film schools. The University of Southern California (USC) tied with New York University (NYU) as the top school (with 4.6 score), followed by the American Film Institute (AFI) and the University of California at Los Angeles (UCLA) (each 4.00) and the California Institute of the Arts (3.80). Rivalry among the big schools is fierce and the competition among students to get into them increasingly tougher. Technical resources for instruction are available at community colleges, but the most desirable asset offered by major schools is prestige.

With one of the oldest programs, USC boasts that each year since 1950, at least one of its graduates has been nominated for an Academy Award, and ten out of the twenty top-grossing films have had USC alumni in key creative positions. Ironically, Spielberg (who has a building named after him) was rejected by USC because of bad grades. "Standards were so high," Spielberg once remarked, "that many of today's finest filmmakers were unable to attend."

Concerned that students leave the program with degrees but no jobs, USC's Dean Elizabeth Daley bridged the gap by hiring Larry Auerbach, a former William Morris agent, to help ease graduates' transition into the industry; 75 percent of USC graduates reportedly walk into Hollywood jobs. John Singleton is a cult hero among USC students, not only for having directed a successful movie, Boyz 'N' the Hood, but for making it without "selling out."

By graduation, most students have made at least one film of their own and have worked on several others. Film school output is prodigious, with thousands of shorts produced every year. The hope is that somewhere in those thousands, genuine talent lurks. The film community is like a small town: Word about promising directors spreads quickly. Film schools make it their business to display their best to the industry through various channels. Successful films make it to regional or national contests, such as the one sponsored by the Academy of Motion Picture Arts and Sciences, and to regional festivals. Good student films find their way also to film festivals, some dedicated entirely to shorts. At the Sundance Film Festival, about half of the short films in competition are made by students.

NYU, with an illustrious alumni list that includes Martin Scorsese, Oliver Stone, Spike Lee, Jim Jarmusch, Susan Seidelman, and Martin Brest, has moved to the forefront in the past two decades. The emphasis is on production, not on theory; students arrive expecting to make movies. Of the hundred of applicants to NYU's Film School, the 5 percent accepted pay more than $15,000 in tuition for the first year, then pay an additional $40,000 to $100,000 to finance required projects during the three-year program. Attending film school is an expensive proposition, costing in excess of $100,000 for a three-year stint.

Funding for student films comes from grants, loans, family, and credit cards. Actors often provide free services, a practice that the Screen Actors Guild dislikes but tolerates. Sometimes students are able to sign up well-known actors, tempted by the high quality of writing and the relatively short shooting schedules. Most students start out with ambitions to direct but later become producers or executives. Only a small percentage actually get to direct a feature within a decade after graduation, a fact that forces schools both to prepare students for disappointment and to encourage more commercially oriented films.

UCLA's film program started in 1947 and initially concentrated on nonfiction and experimental film. Under pressure to increase its connection to the industry, however, UCLA has undergone major changes. Columbia University has also reexamined its approach to film-making education, with a sharper eye to providing its students better employment prospects. Film schools operate under constant fear of losing touch with the industry for which they ostensibly train students. In fact, most film schools have changed, allowing more hands-on training and actual moviemaking into their curricula. They try to help students get a leg up in the business, with activities ranging from hosting job fairs to signing first-look contracts with agencies. Encouraging its students to show their work publicly and to interact with agents and executives, NYU sponsors the annual Haig Manoogian Screening in Los Angeles and lends its support to international festivals.

Agencies are always searching for new talent, and, like major league scouts, they are looking for early signs. While student films are fertile ground, agents often ask students if they have a script; smart students have a finished script in hand. The consensus is that two solid scripts can lead to a directing job on the third.

The industry, both mainstream and independent, uses schools as development pools, providing them with scholarships and new equipment. All the major schools have developed strategies to tap industry money and are becoming mired in a debate about the proper relationship between Hollywood and the academe. Schools are intensely involved in examining their educational philosophy, specifically the relationship between theory and praxis. The line between student filmmaking and professional careers has blurred, aided by Hollywood's appetite for "product" and abetted by the schools themselves. The big schools promote their students aggressively, but problems persist: Does early success by Hollywood standards stunt a filmmaker's creativity? Film schools are a place to experiment, but the message doesn't always come down that way.[37]

Schools have traditionally seen themselves as safe places where students can pursue personal visions. Some schools protect their students from the taint of careerism by encouraging them to make films that defy commercial considerations. Students' projects may be their only opportunity to exercise freedom of expression without economic constraints, without bowing to audience tastes, without compromising their beliefs. At the same time, students know that their films will be screened publicly and that the guests will include Hollywood power brokers.[38]

Top schools are courted by the Hollywood studios eager to sign "first-look" deals that give them an exclusive first crack at students' films in exchange for grant money to the program. Faculties are split on this idea; it crystallizes the academic-versus-professionals dilemma. Professors worry that students are producing commercial films just to fit the studio mold.

The debate over the value of film schools continues. Perhaps the greatest value of schools is that they give filmmakers the opportunity to take artistic chances. "It's about doing," said Gillian Armstrong, who attended film school in Australia before making *My Brilliant Career*. "You rarely in the professional world have the chance to express yourself as an individual."[39] The director Emir Kusturica

(*Underground*), who teaches at Columbia, is concerned about the focus at some schools on preparing students for the industry. For him, movies are first and foremost an art form, and students may "lose their religion" in their preoccupation with commerce.

Film education has glamour, but it is also one of the more trouble-fraught corners of American universities. Costs are rising, competitive pressures are fierce, and contentious debates flare about ethics and educational mission. Schools have become a powerful force for rejuvenating Hollywood—a kind of laboratory for the industry. Yet, critics claim that by moving closer to industry, schools have made it increasingly difficult to distinguish deal-hungry would-be filmmakers from young investment bankers. Additionally, some observers are convinced that being a good filmmaker is more a matter of natural talent. Schools can shore up the weak parts, but the ability to move the camera and get good performances may be more instinctive. Often schools seem hard pressed to describe the difference between their students' work and that of filmmakers who came up through the ranks.

Still, the recent growth in film schools is a testament to their acceptance as a legitimate path into the industry. Despite the success of some graduates, only a small number of alumni hit the big time. Half of students from the big schools work in the industry after graduation. About one-third of USC's annual graduates get full-time film work, often as low-paid script readers; one-third may work part-time; and the rest probably won't get anywhere in the business. Schools can't guarantee jobs, but they brag about their alumni's employment rates, carefully pointing out that their graduates are working in "some aspect" of film. However, this success rate may have little to do with anything taught in schools. By choosing the top of an already talented crop, schools may just be selecting people likely to succeed even without the benefit of formal education.

Despite the controversies, film schools have become the dominant way to get into the industry. The small core of prestige schools is beginning to "institutionalize" access to movie and TV work, much like schools that have become the valves that admit (or shut out) talent seeking entry to the medical or legal professions. Unprecedented success in placing graduates in the industry reaffirms the cachet of top schools.

Film schools' control over access is problematic: Burgeoning cost has made it tougher for bootstrap directors to compile sample work without institutional support.[40] There is a growing fear that the best schools are restricted to a small, homogenous group, many of whom have already attended Ivy League colleges and can afford the financial burden of schooling. Not surprisingly, prestigious schools serve predominantly white, male, upper middle-class students, with the percentage of ethnic minorities quite small.

THE SUNDANCE FILM FESTIVAL

Every major city in the United States has a film festival, but there's little doubt that the Sundance Film Festival is the premiere showcase for new American indies. Indeed, as far as industry heat and exciting discoveries are concerned, Sundance now ranks second only to Cannes on the film map. Celebrating new talent, Sundance has become a Mecca for aspiring independents.

Robert Redford, credited with launching the new indie movement, has split himself in two, pursuing a high-road strategy of starring in glossy studio movies (*Up Close and Personal, The Horse Whisperer*), while directing edgier, smaller studio movies (*Ordinary People, Quiz Show*). Redford is still a movie star, but he is better known as the guiding spirit of the Sundance Film Festival, Sundance Institute, Sundance Channel, and soon a nationwide chain of Sundance theaters.

Redford's role in the indie world began in 1980, when he established the Sundance Film Institute. In 1985, he took over the ailing U.S.A. Film Festival and turned it into a first-rate exhibition platform for independents. From the beginning, Redford envisioned the festival as a complement to Sundance's Screenwriting and Filmmaking Labs. "I just put one foot in front of the other," he recalled. "We have this development thing, so let's provide an exhibition. I simply wanted to get the movies seen."[41] Redford situated the festival in the picturesque ski resort of Park City, Utah, where "both the air and the values seem purer than in Hollywood." As conceived by Redford, the festival's function was to detect and display fresh talent.

For Redford, "the narrowing of the main part of the industry opens up the other part, which is diversity, which is what independent filmmaking is all about." Multiculturalism was meant to be Sundance's raison d'être; the festival presented works by women, African Americans, and other ethnic minorities whose voices have been ignored in mainstream cinema. Redford hoped that "what will emerge in independent film is a counterreaction against what's going on."

Michelle Satter, director of Sundance's Feature Film Program, believes that "more and more emerging film artists look to the Sundance Screenwriters and Filmmakers Labs to help them develop and refine their vision." The body of work created by them has an increasing impact on contemporary American cinema. Many of the individuals groomed by Sundance (Allison Anders, Gregg Araki, Tarantino) have been acknowledged as the Next Wave.

Sundance has grown enormously since the discovery of *sex, lies, and videotape* in 1989 and the emergence of its director, Soderbergh, as the hottest filmmaker around. But growth has its costs. Soderbergh now grumbles about the "encroachment of commerce," which eclipses art. When he debuted his film, Sundance wasn't "overrun by agents and wasn't a deal market or a sales place." There's no doubt that *sex, lies, and videotape* was a turning point, as Ira Deutschman points out, after which "everyone started taking the festival seriously." "The shift came in 1990, when suddenly the festival became this feeding frenzy; inundated with agents, executives, and deal makers, it was no longer about art."

With its phenomenal commercial success, *sex, lies, and videotape* ushered in the Age of Sundance, when first-time filmmakers could become overnight celebrities. Indeed, each January, Park City becomes a magnet for distributors looking for pickups, executives checking out new talent, international media eager for new heroes, and agents seeking clients. William Morris alone sends two dozen agents, scouring the festival for the next breakthrough filmmaker. With the studios continuing to back risk-free entertainment, and with prices for established talent rising fast, Hollywood is hungry for cheap writers and directors.[42]

The premiere of films like *River's Edge*, *sex, lies, and videotape*, and *House Party* catapulted Sundance to the status of America's most important festival. As sexy starlets used to go to Cannes to be discovered, non-Hollywood filmmakers arrive in Park City to catch the industry's eye. In 1993, 225 features were submitted to the Sundance dramatic competition, representing a 30 percent increase from just two years earlier. In 1997, 500 dramatic features were submitted, with an additional 200 films vying for a spot in the documentary competition. This makes the programming extremely competitive and the final selections vulnerable to criticism. The emphasis is on the two competitions, the dramatic and the documentary, which jointly present about thirty-four films. Since most of the documentaries are not screened elsewhere, the chance to see a large number of documentaries is one of Sundance's distinctive aspects. But the main event—what really draws the Hollywood establishment—is the dramatic competition.

Traditionally, Sundance represented a chance for no-name filmmakers and no-budget features to land distribution deals; the festival was the happy destination after a long journey. The perennial Sundance story revolves around the difficulty of raising the money, the years it took to make the film, the struggle to find a public. The hardships are still the same, but in the 1990s, the tradition is changing, and many films at the festival arrive with distribution deals. Competition for hot indies is so fierce that many contracts are signed before Sundance. Said one agent: "If you haven't seen the films before the festival, the ship has sailed by the time you get there."[43] Nonetheless, even films screened for distributors prior to the festival get special attention at Sundance, because there's still a need to test audiences' reaction.

But Sundance doesn't simply bring exposure to preexisting indies; it also brings added professionalism. Harvey Weinstein commented that young filmmakers are becoming more cognizant of the opportunities a showcase like Sundance provides: "It's not like they can just go make a home movie. The stakes are a little higher now that there's a forum for it. This really is a world stage."[44] In the 1990s, Sundance developed the critical mass of a major international event, and as with Cannes or Toronto, the press attention to the popular hits and the prize winners now means not only a major career boost and likely distribution but also free publicity for what might otherwise be strictly specialized fare.

While the growing prestige and hype from Hollywood have outweighed the charm and intimacy of Sundance's first years, the films themselves have changed, too. If there was a stereotypical indie in the 1980s, it could be described as a "sensitive" coming-of-age story about a Midwestern farm girl. A low point of Sundance was Rob Nilsson's 1988 top prize for his black-and-white video transfer, *Heat and Sunlight*, a rather weak film. Then, in 1989, *sex, lies, and videotape*, *True Love*, and *Heathers* exploded from the festival, and nothing has been the same since. In the 1990s, the images are almost entirely urban and multiracial, suffused with violence and dark humor.

Discernible cycles and trends can be observed. In 1991, Sundance buzzed with new African American directors—a black new wave—

with *Straight Out of Brooklyn, Hangin' With the Homeboys,* and *Daughters of the Dust.* The "movement" that emerged in 1992 was the new queer cinema, with an unprecedented number of gay directors making radical films with little concern for positive role models. Three gay-themed films grabbed attention in that year: *Swoon, The Living End,* and *The Hours and Times.*

Each year, attendees come away from the festival with a list of filmmakers who bear close watching. In 1992, in addition to the gay movies, there were films by Tarantino, whose stunning heist movie, *Reservoir Dogs,* stirred debate about its violence and guaranteed him a Hollywood future; Allison Anders's *Gas Food Lodging,* a fresh look at a mother in a New Mexico town trying to raise her unruly daughters; and Alexander Rockwell's *In the Soup.*

In 1993, the most innovative movies, those that aroused strong emotions, were in the documentary, not the dramatic competition. Announcing the renaissance of first-rate nonfiction, they may not have caught agents' attention, but for riveting drama and substantial issues they left the dramatic films in the dust. As Kenneth Turan observed, it was the year the understudy went out there and came back a star. Nonfiction films, always in the shadow of the more glamorous dramatic competition, found themselves center stage. The 1993 documentary jury split the grand prize, not because the jurors were divided but because they admired equally two films, *Children of Fate: Life and Death in a Sicilian Family,* about the culture of poverty in Palermo, and *Silverlake Life: The View from Here,* a wrenchingly honest depiction of AIDS.

A large percentage of the dramatic competition films in 1993 were made by first-time directors in their twenties. As such, they display the tentativeness and anomie that go along with that age, together with a peculiar fear of engaging the viewers emotionally. If there was a unifying theme, it concerned young people having to face adulthood. The anxieties of the younger generation were explored in these features by directors who were themselves twenty-something. Documentaries, on the other hand, were not shy about venturing into emotional territory. Viewers were reduced to tears in *Silverlake Life: The View from Here,* the video diary of two HIV-positive men. And when *Earth and the American Dream* received an unprecedented five-minute standing ovation, it was one of the high points of the director Bill Couturie's life.

Over the years, what was once a laid-back, non-Hollywood festival has become a tension-filled auction block, a talent bazaar with long waiting lines for hot screenings and nervous filmmakers whose careers are on the line. Sundance may have lost the communal, alternative spirit that prevailed during the first years, but for the filmmakers and filmgoers who revel in ten days of nonstop pictures and movie talk, passion for movies remains the issue. The goal is still to celebrate the maverick visions of indie directors. Indeed, despite the fact that Sundance is no longer an intimate place, audiences still get to vote on their favorite films, and the preponderance of parkas, sweaters, and cowboy boots continues to gives the place a semicasual feel.

Although Sundance is now a polished operation, Redford refuses to let the festival get too smooth, to grind out grist for the studio mills. "It's a very rough and dynamic experience, and it should stay that way," he says. Year after year, Redford restates the original goal: "This festival is about supporting the independent filmmaker. We don't want to lost track of that sight. If you want to go to Hollywood, great, we support that. If not, we support that too. The *New York Times* called us the last stop before Hollywood. But we're not. Nor are we anti-Hollywood. We're a bridge."

The festival's problems are the kinds that often nag at movie stars: How to survive the pressures of fame? How to avoid being typecast? "Success is a tricky mistress," Redford once observed. "It's nice to have, but it's a tricky thing to embrace.[45] Sundance continues to face serious challenges. As it gets more popular, there are temptations and even pressures to expand. "When you start expanding on something," Redford said, "you run the risk of losing quality, you begin to lose control." Redford is adamantly against expansion precisely because Sundance has caught on in such a big way. "When the mainstream industry realized there was financial profit possible here, that started the ball rolling," Redford acknowledged. "Hollywood comes here for a very clear reason—to discover talent they think will be profitable, or to buy films they think will be profitable." Nonetheless, Redford is aware that excitement generated at Sundance doesn't always translate into box-office success.

Year after year, Sundance films teach Hollywood a valuable lesson: There's no need for a huge budget to make interesting movies. Often, the less filmmakers had to spend, the more they had to say.[46] Most films at Sundance still suggest the festival's low-budget grass roots. About half of the dramatic competition entries are made for less than $100,000, which is lunch money in Hollywood. Every year, a

few pictures generate some buzz, build excitement around their directors, and develop reputations within the industry. In this respect,
the festival has not changed: Novice filmmakers continue to covet the
attention they receive at Sundance from Hollywood, foreign buyers,
and the national press, because it increases the likelihood that they
will land a deal, get their movie into the marketplace, and help ensure their continued productivity.

Of course, no single festival can accommodate the indie explosion.
In 1985, about fifty independent films were made in the United States;
in 1998, the number was estimated to be more than 1,000. Sundance is
the mecca for indies, but, inevitably, many directors aren't invited to the
"holy land." The competition is so tight that decent films are bound to
be rejected. On 1995's snub list were John Fitzgerald's *Self Portrait*,
Shane Kuhn's *Redneck*, and Dan Mirvish's *Omaha: The Movie*. When
Sundance failed to show interest in their low-budget features, instead
of taking no for an answer, these directors created their own festival.

Slamdance, the first guerrilla festival, was born in January 1995, audaciously running head to head with Sundance. The twelve films
screened were made for a combined total of less than $1 million. The or-
ganizers rented theaters around the University of Utah and made sure
that producers and agents who couldn't get into the sold-out Sundance
screenings came to their free showings.

In three years, Slamdance, which began as a renegade, ragamuffin
festival, has gained respect for its resourcefulness—and chutzpah. In an
era when critics fear Sundance might go too mainstream, Slamdance is
a reminder that the indie spirit is still alive. Building on a deepening alliance with former Sundance darling Soderbergh (whose *Schizopolis*
screened at Slamdance), it has doubled its budget to $125,000, bought
new projectors, and refitted screening rooms. In the first year, distributor presence was thin—the general attitude was "send me a tape"—but
in the third year, its visibility increased.[47]

The formerly poverty-stricken festival now boasts sponsorships (in
cash and equipment) from Dolby, Thrifty Car Rental, and some businesses that support Sundance, such as Panavision and Fotokem. It also
created a Web site, which includes a virtual marketplace ranging from
Slamdance paraphernalia to clips from competition films. Among the
ten premieres in 1997 were Stefani Ames's *A Gun, a Car, a Blonde*, starring Billy Bob Thornton, Anthony and Joe Russo's *Pieces*, Joelle Bento-
lila's *The Maze*, and Alexander Kane's *The Gauguin Museum*.

Slamdance came into its own in 1998 with a strong lineup of features, sell-out crowds, and increased attention from the industry. *Surrender Dorothy*, a hard-edged saga about a bisexual drug addict, was the grand jury prize winner. The audience award was given to *20 Dates*, a comedy about making a first feature, and the documentary award went to *Goreville, U.S.A.*, about an Illinois town in which locals are required by law to own firearms.[48]

Slamdance was conceived in protest against Sundance, the "Good Housekeeping seal of approval for indies." Created by frustrated filmmakers, the gathering was a tongue-in-cheek commentary on the bigger festival. But Slamdance is more of a complement than a rival to Sundance. Maureen Crowe, vice president at Arista, thinks the venerable organization and the scrappy newcomer work in tandem. "Sundance has become a little bit Park Avenue, or Top 40, to use a music term," she said. "Slamdance is a little bit more raw in spirit—more `street.' You can't go straight to Top 40 without getting the street credibility. It's not a second choice; it's a necessary step."

Slamdance has grown up, buoyed by both corporate sponsors and a record 1,300 entries for the thirty-one competition slots. It serves a vital purpose that Sundance can't accomplish alone: showcasing limited-budget films. "They started out not even in Park City, with three or four kids in tennis sneakers handing out fliers. Now Slamdance has become an important festival unto itself," says producer rep Jonathan Dana.

The festival has had some successes. The 1997 Jury Prize winner, *The Bible and Gun Club*, Daniel Harris's comedy about five Orange County Bible salesmen in Las Vegas for their annual convention, received three nominations for the Spirit Awards, the Oscars of the indie world. And Greg Mottola's *Daytrippers*, which premiered at Slamdance in 1996 after being rejected by Sundance, went on to Cannes. Released by CFP, the well-received film grossed more than $2 million.

Unknown artists are Slamdance's major draw. As festival director Baxter stresses, "We're about first-time filmmakers, undiscovered talent." Rejected by Sundance, the director Myles Berkowitz (*20 Dates*) was grateful to compete at Slamdance. "Sundance has changed the film world for the better. They created an independent market. But the movies in Sundance now I could not direct and star in," he said, pointing to films with name actors and sizable budgets. For Berkowitz, Slamdance fills a gap for first-time filmmakers. However, asked if he wants to be a part of Sundance in the future, Berkowitz is quick to respond, "Absolutely!"

For Christian Gore, who publishes the weekly E-mail *Film Threat*, Slamdance is less affiliated with the "corporate" indies. "I don't consider Miramax an independent film company. They're funded by Disney and are a studio. The opening film at Sundance, *Sliding Doors*, had a budget of about $11 million and is being distributed by Miramax and Paramount." For Gore, most of what's called independents now are basically "low-budget studio pictures." About half of the 103 features at Sundance in 1998 were "truly" independent, funded and made independently. But Slamdance screens such films exclusively. Besides, Slamdance offers a mellower scene. Many of the Sundance isms—the cell phones, the beepers, the Armani suits—are looked down upon at Slamdance, which caters to "the coffeehouse crowd."

But with more than 1,000 submissions a year, the Slamdance organizers have found themselves facing the same problem that led to Slamdance in the first place—the need to reject decent low-budget films. Hence, in 1997, yet another guerrilla festival, Slumdance, came into being. Which proves the point that as soon as a festival becomes too established, a new, more audacious venue will emerge to fill the gap created at the bottom.

ORGANIZATIONAL SUPPORT FOR INDIES

The independent cinema is a grass-roots movement supported by an extensive network of organizations. While limited funding remains a pervasive problem, guerrilla filmmakers on both coasts draw on the Independent Feature Project (IFP and IFP/West), the Association of Video and Filmmakers (AVF), the Black Filmmakers Foundation, several nonprofit media centers, and indie-friendly labs and vendors.

"A number of institutions are terribly helpful to the independent director," noted *Metropolitan* helmer Whit Stillman: "Sundance is one; the Independent Feature Project is another. And there are now a lot of festivals that have taken a special interest in supporting these films, various sections of Cannes, the New Directors series in New York, the San Francisco and Seattle film festivals. These have given a way for independent films to reach their audience."

The Independent Feature Project (IFP) has been acclaimed as the launching pad for a bevy of indie hits as well as for lending support to those falling through the cracks. At first, it served as a clearinghouse for makers of personal films like *Northern Lights* and *Heartland*. One of IFP's purposes was to allow those already within the industry who have been overlooked to "take their shot." Over the years, IFP has evolved from a quickly organized sidebar to the New York Film Festival to its present status as a large confab, boasting not only screening of pictures for sale but panels and workshops.

IFP is now the country's largest association of independent film-makers, having grown from 600 to 3,500 members within a decade. Its budget has increased from $500,000 to $2 million, and corporate funding has risen from $150,000 to $1.3 million. IFP's annual Gotham Awards attract the support of sponsors such as Bravo, CAA, Fox Searchlight, Miramax, and Absolut vodka.

Correspondingly, the number of submissions to the annual Independent Feature Film Market (IFFM) has risen from 390 in 1990 to 600 in 1997. The IFFM has adjusted to filmmakers' needs, offering more works-in-progress and creating better opportunities for agents, executives, and buyers to interface with new filmmakers. Over the years, the market has launched the premiere of such indies as Linklater's *Slacker*, Whit Stillman's *Metropolitan*, Michael Moore's *Roger and Me*, Kevin Smith's *Clerks*, and Ed Burns's *The Brothers McMullen*, all of which later achieved a measure of commercial success.

"People used to join just to come to the IFFM," said former chief Catherine Tait. "That was the only benefit."[49] But with yearlong programming and the development of new services, the annual turnover in membership was cut from 75 to 40 percent. IFP expanded its resource program, and members now have access to free consultations with established producers, distributors, and lawyers. IFP's training sessions in financing, writing, and marketing help members improve their skills and gain understanding of the business.

In 1997, former Deputy Director Michelle Byrd assumed the leadership of IFP, taking over an organization that has grown from a "collective" with a small staff to a nonprofit association with a $2 million budget and fourteen employees.[50] Along with the burgeoning interest in "independent" film as a brand name in the commercial marketplace, IFP owes its expansion to the high-profile success of the IFFM, its most vital program, as well as to prodigious fund-raising from corporate sponsorship.

IFP wasn't founded on any business principle; it was a project born with a post-1960s spirit: "Let's all get together and have a voice." The initial mandate was to educate the industry about filmmaking outside Hollywood. The idea was to be a solution to a specific problem that would disband when the problem was resolved. But IFP is not a project anymore; it's a full-fledged organization whose founding goals have been achieved—indies are no longer going to be passed over. Clearly, Hollywood wants to get near independents, as evidenced by its involvement in Sundance, but IFP continues to make concerted efforts to get indies to other festivals and to the marketplace. Established filmmakers, despite critical recognition, still struggle to secure funding. It still takes Victor Nunez and Charles Burnett years to get projects off the ground.

There is no discernible aesthetic or philosophy at work; IFP supports all shapes and sizes of creation. For the 1997 Berlin Festival program, it sent a cross-section of films, such as the more commercial *Puddle Cruiser* and the gay-themed *The Delta*. Both were independently made, both by filmmakers struggling to be heard, but they have different points of view and different target audiences. These films are the extremes, and it's important for IFP to represent those extremes.

Nor is IFP solely concerned with commercial success—it's more about discovering talent. Ed Burns was around a long time before *The Brothers McMullen*, an IFP discovery, became a commercial success. Kevin Smith has been extremely supportive of the organization, grateful that it helped him transform from a "nobody" (as he said) to someone with a career.

There has been talk about having the IFP branches form a national organization, which is a good idea. From an audience-building standpoint, the opportunity is there, and the timing is right for an effort to work together, instead of representing the filmmakers region by region. Nationwide, the five separate organizations have a membership of 8,000; this membership represents a powerful tool that hasn't been fully used.

IFP/West, which accounts for 4,500 people out of the national membership, is the largest branch. It presents the annual Independent Spirit Awards during Oscar weekend. What better indicator of the institutionalization of indies than for them to sponsor their own "Oscars"? The Spirit Awards have mirrored the history of indie filmmaking, growing from a small get-together at a West Hollywood restaurant to a large seaside blowout, televised on Bravo and attended by Hollywood's elite. Many in the creative community now commute regularly between Hollywood and indie films.

The Association of Independent Video and Filmmakers (AIVF), which moved in 1997 to more spacious headquarters with a screening room, recently received a $100,000 NEA challenge grant. Headed by executive director Ruby Lerner, AIVF is in more stable financial shape than other nonprofit groups in filmmaking. But it has been hurt by the termination of NEA's small-grants program; numerous careers were founded on those $3,000 to $5,000 grants.

Nonfiction films are aided by the International Documentary Association, a nonprofit organization established in 1982 to promote nonfiction film and video and to support the efforts of documentary filmmakers around the world. The association publishes its own magazine, *International Documentary*, and presents its own annual awards.

Premium cable channels, such as Bravo, the Independent Film Channel, and Sundance specialize in airing indie fare. Bravo, the first channel to promote art fare, is the largest, reaching 22 million subscribers on 550 cable systems.

The Independent Film Channel (IFC), which launched in 1994, has quickly emerged as a major force, its growing indie library fed by deals with Miramax, Sony Classics, Orion Classics, Goldwyn, and Fine Line. In 1995, the twenty-four-hour channel, owned by Cablevision Systems Corporation and NBC and distributed by Bravo, was available in 2 million homes. Three years later, its reach had doubled.[51] IFC has parlayed its growing subscriber base to a more aggressive title expansion through deals with a wide array of distributors.

Though dedicated to independent films and their creators, IFC programming includes retrospectives on the works of foreign directors like Kurosawa and Truffaut, and it also provides live coverage of film festivals such as Cannes and Sundance and its own original shows. Because the network is not looking for first windows or for exclusivity on titles, it pays an average price of between $15,000 and $20,000 a picture. At that rate, IFC can buy about 200 movies for less than the price paid by premium networks like HBO or Showtime.

After enjoying a virtual two-year monopoly on independent film broadcasting, however, IFC is now competing for viewers with the

Sundance Channel, which launched in February 1996 in select cities and is spreading quickly. The Sundance Channel is a cable and satellite pay channel, which gives a platform to films that have not found a release in theaters. In 1998, the Sundance Group, the commercial spinoff of the nonprofit Sundance Institute, entered the exhibition business by partnering with General Cinema. Operating a cable channel in partnership with Viacom and PolyGram, the Sundance Channel wants to leverage the brand awareness created by the Sundance Festival by establishing what some call the "Starbucks of indie film exhibition."[52] The first Sundance Cinema, a joint venture of Redford and General Cinemas, is in Portland, Oregon, but there are plans to build sites in other cities, which will increase the exposure of indie fare.

INDIES' COMMERCIAL SUCCESS

It's no longer a "secret" in Hollywood: There's money to be made out of "small" indie films. In 1986, the blockbuster success of the Vietnam epic *Platoon*, which amassed over $100 million at the box office before it won the Best Picture Oscar, and the solid returns of *A Room With a View* and *Kiss of the Spider Woman* proved that quality art films had commercial viability.

The box-office success of *sex, lies, and videotape* in 1989 was further proof that there was vibrant life outside the mainstream. *sex, lies, and videotape* was not an avant-garde film, but neither was it the product of consensus movie making. The film showcased a talented, self-assured director who came (in Hollywood terms) out of nowhere to win the Palme d'Or at Cannes. With production costs of about $1 million and profits of $25 million, *sex, lies, and videotape* produced a better rate of return than many hugely successful Hollywood blockbusters. Relative to its cost, the Miramax release was one of the most profitable movies of the entire decade.

In 1992, *Howards End*, *The Crying Game*, and *The Player* were all box-office smashes, in addition to garnering more Oscar nominations than the big-studio releases. According to Barbara Boyle, "independent films became fashionable in the 1990s, because the profit ratio on movies like *The Wedding Banquet* and *Four Weddings and a Funeral* made investors sit up and take notice."[53] When a movie like *Dead Man Walking*, which received Oscar nominations for Best Picture and Best Director and yielded a Best Actress award for Susan Sarandon, grosses in excess of $40 million, Hollywood listens. "Audiences have become more sophisticated and receptive to the personal story that is the hallmark of independent movies," said Harvey Keitel in 1995. "Even in remote areas that still don't show indie films in theaters, video stores now stock these titles."

Miramax's co-president Harvey Weinstein was selected as one of *Time* magazine's twenty-five most influential Americans in 1997. The official occasion was the success of *The English Patient*, the romantic epic that Miramax financed when Fox pulled out. Surprisingly, the movie became a big hit and went on to win nine Oscars, including Best Picture. That year, Miramax copped twelve Oscars, a feat not achieved by any studio since MGM in 1939. For Weinstein, "the special effects in Miramax movies are words."[54] With fondness for smart scripts and challenging images, he and his brother Bob hustle in movie-mogul tradition, proving that you don't need bloated budgets if you have savvy taste and good marketing skills.

The highest praise for Weinstein came from Robert Redford in 1997: "This is a man who is truly a pioneer and has spirited the entire independent film movement for the last ten years—fighting as hard as possible so that independent films get seen."[55] Miramax has turned oddball films—*The Crying Game, Like Water for Chocolate, Pulp Fiction*—into resounding hits. With all the criticism of Miramax's ultra-aggressive marketing, few would question Harvey Weinstein's drive, intelligence, and enlightened movie mania. And no critic would challenge his claim that, "we've taken films out of the art house ghetto and brought quirky new sensibilities to mass America."[56]

2

Cinema of Outsiders

THE MAIN ARTISTIC impulse of the new independent cinema has come from "outsiders." That the indie cinema is very much the cinema of the "Other" America can be validated in two ways. First, the characters of most indies are outsiders. In John Waters's shocking satires, the protagonists would be considered "deviant," or at least garish and grotesque, from a mainstream perspective. The characters in David Lynch's films inhabit the outer fringes of society, and all of John Sayles's films are about outsiders.

Second, the filmmakers themselves are outsiders: members of ethnic minorities, gays and lesbians, and women (who, despite their majority numbers, still qualify as a minority in terms of their actual impact on film production). But outsiders also include white male filmmakers who do not belong to the mainstream. Indie cinema is committed to cultural diversity, showcasing new works by filmmakers whose voices have been unheard or ignored in dominant culture. The portrait of America drawn in these films is both more idiosyncratic and more realistic than that evident in mainstream Hollywood fare.

The Sundance Film Festival serves as a useful barometer of indie film-making trends. The percentage of filmmakers at Sundance who are gay and lesbian, black, Hispanic, or from other ethnic minorities is substantially larger than the corresponding percentage of minority filmmakers in Hollywood. The main progress at Sundance has been made by women, who constitute no less than 20 percent of the filmmakers in competition.

The new American independent cinema is not a movement, if "movement" is defined as a neat category with an official organization and a formal leadership. However, if "movement" suggests a shared creative process and unity of spirit or vision, then perhaps one can think of the indie films of the last two decades as comprising a loose artistic movement, an art world with its own institutional structure, values, and goals. The artistic drive behind the indie movement continues to be born out of a creative need to explore new themes, new forms, and new styles, as well as a politically motivated need to render unfamiliar or "hidden" experiences previously ignored. New cinematic forms often emerge as a reaction against the oppressive nature of American society and the restrictive rigidity of dominant culture and mainstream cinema.

How does innovation occur?[1] Films as art works require elaborate collaboration among specialized personnel. The terms of cooperation have been established and routinized by Hollywood in conventions that dictate the concepts, forms, and materials to be used. Conventions also regulate the relations between filmmakers and audiences, specifying their rights and obligations. Because filmmakers and audiences share similar norms and conventions, most films evoke predictable emotional effects. Arguably, the most important element in innovation is playing *against* audiences' expectations, since most American filmmakers go out of their way to fulfill those expectations.

Artistic innovation occurs when existing conventions are violated, when artists make—and audiences appreciate—new kinds of film. The film world provokes some members—often from ethnic minorities—to innovate. Some innovations develop worlds of their own, others remain dormant for a while and then find acceptance from a larger world, and still others remain curiosities. As discussed in Chapter 1, most indie films belong to the first category; they are supported by an institutional network that runs parallel to, rather than against, the Hollywood industry.

Revolutionary innovations disrupt routine patterns and involve deliberate changes in film language. Radical changes differ from gradual shifts in paradigms and conventions, attacking thematically, ideologically, and organizationally the standard activities of mainstream cinema. Ideological attacks, such as Italian neorealism and the French New Wave, take the form of aesthetic manifestos and revisionist use of the medium's technical possibilities. They denounce old paradigms and adopt new aesthetic values. Organizational changes, which aim to alter the prevalent modes of finance, distribution, and exhibition, are motivated by the fierce competition for scarce resources: funds, screens, and audiences.

Cinematic revolutions introduce basic changes in conventions: new ideas, new techniques, and, above all, new ways of seeing. In the same way that Impressionist and Cubist painters altered the existing ways of seeing, new themes, new stock and equipment, new stylistic devices change our cinematic ways of perceiving reality. The fate of innovations depends on the artistic judgment made by critics and on the degree of acceptance from audiences. The process by which deviations become accepted in their own right is an intriguing one.

Ultimately, innovations involve audience expectations, with viewers needing to learn to respond to new or unfamiliar languages. Visionary filmmakers encounter resistance to their innovations from older practitioners and conservative audiences. It's always interesting to observe what the established order—mainstream Hollywood—accepts, incorporates, or rejects. This factor explains why some indie directors, but not others, are more easily coopted by Hollywood. It's easier for Steven Soderbergh to move closer to the mainstream or go back and forth between Hollywood and indiewood than for John Waters or David Lynch.

Innovation, however, has its constraints. One may ask how a film can be truly independent, let alone subversive, if it's distributed within a system whose structures are determined by patriarchal capitalism. As John Sayles has observed: "There is no way to make movies that are seen in more than a handful of commercial theaters and be totally independent of the machinery of the mainstream movie industry."[2] At the same time, Sayles holds that directors don't have to internalize Hollywood's values: "If you're clear that the point is the work itself, not the economic gains or celebrity glory, you have the focus necessary to at least try to tell a story with an independence of spirit." Hence the book's focus on the independent spirit, as allusive as it may be.

The "rebellion" of the indies is targeted against Hollywood's safe, calculated, formulaic fare—innocuous entertainment. Daring directors wish to deviate from classic paradigms, which favor a limited number of "psychologically driven" characters; motivated actions; predictable narratives with beginning, middle, and end; and happy, upbeat resolutions. The new indie directors perceive Hollywood as an institution that has achieved a high pitch of technical excellence but that in the process has lost its heart.

Despite visionary claims, the indie cinema boasts few practitioners whose films are truly avant-garde or whose works are as eagerly anticipated as the films of Bresson, Godard, Ozu, Tarkovsky, and Cassavetes a generation ago. The absence of prominent followers of an earlier American avant-garde—Stan Brakhage, Robert Frank, Shirley Clarke,

Ed Pincus, Jonas Mekas, Rick Leacock, and Andy Warhol, to mention a few—is highly evident in the new indies.

Indie films, as a whole, are not artistically ground-breaking or politically provocative. Despite offbeat characterizations, most indies lack unusual stories, experimental pacing, fractured narratives, or kinetic editing, to mention a few radical devices. By this definition, a filmmaker like Nick Gomez (*Laws of Gravity, Illtown*) is truly innovative, whereas Ed Burns (*The Brothers McMullen, No Looking Back*) is not. Though financed and produced independently, Burns's movies are thematically conventional, leaning on standard plots and narratives.

Indie cinema has been more innovative in subject matter than in style, often by default. In the 1990s, serious, provocative issues long abandoned by Hollywood, have become the indies' centerfield: homophobia (*Poison*), schizophrenia (*Clean, Shaven*), capital punishment (*Dead Man Walking*), obesity (*Heavy*), misogyny (*In the Company of Men*), and disability (*The Waterdance*).

The new independent cinema combines elements of modernism and postmodernism. It continues the modernist tradition of the New American Cinema of the late 1960s, which owes much to the French New Wave. The basic tenets of this tradition are:[3]

1. Recognition that the aesthetics of representation are inherently problematic and inevitably political.
2. Focus on the distinctive properties of film grammar.
3. Dense allusiveness, self-reflexivity and intertextuality.
4. Heightened awareness of the political implications of issues previously assumed to be technical or aesthetic.
5. Distrust of established genres and efforts to blend creatively the conventions of different genres.

There has been a continuous debate over what constitutes postmodern cinema since it's not always easy to distinguish a modern from postmodern film. Postmodernism is thought to refer to highbrow and avant-garde film, but in the United States, postmodernism began as a middlebrow phenomenon, with practitioners like Andy Warhol in painting, Norman Mailer in fiction, Tom Wolfe in journalism, and Robert Altman, Woody Allen, and Martin Scorsese in film, all figures who created accessible art for an educated but nonacademic public.[4]

Several definitions of postmodernism prevail in the literature.[5] First, the organization of the film industry itself exemplifies postmodernism in its transition from Fordian mass production (the studio system) to more flexible forms of independent production (the New Hollywood). The incorporation of Hollywood into conglomerates with multiple entertainment interests reflects the postmodern blurring of the line between industrial practices and cultural forms.

Second, films have exemplified themes and images of postmodern society. Scholars have pointed out that the changing representation of men in postmodern films is connected to the breakdown of confidence in metanarratives about masculinity and patriarchal authority.[6] The decline of metanarratives is expressed in the loss of a sense of history as a continuous and linear sequence of events. Since it's difficult for people to organize and interpret their lives in terms of the old metanarratives, the validity and legitimacy of these concepts have declined.[7] Postmodern culture is a culture without frontiers and outside history. The diverse, referential, self-reflexive, collagelike character of postmodern film draws inspiration from the decline of classic Hollywood metanarratives.

Third, films have displayed aesthetic features associated with postmodernism, such as eclecticism and the collapse of traditional artistic hierarchies. Since the early 1970s, there has been an increasing self-consciousness in American films, manifest in explicit references to film history and extensive quotations from various styles. Postmodernist thinking calls for breaking down the distinction between high and popular art, mixing the conventions of various genres, blending European art films with Hollywood commercial movies.

Fredric Jameson has suggested that both parody and pastiche are associated with postmodernism, although pastiche is more dominant.[8] Like parody, pastiche involves criticism of the text, but it's a more neutral and blank parody, without parody's ulterior motives. Hence, Altman's *The Long Goodbye* quotes from film history and reworks genre conventions with an obvious parodic intent to debunk the myth of the private eye and the values he represents. But in Brian De Palma's *The Untouchables*, the use of film quotations is marked by pastiche, a clever but politically blank reconstruction of the famous Odessa Steps sequence from *Battleship Potemkin*. Similarly, the use of pastiche is less of an ideological critique in *Independence Day*, a movie that invests its conservative politics with tongue-in-cheek knowingness.

Critics have argued that in postmodern film there is emphasis on style over substance, a consumption of images for their own sake, rather than for their usefulness or the values they symbolize, a preoccupation with playfulness and in-jokes at the expense of meaning.[9] As a result, qualities like integrity, coherence, seriousness, authenticity, and intellectual depth are undermined. Indie films and some atypical Hollywood productions, such as *Zelig, The Purple Rose of Cairo, Blade Runner, Blue Velvet,* and *Reservoir Dogs,* have "subverted" American films from within, by challenging audiences' expectations of narrative and visual representation.

This book is mostly about modern and postmodern filmmakers who are committed to innovation and change but are not extremely radical in their criticism of mainstream cinema. Few filmmakers in American cinema have totally repudiated the conventions of narrative film and have enjoyed sustained careers, a sad commentary about the pervasive nature of commercial cinema. Still, the work of many indie directors discussed in this book can be described as innovative, displaying new kinds of narratives (*Slacker, Dazed and Confused, Clerks*), new sensibilities (*Poison, Go Fish*), new thematic strategies (*Blue Velvet, Swoon*), new visual styles (*Eraserhead, Nadja*).

FIVE OUTSIDERS

The five filmmakers profiled in this chapter—Jon Jost, John Waters, David Lynch, John Sayles, and Steven Soderbergh—differ greatly in social background, film work, and career pattern. Yet, each has been an outsider at a crucial point in his career. Some directors began in the indie milieu as outsiders, then moved to the mainstream, never to return. Others go back and forth, transformed or untransformed by the indie experience to varying degrees. Still others began and stayed on the fringes, operating totally outside dominant cinema.

Working in a medium that cherishes mainstream entertainment, outsiders are out of synch in a society where conformity reigns supreme. Outsiders approximate a social type described by German sociologist Georg Simmel as "the stranger." As social types, outsiders enjoy a peculiar combination of nearness to and distance from their surroundings. Their position is determined by the fact that they do not really belong, they are an element of the system but not fully part of it.

The outsiders' perspective benefits from being in and out at the same time, from not being fully integrated. Because of their partial involvement, outsiders can attain a degree of freedom that allows them to deviate from the norms. Unbound by conventional commitments, which taint the perception of reality, they're more liberated. In the American cinema, being an outsider is defined by the attributes of gender, race, sexual orientation, and political outlook.

Four of the five directors belong to the same generation: Jon Jost was born in 1943, David Lynch and John Waters in 1946, and John Sayles in 1952. Coming of age in the late 1960s, during the Vietnam War and the New American Cinema, these directors reacted to the existing artistic and political values in radically different manner. The youngest in the group, Soderbergh, was born in 1963, and hence belongs to a different generation.

AVANT-GARDE OBLIVION—JON JOST

Born in Chicago in 1943, Jon Jost is a ruggedly independent filmmaker whose appeal has been confined to the alternative cinema and festival circuits. Unlike most of his contemporaries, Jost exhibits a voice that is uncompromisingly personal. Self-taught and consistently working on the fringes, he has made his films as cheaply as possible. Though Jost has been directing for thirty years, only a few of his works have found theatrical release. Remarkably, despite scant exposure and little money, Jost has been able to sustain a full-time film career.

Several of Jost's early films, *Speaking Directly: Some American Notes* (1973) and *Last Chants for a Slow Dance* (1977), were shown at European festivals, where critics compared him to Jean-Luc Godard; Godard himself once called Jost the best current American filmmaker. An experimental filmmaker who puts an idiosyncratic stamp on his work, he combines a quasi-documentary style with formal devices. His fluid, unpretentious camera is marked by long takes suffused with meaning and expressive of the inner psyches of his characters.

Jost's contempt for Hollywood is based on his belief that commercial films are the entertainment wing of the military-industrial complex. During the Vietnam War era, he served two years in prison for refusing military induction. Jost defines his identity as nomadic, claiming that he comes from nowhere. He separated himself from the formalist abstractions of the avant-garde; in turn, he has been rebuffed by that community for being "too narrative." His movies have benefited from his marginal position—his sustained creativity shows scant connection to either the mainstream or the indie milieu.

Jost's films are both formal and political, improvised yet carefully planned, pushing narrative to the brink while using formal devices and Brechtian alienation. Few directors have captured so accurately the blunt tedium of ordinary existence and the violence that it can breed. The beauty of Jost's features lies in the ways they evoke the kind of apathy that typifies everyday lives and in their ability to convey real-time monotony.[10]

In a self-revelatory article, "Jost Speaks Directly," published in *Film Comment*, he observes:

> Big, bigger, biggest, best . . . this most American mantra reverberates across the cultural landscape. Big architecture, big science, big sport, big politics, big business, big art, and, of course, big movies. Nothing draws America's attention and its perverse respect like a long line of zeros affixed to an object. Conversely, to not go Big is to fall into a purgatory of disdain and neglect. It is to fail. Only Big things count, and bigness works symbiotic wonders. The big movie begets the big promotional budget, and will have big stars drawing big attention—the cover of *Time* or *Newsweek*, head billing on all the talk shows, five minutes on *Siskel & Ebert*.[11]

Jost makes his films with a minimal crew. He writes, directs, photographs, edits—and sometimes even composes and performs the soundtrack. As he says in his manifesto:

> For nearly three decades, knowingly, consciously, I have worked "small." My entire career has been mounted on a fiscal sum—less than $500,000—that in L.A. would scarcely be imagined suitable for an episode of a lame half-hour sitcom. This being America, over the years I've been told I ought to shape up, get smart, go big. . . .
>
> The thought that there might be virtue in modesty, that having a crew of just two or three might actually have its benefits—and not merely fiscal—is perceived as lunacy. . . . To suggest that the naturalness gained by improvisation is worthy, or that the intimacy of working with as few people as possible yields something positive and

unattainable by large-scale production methods, is to invite its counter: your dialogue isn't snappy and wise-ass, and besides, nobody wants to see your nobodies—what you need is a major star (and writer, and effects, and John Williams). Only one train of logic applies: big production, big money, big promotion. To suggest that this train has nothing to do with art or with human values is to point out the obvious and the tragic.

. . . The American Way has no place or time for smallness, because it is all too desperately busy trying to mask its emptiness with bombast. The function of bigness is not only to attest to its own importance, but also to drown out any possibility that small voices will be heard.

A poet-crusader, Jost has confronted the kind of reality that most American movies ignore. His films are mostly about losers, the kind of protagonists considered "unappealing" by mainstream standards. As a critique of American culture, Jost's work centers on the American male psyche as it is shaped by the zeitgeist. Jost's oeuvre consists of three kinds of films: essays, Westerns, and urbans. His film essays include the acclaimed *Speaking Directly: Some American Notes* (1973), which deals with the intersection of the personal and the political in the context of the American involvement in Vietnam. *Stage Fright* (1980-1981) and *Plain Talk and Common Sense* (1986-88) are his most politicized films; yet they are also lyrical and experimental in their cinematography, editing, and sound. In the ten-part documentary series *Plain Talk and Common Sense*, Jost's sense of marginality and frustration came to a point of crisis.[12]

Last Chants for a Slow Dance (1977), *Slow Moves* (1983), *Bell Diamond* (1985), and *Sure Fire* (1988-1990) are among Jost's modern Westerns. Jost examines the inheritors of the mythic cowboys, left adrift after the closing of the frontier and the demise of the code of honor, living with false hopes of expansionism and individualism. His characters go on long, aimless drives through vast, barren landscapes. The only emotion left for them seems to be rage; most of his Westerns end violently, with pointless deaths.

Jost's urban films include *Angel City* (1977), *Chameleon* (1978), and *Rembrandt Laughing* (1988). *Angel City* attempts to synthesize radical form and political content; its fragmented structure, alienation effects, and documentary overlay owe much to Godard.[13] *Rembrandt Laughing* points to a renewal of artistic sensibility, evident in *All the Vermeers in*

New York (1992), Jost's most accessible work, which won the Los Angeles Film Critics Award for best experimental film.

Unmistakably urban, *All the Vermeers in New York* imports the lyrical camera of Jost's essays and the violence inherent in his Westerns. Enjoying a bigger budget ($250,000), the film was made with support from PBS's *American Playhouse* and was shown on public stations around the country. For a while, it felt as if Jost would finally break out of his "ghetto," but that didn't happen.

A wistful, elegant meditation on art and finance in New York, *All the Vermeers* is a poignant fable about the instabilities of the 1980s and the discrepancy between art and spiritual decay. Capturing the dissolution of an era, the movie blends dreams and reality until they merge and glow with equal beauty. Jost's city dwellers seek solace, but Jost casts an ironic eye over their attempt to find refuge in art. Like all of his films, *All the Vermeers* explores the boundaries between narrative and experimental cinema. In telling a story of stockbrokers and actresses, painters and gallery owners, he presents a world that's both beautiful and decadent, calm on the surface but riddled with anxiety. Jost depicts the desire for visual beauty only to subvert it, showing how futile it is to try to escape the pain of the mundane in the transcendent beauty of art.

At the Metropolitan Museum, Mark (Stephen Lack), a middle-aged man, stares at a young woman posed in front of Jan Vermeer's "Portrait of a Young Woman." The young woman, who looks like the subject of the painting, is Anna (Emmanuelle Chaulet), an aspiring French actress who is seeking insight for a Chekhov play she's studying. Mark is so taken by her resemblance to the woman in Vermeer's portrait that he gives her a note with his phone number. Their first meeting in a coffee shop is strained, as Anna brings her roommate, Felicity, pretending she needs a translator. But later, they start seeing each other and become lovers. When Mark offers to help with her rent, Anna asks for $3,000—a metaphor for the greedy, transaction-minded 1980s. "Three thousand dollars to share that hole in the wall?" Mark says, but he gives her the money anyway.

The deceptively simple story conceals deeper, more intriguing themes. It's a meditation on the inner and outer worlds of two mismatched characters who represent the cultural bankruptcy of America's upper-middle class. Jost is not interested in plot; he wants to immerse the audience in the world of his self-absorbed characters, to make their lives meaningful, as he had done with the lives of the lower class in his previous movies.

A stressed-out Wall Street stockbroker with a passion for art, Mark frequents the Metropolitan to assuage his alienation. In the world of commerce, Mark uses the telephone as a weapon to achieve wealth and power, spending enormous time communicating in what Wall Street calls the cycle of "smile and dial, phone and groan." Mark seeks respite from stress by immersing himself in the serenity of Vermeer's art. The spirituality of the portrait is an antidote to his life: The calm retreat of Vermeer's gallery stands in direct opposition to the crassness and frenzy of his work.

The characters are deliberately archetypal, but the ironies are overt and the politics disturbing.[14] Felicity (Grace Phillips), Anna's wealthy roommate, who works at the Gracie Mansion Gallery, represents the Downtown bourgeois with solid trust funds and vaporous careers. She argues with her wealthy father about whether his investment in her is socially responsible. There's moral outrage when her father (played by former Judge Roger Ruffin) patronizingly dismisses her social concerns. Later in a comic interlude, a painter (Gordon Weiss) demands a huge advance from the gallery owner, Gracie Mansion, then knifes out a frame and walks off with one of his paintings.

A visual style of long tracking shots and disorienting cutting creates an intense mood. The scenes are soaked in absurd, tragic-comic desperation beneath the carefully composed surfaces. Jost invests the gallery and Anna's apartment with a look that suggests both affluence and sterility, grandeur and decay. *All the Vermeers* becomes increasingly mysterious in its exploration of the intricate relation between art and commerce, fiction and reality. The "artists"—painter, actress, opera singer—are selfish and greedy, and they are treated by Mark and the powered people like children. But Mark is also a child who wants to flee into art and hide in it to escape a disgusting world.

Mark's relationship with Anna combines aesthetic pleasure with emotional longing. Jost shows the deceptiveness of love, its tendency to misinterpret emptiness for mystery, silence for depth. To Mark, Anna's beauty signifies something transcendent, but in reality, she's a confused and callous woman.[15] The film also provides a meditation on the organization and meaning of space. Mark, a voyeur, stares at Anna, his object of desire. Anna, in turn, stares at Vermeer's painting. Then the painting stares back at her and back at the audience. The film's subjects become the objects viewed by the woman in Vermeer's painting.[16]

The film opens with an East Village scene, where Gracie Mansion is doing business with an artist who is demanding a cash advance to feed his junk habit and with a collector eager to fill out her collection. Every social interaction is a transaction measured by money. Jost contrasts the cash-fueled frenzy of the art world with the tranquility of Vermeer's room. The camera condemns the contemporary scene, while glorifying the environment of the Dutch masterpieces. Jost's romantic vision of the museum is expressed in Mark's idealization of the place. The richly paneled Metropolitan, with its imposing portico, smooth floors, and muted galleries, is contrasted with the harsh angles and white walls of East Village galleries.

The particular environments that define the characters are far more revealing than the dialogue. In a long tracking shot, the camera records bookshelves, where two books stand out: Tom Wolfe's *The Bonfire of the Vanities* and James Gleick's *Chaos: Making a New Science*, ubiquitous presences in 1980s upper-middle-class homes. The books link the narrative to the broader context of 1980s art markets: Nothing fuels art consumption like cash.

There's another significant context: The Dutch Empire collapsed in Vermeer's day as a result of speculation in the tulip market. The historical parallel with the 1987 stock market crash makes Jost's critique of the present more poignant. *All the Vermeers* underlines the tension between the greed of the 1980s financial markets and art's eternal, spiritual qualities.

The story proceeds to a strong conclusion, which crystallizes the emptiness of the central relationship. After a bad day in his office, Mark retreats to the Met, where he suffers a brain hemorrhage and ultimately dies. His last act is to call Anna and declare his love to her answering machine. Anna, about to return to France, goes back to the museum, where she finds Mark's body. She runs back to "their" Vermeer portrait, and the final shot dissolves her into the painting, uniting her and the woman in the portrait.[17]

The elegance of *All the Vermeers* suggested a new direction for Jost, a path he later chose not to follow. *Frameup* (1993), a tragic-comic road movie about losers traveling through the Northwest, is a reworking of a classic American genre. The two characters—Ricky Lee, a cocky ex-con, and Beth Ann, a ditzy waitress—are played by the husband-and-wife actors Nancy Carlin and Howard Swain. The couple come to a requisite bad end, but there is redemption. As Beth Ann puts it, "Death really isn't so bad; it's getting there that is." Jost combines elements of avant-garde, exploitation flicks, and pulp fiction, with specific allusions to *Bonnie and Clyde* and *Badlands*. Set against the gorgeous landscapes of the Northwest and the banal interiors of motel rooms, *Frameup* is imbued with intense undercurrent of eroticism.

Offbeat and disturbing, *The Bed You Sleep In* (released in 1993) is a visually striking film that eschews the pacing of mainstream movies. The style is deceptively quiet, closer to life's unforced flow, but in Jost's vision, the terror shoots right through the calm. At the center of *Sure Fire* (released in 1995) is a portrait of a uniquely American character—the aggressive, authoritarian salesman. It presents an unsparing look at an archetypal patriarch, a wheeler-dealer in Utah real estate. *Sure Fire* evokes the dark underside of American life with the resonance of a Eugene O'Neill play. Jost's minimalist technique creates a rich sense of place. Shot entirely on location, with a cast of local residents and only a few professionals, the film boasts an almost documentary authenticity.

In the mid-1990s, Jost moved to Rome, where his work has received greater respect and won easier funding from state television. Another motivation behind his expatriate status is his reluctance to pay taxes to the U.S. Government.

THE JIMMY STEWART FROM MARS—DAVID LYNCH

David Lynch may be the only independent filmmaker to bring an avant-garde sensibility to the commercial cinema. A home-grown surrealist, he has traveled the unlikely odyssey from the midnight circuit, where he achieved notoriety with *Eraserhead*, to art house celebrity with *Blue Velvet*, to a *Time* magazine cover during the run of his popular TV series *Twin Peaks*, to an almost inevitable decline in his most recent pictures.

A peculiar combination of perversity and frivolity informs Lynch's work, which can be described as a cinema of anguish, based on the notion of propriety gone awry. From the very beginning, viewers of a Lynch film expected to be shaken up, to be astonished by the tension, mood, and sensation in his work. This may be the reason why the adjective "Lynchian" has become a catchall phrase for every kind of cinematic deviation.

Like Jost, Lynch is dedicated to obsessive exploration of the violent essence of American life, but, unlike Jost, Lynch has the ability to transform scary nightmares into pleasurable sensations. Lynch folds Eagle Scout and Peter Pan qualities into his baroque cinema, blending stylistic excess and devious humor with a peculiar earnestness and innocence about the ways of the world. The Lynch touch is marked by painterly style, bizarre camera angles, offbeat composition, and odd rhythm, all refreshing devices after a decade of MTV hyperkineticism, glitzy imagery, and fast cutting.

Lynch's best films are coming-of-age stories, reflecting the sexual anxieties of a high school nerd. Kyle MacLachlan, who has appeared in several of Lynch's movies and TV series, is the ideal personification of Lynch's depraved fantasies. Lynch has shown concern with odd textures, severed body parts, bleeding orifices, and women's anatomy. His dread of women is reflected in his study of the model-actress (and former wife) Isabella Rossellini.[18]

Lynch's creativity manifests itself through a disconnected series of images and moods. "I believe that ideas come from outside us," he once said. "It's as if they are being broadcast in the air and we tune into them like our mind is a receiver."[19] Lynch's muse takes him beyond logic and beyond narrative, his art vents personal fantasies that, when placed at the service of general themes, become more resonant.

A provocateur, though not a poseur, Lynch is obsessed with stark images of decaying organic matter. His films suggest that nothing in life is fixed, that everything is relative. It's a matter of disorienting scale, of emphases out of kilter. The meaning of an object depends on whether it is seen in a long shot or in a close-up: Cockroaches examined at their own level are as big and menacing as jackals.

As a boy delivering newspapers, Lynch had a route that took him through back alleys, where he would sort through the garbage, hoping to find something exciting. Later, in art school, Lynch was intrigued by burning the skin off a mouse to study its inner parts. Lynch sees the world as a compost heap with something tumorous lurking beneath the surface. In his movies, the physical world is unstable, mutating, breaking apart. David Denby has labeled Lynch "the high priest of industrial detritus, for whom the perversion of the organic becomes a fact of life both feared and admired."[20]

Lynch was born in Montana in 1946 to "normal" parents. He lived a fairly uprooted childhood: His nature-loving father, who worked for the Department of Agriculture as a research scientist, moved the family from place to place. Lynch spent his adolescence in placid, all-American towns like Missoula and Spokane. "When I was little," he recalled, "there were picket fences, beautiful trees, real quiet dreamy afternoons, real good friends, lakes, camping trails, fires. I enjoyed all these things, but there was also something else under the surface."[21] That something was fear, a primordial sense of dread first felt when his mother took him to New York. "I always had one eye looking somewhere else," he recalled.

Consumed with an ambition to paint, Lynch attended Boston's School of the Museum of Fine Arts and Pennsylvania's Academy of Fine Arts. Inspired by *The Art Spirit*, a book written by the painter-educator Robert Henri, he dedicated himself to "Art Life": "In the 'Art Life,' you don't get married and you don't have families and you have studios and models and you drink a lot of coffee and you smoke cigarettes and you work mostly at night. You think beneath the surface of things and you live a fantastic life of ideas."[22]

Deep-seated anxieties goaded Lynch into art, growing out of his fear of big cities—first New York, then Philadelphia. Like the human ear that *Blue Velvet*'s hero finds in a littered field, a visit to a Philadelphia morgue impelled Lynch to go beneath the surface of things. "Getting invited to the morgue was a big deal, the turning point," he said. "Seeing a dead person was proof that something can happen."[23]

Lynch moved to Los Angeles in 1970 to attend the American Film Institute (AFI). At AFI, he made a short, *The Grandmother* (1971), about a lonely, abused boy who grows a loving grandmother from seed. The two are briefly happy, but then she dies, and, shortly after, he does, too. In 1972, Lynch began working on *Eraserhead*, a nightmarish vision of life on the weird fringes of the urban industrial wasteland. The movie took several years to make, but it was brought to the screen uncensored from Lynch's unconscious.

A recluse, Henry Spencer (played by the cult actor Jack Nance), lives in squalor, moving through a creepy, foreboding landscape. Henry's towering pompadour is the eeriest coiffure to be seen since Elsa Lanchester's in *Bride of Frankenstein* and Dean Stockwell's in *The Boy with Green Hair*. A spaced-out daydreamer, Henry fantasizes about having his head used as an eraser. He courts Mary X (Charlotte Stewart), a shy, traumatized girl who lives a cloistered existence with her obnoxious parents. After their marriage, Mary gives birth to a "baby," a hideous thing that seems to have no skin. Nature goes awry, and Mary goes on to give birth to a series of strange creatures. Domestic tranquility is short lived: Mother leaves her anguished husband alone with the creatures. While Henry drifts off into Lewis Carroll dreams of a theater behind his radiator, the baby cries hysterically. At first, Henry's dormant paternal instincts are stirred, but later, in a climax of unbearable intensity, he kills the first and most gruesome of his offspring.

In the final montage, Henry goes from committing infanticide on his mutant, horse-faced love-child to dancing with a white-haired woman who seems to have huge marshmallows implanted on her cheeks. He is decapitated for his crime, and his head is processed into eraser-topped pencils—the organic defeated by the inorganic, realizing his fantasy. Though infused with an atmosphere of intense isolation, Henry's odyssey is leavened with grim humor. Gross comedy dominates a dinner scene, where Henry watches his mother-in-law demolish a squab with orgasmic relish, while bloody mini-chickens writhe on the table.

A stream of subconsciousness packed with grotesque physical deformities and representing a quest for spiritual purity, *Eraserhead* is Lynch's most surreal work to date. Its brilliance depends on nonnarrative elements, particularly imagery: With slight adjustment in lighting, a steam radiator comes to look like the facade of the Metropolitan Opera. Alan Splet's weird, eerie sound and Fred Elmes's and Herbert Caldwell's dense black-and-white photography reinforce the claustrophobic ambience of the gloomy postindustrial landscape.

Eraserhead was greeted with revulsion when it appeared, but, as J. Hoberman noted, the film was so perversely and coherently articulated that it defied comparison to any other film.[24] Its surreal style and narrative ambiguity recalled the early work of Luis Buñuel (*Un Chien Andalou*) and Salvador Dali. A combination of black comedy (grotesquely deformed babies are not a subject for jokes), social satire, and special effects informed the film, which created a nightmare in which successive layers of reality seem to dissolve, with depressing metaphysical overtones. *Eraserhead* pushed the viewers to a terrifying apocalyptic vortex with effects that were amazing, considering the shoestring budget (a grant from AFI). Lynch shot the movie at night in old stables (part of AFI's headquarters), but the inspiration was Philadelphia, which he described as "the sleaziest, most corrupt, decadent, sick, fear-ridden, twisted city on the face of the earth."

First shown at Filmex 1977, *Eraserhead* was not widely seen until 1978, when it came to the attention of the entrepreneur Ben Barenholtz. Despite mixed to unfavorable reviews, it ran for years as a midnight attraction at Greenwich Village's Waverly Theatre. The movie's weirdness developed a cult following in other cities as well. "I wasn't thinking of a midnight audience when I made it," Lynch said, "It was a student film." Eventually, *Eraserhead* became one of the most successful American avant-garde films, establishing a precedent for other eccentric indies to be seen.

After *Eraserhead*, Lynch wrote the screenplay for *Ronnie Rocket*, a film about the adventures of a Candide-like scientist who may be an alien from outer space, but Lynch couldn't interest a producer in it. Mel Brooks, who had seen *Eraserhead*, came to the rescue with an offer for Lynch to direct a film about John Merrick, a man whose exterior was as hideous as his interior was beautiful. An elegy to freakishness, *The Elephant Man* was disguised as a Victorian morality play. Exhibited as a carnival freak, Merrick had an abnormally large, disfigured head, a twisted spine, and an otiose right arm, but his physical repulsiveness belied a gentle soul. Before dying in his sleep (of self-strangulation), he was lionized by Britain's high society.

Revisiting a terrain similar to that of *Eraserhead*, Lynch exposed undercurrents of metaphysical anguish and absurdist fear, along with an accessible tale of Merrick's nobility. Freddie Francis's forceful black-and-white cinematography accentuated a lyrical evocation of the sensitive soul of a physical monstrosity with another unflinching depiction of a grim industrial landscape. For Pauline Kael, *Elephant Man* had the power of a silent film, with wrenching, pulsating sounds (the hissing of steam suggesting the pounding of the new industrial age).[25]

Winning critical acclaim (and an Oscar nomination), Lynch became regarded in Hollywood as a "bankable commodity." For his next film, he chose *Dune*, a baroque tapestry based on Frank Herbert's sci-fi novel. With expectations as swollen as its budget, *Dune* became an expensive fiasco that might have wrecked his career, but Lynch used it as a learning experience. Realizing that Lynch's talents are better suited to making personal films, *Dune*'s producer, Dino De Laurentiis, promised to finance *Blue Velvet* on the condition that Lynch work on a modest $6 million budget. Exercising total artistic control, Lynch made what became the most-talked about film of the decade—and his most accomplished film.

In top form with a film that had touches of Kafka, Bosch, Buñuel, Capra, and Hitchcock, Lynch approached the material as if he were "reinventing movies." He described *Blue Velvet* as "The Hardy Boys Go to Hell,"[because the protagonist stumbles upon an array of social ills—child abduction, drug wars, voyeurism, sexual abuse, corruption—and develops a compulsive need to find truth in a world devoid of meaningful values.]

A coming-of-age tale, *Blue Velvet* centers on Jeffrey Beaumont (Kyle MacLachlan), a student as earnest and innocent as a Hardy Boy. Jeffrey is forced to return to Lumberton, his home town, when his father, a proprietor of the local hardware store, is felled by a cerebral hemorrhage. Returning from a hospital visit, Jeffrey chances upon a severed, ant-infested human ear in the fields. The tantalizing ear resembles a seashell; when the camera enters its dark aperture, it reveals a rare view of the crevices around the hole. Jeffrey launches an investigation that leads him beneath Lumberton's placid surface into an underworld of sleazy drug dealers and corrupt cops.

Jeffrey is assisted by Sandy (Laura Dern), a high school senior whose detective father is also investigating the mystery. As a comic-book character, Sandy is the wholesome "Betty" to Jeffrey's morally ambiguous "Archie." Jeffrey's sleuthing leads him to Dorothy Vallens (Isabella Rossellini), a nightclub chanteuse and the sexual slave of Frank Booth (Dennis Hopper), who has kidnapped her son and her husband and cut off the latter's ear.

The film's title, taken from a popular 1960s song by the crooner Bobby Vinton that was played in school proms, befits the setting. Lynch's Lumberton is a sleepy town—Anytown, U.S.A.—where the local radio station, WOOD, marks the beginning of the hour with the sound of falling timber—Lumbertonians know "how much wood a wood-chuck chucks." In a brilliant opening sequence, the camera pans slowly across whiter-than-white picket fences and red roses, framed against indigo blue skies and chirping birds. Clean-uniformed policemen smile as they help children cross the street safely. A bright red fire engine, with its smiling firemen, moves slowly down the street. The sequence has a dreamy, surrealistic quality, with yellow tulips swaying in a warm afternoon breeze. The camera suddenly cuts to the ground level of grass, and ominous sounds well up as black insects crawl in the darkness. This powerful image sets the film's tone, announcing the duality of beautiful surfaces and horrible things beneath.

Dressed in khaki trousers, canvas shoes, and straw hat, Mr. Beaumont is watering his grass with a hose. At the same time, Mrs. Beaumont is curled up on the couch, smoking a cigarette and enjoying her daytime soaps. Suddenly, Mr. Beaumont is hit with a seizure and falls to the ground—the abrupt eruption of violence in this peaceful setting underlines the precariousness of human life.

Jeffrey lives in a mythic present that feels like the past. Although the setting is contemporary, Lynch fills every frame with signifiers—household furnishings, cars, and even sounds—that evoke the past forty years of American pop culture. Blending the real and the surreal, Lynch merges melodrama, comedy, and noir with both naiveté and pulp kinkiness. Indeed, viewers had no idea whether the film was supposed to be funny or malignant, naive or knowing, emphatic or inhuman. The answer, of course, is all of the above.

Lynch's hypnotic style is achieved not by means of gliding camera or sharp editing but with painterly vision and composition. So disquieting and artfully composed are Lynch's images that when Jeffrey discovers two corpses, one still standing, the other bound to a chair, the vision is arresting in the manner of Duane Hanson's or Edward Kienholz's lifelike figural sculptures. Sensuous details blend with a painterly, neo-Gothic style of the bizarre. Almost everything is the opposite of what it seems: Neat, placid surfaces cloak macabre reality, and the outwardly horrible is ultimately the most benign. Malignant impulses fester deep within people and things. Lynch creates a hallucinatory atmosphere, unfolding the story with the logic of a nightmare. The surreal texture gives audiences pause, wondering where the dream ends and the temporal world begins.

Sneaking into Dorothy's apartment, Jeffrey finds an empty child's room. He observes with fascination how she undresses, slips into a blue velvet robe, and begins to entertain Frank. An obscenity-spouting, drug-warped sadomasochist, Frank brutalizes Dorothy in "games" of sexual bondage, then calls her "mommy" in a pathetic whine. Dennis Hopper's disturbing performance catapults his sleazy drug kingpin into one of the cinema's most repulsive psychos. Later, caught watching, Jeffrey is commanded by Dorothy, "Get undressed, I want to see *you*." She pulls his underpants down to his knees, holding a knife to his genitals. Rarely in American films does a woman command a man to undress. Here, in an unusual role reversal, Dorothy gazes intensely at Jeffrey's penis. Initially, Jeffrey's naiveté is juxtaposed with Frank's raw sexuality. But later, when Dorothy asks Jeffrey to strike her as a prelude to lovemaking, he complies, realizing he is not altogether unlike his nemesis.

[Unlike most small-town films, in which the attitude toward sex is hygienic or hypocritical, *Blue Velvet* depicts sex as an act of risk and adventurism. Huge flames and roaring sounds highlight the lovemaking; the linking of desire and fire is a recurrent motif in Lynch's work. The] rites of passage in this coming-of-age film go way beyond Norman and Allison's innocent kiss in *Peyton Place*. In *Blue Velvet*, sexual initiation is intense, carried out by a mature, uninhibited woman in scenes that contain the most eroticized energy ever displayed in American film.

When Jeffrey decides to spy on Dorothy, he tells Sandy, "There are opportunities in life for gaining knowledge and experience, and in some cases it's necessary to take a risk." The world is seen from an adolescent point of view, underlining the allure of the unknown and the horror when it is encountered. "I'm seeing something that was always hidden," Jeffrey says, acknowledging the dark side of his personality.

Throughout, moral and visual ambiguity prevail. Despite a clean, wholesome look, Jeffrey has the curiosity and the urge for danger. Early on at the college dance, hiding behind a furnace, he watches a student trying to rape his girlfriend. Jeffrey waits before intervening—voyeurism offers its own pleasure. Visually, too, the imagery is ambiguous: When a robin arrives on the kitchen window, it has an insect in its beak.

Sandy recounts a dream in which the world is dark, with no robins, but, all of a sudden, thousands of robins fly down and bring the blinding light of love. The narrative reaffirms that "love is the only thing that would make any difference, but until the robins come, there is trouble." Lynch has said that "finding love in hell may be a theme in all my movies."

Since the narrative deals with subconscious fantasies that are considered perverse in mainstream culture, the film's coda shifts from the subconscious to the conscious, suggesting a tentative return to a normal, ordinary life. In the last scene, Dorothy is seen with her son, but, in Lynch's universe, the restoration of order and legitimate motherhood are at best precarious.

Inspired by Barry Gifford's novel, Lynch's next movie, *Wild at Heart* (1990), is a paean to *The Wizard of Oz*, with a romantic couple, Lula Pace Fortune (Laura Dern) and Sailor Ripley (Nicolas Cage), taking their own Yellow Brick Road in search of the Wizard. Ripley has just served twenty-two months and eighteen days in prison for manslaughter committed in self-defense. Driving from Cape Fear, North Carolina, to the end of the line in Big Tuna, Texas, the couple are followed by Marietta (Diane Ladd), Lula's monstrous mother. Fearing Sailor's knowledge of her plot to murder her husband, Marietta mobilizes "black angel" Bobby Peru (Willem Dafoe) and Perdita Durango (Isabella Rossellini) to track him down.

In outline, *Wild at Heart* recalls *Badlands*, though it lacks Terrence Malick's detached irony. Lynch took a slim work and pumped it up into a pop epic. The dopey Lula and Sailor realize their destiny through intense lovemaking, smoking Kools and Camels, eating burgers, and drinking beer. Sailor likes to kick-box in crowded discos to loud guitar music, pick fights (he smashes a man's skull with his bare hands), and then take the mike and croon Elvis songs to his girl. Once they land in Big Tuna and Lula gets pregnant, the film changes gears. In the motel, Lula is in bed, listening to classic music on the radio, while Sailor commits a bank robbery that will send him back to jail. In the film's scariest scene, shown in menacing close-up, Bobby Peru invades Lula's room and insists that she say, "Please, fuck me."

Flashbacks reveal Lula's incestuous Uncle Pooch and Cousin Dell, a man so obsessed with Christmas that he wears a soiled Kris Kringle suit and counts the days all year round. Mother and daughter temporarily unite, though at the end (five years, two months, and twenty-one days later), Lula defies her mother and goes with their son to greet Sailor.

The point of reference is *The Wizard of Oz*: Marietta is the Wicked Witch, and, at the end, the Good Witch Glinda floats down on a large soap bubble to tell Sailor, "Lula loves you, don't turn away from love." Sailor goes back and sings Elvis Presley's "Love Me Tender" as the end credits roll down. Unlike *Blue Velvet*, the bizarre inventions in *Wild at Heart* become ends in themselves. Not much is made of a fleeting image of a severed head or a solemn look at a toilet bowl. The shocks have little resonance, and the weirdness is trivial: Cousin Dell walks around with cockroaches in his underpants. Once again, fire is the dominant metaphor: In the opening credits, a kitchen match is struck, and the screen erupts into intense flames with the roar of a blast furnace.

The picture's hyperkinetic wildness is mostly on the surface; the images are elaborately conceived but meaningless. The script, basically a series of vignettes, needs more dramatic tension. Lynch infuses the story with menace, but he can't escape the lurid nature of the material. Lynch stylizes Sailor's and Lula's innocence, but their dreams are so infantile that viewers respond with condescension. In this film, all the characters, not just the villains, are schematically constructed as cartoons.

In 1990, Lynch ventured into TV with *Twin Peaks*, a variation on the *Blue Velvet* texture. His foray into television was unique, uniting viewers into an eccentric community that replicated the community onscreen. After making a disappointing prequel feature to *Twin Peaks*, *Fire Walk with Me* (1992), Lynch was back in form with *Lost Highway* (1997).

The movie begins promisingly, when a young married couple, Fred (Bill Pullman) and Renee (Patricia Arquette), become paranoid about intrusions into their privacy, which they learn about through videos sent to their home. Renee is murdered, and Fred goes to jail for the crime. The film then takes up a new set of heroes, Pete (Balthazar Getty), a gas attendant, who dumps his girlfriend and takes up with a gangster (Robert Loggia) and his moll (also played by Arquette).

The narrative takes one character to the end of the line, then sets another one on a parallel track. Fred gets a second chance—a new identity as Pete—that noir heroes never get, but it's not clear whether it's the same man.[26] The requisite Lynch scare show is embodied in the spooky presence of Robert Blake (with white face, shaved eyebrows and sickly smile, like the dwarf in *Twin Peaks*). A mystery figure guiding the characters toward their destinies, he is the director's creation, a manipulator who navigates the film in an arbitrary manner.

An enigmatic thriller with complex formal strategies and intriguing metaphors, *Lost Highway* lacks a potent narrative. Noir's perennial issues of paranoia and fatalism are peppered here with touches of the fantastic. As always, Lynch's technical mastery is impressive: The images and editing rhythms are alarming, but they bear little meaning because they are not conceived in the coherent spirit of *Blue Velvet*.[27]

Described by Lynch as "a twenty-first-century noir horror," *Lost Highway* makes many references to classic noir. But, for all the sordid sex and vengeance, the self-reflexive narrative feels tidy and hermetic, an elegant exercise that blends supernatural and noir elements. As long as Lynch's journeys have the visual audacity of *Eraserhead* or the playfulness of *Blue Velvet*, they are satisfying. As Richard Corliss observed, if *Lost Highway* had preceded *Wild at Heart*, it might have had some novelty, but the turf, with its obsessions and grotesqueries, has become familiar and lacks menace.[28] Lynch is the poet laureate of harebrained Americana, but his work is not shocking anymore; his motifs have been exploited in nightclubs and gift shops across the country.

Lynch has always been more interesting when placing issues of order within a framework of deviance. In his recent work, however, he has strayed into bizarreness for its own sake, making movies that burst into climactic sensations without first establishing engaging narrative premises. Too bad, the American cinema needs a visionary filmmaker like Lynch.

THE POPE OF TRASH—JOHN WATERS

John Waters became a cult figure in the early 1970s, when he began making films of dubious taste or, to use his own words, "exploitation films for the art house." An auteur of outrage, Waters has directed shockingly modern satires with garish characters and grotesque imagery. William Burroughs, godfather of the Beat era, once labeled him "the Pope of Trash," and the novelist Bret Easton Ellis described his work as "demented but endearing."

Waters's tackling of taboo issues makes him more than a priest of trash culture. He has populated his films with people whose appearance and demeanor are deviant and abnormal: "My films are about people who take what society thinks is a disadvantage, exaggerating their supposed defect and turning it into a winning style."[29] Along with gross-out moments, Waters's films are imbued with irony, which for him is "the best kind of humor." Subverting conventional plots, Waters's movies are designed to outrage viewers, building on his belief that "the fantastic is beyond the realm of observable reality." Waters's goal is achieved by employing conventions that mainstream movies have prepared audiences *not* to expect.

Acknowledged as a renegade independent, Waters has survived for three decades, despite changes in the country's political and cultural climate. "Even if you hate my films," he said in 1994, "you have to at least say I've created my own genre."[30] It may be hard to define precisely what that genre is, but it's distinctive enough for him to be identified with it. Waters's work is better appreciated and enjoyed by viewers who know movies and pop culture well enough to experience a new perspective on them—making intertextual references is the name of the game.

Like David Lynch and the Coen brothers, Waters is not really a subversive filmmaker, because he shares most of the bourgeois values he satirizes. And, unlike the Jewish comic and filmmaker Albert Brooks, Waters is not an enraged comic, because deep down he wishes life were as simple as it seems to be in *Leave It to Beaver*.

Although Waters has not achieved the mainstream success of Barry Levinson, Baltimore's other native son, Baltimore's mayor proclaimed February 7, 1985, "John Waters Day."[31] Waters has stayed in Baltimore for practical reasons: "I have a whole crew there, and we know the city better than anywhere else." Indeed, with a few additions, Waters has repeatedly worked with the same crew. Pat Moran supervises the casting, Vincent Perenio the sets, and Van Smith the costumes, which gives Waters a sense of security and continuity. Waters had also formed an acting ensemble, holding that audiences like to see the same actors go from one film to another. Mink Stole has been in all of his films, and Divine, too, until he died in 1989. Another reason for staying in Baltimore is that it's the only place where he has friends who aren't involved in showbiz, "who aren't always talking about movies, and who aren't trendy."

Enchanted with show business since childhood, Waters staged puppet shows at the age of seven; by thirteen, he was an avid *Variety* reader. While in high school, Waters was in a "beatnik" phase, a tough act to pull off in suburban Baltimore. "My parents didn't know what to do," he recalled. "They dropped me off at this beatnik bar and hoped I'd meet some nice people." But when his mother took a look at the place she said, "Is this camp or just the slums?"[32]

Raised in a comfortable Catholic family, Waters schooled himself in marginal cinema at the local XXX houses and made some 8mm exploitation shorts (*Hag in a Black Leather Jacket, Eat Your Makeup*). He circumvented film school to write and direct *Mondo Trasho* and *Multiple Maniacs*, crude movies, shot in 16mm and in black and white, which introduced the "offensive" satire mode that would become his specialty. Waters burst to prominence in 1972 with *Pink Flamingos*, a bad-taste classic, which contained what would become the most (in)famous scene of his movies: Divine stooping to eat dog excrement. In the same movie, viewers were exposed to the spectacle of an "Egg Lady" begging for poultry from her crib and to the rape and murder of a chicken.

Pink Flamingos featured Divine, a flamboyant, 300-pound transvestite whom Waters cultivated as his favorite star, and who was in reality a former high school friend named Harris Glenn Milstead. Divine began his career as a joke on drag queens, mocking their desire to be pretty. There was always anger in Divine, but not hostility. "Divine was hassled a lot," Waters said. "I'm proud that I gave him an outlet for his anger and revenge. The people that used to beat him up later stood in line and asked for autographs."

Giving middle-class audiences a good shake-up, *Pink Flamingos* also had an effect on punk culture with its royal-blue hairdos and half-shaved heads. As a $10,000 effort about "the filthiest person alive," *Pink Flamingos* gained national distribution and a following on the art house circuit. Cherished by midnight moviegoers, it ran for years in New York and Los Angeles.

In a dismissive review, *Variety* described the film as "one of the most vile, stupid and repulsive films ever made." Instead of being offended, Waters took the review as a compliment, adding that *Pink Flamingos* was vile, as *Variety* had said, but "joyously vile." Negative reviews didn't faze Waters, because "there was a cultural war going on; it was them versus us." He knew that critics who panned his work simply didn't get him. It's always been that way: "You just get it or you don't, there's not much in the middle."[33] Waters's reputation for excess enthralled the cognoscenti, but not studio executives; "*Pink Flamingos* is still the movie that gets me in the door, and then thrown out the door," Waters said. He lost years of work in failed attempts to make a sequel to *Pink Flamingos*.

His next features, *Female Trouble* (1974) and *Desperate Living* (1977), reinforced Waters's outlaw reputation with their satiric skewering of middle-class values and their shattering of the suburban status quo. *Female Trouble* spotlighted Divine in a dual role, as a headline-seeking criminal named Dawn Davenport and as her illicit welder-lover, Earl Pertson. After seeing *Female Trouble*, the critic Rex Reed is reported to have groaned: "Where do these people come from? Where do they go when the sun goes down?"

Billed as "a lesbian melodrama about revolution," *Desperate Living* was also disliked by mainstream critics. Janet Maslin described it as "a pointlessly ugly movie that found high humor among low life."[34] Waters pointedly ridiculed bourgeois manners; the credit sequence featured a dead rat served on fine china at a fancily set dinner table. But, later, he himself conceded that the problem with *Desperate Living* was that "everyone was insane and there was nobody for the audience to identify with." Waters always knew that his humor was funnier when situated in context, when Divine was placed next to a straight person.

Polyester (1981), which followed, was not quite as foul as Waters's previous movies. Nonetheless, it was notable for casting the faded movie star Tab Hunter and for introducing a gimmick, a set of scratch-and-sniff cards called Odorama, which contained a range of stimuli matching the sensations experienced by Divine's housewife. Waters flirted with the mainstream with *Hairspray* (1988), his first film in seven years and, by his admission, one of the few of his obsessions that was "palatable" to any studio. He altered his style with a musical comedy that gathered faded stars and offbeat celebrities for campy pursuits. Rated PG, the film was suitable family fare, despite the weird hairdos. The lavish $2.6 million budget for *Hairspray* brought about major changes: It allowed for cappuccino in the editing room, it meant Waters didn't have to pick up the cast in the morning, and when it rained the cast got ponchos.

Based on an essay that appeared in one of Waters's books, *Hairspray* dissects the arrival of racial integration in 1960s Baltimore through a local dance program, "The Corny Collins Show." In the surprisingly sweet-tempered spoof, Ricki Lake plays Tracy Turnblad, a chubby teen who rockets to stardom as the new queen of a TV dance show. In addition to Divine, who plays two roles (Tracy's mom and a nasty male TV station owner) the film featured Sonny Bono, then the mayor of Palm Springs, and the pop star Debbie Harry.

Hairspray was more than a nostalgic romp filled with ratted hairdos and goofy hits. Its key subplot reveals Waters's obsession with the incendiary politics of style. When Tracy is radicalized by the dance's all-white policy, she doesn't join the Weathermen; she starts ironing her hair. "When the straight-hair fashion first hit our neighborhood, it caused panic," Waters recalled. The film is based on his experiences watching and occasionally appearing on "The Buddy Deane Show."

"Your whole values changed: Hair was politics. If you had ironed hair, you became a hippie. And if you kept your teased hair, you got married at twenty and had four kids."[35]

Cry Baby (1990) was an equally sweet-natured yarn of teen rebels and distraught parents. Set in Baltimore in 1954, it's about a good girl (Amy Locane) torn between her pristine roots and a black-leathered Elvis-type hunk (Johnny Depp). More polished than *Hairspray* but less focused or funny, *Cry Baby* failed despite charming performances from its cast.

After making a movie about every decade he has lived in, Waters wanted to get back to contemporary humor with a story that took place in the "real" world. The result was *Serial Mom* (1994), an accessible satire of suburban Baltimore. Waters built into *Serial Mom* the affection audiences felt for TV shows like *Leave It to Beaver* and *Ozzie and Harriet*, encouraging viewers to fantasize what the shows' characters might really be like. The movie is as much a satire of TV sitcoms as an ode to them. Juxtaposing bloody murders with Beaver backgrounds, it reflected a compromise between the early gross-outs and a new, cleaner look. In courting mainstream audiences, which had worked in *Hairspray* but failed in *Cry Baby*, Waters softened his jabs, playing it too safe.

Beverly Sutphin (Kathleen Turner), a middle-class housewife fiercely devoted to her family, is a Supermom in the mold of June Cleaver and Margaret Anderson. Thriving at her chores, she cooks meatloaf, keeps the house spic and span, and goes to PTA meetings. Happily married to a meek dentist (Sam Waterston), she is ultrasensitive to her children's growing pains. Misty (Ricki Lake) is in college, but she is more interested in boys than in studies. Her brother, Chip (Matthew Lillard), a high school senior, works at a local video store, where he cultivates an insatiable appetite for horror flicks—the kind Waters adores. Beverly can't tolerate any criticism of her family. When a teacher recommends therapy for her son, when her daughter is stood up by a beau, when a neighbor is not recycling, she takes the kind of action that's more cleaver than Beaver.

Serial Mom is not as dark or macabre as the deliciously nasty *Parents* (1989), Bob Balaban's horror comedy set in the 1950s, in which Randy Quaid and Mary Beth Hurt play conformist parents with only one flaw: cannibalism. With his move toward the mainstream, Waters began to lose the subversive sensibility that had marked his underground films. As he revealingly disclosed: "In the old days, I wanted to make people nervous about what they were laughing at. In *Serial Mom*, there's a stream of good hearty laughs, but the nervousness is missing from the humor." The least original sequences deal with the media coverage of Beverly's trial and how the family exploits the case via agents, book rights, and TV movies.

Serial Mom reflects a compromise between the outrageousness of Waters's early work and the lighter tone of his later films. With more of an edge than *Hairspray* or *Cry Baby*, *Serial Mom* was seen by Waters as a return to the R-rated territory of his earlier work, with humor that's filtered through the showcase of a big-budget Hollywood movie. For Waters, this was a highly subversive act, because *Serial Mom* was booked into neighborhoods that never let his movies in before.

For the first time in his career, Waters worked with a star of the caliber of Kathleen Turner, who played her role with gusto. Waters wanted people to like Turner and to see her as a heroine, not a villain, to the point where they wouldn't mind how many she killed. Most critics, however, thought Waters showed too much restraint, perhaps *because* of the higher budget and the presence of a major star.

Waters latest film, *Pecker* (1998), is a pleasant but ephemeral tale of a working-class teenager who becomes a celeb photographer despite himself. Shot on Waters's home turf, Baltimore, this amiable satire doesn't have much to say about the culture of celebrity, nor is it biting in the manner of Waters's previous efforts. With the exception of a few shots of rats having sex—a motif in Waters's work—*Pecker* is more in the vein of the nostalgic *Hairspray* and *Cry Baby* than that of the black comedy *Serial Mom*. In fact, if *Pecker* had been made a decade ago, it would have starred Johnny Depp (who starred in *Cry Baby*), a better choice for the hero than Edward Furlong, who played the part. Lagging behind the zeitgeist in terms of what the public already knows about the vagaries of fame, *Pecker* induces some smiles but is utterly forgettable.

Furlong plays Pecker, so named for his childhood habit of "pecking" at his food. A congenial adolescent, Pecker works in a sandwich shop, where he cultivates his hobby, snapping photographs of his customers and family. Congruent with the abundance of dysfunctional families on the American screen, Pecker's family is labeled "culturally challenged" in the text: His mom (Mary Kay Place) dispenses fashion tips to the homeless clientele at her thrift shop; his sister Tina (Martha Plimpton) hires go-go boys to dance at the local club, the Fudge Palace; his younger sister, Little Chrissey (Lauren Hulsey) suffers from an eating disorder; and his grandmother, Memama (Jean Schertler), Baltimore's "pit beef" queen, engages in religious prayers with her talking statue of Mary.

Pecker stumbles into fame when his work is "discovered" by Rorey Wheeler (Lili Taylor), a savvy New York art dealer who becomes smitten with him. Never mind that his photographs are amateurish, grainy, and out of focus; they strike a chord with New York's artsy crowd, and soon there is a public exhibit and instant fame. However, Pecker has to learn the hard way the price for sudden stardom and over exposure. Turning into a sensation threatens to destroy the low-key lifestyle that served as his inspiration in the first place. Pecker's new status means that his buddy Matt (Brendan Sexton III) can't continue to artfully shoplift and that his sweetheart, Shelley (Christina Ricci), who runs a laundromat, becomes distressed when the press label her a "stain goddess," mistaking her good-natured "pin-up" poses for pornographic come-ons.

Waters tries to energize *Pecker* as a witty send-up of the contrast between Baltimore's blue-collar milieu and the New York art world, though he sentimentalizes his working-class characters and encourages the viewers to feel superior to them. Since the narrative is slight, Waters surrounds Pecker with a gallery of eccentric characters, played by actual celebs—a staple of Waters's work. The former beauty queen Bess Armstrong plays Dr. Klompus, Patricia Hearst, a newspaper heiress who gained notoriety in the 1970s when she was kidnapped and later joined her kidnappers in committing a bank robbery, is a society lady, and a Waters regular, Mink Stole, appears as the precinct captain.

Waters's identity has always thrived on exaggeration, on a wish for his life to be "torn from the headlines"; he considers the *National Enquirer* "the ultimate barometer of fame in America." Waters's protagonists share his fondness for gaudy and lurid events. His fascination with crime and courtroom trials has to do with the fact that when you do something horrible, you can't change it. "I think it's a matter of things being forbidden," he has said. "That's part of the glory of being raised a Catholic. It makes you more theatrical, and the sex is always better 'cause it's dirty."[36] Waters's moonlighting as a prison lecturer is also an outgrowth of his attraction to the forbidden.

Throughout his three-decade career, Waters has had to walk a fine line. As he has said, "I'm certainly not going to make a Hollywood movie that will never be shown, but at the same time I don't calculate,

I write what I think is funny, I don't censor myself." Waters is not willing to make a mainstream film without the black comedy, because it would reflect someone else's obsessions, not his. His agents don't even send him scripts, because they know he will direct only his own material.

Waters's grotesque films go so far into the bizarre that they become endearing: "I'm never just trying to gross you out—not even at the end of *Pink Flamingos*—I'm trying to make you laugh first." While they make no overt political statements, Waters's films are not devoid of ideas: "I always have something to say, but I never get on a soapbox. The only way I can change how anybody thinks is to make them laugh. If I start preaching, they'll walk out." Hence, *Serial Mom* affirms that Americans enjoy serial killers, without being judgmental about it.[37]

Waters always knew his movies had to make some money so that he could continue directing. "I had to pay back the people who loaned me money, and eventually I would ask them again. There's always that pressure." Living from picture to picture, with wide intervals between them, Waters is not the kind of director with a three-picture deals. Over the years, he has learned how to play the game, how to get through the system. The changing demographics have been in his favor: "People my age who are now running the studios saw my films in college, so it isn't really something I have to battle."

In the 1990s, Waters's work has become more polished, reflecting the difference between a movie that cost $10,000 and one costing $13 million (*Serial Mom*). Working with higher budgets and bigger stars, Waters doesn't consider himself a cult director anymore. He hasn't had a movie playing the midnight circuit since *Pink Flamingos*; in any event, the real midnight market has disappeared.

One of Waters's idiosyncrasies is his penchant for peculiar casting. He chooses actors who don't ordinarily work together, such as Suzanne Sommers and Sam Waterston in *Serial Mom*. He also likes to use personalities who aren't associated with film, like Patty Hearst, who is in both *Serial Mom* and *Pecker*—"We're at the point where kids don't even know she was kidnapped." Ricki Lake has appeared in three of Waters's pictures; her first was Divine's last. The scene in *Hairspray*, when Lake and Divine come out of a beauty parlor, was highly symbolic to him, the passing of the torch from one generation to the next.

In his earlier pictures, Waters satirized Hollywood's ideals of glamour and liberals' ideals of hipness—the limits in taste. In his later pictures, he satirized the all-American institutions of suburbia and nuclear family. But there are different kinds of suburbia in his work: "*Polyester* was plastic-covered—homage to bad taste, but *Serial Mom* is not in obvious bad taste." The latter was filmed in his old neighborhood; Waters said that while he didn't want to live in it, he wasn't against it. Revisiting suburbia, Waters finds a certain irony in the fact that its denizens like his movies. Their parents may have hated him, but the generation that chased him out doesn't live there anymore.

Although some of the grotesqueries prevail, there's a new tenderness in Waters's latest movies, making them more cuddly than cutting. Middle age has not been very kind for Waters, who seems to have lost his audacity in tackling taboo issues and bizarrely moved toward gentler, kinder movies. Time has diluted the extremities of his work. Waters represents an underground phenomenon coopted into the mainstream, a shocking career gradually rendered palatable. Waters himself has acknowledged that the golden age of trash is over, because there are no more taboos.

BRIDGING THE PERSONAL AND
THE POLITICAL—JOHN SAYLES

For the past two decades, John Sayles has been the uncrowned father of the new independent cinema. Thematically unpredictable, Sayles has cut an impressive path for himself apart from both mainstream Hollywood and the indie world. Writing, directing, and editing his movies has enabled him to exercise assertive control over his work, whose best qualities are balance and restraint.

Sayles's diverse output is unified by a distinctly American dilemma: the tension between personal life and social responsibility, or self-interest versus collective interest. In all of his movies, individuals are asked to take responsibility for their actions, an outgrowth of Sayles's belief that people have to sweat for their pleasures as much as master their pain. "My main interest is making films about people," Sayles has said. "I'm not interested in cinematic art." Sayles has also explored the human dimensions of myth making: the "Black Sox" World Series scandal in *Eight Men Out*, the coal mine labor violence in *Matewan*, the mysterious link between children and animals in *The Secret of Roan Inish*.

An unabashedly left-wing director, Sayles has championed blue-collar causes with acute conscience and rueful humor. Interestingly, his countercultural crusades into the world of losers and underdogs were made during the height of the Reagan-Bush years, thus defying the zeitgeist. He may be the prime proponent of the work ethic in American movies, with themes of racial antagonism and intergenerational strife permeating his oeuvre.

Like John Waters, Sayles has been influenced by Catholicism in terms of storytelling. As he explained: "Raised Catholic, you're born with original sin. You haven't done anything and you are already guilty."[38] Since the first tales Sayles heard as a child were sermons, he has been motivated as a filmmaker to seek out "stories that have a moral content to them." Focusing on large communities rather than individuals, Sayles's narratives consist of a wealth of personal stories interwoven around a thin thematic thread. He walks a high moral ground and takes a realistic point of view without relying on standard plots. All of his films are rooted in character studies and social observations, but they are not Freudian or psychologistic in any way.

Sayles has tackled "big" issues (a labor strike, a baseball strike, urban life), but he has been more effective in his intimate work (the disillusionment of a group of friends, the complex relationship between two women). David Denby has observed that when Sayles works on a large scale, he avoids the dramatic conventions of suspense and conflict and winds up undramatizing, taking the raw life out of his subjects. Indeed, *Matewan* and *Eight Men Out* left viewers with the feeling that their targets were predictable and their dramas predetermined. But when Sayles works small, as in *Passion Fish*, he discovers, deepens, and enlarges.[39]

More than anything else, Sayles's is the cinema of outsiders, and it's his work that justifies the title of this book. Each of Sayles's films has paid tribute to an underrepresented and disenfranchised element in American society:

A group of politically disenchanted friends in *Return of the Secaucus Seven*.
A lesbian in *Lianna*.
An interracial couple in *Baby, It's You*.
A mute African American in *Brother From Another Planet*.
Striking coal miners in *Matewan*.

Gullible baseball players who sell out in *Eight Men Out*.
Working-class city dwellers in *City of Hope*.
A handicapped TV star and an unfit mother in *Passion Fish*.
An isolated Irish girl in *The Secret of Roan Inish*.
A community of disenfranchised Mexican Americans in *Lone Star*.
A liberal doctor in a dictatorial country in *Men with Guns*.

Like Cassavetes, Sayles displays a vision that is singular and icon-oclastic, favoring everyday life and ordinary people. Also like Cas-savetes, Sayles loves performers—even in small roles, his actors shine—though acting in his films is less self-indulgent than it is in Cassavetes's work. Following Cassavetes's model, Sayles has built an impressive repertory company that includes Joe Morton, Chris Cooper, Vincent Spano, David Strathairn—and sometimes himself. However, unlike Cassavetes, Sayles uses large ensembles, and his characters are more in-telligent and complex. His pictures are less emotionally draining than those of Cassavetes, and they benefit from sharp dialogue and clear dramatic structure.[40]

Born in Schenectady, New York, in 1950, Sayles studied psychology at Williams College. After appearing in school plays and summer stock, he embarked on a writing career while supporting himself as a day la-borer and meat packer. In the late 1970s, Sayles joined the Roger Cor-man stable, penning *Piranha*, *The Lady in Red*, and *Battle beyond the Stars*. He never wanted to be a writer for hire; his role model was John Hus-ton, who wrote his way into becoming a director. "I never succeeded in writing my way into being a director," he told *Premiere*, "But I made enough money so that I could take the Stanley Kubrick route and make *Return of the Secaucus Seven* with a bunch of people from my old sum-mer-stock company and my own money."[41]

For Sayles, raising money is like hitchhiking: "It could be the first ride; it could be the thousandth. But you gotta stay out there with your thumb out and just wait." Equally important is to know when *not* to get into the car, "because you might make the movie, but it's not going to be the movie you wanted to make and you're going to be miserable."[42]

After a bad experience at Paramount with *Baby, It's You*, Sayles took pains to maintain his autonomy. Most of the money for his films comes from what he earns as a writer on studio pictures (e.g., rewrites like *Apollo 13*) and from his own pocket. Working on *Apollo 13*, Sayles was "amazed" by how many people its director, Ron Howard, had to listen to. It was the first time he observed actors (including Tom Hanks) batting ideas back and forth as they read a scene. This would never have happened on his set.

Though prominent and respected, Sayles has never become a "hot" director like Soderbergh or Tarantino, perhaps because of the sedate nature of his movies and their lack of visual flair. To a certain extent, Pauline Kael's early observation—"John Sayles has many gifts, but not a film sense. He doesn't gain anything as an artist by using film"—still holds true. The absence of visual distinction gives the feeling that Sayles's films are basically photographed scripts.

Despite their neatly placed humor and irony, Sayles's films often suffer from schematic construction. It may be a result of the way he writes, always beginning with a "tight structure" and then filling things in. As he described it: "Each character has a progression. They start with something they need or want at the beginning of the movie, and by the end they've either gotten it or not, or learned something that they didn't know before."[43]

In his first decade, Sayles seemed relatively uninterested in the formal properties of cinema, but the 1990s have brought greater technical assurance. An eager learner, Sayles has improved as a filmmaker. Still, his refusal to employ a personal style results in the lack of visual signature or a distinctive Sayles trademark. Sayles contends that he is not going to go out of his way "to be shocking to get people's attention," because he's not that much of a "yellow journalist." He thinks style interferes with the complexity of his stories; he's interested in style only insofar as it serves the story. Sayles uses jump cuts, quick pans, wide static shots, and other devices only if they're appropriate for a particular film.

At the same time, almost in self-defense, Sayles claims that each of his films has utilized a different stylistic idiom. *Matewan* and *Eight Men Out* are set one year apart, but the rhythm of *Matewan* is like a mountain ballad, with long shots and dissolves and little fast cutting until the final shoot-out, whereas *Eight Men Out* is set in Chicago at the beginning of the Jazz Age, so the music, the cutting, and the camera are much faster. But Sayles has never been a natural or spontaneous filmmaker. His evenhandedness, his refusal to be a provocateur, his avoidance of style have kept his films from breaking out to a wider audience until *The Secret of Roan Inish* and *Lone Star*, his two most commercial films.

What makes Sayles's movies personal is their perspective—in his words, "how you see the world": "The way I see the world is by making human connections between things." Even when he writes a genre picture, he tries to bring life to the human connections in it. Like Spike Lee, Sayles makes movies about a world he knows something about, but it's not necessarily *his* world. Like Scorsese's, his movies are about the guys he saw around but did *not* hang out with. Several of Sayles's stories are set and shot in Hoboken, New Jersey, an "unlikely" place for filmmaking, but a quintessential Saylesian town, and one where he also resides. An authentic sense of place is crucial to Sayles's films, as is evident in *Matewan, Eight Men Out, The Secret of Roan Inish,* and *Passion Fish.*

Return of the Secaucus Seven (1979), Sayles's first film, provides a poignant look at a reunion of 1960s activists. It's Sayles's going away party for the angry idealism of the Johnson-Nixon years. Shot in four weeks, at the cost of a mere $40,000, this talking-heads film used few sets, sparse camera movement, and little action. But the movie became influential, launching a cycle of "reunion" films, which included *The Big Chill* and the TV series *Thirtysomething.* As a portrait of disenchantment, *Return* was more authentic and more honest than Lawrence Kasdan's star-studded *Big Chill.*

Back in the 1960s, seven restless friends, the ideological children of Kennedy and Abbie Hoffman, were burning with worthy causes like the War on Poverty and Vietnam. They smoked dope, engaged in affairs—and talked politics. They took off for Washington to march on the Pentagon but got only as far as Secaucus, where they were arrested on a phony charge and spent a night in the local cooler. Dubbing themselves "The Secaucus Seven," they missed the big event in the capital, but the experience strengthened their bonds.

Now, a decade later, they come together for a reunion weekend in New England, hosted by Mike and Kate, both teachers. T.J., who still dreams of becoming a folk singer, arrives with his guitar. Irene, who once had an affair with T.J., brings her new preppie lover, Chipp. Maura, having left Jeff, is also alone. Jeff, a former Vista volunteer who now works with drug addicts, is almost tempted to try drugs himself.

Not much happens: Some songs are sung, a few partners change, and the group is falsely arrested for murdering a deer—bambicide, as they describe the charge. Their weekend of nostalgia and soul searching shows that, though only thirtysomething, they are beginning to experience the compromises of middle age. A rueful movie about unexceptional lives that have prematurely grown stale, *Return* is a bit commonplace, lacking genuine drama. But Sayles uses effectively a discursive, episodic format; he constructs strong scenes with resonant dialogue. The characters are complex and individually distinguished by speech, gesture, and manner.

In the more intimate films that followed, Sayles continued to rely on sharp characterization and poignant dialogue, which compensate for a flawed dramatic sense and unpolished technical crafts. Though the film is technically stilted, Sayles succeeded in turning *Lianna* from a coming-out "problem" drama into a comedy about a young woman who unexpectedly discovers resources of wit and confidence within herself.

Married to an adulterous husband, with two children who don't offer challenge or satisfaction, Lianna (Linda Griffith) tumbles into an affair with her older night-school teacher, Ruth. *Lianna* deals with the inner emotional rhythms of a woman whose life is in limbo. As Richard Corliss has observed, the film never addresses the more obvious questions of whether Lianna is in love or just frustrated. Does the affair represent a change in sexual orientation or just a detour? Is the discovery of herself worth the loss of family and friends?[44] But the film offers a realistic portrait of the changes undergone by a woman when she realizes she is lesbian.

A Romeo-and-Juliet tale set in Trenton, New Jersey, circa 1966, Sayles's only studio picture, *Baby, It's You* (1983), depicted a doomed high school romance between a college-bound Jewish girl (Rosanna Arquette) and a working-class Italian Catholic (Vincent Spano). Once again, Sayles's eye for detail and his ear for period lingo give this slice-of-life film solid foundations. Poorly marketed by Paramount, it disillusioned Sayles very quickly about his prospects of working in Hollywood.

A fast writer, Sayles scripted *Brother From Another Planet* (1984) in only six days—"that's the time I had." Telling the story of a mute black alien adrift in Harlem, it offers an engaging look at racial prejudice and drug addiction. Sayles's mild comedy relied on good performances from a tightly knit cast that breathed life into a talk-heavy, visually dull film.

A vast improvement over previous efforts, *Matewan* (1987) explores the personal and political elements of union-making and union-breaking in West Virginia's coal mines of the 1920s. A complex study of individual integrity and community solidarity, the film was assisted by Haskell Wexler's luminous cinematography of Appalachian locations and Mason Daring's blue-grass soundtrack. However, Sayles's unabashed homage to the martyr years of American labor was not sufficiently engaging from a dramatic standpoint.

An account of the 1919 Black Sox scandal that rocked the baseball world, *Eight Men Out* (1988) examines the controversy through the eyes of its individual players. Not conforming to types, each man is portrayed as having his own reasons for agreeing—or refusing—to throw the World Series. Unfortunately, the players seem bland compared to the intricate drama around them.

Sayles's most ambitious film, *City of Hope* (1991), chronicles a decaying town in urgent need of spiritual change. The film confronts a modern urban America, beset with explosive racial and class tensions, as well as crime, political corruption, police brutality, and an absence of leadership. A dense canvas with numerous subplots, the film was shot in Cincinnati for $5 million, using forty locations and thirty-eight characters. The fictional locale—Hudson City, New Jersey—stands in for any average-size city. The multilayered narrative interweaves stories of cops, politicians, contractors, teachers, single mothers, teenagers, hoods, and muggers.

It's a sociological portrait of urban life at the end of the century, when the old political system and old ethnic formations are losing their validity. The Italian-American and Irish-American coalitions are breaking up in the face of a new demographic force, African Americans. Wynn (Joe Morton), a black middle-class councilman who aspires to become the legitimate leader of the embattled constituency, is contrasted with the lazy black former mayor and with the corrupt white mayor.

Nick (Vincent Spano), the substance-abusing, inarticulate son of a powerful contractor, is in desperate need of self-esteem and parental love. Nick's father walks a thin line between corruption, a condition for his survival, and his code of ethics; he lets thugs burn down a building so that he can keep his son out of jail. A minor incident, an attempted burglary of a TV store, sets off a series of events that link all the residents. There are no "heroes," only compromised individuals, each facing a moral dilemma. Two black adolescents, who beat up and mug a white college teacher in the park, falsely accuse him of making sexual advances. But the victim, a happily married professor of urban affairs, is urged to drop the assault charges in order to prevent an explosion in the black community.

Sayles's canvas is admirably wide, even when the treatment is schematic and the reconciliations neat. A socially conscious film in the vein of Hollywood's message films, *City of Hope* is also a touching family drama. To capture the constantly-on-the-move characters, Robert Richardson's alert camera never stands still, drifting among individuals as their paths cross, with long master shots demonstrating the interconnectedness of all of the city forces.

After the sprawling, criss-crossing *City of Hope*, Sayles made *Passion Fish* (1992), a more tightly focused narrative about interior struggles and unexpected changes. An anti-Reagan story, *Passion Fish* is both cynical and critical of monetary success and the inevitability of class distinctions. As Michael Wilmington pointed out, Sayles's matter-of-fact tone diffuses the maudlin, resulting in "a love story without tears, a soap opera with no soap, a political fable about survivors in the ruins of the reign of greed."[45]

Working again in the "woman's picture" domain, Sayles showed he could deal with material usually seen in TV movies of the week in a mature, nonmelodramatic way. Centering on female friendship, *Passion Fish* coincided with a cycle of studio films about female bonding, such as *Thelma & Louise*, *A League of Their Own*, and *Fried Green Tomatoes*.

May-Alice (Mary McDonnell), a soap opera star, is accidentally hit by a taxi cab and is paralyzed from the waist down. Moving back to her childhood home in the Louisiana bayou, she wallows in self-pity and turns to the bottle. She vents her anger at various nurses, who flee her house as soon as they arrive. May-Alice finally meets her equal in strength in Chantelle (Alfre Woodard), a black nurse from Chicago. But it turns out that Chantelle has her own demons: She's running away from her tormented past, a drug addiction that had rendered her an unsuitable mother.

On the surface, the heroines play familiar types, but Sayles again shows his skill in etching deft characterizations, detailing the emotional transformation of each woman and the bond established once they get to know each other. A painstakingly accurate portrait of suffering, the film depicts a woman who's confined to a wheelchair, unable to get to the bathroom on her own. She sits in a big, dark house, drinking and watching TV. Sayles creates a Gothic atmosphere with allusions to

Robert Aldrich's *What Ever Happened to Baby Jane?*, in which a pathetic paraplegic was played by the formerly glamorous star Joan Crawford.

Like much of Sayles's work, *Passion Fish* concerns the dreams and hopes of ordinary individuals who are defeated by big, powerful forces. It revolves around the issue of coming to terms with failure. Since American culture is both success obsessed and youth oriented, for Sayles the question is: "How do you deal with it when you've failed and you know it? Do you crawl up into a ball and get bitter and die? Or do you find some other way to express yourself and like yourself?"[46]

The movie suggests that healing is a mutual process, that the healer needs a large dose of rehab, too. At first, the two women go at each other. Chantelle is relentlessly controlling, a taskmaster trying to change May-Alice, but she also realizes she desperately needs the job. Power, class, and race play their role without suffocating the evolving friendship. Both women are fighting for dignity and survival, and, in the process, each woman discovers what's important to her through the alliance with the other.[47]

Despite a confined indoor setting, the film flows spontaneously. Working with discipline, Sayles takes his time in developing the relationship. The only schematic element are the film's secondary characters, who are used for comic relief: a boozy old uncle, former school friends turned gossipy matrons, self-absorbed actresses from May-Alice's soap-opera days. Chantelle's visitors from her past include a lover from Chicago—the father of her child, with whom she almost died in an accident—and her father, who still treats her like a child. However new men change the women's romantic prospects: Sugar (Vondie Curtis-Hall), a ladies' man, pursues Chantelle, and Rennie (David Strathairn), an old classmate who's married, shows interest in May-Alice.

May-Alice is a quintessentially Sayles outsider: Having moved to New York to pursue her acting career, she has effaced her past—at a price. The resolution suggests a coming to terms with that past. The bayou country—its myths and charms—is integrated into the texture of the film. A boat trip into the swamps represents a journey of renewal backward in time, as the country's folk tradition alters the women's urban consciousness.

Changing gears again, *The Secret of Roan Inish* (1995) is a "corrective" film for a genre in which most characters have been boys. Sayles explores a young girl who's alone in the world—in other words, an outsider. His straightforward approach transforms Rosalie K. Fry's mythic novella about the determination of Fiona Connelly (Jeni Courtney) to unveil secrets of her family's past—the curious disappearances of humans, the strange power of animals.

After the death of Fiona's mother, her father sends her to live with her grandparents on Ireland's isolated coast. The elderly couple, who used to own houses near Roan Inish island, linger over the past. Grandfather Hugh tells Fiona of the disappearance of her infant brother, Jamie, who floated to the sea in his cradle and never came back. And her cousin recounts the legend of Liam, who fell in love with a beautiful selkie, half-woman, half-seal.

These stories motivate Fiona to take action. Although she gets assistance from her cousin, she is a self-reliant heroine, a fairy-tale princess with a feisty spirit. For Sayles, what Fiona wants is fairly traditional—to bring her family back together—but she's doing things that are adult, even though she's still a kid, and she does the hard work without relying on magic, as is often the case in fables. Like all fairy tales, The Secret of Roan Inish underlines humans' links to the physical surrounding ("What the sea will take, the sea must have") and to the animal world. Haskell Wexler, who also shot Matewan, imbues the film with magical lighting.

The idea for Lone Star (1996), Sayles's most popular effort, goes back to his childhood, when he was watching Davy Crockett and The Alamo on TV. Technically, Lone Star is not a factual story, but as with City of Hope, Sayles says he could find documentation in old newspapers for each incident depicted in his film. At its core, Lone Star explores the long-standing strain between the Mexican and the American communities in South Texas: "Texas has always belonged to Mexican-Americans, but only in the last ten to fifteen years have they started to get the jobs that run the place. The Daughters of the Confederacy, who were white, and the Daughters of the Alamo, who were Latino, are still fighting for their version of history." For Sayles, this racial antagonism serves as "a good metaphor for America."

Set in the town of Frontera, Lone Star follows the expedition of a reluctant sheriff to resolve a mystery of the past. It begins with a skeleton discovered among cactuses and a rookie sheriff, Sam Deeds (Chris Cooper), who is trying to figure out whether his father was a murderer. The root of evil, related in flashbacks, points to Sheriff Charley Wade

(Kris Kristofferson), who was run out of town and killed by Sam's father, Buddy Deeds (Matthew McConaughey). *Lone Star* is a movie haunted by a sense of America as a violent country, where uprootedness and lack of collective memory are common problems. Frontera flows in blood; there's no release, no relief from the past: Even the memory of the dead Sheriff Buddy Deeds, a mythic figure, wields more power than the living sheriff.

Sayles turns a criminal investigation into a multilayered epic about intergenerational wars. The white, black, and Mexican characters are mixed up in one another's lives. In most Sayles movies, it's fathers and sons, but here, it's also mothers and daughters and grandfathers, sons, and grandchildren. A schoolteacher, Pilar (Elizabeth Peña), is alienated from her mother, and Delmore (Joe Morton), a black Army colonel, is in conflict with both his son and his father. Characters who seem unrelated are ultimately brought closer until they are all held in a tight net. Impressive as the film's scope is, *Lone Star* still suffers from a diagrammatic construction: Everything is explicit, including the simplistic use of recognizable heroes and villains. Moreover, Frontera's racial history is not only dramatized; it's also discussed by parents at home and lectured about in schools.

That said, the flashbacks are presented inventively, as when the camera studies Sam's face on the bank of a river, pans away to the water, then returns to find that Sam's place has been replaced by his teenage self. For dramatic punctuation, Sayles uses Charles Wade's trigger: Whenever the action flags and the pace drags, the sound of his gun pushes it along.[48] Recalling Peter Bogdanovich's masterpiece, *The Last Picture Show*, *Lone Star* shares visual and thematic motifs with it: a decrepit small town, dusty streets, and a ruined drive-in. And, like the 1971 film, *Lone Star* depicts a town beset by bigotry and unresolved mystery. In *The Last Picture Show*, the secretive love is between Sam the Lion and Lois (played by Ben Johnson and Ellen Burstyn); here, it's between Buddy Deeds and a schoolteacher.

Centering on the discrepancy between the official story as it is constructed by power elites in totalitarian regimes and the personal responsibility of citizens to search for the truth, *Men with Guns* (1998) was a logical follow-up to *Lone Star*. Structurally and stylistically, however, the two movies are different, with *Men with Guns* (which is in Spanish) far less complex and less accomplished. Like *The Secret of Roan Inish*,

Men with Guns is framed as a mythic tale, one in which an old woman tells her daughter the story of an idealistic doctor. And like *Lone Star*, the film adopts the format of an investigation conducted by an aging doctor. Overall, *Men with Guns* lacks *The Secret of Roan Inish*'s visual magic and *Lone Star*'s dramatic momentum.

Inspired by the character of Dr. Arrau (from Francisco Goldman's novel, "The Long Night of White Chickens"), Humberto Fuentes (Federico Luppi), a wealthy doctor whose wife has died, is a proud, dignified man who considers his greatest achievement—his "legacy"—to be an international health program that trains doctors for the impoverished villages. Close to retirement, Fuentes decides to visit his former students, beginning a journey that turns into a revelatory political and moral odyssey.

Unfolding as a road movie, each stop represents a phase in the doctor's political awakening. Along the way, he befriends a young boy, Conejo (Dan Rivera Gonzales), who was raped and then abandoned by his mother. Conejo takes Fuentes to a deserted school, the site of torture and the spot where one of Fuente's students was murdered. The tale gets more interesting when Fuentes and Conejo are joined by Domingo (Damian Delgado), an army deserter, and Padre Portillo (Damian Alcazar), a defrocked priest, who recount their traumatic experiences through flashbacks. Domingo is haunted by memories of having stabbed a prisoner to death, under peer pressure, as part of his initiation into the group.

Wearing its liberal-humanitarian doctrine on its sleeves, *Men with Guns* is too didactic. Sayles's decision not to ground the story in any particular historical context makes it vague; the generic title suggests that the tale could take place in any authoritarian regime. The journey taken by the doctor is metaphoric, stressing the importance of alertness and search for the truth. In message, the film is similar to the Oscar-winning Argentinean film *The Official Story*, which revolves around a bourgeois couple blind to the atrocities around them. A sharp observer, Sayles makes an important distinction between a naive and a willful innocence. Fuentes is blind to what's happening around him, not only because he is manipulated but also because it's convenient *not* to know; his comfortable life has precluded perception of political ills. Plodding along with pedestrian tempo, *Men with Guns* does not benefit from its inherently dramatic format of a murder investigation.

INDIES' POSTER CHILD—STEVEN SODERBERGH

It's hard to think of a more influential indie than Soderbergh's first feature, *sex, lies, and videotape*, one of the most stunning debuts in American film history. The film forever changed the public perception of independent movies—and of the Sundance Film Festival, where it premiered. It also established Soderbergh as the most promising director of his generation—a poster child for indie filmmaking.

In addition to directing seven films, Soderbergh has executive-produced *Suture*, *The Daytrippers*, and *Pleasantville*, but he's still pigeonholed as the man who made *sex, lies, and videotape*, largely because it's his only movie that earned money. "In retrospect, I think that's the most memorable thing about it," said Soderbergh. "It's time for me to get a new middle name."[49]

Soderbergh began his directorial career in 1989, a decade after Lynch and Sayles. His universe is not as rich or complex as that of Sayles, although he's more in control of film's technical facilities. With seven films to his credits, Soderbergh has shown versatility, hopping from genre to genre. But to what effect? After a decade's work, the verdict is still out on the caliber of his talent, and a baffling question persists: Who is Soderbergh as a filmmaker? His choice of material has been dubious, revealing a strong need for a writer-collaborator.

Born in Georgia in 1963, Soderbergh seemed destined to become a filmmaker. He began making movies at age 14 when his father, a college dean, enrolled him in a summer class at Louisiana State University. Upon graduation from high school, he headed for Hollywood. It never occurred to him to go to film school. There was no need: He had spent his adolescence hanging around film students, borrowing equipment, arguing about movies. He had already cut his teeth making Super-8 shorts.

Soderbergh experienced a frustrating spell in Hollywood with a routine job, holding cue cards for a talk show. Trying to sell a script, he returned to Baton Rouge a year later, feeling a failure. Soon after, he got a job at a video arcade, wrote a number of scripts, and made shorts. Soderbergh's break came in 1986, when the rock group Yes asked him to shoot concert footage, which was later shaped into a Grammy Award–winning video. In 1987, Soderbergh put an "abrupt halt to all the bad personal stuff" that would be the basis for *sex, lies, and videotape*.

He wrote the screenplay in motels as he drove west cross-country. With backing from RCA/Columbia Home Video, he completed the $1.2 million movie a year later, freeing himself from the destructive emotions he had been carrying with him for years.[50]

The most remarkable thing about *sex, lies, and videotape* was its freshness; it didn't recall any other film. Soderbergh spoke with a distinctive voice about issues that mattered. Intimate in scale, the film is a finely crafted, modern-day morality tale. Set in Baton Rouge, it revolves around an outsider, a handsome young man named Graham (James Spader). Sexually impotent, Graham derives gratification from recording women talking about their sex lives.

A success at Sundance and a triumph in Cannes, *sex, lies, and videotape* made Soderbergh, at age 26, the youngest director to ever win the Palme d'Or. The movie also won the Cannes acting award for Spader and was later nominated for an Academy Award for Best Original Screenplay. Soderbergh was stunned at people's response to his movie; he thought it was "too internal, too self-absorbed." While not autobiographical, the film is personal: Soderbergh was not a sexual interrogator, but he was in a relationship where he behaved much like the film's adulterous husband, hurting someone he was close to.

As the movie begins, a beauty in a long, flowered dress, Ann Millaney (Andie MacDowell), sits in her psychiatrist's office and talks about her fear: What will happen to all the garbage piling up in the world? Her soft Southern voice floats over the image of Graham, her husband's friend, who stops for a shave in a men's room, splashing water under his armpits before driving on to Baton Rouge. At the same time, Ann's husband, John (Peter Gallagher), takes off his wedding ring and heads for a sexual interlude with Ann's sister, Cynthia (Laura San Giacomo). By the end of the opening sequence, when Graham takes his duffle bag from his trunk, Soderbergh has mapped out the film's smooth style and mature tone.

A *Liaisons Dangereuses* for the video age, *sex, lies, and videotape* is an absorbing tale of desire and anxiety in which Graham's camera becomes the lead player. The film is structured as a layered labyrinth, in which the links among the partners are initially based on self-denial and deception. Documenting the video generation, Soderbergh shows an insider's sense of his characters' mental world, directing the camera as if it were a natural storytelling device. The camera cuts fluidly from one pair to another, showing precision for details that are both funny and chilling. Dialogue driven, the movie contains long sequences shot in close-up. Technically, Soderbergh's debut was more accomplished than most first efforts.

Smart but confused and hiding behind her good-girl demeanor, Ann never descends into coyness. She tells her psychiatrist, "I'm kinda goin' through this thing where I don't want him to touch me." Her fragile look hides a sexuality whose existence she can hardly admit. Her description of her sister as "an extrovert, kind of loud," turns out to be accurate. Cynthia sports a sharp nose, a randy gap between her teeth, and a husky voice that suggests risk taking. Sexually confident, she flaunts her shapely body in tight shirts and miniskirts. Cynthia's affair with John is built as much on sibling rivalry and the thrill of deception as on sexual heat. "The beautiful, the perfect Ann," Cynthia says with contempt, suggesting a manic edge beneath her self-possession.

Every character in the film is precisely constructed. From his wire-rim glasses and suspenders to his compulsive womanizing, John represents a shallow, amoral 1980s yuppie. But it's Graham who is the most intriguing character, a "nightmare" product of the video age. Impotent, he derives physical satisfaction from watching tapes of women revealing their sexual histories. With hesitant smile and tentative voice, Graham is both sweet and sinister. Upon arriving at Ann's house, he instantly starts questioning her: "What do you like best about being married?" He is a cool observer, so detached that voyeurism hardly matches his personality. Ann, the film's most sympathetic character, sees in Graham vulnerable qualities, perceiving him as a kindred repressed spirit. She responds to him sexually but runs from friendship when she learns about his tapes.

Graham distances everyone with his camera, an apt metaphor for people who can relate only through mediated images. Like Antonioni's *Blow-Up*, beneath the adultery intrigue the film poses serious questions about the potency of the video camera as an alternative to real and direct experience. The bright windows that frame the characters reinforce the idea of voyeurism, while preventing the drama from becoming too claustrophobic. With a delicate serio-comic tone, Soderbergh demonstrates his authority over every detail. Ann sees John as the Husband and he sees her as the Wife; Cynthia sees every male as a sex object. Soderbergh's camera, like Graham's, is more concerned with talk than sex—it's the dialogue that carries the erotic charge. All the characters are problematic: the dark deception of John and Cynthia, the buried passion of Ann and Graham.

The film is by no means perfect. The characters' motivations are too simple: Cynthia needs to set herself apart from Ann, and Ann rejects sex partly because of Cynthia. The resolution is too neat for these messy lives, and the formation of a new couple at the end, while tentative, is too upbeat for this kind of tale. Those aspects, combined with a cast of name actors (rather than unknowns), positioned Soderbergh as a filmmaker who wants to do personal work but stay close to the mainstream.

It would have been more dramatic, but also more predictable, if the film assumed Graham's distorted point of view, but Soderbergh's detached strategy is more challenging. Soderbergh should also get credit for not allowing the viewers any distance, urging them to weigh the characters' morality while evaluating their own motives. As Janet Maslin pointed out, the moral transgressions committed by the characters are measured on a sliding scale: Is cheating on a sister worse than cheating on a spouse? Is lying to oneself as bad as lying to others?[51] It's all relative, with gray shading and moral ambiguity. "I look around this town," Graham tells Ann, "and I see John and Cynthia and you, and I feel comparatively healthy." Graham's ritualistic recording of women's confessions is his means of seeking truth, but, as the movie's title indicates, it's the dishonesty in *sex, lies, and videotape* that gives the film its edge. As Maslin suggested, each of the four principals turns out to be a liar of one sort or another, and weighing the different dishonest acts becomes the audience's responsibility.

After his breakthrough, Soderbergh made the visually striking but intellectually vapid *Kafka* (1991), which inadvertently gave credence to the theory of sophomore jinx. A paranoid thriller, whose style was deliberately artificial, *Kafka* felt much more like a first film than *sex, lies, and videotape*. Shot in black and white, with an impressive international cast, it was neither a biopicture nor a mystery. Hampered by a conventional plot, *Kafka* is neither stylized nor radical enough to convey the spirit of Kafka's outsider status as a modern, troubled Jewish intellectual.

Lem Dobbs's script describes Kafka (played by a miscast Jeremy Irons) as a quiet insurance company clerk, who lives a routinely ordered life; at night, he writes stories for esoteric magazines. At his vast, impersonal office, he is oppressed by a snooping overseer (Joel Grey) and criticized as a "lone wolf" by his boss (Alec Guinness). When a series of murders plagues the city, a police inspector (Armin Mueller-Stahl) begins an investigation. Through some puzzling events, Kafka finds himself with a briefcase bomb on a secret mission to an ominous castle where a fascistic government resides.

Failing to evoke Kafka's literary world, Soderbergh's melodrama evokes old film styles. The tone vacillates among art film, absurdist comedy, horror movie, and self-conscious thriller. Placing Kafka in Prague, a sinister milieu that echoes the author's fictional universe, proves to be a gimmick. As David Ansen has pointed out, conceptually the story is schematic, and the artist's portrait is too shallow to qualify as a convincing evocation of a complex psyche or paranoid mind.[52] The villain is named Murnau (after the German director), and the shadowy black-and-white imagery is an obvious homage to German Expressionism. The film is a pastiche, whose most obvious influence is *The Third Man* (in location as in Cliff Martinez's score), starring Orson Welles, who directed the film of Kafka's novel *The Trial*. Ironically, Soderbergh scores a visual coup when he switches to color in the castle sequences, whose design recalls Terry Gilliam's *Brazil*.

Soderbergh's third outing, *King of the Hill* (1993), an adaptation of A. E. Hotchner's Depression-era memoir of his childhood in St. Louis, was a return to form, though few people saw the film. When the finances of the Kurlanders (played by Jeroen Krabbe and Lisa Eichhorn) reach their limit, the couple send their younger son, Sullivan, to live with relatives. Mrs. Kurlander's poor health deteriorates, she is sent to a sanitarium, and her salesman husband leaves town for a job. This coming-of-age story revolves around the bright twelve-year-old Aaron Kurlander (Jesse Bradford), who perseveres in the face of danger. Aaron is left alone in a spooky transient hotel that evokes Southern Gothic tradition. With plenty of time on his hands, the ever curious boy observes with fascination the strange people around him and soon finds himself entangled in their adventures.

As a survival study of a kid who relies on his intuition and smarts, Aaron recalls the young protagonists of Mark Twain and Charles Dickens. The movie was intended as a tribute to the indomitable spirit of many Jews who have fallen on hard times. An assured, well-acted film, *King of the Hill* displays Soderbergh's penchant for realistic portrayals of intimate dramas, but it is less effective in creating an authentically Jewish milieu.

Soderbergh's next film, *The Underneath* (1995), was an unsuccessful exercise in noir, a remake of the 1949 classic *Criss Cross*. The weak dialogue and the formulaic plot underlined again Soderbergh's need for stronger, more original material. Besides, as John Powers noted, Soderbergh is a realist, with strong feel for textures of domesticity and blessed with a sensibility that's closer to Eugene O'Neill's and Woody Allen's than to pulp fiction, which is what the material calls for.[53]

"I'm obviously coasting on the success of one film, and it's always fun to see how long that lasts," Soderbergh said in 1995. "Luckily, the films I've made weren't really expected to be wildly successful. Whether or not I'm perceived as a commercial filmmaker, or bankable really doesn't matter to me, I can always write something extraordinarily contained and shoot for very, very cheap."[54] Nonetheless, he later admitted that, after *The Underneath*, "I was at the end of my career, drifting into a place that wasn't very interesting or challenging."

To break through the stagnation, Soderbergh made the low-budget *Gray's Anatomy*, a visually inventive version of the Spalding Gray stage monologue, about an eye problem that sends an artist on a wild journey through alternative medicine before he succumbs to surgery. The material is less funny than Gray's previous monologues (e.g., *Swimming to Cambodia*), but Soderbergh compensates with creepy visuals and Lynch-like interviews with individuals who have suffered optical problems.

Soderbergh then put his own money into the screwball stylistic oddity *Schizopolis* (1997), a personal satire that he wrote, directed, lensed, and starred in. With its disdain for narrative coherence, this satirical critique of modern life seemed to have come straight out of the director's head, a sharp departure from the meticulous craftsmanship of *King of the Hill* and *The Underneath*, which were weighted down by the intense concentration of form.

Schizopolis turned out to be a wake up call. Just when Hollywood was ready to write off Soderbergh as a major film artist, he rebounded with his best film to date, *Out of Sight* (Universal, 1998), demonstrating again what a good actor's director he is when working with the right material—and also showing that he is one of the few filmmakers who can navigate smoothly between Hollywood and indie projects.

Soderbergh was concerned about finding a film with a big budget that would allow him to exploit his creative energy. In *Out of Sight*, he found a high-profile project that won him the largest audience of his career. According to conventional Hollywood wisdom, you don't just hand over a $49-million star vehicle like *Out of Sight* to someone with an art house reputation and a commensurate box-office track record. Soderbergh had to convince Universal that, as he said, "I really know how to do this." Once assigned, he was given free rein; the only pressure about making a big-budget movie came from within: "I wanted it to be good, because potentially more people would see it than any other film I'd made, and you don't want to blow that."[55]

Out of Sight was an opportunity "to put into use some things I had learned in other movies, which were testing grounds for me." Soderbergh approached *Out of Sight* as the continuation of creative rebirth, with playful energy, jump cuts, freeze frames, saturated colors, and gritty textures. A sly, sexy version of Elmore Leonard's crime novel, *Out of Sight* contains a dozen offbeat characters and bright, snappy dialogue rarely heard in mainstream pictures. The complex structure, subtle humor, and deliberate pacing all contribute to the overall artistic impact. While lacking the more facile commercial appeal of *Get Shorty*, which after all spoofed Hollywood, *Out of Sight* is more satisfying than Tarantino's *Jackie Brown* (based on Leonard's *Rum Punch*), which was low-key and lacked a strong romantic angle.

In Soderbergh's film, an eccentric romantic couple is front and center. Standing on opposite sides of the law, the mismatched vet criminal Jack Foley (George Clooney) and Deputy Federal Marshal Karen Sisco (Jennifer Lopez) begin a courtship in the tight space of a car's trunk. Scott Frank's witty, densely rich script is character driven and performance reliant. Soderbergh understands that Leonard's forte lies in his sharp, nonjudgmental portraits and in the authentic lingo of low-lifers who are immensely appealing. With unmistakable ease and subtle humor, the film consists of priceless scenes, including a brilliantly staged romantic interlude. Not since *Boogie Nights* has there been a Hollywood movie with so many characters, each perfectly portrayed by the likes of Ving Rhames, Billy Zahn, Don Cheadle, Dennis Farina, Catherine Keener, and Albert Brooks.

CONCLUSION

Of the five outsiders profiled in this chapter, the first, Jon Jost, is out of the country, living in Europe where he reportedly works on video.

David Lynch's last movie, *Lost Highway*, was a commercial failure, earning $4 million against its $16 million budget, but a talent like his can't be hindered by the box-office. John Waters has softened and moved closer to the mainstream in sensibility, though his audience has not grown, as *Pecker*'s poor showing (a take of barely $3 million) demonstrated.

John Sayles is likely to stay within the independent milieu. Unlike other filmmakers, who tend to develop a single style and work in a single genre, Sayles has spread his work over several genres, with locations as different as his narratives.[56] Sayles is one of the few filmmakers, indie and Hollywood, who is concerned with the diverse and complex structure of American society and the intricate ways in which various groups of people are interlinked. His ambitious approach often calls for large, ensemble casts, sprawling narratives, and multilayered plots.

While Sayles continues to improve technically, the only one in the entire group who is truly experiencing artistic growth is Soderbergh. Cited as the best film of 1998 by the National Society of Film Critics, *Out of Sight* was a terrific studio movie, made without selling out. "It doesn't seem greedy to make a movie once every nine years that people show up to go see," Soderbergh noted. "If I'm the cinematic equivalent of the locust, it seems like I'm coming up on that time. And if so, that's great, because then I'll be able to coast for another eight years and make some more interesting movies."[57]

Indicative of the stature of these filmmakers—and the visibility of indies in the global film world—is the fact that three of them are represented in the 1999 Cannes Film Festival: Lynch with the *Straight Story*, Sayles with *Limbo* (both in competition), and Soderbergh with *The Limey*, an independent film financed and distributed by the new kid on the block, Artisan.

3

Fathers and Sons

THE NEW AMERICAN wave may be independent in spirit, but it's highly dependent on the past; it rests on the shoulders of giants. Continuity as well as change in paradigms, themes, and styles have marked the new indies. A number of iconoclastic filmmakers who began working in the 1960s and 1970s have influenced contemporary indie cinema. Among these, the most prominent figures are John Cassavetes in dramatic realism, Robert Altman in his maverick, ever-changing strategies, and Martin Scorsese in the crime-noir genre.

THE LEGACY OF JOHN CASSAVETES

John Cassavetes's film output still stands as a monument in the independent canon. One of the first modern American filmmakers, Cassavetes shared many concerns with the directors of the French New Wave. In fact, he *was* the American New Wave, with one basic difference: Instead of bringing a critic's perspective to his films, as the French did (Godard and Truffaut were critics before embarking on directorial careers), Cassavetes brought an *actor's* understanding.[1]

For three decades, Cassavetes held a unique position in American film, maintaining dual careers as a respected actor in Hollywood movies and as a fiercely iconoclastic director. Acting gave Cassavetes the financial security to make eccentric films, many of which explored the art of acting. Like Orson Welles before him, Cassavetes fused his various roles in a way that exerted tremendous influence on a younger generation of actors-directors. Tim Robbins, Steve Buscemi, John Turturro, and Sean Penn have all first distinguished themselves as actors before turning to directing.

Cassavetes began his experiments in 1957 with a hand-held camera, shooting in 16mm and in black and white. He used earnings from his

TV series *Johnnie Staccato* to finance *Shadows*, a semi-improvised film about a love affair between a white boy and a black girl, which he made for $40,000. A cast of then-unknowns brought a new dimension of realism. When shooting was over, United Artists gave him only two weeks to edit; the studio then did further editing, resulting in a compromised picture that did not reflect Cassavetes's vision. *Shadows* taught Cassavetes a lesson: He decided that in the future he would have to be his own master, even if it meant waiting years before making another picture. Still, even a conservative critic like Bosley Crowther of the *New York Times* appreciated *Shadows* as "fitfully dynamic, endowed with a raw but vibrant strength, conveying an illusion of being a record of real people."

After two frustrating Hollywood films (*Too Late Blues, A Child Is Waiting*), Cassavetes made *Faces* (1968), a brutally intimate look at a marriage whose partners can't communicate with each other. The narrative was based on a single day and night in the life of a middle-aged couple (played by John Marley and Lynn Carlin) whose marriage is on the verge of collapse. Like *Shadows*, *Faces* was shot in black and white and in 16mm (later blown up to 35mm). It took eight months to shoot (in sequence) and two years to edit. Cassavetes encouraged his actors to freely interpret the emotions suggested in his script, resulting in a work that was spontaneous in form and "the realest dramatic movie ever produced," according to Crowther.

In *Faces*, and later in *Husbands*, Cassavetes depicted marital problems with harsh realism and hand-held camera. Manifesting his directorial signature, these movies were overlong and indulgent, but the excess was motivated by honesty, not greed. Cassavetes's pictures, which dissect relationships from different perspectives, deal with the kinds of feelings people can't express. Some of his films are thoughtful celebrations of the art of acting, centering on the bonds that define a family of players. Arguably no American director has so powerfully illuminated the complexity of these relationships as they prevail on stage and off.

A powerful realism informs Cassavetes's work: The raw material on screen gives it the look of cinema verité. His characters, mostly obsessive talkers on the brink of hysteria, reveal themselves through their small worlds. Cassavetes dwells on the messy feelings and relationships that limit individual freedom, showing the confusion and clutter that riddle the yearnings and frustrations that define the American experience. Distrustful of fixed style, Cassavetes's films violate

Hollywood's elegant framing and smooth pacing. His films are often mistaken as improvisational, but they are usually shot from precise scripts with rough camera techniques and long takes that are meant to expose the shakiness of middle-class life.

At a time when American movies were becoming increasingly standardized, Cassavetes succeeded in maintaining a singular voice. To the end, he moved in uncharted territory, refusing to work in any identifiable tradition. His films were not easily categorized or liked; they shared no thematic or stylistic concerns with the work of other filmmakers.[2] As disturbing as they are erratic, Cassavetes's films leave no one indifferent: Critics and audiences alike either embrace or reject his work. Amazingly, Cassavetes was able to garner a much wider audience for his films than one would expect.

Raymond Carney has noted that Cassavetes's daring experiments with dramatic pacing and with the duration and complexity of shots supported the double tradition of his work as both theatrical and distinctly cinematic. His best films are intimate chamber pieces, revolving around a small number of characters engaged in seemingly simple domestic stories. These domestic dramas subject their characters' behavior to microscopic scrutiny.[3] Cassavetes's studies of relationships between husbands and wives, lovers and friends run against the systematization of experiences; they explore the emotional messiness and people's tolerance for personal and social disorder. A romantic, Cassavetes searched for signs of love beneath mundane and hellish surfaces.

Cassavetes made his films as if he were wrenching them out of his gut, favoring, as Hoberman pointed out, performances over script and actors over stars.[4] Cassavetes shot his narratives with inventive mise-en-scène, actor-driven writing, theatrical concerns, and bravura role-playing. The originality and intensity of his work make him America's most idiosyncratic and least categorizable filmmaker. His films resist static, formulaic ways of ordering and presenting interactions, attempting a new way of seeing and of visualizing human experience. A visionary, he managed to hold onto his freedom and self-expression in an increasingly hostile environment that favored bureaucratic filmmaking.[5]

Cassavetes created vehicles for himself (*Husbands*), his wife, Gena Rowlands (*Minnie and Moskowitz, A Woman Under the Influence*), and a select group of actors. *Husbands*, starring Peter Falk, Ben Gazzara, and

Cassavetes, is about three suburban commuters who are shocked into the recognition of their own mortality when their friend dies during an intense three-day trans-Atlantic alcoholic binge.

In *A Woman Under the Influence* (1974), an insightful essay on sexual politics, Mabel is a housewife who crosses the line into insanity. With a light feminist touch, she is perceived as a victim of a repressive patriarchal order and imposed social roles. Cassavetes sees Mabel as a desperate woman, yet courageous enough not to pull back from madness but to descend into it, confronting every facet of life with her husband, Nick (Peter Falk). Cassavetes never considers Mabel insane; he sees her as just a woman who has her subjective way of perceiving the world and who insists on the validity of her feelings.

Cassavetes allows no distance: Like Mabel's family, the viewers are forced into the troubling experience of her life. As Michael Ventura has pointed out, for Cassavetes that was the meaning of family; he refused to compromise his portrayal with comfortable cuts and smooth scene changes. Even in her worst pain, Mabel possesses a transcendent beauty that affects those around her. This is Cassavetes's strong point: He demonstrates that love can exist in the most horrible circumstances, an idea that would later be embraced by David Lynch.

Contrary to popular notion, the film's underlying structure is so rigorous that every aspect of Mabel's conduct receives equal attention. Even so, Cassavetes's approach depends more on the actors' personalities than on predetermined scripts and camera technique. He provided the essential key to his philosophy when he said, "I'm more interested in the people who work with me than in film itself."[6] That's why his films go deeper than most in their explorations of the emotional truth of their participants.

A Woman Under the Influence was innovative in another way. Dismayed by the poor distribution of his previous films, Cassavetes, Falk, and Rowlands traveled from coast to coast to promote and book their movie directly with theaters. This pattern would encourage other indie filmmakers to take greater control over the distribution of their movies.

Opening Night (1977) concerns more directly the art and life of actors, with Rowlands superbly embodying the complex relationship between actor and character, actor and colleagues, actor and director. Cassavetes's final film, *Love Streams* (1984), provides a free-form, offbeat look at the emotional codependence of two siblings, played by him and Rowlands.

Significantly, Cassavetes's style was so powerful that even his acting vehicles made for other filmmakers seem as if they were directed by
him. A case in point is Elaine May's maverick *Mikey and Nicky* (1976),
starring Cassavetes and Falk, which feels like a sequel to *Husbands*, with
a touch of *The Killing of a Chinese Bookie* thrown in. Though May put her
own stamp on the material, the gritty, improvised observations have a
Cassavetes-like realism. Relying on evocative dialogue and intense acting, the narrative weaves a love-hate bond between two men during
one fatal night in Philadelphia's lower depths. In Paul Mazursky's reworking of Shakespeare, *The Tempest* (1982), Cassavetes the actor also
overwhelms the director and the movie.

No one in today's cinema works directly in Cassavetes's tradition,
but a number of filmmakers were influenced by him: Robert Altman,
Martin Scorsese, Elaine May, and John Sayles. Among the younger generation, Sean Penn, John Turturro, Steve Buscemi, Alexander Rockwell,
and Cassavetes's own son, Nick, owe a debt to Cassavetes.

VISCERAL INTENSITY—SEAN PENN

Sean Penn brings the same visceral intensity and raw emotionalism to
his filmmaking as he does to his acting. His directorial efforts, *The Indian Runner* (1991) and *The Crossing Guard* (1995), both honorable failures, have a brooding, claustrophobic ambience that aims at getting
deep inside their anguished characters. As director, Penn displays the
boldness evident in his acting, taking risks with difficult material, but
he seems to mistake pain and intensity for art and truth. His movies are
not bad, but they are derivative, based more on amalgams of attitudes
than on fully developed narratives. At their best, they represent a troubling exploration of American manhood, rendered in stark yet lyrical
tones; at their worst, they are pompous and lugubrious.

It's no surprise that as a director Penn is most impressive in his
work with actors and that his films focus tenaciously on performance.
In both pictures, high-caliber casts generate charged tension. The
downside is that, like other actors-turned-directors, Penn holds the
camera on his actors far too long, as if waiting for something miracu-
lous or extraordinary to happen.

Indian Runner was inspired by Bruce Springsteen's popular ballad
"Highway Patrolman." Extending a five-minute song to a two-hour,

five-minute film, Penn tells a biblical allegory about the bond between two brothers, Joe (David Morse) and Frankie (Viggo Mortensen). "I got a brother named Frankie," says Joe in the ballad, "and Frankie ain't no good." Nominally, the story probes the psyche of a wounded, incorrigible loser, Frankie, but it's also about troubled relationships between father and sons. Quiet and upright, Joe is a cop struggling to reconcile his professional duty with the personal responsibility he feels for Frankie, a violently unpredictable Vietnam vet. Joe radiates both kindness and repressed yearning in his interactions with Frankie and with his loving wife, Maria (Valeria Golina).

In ambition, though not in execution, Penn goes for Cassavetes's ragged emotional intensity, attempting to construct a painful family portrait. Some scenes, such as the one in which the brothers talk in a bar, recall the way Cassavetes used to throw his actors into unscripted situations. However, the loose, rambling *Indian Runner* has only a few moments of substance and many more of excess and self-indulgence. Penn's dialogue is stilted and simplistic, as when the father says, "He's a very restless boy, that Frankie. That's what got him into trouble, you know." Or when Joe observes, "There are two kinds of men, the strong and the weak."

Moody and volatile, Frankie is capable of both ferociously scary outbursts and eerie calm. Joe observes with fascination his brother's frightening conduct as he displays alternately viciousness and sweetness toward his childlike girlfriend, Dorothy (Patricia Arquette). With her baby-faced innocence, the blonde Dorothy serves as a visual counterpoint to the darkly menacing Frankie.

The glum, earnest film starts off with a killing and sustains a threat of violence throughout, even in its gentler episodes. There are montages that don't connect, such as a graphic childbirth sequence. The title figure, from a Plains Indian legend, commingling the hunter with his prey, runs through the film in whiteface. And a man whose son has been killed bursts into an angry, defiant chorus of "John Henry." These touches make *The Indian Runner* more haughty than heartfelt or soulful.

The sorrowful account of the aftermath of a tragedy, *Crossing Guard* is another pretentious movie whose improvised structure displays powerful passions but is dramatically shapeless. Artful cross-cutting introduces three people as they deal six years after the fact with the death of a small girl in a car accident. A study of an obsessive father (Jack

Nicholson) who won't give up until he confronts the drunk driver (David Morse) who killed his daughter, the film is overbearing and often painful to watch. Structured as a journey of reconcilement—the father with grief, the killer with guilt—the material escapes Penn's grasp as a director. The result is an intense but flat drama that's sporadically punctuated by moments of raw emotionalism and bravura acting by Nicholson and Anjelica Huston (as his former wife).

CELEBRATING CRAFTSMANSHIP—JOHN TURTURRO

Cassavetes's films reflect great understanding and sympathy for their characters as well as the actors who play them. Similarly, *Mac*, John Turturro's 1992 directorial debut, expresses as much affection for the craft of the actor as for the craft of the film's blue-collar laborer-hero. The film pays homage to Turturro's late father, a carpenter who took tremendous pride in his work. Set in Queens in the 1950s, it's a eulogy to a kind of immigrant experience that's gone forever from the American experience. *Mac* recalls Ken Loach's *Riffraff*, a British comedy about construction workers, but Turturro's film is more romantic and less political, perhaps a reflection of the differences between American and British labor.

The movie perceives carpenters as modern Van Goghs, who work in brick and mortar, spackle and beam—"people who are artists and don't even know it." Celebrating craftsmanship, *Mac* concerns the costs of technological progress, the slipping standards of excellence in manual work. It's about the end of the craftsman—a man who dreams of being independent and all the battles he has to go through to achieve that.[7] Turturro is aware that "not everyone works with their hands, but the ones who do, there's a sense of worth and they know who they are. People who just make money are always hysterical and they're never at ease with themselves."[8]

Turturro conceived the idea in 1980, first writing a play with Brandon Cole, then rewriting the script over an entire decade. Scenes from the play were continuously revised with the actors' collaboration. In honing his craft, Turturro picked up a few tips from the indie directors he'd worked with, notably Spike Lee and the Coen brothers. He also credits the Italian neorealist director Vittorio De Sica as an influence.

But, above all, his work derives from Cassavetes: *Mac* is unmistakably an actor's film. Like most actors-turned-directors, Turturro relies too heavily on long monologues and close-ups.

It's rare for an American film to knowingly extol working-class life, which *Mac* does with great ease. The film charts the labors of Mac Vitelli (Turturro), a Queens carpenter who quits his job with an abusive contractor to go into business for himself. Set during the post–World War II suburban housing boom, when financial opportunities were abundant, *Mac* follows three brothers who start a partnership that eventually shakes up their personal relationships. Mac, the leader, is a taskmaster whose perfectionism alienates his siblings. His hardspokenness can't keep his brothers (Michael Badalucco and Carl Capotortol) in line, and eventually he executes his dream bitterly alone.

Turturro's directing stumbles in the neophyte's danger zone of structure and pace. His sensitive understanding is occasionally marred by a crude portrait of ethnicity and a tangled narrative. Nonetheless, there are some small, delightful scenes, as those in which Ellen Barkin, playing a beatnik, lures one of the brothers into her bohemian world.

The product of a working-class Italian-American family in Rosedale, Queens, Turturro started working summers with his father when he was ten. Since Turturro père was too busy to teach his son the finer work, young John was allowed to do only minor jobs, framing, wielding a hammer, mixing cement. Turturro recalled: "As a kid, I thought, 'I'm not gonna be doing this,' but then I got to appreciate it."[9] Turturro's acting ambitions met with resistance; his father urged him to have something to fall back on, like teaching. It was a typical concern of an immigrant who, having come from Italy as a boy, always worried about financial security.

The romantic tones in *Mac* are also evident in Turturro's second feature, *Illuminata* (1998), a farce about the fables and foibles of a tightly knit acting troupe. Recalling Cassavetes's films (specifically *Opening Night*), *Illuminata* offers a serious meditation on love—its compromises, imperfections, sacrifices, and rewards. It's a personal film in which Turturro and his real-life wife, the actress Katherine Borowitz, disclose intimate issues that beset a marriage when one partner is more successful than the other.

Mac was obviously influenced by Cassavetes in theme and style. *Illuminata* continues to draw on Cassavetes (including the casting of

Cassavetes veteran actor Ben Gazzara), but it is more specifically inspired by the classic French tradition of Feydeau's bedroom farces, Jean Renoir's masterpiece *Rules of the Game*, Marcel Carne's poetic *Children of Paradise*, and other works about the magical, all-consuming life in the theater. Robin Standefer's design and Donna Zakowska's costumes are colorful in the manner of those found in 1940s pictures like *The Red Shoes*.

Set in 1905, when theater was the dominant form of entertainment, the movie expresses as much affection for the wizardry of actors on stage as it does for their tempestuous, neurotic personalities offstage. Turturro plays Tuccio, the ambitious resident playwright of a struggling repertory company, eager to stage his new play, *Illuminata*, which he specifically wrote for Rachel (Borowitz), the company's leading actress and the daughter of Flavio (Gazzara), the senior actor in the troupe, who's lost his memory. The theater owners claim the piece is unfinished, but when an actor collapses during a performance of *Cavalleria Rusticana*, Tuccio unscrupulously connives to substitute his play. Unbeknownst to him, the audience that night includes the powerful drama critic Bevalaqua (Christopher Walken), who venomously savages the play.

Turturro and his co-scripter Brandon Cole (who also worked on *Mac*), arrange an amorous rendez-vous for each of the characters. Through cross-cutting, the film jumps around from the salon of Celimene (Susan Sarandon), the celebrated star who's seducing Tuccio with promises of international fame if she does his play, to the bedroom of the foppish critic Bevalaqua as he none too subtly seduces Marco (Bill Irwin), the company's clown, who is sent to him as a messenger. It's here that *Illuminata* misfires, for Turturro lacks (as an actor and as a director) the light touch necessary for staging a farce.

Surprisingly, the story regains its emotional and dramatic focus in the last act, which brings together its central issues: the difficulty of sustaining love once physical passion has subsided and the insecure relationships that encompass love and work, with no separation between the private and public domains. Tuccio and Rachel deliver several touching monologues about the bittersweet nature of love, with the egotistical playwright forced to acknowledge his imperfections and Rachel revealing herself as a loyal woman whose life has been dedicated to him.

THE WHIMS OF FILMMAKING—ALEXANDER ROCKWELL

Seymour Cassel's appearances in Cassavetes's films (*Faces*, *Minnie and Moskowitz*) prompted Alexander Rockwell to write the part of Joe in his comedy *In the Soup* (1992) specifically for him. The improvisation of Cassel (and the other actors) and Phil Parmet's black-and-white cinematography make the movie feel like a tribute to Cassavetes.

Like Tom DiCillo's *Living in Oblivion*, *In the Soup*, a playful film with darkly comic twists, also concerns an idealistic indie filmmaker who dreams of glory. Living in a low-rent, walk-up tenement, Aldolpho Rollo (Steve Buscemi) displays on his walls a poster of the Russian filmmaker Andrei Tarkovsky. He envisions a future when tour buses will visit his apartment and a plaque will commemorate his struggles, a time when Angelica (Jennifer Beals, Rockwell's wife), his beautiful neighbor, will be nice to him. For now, though, with his landlord on his case, he's desperate for money.

Aldolpho's meeting with the underground producers Barbara and Monty (played by Carol Kane and Jim Jarmusch) doesn't turn out the way he expected. When his mother can't help him financially anymore, Aldolpho is forced to sell his favorite books, the most precious of which is a massive screenplay for a film called *Unconditional Surrender*. He places an ad for his script, which brings Joe (Cassel) into his life. Refusing to recognize any social, moral, or legal constraints, Joe lives by his own rules. Says Aldolpho in his voice-over narration: "Joe had his way of making people feel important, even though you knew he was taking you for a ride."

In their first meeting, Joe introduces the nervous director to his sexy girlfriend, Dang (Pat Moya), hands him $1,000, and threatens him with a gun, all in a matter of seconds. Before Aldolpho can even breathe, Joe announces that the two of them are "in the soup" together. "I've decided," Joe announces, "I want art to be an important part of my life." Aldolpho can't help giving in to Joe's energetic enthusiasm, which means hanging out with Skippy (Will Patton), Joe's psychotic hemophiliac brother, and getting involved in illegal schemes, growing out of Joe's belief that "before you make films, you have to make money."

Rockwell, whose previously disappointing features were little seen, made the film on a shoestring, borrowing money from his mother-in-law's pension fund. Basing *In the Soup* on his own experience, he and his co-scripter Tim Kissel have constructed a light tale about the "emotional education"—basic training—of a young artist. Like DiCillo's screen heroes, Aldolpho is not only a tyro director but an immature man; his friendship with Joe forces him to engage in "real" life and ultimately to get a life of his own. At once tough and funny, irresistible and impossible, a lover one minute, a potential killer the next, Cassel gives an eccentric performance that overwhelms the picture. But somehow Cassel's self-indulgent acting is an asset in a film marred by narrow vision, meandering pacing, and arbitrary resolution.

THE COMEDY OF DEFEAT—STEVE BUSCEMI

A serio-comedy about a ne'er-do-well barfly, Steve Buscemi's *Trees Lounge* (1997) is also in the vein of Cassavetes, a rueful look at the petty feuds and uneventful existence of working-class people in a New York suburb. Seymour Cassel, Buscemi's co-star in *In the Soup*, provides a further link to Cassavetes, here playing Tommy's Uncle Al. The film's greatest virtue is Buscemi's thorough knowledge of the characters. His autobiographical film is a projection of what life might have been had Buscemi never left Valley Stream, Long Island, to pursue an acting career. Judging by *Trees Lounge*, it would have been a sorry life marked by irresponsible behavior and underachievement.

At age 31, Tommy (Buscemi) is a loser who is described by his own friends as a screw-up. Tommy is fired from his job as an auto mechanic after "borrowing" money without informing his boss. Tommy's former girlfriend (Elizabeth Bracco), who may or may not be pregnant with his child, has moved in with his angry former boss (Anthony LaPaglia). Living in a tiny apartment above a bar, Tommy has no money to fix his car or to buy drinks. Further complicating life is Debbie (Chloe Sevigny), an adolescent with a crush on Tommy. Temptation overcomes Tommy, and their ill-advised night together infuriates Debbie's hotheaded father. Tommy must face up to the repercussions of his mischief, which ultimately damages him more than those around him.

Epitomizing the working-class milieu is the neighborhood bar, Trees Lounge, in which neither the furnishings nor the jukebox songs have changed in years. Spending his time hustling drinks and engaging in one-night stands, Tommy gets kicked out of the place for excessive behavior. The only person who spends more time at the bar is old Bill, who never moves from his stool. At a crossroads, without even knowing it, Tommy is young enough to break out and make something of his life. If he doesn't, he can see his future down at the other end of the bar, where Bill drinks himself to death. Uncle Al, an ice cream vendor, presents Tommy with a "demeaning opportunity" to take over his route in the neighborhood, which draws Tommy out of the bar.

Neither the comic nor the melodramatic elements are punched up by Buscemi in a manipulative way. Taking his cue from Cassavetes, Buscemi roots his film in characterization and acting, with the humor stemming directly from the characters. Without forcing a dramatic structure or an obvious climax, and without condescension, Buscemi conveys the dead-end nature of aimless lives. He refrains from giving his film the self-conscious "downtown hipness" typical of the indie pictures in which he has appeared as an actor. The realistic setting and the characters' verisimilitude keep *Trees Lounge* afloat, despite its limited scope.

Buscemi handles the material with casualness; his characters are caught up not in a big dramatic crisis but in petty quarrels. There are no bad or good guys, just people struggling to get by. For Tommy, this means getting his car fixed so that he can go back to work and buy drinks. Laced with the kinds of scenes and performances that define Cassavetes's work, *Trees Lounge* boasts a cast of such indie staples as Samuel L. Jackson, Mimi Rogers, Chloe Sevigny, and Elizabeth Bracco. Above all, it's Buscemi's triumph as an actor that makes Tommy both pathetic and sympathetic. Buscemi has specialized in playing losers whose intelligence can't save them from humiliation and defeat; he's often funny because of his profane complaining.

In *Trees Lounge*, Buscemi successfully transfers his saturnine character and sensibility to a bar that is a cave for losers in a lawn paradise. Observed with a compassion worthy of Eugene O'Neill, the movie shows how the young and restless Tommy struggles to distinguish himself from this drinking community. Despite its grim subject, the film maintains a rambunctious tone: The drinkers are funny, because each one has an ego to defend. A low-key comedy, *Trees Lounge* is Buscemi's testimonial to the gallantry of failure.

BLOOD TIES—NICK CASSAVETES

The son of John Cassavetes and the actress Gena Rowlands, Nick Cassavetes gives the symbolic title of this chapter, "Fathers and Sons," a literal meaning. His feature debut, *Unhook the Stars* (1996), celebrated the
acting grandeur of his mother, and his sophomore effort, *She's So Lovely*
(1997), paid tribute to his iconoclastic father, who wrote the screenplay
in the 1970s.

As if to compensate for all the abused, emotionally intense women
Rowlands embodied in his father's films, Nick has constructed a star
vehicle that showcases her warmth and generosity. Rowlands plays an
aging but still beautiful widow, who suddenly realizes that life goes on
and she can't rely on anyone but herself. The narrative premise may not
be new, but the old-fashioned, sweet nature of the tale, cowritten by
Cassavetes and Helen Caldwell, defies all fashions of indie cinema.

Mildred is a financially secure widow whose husband has left her
a comfortable house, shared with her rebellious teenage daughter,
Ann Mary (Moira Kelly). She gives the impression of an accommodating woman who has devoted all her life to pleasing others. After
yet another argument, Ann Mary takes off with her boyfriend, leaving Mildred alone in the oversize house. But unexpected company
appears in the person of Monica (Marisa Tomei), a working-class
mom whose physically abusive husband departs, leaving her with
the responsibility of raising their young son, J.J. Mildred takes an immediate liking to J.J., soon becoming his surrogate mother, picking
him up from kindergarten, babysitting, and teaching him language
and art history.

Nick provides a more benevolent view of suburban life and lonely
widows than is found in most American films, such as Douglas Sirk's
melodrama, *All That Heaven Allows*. Accepting her new existence with
dignity and pride, Mildred forms a new friendship with Monica and
even engages in a romantic affair with Big Tommy (Gerard Depardieu),
a French-Canadian truck driver. Nick tackles some taboos in our culture, like the notion that parents are supposed to like their children
equally; Mildred has no qualms about favoring her son.

The production designer, Phedon Papamichael Sr., who had
worked with Cassavetes père, provides continuity, although, consciously or not, Nick avoids the stylistic devices associated with his father. With respect for the smoothness of a well-constructed narrative,

there are no mega close-ups, no grueling realism; the tempo is relaxed and the characters properly introduced.

As a serio-comic meditation on love and madness, *She's So Lovely* is a slight romp that lacks the profound ideas and rich subtext of John Cassavetes's work. A curiosity, it stands more as an homage to Cassavetes than on its own merits. In the context of today's cinema, both Hollywood and indie, *She's So Lovely* is such an anomaly that the film betrays its 1970s origins, when it was written. Twenty years ago, the triangle played by Sean Penn, Robin Wright-Penn, and John Travolta would have been cast with Rowlands, Peter Falk, and Ben Gazzara. There's also thematic continuity: the female character played by Wright-Penn would evolve into Rowlands's mad housewife in *A Woman Under the Influence*.

Cassavetes's prevalent themes are present in *She's So Lovely*, a movie that belongs to his microscopic studies of husbands and wives who love each other intensely but are incapable of expressing their feelings articulately. The film also displays Cassavetes's romantic view of insanity, his belief that a fine line separates those who are "really" mentally ill from those who are so labeled by society. The central messy existence here belongs to a young working-class couple, Eddie (Penn) and his pregnant wife, Maureen (Wright-Penn). In the first scene, Maureen is hysterically looking for her husband, who's been missing for three days. A couple of drinks with her next-door neighbor lead to an attempted rape that leave Maureen shattered and bruised. Knowing Eddie's dangerously unstable temper, Maureen avoids telling him the truth. When she does, he predictably loses control and goes on a wild spree, shooting a police officer, for which he's thrown into an asylum.

Jumping ten years ahead, the second act finds Maureen happily remarried and the mother of three children, including the daughter Eddie had fathered. Maureen's life is disrupted when Eddie is released from the hospital and a meeting is arranged between the former mates, who have not kept in touch. Heated arguments about true love versus compromised marriage lead to a rushed ending in which Eddie and Maureen's second husband, Joey (John Travolta), battle over Maureen. In the end, she departs with Eddie, which is neither dramatically nor emotionally satisfying.

Cassavetes clearly wants to show there's nothing like the purity of first love, but the underwritten script feels unfinished and is severely marred by missing a third act and by the lack of a discernible point of view. Visually, too, the movie is incoherent, with two clearly distinguishable styles. The first act displays stylistic devices associated with the senior Cassavetes: raw, dynamic staging, a restless and brooding camera, megaclose-ups, and self-indulgent acting, whereas the second, with its fluid framing and smooth pacing, represents a more conventional film.

THE HERITAGE OF MARTIN SCORSESE

Scorsese has repeatedly acknowledged his debt to Cassavetes's dramatic realism and boldly inventive style. Uncompromising, he is arguably the most brilliant filmmaker working in American film today. Over the past thirty years, Scorsese has directed an impressive canon of innovative and controversial films. He combines a cineaste's passion for film noir with an appreciation of rich characterization and an evocation of precise sense of time and place. Scorsese's impressive, if also erratic, career has been emulated by young indie directors. His intoxicating belief in the infinite possibilities of the film medium is most apparent in the work of Abel Ferrara, Quentin Tarantino, Nick Gomez, and, most recently, Paul Thomas Anderson.

Scorsese's films display such bravura with their dazzling camera, jump cuts, and vivid frames that the filmmaking itself becomes a subject of his movies. Even his weaker movies boast stylistic audacity, self-reflexivity, and rich commentary on narrativity. A small-scale film like the black farce *After Hours* (1985) is rewarding because of its mixture of Kafkaesque ambience, realistic dialogue, delirious expressionism, and sketch comedy from *Saturday Night Live* (through the presence of Cheech and Chong).

Scorsese's first film, *Who's That Knocking at My Door* (1968), was a semi-autobiographical drama about the relationship between a streetwise man (Harvey Keitel), heavily influenced by his strict Catholic upbringing, and an independent young woman (Zina Bethune). He then made the exploitation flick, *Boxcar Bertha* (1970), a minor gorefest that nonetheless gave him the opportunity to get closer to the Hollywood system.

Few observers could have predicted that *Mean Streets* (1973), Scorsese's first significant work, would become the most influential film of the 1970s. Interestingly, despite ecstatic reviews from major critics,

Mean Streets was a box-office flop that didn't recoup its small $3.5 million budget. Still, it's hard to think of an American film that has had greater impact. In the 1990s alone, there have been at least half a dozen offshoots, including Tarantino's *Reservoir Dogs*, Nick Gomez's *Laws of Gravity*, Rob Weiss's *Amongst Friends*, Michael Corrente's *Federal Hill*, John Shea's *Southie*, Ted Demme's *Monument Avenue*, and Eric Bross's *Ten Benny*.

A sort of Little Italy version of James Joyce's *Ulysses*, *Mean Streets* explores male camaraderie, a perennial theme in the new American cinema as young directors embrace Scorsese's tough turf—macho rivalries and betrayals, brutal violence, and Catholic guilt. Set in the neighborhood where Scorsese grew up, *Mean Streets* is the story of two Italian-American hoodlums at odds with their seedy environment. Charlie (Keitel) must juggle concerns for his crazy friend Johnny Boy (De Niro), a secret romance with Johnny's cousin, and an ambition to run an uptown restaurant. The film's visual style is marked by a restless, jittery camera that reflects the tension of city life, a topic that would find a more elaborate expression in Scorsese's *Taxi Driver* (1976), based on Paul Schrader's script.

An iconographic street opera, *Taxi Driver* centers on Travis Bickle, a Vietnam vet turned psychotic vigilante fighting against New York city's "scum," pimps, whores, muggers, junkies, and politicians. The film generated controversy due to its bloody denouement—a hallucinatory, brilliantly sustained sequence of carnage involving a twelve-year-old prostitute (played by Jodie Foster). A disturbing expression of seedy city life, *Taxi Driver* was filtered through the distorted personality of a troubled cabbie, superbly played by Robert De Niro.

For his next and finest film, *Raging Bull* (1980), Scorsese chose black-and-white cinematography to lend stark realism, brutal vigor, and psychological intensity to the story of the middleweight boxing champion Jake La Motta, who rose from squalor to the height of his profession, only to be destroyed by his own paranoia. In a switch of genres, but in keeping with his continuing concern with the darker side of urban life, Scorsese turned next to *The King of Comedy* (1983), an incisive black comedy about an obsessive fan (De Niro) who wreaks havoc by stalking a comic celeb (Jerry Lewis). Bizarre aspects of city life during a seemingly endless night are also evoked in the nightmarish comedy *After Hours*.

Emphasizing characterization rather than plot, *Mean Streets* assured Scorsese a central role in contemporary film history. Densely rich and angst ridden, Scorsese's films are rooted in his Italian-American Catholic experience and confront themes of sin, guilt, and redemption in a fiercely contemporary yet universal fashion. His explorations of male camaraderie, violent behavior, and men's deep fear of women have left a significant imprint on the work of numerous directors.

Scorsese doesn't go for ironic detachment. As David Denby has pointed out, Scorsese stresses the lyrical, opera-like possibilities of gangster life (*GoodFellas*); his mobsters are emotional, unlike Tarantino's cool, sardonic heroes.[10] Scorsese should also be credited with inventing a new street language; his hoodlums talk in fresh, deliriously spontaneous lingo. In Scorsese's world, violence is expressed in sudden eruptions of aggression in seemingly peaceful surroundings. In *Mean Streets*, Charlie starts a fight with a girl's boyfriend simply because there's nothing better to do. Later on, Johnny Boy throws a bomb into a mailbox, slugs a stranger in the street, picks a fight with Charlie, and badgers another man with a gun. Scorsese portrays violence with shocking sadism; his men use primitive tools like hammers and baseball bats rather than guns.

Scorsese's problematic treatment of women in his movies has also influenced the work of younger directors. Scorsese places certain women (usually mothers) on a pedestal to be revered, but more women in his films are depicted as deceitful whores.[11] In *Mean Streets*, Charlie loves Teresa and wants to marry her, but he calls her a cunt because they have slept together. Prostitutes abound in *Who's That Knocking*, *Big Bertha*, *Mean Streets*, and *Taxi Driver*. In *Raging Bull*, La Motta asks his brother to keep an eye on his wife, Vickie, implying that, given the chance, all women cheat on their husbands.

This virgin-whore dichotomy is sometimes embodied within the same female figure, who's visually presented in a fragmented manner. In *Taxi Driver*, the teenager Iris is a child-woman who's an object of idealization for Bickle but a sexual object for her customers. A blonde campaign worker, Betsy (Cybill Shepherd), is first perceived by Bickle as a goddess to be protected, but when she rejects him he calls her a cunt. In *After Hours*, Paul becomes infatuated with a seemingly shy and fragile woman (Rosanna Arquette), who turns out to be sexually promiscuous and emotionally unstable. Women's first appearance onscreen reflects only parts of their bodies; if their entire bodies are shown, they're masked in a disharmonious way.

Mean Streets marked the beginning of one of the most creative pairings in American cinema. De Niro would loom prominently in future films as an embodiment of Scorsese's vision of urban society's neuroses. This kind of intimate director-actor collaboration would influence other indie directors: Abel Ferrara and Christopher Walken, Alan Rudolph and Keith Carradine, Whit Stillman and Chris Eigeman.

Based in New York, Scorsese has largely worked outside the establishment, pursuing his own path (with Hollywood money) by making personal movies such as *The Last Temptation of Christ* and *Kundun*. Scorsese has never enjoyed the box-office success of Francis Ford Coppola (*The Godfather*), Steven Spielberg (*E.T.*), or George Lucas (*Star Wars*). Weary of not getting public recognition for his versatility after directing *The Age of Innocence* and *The Last Temptation of Christ*, Scorsese returned to more familiar grounds with vivid portraits of mob life in *GoodFellas* (1990), which was successful, and *Casino* (1995), which was not. Then, totally disregarding commercial considerations, he made one from the heart, *Kundun* (1997), a box-office failure.

Scorsese has attained the goal of authorship more fully than his peers by maintaining high artistic quality. He may be the only director of the film generation who still passionately cares about film.[12] However, this artistic freedom and bold experimentation have come with a price: Despite his prestige and critical kudos (e.g., the AFI Life Achievement Award), Scorsese has never become part of the mainstream industry and has never won an Oscar, and his recent movies suggest that he is no longer a major player in Hollywood.

AT THE EXTREMITIES—ABEL FERRARA

Abel Ferrara has taken Scorsese's thematic and stylistic concerns to an extreme, which is why he has never gained wider acceptance. Labeled a low-rent Scorsese by some critics, Ferrara is known for his stylized portraits of urban violence in a crime-ridden New York, with its blue-lit, rain slicked streets. Ferrara has confronted audiences with the shady, contemptuous side of urban life, showing the ineffectual underbelly of the American justice system in such films as *Ms. 45*, *King of New York*, and *Bad Lieutenant*. His extremes stand for a mad society in which the boundaries between good and evil have been irretrievably erased.

From his first feature, the low-budget cult movie *Ms. 45*, about a rape victim seeking vengeance, Ferrara continued to perfect his incendiary methods with gory thrillers. A chronicler of the "sick" nature of modern life, Ferrara perceives himself as a rowdy outsider, a rules breaker. His combative personality is reflected in films that fall into the crack between exploitation and art, hype and hip. His audience has been small but appreciative, a peculiar mix of the action and art house crowds. Ferrara began to be taken more seriously with *King of New York*, which was shown at the 1990 New York Film Festival, where it elicited walkouts (including Ferrara's own wife) along with praise.

Ferrara's movies are all morality tales, explorations of good and evil that offer only slight suggestions of redemption.[13] These themes receive their most schematic and religious treatment in *Bad Lieutenant*, arguably his *chef d'oeuvre*. Thematically, if not stylistically, *King of New York* (1990), *Bad Lieutenant* (1992), and *The Funeral* (1996) form some sort of urban trilogy. Probably no other director in the contemporary American cinema has exhibited in his work such a gap between the dictates of his head and those of his gut. In film after film, Ferrara's high art and philosophical ambitions clash with his more natural disposition for lowlife sleaze. This may be a result of his collaboration with an intellectual screenwriter, Nicholas St. John, but is also a function of undeniable pretensions, as evidenced in the "existential" vampire film, *The Addiction* (1996).

A native New Yorker, Ferrara began making shorts during high school with St. John, a classmate, launching a long-enduring cooperation. The producer Mary Kane joined the team when they were in college, and later additions included the associate producer Randy Sebusawa and the editor Tony Redman. "When you have no money, you gotta shoot in the places you live with people you know," Ferrara has said.

Like Scorsese, who has cultivated a special relationship with De Niro, Ferrara has his own favorite ensemble. Christopher Walken is Ferrara's quintessential actor, an eerily entertaining mannerist whose specialty is the delivery of long monologues filled with weird intellectual and moral overtones.[14] Combining a scary temper with balletic grace, good and bad impulses coexist within Walken's battling soul. In *King of New York*, Walken plays a crime lord out to regain his turf, and in *The Addiction*, a tough-minded vampire-mentor of a female recruit. As the family's leader in *The Funeral*, Walken plays a murderer who declares contempt for the flaws of the criminal mind just as he is about to kill someone.

A virtuoso of grunge, Ferrara neglects narrative coherence, dramatic logic, and empathy. Technically, *King of New York* is his most stylish film, but emotionally it's as vapid as *Ms. 45* or *Fear City*. A lurid drama steeped in the bright lights and noisy rhythms of urban decadence, it's the story of a drug kingpin (Walken), who operates with venality and pragmatism. But he's also blessed with a streak of idealism and plans to strong-arm the city's drug lords into redistributing their money to the poor and building a hospital for them. These "moral" concerns are embedded in an ultraviolent movie, which is Hollywood's time-honored strategy: Make antiviolence pictures by showing more of it onscreen.

Ferrara's instincts are clearly on the side of mayhem, juicing everything up, exploiting urban fears; his expository, nonviolent sequences often lack dramatic sense. He rehashes a perennial theme of crime films: the thin line between cops and criminals (although his screen cops exceed the norm of screen brutality). In Ferrara's world, deep ambiguity abolishes the distinction between cops and the debased world in which they function.

The scabrously powerful *Bad Lieutenant* offers an excursion into the addictive psyche, mixing Ferrara's favorite elements of sex, drugs, and mayhem. An intensely religious film, *Bad Lieutenant* lacks the balletic butchery of *King of New York*, but it's basically the same morality play, reflecting Ferrara's fascination with reclaimed sinners who are desperate for salvation in a world devoid of love and decency. However, this movie stands out in presenting soul-scorched sordidness and moral disintegration without the usual Ferrara's visceral thrills.

Harvey Keitel plays a strung-out cop who has crossed the border between law and disorder. He is so abhorrent that he doesn't even have a name. Known only as the Lieutenant, he spends his days drinking, snorting, freebasing, shooting up, gambling, and harassing women. The lieutenant abuses his power in every possible and perverse way, doing everything a cop isn't supposed to do. Arresting two teenage girls from the suburbs, he subjects them to sexual humiliation in their car while engaging in masturbation. On his final descent into hell, he threatens to take with him all those within reach.

As heavily steeped in Catholicism as it is in street life, *Bad Lieutenant* represents an unwieldy mix of the sordid and the spiritual, eliciting further comparisons between Ferrara and Scorsese. Like Scorsese, Ferrara's childhood instruction in Catholicism surfaces in his films. *Bad Lieutenant*, like *Taxi Driver*, represents a harrowing journey through the ugliest ruins of civilization. The pitch is close to Scorsese, but the mood may be Polanski. Unlike Scorsese, Ferrara perceives violence as a metaphor: "A lot of this shooting is just symbolic of interpersonal violence, and how people who love each other hurt each other the most." Ferrara sees it as his mission to arouse compassion and forgiveness in a society dominated by hatred and violence.

Indeed, just as the lieutenant is about to hit bottom, he is drawn to a rape case involving a nun (Zoe Lund) in Spanish Harlem. When he first hears of the Church's reward for capturing the rapists, he says, "Why should it make a difference if she's a nun? Girls are raped every day and the church doesn't care enough to offer a reward." Initially, he pursues the case to get the reward, but, as a once devout Catholic, he finds that his religious training and moral upbringing begin to torment his numbed conscience. Obsessed with the nun's sublime forgiveness for the rapists, he undergoes a crisis of faith and becomes consumed by the prospect of redemption.

In what's close to a one-man show, Keitel gives a bracing performance, stripping himself down to raw emotional desperation. Keitel is at his best when he's reined in—when the audience sees his internal battle between good and bad—but he's at his silliest, when he goes all out as a modern Christ, arms outspread, as he stands naked in the middle of an orgy. There are visceral scenes of despair and anguish that bear Christian overtones: In the climax, the lieutenant crawls across a church floor, cursing Jesus with "you fuck, you ratfucker, you fuck," providing shock value that is more theoretical than realistic.

Ferrara and his cowriter, Zoe Lund, confront transgressive issues, redemption, and defeat in a film that divided critics more for its intellectual pretension than for its sacrilege or violence. *Bad Lieutenant* feels like an academic exercise, taking the concept of the antihero to an extreme. The logic of the film seems to be determined by the desire to shock, as if the director were compiling a list of offensive acts never before seen on the big screen. *Bad Lieutenant* didn't mark the first time Ferrara had a tangle with the ratings board, but it was the first time a film of his bore the NC-17 rating. The rating fits Ferrara's film to a T. "It was designed to be NC-17," he said. "If it wasn't, we'd have nothing to sell."[15] Ratings helped: *Bad Lieutenant* didn't become an emblematic document of the 1990s, but it did become Ferrara's most commercial film to date.

If *Bad Lieutenant* is about one corrupt cop, Ferrara' next picture, *The Funeral*, is an ensemble piece about three racketeering brothers: Ray (Walken), the oldest and the most rational, Chez (Chris Penn), the middle and the most volatile, and Johnny (Vincent Gallo), the youngest and the least responsible. Though close to one another, the siblings differ in their outlook on life. Ray, the most dangerously cruel, is contrasted with the temperamental, violence-prone Chez and with the reckless Johnny, who's committed to leftist politics.

A clip of Humphrey Bogart from *The Petrified Forest* and a Billie Holiday song establish the Depression setting of the drama, which begins with the placement of Johnny's coffin in Ray's living room, surrounded by bouquets of flowers from every element of the community. In a labyrinthine narrative, interspersed with lengthy flashbacks, Ferrara and St. John relate the multigenerational saga of the Tempios, a family marked by a tradition of violence and revenge that began with their Sicilian ancestors.

The novelty here is Ferrara's concern for women. Ray is married to Jean (Annabelle Sciorra), a bright, educated woman who is unafraid to express her opinions. Understanding better than any of the men the vicious circle of violence as it moves from one generation to the next, Jean tells Johnny's fiancee, "There's nothing romantic about them. They're criminals because they've never risen above their heartless, illiterate upbringing."

Dramatically, the movie centers on the self-destruction of a Mafia family after its youngest is killed. But the structure is loose enough to allow for the examination of weightier themes than revenge: the burden of family ties, the nature of "fair" justice, the possibility of terminating evil after generations of violence. Ferrara's past inability to harness his eccentric artistic impulses in the service of a more coherent narrative is reined in here. *The Funeral* lacks the operatic style of *King of New York*, the thematic audacity of *Bad Lieutenant*, or the visual boldness of *The Addiction*, but it's a more mature and solid work. It's Ferrara's attempt to make *The Godfather* on a modest scale, without Coppola's epic vision and visual grandeur.

For David Denby and other critics, Ferrara is a moment-by-moment director who can frighten, amuse, or astound but who can't pull a whole movie together.[16] Ferrara creates startling scenes of sordid life—wild parties, decadent sex, joyful killings—but the sequential presentation of events seems arbitrary and the drama vaguely developed, lacking a much needed narrative momentum.

POSTMODERN PULP—QUENTIN TARANTINO

Like Scorsese, Quentin Tarantino does not feel superior to Hollywood's "debased" genres, such as crime movies. Quite the contrary; Tarantino has used the conventions of B-movies to make personal A-films. Situated in Scorsese's thematic turf, *Reservoir Dogs* and *Pulp Fiction* are serio-comic meditations on manhood, honor, loyalty, and redemption. Like Scorsese's best, Tarantino's movies are essentially European art films disguised as American crime movies. Indeed, Tarantino's work is not just a homage to B-movies; it's respun with an art house veneer.

Despite the thematic links, Tarantino's films have a different tone and sensibility from Scorsese's films. Tarantino is an ironist who doesn't believe in emotionalism, fearing that he might lose his edge or perhaps his audience. Tarantino's heroes are as hip, lurid, and self-reflexive as characters in the pulp literary tradition that inspired them. He refuses to sentimentalize his characters or force them to repent, the way Scorsese does in his more spiritual films. Unlike both Scorsese and Ferrara, Tarantino creates an unsentimental world that has little use for conventional notions of good and evil. Defying both realism and noir fatalism, Tarantino sees no problem in granting his antiheroes a second chance.

Nonetheless, Tarantino's dissection of the macho code has not yet achieved the emotional richness or mature depth of Scorsese's work. His idol is Jean-Pierre Melville, the maverick French director for whom style was a kind of morality. Tarantino's production company is named "Band Apart," after Godard's landmark movie, but, as John Powers has noted, so far Tarantino hasn't shown Godard's (or other New Wave directors') sophistication about politics and philosophy.[17]

Placed among his contemporaries, Tarantino stands in diametric opposition to Jim Jarmusch, who has contempt for entertaining the mass public. Tarantino is a natural-born entertainer who sees it as a challenge to captivate his audience with frolicsome movies. He understands that his movies are as much a reflection of pop culture as they are pop culture themselves. *Pulp Fiction* is a frisky postmodern commentary on old movies that consciously plays with audience expectations.

Before *Reservoir Dogs*, Tarantino wrote the screenplay for *True Romance*, intending to raise money and direct it himself. However, unsuccessful at attracting investors, he wrote another violent script, *Natural Born Killers*; again, rejections followed.[18] Warner bought *True Romance* as a big-budget movie for Tony Scott and lost a bundle on it. Then Oliver Stone optioned the script for *Natural Born Killers* and turned it into a vicious, coldhearted farce. Even so, the highlights in both movies are arguably the characters and their monologues, which are Tarantino's trademark.

Though self-conscious about the noir tradition and based more on old movies than on real life, *Reservoir Dogs*, Tarantino's first directorial effort, flaunted a sparkling script and superlative performances. The movie created a buzz in the festival circuit, winning the international critics award in Toronto for making "a spectacular debut that combines a brilliant narrative sense, an expressive use of space, and insightful direction of actors." A moral tale suitable for a jaded, topsy-turvy world, *Reservoir Dogs* is full of dark humor and boasts bravura stylistic command.

Centering on a group of men who, unbeknownst to one another, are brought together to assist a criminal mastermind in a jewelry heist, the movie explores the dynamics of the white male psyche—identity, camaraderie, paranoia, and sexual ambiguity—under conditions of crisis and stress. Structurally, *Reservoir Dogs* bears a resemblance to Stanley Kubrick's heist film, *The Killing* (1956), with Tarantino using a similarly complex narrative format (although, after its release, some critics claimed that *Reservoir Dogs* borrowed heavily from the Hong Kong film *City on Fire*).

The tale opens with seven mugs—played by Michael Madsen, Harvey Keitel, Tim Roth, Chris Penn, Steve Buscemi, Lawrence Tierney, Eddie Bunker, and Tarantino—sitting in a restaurant and arguing about the meaning of Madonna's song "Like a Virgin." They sound like macho blowhards, but they are in fact a bunch of crooks on their way to a bank job. The heist that follows goes very wrong when it turns out the cops have been forewarned. The gang members slowly regroup in an empty warehouse, where they try to determine which of their members squealed. The story is pieced together through sharp dialogue and inventively placed flashbacks.

Wearing black suits, white shirts, black ties, and sunglasses, Tarantino's guys are the epitome of cool. Early on, when they are assigned code names, one (Buscemi) objects to being called Mr. Pink and asks why they can't choose their own names. Answers the boss, "I tried that once. It don't work. You get four guys fighting over who's gonna be Mr. Black."

The Tarantino touch is also evident in a scene in which the undercover cop (Roth), who has infiltrated the gang, experiences a panic attack before the heist, fearing he will be unmasked. Recalling De Niro's self-reflexive scenes in Scorsese's *Taxi Driver* and *King of Comedy*, the cop stands in his apartment and talks to his reflection in the mirror. "Don't pussy out on me now," he says, "They don't know. They don't know shit. You're not gonna get hurt. You're fucking Baretta, and they believe every word, 'cause you're supercool." *Baretta* was a popular 1970s TV show, with a hero who was an undercover cop and master of disguises. One of the crooks, Mr. Blue, is played by Eddie Bunker, known for the crime novels he wrote while in prison.

A brutal torture scene, in which a cop's ear is slowly cut off, had squeamish audiences fleeing the theater. But, for all the gore, the film's most striking image may be that of a wounded Keitel holding in his arms the fatally wounded Tim Roth and combing his hair. The graphic violence, as Amy Taubin observed, not only exposed the sadomasochistic bond between the filmmaker and viewers but also expressed the violence of the underclass and its paranoid abhorrence of other groups.[19] The all-male, white cast suggests that violence is the only recourse for the white underclass to assert superiority over non-whites—including women and homosexuals.

Tarantino's follow up, *Pulp Fiction* (1994), displayed even more of an entertainer's talent for luridness—"a funky American sort of pop, improbable and uproarious with bright colors, danger and blood," according to David Denby.[20] Pauline Kael astutely put her finger on the special appeal of *Pulp Fiction* when she described it as "shallow but funny. And it's fresh. It was fun and there aren't that many movies that are just fun."[21]

Indeed, Tarantino is not an original in the way that David Lynch is; he lacks Lynch's powerful imagination. His stories are not taken from real life, but rather from previously existing films, books, and TV shows.[22] Tarantino does not so much create his stories as reconstruct them, using material that already exists. But it's not the stories that he tells; it's how he tells them. More than other directors, Tarantino understands that in a society that takes all its points of reference from pop culture, Americans' sense of identity is largely based on media images, which explains his appropriation of the most common artifacts of our culture.

Lurid, low-life characters in cheap crime novels of the 1930s and 1940s provide the inspiration for *Pulp Fiction*, which is set in a modern-day Hollywood populated with hoods, gangsters, corrupt cops, and black widows. Boasting an audacious structure, *Pulp Fiction* comprises three interconnected stories that don't match up evenly. Tarantino breaks Hollywood's honored norm of presenting events in sequence. Yet, by the end, the chronology falls into place.

Each story centers on two characters. The first duo are lovebirds Honey Bunny and Pumpkin (Plummer and Roth), who are in a coffee shop contemplating a career change—whether to hold up restaurants instead of liquor stores. The second pair forms the central core of the film; Vincent Vega (John Travolta) and Jules (Samuel L. Jackson) are talkative hit men who work for a crime boss, Marsellus Wallace (Ving Rhames). The jealous Wallace is married to the exotic heroin-addled Mia (Uma Thurman). There's also a double-crossing prize-fighter, Butch (Bruce Willis), and his girlfriend (Maria de Medeiros); Butch is supposed to take a dive but instead grabs the money and runs. The movie ends with Vince and Jules dealing with a drug hit that goes uproariously awry.

The thematic novelty of *Pulp Fiction* is that it's less about the depiction of crime than about what happens before and after crime—how one copes with the bloody mess of a man killed in the back seat of a car. Tarantino creates a character named Wolf (Keitel), a mobster cleanup man who instructs others on how to do the job. What holds the movie together is its inspired playfulness and its cool nihilism in stories that are pitched at a resolutely human scale. Tarantino neglects plot mechanics and linear narrative in favor of lengthy, sustained scenes which are presented out of sequence. Like *Reservoir Dogs*, there's very little action in *Pulp Fiction*: Tarantino's hit men spend more time talking than killing. At the end, a sociopath killer is transformed into a spiritual shepherd; earlier, Jules quotes Ezekiel 25:17 to his victims before blasting them.

In the self-enclosed world of *Reservoir Dogs*, there is no room for women, except for a cameo of a woman who shoots Keitel's character.

But in *Pulp Fiction*, one of the central figures is Mia, Marsellus's attractive wife, whose date with Vince provides an exhilarating scene. Knowing that her husband once threw a man out a window for giving her a foot massage, Vince escorts her with trepidation. A leisurely buildup of their date culminates with the memorable sight of Travolta and Thurman twisting on the dance floor of a 1950s-themed restaurant.

Once again, Tarantino shows his penchant for the rhythm of words—the talk has the drollery of gangland Beckett with exuberant verbal riffs. As Vince and Jules drive to their first "mission," they talk about fast food in Europe. "Do you know what a Quarter Pounder is called in Amsterdam?" Vince asks. "A Royale with cheese." The two bicker endlessly about whether a foot massage counts as a sexual act. Tarantino is a master at taking trite situations and giving them a sudden, vertiginous twirl, as the farcical scene of Mia's drug overdose demonstrates.

The three overlapping stories brim with anecdotes, debates, profanities, and biblical quotations. Tarantino's scripts contain so many stories that it's easy to overlook the restrained lucidity of his style and his respect for actors. Unlike most action films, in which actors compete with—and are upstaged by—special effects, Tarantino's movies are centered around the actors. In *Pulp Fiction* Tarantino builds the entire film around the cadence of the actors' performances. When characters converse, Andrzej Sekula's camera gracefully observes the dialogue, without much movement or other distractions.

Stylistically inventive, *Pulp Fiction* differs from the conventional landscape of film noir; it shows a different side of Los Angeles. Most noirs are set at night, but Tarantino's action is set in a sun-blasted sprawl with no palm trees, no shots of the ocean, no montage of Rodeo Drive shopping, no reference to the Hollywood sign. Pointedly avoiding a slick look, Tarantino replaces these icons with squalid settings of barren streets, dilapidated buildings, and plain coffee shops.

Many directors have borrowed from classic Hollywood genres, but the achievement of *Pulp Fiction* is its coherence despite its secondhand parts. Tarantino takes familiar situations and subverts them with sudden outbursts of violence and radical changes of tone. As a postmodern work, *Pulp Fiction* succeeds where Soderbergh's *Kafka*, which was also made of borrowed elements, fails. David Denby has observed that Tarantino works with trash, but, by criticizing and formalizing it, he emerges with something fresh: an amalgam of banality and formality.[23]

The movie contains weak scenes, such as the flat romance between Butch and his girlfriend, or Butch's gaudy encounter with rednecks, replete with S&M and male rape that recall the Gothic of *Deliverance*. As in the torture scene in *Reservoir Dogs*, Tarantino indulges in unadulterated villainy. His adolescent delight at showing physical torment and his uncertainty about female characters may derive, as John Powers has noted, from the fact that his primary experience comes from movies; he still doesn't know much about human behavior.[24]

Released by Miramax (which in 1993 was bought by Disney), *Pulp Fiction* became the most morally subversive movie to come out of the Disney empire. But the public reacted with unprecedented enthusiasm, elevating Tarantino and his picture to a cult level. Of course, it didn't hurt that Miramax planned a brilliant campaign. Sweeping most of the critics' awards in 1994 and winning seven Oscar nominations, *Pulp Fiction* became one of the few independent film to cross the magic $100 million mark at the box-office.

Less outrageous, if also more mature, *Jackie Brown* (1997), Tarantino's third feature, pays tribute to two creative influences on his career, the crime novelist Elmore Leonard and Pam Grier, star of such 1970s blaxploitation films as *Coffy*, *Foxy Brown*, and *Sheba Baby*. Tarantino takes the twisty plot of Leonard's *Rum Punch* and runs it through his sensibility, which results in a leisurely paced movie. Transplanting the book's action from Miami to South Bay Los Angeles means that there are jokes about Roscoe's Chicken & Waffles and crucial scenes set in the Del Amo Fashion Center.

This time around, Samuel L. Jackson is the star, playing Ordell Robbie, a smooth, garrulous gun runner who operates out of a Hermosa Beach house he shares with his stoned girlfriend (Bridget Fonda). Ordell intends to get out of the gun business after stashing away 500 grand in Mexico. One of Ordell's pawns is a flight attendant, Jackie Brown (Pam Grier), who, as the film begins, is busted at LAX by a federal agent and a cop, while smuggling $50,000 into the country. The authorities put pressure on her to turn Ordell in, but Jackie, aided by a bail bondsman, Max Cherry (Robert Forster), decides to play each side against the other in order to get a crack at Ordell's stash. Jackie tells Ordell she's going to put one over on the authorities by orchestrating an intricate money exchange in which he will get his money back. In the film's most intriguing sequence, Tarantino stages a twenty-minute set piece, showing the same act from three distinct points of view, each revealing different aspects of the transaction.

Revisiting the crime turf in this film, Tarantino examines again the issues of deceit, trust, and cunning among small-time crooks, but he gives the familiar material a distinctive feel through profane street lingo (the overuse of a racial slur irritated Spike Lee), soul and funk music, and other pop artifacts. In a sequence that illustrates Tarantino's talent for combining comedy and startling violence, Ordell puts an errant associate (Chris Tucker), who has violated his parole, in his car's trunk, drives away, and coldly shoots him at a vacant lot.

Jackie Brown is Tarantino's first film about how people connect to each other. The film is not really about a femme fatale's trying to outsmart the cops or the crooks. It's about her relationship with a beat-up old guy, who falls for her, risks his life to help her, and asks nothing in return. Some critics have complained that there is not enough knowledge of Jackie's past—but what gives Jackie power as a character is precisely this lack of information, the fact that the audience's only cues derive from her immediate behavior.

Suffering from lack of dramatic excitement, the picture offers compensations in the imaginative casting and performances. Holding there are no small or insignificant sequences, Tarantino endows each of the film's longeurs with humor, color, and observation. And there's an element of surprise in the mature romance between two unlikely partners, bail bondsman and Jackie, both of whom are at midlife crossroads, which provides quiet emotional undercurrent. As in every Tarantino movie, there are explicit references and tributes, here in the form of a sustained close-up of Jackie driving in her car at the end of the movie, which recalls the final celebrated shot of Garbo at the bow of a ship in *Queen Christina*.

NIHILISM—NICK GOMEZ

A terrifying nihilism, an out-of-control normlessness, marks all of Nick Gomez's movies. *Laws of Gravity* (1992), his first and most emotionally effective picture, is a Brooklyn variation of *Mean Streets*. Tightly focused and intensely dramatized, it's a bleak, hard-edged, ultra-realistic exploration of the reckless lives of small-time hooligans. Gomez's down-and-out characters are the offspring of *Mean Streets*'s Charlie and Johnny: Like them, they are too anarchic and dumb to get anywhere. They bluster or shout, unable to articulate any discernible emotion or mental activity.

The Shooting Gallery, a New York production company, gave Gomez, a cinematographer, the chance to direct his own screenplay provided that he did it on a $38,000 budget. Out of financial necessity, Gomez turned to his neighborhood streets, where he shot the film in only twelve days. He treated his script as a "blueprint," inviting the actors to freely improvise on the dialogue.

Set in Brooklyn's Greenpoint, the film provides an authentic look at a volatile criminal environment and violently haphazard lives. Gomez underlines the characters' cockiness and foolishness, showing how tragically sad their lives are beneath the macho bravado. With a relentlessly narrow focus, the movie illuminates the instant, endless quarrels that often result in senseless killing. That violence grows out of intimacy resonates throughout the film: In Greenpoint, everyone knows everyone else, and no expression of emotion goes without notice.

The movie is personal, if not autobiographical. Like his characters, Gomez was a "knucklehead" who did "a lot of stupid stuff" as a kid.[25] Growing up in an Irish-Italian neighborhood on the fringes of Cambridge, Massachusetts, Gomez didn't attend school from the sixth grade on; later, a couple of assault charges put him on probation. "There was a long period when I was kind of crossed-off the list, a goner," he recalled. However, an interest in music pulled him out of his adolescent tailspin, leading to the formation of a punk-rock band with friends. Eventually, Gomez earned a high school equivalency diploma and attended State University of New York at Purchase, a school Hal Hartley and other indie directors have come from.

Laws of Gravity is a depressing depiction of modern-day Dead End Kids whose world consists of stealing, selling, drinking, and fighting. Living utterly directionless lives, they rip off cartons from a parked van, lift tape decks from unlocked cars. The sketchy, fatalistic story revolves around Jimmy and Jon, who pull off petty heists and finally get in a jam over a bag of hot revolvers being fenced by Frankie (Paul Schultze), a volatile street hustler. The title of the film accurately suggests that losers are bound to fall.

Lean and tattooed, Jimmy (Peter Green) acts as a big brother to the wild Jon (Adam Trese), but he has his own problems. He's on parole but must steal to live. However, with a working wife, Denise, the film's most mature and intelligent character, Jimmy at least has someone to count on. Charged with a crazy energy, Jon is out of control, failing to make his court date on a shoplifting charge. The narrative turns on Jon's arrest after he attacks his girlfriend, Celia (Arabella Field), on the street and on Jimmy's quest to bail him out.

The primary plot device stems from an incident in Gomez's life, though *Laws of Gravity* was not prompted by any burning desire to comment on the plight of his buddies or to advance any theories on how to escape the 'hood. Occasionally, the film is softened with comic bit, but nearly every scene degenerates into a verbal argument and physical brawl. A sense of dread pervades as the film gets more and more intense, marching toward its inevitably tragic conclusion.

Heavily influenced by the urban grit and lingo of *Mean Streets* and the obscene poetry of David Mamet (specifically, *American Buffalo*), Gomez has created a film that surpasses both his masters in its relentless realism. He depicts lowlifes who are prone to feverish outbursts and who converse in limited vocabularies that are bizarrely eloquent.[26] Jon tells Jimmy's no-nonsense wife, Denise: "I'm trying to do what I like to do, trying to live." And when he overextends his guest privileges at their home, the resentful Denise says: "You're sitting on it. You're looking at it. You're drinking it."

Realism dominates in the images of littered streets, graffiti-tattooed buildings, primed but not repainted cars. The cinema verité style—Jean De Segonzac's jittery, hand-held camera and semi-improvised dialogue—gives the film the rough surface and immediacy of a documentary, with its painfully accurate depiction of the drab streets, the greasy bars, and the depressing apartments. The rap, hip-hop and Hispanic soundtrack echoes the film's vision of the grimy, crumbling nature of American cities in the 1990s.

Gomez's second effort, *New Jersey Drive* (1995), was also hyperrealistic in its depiction of black teenagers in Newark who jack cars for kicks. Focusing on the personal odyssey of one youngster, the film takes a hard look at the criminal justice system—the courts, probation officers, social workers, and even the police. As an evocation of black youth, stuck living in a combat zone, *New Jersey Drive* is vibrant. Gomez creates a vivid portrait of street culture, but the film lacks a discernible point of view to make it more poignant dramatically.

The project began when Spike Lee asked Gomez to make a film for Universal. It was budgeted at $8 million, quite a jump from the minuscule budget of *Laws of Gravity*. But, according to Gomez, Universal didn't like things that were "germane" to the story, pushing instead the "more obvious action moments."[27] There was a lot of talk about "narrative signposts," and subsequently the budget was cut to $5 million. In retrospect, Gomez thinks he should have pulled out, but he had already spent months working on the script and was reluctant to start all over again at another company. Gomez felt he didn't have a sufficient budget for the endless car chases envisioned by him. He thus found himself caught in the perverse logic of American filmmaking: new directors tangled up in big-budget projects that prevent them from making the kind of personal movies that caused them to be noticed in the first place.

Illtown (1996), Gomez's third and most experimental feature, came out of the dark place in which he found himself after losing control over *New Jersey Drive*. He told the *Village Voice*: "The mood and tempo of *Illtown* express what I felt like going into it. I had to make it to come out the other end. It was incredibly hard, but it was really satisfying working on a more intimate scale again."[28] The intent was to go to Florida to make a "Hong Kong thriller," but insufficient funds forced Gomez to take risks and be more daring. Indeed, the film's radical form represents a stylistic antithesis to *Laws of Gravity*. It shows again Gomez's attraction to outcasts and criminals, but this time, his haunting look at a Miami drug-dealing circle is staged in a dreamlike, hallucinatory manner, infused with the fatalistic noir notion of one's inability to escape the past.

The stylistic influences of the films of the Japanese renaissance man Takeshi Kitano (*Sonatine*, *Fireworks*) and the Chinese ghost films are evident. The dreamlike rhythm differs from the frantic pace of *Laws of Gravity*; here the pace is more reflective and calculated. Gomez transmutes genre conventions, combining formalism (the conclusion bookends the beginning) with disjunctive editing that sometimes races and sometimes lingers leisurely and moodily. The mise-en-scène juxtaposes static compositions with Gomez's trademark dynamically kinetic action sequences.

More violent than Gomez' previous films, *Illtown* presents crime life from a street point of view. The story follows Dante (Michael Rapaport), his girlfriend, Mickey (Lili Taylor), and the illicit, if profitable, world they developed as street kids. But what was once an exciting life is now taking a physical and emotional toll. Dante and Mickey want out, they yearn to start a normal family life (have a baby), but they're caught up in a vicious circle with no exit. Like *Laws of Gravity*, the narrative impetus is provided by a character from their past, Gabriel (Adam Trese), an old business partner who has just been released from jail. Bent on revenge, Gabriel slowly poisons Dante's business with the help of a crooked cop.

Unfortunately, Dante's and Mickey's "normal" aspirations don't ring true in the dramatic context of their personal histories. And, with the exception of Mickey and her younger deaf brother, the characters are not as engaging as those in *Laws of Gravity*. Still, Gomez's talent for mixing violence and tenderness is evident. He adds to the more familiar tale of betrayal and vengeance the theme of generational gap. The veteran drug dealers, who have gone too soft, are now challenged by more ruthless upstarts; Florida schoolchildren play the low-level dealers with scary authenticity.

Suffused with devices that generate ambiguity, the story is told in flashbacks, which themselves are punctuated with snippets from the characters' pasts. As Dante's nemesis and doppelganger, Gabriel resembles a fallen angel; his entrances and exits are depicted through dissolves. Slowly fading into scenes, he's like a ghost who materializes in the lives of the others.[29] The stylized staging and cutting suggest that some of the confrontations might exist only in the characters' imagination. Isolated moments of daily life are conveyed in fractured time frames, and certain sequences achieve brilliance, such as one hallucinatory foreboding view of Mickey going out to check the club's surroundings. Jim Denault's roving camera, at once rough edged and dreamlike, highlights the visual contrast between Florida's glaring sun and the night glow of its street lamps.

CARTOONISH VIOLENCE—ROBERT RODRIGUEZ

Younger than Tarantino, and just as much a teenager in his sensibility, Robert Rodriguez subscribes to the belief that neoviolence is the ultimate hip. Like Tarantino, he makes movies that are viciously violent, but his violence is more casual and cartoonish. Unlike Scorsese or Tarantino, Rodriguez doesn't believe in developing characters or setting the ground for action. From his first film, *El Mariachi* (1992), he specialized in staging wildly elaborate comic-book action sequences based on grotesque poses.

Rodriguez spent years making shorts with his parents' video camera, a training ground for many filmmakers. Instead of paying attention to his courses at the University of Texas (Austin), he worked on a comic strip that ran for years in the campus's newspaper. Rejected from production classes because of his low grades, he nonetheless managed to make a short that won a local competition. His teachers let him back into class, but they cautioned that it was impossible to make a feature-length movie with no budget.

Making his debut at age 23, Rodriguez, a native of the Mexican border town of Acuna, is still wide-eyed about his sudden success. He relishes telling how he did exactly what his professors thought could not be done: shoot a feature for under $10,000 with a one-man crew—himself—and two 250-watts bulbs for lighting. To raise the money for *El Mariachi*, Rodriguez volunteered to be a subject for a cholesterol-lowering drug experiment at a research hospital, using the month he spent there to write a script.

With no technical help or equipment, Rodriguez used a silent 16mm camera. He dubbed in the sound from recordings made of the actors speaking their lines right after each scene was shot. Rodriguez originally made *El Mariachi* as a learning experience, hoping to recoup his investment by selling it to the Spanish-language video market. He never expected his film to appear with English subtitles in festivals and art houses. However, on the basis of this success, he landed a two-year contract and a distribution deal with Columbia.

Rodriguez's work combines elements of the lurid, low-grade Mexican cinema with the absurdist atmosphere of Austin (which after all produced *Slacker*). A whimsical action-adventure, *El Mariachi* concerns a guitar player who travels Mexico's dusty roads on a motorcycle. The comedy of mistaken identities begins when the player walks into town at the same time that an escaped convict, carrying a similar-looking guitar case filled with weapons, crosses his path. For the lead, Rodriguez enlisted his school chum, Carlos Gallardo, instructing him and the other actors not to rehearse. The intimacy of a one-man crew helped to relax the amateurish cast, and the natural acting, so unexpected in an action movie, became one of the film's most charming qualities.

The sequel to the 1992 hit, which premiered at the Telluride Festival, was *Desperado* (1995), which also had the giddy, gross-out cartoonish quality of a Hong Kong actioner, though without the latter's elegance or grace. The picture got its edge from Antonio Banderas, who brought abundant sex appeal to the avenger's role, proving that an action hero can be more than a beefcake in the mold of Sylvester Stallone. In the new story, the mariachi plunges into the border underworld while pursuing an infamous Mexican drug lord, Bucho (Joaquim de Almeida). In a bloody showdown, with the help of his white friend (Steve Buscemi) and a beautiful bookstore owner (Salma Hayek), he takes on Bucho's army of desperados.

Rodriguez's goal was to make a new kind of movie, one that adds "humor, a strong female character, and a clean-cut good guy who is Mexican" to the action mix.[30] Most of all, he wanted to challenge the cliché that "Mexicans are always the bad guys in movies." Having grown up wanting to be Indiana Jones and Luke Skywalker, Rodriguez felt it was time to provide new role models for Mexican-Americans. Indeed, Salma Hayek became the first Mexican to play a female lead in a Hollywood movie since Dolores Del Rio, back in the 1930s.

Desperado was a slicker, more expensive version of the original—except that what was promising at $7,000 looked tiresome at $7 million. Rodriguez again showed a facility for comic action and cartoonish violence. More than 8,000 pounds of ammunition, thousands of gallons of "blood," and various oversized weapons were used during the shoot to stage the huge explosions and show people getting sliced and diced in various ways—as if the director were telling the audience, "here's another way to shoot a bad guy."

Based on an early, underdeveloped script by Tarantino, Rodriguez's next movie, *From Dusk Till Dawn* (1996) begins as an amusing put-on gangster film, with Rodriguez's signature gunfights and explosions splashed onscreen even before the opening credits. A pair of bank robbers, Seth Gecko (George Clooney) and his psychotic brother, Richie (Tarantino), streak through the Southwest toward the Mexican border. At a scuzzy motel, they capture a widowed former preacher (Harvey Keitel) and his two kids.

The story makes a sharp, unexpected swerve midway, switching from an action to a vampire movie, with naked ladies and plenty of melting flesh. Nominally, the film is a collaboration between Rodriguez and Tarantino, but their sensibilities don't mesh. The movie takes turns: The first half is Tarantino's, the second Rodriguez's. The early sequences consist of long, tense scenes, displaying Tarantino's digressive verbal riffs.[31] Tarantino's indelible dialogue prevails when a Texas Ranger (Michael Parks) gives an uproarious reading of a redneck speech before Tarantino blows him away. Until the crooks and their prisoners reach Mexico, the film sticks to Tarantino's style.

In Mexico, the fugitives reach a garish, raunchy roadhouse, the Titty Twister. Once inside, all hell breaks loose. A curvy dancer (Salma Hayek) does a sultry number with a snake wrapped around her, then sprouts fangs and turns into a vampire. The main characters and other patrons, including Frost (Blaxploitation's Fred Williamson) and Sex Machine (special effects meister Tow Savini), fight off the undead.

The abrupt shift to lurid horror-comics style bears Rodriguez's signature: The second hour is cheesy and derivative of *Night of the Living Dead* and its sequels and of John Carpenter's *Rio Bravo* ripoff, *Assault on Precinct 13*. With its elaborate special effects and heavy ammunition, it's a 1970s exploitation flick, unpretentious but also wearisome. Rodriguez's penchant for weird weaponry, nonstop stunts, and fast-speed editing keep the eyes busy but the mind numb.

Rodriguez has been compared to Sam Peckinpah, but the comparison is unwarranted. The violence in Rodriguez's films doesn't carry any moral or psychological weight. *Straw Dogs* (1971), Peckinpah's most controversial film, was not just violent; it showed the transformation of a rational man (Dustin Hoffman) into a beast, a metaphor for the horrific potential of the human psyche when it feels threatened. Rodriguez recalls Peckinpah only on a superficially stylistic level. Peckinpah was celebrated for his slow-motion montages, cathartic violence, and iconoclastic postures. But, whereas Peckinpah's violence evokes strong emotional response and ambiguous readings, there's only one way to read Rodriguez. Unlike Peckinpah's movies, which have dense texture, Rodriguez's work doesn't hold up on a second viewing.

Peckinpah was berated for demeaning women and glorifying men's exploits, but his work also exhibited philosophical concerns: the violent displacement of a false code of honor by another one. Propagating outlaw mythology, Peckinpah's pictures display a tragic vision in lamenting the demise of the Old West and its noble way of life. In contrast, Rodriguez's work, as Todd McCarthy has pointed out, is juvenilia, staged with visual flair and relentless energy that amount to trashy exploitation.[32]

THE STORYTELLER—PAUL THOMAS ANDERSON

Paul Thomas Anderson's striking command of technique, bravura film-making, and passion to explore new kinds of storytelling recall the young Scorsese. His darkly comic *Boogie Nights* (1997) was one of the most ambitious films to have come out of Hollywood in years. Spanning the height of the disco era, the years from 1977 to 1984, it offers a visually stunning exploration of the porn industry, centering on a hard-core movie outfit that functions as a close-knit family. Risqué subject matter excited critics but divided audiences and tarnished box-office results. Budgeted at $15.5 million by New Line, *Boogie Nights* didn't do well at the box office (about $26 million), but it established Anderson as the hottest director of the year.

Anderson dropped out of NYU film school to shoot a short, "Cigarettes and Coffee," which showed at the 1993 Sundance Festival, leading to an invitation for Anderson to attend Sundance's Filmmaking Lab. His first feature, *Sydney*, was bankrolled by Rysher Entertainment, which interfered with his work. Anderson was able to get his movie back when Rysher agreed to release his cut provided that he retitle the film *Hard Eight*.

Like Scorsese's *Casino*, *Hard Eight* (1997) is set in a gambling mecca, and, like Scorsese, Anderson skillfully conveys the lurid, tawdry atmosphere of all-night casinos and restaurants. Though it premiered at Sundance and successfully played at Cannes, the film never found its audience. Following the rave reviews for *Boogie Nights*, *Hard Eight* became known as Anderson's "other" film.

Anderson grew up in the San Fernando Valley, where he became aware of porn movies. He wrote *Boogie Nights* when he was seventeen, after watching a lot of porn in that "half-juvenile horny-young-man way."[33] He first scripted the story as a short and filmed it on video, but the idea stuck with him, and years later he wrote first a documentary version and then a feature.

In the exquisitely produced *Boogie Nights*, Anderson made a quantum leap forward. The opening sequence owes a debt to Scorsese's

Mean Streets and to Scorsese's noted Steadicam shot in *GoodFellas* of Ray Liotta and Lorraine Bracco entering the Copa through the kitchen. And *Boogie Nights*'s last scene, in which the porn star Dirk stands in front of the mirror flaunting his penis and saying, "I'm a star, I'm a star," recalls *Raging Bull*, when Jake La Motta rehearses movie dialogue in front of the mirror.

In its approach to the porn industry as a unique social milieu, with its own heroes, norms, and lifestyle, *Boogie Nights* resembles *GoodFellas*, Scorsese's chronicle of organized crime, and Altman's take on studio politics in *The Player*. All three movies document "exotic" subcultures (at least from mainstream society's perspective), with their duality of values: the seamy, sordid elements as well as the more humanistic and familial ones. The porn industry is even more ruthless and cutthroat than Hollywood, for its stars are totally dependant on their youthful looks and physical attributes. Of course, the use of sex as a commodity can breed alienation, reducing participants in porn to merchants effective at trading their goods at the marketplace so long as there's demand for them.

Relying on the rags-to-riches format, *Boogie Nights* follows the rise and fall of Eddie Adams (Mark Wahlberg), a handsome, uneducated teenager who works in the kitchen of a San Fernando club. Back at home, Eddie has to face the oppressive company of a passive father and a domineering mother who perceives him as a failure. However, spotted at the club by Jack Horner (Burt Reynolds), a successful porn producer, Eddie is instantly lured to a promising career in the adult entertainment industry. Naive and gullible, Eddie immerses himself wholeheartedly in the new world, which offers a substitute family for the biological one he deserted and the seductive lifestyle of sex, music, and drugs. Adopting a new name, Dirk Diggler, and a new look to match, he soon becomes a hot property, rising to the top. From his point of view, it's the American Dream, with all of its success symbols: a luxurious house, a fancy wardrobe, a red sports car. Hard-working, Dirk comes up with a novel concept, a film series that flaunts his skills as an action hero—a porn James Bond.

As the tale moves into the 1980s, Dirk's excessive drug use, endless partying, and enormous ego begin to interfere with his work. Failing to understand the industry's competitive nature, and not realizing that he's easily replaceable by the next stud around the block,

Dirk confronts Jack with outlandish demands and is humiliatingly removed from the set. Diminished, Dirk becomes a hustler selling his services to a male customer in a parking lot, where he is brutally assaulted in a vicious gay bashing.

Anderson goes for something broader and more ambitious than an account of the inner working of the adult industry at a time of change precipitated by the video revolution. Like Scorsese's *GoodFellas* and *Casino*, *Boogie Nights* is a parable of the greedy, decadent 1980s. Yet, considering the material's potentially explosive nature, Anderson's strategy is nonsensational. The erotic scenes—the films within film—flaunt nudity, but they are handled with discretion and sardonic humor. Structured unevenly, the film's first hour, which is devoted to one year (1977), is nothing short of brilliant, narratively and technically. However, subsequent chapters, which get increasingly shorter, make the saga sprawling and messy.

A well-crafted, overextended canvas, the picture comes across as a piercing, serio-comic inquiry into the personal lives of the players involved. Superbly cast, there's not a single flawed performance, beginning with Wahlberg as the gullible lad who truly believes that he should be "generous" with his natural biological gifts and Reynolds, as the moral center, a surrogate father-filmmaker who takes pride in his metier, attempting to elevate the crassly commercial into the genuinely artistic. Each individual is given a distinctive profile—and a bag of problems to handle: Amber (Julianne Moore), the company's female star and surrogate mother, who loses custody of her boy due to her "irresponsible" lifestyle; a cuckold husband (William H. Macy), who ends up killing himself; a blonde rollergirl (Heather Graham), who demands respect from her sex partners; a decent man (Don Cheadle), who dreams of opening a stereo store; and a rich druggie (Alfred Molina), who's smarter than he appears to be and whose scenes are the film's most brilliantly staged.

OTHER *MEAN STREETS* OFFSHOOTS

Robert De Niro, Scorsese's frequent actor-collaborator, also chose for his directorial debut, *A Bronx Tale* (1993), a *Mean Streets* type of movie, except that his protagonist is a nine-year-old boy trying to fathom the codes of adult behavior. Sitting in front of his house in the Bronx, circa 1960, Calogero witnesses a shooting by a neighborhood gangster, Sonny, but he refuses to name him. "You did a good thing for a bad man," says his father, Lorenzo (De Niro), an honest, hardworking bus driver. *A Bronx Tale* is a variation on the familiar struggle for a boy's allegiance—the good father versus the bad father—except that, in tune with the times, the moral turf is ambiguous. The good father, stands for hard work, honesty, and love. But, as written by Chazz Palminteri, Sonny is not a monster but a thug who becomes the boy's surrogate father and guardian angel. De Niro shows warmth and feelings often lacking in his master's work, but, like most indie directors inspired by Scorsese he doesn't know what to do with the female characters.

Rob Weiss's *Amongst Friends* (1993) is a kind of a Jewish *Mean Streets*, except that the protagonists are not Scorsese's lowlifes but upper-middle class youngsters who choose crime as a way of life. Unlike their peers, who went to college, they decide to stay home. Weiss sets his tale of Generation-X angst near the affluent Five Town area and Hewlett Harbor, not far from where he was born, in Baldwin, Long Island. He wrote the script for *Amongst Friends* quickly, in two weeks, later boasting to the press, "I had never written anything before in my entire life."[34]

Andy, Trevor, and Billy have been inseparable friends until Trevor gets thrown into jail for selling drugs in a deal in which all three were involved. When he returns home, three years later, it's not exactly a happy homecoming. During his absence, Billy has become a wiseguy, with Andy as his lackey, and he's dating Laura, Trevor's girl, who has transferred her affection to him during Trevor's absence. Trevor intends to stop by long enough to find Laura and take her with him.

Billy and Andy are engaged in small-time crime, but they aspire for the big league. Billy is goading his friends into taking big risks, but, desperate for a score of his own, Andy arranges for a drug deal, which he plans to bankroll by robbing a nightclub. He persuades Trevor to get involved; the robbery is pulled off without a hitch, and the down payment is delivered to a fast-talking duo. Unfortunately, the club robbed belongs to a tough, old-time gangster, Jack Trattner, who punishes the violators, forcing them to work for him until their debt is paid. Jealous of Trevor's reunion with Laura and of Trevor's success in the heist with Andy, Billy makes plans to drive Trevor out of town. He arranges for a diamond shipment to Trattner to be replaced with fakes and implicates Trevor in the deal. Things escalate, and the moment of truth arrives in a final confrontation that ends with Andy's senseless death.

In a voice-over narration, Andy says: "My grandfather was a bookie to send my dad to law school, and my dad made money so I could do whatever I wanted, and all that me, Trevor, and Billy ever wanted was to be like my grandfather. We were ashamed of how easy we had it. We felt spoiled. We felt like pussies." Weiss never makes clear why teenagers who have everything would turn to crime. Is it out of contempt for their parents? Boredom? Adventurism promised by crime life? Nor does *Amongst Friends* illuminate the boys' stronger emotional bond with their grandparents. Weiss reportedly feared that elaborating on the intergenerational conflict would turn his film into a conventional family melodrama. The film suffers from other problems: The milieu lacks a distinctly Jewish flavor.

What is effective, however, is the portrayal of peer pressure in yet another story of camaraderie, loyalty, and betrayal. Weiss's superficially sharp style clearly grabbed some viewers. "He's a stylist, a born storyteller," declared Ira Deutchman, after picking up the film for Fine Line distribution. "This film twists conventions around and deals with a culture we've never seen on film before."[35] But *Amongst Friends* received mostly negative reviews, all of which labeled Weiss a pale imitator of Scorsese. Echoing a number of critics, Peter Rainer wrote in the *Los Angeles Times*, "There are far worse models for a new director than *Mean Streets*, but Weiss misunderstands the nature of that film."[36]

Released in the same year, and also suffering from comparisons with Scorsese, was Michael Corrente's *Federal Hill*, an exploration of male camaraderie among young Italian-Americans in the 'hoods of Providence, Rhode Island. Despite a familiar *Mean Streets* ring, *Federal Hill* is well acted and well structured, with unexpected twists. The film has a romantic angle in the story of Nicky (Anthony De Sando), the local hunk who becomes infatuated with a blonde archeology student (Libby Langdon) who's way out of his class. True to form, however, most of the proceedings are about Nick's friendship with his cronies—firecracker-tempered Ralphie (Nicholas Turturro) and Freddo (played by director Corrente).

In this movie, too, the influence of *Mean Streets* is thematic, rather than stylistic. *Federal Hill* is best when it keeps to the street rhythm of its desperate tough guys. There's energy in the staging and performances, but there is nothing terribly exciting about the film, except perhaps the struggle to make it: Corrente shot the movie in black and white on a meager $80,000 budget.

Ted Demme's *Monument Avenue* (1998), a bleak, downbeat, but compelling movie, based on a Mike Armstrong script, is the latest of the *Mean Streets* offshoots. Like Scorsese's work, it's a movie imbued with raw power, suspense, and looming dread. A street divides the old Boston neighborhood of Charlestown, where Irish working-class people settled a century ago, from the surrounding gentrified area. Bobby O'Grady (Denis Leary) and his pals, whose aimless lives consist of hanging out in the local bar, resent the intrusion of yuppies into their region. At age 33, Bobby still lives with his parents, passively accepting his position in life. Bobby is more intelligent than his friend, Mouse (Ian Hart), or Seamus (Jason Barry), his cousin from Dublin, and while he is too smart not to see that his life disintegrating, he is not strong enough to do something about it.

All the familiar types of this subgenre exist, including a veteran Irish cop (Martin Sheen) from across the bridge. The code of silence in Charlestown allows most murders to go unresolved. When one of Bobby's cousins, Ted (Billy Crudup), out of prison and high, talks loud and loose in a crowded bar, the local crime boss, Jackie (Colm Meaney), guns him down. Celebrating male bonding, this society basically excludes women; there's only one woman over whom there's rivalry. Bobby has an affair with Jackie's girl, Katy (Famke Janssen), but neither Bobby nor Jackie has time for her. Forming a clique of criminals closely tied to one another by kinship or friendship, they're imprisoned by rigid codes of behavior that exclude any possibility for change. When they spot a black man walking on the turf, Bobby displaces the rage of his frustrations to some disastrous effects.

It's not a coincidence that young, ambitious male directors choose for their debut a dynamic crime movie modeled on *Mean Streets*. As Eric Bross's *Ten Benny* (a.k.a. *Nothing to Lose*), set in New Jersey, and John Shea's Boston-set *Southie* (both shown in 1998) demonstrate, the thematic and stylistic format of *Mean Streets* allows enough flexibility to flaunt dramatic and visual chops. What these young directors don't realize is that, with the exception of *A Bronx Tale*, this genre's commercial appeal is limited.

THE TARANTINO EFFECT

The American "pulp-fiction" school of filmmaking has shown appreciation for cool, stylish directors like the late Frenchman Jean-Pierre Melville, the Hong Kong filmmaker John Woo, and the Japanese stylist Takeshi Kitano. The bank heist genre has made it into a new generation with a vengeance—and ultraviolence. Two of the most prominent screen types in 1990s indie movies are hit men and con men, placed in cool, ironic noir comedies.

Numerous filmmakers have shamelessly emulated Tarantino, copying his notorious blood-and-guts-and-brain style. His imitators think that all they have to do is write ultraviolent scenes and long, irreverent arguments colored with profanity. These copycats, spinoffs, derivations, and homages have brought the adjective "Tarantinoesque" and the noun "Tarantinees" into film vocabulary. Included among the Tarantinees are *Killing Zoe* (1994); *Coldblooded, Parallel Sons, Swimming with Sharks, The Usual Suspects, Things to Do in Denver When You're Dead* (all in 1995); *Feeling Minnesota* (1996); and *Keys to Tulsa* (1997). Most of these derivative movies owe their existence to *Reservoir Dogs*, which has assumed the importance of *Mean Streets* among the newest crop of filmmakers.

Keith Gordon, an ambitious director who made some original and complex films about men in war (*A Midnight Clear, Mother Night*), has described the new trend this way: "Everybody in town is looking for the next gritty-bunch-of-people-who-are-lowlife-criminals-and-are-kind-of-satirically-funny-with-a-lot-of-violence-script." The idiosyncratic Gregg Araki concurs: "It's a fucking jungle out there. Everyone and his grandmother wants to be Quentin Tarantino, and there's like five sources of money out there, and 60 million projects."[37]

That *Killing Zoe*, written and directed by Roger Avary, is a Tarantino-like picture is no surprise. Tarantino served as executive producer, and Avary, Tarantino's co-worker at Manhattan Beach's Video Archives, collaborated on the scripts of *True Romance* (a shared daydream of two video-store clerks) and *Pulp Fiction*. Much less subtle than Tarantino, Avary relies on an aggressive, in-your-face style.

The script for *Killing Zoe* was done quickly in order to use a bank location in downtown Los Angeles, standing in for Paris, where the story is set. A relentlessly over-the-top, ultrabloody crime caper, it owes its existence to French noir. As Hoberman observed, "Like *Reservoir Dogs* and other male adolescent fantasies, *Killing Zoe* is a feast of high-octane gibberish and badass attitude, rampant female masochism and routine misogyny."[38] Avary replaces Gomez's terrifying nihilism with comic nihilism in a bank heist yarn gone disastrously awry.

An American safecracker, Zed (Eric Stoltz), lands in Paris to hook up with Eric (Jean-Hugues Anglade), his buddy, who's planning a bank robbery on Bastille Day with his heroin-addicted gang. As soon as he arrives, a cabdriver fixes Zed up with Zoe (Julie Delpy), a hooker, or as the cabbie says, "a wife for a night." For all his tough-guy facade, Zed is an innocent abroad, and much of the humor is directed at his passivity: Zed can't even prevent the naked Zoe from being thrown out of his room when Eric shows up.

A would-be criminal mastermind, Eric is a crazed philosopher with a theoretical axiom for every occasion. Dissuading Zed from taking a shower, Eric says, "In Paris, it's good to smell like you've been fucking—it will make them respect you." Zed is welcomed by the rest of the gang with a dead cat, dirty dishes, marijuana, and endless squabbles. The gang spends a long evening driving around Paris under the influence of drugs. With visual flair, Avary and the cinematographer, Tom Richmond, use a mobile camera to present Zed's journey through the night. The dissolute team shoots up and pops pills in a ritualistic male bonding in an all-night Dixieland cavern.

Although Avary, Stoltz, and the other actors are American, and although a Los Angeles bank doubled for the interiors, the film has the lurid tone of a French neo-noir, like Luc Besson's *Subway*, with all the existential pretentiousness. According to Avary, *Killing Zoe* was meant to be an allegory: "Eric can be likened to the Reagan-Bush years, when they kept everyone happy through hysteria. Just saying that things are good doesn't necessarily make everything good, but it fools a lot of people into following you."[39]

Avary keeps things loose and visually exciting: Zed's robbery joyride turns into a delirium. But it's a letdown when the bank heist takes center stage. As robbers, the gang members are such out-of-control incompetents that there's no doubt the heist will go awry; the only question is how messy the bloodbath will be. Zed's realization that Eric is a psychopath comes too late. As Peter Rainer has pointed out, Avary juices the screen with ultraviolence because he can't figure out a clever way to get his guys out of there.[40]

An arty neo-noir in color, *Killing Zoe* promises to take off in unexpected directions, but its major distinction is Avary's gift for hysteria and pompous existentialism. Most critics acknowledged the blatantly flashy style but dismissed the film as lifted from the Tarantino school. Released by October while *Pulp Fiction* was still in vogue, *Killing Zoe*'s disappointing grosses ($400,000) couldn't even recoup its $1.6 million budget.

Bryan Singer's *The Usual Suspects* (1995) is another derivative film wrapped in a seductively slick style. The film's merits have less to do with a display of a singular voice than with its place in post-Tarantino Hollywood. A well-acted, highly ironic thriller about the wages of crime, *The Usual Suspects* revolves around a complicated but superficial puzzle that doesn't pay off emotionally. As polished as the filmmaking is, it's second-rate Tarantino, but, with the help of good reviews, the film found an audience.

In the *Los Angeles Weekly*, the critic Manohla Dargis perceptively singled out the ingredients of the Tarantino-driven formula:

> Take a company of actors, among them the cool, the somewhat cool and the thoroughly hopeless, which in the case of this picture means newcomer Benicio, the fast-rising Palminteri and a handful of well-known faces, including Stephen Baldwin, Gabriel Byrne and Kevin Spacey. Add to this mixture a self-consciously tangled plot, plenty of loose tough talk ("Oswald was a fag"), loads of casual sadism, and the occasional misplaced reference to some pop-cultural fetish or other. Throw it at the screen and pray that the deities that smiled on Quentin Tarantino take your sorry ass and turn you into the next great hope of God, country, and Hollywood.[41]

Five professional thieves, rounded up by the New York police in an effort to identify a voice, are placed in a lineup, each taking turns speaking the same profane words, each actor emphasizing a different word in the string of obscenities. The narrator, Verbal (Spacey), is a con man with a gimpy leg whose voice variously shifts rhythms. Verbal's friend and mentor, the enigmatic Keaton (Gabriel Byrne), has a tendency to melancholy moroseness. Two hardballs—Hockney (Kevin Pollak), whose quickness has an edge of paranoia, and McManus (Stephen Baldwin), a cocky killer—and a handsome Latino, Fenster (Benicio De Toro), round out the clique. After the lineup, the men begin working together, gradually evolving into a tightly knit gang with coalitions and rivalries.

There's a front man, Mr. Kobayashi (Pete Postlethwaite), who may or may not be Japanese and speaks with formality, and a mysterious Keyser Soze, also of uncertain nationality (Turkish or Hungarian). Characters utter his name with trepidation, but it's unclear whether he actually exists. The movie begins five weeks after the lineup, when most of the protagonists have been destroyed while storming a ship allegedly filled with cocaine. Verbal, the only survivor, is interrogated by a Customs agent (Chazz Palminteri) and he goes back in time, before the lineup, and then comes back to the present again. Is he telling the truth? Are we seeing what really happened or what Verbal subjectively wishes the agent to believe?

Stylishly playful, the film offers a Rashomon-like maze in which it's impossible to determine the truth. An accomplished ensemble of actors elevates the film, adding perversity, particularly Kevin Spacey, who won a supporting actor Oscar for his brilliant turn. Spacey's deliciously ironic manner keeps the story off balance whenever it threatens to become conventional.

David Denby has observed that Singer's style is elegant but empty, using pop culture without much wit.[42] Singer shoots in chiaroscuro, with obsessive close-ups of objects; like Lynch, he zooms in on a lighter, a cigarette, a coffee cup. Like Tarantino, the scripter Christopher McQuarrie shows a flair for theatricality and knowledge of the crime genre. Singer shares with Tarantino a movieish playfulness, the tough-guy bravado, the mystique of macho power, but his work is less spontaneous and more studied than Tarantino's. Like his model, Singer is good at creating tension, and, like him (and most indie directors), he has little use for women; there's only one female character, and a minor one at that.

Slickly made, Gary Fleder's *Things to Do in Denver When You're Dead* (1995) recounts the ill-fated reunion of another ruthless gang. The screenwriter, Scott Rosenberg, reportedly made a bet with Tarantino, promising to give him $10 for every review of the movie that did *not* mention Tarantino's name. The reasons for the inevitable comparisons are abundant: the familiar milieu of organized crime, the tough-guy heroes, the snappy, self-conscious macho talk.

Though the film doesn't feel like a personal work, it was meant to be. The death of Rosenberg's father from cancer allegedly inspired the story of a man with another kind of death sentence, a man who's the target of a hit. "This guy is incredibly decent, and he becomes part of the lore," Rosenberg explained. "He's spoken of in heroic terms, which is how I always talk about my father. There are guys who are so successful and make so much money, and they're miserable pricks and not a tear is shed at their funeral. My movie is about the value of a man."[43]

The mythically named hero, Jimmy the Saint (Andy Garcia), is a former seminarian who soured first on the church and then on crime. He hangs out in a malt shop, "Thick 'n Rich," and runs a dubious video operation, Afterlife Advice ("Just Because They're Gone Doesn't Mean They Can't Guide"), in which dying parents record their advice for their survivors. A rhapsodic talker, Jimmy is a wizard with a slang laced with words like "buckwheats" and "boatdrinks."

Fleder and Rosenberg take the conventional themes of loyalty and honor and try to twist them in darkly humorous ways. The film's gallery of characters includes a bluff narrator (Jack Warden) and a terrifying crime lord known as the "Man with the Plan" (Christopher Walken), who is paraplegic from injuries sustained in an attempted rubout. The most artificial and preposterous figure is a hoodlum named Critical Bill (Treat Williams), so named because he leaves everyone he meets in critical condition. A mortuary driver who uses corpses as punching bags ("I haven't touched a live person in years," he says), Critical Bill reveals a guileless boyish quality that covers his psychopathic actions with an eerie calm.

Trying to correct the genre's bias against women, Fleder creates a romantic interest in the figure of Dagney (Gabrielle Anoir), a ski instructor whom Jimmy pursues with seductive lines like "Girls who glide need guys who make them thump." Juggling different roles, all at the same time, Jimmy tries to manage his fragile relationship with Dagney, look after his crew, and, in a subplot lifted from *Taxi Driver*, straighten out a troubled hooker, Lucinda (Fairuza Balk in the Jodie Foster role).

The plot gets into high gear when the powerful Man with the Plan, who dotes on his son Bernard, asks Jimmy to put a scare into the boyfriend of Bernard's former girl. "It's just an action, not a piece of work," he says, meaning no one is to get killed. To do the job, Jimmy rounds up the usual suspects from the old days, including Franchise (William Forsythe), a tattooed trailer park manager. Not surprisingly, things go wrong, as they always do in such movies.

The film is directed in a brisk, stylish manner, but the talented performers can't propel the film over its rough spots. Excessively graphic violence—bloody shootouts and brutal beatings—assumes center stage, accentuating all the more the senseless narrative. As a noir comedy, *Things to Do in Denver* flaunts an arrogant style, but, like *The Usual Suspects*, it's hollow at the center.

A cross between Robert Altman's *The Player* and Tarantino's *Reservoir Dogs*, George Huang's darkly cynical comedy *Swimming with Sharks* (a.k.a. *The Buddy Factor*) was supposed to present a "realistic" take on Hollywood. Disenchantment with the industry's establishment provides the inspiration for a black comedy about a young man's ruthless rise to the top. Focusing on the relationship between Buddy Akerman (Kevin Spacey), an egomaniac executive, and Guy (Frank Whaley), his neophyte assistant, the film is meant to be an exposé of the industry's venality. But it comes across as a Tarantino-like revenge fantasy, in which a rookie holds his obnoxious boss hostage and tortures him for all the "indignities and hardships" the rookie has suffered while working for him.

A film school graduate, Guy reels in disgust when his friends react with indifference to his analysis of Shelley Winters's career. This opening scene borrows from the sequence in *Reservoir Dogs* in which the gang members discuss the meaning of Madonna's song "Like a Virgin" in a coffee shop. Guy lands a fast-track job as assistant to a high-powered exec, Buddy, an egotist known for his abusive relationships with women and employees. On the job, Guy endures ceaseless verbal and physical abuse; Buddy prevents him from taking lunch, then forces him to remove from local newsstands every copy of a *Time* magazine issue that includes a derogatory mention of him.

The script loses its bite when Guy begins to date Dawn (Michelle Forbes), a producer whose ambition is to get Buddy's support for her new project. Buddy initially responds with a lack of enthusiasm, but

Guy is able to turn him around. Though the film centers on a triangle with a major female role, it's hard to ignore its misogyny. When Guy has to choose between his mentor and Dawn, his decision suggests that in Hollywood women are easily disposable.

In the phony climax, Guy forces Buddy to confront his sadism, torturing him in the manner of *Reservoir Dogs*. The coldly calculated ending does *The Player* one better in its take on how self-centered and insular Hollywood can be, illustrating Guy's transition from a gullible victim to a shrewdly manipulative insider. Like *The Usual Suspects*, the film's major asset is Kevin Spacey, who lifts the conceit with his bravura poisonous performance. Too cynical and knowing for his own good, Huang makes some missteps—in an inside joke, he names a director Foster Kane. The showbiz strivers in *Swimming with Sharks* simultaneously romanticize and demonize Hollywood—the ultimate cool. Basically an exercise, the film is a gimmicky kiss-off to Hollywood, meant to facilitate Huang's entry into Hollywood's select group of hotshot directors.

CONCLUSION

The Tarantino effect seems to be in decline, judging by the failure of such offshoots as *Keys to Tulsa* (1997) or *Very Bad Things* (1998). Harley Peyton's script from Brian Fair Berkey's novel is deft and witty, but Leslie Grief's awkward direction in *Keys to Tulsa* lacks modulation and visual style. This comic crime, a late-in-the-cycle Tarantino retread, mixes genre ingredients with fresh observations on class disparity, Great Plains lifestyles, and generational and family strains. However, Gramercy could not distinguish this entry from other comic thrillers, which sent it to video stores rather quickly.

Tulsa's Richter Boudreau (Eric Stoltz), a "black sheep son of a black sheep," is about to lose his job as a film critic for the local paper. Although he is penniless, his eccentric, much-married socialite mother (Mary Tyler Moore) refuses to bail him out. This makes him vulnerable to the schemes of Ronnie Stover (James Spader), a drug-dealing low-life married to Richter's sexy childhood friend, Vicky (Deborah Unger), who was disinherited when she married Ronnie. Suffused with sexual innuendo and dark humor, the film's as concerned with Richter's maturation as it is with resolving a murder. The tale runs the gamut of Oklahoma City's social hierarchy, from the country club set to the trailer trash, as well as the downwardly mobile offspring of privileged families who have failed to uphold their ancestors' traditions.

In *Very Bad Things*, actor-director Peter Berg makes the mistake of thinking that his politically incorrect tale is clever and hip; he even casts a real porn star to play the hooker. Centering on five friends and their disastrous bachelor party in Las Vegas, the film aims at criticizing bourgeois hypocrisy and complacency. But instead of examining this phenomenon, the movie sinks to a level of smugness that only a young, immature writer-director like Berg (better known for his role in TV's *Chicago Hope*) could have created.

The new trend in indie cinema, replacing Tarantino's profane, ultraviolent movies, is manifest in cynical, nihilistic exposés of social relationships, where the violence is more behavioral and emotional than physical. This is reflected in the work of Neil LaBute (*In the Company of Men, Your Friends & Neighbors*) and Todd Solondz (*Happiness*), which is examined in Chapter 8. Tarantino's shock value is still present, but it is contained in a different type of film, one that's amoral rather than immoral.

4

Regional Cinema

THE LANDSLIDE VICTORY of Ronald Reagan in 1980, and the corresponding defeat of Democratic candidates and causes, signaled that
American society was shifting to a more conservative mood. Reacting
against the cultural and political liberalism of the 1960s, Americans
were turning toward more traditional values. The new conservatism
was seen as a reaction to rising divorce rates, the Me generation and its
cult of intimacy, and sexual promiscuity. With Reagan's blessing, the
glories of the good ol' days—which may or may not have ever existed—
became a potent myth. The resurgence of a patriotic mood led to the
production of films that strongly reaffirmed the centrality of the nuclear
family. These films expressed nostalgic yearning for traditional values
in reaction to both the domestic and the international problems that
beset American politics at the time.

Country-and-Western music, a fast-growing industry that reflected
the zeitgeist, was suddenly discovered by Hollywood, and country
music themes began surfacing in big-studio films. *The Electric Horseman*
(1979), starring Jane Fonda and Robert Redford, featured the country
singer Willie Nelson on the soundtrack and in a small role. *Coal Miner's
Daughter* (1980), a biopicture about the singer Loretta Lynn, became a
blockbuster and Oscar winner.[1] The "country" motif was also reflected
in a new fashion that combined cowboy boots with Ralph Lauren Western wear.

The 1980s saw the release of a large number of country-themed
films. After a decade of ignoring rural America, the American cinema
seemed to have rediscovered the dramatic potential of small-town settings. Horton Foote, who wrote the script for *To Kill a Mockingbird* (1962)
and the play upon which *The Chase* was based, enriched the small-town
tradition in the 1980s with impressive works for the stage (*The Widow
Clare*), the screen (*The Trip to Bountiful*), and television (a miniseries
based on the film *1918*).

It is not a coincidence that Sam Shepard flourished as both a playwright and a screen persona in the late 1970s and 1980s. As a playwright, Shepard created a new kind of drama filled with violence, lyricism, and intensity and marked by vivid theatricality and brutal honesty. A poet laureate of the inarticulate, Shepard writes by instinct; his work doesn't necessarily improve when made more shapely and orderly. As a movie star, Shepard recalls a modern Gary Cooper, the tall, solitary, reticent American on horseback.[2] In *Country* (which is discussed later), Shepard plays a struggling farmer who shows the vulnerability beneath the icon.

Shepard has devoted his entire theater and screen career to rural settings and characters. In Terrence Malick's *Days of Heaven* (1978), he plays the wealthy, mortally ill farmer who gets into a fatal triangle with Brooke Adams and Richard Gere. In *Resurrection* (1980), Shepard is the fanatic lover of a spiritual woman whose husband has died in a car accident. In *Fool for Love*, which he wrote as a play and was independently filmed by Altman in 1983, Shepard plays a rodeo cowboy who's traveled miles with his pickup and horses to find May (Kim Basinger), his lover and half-sister with whom he's had a tormented relationship. The drama concerns their explosive, elemental, fateful love, marked by contradictory feelings of anger and yearning. Shepard gives a scary yet touching performance, helped by Basinger as May, Randy Quaid as May's gentleman caller, and Harry Dean Stanton as the father of the lovers.

Shepard's trilogy, *Curse of the Starving Class*, *Buried Child*, and *True West*, is a searching exploration of family dynamics, dramas about bad blood ties, betrayals, and battles over unpaid land. As a playwright, Shepard neglects plots in favor of dramatizing agonizing relationships. He transplants his dysfunctional families to the old West in *Silent Tongue*, a bizarre film directed by him in 1994 that represents an unpalatable mixture of prairie melodrama, Greek tragedy, Japanese ghost tale, and travel minstrel show. A hodgepodge of acting styles and influences, it is a Western as disappointing as Shepard's directorial debut, *Far North* (1988), a drama about the effect on a Minnesota family of the near death of the family patriarch, who is almost killed by a wild horse.

In 1980s pop culture, small-town America was far from a barren land; bizarre and mischievous characters breathed new life into the heartland. In 1986 alone, several movies celebrated the idiosyncrasies of small towns and the eccentricities of their inhabitants: Jonathan Demme's

Something Wild, Francis Ford Coppola's *Peggy Sue Got Married*, David Byrne's *True Stories*, Evelyn Purcell's *Nobody's Fool*, David Lynch's *Blue Velvet*, and Bruce Beresford's *Crimes of the Heart*. Each of these films depicts reserves of energy and imagination hidden beneath traditional facades.

At the same time, these films concern a moral and emotional vacuum and the lack of organized communal life, with characters pretty much left to their own devices. The new movies stress the need of individuals to distinguish themselves from mainstream mores, but, as Janet Maslin has pointed out, Main Street still exists as a set of values that demands conformity—"in those ways, Main Street will never change."[3]

Notwithstanding the title of *My Own Private Idaho* (taken from a song by the rock group B-52s), Gus Van Sant shot several of his pictures in Portland, Oregon, where he lives in a large Victorian house in the West Hills district. "Portland is how the movie is," Van Sant told *Newsweek*. "Everything's tame and sort of friendly."[4] After toiling in Hollywood for years, Van Sant realized his unique filmmaking voice in Portland. Van Sant is one of several artists—others include David Lynch and the cartoonists Matt Groening, Lynda Barry, and Gary Larson—who delineate the eccentricities of life in the Pacific Northwest. "People in the Northwest," Van Sant said, "tend to be more eccentric than people anywhere. This place is full of folks who disdain the things you might go to L.A. for: a big house, a lot of money, ego."

Most American independent movies are set in New York or Los Angeles, the country's two cultural centers. But in the late 1970s and 1980s, a number of filmmakers explored indigenous subcultures, drawing on their firsthand familiarity with their regions' distinctive look and feel. Several regions were put on the national cinematic map through the work of their local directors. Based in Austin, Richard Linklater has used Texas as a setting for most of his work (*Slacker*, *Dazed and Confused*). Robert Rodriguez (*El Mariachi*) has also drawn on his origins in a border Texas town. Florida is richly reflected in the work of its premier filmmaker, Victor Nunez (*Ulee's Gold*).

JONATHAN DEMME AND REGIONAL COMEDY

Jonathan Demme is a popular entertainer who knows that a director can't criticize culture unless he understands its meanings to people.[5]

Rosanna Arquette as the drab New Jersey housewife about to be transformed and Aidan Quinn as a Downtown projectionist in his loft in Susan Seidelman's *Desperately Seeking Susan* (1985). Courtesy of the Academy of Motion Picture Arts and Sciences.

Madonna positioned on the floor (Seidelman likes to keep her flighty heroines down to earth) in New York's Port Authority in *Desperately Seeking Susan* (1985). Courtesy of the Academy of Motion Picture Arts and Sciences.

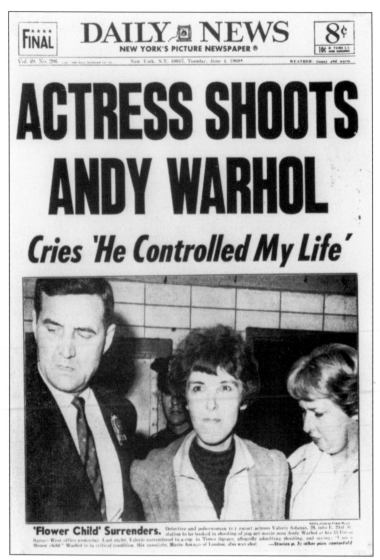

FINAL

DAILY ☐ NEWS
NEW YORK'S PICTURE NEWSPAPER ®

8¢

Vol. 29, No. 296   New York, N.Y. 10017, Tuesday, June 4, 1968*   WEATHER: Sunny and warm

ACTRESS SHOOTS
ANDY WARHOL
Cries 'He Controlled My Life'

'Flower Child' Surrenders. Detective and policewoman (r.) escort actress Valerie Solanas, 28, into E. 21st St. station to be booked in shooting of pop art movie man Andy Warhol at his 33 Union Square West office yesterday. Last night, Valerie surrendered to a cop in Times Square, allegedly admitting shooting, and saying: "I am a flower child." Warhol is in critical condition. His associate, Mario Amaya of London, also was shot. —*Stories p. 3; other pics. centerfold*

The real Valerie Solanas on the cover of *Daily News*, June 4, 1968, which revealed the shocking story of her attempt to kill celebrity Andy Warhol. Courtesy of the Academy of Motion Picture Arts and Sciences.

Bearing a striking resemblance to the real Valerie Solanas, Lili Taylor strikes a pose in front of Warhol's famous image of Elvis Presley in Mary Harron's *I Shot Andy Warhol* (1996). Courtesy of the Academy of Motion Picture Arts and Sciences.

Tom Waits *(left)* is Zack, John Lurie *(center)* is Jack, and Roberto Benigni is Roberto in Jim Jarmusch's second indie comedy, *Down by Law* (1986), which opened the 1986 New York Film Festival. Courtesy of the Academy of Motion Picture Arts and Sciences.

In Alan Rudolph's best film, *Choose Me* (1984), Dr. Nancy Love (Genevieve Bujold) descends from the isolated sterility of her radio show for an unexpected interlude with a hunky Mickey Bolton (Keith Carradine). Courtesy of the Academy of Motion Picture Arts and Sciences.

An utterly transformed Dr. Nancy Love (Bujold) talks with her own phone-in analyst in *Choose Me* (1984), a romantic film that, among other targets, pokes fun at shrinks, showing them to be just as problematic and needy as their patients. Courtesy of the Academy of Motion Picture Arts and Sciences.

A light feminist streak runs through Joan Micklin Silver's *Hester Street* (1975), in which a religious Russian immigrant (Carol Kane) arrives in the New World at turn-of-the-century New York and has to face new realities. Courtesy of the Academy of Motion Picture Arts and Sciences.

Three beautiful working-class women dominate Allison Anders's most accomplished film, *Gas Food Lodging*: a waitress mother (Brooke Adams, *right*), a sensitive teenager (Fairuza Balk, *second right*), and a rebellious daughter (Ione Skye). In the course of the film, each discovers or rediscovers her sexuality and realizes she can't live without men—a recurrent motif in Anders's work. Courtesy of the Academy of Motion Picture Arts and Sciences.

RIGHT: Frances McDormand as the errant wife in the final, stylized shootout in the Coen brothers' *Blood Simple* (1985), one of the most stunning debuts in indie history, which is also responsible for the resurgence of film noir among young filmmakers. Courtesy of the Academy of Motion Picture Arts and Sciences.

BELOW: As the tormented, utterly corrupt cop, Harvey Keitel experiences revelation—and moral redemption—in Abel Ferrara's scandalous NC-17 *Bad Lieutenant* (1992). Courtesy of the Academy of Motion Picture Arts and Sciences.

Michael Rooker plays the title character in John McNaughton's terrifyingly uncompromising *Henry: Portrait of a Serial Killer* (1990). Courtesy of the Academy of Motion Picture Arts and Sciences.

Rose (Annabeth Gish) dances with her stepfather, Jack Chismore (Jon Voight), a troubled WWII vet, in the coming-of-age saga *Desert Bloom* (1985), which captured the "A-Bomb culture" of the 1950s. Courtesy of the Academy of Motion Picture Arts and Sciences.

Guatemalan refugee Enrique (David Villalpando) discusses his plans of journeying up North with his close friend, Ramon Munoz (Rudolfo Alejandre) in *El Norte* (1984), Gregory Nava's melodrama which brought Third World painful realities to Western audiences. Courtesy of the Academy of Motion Picture Arts and Sciences.

Tim Robbins as Bob Roberts, a singer/entrepreneur turned right-wing politician in *Bob Roberts* (1992), a satire that was not biting or audacious enough. Courtesy of the Academy of Motion Picture Arts and Sciences.

In the lesbian drama *Desert Hearts* (1986), a stiff, repressed Columbia professor, Vivian Bell (Helen Shaver, *center*), is contrasted with a liberated lesbian (Patricia Charbonneau, *center, in shorts*). As Reno locals, Alex McArthur *(left)* and Gwen Welles add color to this earnest coming-out tale. Courtesy of the Academy of Motion Picture Arts and Sciences.

In Lisa Cholodenko's impressive debut, *High Art* (1998), Ally Sheedy *(top right)* gives a mesmerizing performance as Lucy Berliner, a disenchanted photographer whose accidental meeting with a young, ambitious editor (Radha Mitchell) radically changes both her professional and personal lives. Courtesy of the Academy of Motion Picture Arts and Sciences.

A typical David Lynch composition: an old man has just had a stroke *(on the ground)*, the water is running, a dog is barking, and an innocent baby is standing behind white picket fences witnessing the bizarre occurrence in *Blue Velvet* (1986), the most talked-about indie of the entire decade. Courtesy of the Academy of Motion Picture Arts and Sciences.

In *Blue Velvet* (1986), through voyeurism, boy scout Kyle MacLachlan discovers not only a dark outside world of drugs, violence, and perversity, but also his inner dark self. Courtesy of the Academy of Motion Picture Arts and Sciences.

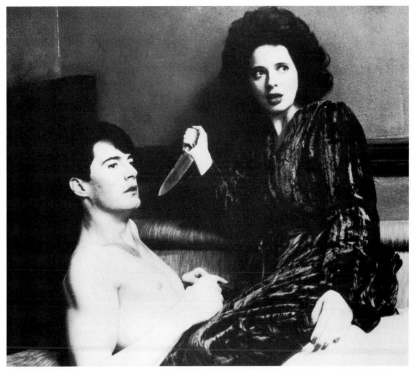

Violent sexuality is one of the many themes of *Blue Velvet* (1986), in which a naive adolescent, Kyle MacLachlan, is initiated into sex by a mature, alluring, and victimized chanteuse (Isabella Rossellini). Courtesy of the Academy of Motion Picture Arts and Sciences.

Sitting and talking is a staple of John Sayles's work from his very first film, *Return of the Secaucus Seven* (1980), with Maggie Renzi *(left)*, Bruce MacDonald, and Jean Passanante as disenchanted 1960s radicals facing early mid-life crises. Courtesy of the Academy of Motion Picture Arts and Sciences.

The dissolution of old couples and the formation of new couples are the central principles in Steven Soderbergh's stunning debut, *sex, lies, and videotape* (1989), the film that changed the public image of American indies. Repressed wife Andie MacDowell and outsider-impotent James Spader *(left)* fall in love, as her crass sister Laura San Giacomo and adulterous husband Peter Gallagher fall out of love. Courtesy of the Academy of Motion Picture Arts and Sciences.

Sacked out in a cheap Florida motel, Eddie (Richard Edson, *center*) and Willie (John Lurie, *right*) plot a day at the dog races, while Eva (Eszter Balint) dreams of surfing and sand in Jim Jarmusch's first—and best—film, *Stranger Than Paradise* (1984). Courtesy of the Academy of Motion Picture Arts and Sciences.

Florida, Ohio, and the East Village all look and feel alike to the romantic trio Eddie (Richard Edson, *left*), Eva (Eszter Balint), and Willie (John Lurie) in *Stranger Than Paradise* (1984). Courtesy of the Academy of Motion Picture Arts and Sciences.

Notorious John Waters star Divine, surrounded with flamingos, in the shockingly bad-taste satire *Pink Flamingos* (1972), one of the longest-running midnight movies. Courtesy of the Academy of Motion Picture Arts and Sciences.

Demme has probed small-town America with the same intensity that Scorsese has applied to his explorations of "urban nightmares" (*Mean Streets, Taxi Driver, After Hours*) or Woody Allen to his bitter-sweet portraits of New York (*Manhattan, Hannah and Her Sisters*). Demme's trilogy of serio–folk comedies, *Citizens Band* (a.k.a. *Handle With Care*) (1977), *Melvin and Howard* (1980), and *Something Wild* (1986), portrays the idiosyncratic varieties of American life. With the exception of *Something Wild*, which was released by Orion, they were studio movies, the kind that would never be made by Hollywood today.

In his lyrical sketches of rural America, Demme uses a relaxed, diffuse style to capture the innocent quality of American hopefulness. He provides uncondenscending insights into a working class that, despite poverty, is still buoyed by dreams of striking it rich. Demme has shown an intuitive feel for the texture of life outside the mainstream, suffusing his characters with warm acceptance devoid of criticism.[6] Rich in commonplace detail and nonjudgmental humor, Demme's approach combines the satirical percept of the very American Preston Sturges with the humanist compassion of the very French Jean Renoir.

The hallmark of Demme's populism is his taste for kitsch; he rummages around the American landscape like an antique hound in a thrift store. The critic David Edelstein has described it as "the moral uses of kitsch," or how bad guys use kitsch to insulate their souls and good guys use it to liberate them.[7] Demme's movies are laden with tacky interiors and garishly tasteless costumes that reach their best expression in *Married to the Mob* (1988), in which working-class gangsters live in a fake world, parading around in long white overcoats that serve as a mask for their lack of subtlety. Demme's America is a colorful place, as in "dress-up and be what you want to be, but don't think that clothes by themselves make the person."

Handle With Care explores the psychology of CB radio operators obsessed with talking on the airwaves. Radio is a medium that allows them to maintain their anonymity and at the same time reinforces belongingness. The characters' anonymous public names are all icons of pop culture: Spider, Electra, Warlock, Cochise, Chrome Angel, Smilin' Jack.

The movie illustrates how individuals can transform themselves— with CB radios—into close-knit communities. By contrasting people's unrepressed ids with their more socialized egos, the narrative shows how people use CB radios to express their sexual fantasies to strangers in a manner they would never dare in personal interactions. The radio helps unleash their hidden, subconscious desires. In a quintessential scene, Electra, an otherwise ordinary girl named Pam, unleashes onto the airwaves such outrageous sexual profanities that an overly excited driver reaches orgasm in his truck.

Spider (named Blane), a mechanic who runs a CB repair shop, is a self-styled crusader who cuts off the wavebands of those who violate the FCC regulations—parasites like a redneck obsessed with Communism and a priest who sees danger in America's secularization. There is no communication between Spider and his retired, drunken father, who comes to life only when he uses the CB. Failing to wake his father, Spider walks to another room and calls him on the radio, and the old man wakes up immediately.

At the film's climax, when an old man is lost in the woods during torrential rains, all the members of this newfound community search for him over their CB. This magical forest sequence recalls Shakespeare's *A Midsummer Night's Dream*. Holding hands, strangers participate in a collective, quasi-religious ritual. The film's eccentric characters derive from those of Preston Sturges, though Demme's touch is lighter, less frenzied. Where else but in a Demme film can two women accidentally meet on a bus and realize they are married to the same man? The casting of Paul LeMat and Candy Clark, of *American Graffiti* fame, suggests some continuity between the two films, though, defying genre conventions, *Handle With Care* is more original than George Lucas's film.

Loosely based on real-life characters, *Melvin and Howard* provides one of the 1980s' most perceptive looks at how the American Dream can become entangled in an obsession with jackpots and prizes—the last-ditch hope of the little people. More lyrical than *Handle With Care*, the film's vision has been described by the critic Michael Sragow as "robust and generous as Walt Whitman's."[8]

The narrative begins with a bizarre meeting in the Nevada desert between one of America's richest men, Howard Hughes (Jason Robards), and one of its poorest, Melvin Dummar (Paul LeMat). Melvin finds the white-haired, long-bearded Hughes on the ground, thrown from his motorcycle. Trying to cheer him up, Melvin sings "Santa's Souped-up Sleigh," and soon Hughes joins him with "Bye Bye Blackbird." When Melvin expresses his dream of getting a better job at an airplane factory like Hughes Aircraft, the old man says, "What a shame. I might have done something. I'm Howard Hughes." In Vegas, Melvin drops Hughes at the Sands Hotel and gives him all his money—a quarter. In this unlikely encounter, the two interact as equals, and the media-created, monstrous Hughes emerges as a human being. The meeting reflects the American egalitarian, optimistic spirit in its conviction that it's still possible for people at opposite ends of the social spectrum to interact.

Melvin returns to his trailer-home in Gabbs, where he lives with Lynda (Mary Steenburgen) and their daughter, Darcy. When repossession men haul away his truck and his new motorcycle, Lynda leaves him, with help from her friend Taylor. Later, deserted by Taylor in a low-rent motel, she struggles through a procession of nowhere jobs, dancing in a sleazy Reno club and waitressing in a topless joint. Melvin gets impatient, files for divorce, and is granted custody of their daughter. Ultimately, Lynda and Melvin reconcile and remarry in a $39 Vegas wedding chapel service. But when Melvin recklessly buys a Cadillac and a huge motorboat (which he parks on the ground), Lynda leaves him again. Listening to her farewell speech, Melvin protests only when she says they are poor: "Broke maybe, but not poor."

The most illuminating scene involves a TV game show, which captures the American obsession with winning. What's left of the elusive American Dream of hard work is the urge to share the national spotlight and appear on TV, if only for a few seconds. Modeled after *Let's Make a Deal*, the film's *Easy Street* has a smooth host, Wally (Mr. Love) Williams, whose soothing voice fits his function as a pastor in another collective ritual.

Demme doesn't criticize TV as an impersonal medium. For Melvin (and his like), TV game shows offer a bond with millions of anonymous strangers, united by their love of TV and their fantasy of winning. A modern example of Capra's "little people," without Capra's sentimentality, Melvin is a quintessential American hero: innocent, kind-hearted, and generous. Genuinely happy for those who win, he hopes that the next time it will be his turn.

Demme shows a sharp eye for the offbeat in rural America, the subjective perceptions of the American Dream. The movie depicts people's attempts to rise above their limitations; the characters are not fully aware of their class and don't see their background as an obstacle. Although they face one crisis after another, they continue to be hopeful and always land on their feet. Melvin is selected "Milkman of the Month," and, after a second divorce from Lynda, he finds happiness with another woman. *Melvin and Howard* was billed as a romantic comedy, "a fiction based on fact," but the writer, Bo Goldman, was not concerned with whether Melvin was telling the truth about the encounter (according to the film, Hughes's will was left at Melvin's gas station). For him, the film is about "what if Melvin was telling the truth."[9]

Continuing his exploration of a culture addicted to fantasy and escapism, Demme next directed *Something Wild*, which featured a prevalent 1980s type: the yuppie. At the center, once again, is an unlikely pair: Charlie Driggs (Jeff Daniels), an uptight Wall Street tax accountant, and Lulu Hankel (Melanie Griffith), a recklessly sexual woman. They meet in a downtown Manhattan luncheonette, when Lulu spots Charlie beating a check. Charlie, a vice president at a consulting firm, claims that he has meetings to attend, reports to write, a wife and children waiting in their suburban house. Ignoring his objections, Lulu takes him to a New Jersey motel, handcuffs him to the bedpost, and makes love to him in ways he has never before experienced.

Like other "yuppie angst" movies (*Desperately Seeking Susan, Lost in America, Blue Velvet, Into the Night*), *Something Wild* suggests that appearances are deceptive, that people should not be trusted simply on the basis of their look or their verbal expressions. Although they are seemingly opposites, Lulu and Charlie turn out to be kindred souls. Charlie starts out as a conservative starched shirt, a 1980s version of "The Man in the Gray Flannel Suit," and becomes more nonconformist as the story progresses, whereas Lulu's transformation moves in the opposite direction.

Something Wild, like *Blue Velvet*, was inspired by a popular song, and also like Lynch's movie it concerns the delicate balance between the normal and the abnormal. As in *Blue Velvet*, role reversal is a key element: Here, a sexually aggressive female initiates an innocent white male. Lulu's sexual practices and transgressive desires shock the Yuppie in much the same way that Dorothy's shocked Jeffrey. More significant, in both films the women are restored by the end to more traditional, domestic roles. In *Blue Velvet*, Dorothy is revealed to be a good mother, and by the end of *Something Wild* Lulu shows signs of domesticity.

Sporting a kinky black outfit, Lulu dons a Louise Brooks pageboy wig. Her real name, Audrey, also seems to be drawn from movie lore, perhaps representing a link to Audrey Hepburn, whose role in *Breakfast at Tiffany's* she slightly resembles. In this and other aspects, Demme reveals pop culture as America's secular religion, permeating every aspect of our lives. Lulu drags Charlie to her mother's Virginia home, then off to a tenth high school reunion, a joyful occasion that turns into a nightmare when Audrey's psychotic former husband shows up. Abruptly changing gears, the film turns into a violent drama, with the two men vying for Audrey. Again recalling *Blue Velvet*, the sequence asserts that crime is no longer the exclusive territory of urban America. Despite its disquieting melange of genres, the movie plays like a modern version of a Depression screwball comedy—*It Happened One Night*, in reverse. Instead of Clark Gable's aggressive, boozy, self-centered newspaperman, there's Audrey, the unemployed sexual aggressor. And instead of traveling from Florida to New York City, Demme's couple drives from the city to the country.

Something Wild also shares thematic similarities with *After Hours*; it's like a rural counterpart to Scorsese's nightmarish view of SoHo. In both films, the hero is a square, upright, and uptight professional, but, unlike *After Hours*, wherein the hero goes back to "normal life" at the end of his ordeal, Charlie undergoes a more radical transformation, and his future is uncertain.

The multiracial skew in *Something Wild* stood out in the landscape of 1980s movies. While the leads are white, Demme populates the background with black musicians, waiters, and gas attendants. Their conspicuous presence offered an ironic commentary on Reagan's separatist ideology with its "white supremacy" implications. They reminded viewers that ethnic minorities were still at the bottom of the hierarchy; in fact, it would take another decade for African Americans to take center stage in their own movies.

Demme's work set the tone for a number of idiosyncratic comedies; both indie and mainstream, peopled by eccentric personalities in seemingly ordinary locales: Francis Ford Coppola's *Peggy Sue Got Married*, Bruce Berseford's *Crimes of the Heart* (based on Beth Henley's stage play), and David Byrne's *True Stories*, cowritten by Byrne, Henley, and Stephen Tobolowsky. Henley's comic characters, in both *Crimes of the Heart* and *The Miss Firecracker Contest* (filmed as *Miss Firecracker* by Thomas Schlamme in 1989), are marked by wild individuality, a trait more applauded in the South than in other regions of the country.

Despite Beresford's attempts to open up Henley's play, the sensibility of *Crimes of the Heart* remains theatrical. The film offers a vivid portrait of three Chekhovian sisters in Hazlehurst, Mississippi. Lenny

MacGarth (Dianne Keaton), the oldest, is a modern version of the spin-ster (her problem is a shrunken ovary). The family's black sheep, Lenny has grown bitter but is not entirely devoid of humor. Meg MacGarth (Jessica Lange) is the small-town girl whose acting ambitions have car-ried her to Los Angeles. Life in the Big City, where she suffered a nerv-ous breakdown, has made her harsh, and she is now working for a man-ufacturer of dog food. Babe MacGarth (Sissy Spacek), the youngest and the most eccentric, is a child-bride in the mold of Tennessee Williams's heroine in *Baby Doll*. Babe shoots her husband in the stomach—because she hates his "stinking looks"—then gracefully offers him an iced lemonade.

The sisters spend their time reminiscing about their childhood and sharing sexual secrets. They are actually three faces of the same woman, three sides of female sexuality: shyness and asexuality (Lenny), ripe, overt sexuality (Meg), and childishly naive sexuality (Babe). In another era, their naughtily crazed behavior might have been offensive, but here, as the title suggests, the characters are presented as all heart and feeling.

Babe is concerned mostly with the media coverage of her murder case. When her mother committed suicide, she received national atten-tion in the *National Enquirer*, but, now married to a prominent politician, Babe worries that her story might get only local coverage. Obsession with fame and celebrity and desire for acknowledgment by the media, particularly through TV appearances, became new national concerns in the late 1970s. Christopher Lasch, in his seminal study, *The Culture of Narcissism*, observed: "All of us, actors and spectators alike, live sur-rounded by mirrors. In them, we seek reassurance of our capacity to captivate or impress others, anxiously searching out blemishes that might detract from the appearance that we intend to project."[10]

Similar narrative logic, carried to a more schematic extreme, pre-vails in *True Stories*, produced by Karen Murphy, who is also the copro-ducer of the sublimely goofy *This Is Spinal Tap*. The film pays homage to the boundless inventiveness that small towns— here Virgil, Texas—in-spire. The occasion for celebration is Virgil's commemoration of the state's Sesquicentennial, an idea that would also be used by Christo-pher Guest in *Waiting for Guffman* (1997).

Byrne's *True Stories* opens and closes with the image of a narrator (played by Byrne), dressed in stetson and string tie and driving a fire-engine-red convertible against a flat and barren horizon. The austere landscape magnifies the quirkiness of the characters, who derive from tabloids' human interest stories. The narrator performs the same role as the druggist in *Our Town*, wandering through town and observing its habits. But, unlike *Our Town*, in which the narrator encounters the commonplace, Byrne never ceases to be surprised by what he sees. *True Stories* is a glorification of kitsch as it invades the commonplace, a democratic celebration of the unique qualities that transform the ordinary into the extraordinary.

Following a montage that encapsulates the history of Texas, the characters, all icons of pop culture, are introduced, including the Cute Woman (loosely based on a TV show hostess who likes to paint pictures of puppies); the Lying Woman, (who claims to have written half of Elvis Presley's songs); the Lazy Woman (a TV addict who never gets out of bed); the Innocent (who is in constant search of Love); the Computer Man; and the Visionary Businessman.

Everybody's looking for America, a quest that would appear in many works of pop culture as the country nears the millennium. The implication is that Americans have lost their identity, and their direction. Of the contemporary questers for the national soul, Byrne, the author of quirky American lyrics, is one of the cleverest.[11] Byrne has said he was attracted to the characters "because they had their own eccentricities but they weren't ashamed of them."[12] In films of the 1980s, America has a center, a Main Street, but it's looser, less confining, allowing for the coexistence of alternate lifestyles. An "appreciation of people and things," *True Stories* is a tribute to "openness and willingness to see things differently, to try things, to experiment."

Byrne attests that "there are a lot of places like Virgil," but *True Stories* is not so much about Virgil as it is about consumerism, the way pop culture is reflected in every aspect of our lives. The centerpiece, a "Celebration of Specialness," consists of 130 unusual talent acts: disco-dancing goldfish, glass-harmonica players, yodelers, a precision dance team, the Tyler Junior College Apache Belles. A fashion show at a shopping mall is staged with a life-size wedding cake, living grass suits, trompe l'oeil brick wall suits, and local clubs with matching uniforms.

True Stories expresses Byrne's postmodern sensibility, a "high-tech cum postcard America, well-stocked supermarket shelves, tract houses under the sky, rat-a-tat-tat TV channel zapping."[13] Influenced by Ken Graves and Michael Payne's "American Snapshots," the cinematographer, Ed Luckmann, gives the movie the quality of a snapshot, mixing styles of the corner drugstore, Bauhaus functional imagery, and Japanese calligraphy all in one film.[14]

FARMING: MYTH AND REALITY

Ruralism and regionalism are in, cosmopolitanism and sophistication are out, wrote David Denby in a critical piece in *New York* magazine in the late 1980s, noting that independent films have stayed out of Hollywood and the big cities, concentrating instead on the "common man."[15] In Denby's view, independents were arming themselves with earnest fare as much for the institutional support it garners (from, e.g., the National Endowment for the Arts, *American Playhouse*, or the Sundance Institute) as for its assumption of virtue and righteousness. In the arts, however, virtuous thinking and anti-Hollywood sentiment, like all forms of high-mindedness, encourage solemnity and dullness. Too many indie films of this ilk wander around aimlessly as if setting diffident characters in rural areas absolves the screenwriter of the responsibility for writing good, articulate dialogue.

Until the late 1980s, if there was a stereotypical independent movie, it would be an earnest coming-of-age story about a sensitive girl. Rural movies, with their closeups of noble and weathered faces, became icons of bygone American innocence; they were labeled "granola movies" by some critics. Robert Redford reportedly bristled at the association of granola movies with Sundance, making every effort to distance the Sundance Institute and Festival from *American Playhouse*, which was known for such fare.

Viewers don't go to mainstream Hollywood pictures to see losers or underachievers, the typical characters in regional cinema.[16] The portrayal of such people has been left to low-budget indies. During the Reagan-Bush era, American indies attempted to combat Republican triumphalism with nostalgia for rural simplicity. In these high-minded movies, the bright golden haze on the meadow was darkened by clouds of corporate greed, and youngsters came of age while their parents struggled to save the family farm.

Richard Pearce's *Heartland* (1979) set the pattern for many rural films of the era in its story of Elinore Randall (Conchata Ferrell), a young widow who moves out West to work as a housekeeper on a ranch. Based on diaries of an actual pioneer, the film examines the challenges and hardships of frontier life, celebrating the American spirit of fierce independence. Unlike later Hollywood films of this kind (*Places in the Heart, Country, The River*), *Heartland* has as its protagonist a new-comer who did not look like an actress, which contributes to the film's authenticity; a big-boned, wide-hipped woman, Ferrell looked like an ordinary woman.

Heartland begins with the arrival in the West of Elinore aboard a train crammed with people. She has come to meet her employer, Clyde Stewart (Rip Torn), a harsh man of few words. At first, their interaction is restricted to work: She commits herself to give "a full day's work for a full day's pay." But she ends up working harder than she did in Den-ver, where at least she had her Sundays free. Women in *Heartland* do their share, but they don't get the same recognition as the men. Elinore would like to own her own ranch because, as she puts it, "all my life I've been working for somebody else."

The film records Elinore's daily routines: cleaning, cooking, sewing, milking, and sometimes even reading (*Dryland Homesteading*). The other women in the film are just as tough as Elinore. Grandma (Lilia Skala) arrives on a horse wearing a cowboy hat. "You don't play with these winters," Grandma warns Elinore, recalling how her own baby froze to death. Aside from brutal storms (the painful sight of a dead horse in the blizzard), there's a food shortage, and the men are leaving.

The film has little dialogue; for long stretches, the visuals carry the story without need for words. Emotions are vastly understated; Clyde's proposal to Elinore is brief and unsentimental. For her wedding (filmed with local residents), Elinore wears her apron and work boots. Later, the pregnant Elinore waits as Clyde goes to fetch a midwife from another farm, but a storm prevents him from returning in time. She gives birth alone, but the baby dies. Celebrating the singleminded commitment to life in the wilderness, *Heartland* abounds with matter-of-fact scenes that show in graphic detail pigs being slaughtered, cattle skinned, cows giv-ing birth. However, the very last image, a hopeful shot of a sunny day, reaffirms Clyde and Elinore's attachment to the land. In its emotional power and stark realism, *Heartland* boasts a lyrical effect similar to that of Jean Renoir's American film, *The Southerner* (1945).

Indies were not the only movies to glorify the Land. Three studio movies in 1984 depicted farming from a female perspective: *Places in the Heart*, starring Sally Field; *Country*, with Jessica Lange; and *The River*, with Sissy Spacek. The appearance of three farm movies in one year, as if suddenly the farmers' plight were the hottest issue on the national agenda, was probably a coincidence. What was not a coincidence was that all three revolved around strong heroines. In the 1980s, every major actress in Hollywood sought "substantial," preferably moralistic, screenplays. After decades of underrepresentation, women were finally getting better screen roles.

The least sentimental of the three, *Country* was inspired by newspaper articles about the economic hardships faced by farmers in the Midwest. Although Reagan was in power, the film attacks the farm policies set by the Carter administration. The problems are seen as the fault of government: Farmers were encouraged to expand, having adopted wholeheartedly Carter's slogan "We're gonna feed the world!," but, soon after, the administration placed an embargo on foreign sales.

A tornado during corn harvest destroys the crops, and with the FFHA (Federal Farmers Home Administration) calling in loans, the farmers face bankruptcy and the loss of their land. Tom McMullen, the FFHA's county representative, charges that "something is wrong" with the farmers' way of doing things and suggests partial liquidation of their holdings. But the proud and stubborn Gil (Sam Shepard) claims that McMullen can't look at it "short-term." He argues that farming is a way of life, not a business, and dismisses Tom as "a college boy who knows nothing but numbers."

The tension between romantic individualism and collectivism is expressed in the intergenerational conflict between Gil and Otis (Wilford Brimley), his father-in-law. "Our blood goes deep as the roots of that tree in this ground," Otis says. "Nobody can yank us with a piece of paper." As a boy, watching his father plow, Otis vowed to never leave the place, which he never did, except to fight in World War II. But impersonal bureaucracy has replaced personal relationships between officials and farmers. The bank's president, Walter Logan, is a cold-blooded bureaucrat who views farming as big business. Gil misses the times when the bank used to loan money on the man, not the numbers, and Jewell tells the banker she would rather be a thief than do what he does for living.

The scene is depressing. In Allison, a town with only 2,064 people, "Out of Business" signs are common, along with mass sales of tractors and plows. Gil doesn't know what to do, and, under pressure, he collapses emotionally. He starts drinking heavily, becomes abusive with his children, and finally walks out on his family. It's Jewell who saves the farm by realizing that collective action is the only viable solution. An earth mother (a modern, attractive Ma Joad), she's also the one who holds the family together. Throughout the film, an emphasis is placed on the centrality of the nuclear family in providing love, support, and unity. The story begins appropriately enough in the kitchen, with Jewell holding her baby in her arms while cooking hamburgers.

In the climax, the farmers rebel against the government-sponsored auction, but the film can't conceal the cracks in the mythology of "the land." "We're maybe the first generation in the country," says a farmer, "who don't necessarily believe life's gonna be better for our children than it was for us." But at the end, it's unclear who the "villains" are: Is the film against Carter and/or Reagan's policies? Made with restraint, and shot in Iowa with local farmers, *Country* is grounded in specific reality, although, with all its attention to detail, it perpetuates the American myth of the sacredness of "the Land."

In fact, this myth has become so powerful that it doesn't allow for any deviation. In *The River*, a rich farmer, Joe Wade, pressures a state senator to build a dam to irrigate Wade's massive land holdings. He hires farmers to break up the levee Tom Garvee (a contemporary Tom Joad of *Grapes of Wrath*?) has built to protect his land. But in the end, the workers switch allegiance and help Tom. Rationally speaking, Wade is right, but he is portrayed as a greedy villain. In the emotionally rousing climax, Tom and his friends succeed in protecting the land from flood. Like *Country*, *The River* perceives farming as a dignified way of living, rather than an enterprise.

Places in the Heart was the most commercial of the cycle. It grossed domestically over $16 million, while *Country* and *The River* each made about $4 million. The first to be released, *Places in the Heart* was a prestige production: The director Robert Benton, and the star, Sally Field, were both Oscar winners. The film is an ode to togetherness; the central community in *Places in the Heart* is headed by a young widow and consists of society's "weak" elements: children, a black man, and a blind resident.

The success of *Places in the Heart* could be attributed to the fact that it was set safely in the past, during the Depression. Thus, it was less overtly political than the other two farm movies. Benton meant it as a mythic evocation, a film memory rather than a problem picture. *Country*, in contrast, was made in the tradition of the "living newspaper" and hard-edged journalism to show that hard work is not enough to save farms from foreclosure. Even so, *Country* was released in October 1984, one month prior to the national elections, and the filmmakers were nervous about its implied criticism of Reagan's policies. They allegedly refused to hold benefit showings to avoid politicizing the film, insisting that the villain was not Reagan but "monolithic bureaucracy and government apathy."[17]

Of a number of rural documentaries, made during the past decade, *Troublesome Creek: A Midwestern* (1995), a chronicle of the struggle of one Iowa family to hold onto its farm, stands out not only for being deeply personal but also for its amazing similarity to the plot of the fiction film *Country*. A husband-and-wife team, Jeanne Jordan and Steven Ascher, began shooting shortly after learning that Jeanne's father, Russell, might lose the farm that had belonged to his family for more than a century. The crisis had begun when new bank owners, less sympathetic to Russell's plight than the former owners, called in his accumulated debt of $200,000, which he could not pay.

The film concentrates on the Jordans' efforts to raise money by liquidating their farm machinery and selling at auction all but the most essential household items. The Jordans receive support from their neighbors (who have had their own farms foreclosed), who drive miles through snow just to be with them on auction day. Russell and his wife, Mary Jane, maintain a stoic dignity as they oversee the sale, sporadically punctuating the proceedings with mordant humor. Mary Jane occasionally raises an objection, demanding that certain cherished items be saved.

Jeanne narrates the bittersweet history of the farm and the family that lived there. Back in the 1880s, her great-grandfather fought off the notorious Crooked Creek Gang. Named after a twisty waterway on the Jordan farm, *Troublesome Creek* uses clips from classic Westerns (e.g., *Red River*) to underscore its views of the farmers' struggle as a universal conflict of good versus evil. Drastic steps are needed to turn the farm over to Jeanne's older brother, Jim. But, unlike Hollywood's farm movies, *Troublesome Creek* has no happy ending: The Jordans pay their debt, and Jim admits that there will be rough times ahead for him. Still, like most of the farm movies, it's an eloquent elegy to the demise of a way of life.

In recent years, there have been few farm movies. Like *Country* and *Places in the Heart*, *Stacking* (1988) centers on a female, in this case an adolescent, who's trying to comprehend the morass that constitutes the

adult world. Set in the summer of 1954, in Montana's beautiful meadows, the film uses elements that are overly familiar: A strong-willed girl
(Meagan Follows), who is coming of age; a stranded woman (Christine
Lahti) who wants excitement; a beer-guzzling handyman (Frederic For-
rest); and an itinerant outsider-photographer (Peter Coyote). Made
under the auspices of *American Playhouse* and Sundance Institute, two
outfits prone to mistake virtue for virtuosity, the film does have an unmistakable homespun honesty.[18]

Set in a Wisconsin farm, Paul Zehrer's *Blessing* (1994) may be the exception in its antiromantic view of the heartland. A moody family
drama, the film captures the rhythms of Midwestern farm life in acute
detail, with the damp morning air, the barn smell, the austere beauty of
the countryside.[19] The members of the dairy-farming family are
gripped by boredom and claustrophobia. The autocratic Jack (Guy
Griffis) is an embittered patriarch who is barely able to make ends meet;
in fits of frustration, he beats his cows. His frightened wife, Arlene (Carlin Glynn), fends off despair by entering newspaper lotteries and tend-
ing her religious statues. Whenever Jack climbs to the top of the silo (to
take snapshots), she is convinced he is spying on a neighboring woman.
Occasionally, when Arlene voices her suspicions, Jack flies into a rage,
digs a gaping hole in the backyard, and orders her to fill it up just to give
her something to do.

Of their three children, the oldest son has already fled, and the
youngest, ten-year-old Clovis, is on the sidelines. The central character
is twenty-three-year-old Randi (Melora Griffis), who dreams of becoming a marine biologist. Family tensions arise when Randi becomes involved with Lyle (Gareth Williams), a milkman and freelance astrologer.
They meet at the general store and strike up a friendship that quickly becomes romantic; the fact that Lyle has a wife and child back East doesn't
faze Randi. In a tone that suggests a contemporary echo of *Wisconsin
Death Trip*, Michael Lesy's collection of grim photographs, news stories,
and obituaries, *Blessing* shows the devastating impact of socioeconomic
change on a way of life that is out of step with modern technology.

REGIONAL FILM CENTERS

Before there were *Fargo* and TV's *Northern Exposure*, both about the lives
and struggles of Americans living in cold, rural climates, there was

Northern Lights (1978), codirected by John Hanson and Rob Nilsson, a quietly moving, dignified drama about the harsh life in early twentieth-century North Dakota.

Several of David Burton Morris's films were made in his native Minnesota. *Loose Ends* (1974), which cost only $30,000, was one of the first efforts at regional filmmaking in the Twin Cities, a blue-collar drama shot by Morris and his wife, Victoria Wozniak. In *Purple Haze* (1981), Morris and Wozniak returned to Minneapolis to direct a serio-comedy set in the 1960s. Made on a bigger budget ($350,000), *Patti Rocks* (1988), a sequel to *Loose Ends*, revolved around a romantic triangle.

John Hanson's *Wildrose* (1985) was a compellingly realistic drama about heartland folks, using the particularities of place to enhance the story of June Lorich (Lisa Eichorn), a sturdy young woman, and her choices regarding work, love, friendship, and community. The setting is Northern Minnesota's Mesabi Iron Range, where mining is the chief occupation. June goes to work in the mines, after a decree opens these jobs to women, but the economy is ailing, and she and the other women are resented. She befriends an elderly Finnish woman, who lives alone in the woods and once worked in a lumber camp. Together, they swap anecdotes about the roughness of getting along in a male-dominated world.[20]

Rachel River (1988), the debut of Sandy Smolan, is set in northern Minnesota and tells several intertwined stories of small-town American life. The film won critical acclaim for its vivid, touching, and comic portrayal of life in rural Minnesota. Judith Guest's script captures local flavor with effective character portraits: A single thirtysomething divorced mother and journalist (Pamela Reed), whose choices are to remain lonely or accept one of her misfit suitors. The other characters include a distinguished lady (Viveca Lindfors) facing the impending death of her husband, and the village idiot (Zeljiko Ivanek), who may know the truth of rumors that a horde of cash was hidden on the property of a deceased townswoman.

FLORIDA—VICTOR NUNEZ

Victor Nunez has been exploring the unique landscape, culture, and myths of Florida for his entire professional career. From the Depression romance of *Gal Young 'Un* (1979) to the Kennedy-era drama *A Flash of*

Green (1985) to the contemporary *Ruby in Paradise* (1993) and *Ulee's Gold* (1997), Nunez's films have focused on characters yearning to come to terms with living in a specific world. In each story, Florida plays a central role in defining and revealing the human characters. The coastal areas of mangrove swamps and mud flats are unlike the geography of any other place in the country. Nunez loves this back country, which he photographs in precise but plain manner.

While a student at Ohio's Antioch College, Nunez forged his ambition to become "a Southern writer in film." He was particularly inspired by "the linkage of character, place, and story" in the Italian neorealist cinema of the 1940s. Indeed, Nunez directs multilayered, character-driven narratives that lack visual excitement but are emotionally resonant. He imbues his films with the emotionality of a foreign film: Characters in his work unabashedly think and feel, as they never would in conventional American movies. Nunez holds that "it's possible to create a kind of universal feeling through the use of very specific place and time with sounds and textures that are there for a definite reason." For example, Florida's Panama City, where *Ruby in Paradise* is set, is perceived as "the perfect metaphor" for America at the end of the century, a culture that seems for better or worse, intentionally or not, to be choosing "life without a past."

Nunez's first feature, *Gal Young 'Un*, which he wrote, directed, shot, and edited, helped shape regional cinema within the independent movement. The film is set in the Prohibition Era of the 1920s, in Florida's backwoods country, light-years away from the fancy resorts along the Atlantic and Gulf Coasts. The period details are striking, particularly Nunez's camera work and Charles Engstrom's country music score.

Based on Marjorie Kinnan Rawlings's 1932 story, *Gal Young 'Un* is a comedy about a robust woman of substantial reserves. Mattie (Dana Preu, an English professor who had never acted before), a middle-aged widow, lives alone in the pinewoods, having given up society. Mattie works for her immediate needs, pays her bills on time, smokes a pipe to relax, but lives a solitary life. Into her life comes Trax (David Peck), a no-good womanizer with a gift for gab and gallantry. Trax courts Mattie, who's old enough to be his mother, for her money, and she, charmed by his courtship and youthful energy, accepts his proposal. It is a peculiar marriage; Trax is always threatening to leave, essentially blackmailing Mattie. He spends his time in the big cities, living high on her profits, coming home only to pick up another load of liquor and leave his laundry. Mattie bides her time, but it's clear that she won't be bested by him.[21]

For his second film, Nunez again turned to fiction set in Florida, this time adapting John D. MacDonald's 1962 novel, *A Flash of Green*, to the screen. In another display of low-budget, high-quality filmmaking, the character-driven ecological thriller, set on Florida's West Coast, uses "name actors"—Ed Harris, Blair Brown, and Richard Jordan—in a regionally based production. The title derives from a phenomenon that occurs when the Western horizon is totally free of haze and a clear green light appears.

Jimmy Wing (Harris), a Palm City newspaper reporter, accepts a bribe to provide information with which his boyhood friend, Elmo Bliss (Jordan), an ambitious county commissioner, can blackmail opponents of an ecologically disastrous land development scheme. Otherwise, Jimmy is an honorable man. He's loyal to his hospitalized young wife, who's dying of a brain disease, and acts as a responsible surrogate father to the children of Kat (Brown), his best friend's widow.

Conveying effectively the specific time and place, this offbeat drama excels in defining the characters' contradictory feelings for one another, especially Jimmy's for the conniving Elmo, the film's most vivid character. It's never clear why Jimmy accepts the bribe, nor is it important. Nunez is more interested in character exploration—in Jimmy's fall from grace. The cynical Elmo says: "The world needs folks like me, folks with a real love for power." Later, Elmo rationalizes his actions with "all the wild things and the magic places have already been lost forever." It takes Jimmy a long time to see the light—before that can happen, several lives are wrecked and other people injured. Jimmy's ultimate rehabilitation provides the most complex part of *A Flash of Green*.

Nunez did not make another film until 1993. After years of going to meetings, taking long shots, and trying to pitch projects to various producers, he was ready to quit filmmaking altogether. But he decided to hang on—to affirm, as he said, the "micro-budget level" of production.[22] The result was a small inspirational study, *Ruby in Paradise* (1993), his best film to date. Nunez had only to look ninety miles west of his Tallahassee home to find the setting. "I grew up vacationing in Panama City Beach," he said. "The beach is a working-families resort fast being transformed into the condo-lined coast of the rest of Florida. It still has a wonderful mix, however—Fort Lauderdale and Alabama in the same room."

Like the locale, the main character is unusual by Hollywood standards. American films have rarely centered on working-class women without pandering or condescending to them. It's even rarer for male directors to paint insightful psychological portraits of female protagonists. But Nunez gets inside his heroine's psyche with the vision and nuance of a richly dense novel. Few male directors would base a whole film on a woman's inner odyssey, but in *Ruby in Paradise*, Nunez does just that with both simplicity and eloquence.

Nunez has adapted the works of Southern women writers before. His 1977 short, "A Circle in the Fire," was based on Flannery O'Connor's story, and *Gal Young 'Un* was an adaptation of a work by Marjorie Kinnan Rawlings. He continued his exploration of women in his original script for *Ruby in Paradise*, which revolves around an ordinary woman who gradually becomes extraordinary. Ruby Lee Gissing (Ashley Judd), just past her high school graduation, leaves Tennessee for a better life in Panama City, "the redneck Riviera." But she faces a number of obstacles in realizing her dream. She arrives in the resort town at the end of the tourist season, which enables her to find an apartment but no work.

Nonetheless, plucky and resourceful, she lands a job as a sales clerk at a gift store. A free spirit, but a woman with standards and morals, Ruby has a native intelligence that serves her well. Despite some melodrama surrounding the sexual advances of her boss's loathsome son (Bentley Mitchum), the narrative is low key, almost uneventful. A realistic update of Ginger Rodgers's working heroine in *Kitty Foyle* (1940), *Ruby in Paradise* avoids the fairy-tale optimism of Mike Nichols's fantasy-fable *Working Girl* (1988), which starred Melanie Griffith. Indeed, the nominal plot is less important than the film's observation of how Ruby deals with life's inevitable frustrations. Much of the text relies upon Ruby's struggle to regain her inner tranquility. The tacky landscape, the backdrop to Ruby's self-discovery, gives the film poignancy. Nunez never imposes any ideological or moral positions on his deftly observed tale of a young woman's passage into adulthood.

Through his subtle mise-en-scène, which relies on voice-over narration as Ruby makes entries in her journal, Nunez captures the workings of Ruby's inner soul, the gaining of consciousness—issues that are usually easier to handle in literature than in film. Nunez places Ruby under a magnifying glass, although his camera is not oppressively close to her. As in Todd Haynes's *Safe*, there are no lingering close-ups, as would be the norm in Hollywood's more typical women's movies.

A story of "soul work" (to use Nunez's words), *Ruby in Paradise* finds universal meaning in a most particular existence. With a touch of female bonding, a new friend tells Ruby, "The important thing is to learn how to survive with your soul intact." Ruby attempts to reach a calm, stable point in her life before making any decisions, which explains her rejection of Mike McCaslin (Todd Field), a sensitive gardener who introduces her to Jane Austen and Emily Dickinson.

Like John Turturro, who celebrates construction workers as artists in *Mac*, Nunez holds in high regard his beekeeper hero in *Ulee's Gold* (1997). Beekeeping is used as a metaphor for all the specialized crafts abandoned in the modern, postindustrial world. Old-fashioned and emotionally quiet, the film offers a rewarding psychological portrait of a taciturn, aging beekeeper (Peter Fonda in an impressive, Oscar-nominated comeback performance). Pushed out of his solitary life, Ulee is forced to face his responsibilities as the father of an imprisoned son and the grandfather of two young girls who were ruthlessly deserted by their drug-addict mother.

Highbrow critics continue to complain about Nunez's restrained, unexciting film approach, and, indeed, it's easy to overlook the qualities of *Ulee's Gold* in today's overhyped market. *Ulee's Gold* doesn't match *Ruby in Paradise* in psychological depth or emotional impact, but its coherence is unparalleled in both Hollywood and indiewood. Ulee's work is silent, repetitive, and undramatic, and so is the film. Integrating Florida's unique landscape and spirit, Nunez's fully realized drama represents American regional cinema at its very best.

TEXAS—RICHARD LINKLATER

Although Richard Linklater is Texas's premier filmmaker, the big state that has given American culture the Alamo, the setting for the popular TV show *Dallas*, and oil fortunes has also produced a number of idiosyncratic directors, such as Eagle Pennell, who made some interesting, low-budget pictures before indie cinema hit its stride in the late 1980s.

Shot on a budget of $30,000, Pennell's *The Whole Shootin' Match* (1978) is a humorous portrait of two hapless Texas buddies who grasp

at life and constantly come up empty, yet still maintain their hopefulness. His second feature, *Last Night at the Alamo* (1984), is marked by the
simplicity and ease with which he brings ordinary blue-collar existence
to vivid screen life. Sonny Carl Davis and Louis Perryman, who played
similar characters in *The Whole Shootin' Match*, are cast in this film as
Cowboy and Claude. Made in three and a half weeks, *Last Night at the
Alamo* was produced for $50,000, half of which was provided by the Na-
tional Endowment for the Arts and the rest by the Southwest Alternate
Media Project (fondly known as "SWAMP") in equipment and office
space.

The first shots of Houston's glass-and-steel skyscrapers represent a
vision of high-tech at its most inhumane, but the people themselves still
live in buildings where it's possible to open the windows. The Alamo's
regulars gather to celebrate the bar's last night, which means drinking
beer and awaiting the appearance of Cowboy, a favored son who may
be able to save the place from destruction. The customers speak of
Cowboy with awe, especially Ichabod, a hotheaded youngster who
wishes he had a "neat" nickname like Cowboy, instead of Ichabod (his
real name is William). Cowboy's major admirer is Claude, an unhappy
middle-aged man who spends much of his time arguing on the pay
phone with his wife, Marcie, an off-screen character. When he receives
another furious call from Marcie, he says, "I guess I better be getting
home, I ain't never going to hear the end of this."

The film's vulgar, down-to-earth dialogue, as Vincent Canby
has observed, rings utterly true.[23] Claude's friend, Mary, thinks he
shouldn't blame people for being fat, which leads to a serious discussion of whether someone with a beer belly can accurately be called
fat. Later, mad at Ichabod's behavior, Mary screams, "When you talk
to me, keep that eye open. I don't want it twitching at me!" Abstract
notions never enter the minds of the characters, who are completely
absorbed by things and events of the present.

Cowboy finally appears as a good-looking, smooth-talking guy,
who has just told off his boss and is once more out of a job. Cowboy's
plan to save the Alamo, by contacting a Texas legislator with whom he
roomed during his one year at college, fails. But nobody gets upset or
disturbed for too long. The old Alamo gang simply shifts its gathering
to another bar, the B&B, and life goes on in the same laid-back, uneventful manner as it did before.

■

Richard Linklater is a Houston-born college dropout who eschewed film school in favor of playing around with a super-8 camera. After studying literature and philosophy, he drifted around for a while, then founded the Austin Film Society in order to screen his favorite films, made by Tarkovsky, Fassbinder, Godard, all the while making experimental shorts.

His first feature, *It's Impossible to Learn to Plow by Reading Books*, is a brooding, nearly nonverbal super-8 film, which takes place on a train. The film was not released theatrically, but, undeterred, Linklater forged on. His next two films, *Slacker* and *Dazed and Confused*, are inspired satires about apathetic American youth. Linklater then directed a more mature romantic drama, *Before Sunrise*, about the meeting of two privileged soulmates; a depressing youth-angst indie, *SubUrbia*; and a big-budget Western-adventure, *The Newton Boys*. Like Nunez, Linklater favors character development over plot-driven narratives. His films are radically different in tone, though most take place within a short, intense period of time, usually a day.

Having attended high school in the 1970s, Linklater was still close enough in age and spirit to draw that experience out. His perpetually waiting characters are not committed to careers yet and lack a firm political orientation and sense of self. "You have to go through the same old shit anyway," says Celine in *Before Sunrise*, which is the point of all of Linklater's movies. Even if there's nothing specific to rebel against, it's still tough to go through adolescence.

In 1990, *Slacker* put Linklater—and Austin—on the map. The movie made Linklater an instant, if reluctant, spokesperson for a whole generation. It was about the time that the Canadian writer Douglas Coupland's book *Generation X* came out, and the mass media embraced the concept as an anthropological discovery. A new generation had been found and it became a duty to label, package, and sell it. Linklater emerged as the uneasy standard-bearer for a generation that doesn't even want standards, let alone anyone to bear them. He still resents the marketing shorthand that reduced his work to generational tract. "I never saw myself as a spokesperson," he said. "Filmmakers make bad spokespeople for generations or politics. You might intersect with something in the air for one moment in time, but it's not gonna last, because filmmakers' agendas are always film."[24]

College towns have provided friendly environment for indies, but, as Hoberman observed, *Slacker* may be the first to return the favor.[25]

Made in the area around the University of Texas, Austin, the film is an ensemble piece about media-fixated, affectless youngsters—the ultimate campus comedy. The title derives from the subculture of deadbeat youth: As the successor to beatniks, hippies, and eternal students, *Slacker* elevates the anti-yuppie heroes of Jarmusch's *Stranger Than Paradise* into something of a collective movement. Jarmusch's deadpan influence is evident in the pervasive wackiness, though it's neither cynical nor tolerant.

Slacker boasts a bold concept, structural daring, and clever dialogue. Moving from one random conversation to another, the film induced discussions about the twentysomething crowd, deadened by meaningless work, aimless activity, and a lack of beliefs. An end-of-the-road movie, *Slacker* begins with the arrival of a Greyhound bus in Austin, where a garrulous passenger (played by Linklater) gets into a cab. Inside, he delivers a monologue about the separate realities that exist in the things we decide not to do (like the road Dorothy chooses not to travel in *The Wizard of Oz*). He tells his theory of bifurcating realities and proliferating alternate universes to the uninterested driver. A few seconds after the taxi disappears, the camera observes another cab pulling into place, representing the possibility of another story about to start.

Linklater's soliloquy sets the tone for a film that drifts down the road of individual but parallel worlds. *Slacker* sweeps through Austin's coffeehouses, bookstores, bedrooms, and nightclubs to discover a world of philosophers, bored romantics, conspiracy enthusiasts, people who leave behind political explanations written on postcards, people who are catching up on a lot of sleep. The film derives its look from the college's melting-pot atmosphere. "West Campus is where all the students who either quit or have already graduated but haven't moved on to what they're gonna do are hanging out," Linklater explained.[26] "Their education continues, but along unsupervised paths. The quest for knowledge is still there—but there's no action. It's all ideas and words but nothing happens."

With a form similar to that of Arthur Schnitzler's *La Ronde*, *Slacker* is structured so that one character leads to another. But, unlike *La Ronde*, *Slacker* never circles back or returns to any character. It travels across the lonely, eccentric trajectories of dozens of people over a single day (from dawn to dawn), dropping some characters just as they become interesting, finding something peculiar in nearly every episode.

The novelty of *Slacker* is that it encompasses material that usually happens offscreen, scenes of tedium that in Hollywood movies disappear in the name of a cleaner, linear plot. Since the film is basically plotless, nothing is extraneous—and everything equally important. People keep moving from one place to another, never ceasing their torrent of talk. Linklater shoots scenes in long takes, allowing his characters to find their distinctive rhythm and avoiding as much as possible editorial comment through camera movement or music.

The film offers a deadpan portrait of Austin's laundromat philosophers, lumpen intellectuals, college dropouts, and eternal students stuck in their dope habits and bizarre "theories." The shaggy-dog story is organized serially from anecdote to anecdote, from rap to rap. An expert in JFK assassination conspiracy theory corners a woman in a bookstore and delivers a monologue about Lee Harvey Oswald. A neo-punk tries to sell a cultural relic—a Madonna pap smear. A UFO spotter lays out a theory linking moon landings, American-Soviet relations, and missing children.

Paranoia is rampant among the alienated do-nothings, who listen to each other with amusement or indifference, although no one gets excited or upset for too long. "I just thought you ought to know," one man says to his captive listener, a line that captures the movie's curious attitude. In a memorable sidewalk scene, an Indian woman describing her homeland pauses to tell a companion that "the next person who passes us will be dead within a fortnight." Down the sidewalk and into the frame comes a poor, hapless fellow (Frank Orral, a singer), whose subsequent encounters at a coffee shop suggest that his days are numbered. An offscreen sound of a car screeching to a halt, roughly from the place he walked into the street, affirms her prophecy.

The encounters of the endless parade of eccentrics are randomly organized and linked. Despite the film's improvised look and its use of street people, *Slacker*'s dialogue is based on notebooks Linklater kept over several years in which he recorded the wacky junk he heard from hangers-on around the university district. *Slacker* weaves its way through a group of people who cling to whatever will get them through the day, whether it's an honorable cause or a far-out conspiracy, a cup of coffee or a newspaper—anything to fill in the time. But the film has an unexpectedly giddy ending: A character who declares he has given up on humanity says, "I can only address myself to singular human beings now."

Linklater's next film, *Dazed and Confused* (1993), is also genera-tionally specific. It is the tale of one eventful night in May 1976 (the last day of high school), contained within the otherwise uneventful lives of suburban teenagers. With a larger budget ($6 million) than *Slacker*, it displays *Slacker*'s distinctive vision but has a more accomplished visual style. Linklater's wish was to make a film about diverse characters who are not connected except by the movement of the narrative itself. The movie deftly juggles a dozen characters, nearly as many locations, and a historically specific soundtrack (Foghat, Peter Frampton, Aerosmith). Linklater's offhanded style is deceptive; each of his films is a product of lengthy planning. Like *Slacker*, which was shot over a couple of months after extensive research and interviews, *Dazed and Confused* took years to make.

With *Dazed and Confused* (the title comes from an early Led Zeppelin anthem), Linklater was determined not to make a movie that imitated *American Graffiti*. Like Lucas, he goes back to his youth, although he's free of nostalgia, aware that it can function as escapism from the pres-ent. The early 1980s were an era of dark cultural plague—1950s nostal-gia—reflected in such films as *American Graffiti* and *Grease* and in TV shows like *Happy Days*. But, for Linklater, "there's something unpro-ductive about nostalgia, about thinking backwards instead of for-wards."

Set in 1976, when American youths were stranded between 1960s political activism and 1980s materialism, *Dazed and Confused* is about kids who lack both causes to fight for and personal ambition. Waiting for something to happen, they endlessly ask, "Hey, man, what's hap-pening?" to which the answer is always the same, "Nothin', man, nothin'." This repeated pattern gives the film a familiar but uncomfort-able feel.

American Graffiti has a geographical center (Mel's Drive-In), a mythic hero (Wolfman Jack), a special look (red and blue neon), and a layer of dreams. In contrast, Linklater sets his movie nowhere in partic-ular—Suburbia—which, in fact, became the title of a later movie. *Dazed and Confused*, which describes events that could happen in any high school, is an acute period film about a time most people would rather forget; as Pink says, "If I ever start calling these the best years of my life, remind me to kill myself." For his cast, Linklater interviewed young-sters who were barely born in 1976. But they all told him, "We all hang out in the 7-Eleven parking lot, and when the cops come, we go to this place called the turnaround under a freeway and then we go back to the 7-Eleven."[27] This reaffirmed Linklater's feeling that "times haven't changed, it's a loop."

Linklater measures artistic success by how closely a film matches his initial design. By that count, *Dazed and Confused* is a success. "I was trying to recreate the feeling and texture of the time I grew up. There are scenes in the movie that are 100 percent of what I had in mind, from the music to the atmosphere." Like his characters, Linklater was forced to participate in that singular ritual, "a greaser day." He recalled: "My school was having a 1950s day. My uncle was helping me put my hair back in a grease ducktail and he was saying 'You know, you kids think the fifties were really cool, but let me tell you, they sucked.'"

Like *Slacker*, *Dazed and Confused* has a large ensemble, no dramatic plot, and great music. Thematically selected tracks—from Nazareth, Aerosmith, Peter Frampton, Kiss, Ted Nugent, and Led Zeppelin—drive the narrative forward. Alice Cooper's end-of-year anthem, "School's Out," blares over a shot of blue-gray aluminum lockers being flung open, their contents pitched into the air. Linklater's camera follows the kids through a day and an all-nighter as they get stoned and drive around looking for a party or other ways to kill time and mark their rite of passage. He lavishes detail and insight on the eight-track, dope-smoking, bell-bottomed, Pontiac-GTO generation.

What unifies both the episodic *Slacker* and the more ambitious *Dazed and Confused* is the near-documentary feel with which they report about mundane reality. However, they are based on different formal designs, and their styles diverge. "*Slacker* was about the internal pace of the scene itself; the rhythm came from the characters' speech patterns. *Dazed and Confused* was all in the editing. The music was very up front and everything else fell into place behind that." *Slacker* is not a genre film, but *Dazed and Confused* is with standard types (the nerd, the jock, the stoner) and typical situations.

Both *Slacker* and *Dazed and Confused* are shaped by a foreboding sense that something is basically wrong for youngsters coming of age today. The movie is about rites of passage that celebrate aimlessness, thematic concerns that Linklater shares with Gregg Araki (see Chapter 12), though their sensibilities are different. Some critics misinterpreted *Slacker* as propagating nihilism—but Linklater insists that he was trying "to show a way out." In this respect, *Dazed and Confused* is more upbeat than *Slacker*.

Linklater is aware that his characters are flawed, but he also knows that in time they'll learn. "I'm interested in people who are still forming, still deciding what kind of person they're going to be," he said. "Of all the characters in *Dazed and Confused*, there's maybe five or six who could end up in *Slacker*. Right now, they're intuitively smart, but they need to read the great books, see the great movies."

Linklater doesn't structure his movies tightly: *Dazed and Confused* is a collective portrait casually organized as a series of interlaced tales—pranks, hazing—taking place on the last day of school. Linklater accentuates the spontaneous elements in anecdotes and passing moments: a pothead's way of using his hands when he talks, a phrase rising out of youth jargon, a touch of poetry.[28] The teenagers bash mailboxes with garbage cans, smoke dope, and spend a lot of time talking about getting laid. The main goal is humiliating other people while avoiding humiliation yourself. Since feminism has not yet taken hold, the girls engage in hazing rituals with younger girls, covering them with sugar or ketchup, getting them to propose to the boys on their knees.

In 1976, America was 200 years old, an event memorialized in *Dazed and Confused* by the fantasy of the pothead Slater (Rory Cochrane), who's convinced that George Washington cultivated weed as a southern cash crop. In a gesture of mock revolution, the handsome football player, Pink (Jason London), refuses to sign a demeaning document that calls for players to abjure drugs and alcohol. Other signs of spirit are shown by the two self-conscious nerds who reject the norm of mediocrity and try to escape. Articulate, these boys feel like freaks, and they're heading out; everyone else is trapped.

The high schoolers go through changes, but without dramatic punctuation. The personal stories aren't overdramatized, because Linklater keeps everything on the same level: keg parties, scuffles, dope smoking. Most movies are made by adult filmmakers who don't realize that youngsters don't perceive their lives as a series of rites of passage; they're too busy being dazed and confused.[29] Linklater feels too much affection for his characters to classify them as types, yet they're immediately recognizable: the star quarterback (Ben Affleck), the bully who hazes freshmen (Rory Cochrane), the doper (Matthew McConaughey), the graduate who still hangs around high school, the red-headed brain who falls for the hood, the junior who wants to become a lawyer and join the ACLU except he can't stand the people he's supposed to help, the footballer who can't resist dispensing headlocks to the less fortunate.

One of the film's surprises is how close these kids seem to contemporary teenagers. The fashions are back in style and the tribal rituals are essentially the same. Set a few years earlier or later, the mood would have been altered. These students live in the era of lowered expectations, the years between the rebellious 1960s and the greedy 1980s. They're in limbo, but they seem to accept their fate, waiting for a new era to define them.

Revisiting the idea of Linklater's first film, *Before Sunrise* depicts a brief encounter between an American boy, Jesse (Ethan Hawke), and a French girl, Celine (Julie Delpy), who meet on a train. Rather than continue home to Paris, Celine gets off the train with Jesse in Vienna, and they spend the night talking about family, love, sex, and death. With the earnestness of intellectual youth—so atypical of contemporary American youth—they say awkwardly candid things that only young people say. On the surface, the situation is movieish (will they become lovers? will they see each other again?), yet the movie depicts quite realistically a unique adventure, a free-of-worries night in a foreign city.[30]

The film lacks the playful spontaneity of Godard's lyrical movies about smart youth, *Band of Outsiders* and *Masculine-Feminine*, which mixed American movies with contemporary fads.[31] Linklater, who collaborated with the actress Kim Krizan on the script, is closer to Eric Rohmer, who's more literal and methodical than Godard. Like Rohmer, Linklater's films have a romantic flare, but there's a warmer hopefulness than is found in Rohmer's films. Linklater shows more maturity and is more generous to his characters here than he was to the layabout potheads and solipsists in earlier pictures.

Coming from different countries, Celine and Jesse cannot assume any mutual ground; they don't even share the same pop-culture references. This means they have to expose themselves, talk about their innermost feelings and fears and important events in their lives, such as their first sexual experiences. Linklater holds the camera on his actors through long shots and lets the scenes proceed naturally with all the hesitations, withdrawals, and tentative advances that define real-life encounters.

A brooding comedy, *SubUrbia* (1996), arguably Linklater's weakest film, fails to blend his directorial talent with Eric Bogosian's script (based on his play). It's a harsh account of twentysomething losers, who act out their miseries in one endless night. The two artists share a concern with youth's discontent and passion for language, but in every other way their sensibilities are different. Reflecting Bogosian's age, the film's point of view feels older, bitter, and more cynical than Linklater's.

The opening shots, set to the tone of Gene Pitney's "Town Without Pity," reveal a typical strip mall with franchise food chains. Three dyspeptic youngsters gather in the parking lot of a twenty-four-hour convenience store: Jeff (Giovanni Ribisi), a college dropout whose nihilism actually covers idealism; Buff (Steve Zahn), a hedonistic goofball who works in a pizza parlor; and Tim (Nicky Katt), a bitter man discharged from the air force after slicing off a fingertip. They are joined by Jeff's girlfriend, Sooze (Amie Carey), and her friend Bee-Bee (Dina Spybey), a nurse's aide who has been to rehab. After demonstrating a new performance piece called "Burger Manifesto Part One," an obscene denunciation of men, Sooze announces her plan to attend art school in New York, to which Jeff reacts with disdain that masks his jealousy.

They are joined by an old schoolmate, Pony (Jayce Bartok), who has formed a band and who arrives in a limo with his sleek L.A. publicist, Erica (Parker Posey). Pony is a likable kid who's just started to hit paydirt, but his modest fortune ignites his friends. Jeff's jealousy turns into hostility when it becomes obvious that Pony is ready to help Sooze and Buff leave town to pursue their ambitions. Drunken and mean, Tim vents his rage on Erica and on the hard-working Pakistani storeowner. Linklater approaches Bogosian's misanthropic material reverentially (the movie is better directed than scripted), keeping the emphasis on the characters—and the actors. However, the confined setting—the whole movie is claustrophobically set in a parking lot—reinforces the text's theatrical nature.

A radical departure from his youth-angst movies, Linklater's next movie, *The Newton Boys* (1998), a studio project, boasted a $27 million budget and numerous outdoor scenes. "I was ready to work with a bigger canvas with action sequences," Linklater said.[32] A chronicle of the four siblings who have entered collective mythology as the most famous bank robbers in history, the film benefits from a handsome production that nicely evokes the 1920s and a likable cast, but the story is too diffuse; it lacks a discernible point of view to make it dramatically engaging. Perceiving the movie as an homage to old gangster and

Western films, Linklater made a sprawling epic. *The Newton Boys* comes to an exciting crescendo at the end, during the credits, when documentary footage of the real-life siblings is inserted. A 1980 *Tonight Show* clip in which Johnny Carson talks to the still feisty Willis Newton and a recorded interview with the aging but lucid Joe illustrate what a movie *The Newton Boys* could have been if it had been based on stronger characterizations.

CONCLUSION

Although the two big centers for indie productions remain New York and Los Angeles, the tradition of regional indies continues. As Sundance's Gilmore recently observed: "Independent film has its roots in regional work characterized by stories about people nobody in a studio deems worthy of attention. There is a much more advanced and sophisticated filmmaking community existing all over, not just bi-coastally. The tools of filmmaking have become much more available, even to small communities."[33]

Space limitations prohibit consideration of other regional centers, such as Boston, where the director Brad Anderson has anchored his two excellent movies, the serio-comedy, *The Darien Gap* (1996) and the romantic comedy *Next Stop Wonderland* (1998), in distinctly Bostonian milieux. Anderson was raised in Connecticut and lives in New York, but he considers himself a Boston filmmaker. "These days a lot of people call themselves Boston filmmakers, but we're the real thing," he said, referring to himself and Lyn Vaus, his cowriter.[34] "Not only did we make a film imbued with the spirit of Boston, but we know this town inside and out. I've probably shot on every street in this city."

A charming comedy about the eternal search for true love, *Next Stop Wonderland* was snapped up by Miramax for $6 million at the 1998 Sundance festival. "It's great that Boston is being heralded as a new venue for film," Anderson said. "Boston has a look, a tone, and a feel unlike any other city. With this film, we wanted to make a valentine to Boston."

π was not filmed in Boston, but the writer-director Darren Aronofsky is a Harvard University graduate, and the actor Sean Gullette is from Newton. The best-known indie with its heart in Boston is *Good Will Hunting* (1997), the film that turned two Cambridge natives, Matt Damon and Ben Affleck, into Oscar-winning stars (they won for best original screenplay). Damon said he and Affleck had always known that if they wrote a film it would have to be set in their hometown. Miramax financed that film, which became its highest-grossing movie ever. *Good Will Hunting* brought prominence to the Boston area, where the incentive of "fee-free locations" allows filmmakers access to state-owned facilities at no cost.

5

The New York School of Indies

A DISPROPORTIONATELY LARGE number of indie directors are from New York, exhibiting in their work what might be called a distinct New York sensibility. Not surprisingly, most of these directors are graduates of film schools, with NYU and Columbia leading the pack. NYU has produced Jim Jarmusch, Spike Lee, and Susan Seidelman, to name only a few indie celebs. And Columbia boasts, among others, Kathryn Bigelow, Stacy Cochran, and, most recently, Lisa Chodolenko.

During the 1980s, an innovative cinema emerged from the streets of the East Village and the Lower East Side. A Lower East Side basement, known as Club 57, functioned as a hangout and breeding ground for painters, performance artists, and filmmakers, whose attitudes were expressed in such quintessentially New York films as Kathryn Bigelow's *The Loveless* and Slava Tsukerman's cult picture, *Liquid Sky*.

Jarmusch's *Stranger Than Paradise* (1984) was a turning point in the codification of the New York sensibility, for reasons that will become clear later in this chapter. As Richard Edson, one of Jarmusch's actors, noted: "We all had a similar sensibility, a combination of alienation and humor and a kind of low-key passion." Jarmusch's hip, urban comic jags arose from the same East Village-NYU explosion that nurtured the relentlessly contemporary films of Susan Seidelman (*Smithereens*, *Desperately Seeking Susan*) and Spike Lee. Lee's work, from his first film, *She's Gotta Have It*, through the controversial *Do the Right Thing*, is set in Brooklyn.

This downtown New York sensibility is reflected mostly in disdain for the ordinary and the routine, a motif that runs through most of the New York movies. The diversity of the New York school is also evident in the work of Hal Hartley, whose dry, precise, Oedipally obsessive comedies (*The Unbelievable Truth*, *Trust*) display a style as instantly identifiable as Jarmusch's. Before Tom DiCillo struck out on his own as a director (*Johnny Suede*), he served as cinematographer for Jarmusch's

Permanent Vacation and *Stranger Than Paradise*, as well as for Eric Mitchell's *Underground USA* and Bette Gordon's *Variety*.

Lech Kowalski, a uniquely New York filmmaker, made *D.O.A.* (1981), about the Sex Pistols' American tour, and *Gringo* (1983), about the life of a Lower East Side junkie. In his lyrical documentary *Rock Soup* (1992), Kowalski captures the Lower East Side through "the sounds and textures of hundreds of people ostracized into communal dependency in the shadows of Wall Street."[1] Much of *Rock Soup* is devoted to meticulously shot urban details—street puddles, crude shelters, trash-clogged gutters.

David Lynch is decidedly not a New York filmmaker, but there's no question that *Eraserhead* could not have become a cult midnight movie without the support of the hip, downtown New York crowd. Similarly, it's hard to think of a midnight movie in the early 1980s that was more rooted in New York than *Liquid Sky*, which, like *Eraserhead*, appeared out of nowhere.

A low-budget fantasy, *Liquid Sky* is a perversely beautiful sci-fi movie. Unseen aliens in search of heroin land in their flying saucer on the roof of the downtown apartment of Margaret (Anne Carlisle), a decadent fashion model. The greedy aliens are after a euphoria-inducing chemical produced by the brain during orgasm. Besieged by seducers and rapists of both sexes, Margaret produces a lot of chemicals. There's a twist, however: When Margaret's pursuers make love to her, they dematerialize in an explosion of iridescent orange-green-blue light. Realizing her power, Margaret becomes a sexual avenger (killing off her lovers and tormentors) before ascending to heaven in the saucer.

Margaret and her self-destructive friends live for their ritualistic fantasies of turning themselves into works of art. Much of their energy is focused on their clothes, a mixture of Kabuki, punk, and rags. They project the image of punk narcissists living life fully at the risk of death. The androgynous-looking Anna Carlisle, with the spiked hair and transparent blondness of David Bowie, plays two roles: Margaret—as well as a sulky male model—which enables her to make love to herself.

Similar in manner and humor to a comic strip about punk culture, *Liquid Sky* was produced, directed and cowritten by Slava Tsukerman, a Soviet emigré who arrived in New York in 1976. Like the aliens, the filmmaker was an explorer of exotic pleasures denied him in his native country. Celebrating every antisocial attitude imaginable, *Liquid Sky* is the kind of movie that could never have been produced in the Soviet

Union. Tsukerman satirizes the New York demimonde of spaced-out models, junkies, and performance artists. With style to burn, he and the photographer Yuri Neyman give the film a slick, colorful look, showing a New York in which the Empire State Building glows against turquoise and lavender skies.

EAST VILLAGE SUBCULTURE—JIM JARMUSCH

An American original, Jarmusch, with his darkly comic minimalist sensibility, has been compared to Robert Frost and Sam Shepard. Jarmusch has developed a singular style over which he maintains complete control. "I do it my way or I don't do it," Jarmusch told *Filmmaker*.[2] "It helps me in negotiating to know that I will walk away if I don't have control. The only thing that matters to me is to protect my ability to be the navigator of the ship. I decide how the film is cut, how long it is, what music is used, who the cast is. I make films by hand."

Jarmusch's shaggy-dog style is evident in his feature debut, *Permanent Vacation* (1980), which depicts the life of a young guy who doesn't have any ambitions or responsibilities. Distributed on the art circuit, *Permanent Vacation* gained a small following but didn't do much for the director's career. The three features that followed, *Stranger Than Paradise* (1984), *Down by Law* (1986), and *Mystery Train* (1989), however, form a trilogy of sorts that placed Jarmusch in the pantheon of indie filmmaking. They all take place in blighted cultural landscapes: bleak wintry Ohio in *Stranger Than Paradise*; shiny New Orleans in *Down by Law*; Memphis's tawdry, clapboard decay in *Mystery Train*.

Jarmusch's characters carry little in the way of history. Their pasts are unimportant, their conduct motivated strictly by the present. A Jarmusch film typically begins with characters who are living a quiet existence and are unable to communicate. An early shot might show a person staring offscreen until the screen fades to black. This lethargic atmosphere is usually interrupted by an outsider who exposes the shallow emptiness of the American characters. It's always a foreign presence: a Hungarian girl in *Stranger Than Paradise*, an Italian tourist in *Down by Law*, Japanese teenagers in *Mystery Train*.

Not surprisingly, Jarmusch's central theme is culture collision, an outgrowth of his notion of America as a "throwaway culture." As he explained: "To make a film about America, it seems logical to have at least one perspective that's transplanted, because ours is a collection of transplanted influences."[3] Over the years, Jarmusch's comic vision has become darker and more despairing. Indeed, at the end of *Stranger Than Paradise*, Eddie and Eva still have a chance at happiness, and in *Down by Law*, Jack and Zack are still on the run, as Roberto plans for a promising future. But in *Mystery Train*, as dawn comes up in Memphis, the three sets of characters race off in unknown directions.

A postmodernist (mis)communication informs the interaction among Jarmusch's characters. Sealed off from one another, their only link is through pop culture. In Jarmusch's world, characters connect by sharing TV dinners, chanting ice-cream jingles, revering Elvis Presley. Living in a world devoid of values, his characters seek the shelter of comfort and familiarity, blanketed by the blaring music of Screamin' Jay Hawkins and Irma Thomas. Jarmusch's talent lies in locating the weird among the mundane, highlighting the ordinary side of abnormality. But despite his postmodernist sensibility, a benign, socially conscious poetry sneaks into his formal minimalism.

The austere, black-and-white *Stranger Than Paradise* consists of single, long-lasting shots. Not much happens by conventional standards of plot in the three vignettes that make up the tale. In the first act, "The New World," Willie is visited by his Hungarian cousin, Eva. In the second, "One Year Later," Willie and Eddie go to Cleveland to visit Eva. In the conclusion, "Paradise," all three go to Florida. Change of locale doesn't necessarily mean change of look. "It's funny," says Eddie, looking at Ohio's Lake Eerie, "You come to something new, and everything looks the same."

Willie (John Lurie), who emigrated from Hungary a decade ago but has since sunk into American passivity and banality, sits in his room watching TV all day. Tall and skinny, with a flattened nose that extends to his lips, he wears suspenders and a hat. His skinny buddy Eddie (Richard Edson) is virtually a twin, sporting the same nose and the same hat. The two men seem self-assured in their odd, hopelessly out-of-it style. Into their lives comes the sixteen-year-old Eva (Eszter Balint), just off the plane from Budapest. Smarter than either man, Eva stirs the dimwits, and the yarn turns into an oddly touching road comedy in which the trio wanders aimlessly from Lake Erie's freezing whiteness to Florida's motel wasteland. The surprise denouement, in which Eva accidentally lands money and proves that America is a land of opportunity, offers a perfectly absurdist finale.

A black-clad neo-hipster, Jarmusch possesses unusual technical skills and an offbeat sensibility. Pauline Kael likened Jarmusch to "a comic-strip" lightweight Beckett: His ordinary characters exhibit the same patience as Beckett's toward a huge blundering universe.[4] The reticence of Jarmusch's style creates a peculiar sense of suspense; one never knows what to expect.

At NYU, Jarmusch worked as a production assistant on Wim Wenders's *Lightning Over Water*, and the German director gave him some leftover stock. *Stranger Than Paradise* began as a five-minute short, which was then expanded into a thirty-minute film. Eventually, the original half-hour, which cost $8,000, became a ninety-minute feature with a $110,000 budget.

Jarmusch's goal was to make a simple but innovative film: a deadpan comedy about deadbeats. It was critical that *Stranger Than Paradise* avoid categorization as a New Wave film or be aligned with any kind of fashion or trend. Aiming at incorporating foreign influences without being derivative or imitative, Jarmusch espoused a new kind of American film, one that boasts a cool, fresh comic tone. *Stranger Than Paradise* cannot be mistaken for TV, which Jarmusch perceives as the worst threat to innovation in American film.

Unlike other indies, *Stranger Than Paradise* was not made for a niche or a preexisting audience. Winning the 1984 Camera d'Or in Cannes and later shown at the New York Film Festival, it established Jarmusch as the most hip indie director of the 1980s, a position Quentin Tarantino would occupy a decade later. Enjoying a long run at New York's Cinema Studio, the movie attracted a large following in other cities, eventually turning a profit for its investors.

In the wake of his success, Jarmusch was courted by Hollywood producers, who sent him numerous scripts to read. "They were mostly teenage sex comedies," Jarmusch told the *New York Times*. "It made me wonder if anyone had even seen *Stranger Than Paradise*."[5] Beyond his aversion to sex comedies, Jarmusch disdains the overdramatic style of American cinema, "where you're always thinking about the actors as actors and not really as characters."

For his next film, *Down by Law*, Jarmusch chose to make a "neo-noir comedy." The title is an idiomatic expression that means to be "taken down" by the legal system. With a budget of $1 million, provided by Island Pictures, he hired the cinematographer Robby Müller and again filmed in black and white. Jarmusch cast the surly, laconic John Lurie as

Jack, a New Orleans pimp sent to prison, where he shares a cell with Zack (Tom Waits), an unemployed disc jockey arrested for vagrancy.

Zack and Jack, who are more alike than either can bear, detest each other. They sullenly live together until a magical presence, Roberto, intervenes. A cheerful Italian tourist, Roberto cheats at cards, loves American culture, and is the only one of the three to have killed anyone, though in self-defense during an incident that involved the use of a billiard ball. Roberto, played by the comedian Roberto Benigni in a manner evoking Stan Laurel and Chaplin, stages an unlikely prison break and eventually humanizes the dour, irascible Americans. Gradually forging a friendship, the trio escape into the Louisiana bayou, where they chance upon a roadhouse run by a ravishing Italian emigree (Nicoletta Braschi), who falls in love with "Bobo."

Down by Law plays like a comic reversal of the typical Hollywood movie, in which a high-spirited American shows dejected Europeans how to get something done. Chosen to open the 1986 New York Film Festival, *Down by Law* was consciously a more cheerful and entertaining film than *Stranger Than Paradise*. "I am tired of the cinema of despair and existential angst," Jarmusch said. "I'm interested in comedy in a new kind of context. Not just sight gags. Not just linguistic jokes. But humor based on small details, things from daily life that are funny."[6]

A poetic fable, *Down by Law* was photographed by Müller in rich black-and-white tones and deep focus, which enabled the audience to see the actions and reactions to the characters, a change from the standard Hollywood angle-reverse angle, in which the camera intercuts between actors. The excitement in watching a Jarmusch film derives less from its subject than from its use of film language in a manner that differentiates it from both theater and literature.

After *Down by Law*, Jarmusch's work declined severely. His third feature, *Mystery Train*, tells three stories that take place at the same time but are told sequentially, end to end, rather than through intercutting, which is the Hollywood norm. There is no significant connection among the stories, except at the level of whimsy. Once again, the lost characters are floating among the driftwood and candy wrappers.

Jarmusch imbues a weak anecdotal narrative, entirely set in a hotel, with style. Muller's daylight cinematography is clear-textured, with a steady and gently moving frame. The night scenes are luminous; everything in Memphis glows, even the streets. Elvis Presley, the myth and the person, hangs over the comedy, providing the bridge that connects the three vignettes. As the odd events and eccentric details accumulate, Jarmusch's vision becomes recognizable. The material is fragile: Each story is an amalgam of attitudes, images, and songs, meant to evoke something larger, but the dialogue is mostly trivial.

In *Mystery Train*, Jarmusch came close to crawling in place, and critics who earlier had championed him were disappointed. David Denby pointed out that while drawling pace is integral to Jarmusch's style, a director who depends on people talking past one another can not develop much momentum.[7] Charging that Jarmusch was "interested in the look of the actual world, but not in the world itself," Pauline Kael claimed that there are limits to how much lethargy audiences will take, urging Jarmusch to expand his scope.[8]

No less bleak than Jarmusch's earlier films, though more episodic, *Night on Earth* (1992) is composed of five stories, set in Los Angeles, New York, Paris, Rome, and Helsinki, always maintaining an outsider's distance. Revisiting his interest in oblique comedy, Jarmusch explores a primal urban relationship, that of man and taxi driver. The cab is a temporarily shared world, from which one of the parties emerges shaken up. *Night on Earth* tries—but fails—to transform the commonplace into a haunting, mysterious experience.

Jarmusch's experimentation in the film offers neither visionary nor formal boldness. Instead, what emerges is urban depression, in harsh, dark colors, flaked with bits of sardonic wit. Using his usual jokes about alienated outsiders meeting and bashing one another, *Night on Earth* illustrates Jarmusch's recurrent idea of life's failure to fall into dramatic shape. His detractors pointed out that what used to be a fresh, unique rhythm has not translated into a new perception of reality. For them, the curtness of Jarmusch's method marks the limits of his interest in real life, and his low-key minimalism and stylized ennui mark artistic enervation.

Minimalism also defines the noir-Western *Dead Man* (1996), a welcome artistic departure from Jarmusch's increasingly tiresome downtown sensibility. William Blake (Johnny Depp), a mild-mannered accountant, travels across the frontier to work for a bookkeeping firm run by a crazed man (Robert Mitchum). But when he arrives at what appears to be a harsh, alienating town out of a Kafka novel, the job vanishes. Accused of a murder he didn't commit, Blake escapes into the country, where he falls under the spell of a philosophical Indian named

Nobody (Gary Farmer), who communes with spirits and treats Blake as if he were the poet William Blake.

Ambitiously, *Dead Man* deals with complex issues—history, language, indigenous culture, and violence. More multilayered than Jarmusch's former films, the film has a central story that does not take precedence over the subplots, which involve a talkative murderer (Michael Wincott) and a Bible-quoting man (Iggy Pop). With its fixation on morality and transcendence, *Dead Man* stood along other death-obsessed movies, like *Leaving Las Vegas* and *Dead Man Walking*. Wishing to evoke the feel of a Mizoguchi film, the stylized black-and white cinematography formalizes and distances the landscape. An excellent beginning alternates shots of the changing landscape, the train wheels, and the interior of a passenger car in a rhythm that suggests both tranquility and anxiety—whenever Blake drifts off, people mysteriously disappear. The earlier sequences combine Jarmusch's distinctive sense of rhythm with poetic symbolism.

But Jarmusch's attempts to link Blake's violent, existential experience with William Blake's poetry, a fusion echoed by Nobody, don't go beyond jokiness. The film suggests that "something mysterious" happens to Blake—a vision quest—for, at the end, he gives up his identity. But audiences are confused by the mystical, absurdist treatment, uncertain whether the film is more than a put-on Western. Sharply dividing the critical community, the movie was deemed an artistic achievement by the alternative press and dismissed by mainstream reviewers. Indifferently distributed by Miramax, *Dead Man* failed at the box office, further demoting Jarmusch from his standing as a major indie filmmaker.

LONG ISLAND'S POET LAUREATE—HAL HARTLEY

In his exploration of the ennui of a generation of disaffected youth, Hal Hartley has been compared to Jarmusch, Linklater, and Whit Stillman. Each of these directors has dealt with alienation and anomie while using distinctive verbal and cinematic language. Arguably, there could be no more opposing milieux than Jarmusch's East Village and Hartley's Long Island, yet Hartley's precise comedies reveal a style as instantly identifiable as Jarmusch's.

Hartley is poet laureate of Long Island, the backdrop for his movies and the place where he grew up. Cruelly impersonal, the setting of his first film, *Trust*, can be described as a cross between Beaver Cleaver's hometown and a prison. Who could have predicted that suburbanism, deplorably depicted in American literature and popular culture as "monotonous," would inspire a whole cohort of filmmakers to make original, even poetic movies? What David Lynch did to the time-worn mythology of Small-Town America in *Blue Velvet*, Hartley, Stacy Cochran, and others have done to the supposedly barren, stifling suburbs—they have found in them new life and humor.

Hartley's point of departure is an emotional situation that goes oddly askew, producing unanticipated, utterly bizarre effects. Displaying murky morality, his characters are charged with repressed sexuality, philosophical overtones, and detached irony. Like Jarmusch and Linklater, Hartley shows an intuitive understanding of what's important both on screen and off. His narratives abound in verbal and visual epiphanies, mixing seemingly incongruent details with precisely edited rhythms. His quirky performers are in tune with their odd characters, enacting their dialogue in a low-key manner.

Hartley represents an odd combination: a baggy-pants comic in a lab coat. Graham Fuller has drawn parallels between Hartley and Buster Keaton: If Keaton's aesthetic was technological and tempestuous, Hartley's is suburban and quotidian, though no less poetic.[9] Like the deadpan Keaton, Hartley's characters seldom smile. Hartley also shares with Keaton the knowledge that emotional precision and self-abnegation, not self-pity or sentimentality, are the valid responses to a cruel, unjust world. A spare style devoid of extraneous words or images has made Hartley a master of economy, as much concerned with minimalism and space manipulation as Jarmusch.

Hartley's inquiries into the burdens of desire and duty are as lyrical as they are comic. His features present the journey of odd characters toward self-awareness and maturity. Each new Hartley film is part of an ongoing process in search of better understanding of the way we live. In his universe, out-of-synch characters bounce off one another, and the offbeat oppositions produce unexpected results. At the end of each film, a new couple emerges rather hesitantly into an unstable relationship.[10]

Precise timing and stylized visuals pull Hartley away from realism, although, unlike Lynch, he seldom yields to weirdness for weirdness's sake. His characters exhibit private obsessions and idiosyncracies, but they rarely descend from the absurd to the grotesque. Hartley makes sure his characters are infused with dignity and sobriety, even when they are placed in the most ridiculous situations.[11]

Able to finance his movies independently, without kowtowing to the studios, Hartley likes to work "fast and cheap." In ten years, he has made seven features, enjoying absolute creative freedom, which he refuses to relinquish. "I would love to have the money to do a crane shot that lasts ten minutes, but I know that I would be the biggest pain in the neck to some studio. I'd refuse to listen to some boss telling me to make this funnier or cut this out. . . . My films are too idiosyncratic to bank a lot of money on. I understand that. I'm willing to make smaller films for the rest of my life."[12] This early statement proved prophetic, for Hartley's self-conscious artistry has restricted his work to a small, rarified audience.

The son of a steel-bridge worker, Hartley studied film at the State University of New York at Purchase. He was answering phones at an industrial video company when his boss agreed to bankroll his first feature, *The Unbelievable Truth*. A black comedy set in the Long Island flatlands, the film revolves around Audry (Adrienne Shelley), a high school senior who has decided not to go to college, and Josh (Martin Donovan), a paroled killer who works as a mechanic at her father's garage. They fall in love but stay apart until they can clear up some misunderstandings. Like Jon Jost, Hartley satirizes commercial transactions, using the "deal" as a metaphor for the ways people negotiate with one another. As Audry asserts: "You can't have faith in people, only the deals you make with them."

For his lyrically offbeat explorations, Hartley takes the audience to familiar-looking yet utterly strange places. Truly Godardian, Hartley's tales are logically constructed; *Simple Men* contains a dance number that pays homage to Godard's *Band of Outsiders*, a quintessential film for indie directors like Hartley, Tarantino, and Araki. Hartley also cites the work of Wim Wenders and Preston Sturges, Robert Bresson's spare style, and Carl Theodore Dreyer's religious overtones as strong influences on him.

Hartley's movies are personal in another way; his leading men are tall and thin just like him (Hartley stands about six-three and weighs 150 pounds). Hartley likes to read, and the characters in his movies read books, too. "I try to eliminate everything that's superfluous in the dialogue and in the gestures," Hartley said about his laconic language. He prefers to think of his films as precise rather than deadpan: "In each moment of the film, I'm trying to get down to something exact." The humor derives from an "inability to see the difference between the serious and funny," Hartley allows. "The comic effect is not a result of intellectual thought but a visceral reaction. I put that stuff in because the characters are having some esoteric conversation and it's difficult to follow."[13]

In all of his films, young people are forced to make decisions and, as he says, "if decisions are the subject, you are going to deal with issues of ethics. The process of making decisions is how our moral selves are evidenced." Hartley's urge for self-expression is "a reaction to questions, the only way to find out more is discourse. My films are a discourse that starts with myself, and then the characters begin to take on more of the load."[14]

The look of Hartley's films is as coherent and as distinctive as their language. The visual consistency derives from working with the same team: Michael Spiller, who provides the precise cinematography, and Steve Rosenzweig, who creates the exquisite design. *Trust*'s hard primary colors owe a debt to Godard, but there's also the cash factor. According to Hartley, the budget is often the aesthetic: "When I know how much money I have, I know how the film will look." *Unbelievable Truth* was made in eleven days for only $75,000. After seeing it, the British company Zenith granted him $700,000 to direct *Trust*. He had $2 million for *Simple Men*, a minuscule budget by Hollywood standards, but Hartley felt he was "slowed down" by the money.

His command of a distinctive lingo enables Hartley to shift from realism to absurdism, from glum despair to blank-faced comedy. For Ira Deutschman, who distributed some of his first films, Hartley is an original whose work is comparable to that of the playwrights David Mamet and Harold Pinter. "It's closer to what people look for in theater, where the author has a particular voice. It's the language of his films that people respond to."[15] Deutschman's hope was that Hartley will turn into a filmmaker like Sayles, "where every time out you can count on a certain level of interest among his fans—which will allow him to make movies on an ongoing and prolific basis, and eventually one of his films will break through to a much broader audience."[16] After a decade of work, however, this has yet to happen.

If Hartley's style and sensibility are European, his thematic concerns are squarely American. His pictures deal with loyalty and betrayal, passion and loveless marriages, ordinariness and transcendence.

But nothing is resolved in his narratives: He leaves the characters in flux, always searching. Hartley looks straight into what Americans fear, what they hope for. He makes films "about things I'm even embarrassed to articulate myself in polite conversation." Like Sam Shepard, Hartley is obsessed with fractured families and the irreconcilable gap between parents and children. But his families don't look or sound like the families depicted in TV sitcoms or Hollywood movies. In one of *Trust*'s memorable scenes, a character intones: "A family is like a gun. You point it in the wrong direction, you're going to kill somebody."

Hartley's agonizing over issues of faith motivated him to write *Trust*, a film in which the heroine, Maria (Adrienne Shelly), is at war with her family. When Maria tells her father she's pregnant, he calls her a slut. She slaps his face, and he drops dead of heart attack. The situation is part nightmare, part bad joke, the perfect deadpan to kick off a movie. In a relationship based on mutual need, Maria enters into a friendship with Matthew (Martin Donovan), a morose electronics genius. Like Maria, he's abused by a sadistic father, who commands him to clean the spotless bathroom over and over again.

Trust chronicles what Hartley terms "the self-actualization of a teenager, conceived as part mall chick, part Cinderella, part Christ." Progressing from a brat to a saint, Maria rises above the traps of working-class suburbia and in the process transforms everyone around her. Framed as a melodrama, *Trust* is replete with sexual assault, baby kidnapping, abortion, a Machiavellian mom, a drinking duel, a fistfight, and a hand grenade that threatens to explode at any moment. It's a droll analysis of family violence and the moral courage needed to defeat it. Though *Trust*'s tone is more sober than the black humor of *Unbelievable Truth*, both films suggest that all individuals are disturbed if one just looks hard enough.

Hartley's high-school themes recall John Hughes's films, but Hartley emphasizes what Hughes leaves out, the core emotions of his teen protagonists. In Hartley's films, the negotiations between parents and children for power are in earnest, and they are not a game; there are real winners and losers.[17]

In *Simple Men*, two brothers, one criminal, the other intellectual, hit the road looking for their father, a former Dodger shortstop turned anarchist who has spent the past twenty years living underground. *Simple Men* features, as Hartley says, "extreme factions of America that are not idealized but stylized." Bill (Robert Burke), the older brother, is a robber-mechanic, an amalgam of a 1980s Reaganomics overachiever and a thug, whereas Dennis (William Sage) is a contemplative scientist-philosopher. Bill defines the world as he moves through it; Dennis questions it.

In all his films, Hartley delineates troubled relationships dominated by crisis and desire. Nominally, *Simple Men* is about two brothers' quest for their terrorist father, but, on a deeper level, the film is about the way men relate to women. Asked to describe *Simple Men*, Hartley said: "It's about a man who tries to hate women. It's about his inexperienced brother, who feels he will lack an identity until he confronts the truth about his father. It's about their father who subscribes to a justice that cannot be codified. And it's about a woman who refuses to lie. In all, it's a romance with an attitude problem."[18]

Having been betrayed by his sexy girlfriend during a computer heist, Bill tells Dennis that "the first good-looking blond woman I see, I'm gonna make her fall in love with me and then I'm gonna fuck her." But when he meets Kate (Karen Sillas), a mature bar owner, he is forced to reexamine his misogynist attitude and to regard women as more than just objects. When they visit the site of a burned house, Bill steals a kiss, and Kate slaps him. Later, in a similar gesture, quite symmetrically, Dennis is slugged in the head by Elina (Elina Lowensohn), a Romanian friend of their father's. In addressing men's attitudes toward women, Hartley reveals the conscience of a New Man without the phony rhetoric.[19]

In *Amateur*, Hartley's silliest film, he uses established talent, adding Isabelle Huppert, a bona fide star, to his ensemble. Huppert plays a former nun who checks out of a convent to write erotic stories, a subject she knows nothing about. Under the most bizarre circumstances, she meets Thomas (Martin Donovan), an amnesiac with a criminal past who's been pushed out a window (and is presumed dead) by his wife Sofia (Elina Lowensohn), "the most notorious porno actress in the world," whose desperate finances force her into a deal with a powerful arms merchant. With digressions that involve Thomas's accountant and two goons who are on Sofia's trail, all the characters end up in upstate New York in a surreal climax.

Less quirky than Hartley's earlier efforts, *Amateur* tries to push humor to the forefront, but the absurd conceit of amnesia and other comic elements are too forced. Amnesia has been such a prevalent theme in American films that it has become painfully banal. Occasionally, though, fresh observations surface about the contrasts between purity and experience and ignorance and knowledge, two of Hartley's perennial themes.

An academic exercise, *Flirt* (1996), a three-part anthology of variations on the same emotional situation, poses a theoretical question about the effect of context on contents, the limits of narrativity, and the possibilities of film language. The film began with a 1993 short, also titled "Flirt," in which a spoiled but good-natured man, Bill, is given an ultimatum by his girlfriend: commitment or termination of their relationship. Bill promises an answer in a few hours, during which he hysterically examines his romantic options. For his bad faith, he's accidentally shot in the face and loses his girl. Set in 1994, the second segment transposes the same dilemma to a gay locale in Berlin; for the third episode set in Tokyo, Hartley lets the context dictate the story. This slight meditation starts out in familiar territory, then moves to a romantic closure with some frivolous autobiographical elements (Hartley plays a filmmaker). A precise sense of place is evoked by Spiller's photography: the New York act is shot in tight closeups, the German in medium range, and the Japanese in a more remote style.

With *Flirt*, Hartley's career plummeted, but he rebounded with the solid, if flawed, *Henry Fool* (1998). A summation movie embracing all of Hartley's thematic motifs, *Henry Fool* is occasionally meditative and touching, but also pretentious, overlong (138 minutes), and dull. It's a tale of two eccentric losers: a garbage man's life is changed by a hobo philosopher. Like Hartley's previous features, *Henry Fool* is a dark comedy about frustrated individuals in blue-collar Long Island, pushed into a journey towards self-awareness through which they discover the meaning of friendship and the unpredictable workings of fate.

Citing Joyce's *Ulysses*, Beckett, and the legends of Faust and Kasper Hauser as inspirations, Hartley reflects on American culture's excessive conformity and conservatism and the vagaries of fate, how individuals can creatively reinvent themselves, and the unexpected ways in which life redefines individuals' identities and tangled relationships. Although some critics declared it a breakthrough movie, *Henry Fool* again showed how esoteric Hartley's appeal is.

The New York directors can be distinguished as much by sensibility as by geography. If Jarmusch is East Village and Hartley Long Island, Whit Stillman is certainly Upper East Side.

IVY LEAGUE INTELLECTUALISM—WHIT STILLMAN

Whit Stillman has written, produced, and directed three films: *Metropolitan*, *Barcelona*, and *The Last Days of Disco*, all ensemble pieces with a large number of characters. Notable for their Ivy League intellectualism, all three are about a rarified type, the privileged upper-class members who often marginalize themselves through self-involvement. Stillman makes cerebral comedies, in which relentlessly verbal characters are expressed in and by ideas and are engaged in circular talk peppered with self-mockery.

Like Hartley, Stillman has developed a stylized dialogue—there's a distinct, unnatural cadence to his talk. Also like Hartley, he has situated his films at the intersection of politics and culture, flaunting a strong authorial voice in depicting issues of career, identity, and love. Stillman burst onto the indie scene in 1990 with *Metropolitan*, a romantic comedy about young Manhattan debutantes socializing in elegant Park Avenue apartments.

Metropolitan boasts a Preston Sturges sensibility, in sharp contrast to the quirky and offbeat indie movies of the Coen brothers and Jim Jarmusch, who were then in high vogue. As Andrew Sarris has pointed out, Stillman emerged as an American Eric Rohmer, making intelligent, dialogue-driven films.[20] Like Rohmer, Stillman's work depends on language, with humor submerged in the text and played deadpan by the actors. But Stillman doesn't shortchange the men as the veteran French director does in his female-themed morality tales.

The fast speech and satirical wit betray Stillman's Harvard education: *Metropolitan* makes explicit references to Jane Austen's *Mansfield Park*, Lionel Trilling's critique of Austen, and Luis Buñuel's *The Discreet Charm of the Bourgeoisie*. In describing his work, Stillman uses the word "novelistic" rather than "literary," because "literary is a way of treating the material, while novelistic implies that the story is somehow bigger than the vessel you're putting it into, that there's more of a world there than you're showing."[21]

The vignettes that describe the debutante scene in the holiday season convey the poignancy of the movie's two levels, the personal and the political. The sense of decline and fall is disguised as a running joke about underachievers in the upper class, but *Metropolitan* never loses its sense of anthropological curiosity about preppies as an endangered species. The WASPish enclaves prevail in the lobbies and ballrooms of the Plaza and the St. Regis hotels, in the Protestant cathedrals of the Upper East Side, and in Sally Fowler's lush apartment. They are an anachronism in a city filled with immigrants and outsiders of every race, nationality, and class. Privileged as they are, Stillman's characters are presented from the inside, without indulging in the class bashing that is the norm in most Hollywood movies about the rich and famous.

Charlie Black (Taylor Nichols), who talks social theory and is given to sweeping generalizations, is convinced that his class is doomed. An overly philosophical but romantically frustrated nerd, he's contrasted with Nick Smith (Christopher Eigeman), the self-confident dandy. For dramatic tension, Stillman creates the main character as an outsider-preppie, Tom Townsend (Edward Clements), who lives on the Upper West Side with his divorced mother. Though Tom doesn't approve of the ethos of the clique, he doesn't hesitate to join it when he's unexpectedly asked to. Tom goes back on his principles, but, avoiding judgment, Stillman treats him with compassion.

Instead of accepting the love of Audrey (Carolyn Farina), a clear-eyed girl with whom he is intellectually compatible, Tom has a crush on the bubbleheaded and flirtatious Selena—until it's almost too late. Stillman shows empathy for Audrey's vulnerability in a scene in which she stands abandoned in a ballroom, a scene that recalls Katharine Hepburn's isolation in a public ball in *Alice Adams*. The idealism of Tom and Audrey is juxtaposed with the banality and disenchantment of Cynthia and Rick Von Sloneker.

As a comedy about young socialites' growing pains, *Metropolitan* came right out of Stillman's own experience. Stillman spent many tuxedoed nights on velvet furniture with puffy dressed, white-gloved women, talking about sociology, literature, and romance. "The subject for the film just fell into my lap," said Stillman, whose film career came after years in publishing, journalism, and film distribution. "I tried writing about that world in college, trying to be F. Scott Fitzgerald, but it never worked. I was too close to the material."[22] With time and distance, Stillman was ready to approach the subject again: "For ten years, I was totally estranged and not involved in that scene, so I could go back to it with a humorous take." Stillman treats the material ironically, making fun of the obsessions of those years, obsessions that involved being lost in the world of Fitzgerald novels, the sociological theories of Charles Fourier, the daydreams of charming socialites.

The movie is autobiographical: In *Metropolitan*, Tom is smitten, just as Stillman was. And, like Stillman, Tom could play both sides when it concerns the debutante set. Although Stillman's family took part in the socialite scene, they were hostile to it, partly because his father was a lawyer with the Kennedy administration. A socialist thinker with one tuxedo, one raincoat, and divorced parents, Stillman was at once an outsider and an insider. This duality influenced Stillman's writing: He decided to spread himself around the other characters: Audrey, the naive heroine; Nick, the aggressive fast talker; Charlie, preoccupied with his doomed class.

The movie's original tag line was: "Doomed. Bourgeois. In Love." Considered to be too depressing for a comedy, however, it was changed to "a story of the downwardly mobile." But the film is instilled with a subtext of failure. Stillman even invented an acronym, UHB, which stands for Urban Haute Bourgeoisie. A UHBie is not a preppie or a WASP but a member of a group that because of its specific status has nowhere to go but down. Again, the concept reflects Stillman's experience: "Before the film, I wasn't a terrible failure, but I was succeeding OK at something I had no identification with at all."[23]

Stillman made *Metropolitan* for $230,000 by cajoling friends and relatives to invest money and by shooting in borrowed apartments. Conditions were very different for his second feature, *Barcelona* (1994), whose $4 million budget was entirely financed by Castle Rock. The film was shot in exotic, cosmopolitan Barcelona, with its broad boulevards and imposing plazas. The city's wildly eccentric architecture features prominently in the narrative.

Jokingly described as *"Metropolitan* meets *Where the Boys Are* meets *Year of Living Dangerously," Barcelona* is a darker, more acidic comedy than *Metropolitan*, given the terrorist element in the story. Set in the early 1980s, it's a tale of two Americans, one a businessman, the other a naval lieutenant, at the end of the Cold War. The duo must make moral choices about love and career, against a backdrop of anti-Americanism and terrorist attacks. As in *Metropolitan*, Stillman constructs characters who are not particularly likable so that he can humanize them. Ted (Taylor Nichols) is an American sales executive, and Fred (Chris Eigeman) is a lieutenant with the Sixth Fleet. They are extensions of the men in *Metropolitan*: Ted is given to odd theories that fail the test of reality, and, recalling *Metropolitan*'s sharp-tongued

Nick, Fred tends to spin extravagantly false yarns, hoping their audacity alone will convince others.

The Last Days of Disco (1997), the last and feeblest in the triptych, loosely connects *Metropolitan* and *Barcelona*. Its young characters use the disco as they would use any other salon; for Stillman, discos are "civilized environments." This is one of the picture's problems: The ambience is wrong, failing to convey the passion, the erotic heat, the decadence that characterized discos as temples. At film's end, when the characters suddenly realize disco is dead, the viewers are left to feel that they never understood what disco was about, what it meant for their lives, in the first place.

Chris Eigeman, Stillman's favorite actor, who moves from picture to picture, articulates the director's voice. Nick, Eigeman's character in *Metropolitan*, becomes Fred in *Barcelona*, and then Des in *Last Days of Disco*. Representing the darker side of the more naive and idealistic characters, in each film Eigeman is both noxious and knowing, arrogant yet self-critical.

Ensemble driven as they are, all of Stillman's films have an emotional center. The Eigeman character disappears from *Metropolitan* too soon, and in *Barcelona* his character is in a coma for a whole act. As if to correct these mistakes, in *Last Days of Disco*, Stillman avoids putting Eigeman's Des out of action, and he also creates a female Eigeman character in Charlotte (Kate Beckinsale). Charlotte and Des are strong characters, present in the story from beginning to end. Only in the last reel does the focus switch to the two "nice" ingenues, Josh (Matthew Keeslar) and Alice (Chloe Sevigny), with the latter serving the function that Audrey is meant to serve in *Metropolitan*, although Audrey is more sympathetic. Initially, Stillman tried to tell *Metropolitan* from Audrey's point of view, but he was more committed to Tom, so it became his film.

Each film in Stillman's trilogy is set against a backdrop of change—the decline of the UHBs in *Metropolitan*, the anti-Americanism of post-Franco Spain in *Barcelona*, and, least pointedly, the end of disco in *Last Days of Disco*. Stillman's consistent theme is decline—his stories are situated in a crucial historical moment when things begin to fade. This bittersweet poignancy, which lends strong dramatic structure to his work, comes from Stillman's own experience of "hooking onto things and getting to like them just as they're going out of fashion."[24]

MOONLIGHT FAIRY TALES—TOM DiCILLO

Tom DiCillo worked as Jarmusch's cinematographer on his first two pictures. However, the comic-nightmarish quality of DiCillo's debut, *Johnny Suede* (1992), is less influenced by Jarmusch than by David Lynch. The film's eponymous hero (Brad Pitt) is an *Eraserhead*-like James Dean, and its Brooklyn exteriors have the menacing German Expressionism evoked by Lynch. As Hoberman points out, DiCillo borrows devices from other indie directors: Jarmusch's deliberate pacing, John Waters's retro kitsch, Lynch's camp and midgets.[25] A stylish exercise in cool, *Johnny Suede* assumes its place along other films that take their titles from symbolically evocative textures—*Polyester, Blue Velvet*.

Combining hard-edge cynicism with compassion, *Johnny Suede* looks like a cartoon, but it's serious enough to raise intriguing questions, specifically about men's deep fear of women. DiCillo populates an urban wasteland, Long Island City, with retro icons of pop culture, casting a *Gilligan's Island* star, Tina Louise, as a record producer and quoting the 1938 all-midget musical Western *The Terror of Tiny Town*, which is shown on television. In a role that suggests James Dean, Elvis Presley, and Ricky Nelson, DiCillo crafts a lyrical portrait of a wannabe, a good-natured poseur mythically named Johnny. Mixing sight gags with deadpan humor, *Johnny Suede* works its magic as a fairy tale about a man who has to lose one shoe in order to find his true identity.

Conveying a 1950s zeitgeist, the film centers on a talentless youngster who aspires to become a teenage idol. Johnny starts with the basics—a monstrous lacquered pompadour, black and white clothes, and a steel guitar. He lives in a ratty tenement where he sits around strumming the guitar, dreaming about forming a band with his friend Keke (Calvin Levels), who also sports an elaborate coif—a tangle of off-kilter dreadlocks. While painting apartments to make a living, the duo fantasize of being onstage, mobbed by throngs of adoring fans. Standing in front of the mirror with his hand provocatively in his underwear, Johnny practices Nelson's "Some People Call Me a Teenage Idol."

In *Johnny Suede*, like the downtown milieu that inspired it, everyone is an aspiring star. Johnny's friend, an airhead musician (the rocker Nick Cave) with a platinum pompadour, is a more degenerate version of Johnny. Even Johnny's landlord breaks into a mockingly toneless dirge when he comes to collect the overdue rent. Basically, Johnny's a loner; he wanders around half-naked in his apartment and through nightclubs with the same self-absorption. Johnny ambles dreamily and innocently through life. The film's running joke is that whenever he gets lost in his dreams, reality smacks him in the face.

Johnny dates Darlette (Alison Moir), a willfully vapid girl who's as lost as he is. She brings him up to her pink ultrafemme pad to read him inspirational poetry, but later dumps him. Things change when Johnny meets Yvonne (Catherine Keener), an older, smarter girl, who works as a teacher for mentally challenged children; by implication, Johnny becomes one of them. The hard-boiled Yvonne cuts through Johnny's solipsism, and it's in their interactions that the movie becomes a poignant satire of male-female relationships. Yvonne has to instruct Johnny about women's sexuality, their anatomy, how to make love, where to touch. She challenges Johnny's misogyny, instilling in his "teenage heart" some maturity, and under her guidance he begins to feel and show real emotions.

The film's cumulative effect is that of a synthesis of 1980s New York indies. Johnny lives in one of those timeless cinematic communities, with no specific dress codes—the movie could have taken place in another era. The streets are always empty, until, suddenly, like a gift from God, a pair of suede loafers falls from heaven with the power to transform Johnny's life. But, first, Johnny has to lose one shoe to feel a sense of loss. The film ends with a heartfelt reunion between boy and shoe.

DiCillo's follow-up, *Living in Oblivion* (1995), offers a smart, amusing look at the perils of filmmaking, low-budget style. It's DiCillo's version of Truffaut's *Day for Night*—a valentine to the independent film world. Of course, the bleak title, which suggests a crime-gangster flick, indicates nothing about the film's clever treatment and intricate structure. Originally designed as a short to showcase the actress Catherine Keener (*Johnny Suede*'s costar) and Dermot Mulroney, who also appears in the film, it's a picture in which reality and fantasy double back on one another.

Highlighting every problem a struggling filmmaker might encounter, each of the three sections involves a scene that the put-upon director Nick Reve (Steve Buscemi), a cineaste who displays a poster of Fritz Lang's *M* on his wall, is desperately trying to shoot. Modest in scale, and sophisticated without being self-absorbed, the film examines the anxieties and mishaps that befall creators of low-budget indies, with observations that apply to any artistic collaboration where egos, libidos, and technology collide.

Chad Palomino (James Le Gros), the heartthrob star of the film within the film, declares upon his arrival: "I'm watchin' you, buddy, like a hawk! I wanna learn from you!" Chad, whose more typical roles are that of a rapist with whom Michelle Pfeiffer falls in love and a sexy serial killer who shacks up with Winona Ryder, wreaks havoc on the set. Despite DiCillo's repeated denials that his character's diffident dudehood has nothing to do with Brad Pitt, the implication didn't escape audiences. When a journalist asked Pitt what sort of character he played in *Johnny Suede*, he said: "He's just an idiot trying to figure out how he can sit comfortably in a chair."

Chad's antics are only part of the trouble plaguing Nick, whose black-and-white nightmare gives the film its opening salvo. In the first sequence, an actress named Nicole (Keener) is forced to repeat the same scene with her mother over and over again while mishaps ruin every take. There's nothing new about seeing a shot go fuzzy, or a sound boom lurch comically into a close-up, but DiCillo turns the accumulation of such screw-ups into funny material.

With endless patience and misplaced optimism about his artistry, Nick plays peacemaker on his strained set. He handles Wolf (Mulroney), a cameraman who wears a beret, an armband, a leather vest—and fake bravado. "I love the shot; hell, I designed it," Wolf says. On the verge of panic, Nick must contend with Wanda (Danielle von Zernick), a cutthroat assistant director who unexpectedly softens when Chad appears; a driver (Tom Jarmusch) loaded with free advice; and crew members with plans to make their own movies. Nicole and Chad become just well enough acquainted to turn their romance into a catastrophe, and Nick learns that real-life love scenes usually turn troublesome on-screen.

The best segment is the central one in which Chad, for all his casual manner, turns out to be a ruthless scene-stealer, sneakily outmaneuvering his director and costar—until he's forced to make the ultimate power play ("I'll pay for it myself!"). The last reel raises serious doubts about Nick's artistry as he stages a dream sequence involving Tito, a indignant dwarf in formal attire. Tito rants against dream sequences and the aesthetic of bizarreness; he is fed up with lending what can be described as the Lynch touch to movies. Resenting the stereotyping, Tito asks, "Have you ever had a dream with a dwarf in it?" If Nick had an answer, he would be making a better film. In a perfect coda, DiCillo shows the longings of his characters, lavish lunches, romantic love, and prizes—including one "for the best film ever made by a human being."

With the fresh spontaneity that signals a labor of love, *Living in Oblivion*'s subject is narrow, but the film is blessed with infectious good humor and a delightful ensemble that keeps its energy high. Inhabiting a world that becomes seductively real, the performers display a shared sense of purpose. Wickedly playful, *Living in Oblivion* celebrates mischief so deliciously that it could only encourage neophyte directors to follow suit.

In *Box of Moonlight* (1997), Al Fountain (John Turturro), an uptight engineer, finds himself with a few days to spare in the middle of nowhere. He hires a car and drives around in circles, encountering along the way a variety of oddballs who show him how wonderful life can be. A central, fateful encounter ensues with the mythical Kid (Sam Rockwell), who wears a Davy Crockett hat, lives in a glade, swims in the nude. Inexplicably, and with only a few contacts with his loyal wife and lazy boy back home, Al stays with Kid and learns to enjoy mashed-up Hydrox cookies for breakfast.

The movie recalls such 1980s yuppie-angst films as *Something Wild* or *After Hours*, in which squares are loosened up by outsiders who preach "hippie wisdom" to them. With its magical touches—fairground lights, a deer head on the seat of a car, an axe-wielding priest—*Box of Moonlight* is meant to be a whimsical romp, but it's miscast, asking the audience to believe in the credibility of a brilliantly eccentric actor like Turturro as an Everyman in Middle America.

Many male directors, not just DiCillo, manifest problems in their movies with the way they handle the female characters. No matter what one thinks of David O. Russell as a filmmaker, he should be credited with dealing with sex and sexuality head on.

MANHATTAN NEUROSIS—DAVID O. RUSSELL

"There will always be libido and sex in my movies," David O. Russell has said, and, indeed, sex, deception, and family-inspired neuroses are his themes.[26] His gift for clever detours reconcile circumcision jokes and beach-volleyball babe twins into a farce. With each movie, Russell has "exorcised certain behaviors," as he said: "With *Flirting with Disaster*, it was fickleness and second-guessing and knocking myself out with obsessing over things. With *Spanking the Monkey*, that whole wanting to just having sex with my mother."[27]

Russell fell in love with film as a teenager, watching *Taxi Driver*, *Chinatown*, and *Shampoo* over and over again. His guiding vision came from "all those great 1970s Hollywood movies that had stars and were commercial; yet they were original and subversive." After graduating from Amherst College in 1981, Russell's John Reed period as an unreconstructed leftist activist took him to Nicaragua to teach in a Sandinista literacy program. At age 28, in a radical shift of careers, Russell switched to catering and to writing self-termed "bad screenplays." Unlike most beginners, Russell had more life experiences to draw on beyond film school or comic books.[28]

His feature debut, *Spanking the Monkey* (1994), was a gleefully subversive, bleakly comic family saga that seethes with misanthropy. A twisted coming-of-age tale, it begins in detailed realism, then pushes its characters over the edge into lunacy. Neurosis-tinged, despite its theme of incest, the comedy is couched as a cautionary yarn. It examines the sexual agonies and gloomy life of Raymond Aibelli (Jeremy Davies), a premedical student who's forced to give up an internship in Washington and stay home in suburban Connecticut to nurse his mother, who has broken her leg. A man who spends more time on the road than at home, Ray's father is a hypocritical, philandering salesman of self-help videos. Prior to his departure, he lays his ground rules, all of which involve his dog, a German shepherd which gets better treatment than either his wife or his son. Ray is not to use the car for walking the dog, and he has to clean its delicate gums with a special toothbrush every day.

Susan (Alberta Watson), Ray's mom, is an attractive fortysomething woman with long hair and a shapely body that gives her a sensual look. Bored and lonely, she's ruthless in her demands for attention from her son. Asking Ray to massage her toes, she sadly notes, "I can never get your father to do these things for me anymore," to which Ray's reaction is both repressed and disturbed. Later, when Ray helps her stand naked in the shower, the scene is neither titillating nor innocent. Russell displays a shrewd way of breaking tension with irreverent humor, as when Ray tells his mother that her buttock birthmark is shaped like a shopping cart.

Ray takes a "rational" approach to sex (hence the title), but the dog presents a continuous problem: Whenever Ray tries to masturbate in the bathroom, the dog howls at the door (a joke repeated too many times). Resentfully bouncing around the house, Ray becomes the fulcrum of emotional cruelty. With no real friends in town, he becomes attached to Toni (Carla Gallo), a sultry teenager who desires him, yet runs to her father-psychiatrist to complain about his advances. "Is this how you like them? Little baby psychobabble?" charges Ray's ferociously jealous mother when she finds Toni in his room.

The incest scene is brief and discreet—Russell makes sure to establish the "proper" context, a night when Ray and Susan have one too many drinks while watching TV in bed. They start tossing bits of cheese at the TV while laughing hysterically, then roll around, and one light physical touch leads to another. Then, there's a quick cut to the next morning and a messy room. The aftermath, as Ray tries to find his road back to mental health, is more comic than the descent into forbidden sex.

For a while, the film's deadpan, understated manner is entertaining, although it seems that Russell consciously sets out to treat a lurid subject audaciously. He handles the incest in an unsentimental, "responsible" manner, as if it were part of a normally painful coming of age. But it's not. The film leaves an uneasy feeling: Did it have to be about incest to precipitate Ray's maturation? The mother-son sex comes across as attention-grabbing gimmick in an otherwise worthy story about the need of children to escape the clutches of suffocating parents.

That Russell is a director of good ideas but unevenly executed movies became clear with his follow-up, *Flirting with Disaster* (1996), an inspired piece of lunacy about the need to establish one's biological roots. Boasting a clever title, the movie thrusts the audience into a giddy adventure of confusion and mischance, brimming with loopy dialogue and anarchic digressions. Like *Spanking the Monkey*, however, it ultimately is undone by problems of tone control.

A Woody Allenish neurotic type, Mel Coplin (Ben Stiller) is a mild-mannered entomologist, who can't bring himself to name his infant son or to have sex with his loving wife, Nancy (Patricia Arquette) until he completes a manic cross-country search for his parents. The adopted son of maladjusted New Yorkers (Mary Tyler Moore and George Segal), Mel convinces himself that his anxieties would vanish if he could locate his biological parents. (A similar premise is used by Albert Brooks in *Mother*, about a middle-aged son who moves back in with his mother to resolve his problems with women.)

Reassured by the adoption agency that "the mystery of your un-known self is about to unfold," Mel and Nancy are joined by a sexy but inept counselor, Tina Kalb (Tea Leoni), who's assigned to videotape the reunion. Like the engineer in DiCillo's *Box of Moonlight*, the trio hits the road on a wild-goose chase that sends them all over the country, meet-ing along the way an assortment of eccentrics and oddballs.

Nancy, at a low point in both her marriage to Mel and in her self-confidence, contemplates an affair with Tony, her best friend, who's openly gay. In a more typical studio movie, there would have been a sex scene between them, but, wishing to "subvert expectations," Russell in-structed Tony to court Nancy by licking her armpit. The journey recalls vintage screwball comedies like Preston Sturges's *The Lady Eve* or *The Palm Beach Story*. Russell creates a physical comedy that moves at a breakneck pace so that there's no time for the audience to reflect on its silliness. He shows a facility for mocking such sacred American institu-tions as bed-and-breakfasts and rental cars, but he is not as witty as Sturges. Throughout, artificially induced physical situations serve as camouflage for lack of inventive writing.

RAUNCHY NEW JERSEY—KEVIN SMITH

Kevin Smith has been called "the King of Gen-X Cinema," a label he embraces with ambivalent joy. A satirist who writes deftly but who lacks any sense of visual style, Smith makes a strong case for attending film school, if only to acquire some technical skills. *Clerks* (1994), a sav-age assault on convenience-store culture, put onscreen the loves and "ambitions" of two cash register jockeys. Ragged and ribald, the studio-made *Mall Rats* (1995), which takes aim at the shopping-malls subcul-ture, was a sophomore jinx—flat and unfunny. The sex comedy-drama *Chasing Amy* (1997) represented a return to form but again showed that Smith is a crude filmmaker with limited understanding of the medium's possibilities.

The son of a postal clerk in Highlands, New Jersey, Smith spent an uneventful childhood in a white-trash town, watching six hours of TV a day. He told *Time*: "I read comics and went to Mass on Sundays. On weekends, we'd hang out and make crank calls and go drinking." Ac-cording to Smith, a defining moment of his generation occurred, when "Fonzie jumped over the shark tank in *Happy Days*."[29]

Smith dropped out of college, returning to the Jersey shore with vague dreams of becoming a screenwriter.[30] He applied for a job in a videostore but ended up working next door, behind the counter of Leonardo's Quick Stop Groceries. On the night of his twenty-first birthday, Smith watched *Slacker*. It was different: The people in it did nothing—they just stood in front of the camera and talked, exactly what they did at the Quick Stop. There was a bizarre trailer for another movie that night, *Trust*, by Hartley, whose debut, *The Unbelievable Truth*, was gathering dust at the videostore next to the Quick Stop. In *Trust*, too, "people talked and nothing happened."

After spending four months at a Vancouver film school, Smith decided to invest the rest of his tuition in making a movie. Back at his folks' house, with his old $5-an-hour job at the Quick Stop, he wrote the script for *Clerks*, about a day in the life of two "do-nothings," who work in a convenience mart and a video store. "I had things in *Clerks* I wanted to say about growing up in the Tri-City area," Smith said, "but my idea to get money for more movies was to say that it was part of a trilogy, which was actually horseshit."[31] Shot in three weeks at the Quick Stop after hours, *Clerks* was made for a mere $27,575.

The anti-hero, Dante Hicks (Brian O'Halloran), plans to sleep late, play hockey, and enjoy his day off, but, instead, he gets called in to the Quick Stop and is stranded when his boss never shows up to relieve him. Pelted with cigarettes by angry customers, he's forced to listen to tales of lung cancers and is later devastated by the wedding announcement of Caitlin, the high-school sweetheart he can't forget. Shocked by the sexual revelations of his girlfriend, Veronica, he blusters, "You sucked thirty-six dicks? Does that include me?" "Thirty-seven," she calmly responds.

Dante quips that his job would be great if "it wasn't for the customers." Randal (Jeff Anderson), Dante's reckless counterpart at the adjoining video store, also insults customers. Together they philosophize about the *Star Wars* trilogy. *The Empire Strikes Back* ended on a down note, Dante says, and that's all life is, a series of down notes. The closest *Clerks* comes to existential truth is Dante's constant refrain, "I'm not even supposed to be here."

Shot in grainy black and white, *Clerks* is cast with beginners. Inspired by Hartley, Smith's script dogpiles absurdity and obscenity on top of each other. The dullness of dead-end jobs is brightened with odd bits—a fat guy asks for softer toilet paper and then dies on the toilet.

When Dante and Randall sneak out to attend the funeral, Randall outrages the mourners by tipping over the casket. "What kind of convenience store do you run here?" a coroner asks as she collects data on a customer's embarrassing demise. It's a relevant question: By the end of the day, the Quick Stop lies in ruins.

The by-the-book Dante represents Smith's id, and the spit-in-your-face Randal his ego, the director once said, though he allowed that it could also be the other way round. More happens on one lousy day than in most years on other jobs—it's a convention of "do-nothing" movies that characters are always busy doing something. *Clerks* contains sex, death, and hockey, but mostly it's about hanging out and talking in the manner of classic American comedies like *American Graffiti* and *Diner*.

Although *Clerks* depicts no graphic sex or violence, the MPAA initially gave it an NC-17 rating, making it the first film to get the restrictive rating solely on the basis of its profane dialogue. But later, when the high-profile attorney Alan Dershowitz and some influential filmmakers (Danny DeVito, Callie Khouri, Cameron Crow) petitioned for reconsideration, the MPAA appeals board granted a softer R rating. Miraculously, the "porno list and sucking your own dick thing" remained intact. No cuts were made except for a new denouement—albeit for different reasons. In the original ending, Dante is killed by an unidentified robber, but, upon reading the script, the producer rep John Pierson told Smith, "Cut it, and I'm in." Smith was happy to oblige.

After premiering at Sundance, where *Clerks* won the Filmmakers Trophy, Smith barnstormed around the global festival circuit, presenting himself as a working-class intellectual who drinks Shirley Temples and wears a long thrift-store overcoat as befits a "true vulgarian." Particularly important was the reception at Cannes, where the film won two prizes and chalked up strong foreign sales. *Clerks* was snapped up by Miramax, which released a ninety-one-minute version, trimmed from 104 minutes. Miramax cleaned up the print, added a new soundtrack featuring Soul Asylum's "Can't Even Tell" and opened the picture with a beefed-up ad campaign that included the tagline: "Just because they serve you doesn't mean they like you." The film pulled in a box-office gross of $2.4 million, alright but not spectacular considering the hype.

"A totally welcome blast of stale air," raved one critic; a "grunge Godot," said another. For Smith, "it's easier to be daring in comedy—to really piss off people—because you fall into a pillow and the pillow is humor."[32] Indeed, despite the grossouts, *Clerks* is disarmingly likable, making even necrophilia seem funny. Smith is aware that his specialty—the verbal gyrations of the randy twentysomething—represents a tough sell for the studios, which don't know what to do with his work.

Although hailed as a New Wave filmmaker, Smith harbors more mainstream aspirations. As strange as it may sound, the career he would like to emulate is that of John Hughes: "There's a hole in the market for smart teen films. That's what I'd like to be, the John Hughes of the 1990s."[33] Mainstream hopes should not be surprising from someone who avoids drugs, attends church regularly, and plans to get married and have a family. Smith grew up "talking about sex, but not having it," which explains why his movies are raunchy, anticlerical, and sexually flamboyant.

A deal with Universal led to *Mallrats*, a Gen-X hang-out movie that takes place in a *Clerks*like universe, where nothing seems to happen, yet a lot does. Marred by inept slapstick and draggy pacing, this $6 million movie was a flop for Universal. In his defense, Smith claimed, "I just wanted to make the kind of kids-lost-in-a-mall type of comedy I grew up watching. I wore the studio label like a badge of honor, but I got crucified for it."[34] Smith was castigated by the indie community for his perceived sell-out, and most reviewers declared *Mallrats* a total failure. But for Smith, the experience was liberating: "I would wish a flop on everybody, because you feel afterwards like you have nothing to lose."

Inspired by his Sundance encounter with the director Rose Troche and the cast of *Go Fish*, a lesbian romantic comedy, *Chasing Amy* redefines the boy-meets-girl formula for a culture where anything goes. "I'm a jaded optimist looking behind the doors of small-town America," said Smith. Peeping behind closed doors links him to Lynch's *Blue Velvet* and *Lost Highway*, although Smith is peering with humor as opposed to menace or bizarreness. Smith is one indie director not seduced by film noir and its somber fatalism. How could he be? "My generation believes we can do almost anything. My characters are free: no social mores keep them in check."[35]

In a spiky film that depicts the stormy, unlikely love affair between two comic-book artists, the twist is that the guy is straight and the girl isn't. Smith turns the lighthearted, sexually charged material into an emotional drama. Deliberately designed to confound expectations, the film begins with the most outrageous lesbian stereotypes, only to explode them. Once again, Smith centers on yearnings—forlorn layabouts looking for love. The title derives from a monologue delivered by Silent Bob (a recurring character in Smith's films, along with Jason Mewes's druggie Jay), who mourns the girl that got away. A comedy with serious overtones, *Chasing Amy* is about sacrifice, or how much one is willing to give up for love.

The lovestruck Holden (Ben Affleck) shares a place with his buddy Banky (Jason Lee) in central New Jersey; they're like college roommates who refuse to mature. The creators of a popular comic book, *Bluntman and Chronic*, they enjoy a laid-back partnership, marked by intuitive understanding and constant sparring. Alyssa (Joey Lauren Adams), the comic-book artist Holden falls for, is lesbian. It takes a lot of "pseudo-dates"—as Banky sneeringly says—for the two to connect. Banky serves as a jealous former suitor, always presenting the negative side of things. It takes some byzantine sexual maneuvering before Alyssa realizes she's in love with Holden.

At first, the cynical but romantic Holden can't believe Alyssa remains sexually unresponsive, but when he finally breaks down and confesses his love, she's furious. For him, to be in love is easy, but for her it means change. The irony is that it's Holden's life, not Alyssa's, that needs to change the most. Holden's curiosity about lesbian courtship and sex (what women do together in bed) begins as leering but then changes into genuine interest. Holden is not upset by Alyssa's lesbianism, because he perceives her love for him as a renunciation of that past. What disturbs him is Alyssa's heterosexual experience (in high school, she had sex with two men at once), because of his desire to be the first man in her life. His double standard can't tolerate Alyssa's promiscuous past. As Peter Rainer has observed, *Chasing Amy* is about a guy who's forced to face up to his own square expectations and to reluctantly acknowledge that he is not as hip as he thought.[36]

Like *Clerks*, *Chasing Amy* is a politically incorrect comedy with casual profanity, but more profound philosophy. To his credit, Smith isn't playing out the stereotype that lesbians are women who haven't met the right guy. And he shows respect for women, thinking, as Manohla Dargis has pointed out, that a woman's mind is as sexy as her body.[37] Nonetheless, although honestly conceived, *Chasing Amy* still reflects a naive, outside view of lesbianism by a white heterosexual male. Curiously, once Alyssa is committed to Holden, she never again experiences doubts about her sexual orientation, never even entertains a thought of having sex with another woman.

"We're not career-driven," Smith told *Time*. "You watch your parents work all their lives, and what do they have to show for it? My generation wants to get the most for doing the least."[38] Like many Gen-Xers who forswear the rat race, Smith still lives in the Jersey suburbs; his View Askew Productions is located a few blocks from his home in Red Bank. He claims that moviemaking—with his girlfriend Adams as leading lady and his friend Scott Mosier as producer—is "an easy way to avoid manual labor."

LONG ISLAND IRISH CATHOLICISM—EDWARD BURNS

As in Hartley's films, working-class Long Island features prominently in the work of Ed Burns. Surprisingly, Burns is one of the few filmmakers to explore the Irish-American Catholic experience. "It would have seemed so natural for people to do stories about Irish-Americans, and I don't know why this hasn't happened," he said.[39] "I grew up on Scorsese and Coppola, and we've had all those films about the Italian-American experience. You have Woody Allen, Barry Levinson, and Neil Simon and plenty of works about the Jewish experience. You have the African Americans and Hispanics. But not Irish."

A crowd-pleaser that raised eyebrows when it won Sundance's top prize, *The Brothers McMullen* (1995) is an old-fashioned, disarmingly straightforward comedy in its disregard for trendiness. Desperate for the Woody Allen touch, Burns pays tribute to *Annie Hall*, *Manhattan*, and *Hannah and Her Sisters*—his movie could be called *Barry and His Brothers*. In a film that's an outgrowth of his personal life, Burns paints the Irish-American brothers as lovingly complicated and utterly confused about women.

Thematically conventional, *The Brothers McMullen* is a test case for films that are indie in budget and production mode but not in spirit or style. Modest in scale, the film was shot at Burns's parents' home in Valley Stream, mostly on weekends. Its initial cost, an incongruously low $25,000, was raised by family friends and relatives. Early cuts of the film were rejected by all the major festivals except Sundance; then, a new distributor, Fox Searchlight, invested $500,000 in postproduction for what became its first theatrical release.

For a twenty-seven-year-old tyro, Burns shows sharp commercial instincts for involving the audience in the amorous adventures of brothers who struggle with the vagaries of the heart and familial commitment. But it's the sprightly, profane dialogue, the "dirty" talk used by the brothers to needle each other, that gives the movie a modern feel and winsome drive, if not exactly an edge. It's this "new" element, the blasphemous banter, that keeps the picture from getting stale.

Battles with faith, love, and masculinity define the lives of three siblings who are temporarily living under the same roof. Although they don't go to church, they are tortured by their Catholicism, their need to reconcile their love lives to their religion. With their abusive father dead and their mother gone to Ireland to rejoin an old flame, they have only one another to turn to as they puzzle out their relationship with women.

Utterly different, the brothers are united by a shared refusal to commit, a belief that "a real guy with a real life" is frightening. This even applies to the eldest, Jack (Jack Mulcahy), the only brother with a wife and a steady job (as a school coach); whenever his wife, Molly (Connie Britton), starts talking about children, Jack gets nervous. Burns plays the middle brother, Barry—hard-drinking, tough-talking, suspicious of women yet yearning for love. An affable rogue, teasingly labeled Mr. Hotshot Noncommittal, Barry is a would-be screenwriter with a wicked tongue and a firm belief that no one should ever get married. He reasons: "Your wife is the last woman you'll see completely naked and be allowed to touch. It's something to think about." Proud of never having been in love, he considers himself an expert in the art of breaking up, dispensing the worst romantic advice possible to his equally mixed-up siblings.

The devout religious commitment of the youngest brother, Patrick (Mike McGlone), makes him the family's moral center. Jokingly called "altar boy," he is the one that the other two come to when they're worried about what "a big-time sin" is. Patrick is involved with a Jewish girl, Susan (Shari Albert), who seriously contemplates marriage, but he's still preoccupied with finding his "true soul mate." Lack of money forces Patrick and Barry back into their old rooms in what's now Jack's house, and that change brings new women into their lives. Patrick starts to notice Leslie (Jennifer Jostyn), a neighborhood girl he admired in high school, and Barry, desperately apartment hunting in Manhattan, finds himself outsmarted by Audrey (Maxine Bahns), a self-reliant actress who resists his charms.

Burns's life changed significantly after the success of *The Brothers McMullen*. He was able to make a second film, *She's the One* (1996), on a bigger budget, $3 million, for Fox Searchlight. Very much in the vein of the first picture, but not nearly as funny, *She's the One* is a comedy-drama about a retired New York firefighter ("verbally abusive but loving") and his two sons: a Wall Street broker in the process of divorce and a cabdriver (Burns), who marries one of his customers hours after meeting her.

Raised in an Irish-Catholic household, Burns wants to show "how your background has a hold on you for life—with disastrous, confusing, and funny consequences." His goal is to create authentic sagas about Irish-American police and their families. "I guarantee my cop films will not have a cop eating a doughnut," he said.[40] "When I see that, I walk out and want to strangle the filmmaker, it's such a cliché. My cops won't be big, fat, bulbous-nosed Irishmen, and they won't be abusive, ignorant racists." Coming from a family of cops, Burns doesn't deny there are cops like that, but he sees it as his responsibility to show "the other side."

A minor, moody character study, Burns's third feature, *No Looking Back* (1998) represents an unexciting, misguided sidestep. While evocative of dead-end small-town life, this working-class drama lacks the complexity, depth, or humor to generate any interest in its familiar theme. This time around, critics gunning for Burns found plenty of ammunition in his simplistically drab woman's picture about a waitress facing a life crisis.

BACK TO THE EAST VILLAGE—MATTHEW HARRISON

This chapter began downtown, with the work of Jarmusch, and it ends downtown, on the Lower East Side, with the gifted Matthew Harrison, whose *Rhythm Thief* (1995) represents urban guerrilla filmmaking at its best, with raw black-and-white cinematography and rigorous minimalism. Shot on a minuscule budget of $11,000 in eleven days, it's a triumph of economy, cutting through all the glamour that surrounds no-budget filmmaking. *Rhythm Thief* blends a bleak, gritty backdrop with strong characters. While the film is funny in its sense of absurdity, it's a tale of a life lived on the edge. Harrison portrays with a fresh, clear vision the dubious, dreary lives of a bunch of ne'er-do-wells.

Set in the mean streets of the Lower East Side, the film revolves around Simon (Jason Andrews), a poor white man who sells bootlegged music tapes on the streets. His meager income barely covers the costs of cheap liquor and kitty litter, the staples of his marginal existence. Simon spends his evenings drinking alone, sifting the cat's litter box, and listening to his neighbors' arguments through his apartment's thin walls. The monotony is broken by Cyd (Kimberly Flynn), Simon's casual girlfriend, who drops by for "sex and nothing else." However, when he insists that they live up to the terms she has set, Cyd gets hysterical.

Simon's survival depends upon his living strictly by his own code, which means detachment. His only confidante is a philosophical neighbor (Mark Alfred), who respects Simon's integrity but wishes he would do more with his life. Simon's simple life is also challenged by Fuller (Kevin Corrigan), a tagalong who pesters Simon to teach him the bootlegging game. Simon exudes the kind of inner resilience and cool discipline that make him attractive to Fuller, who wants to be his pal and partner.

Simon is willing to do anything to keep his routine intact, but when he is accused of stealing a TV set and the band whose music he has bootlegged beats him up, his ordered existence is shattered. A waiflike woman from his past, Marty (Eddie Daniels), suddenly turns up to tell him that his mother, a mental patient, has died. Things go awry, and Simon finds himself on the run. Almost reluctantly, he realizes that he needs Marty and Fuller to help him get his revenge on the band. A series of events propels Simon to Far Rockaway Beach, where he finally reveals his vulnerability and his capacity for feeling. *Rhythm Thief* combines comic sensibility with existential angst and a tongue-in-cheek approach to the conventions of Lower East Side/low-budget filmmaking.

Kicked in the Head (1997), the follow-up to Harrison's highly acclaimed first effort, was not exactly a sophomore jinx but was an ephemeral film that benefited from a solid cast headed by Kevin Corrigan and Linda Fiorentino. Despite some funny situations—parodic gunfights and car explosions in which no one gets hurt—the laughs are too scarce in a slight story overloaded with trivial incidents. Enjoying a bigger budget, the film displayed improved production values but had little to offer beyond modest pleasures.

CONCLUSION

Two recent graduates of Columbia, Greg Mottola and Lisa Chodolenko, demonstrate the viability of the New York school of indies (Chodolenko's *High Art* is analyzed in the Chapter 12). A subtle satire about the intricacies and imbalances of modern relationships, Mottola's *The Daytrippers* (1997) is elevated by a spirited cast that includes old pros like Anne Meara and younger talents like Hope Davis, Parker Posey, Campbell Scott, and Stanley Tucci. Eliza (Davis) and Louis (Tucci) enjoy a blissful marital life in their suburban home, until Eliza finds a poetic love letter addressed to her husband. Shocked and distraught, she rushes to her parents' house for advice. Eliza's dad (Pat McNamara) just listens quietly, but her upset mom (Meara) is determined to take action, urging Eliza to confront Louis at his Manhattan publishing office, whereupon Eliza, her folks, her younger sister, Jo (Posey), and her boyfriend Carl (Liev Schreiber) hit the road in search of the erring husband.

Mottola structures his tale as a road comedy; the quintet encounters obstacles along the way, including a Columbia business student whose irresponsible father takes refuge in his apartment, siblings who argue over their inheritance from their deceased mother, and so on. A good deal of the story is set within the confined space of a car, focusing on squabbles between the parents, nasty exchanges between the domineering mom and her rebellious daughter, and tensions between the young lovers. Mottola shows a sensitive ear for the nuanced dialogue used by vulnerable people on the edge, but his writing is uneven; the "asides" provide a welcome respite, but not all of them are funny. *Daytrippers* gets progressively darker, and the ending, which reveals Louis's mysterious nature, is abrupt and unsatisfying. Mottola mines the same comic turf as Russell does in *Flirting with Disaster*, but his approach is more compassionate; the humor is tinged with tenderness, not derision.[41] He doesn't look down on his bourgeois characters, as Russell does, offering instead gentle understanding of all them.

6

The Resurrection of Noir

IS FILM NOIR a singular genre that recurs over time with an unrestricted life span? Or is it a time-bound cycle, a congealing of forces and attitudes operating in a specific era? Theorists have long been preoccupied with the question of whether noir is a distinct genre or a distinct style that crosses generic boundaries. For Paul Schrader, noir is not a genre because, unlike Westerns or gangsters, it is defined not by conventions of setting and conflict but by the "subtle qualities of tone and mood."[1] This mood was described by J. P. Telotte as a longing for *temps perdu*, "an irretrievable past, a predetermined fate and an all-enveloping hopelessness."[2] Similarly, in his *Film Encyclopedia*, Ephraim Katz defines noir also in terms of mood: "a type of film that is characterized by its dark, somber tone and cynical, pessimistic mood."[3]

Others critics argue that visual style is what unites the diverse body of films that form the noir universe. But if noir is a style, the question is what specifically constitutes that style. Needless to say, each definition of noir leads to the exclusion and inclusion of particular films. But no matter how noir is defined, most scholars agree that it represents a combination of iconographic, stylistic, and thematic elements.

The strongest argument for noir as a genre is its literary origins in the hard-boiled fiction of the 1930s and 1940s. Like those of the Western, noir's literary conventions and thematic concerns went beyond the realm of cinema. As Schrader points out, the hard-boiled school of fiction created a tough, cynical way of thinking and acting, distinct from the world of everyday emotions. It was the American counterpart of European existentialism, a romanticism with a protective shell, with cynical heroes who had reached the end of the line.

Perpetually reborn in American cinema, noir enjoyed a major revival in the 1980s in the work of David Lynch and the Coen brothers. And it is even more apparent in the 1990s, in the films of Tarantino and his imitators. The reason for the continuous fascination may be simple:

218

Noir strikes responsive chords of fear, anguish, and desire that are indigenous to American life. Noir's brutal frankness in dealing with the
primal subjects of sex, greed, and death is as relevant today as it was in
the 1940s.

Neo-noir continues to bewitch young filmmakers, who love its
glamour but often misunderstand its existential consequences. Distinctions should be made in the growing body of neo-noir among directors
who update the genre, those who reinvent it, and those who just use it
as a point of departure. One can detect in the growing body of films pastiches (*Body Heat*), straight remakes (*The Postman Always Rings Twice*),
efforts to resuscitate the noir universe by combining it with another
genre, such as Ridley Scott's *Blade Runner*, which mixes noir and sci-fi,
and even parodies (*Dead Men Don't Wear Plaid*).

Specific political and cultural conditions of the 1940s and 1950s
brought noir to its zenith: Postwar disillusionment, the German artistic
influence, the impact of Freudian psychology, the popularity of hard-
boiled literary characters, and the dread of the atomic bomb and nuclear holocaust. The combination of these conditions helped define the
noir tonality and vocabulary. Noir's antiheroic vision was generated in
response to the horrors of the war and problems that beset postwar
American society, such as urban crime and political corruption. Noir
films dealt with the loss of honor, the decline of integrity, and the rise of
despair, alienation, and disintegration.

The advent of Italian neorealism, with its emphasis on on-location
shooting, gave film noir verisimilitude in portraying dark, sinister environments. The realist movement suited America's postwar mood,
and actual location shooting became the norm. The public's desire for a
more honest, harsh portrayal of life shifted noir from high-class melodrama to the streets of the cities. But Expressionist studio lighting, im-
ported to Hollywood by German directors, was not incompatible with
realistic exteriors. Noir welded seemingly contradictory elements into a
unified style: Unnatural, stylized lighting was directed into realistic settings.

Despite the fact that the label was given by French critics, noir is a
uniquely American form, one that has outlasted Westerns, screwball
comedies, and musicals. Noir is indigenous to Los Angeles, the last
frontier of the American Dream. It's not a coincidence that writers like
Raymond Chandler, Ross MacDonald, James Ellroy, and Elmore Leonard have set their tales in Los Angeles, a city that occupies a special

place in our collective fantasy. To the millions of Americans emigrants, Los Angeles represented the end of the rainbow—the promised land. The land was cheap, the space vast, the weather accommodating. The new economy and emerging culture also encouraged the development of cults and fashions that exemplified the country's achievements and failures.[4]

Los Angeles also became the home of the world's greatest dream factory—Hollywood. As a metaphor, Los Angeles became, on the one hand, the city of eternal sunshine where prayers are answered and, on the other, the end of the continent. Not surprisingly, the gap between expectations and reality has been a major theme of noir. When noir is set somewhere else, the film succeeds if the new location suggests California's sprawling seediness and sunlit vulgarity. *Body Heat* takes place in Florida, but its landscape, architecture, and manner evoke the Los Angeles of the 1940s.

New directors have been intrigued by noir's distinct vocabulary: voice-over narration and subjective camera. As a privileged way of seeing, subjective camera emphasizes point of view, challenging "normal" perspective by forcibly aligning the viewers with a specific way of seeing. Subjective camera is concerned with heightened expression—the complex relationship of external events with inner feelings.[5]

Of the wide gallery of noir protagonists, the most prevalent types in neo-noir continue to be corrupt, neurotic cops, psychotic killers, ruthless con artists, and cynical hit men. However, in neo-noir, the gap between heroes and villains has considerably narrowed: Both are portrayed as cynical, disillusioned, insecure loners, inextricably bound to the past and uncertain of the future.

In classic noir, the seedy, malignant characters in the background made the lead characters (played by major movie stars) shine. But today, the peripheral characters and villains, often played by Christopher Walken, Michael Madsen, or Chris Penn, are more interesting than the central one. Reflecting the moral chaos in American society at large, villains in the new noir have become more sympathetic, their charm masking a malevolent perversity.

Women in noir were cast not as wives or mothers but in overtly sexual roles that allowed them to exert control over men. The linking of women's sexuality with destruction is a reflection of men's deep anxieties and fears of women's sexual power. Noir women present a challenge to the restoration of a patriarchal-capitalist order in which men are in control. Neo-noir continues to draw on women's threatening sexuality, but, if in the past noir rebuked women's independence and looked toward the restoration of traditional family values, at present, traditional patriarchal values are more fractured than ever before.

Attempting to explain why noir has never died in American film, scholars have suggested that whenever there is a deep rift or disruption in values, one way to express it artistically is through film noir. In the 1970s, as a result of the Vietnam War and the Watergate scandal, distrust of government and paranoia became major themes in a cycle of noirish films that included *Chinatown*, *The Conversation*, *The Parallax View*, *Three Days of the Condor*, *All the President's Men* and *Nashville*, all made between 1974 and 1976.

The dark, twisty territory of noir—a shadowy world dominated by fatalism, pessimism, and romantic despair—is the drug of choice for today's filmmakers. Kenneth Turan has observed that hardly a month passes without one filmmaker or another attempting a noir, so strong is the lure of this brooding genre.[6] While most neo-noir films are content to mimic the surface moodiness and stylishness of the classics, the good ones also echo their emotional impact. For Turan, the noir essentials boil down to an intricate plot that ebbs and flows in unexpected places, dialogue that is juicy and wise-ass, and characters whose anguish is easy to connect with.

For the most part, the new noir directors draw on a now codified style with its visual conventions: Deco titles, heat waves, flames, ceiling fans, shadowed window blinds, tinkling wind chimes, rainy nights in neon-city, muted voices, hopped-up dialogue. Often, the double entendre, which was developed in the 1940s as a way around the restrictive Production Code, seems ludicrous in contemporary films that are filled with profanity and nudity. Classic noir's visual codes that continue to define noir today include somber black-and-white photography, low-key lighting, oblique camera set-ups, use of extreme camera angles to emphasize a dark oppressive tone, tight framing to underline themes of claustrophobia and entrapment, compositional tension to create an atmosphere of eerie menace, and deliberately disquieting editing.[7]

Style in Hollywood movies has become more assertive and pronounced, but no more personal. Ambitious indie directors strive for personal and original works, but they often fall victims to clichés. That the noir style has become overcalculated and deterministic is evident in a body of noir clichés, summed up by one critic in the following way: a man drinking black coffee in an isolated roadhouse; a neon sign blinking on and off outside a seedy bar with one letter missing; a ceiling fan revolving, even in the dead of winter; a hero spilling his guts in voice-over narration; rooms dominated by mirrors; unfiltered cigarettes and overflowing ashtrays; men drinking whisky straight in a barroom during the day; wet and glistening streets, with shadowy figures, even when there's no trace of rain; a muted trumpet moaning plaintively in the night; men with pocket handkerchiefs; a body lying face down in a pool of blood.[8]

Pop culture continues to provide young directors with material that stimulates their more serious artistic instincts. American film history has played a little joke on educated American viewers. For moviegoers who wish movies were more civilized, mature, or ennobling, crime films cause dismay. But, as often happens in American film, fresh, creative energy has come up from the bottom, from tabloid thrills, lurid pulp fiction, cheap horror flicks, and comic books.[9]

THE STYLISTS—THE COEN BROTHERS

Arguably no indie filmmaker has benefited—or exploited—the noir tradition more effectively and thoroughly than Joel and Ethan Coen. The Coen brothers are one of the most creative pairings on the contemporary scene. Unconventional and inscrutable, they have maintained artistic control through writing, directing, producing, and occasionally editing their movies. They form a unified team, with their individual contributions so intertwined that no one can say precisely who did what, though nominally they write together, Joel directs, and Ethan produces. With seven films to their credit, including *Blood Simple* (1985), *Miller's Crossing* (1990), and *Barton Fink* (1991), the Coens have created a world that doesn't look like anybody else's, even though they have heavily drawn on other movies.

The Coens' commercial successes, *Raising Arizona* (1987) and *Fargo* (1996), are, as Todd McCarthy has observed, set in recognizable worlds inhabited by more or less ordinary characters. The rest take place in the stylized noir tradition (*Blood Simple*), remote gangster lands (*Miller's Crossing*), or abstract studio sets (*The Hudsucker Proxy*).[10] As formalist filmmakers, the Coens have pushed Hollywood conventions to the point of absurdity. Like those of many young filmmakers, their ideas were formed by pop culture, which means that their work is self-conscious. Each of their films pays homage to a classic Hollywood genre, with a knowingness born of numerous hours spent in the dark. The Coens are clever directors who know too much about movies and too little about real life.

The shallowness of most of their work is a result of their creating sealed universes that have few references outside the world of cinema. The Coens believe that linking form and content is irrelevant, that brilliant style will somehow lure viewers into uncritical acceptance of their schemes. Filled with artifice, their films are both unique and derivative, displaying dazzling camera pyrotechnics, meticulously conceived scenes, elaborate set pieces, brilliant production design, and occasionally deadpan dialogue.

Technically, their ambitious films are full of allusions to old movies, but emotionally they are vapid, calling attention to a huge gap between form and feeling. The danger of extreme stylization, as Peter Rainer has pointed out, is that nothing matters emotionally.[11] Largely constructed as pastiches, the Coens' movies represent wizardly syntheses that leave a hole where human feelings should be. The Coens, not their characters or the actors who play them, are the stars of their movies. Unlike Tarantino, who puts his performers center stage, the Coens pull the viewers away from the actors in order to showcase their own virtuosity. Hence, it's easier to appreciate the Coens' accomplishments from a distance than to enjoy them viscerally.

From the very beginning, it was the Coens' "knowingness" that endeared them to high-brow critics and sophisticated audiences. Box-office failures such as *Miller's Crossing*, *Barton Fink*, and *The Hudsucker Proxy* would have ruined most filmmakers, but in the Coens' case, they have increased their stature. As John Powers has observed, the Coens offer patrons the cachet of artistic respectability.[12] At the same time, there's always a teasing edge, a disdain for audiences who take their stories too seriously. The Coens' work, like the arty *Miller's Crossing* or lugubriously stylized *Barton Fink*, feels sealed off and inert. But this doesn't mean their work is devoid of serious themes or ideas: Unbridled individualism, often translating into greed, runs through most of their films.

When the siblings were kids, the Minnesota winters of St. Louis Park kept them inside with lots of books and TV; they have described their suburban childhood as "unbelievably banal." Joel, a dropout from the NYU film school, acquired a deliberate, borderline exploitation style through his editing work on low-budget features for other directors, such as Frank LaLoggia's *Fear No Evil* and Sam Raimi's *The Evil Dead*. It didn't take Joel long to lure Ethan out of his philosophy studies at Princeton and for the brothers to start writing scripts together.

The Coens' first film, the Gothic noir *Blood Simple*, which premiered at Sundance, remains one of the 1980s' most visually stunning debuts, with sprightly black humor and mordant wit. Joel wrote the script with Ethan, and together they produced the film for a little over $1 million. The movie interjects visual shrewdness and playful moodiness that compensate for a familiar plot of a cuckolded husband (Dan Hedaya) who hires a seedy private eye (M. Emmet Walsh) to kill his wife (Frances McDormand) and her lover (John Getz). Occasionally, the Coens abandon discipline and coherence and let stylishness overwhelm the film, a problem that recurs in most of their work.

The Coens are masters of props, and their angling on graphic details transform this variation on the love triangle into a bizarre nightmare. A thriller with noirish fatalism and great style, *Blood Simple* lacks strong characterization. The protagonists are cardboard creations, manipulated like the other props, but the film demonstrates the Coens' strong authorial vision, with a showy aestheticism that makes the story bleaker and colder. The Coens concoct a plot rich in surprise and coincidence, with roots in the crime stories of James M. Cain, Elmore Leonard, and Jim Thompson. The premise is unremarkable—the reduced core of hard-boiled novels—but the film, as David Denby has suggested, offers an ironic sense of destiny: Life is smarter and more treacherous than we are, and nothing turns out the way it is planned.[13]

From the opening shot of a rain-spattered windshield through the tense, artfully composed finale, *Blood Simple* is soaked with suspense. Barry Sonnenfeld's dazzling camera, which consciously distorts space, becomes an active participant in the game, lending the film's last scene, in which the wife and the detective fight for their lives, bizarre humor. Throughout, there are plenty of fancy moves, as when the camera slowly glides along a bar, then lifts up over a napping drunk.

Blood Simple introduced the Coens' wry, sardonic treatment of stylized violence. The cartoonlike violence is choreographed to produce a visual rather than an emotional effect; it aims to both scare and stun viewers with its gory pulp elements. In the film's most talked-about scene, the husband is buried alive by the lover. In the next scene, a memorable long take shows the lover's car totally isolated in Texas's vast, flat fields. Nonetheless, some criticism of classic noir is implied in the film. Frances McDormand, who later married Joel Coen and went on to star in several of the brothers' films, is an ordinary-looking actress cast as femme fatale, a type traditionally played by glamorous stars. Brighter than all the men around her, she is the only one to survive the ordeal.

In a shrewdly calculated about-face, *Blood Simple* was followed by *Raising Arizona* (1987), a screwball comedy about a childless couple (Nicolas Cage and Holly Hunter) who kidnap a baby from Nathan Arizona Sr., the father of quintuplets. If *Blood Simple* is deliberately slow and spare with words, *Raising Arizona* boasts breakneck pacing and hopping banter. Until the film skids off-road with a *Road Warrior* fantasy at the end, it's a madcap romp designed to showcase the Coens' versatility.

Demonstrating implacable nuttiness, *Raising Arizona* has a couple of escaped convict brothers, surnamed Snopes, in a jolly reminder of Faulkner's Yoknapatawpha County. The picture contains an excellent on-foot chase scene, but in a sequence where the baby quintet is left unattended on the highway, the Coens reveal their calculated heartlessness. Once again, flashy camera and brilliantly conceived scenes—John Goodman literally bursting up out of the earth in a rainstorm—create a milieu totally removed from that of *Blood Simple*. Full of references to the *Road Warrior* films, *Carrie*, and *Badlands*, *Raising Arizona* gave new life to the road comedy of the 1980s.

With *Miller's Crossing* (1990), the Coens did for the gangster genre what their earlier movies had done for noir and screwball comedy. Loosely based on Dashiell Hammett's *The Glass Key* and drawing on Chicago's Capone-O'Bannion gang war, the film pits Irish, Italian, and Jewish gangsters against one another. Set during the Prohibition in an unnamed Eastern city, *Miller's Crossing* is a put-on gangster film, removed from any discernible reality. Morally vague and strictly pop, the film suffers from excessive style, motivated by the Coens' concern to show off their familiarity with the gangster genre. Still, what gives the familiar drama of murder and betrayal a different feel are its rich visuals and dark, melancholy mood.

The movie opens with a comic monologue in which Leo's Italian rival, Johnny Caspar (John Polito), complains about the collapse of ethics. Pompously righteous, Johnny is given to theoretical formulations about honor and loyalty. His grievances disturb Leo's chief adviser and friend, Tom (Gabriel Byrne), a brooding gambler who senses Leo is losing control. Leo (Albert Finney), the Irish political boss, sleeps with Verna (Marcia Gay Harden) and out of loyalty protects her brother, Bernie (John Turturro), who skims the profits from fixed fights. When Leo discovers that Tom and Verna have betrayed him, a full-scale war begins.

The Coens' films usually begin with a strong visual image. In *Miller's Crossing*, Tom describes a dream in which he chases his hat through the woods; the hat is seen flying in slow motion across the ground. In *The Hudsucker Proxy*, it's a circle motif: hula hoops, clocks, the plot's 360-degree shape. In *Fargo*, it's the vision of a single car driving through vast, white snowscapes. Throughout *Miller's Crossing*, the imagery is striking: closeups of heavy guns, black blood slowly dripping to the ground, sunless skies and serene woods, men in black overcoats speaking in coarse voices. The Coens exaggerate the genre's conventions: The mayor and police chief take orders from the gangsters, who maul one another. Unlike Scorsese, whose crime films *Mean Streets* and *GoodFellas* were based on realistically recognizable characters, the Coens are concerned not with the actual conduct of gangsters but with their visual representation: hatched-faced thugs hiding under fedoras, snarling quasi-poetry.[14]

With their next picture, *Barton Fink* (Fox, 1991), a satirical allegory framed as noir, the Coens decoded the myth of the sensitive artist, the mysteries of the creative process, and the ambiguities of authorship. They began writing *Barton Fink* in the midst of a writing block. "We started with the idea of a big seedy hotel," said Joel. "We'd also been reading about that period in Hollywood, and it seemed like an amusing idea to have John Turturro as a playwright in Hollywood," noted Ethan. "We wanted Barton to meet another writer, and we were playing with the kinds of people who came out to Hollywood at that time, like Faulkner and Odets, people from very different backgrounds, and the funny thing is that they were all writing wrestling pictures."[15]

John Turturro plays a self-absorbed playwright with the big hair and round spectacles of George S. Kaufman and the ideological bent of Clifford Odets. After a Broadway hit, he's brought to Hollywood by a studio mogul, Jack Lipnick (a Louis B. Mayer or Harry Cohn type). The theater in the opening scene is meant to be the Belasco and the play *Awake and Sing*, which actually premiered in 1935. Defying history, the Coens set their movie in 1941, when Fink's proletarian ethos—theater for the masses—was already out of date, replaced by anti-Fascism, the then current intellectual cause.

The philistine studio head first proclaims that "the writer is king at Capitol Pictures," then asks Fink to infuse a Wallace Beery wrestling picture with the "Barton Fink feeling." "We need some heart in motion pictures," he says. "Can you make us laugh, can you make us cry?" Lipnick engages in delirious monologues: "I'm bigger and meaner and louder than any other kike in this town. I don't mean my dick is bigger, though you're the writer—you'll know about that better than me."

To prove he still has a social conscience, Fink checks into a seedy hotel, where he experiences an intense creative block. Fink seeks help from another contract writer, W. P. Mayhew (John Mahoney), a novelist modeled on Faulkner, who actually contributed to *Flesh*, a John Ford wrestling movie. Hopelessly naive, Fink is shocked to realize that the literary genius is tended by a secretary-mistress, Audrey (Judy Davis), who claims to have written his novels. The Coens, however, don't challenge the industry's vulgarity or its abuse of artists; rather, they emphasize Fink's comeuppance, the shattering of his vanity. Parodying the self-important artist, the Coens make Fink a caricature, a man pretentiously raving about a new theater for the common man. "I've always found that writing comes from a great inner pain," Fink intones, to which Mayhew replies, "Me, I just enjoy making things up."

Fink spends his time in a dingy hotel room, whose shabbiness mirrors his inner state. Struggling to write a single line, he stares at the peeling wallpaper, which mocks his own creativity, then wistfully looks at a photo of a bathing beauty staring out to sea. Fink meets his neighbor, Charlie Meadows (John Goodman), an insurance salesman who turns out to be a mass murderer metaphorically linked to Hitler. Meadows says he has great stories to tell, but Fink is too absorbed in lecturing about "the life of the mind" and "the common man" to listen to anyone.

For a man described as brilliant, Fink is slow and impervious to his surroundings. The critic Stanley Kauffman raised a series of questions about Fink's character: Would such a man have colluded in hiding a body? Would he then have sat down and written in heat? Would he have remained calm when his hotel was on fire and he was handcuffed to his bed?[16] But rigorous realism is not a yardstick to apply to a Coen film.

The Coens expect viewers to excuse the strained narrative and flawed characterization in the cause of their allegedly brilliant stylistics.

With Dennis Gassner's "distressed Deco" design and Roger Deakins's lighting, the Coens imbue almost every shot with virtuosity: the producer's office, the dank little hotel room, the immense close-ups of the typewriter. To convey a sense of decay, the interior sequences are shot in Rembrandt's sepia tones, and the wallpaper is decorated with rotting banana leaves. Scenes set in the Hotel Earle were filmed in the lobby of the Wiltern Theatre, after the banana trees had been left for days to wither in the sun. When the theater owners became apprehensive about Gassner's plan to "distress" their new carpet, the filmmakers found the same carpeting at the drydocked Queen Mary in Long Beach, where the New York scenes were shot.

Fink's real education takes place not at Capitol Pictures but in the hotel, which is the Coens' most memorable character. The hotel has endless green corridors with symmetrical rows of shoes and feebly lit rooms underlining the dwellers' isolation. The place becomes a physical metaphor for Fink's tormented psyche and, at the end, stands for his hellish metaphysical state. Typically, the Coens provoke Fink's transformation with sudden violence, heralded by a brash visual pun. While Fink makes love to Audrey, the camera tracks from her feet along the floor, up to the bathroom, and then literally down the drain in the sink. When Fink is next seen, his life has taken the same journey; he's sunk into the abyss of darkness and murder.

A hyperbolic vision of 1940s Hollywood gives the film's studio atmosphere a recycled Fitzgerald or Hawthorne ring—some of the settings recall *The Day of the Locust*. A more immediate inspiration is provided by *The Shining* and its hero (Jack Nicholson), a writer locked in a huge Gothic hotel. But *Barton Fink* goes further than Stanley Kubrick in depicting a writer who's first paralyzed by the "unreality" he's asked to write about, then liberated by a severe reality shock. At the end, Fink's eyes have been opened: He sits on the beach with an ambiguous gift, a box that contains human remains—and stares at a real bathing beauty looking out to sea.

Stylistically, *Barton Fink* is influenced by Roman Polanski's surrealistic comic vision, which turns the brooding satire into a horror movie. Employing a subjective camera, the Coens film the tale from Fink's distorted point of view; his experiences are filtered through his claustrophobic sensibility. Echoes of Billy Wilder's *Sunset Boulevard* are also evident: In both movies, the protagonist is a desperate writer suffering from a block. *Sunset Boulevard* opens with a surreal touch—the narrator

is a corpse in a swimming pool—and the Coens use surrealism to register Fink's unconscious.

Throughout, flamboyant camera moves decorate the picture—a
dolly-shot into the bell of a trombone, a shot of Fink sleeping with a pillow over his blank face. The color scheme verges on the psychedelic:
The glue dripping from the fading wallpaper is a sickly yellow, the
ocean in the postcard is a bright blue, Audrey's crimson lipstick fore-
shadows the violent burst of red that will change Fink's life, and the climactic fire is in apocalyptic red.

In the large-budget *The Hudsucker Proxy* (Warners, 1994), the Coens'
biggest commercial failure, Norville Barnes (Tim Robbins) is a bumpkin
from Muncie, Indiana, who comes to New York to pursue his fortune.
Within a matter of days, he finds himself at the top of the corporate ladder when the company's founder, Waring Hudsucker (Charles Durn-
ing), commits suicide. The scheme is orchestrated by the board chair
Sidney J. Mussburger (Paul Newman), who wishes to drive stock prices
down so that he can acquire control of the company. To execute his nefarious design, Mussburger plans to install an imbecile as president. But
the naive, open-faced Norville comes up with good ideas. He draws on
a piece of paper a simple circle, modestly endorsed as "just for kids." He
then stymies the fix by getting the company to market his pet project,
the Hula Hoop. This is not a rags-to-riches story, however; Norville is
about to jump from the forty-fourth floor of the Hudsucker building on
New Year's Eve.

Set in 1958 but evoking the 1930s, *The Hudsucker Proxy* plays like a
Capraesque fairy tale with a Preston Sturges hero and Howard Hawks
dialogue; it borrows from *Meet John Doe*, with Capra's populism turned
inside out. But Norville's comedown has no emotional power; he's like
a puppet. The polished surface and the distant moral superiority pre-
clude any emotional connection. As John Powers has noted, *The Hudsucker Proxy* tries to play its story both ways, but the movie is neither a
sentimental heart-warmer like *Mr. Deed Goes to Town* nor a savvy send-
up of Hollywood's chestnuts.[17] For all the cynical humor and elegant set
pieces, the movie lacks spontaneity or any forward momentum.

Much less vain or flamboyant than their earlier pictures, *Fargo*
(1996) is considered to be the Coens' best feature. Thematically, it bears
the influence of Beckett in its minimalist, deadpan dialogue. Stylistically, in its cool casualness, the movie recalls the Finnish filmmaker Aki
Kaurismaki's sensibility. Jerry Lundergaard (William H. Macy), *Fargo's*

(anti)hero, is a car salesman in desperate need of cash to finance a business deal. When all options fall through, he hires two thugs, Carl (Steve Buscemi) and Gaear (Peter Stormare), to kidnap his wife for ransom; it's the only way to pry money out of her stingy millionaire father. The scheme hits a bump when an investigating cop is killed, and things continue to go awry and get weirder and weirder. Before long, a body is fed into a wood chipper and the criminals are pursued by the small-town police chief, Marge Gunderson (Frances McDormand), who unravels the scheme with disastrous—and hilarious—results.

Much of *Fargo* is a send-up of its local denizens, with gags about snow, Paul Bunyan, and the dimwitted yokels. A comic thriller with a deadpan tone, the humor is at the expense of the characters who stand in for the people of Minnesota and North Dakota; it mocks their broad, flat accents, which connote slowness and stupidity. Instinctively attracted to the offbeat, the Coens begin by cautioning that *Fargo* is a true story; names have been changed "out of respect for the dead." The Coens have always treated their characters with contempt, ruthlessly manipulating and loathing their foolishness. Here their meanness seems inspired by their unpleasant memories of their Midwestern childhoods. Yet, for all their snideness, shocks, and gross-outs, the Coens, like David Lynch and John Waters, ultimately reveal themselves to be decent middle-class citizens upholding bourgeois values.[18]

One notch above a caricature, Marge is slow and polite to a fault. Like her plodding fellow Scandinavians, she drawls out passionlessly lines like "Jeez, that's a good lead, but I'm not sure that I agree with you 100 percent on your police work there." At first, the audience laughs at Marge, but by the end, as she lies in bed with her husband (who paints stamps), one realizes that this seemingly silly woman is the only positive character in the film; she embodies honesty and decency and reaffirms the value of life, underscored by her pregnancy. Ultimately, it's Marge's decency that rescues *Fargo* from deteriorating into a one-note joke.

Going back to their natural instincts, the Coens abandoned *Fargo's* controlled discipline with *The Big Lebowski* (1998), a messy comedy-adventure. Jeff Bridges plays the title role, a character known as the Dude, a slack-brained pothead who gets sucked into a bizarre intrigue involving another man named Lebowski, a millionaire whose promiscuous young wife may have been kidnapped. Hired to deliver the ransom money, the Dude suffers one disaster after another, a cumulative result of his ineptness as well as of the arrogant intervention of his paranoid Jewish friend, Walter (John Goodman). The Dude stumbles through numerous exploits and gets lost in a barrage of surreal episodes, with people and objects flying through the air. Bridges is fine, but it's two cameo appearances that grace the movie: John Turturro as a gay Latino bowler named Jesus urging his ball forward with sexy thrusts of his pelvis, and Julianne Moore as an avant-garde painter.

COWBOY NOIR—JOHN DAHL

Many young directors are drawn to noir, but they tend to overheat rather than reinvent its conventions. John Dahl may be the exception: No matter how complicated his plots are, he succeeds in maintaining a cool, restrained style.[19] Dahl uses the quintessential noir themes of greed and lust without the Coens' self-conscious knowingness and distant formal stylishness. His first film, *Kill Me Again* (1989), staked his claim to "cowboy noir," a genre exemplified by *Blood Simple*. Like Joel Coen, John Dahl has worked with his brother, Rick, and he has also used some of the Coens' actors, such as Nicolas Cage.

Dahl first became exposed to noir after moving to Los Angeles to attend the American Film Institute. "I watched *Sunset Boulevard*," he recalled, "and realized that things I was driving past every day were all part of that movie."[20] Committed as he is to noir, the "good boy" Montana-born director still worries about the reaction of his hometown minister when his darkly cynical movies play in Billings.

Dahl is not interested in a nostalgic evocation of noir. In fact, his films are situated not in a shadowy Los Angeles, the noir capital, but in the country side of Nevada or Wyoming, populated by hapless drifters with ordinary names like Lyle or Wayne. His movies project the laconic tongue of the wide-open plains rather than the fast, nervous banter of city streets. *Red Rock West* is set in a dour little Wyoming town, and *The Last Seduction* in upstate New York.

In Dahl's first, modest feature, *Kill Me Again*, a greedy woman (Joanne Whalley-Kilmer) shrewdly positions her murderous boyfriend (Michael Madsen) against a private eye (Val Kilmer). Dahl's second, and better, *Red Rock West*, is a quirky, low-budget "Western noir." With the assist of a fresh script, cowritten with his brother, Rick, Dahl rounded up a quintessentially indie cast: Nicolas Cage (before he became a star), Lara Flynn Boyle, J. T. Walsh, and the ubiquitous enfant terrible, Dennis Hopper. Sizzling with taut suspense, *Red Rock West* is an intelligent thriller, with eccentric performances and picaresque Southwest American landscapes. Recalling *Blood Simple* and the small-town malevolence of *Blue Velvet*, the film is an edgy trip into the dark side of the American heartland.

Michael Williams (Cage) drives into Wyoming eager to find a well-paying oil job. When the rigging work, which was offered by a former marine buddy, falls through, he drives, unemployed and broke, to Red Rock. At the local bar, its owner, Wayne Brown (Walsh), mistakes Michael for Lyle, a Texas hit man he had hired to "take care" of his wife, Suzanne (Boyle). Before Michael realizes what's happening, and although he has no intention of killing anyone, he has accepted a $500 down payment. Driving to Wayne's house, he warns Suzanne of the impending danger, and she puts another $10,000 in his hand.

A bumbling ordinary guy, Michael is neither corrupt nor greedy but simply cursed with bad luck and bad timing. The film is a twisty tale of mistaken identities and hidden personalities, constantly shifting expectations to the point where the audience is not sure who's to be trusted. A series of incidents keeps Michael in town, and the arrival of the actual hit man (Hopper) further complicates his life.

With a wacky but resourceful fall guy (masterfully played by Cage) at its center, *Red Rock West*'s script unfolds as a blend of greed, betrayal, and revenge. The casting and music echo David Lynch, but Dahl provides a more conventional and engaging noir entertainment, proving that he is a strong actor's director, able to get Dennis Hopper (in a caricature of America's worst nightmare) and J. T. Walsh to modulate their natural flamboyance, though the usually placid Lara Flynn Boyle is miscast as a deceitful femme fatale.

Dahl has done as much for the expansion of women's screen roles as for the revival of neo-noir through his attraction to "really powerful women." In his first two films, the women are licentious, greedy, untrustworthy, and either blown to smithereens or thrown from a moving train. In his third and most popular feature, *The Last Seduction* (1994), Linda Fiorentino plays Bridget Gregory, a brazenly murderous predator who proudly calls herself "a total fucking bitch." *Red Rock West* and *The Last Seduction* should be seen as companion pieces: Much as *Red Rock West* was a vehicle for Cage's hapless loser, *The Last Seduction* is dominated by Fiorentino's femme fatale.

When Dahl first read Steve Barancik's script, he wanted to see Bridget's limo get broadsided by a garbage truck, but then he realized that letting her get away would be "more complicated and interesting." At the end of the film, which echoes *Body Heat*, the immoral Bridget cruises away in a chauffeured limousine. Though considering himself "enlightened male," Dahl never anticipated the impact Fiorentino's character would have on female iconography in the 1990s. He told *Vogue*: "It makes me nervous to think people watched the movie and said, 'God, I loved her!'"[21] Still, Dahl concedes that he has tapped into a hidden male fantasy: strong, sexually potent women.

Dahl packs considerable action into the credits, crosscutting between shots of high-powered executive Bridget, brow-beating her employees, and her medical intern husband, Clay (Bill Pullman), unloading hospital cocaine under the Brooklyn Bridge. Since it was her idea, Bridget takes the money and runs to upstate New York to figure out how to dispose of Clay.

The film's humor derives from the incongruity between Bridget's look and conduct and the mores of small-town America, where she ends up. Most of the action unfolds in a dead-end community where the social life centers around one bar. Compelled to construct a new identity and find a job, Bridget is amused by her own outrageous performances. Bending the rules, playing with people's brains, this superwoman comes up with a scheme for marketing murder to wives betrayed by their husbands. "Murder is commitment," she earnestly tells one smitten stooge.

Bridget is the opposite of Dorothy Valens in *Blue Velvet*, a woman forced to accept her victimized role and smile through her pain. "Are you still a self-serving bitch?" Bridget's corrupt lawyer (J. T. Walsh) asks when she seeks his advice on community-property laws. At once hardfaced and demure, Bridget is manipulative, sarcastic, and tough; she gratuitously stubs her cigarette butt in a home-baked apple pie. She deals with the arrival of a New York detective (Bill Nunn) with the same cool dispatch she employs when seducing an innocent, Mike Swale (Peter Berg), who becomes her "designated fuck." When her husband finally catches up with her, she enlists Mike as an accomplice in murder. Here, Dahl follows noir conventions, where sex is rarely an end in itself.

In classic noir, women seldom play down-and-dirty roles like Bridget, but in this picture, instead of brooding over gender injustice and victimization, Bridget goes for the male prerogative. From her point of view, the rampage is justified: She wants the money her husband obtained in a drug deal she had urged on him. Bridget's character is bracingly constructed—there's no attempt to justify her malevolence or to restore her; her only redeeming quality is her lack of hypocrisy.

No role—feminist or yuppie careerist, prudish housewife or pouty adolescent, barroom slut or abused bride—is too much for Bridget to assume in order to win the game. She changes guises with remarkable speed and single-mindedness. In this film, the target is the eagerness of men stupefied by lust. Richard Schickel has suggested that Dahl has conceived his movie as a parody of "have-it-all feminism," and has done that with plenty of dark humor.[22]

Dahl contrives a danse macabre between domestic partners who are equally dangerous. *The Last Seduction* achieves its hard-boiled quality by dispensing with moral ambiguity. As Hoberman pointed out, since the duplicitous Bridget and Clay are known quantities, the suspense lies in watching their machinations escalate toward an inevitable climax, as the audience wonders whether the sexually out-front and amoral Bridget will get her comeuppance.[23]

After revamping old B-movie formulas, which, by his own description, boil down to "a dangerous broad and a bag full of money," Dahl moved from his modest indies to the $20 million studio-made *Unforgettable* (MGM, 1996), a twisted version of *The Fugitive*. A meek female lab scientist (Fiorentino) helps a husband (Ray Liotta) hunt down his wife's killer by injecting himself with the brain fluids of other people, which enables him to relive their memories. "I'm always apologizing to someone about the female roles in my movies," Dahl admitted to *Vogue*. "I say, 'No, women aren't that mean, they're not that obnoxious.' This is the first one I won't have to apologize for." Unfortunately, the woman in *Unforgettable* is so wholesome, dull, and forgettable that she was perceived as penance for Dahl's earlier and gustier female heroines.

Moving away from noir, Dahl's latest film, *Rounders* (1998), based on a script by Brian Koppleman and David Levien, revolves around Mike McDermott (Matt Damon), a poker genius who's putting himself through law school by gambling. After losing his tuition in a disastrous game, Mike scrapes for a second chance at higher stakes against the sinister Russian, Teddy KGB (John Malkovich). Mike's best friend, a reckless card cheat called Worm (Edward Norton), gets out of jail and pulls him back into the game, putting his life in danger. Although Mike has a girlfriend, in his world male companionship is far more important than love or sex.

The film is inspired by *The Cincinnati Kid* (1965), in which a troubled card shark (Steve McQueen) takes down a veteran (Edward G. Robinson), and *The Hustler* (1961), in which Fast Eddie Felsen (Paul Newman) struggles to earn a marathon pool match with Minnesota Fats (Jackie Gleason) and in the process redeems himself as a pool player and a man. Similarly, *Rounders* is structured as an inspirational morality tale about the professional and personal tribulations of an ambitious striver. Assisted by the great French cinematographer Jean-Yves Escoffier (who has lensed a number of indies), Dahl gives New York's underground gambling a vivid atmosphere, with its specialized rituals and fast macho talk.

Dahl's early movies also set new precedents in their release patterns. His sleeper, *Red Rock West*, was telecast on HBO and was made available on video before it opened in theaters to enthusiastic reviews. And *The Last Seduction* premiered on Showtime before it was released in theaters. With a shrewd marketing campaign, the film became one of the year's most profitable indies, grossing over $5 million and earning an acting citation for Fiorentino from the New York Film Critics Circle.

RETRO NOIR—JAMES FOLEY

James Foley has also worked in the noir tradition, making old-fashioned movies—basically reworkings of 1950s formulas. He has acknowledged his debt to Nicholas Ray's and Elia Kazan's youth melodramas, *Rebel Without a Cause* and *Splendor in the Grass*. Foley is drawn to the working-class milieu; almost all of his films (*Reckless*, *At Close Range*, *After Dark, My Sweet*) are populated by blue-collar characters. His stories revolve around a couple, usually a bad boy and a good girl, very much in the classic tradition.

Reckless (1984), Foley's first film, is a rip-off of *The Wild One*, which starred Marlon Brando, and *Rebel Without a Cause*, with James Dean. Treading the familiar territory of defiant teenagers, it also recalls in its contrivances and clichés more recent films, like *All the Right Moves* and *Risky Business*, both Tom Cruise vehicles. Johnny Rourke (Aidan Quinn), a handsome teenager from the wrong side of the tracks, takes up with Tracey Prescott (Daryl Hannah), a straight-arrow coed. She's attracted to his rebellious sense of danger and excitement, which is very much missing from her comfortable existence. The only new element in the film is its explicit sex scene, which is performed to a pulsating rock soundtrack.

Foley's second feature, *At Close Range* (1986), does not improve much on *Reckless*. In both pictures, rich visual imagery is overstated, to the point of suffocating the story and diminishing its significance. *At Close Range* begins as a tale about alienated youth but quickly devolves into an intergenerational melodrama of a youngster corrupted by his own father in a valueless world. Nicholas Kazan's screenplay is lean, but Foley treats the story of Brad Jr.'s (Sean Penn) fall from grace with excessive visuals and aural ripeness. Everything is lavish and overly stylized: Night shots are perfectly lighted, figures are silhouetted against blue light.

A teenager with no prospects, Brad is enticed into crime by a father (Christopher Walken) who had earlier abandoned him. Brad steals tractors and commits crime not out of rebelliousness but out of a deep emotional need to connect with his father. In this character study, built around the universal longing of sons for their fathers, the father-son relationship is both simple and allegorical. Brad's romance with a farm girl (Mary Stewart Masterson) compensates for dreary family interactions with his mother (Millie Perkins) and his younger brother (Chris Penn). The contradictions in Brad's character could have made him a loser, a defeatist, but Foley stresses the tenacity of his moral convictions, which help him survive a corrupt world. That his triumph is as much moral as it is physical is evident in a preposterous ending in which Brad is riddled with bullets but miraculously survives.

Inspired by a story in the *Philadelphia Inquirer* of a murder that pitted father against son, *At Close Range* was a potentially interesting story that had to wait seven years until Foley found financial backing. Hemdale finally agreed to underwrite the $6.5 million budget, provided that the film's stars, Sean Penn and Christopher Walken, worked for deferments.

In the psychological noir thriller, *After Dark, My Sweet* (1990), Foley's best film, "Kid" Collins, or Collie (Jason Patric), is a desperate former boxer who has escaped from a mental institution. In the first, most impressive scene, Collie is seen walking through the desert toward Indio, California. The cinematographer, Mark Plummer, captures the blinding clarity of the desert light, the way that light leaves one both abstracted and removed. Narrating the film in a tense, nervous manner, Collie contains seeds of smoldering violence. Having killed a man in the ring (shown in slow-motion flashbacks), he now wants to prove himself and to have people trust him. But Collie's new life turns into a nightmare when he falls in with two worthless grifters and pathological liars: Uncle Bud (Bruce Dern), a pathetic con man, and a widow, Fay (Rachel Ward), a beautiful woman who taunts Collie. Uncle Bud and Fay use Collie as the strong arm in a hapless kidnapping scheme they've been planning for years.[24]

An intense, occasionally moving portrait of losers, *After Dark, My Sweet* is an adaptation of the pulp writer Jim Thompson's 1955 novel. As cowritten by Robert Redlin and Foley, the script keeps Thompson's tough-guy fatalism and his characteristic themes of paranoia and the life of a dangerous man on the edge. Deviating from the style of his first pictures, Foley doesn't settle for obvious emotions, putting the audience inside Collie's head to experience life as he does, as a series of traps and frustrations. True to the noir tradition, the central couple consists of a stubborn, implacable antihero and a glamorous, insincere, confused woman caught between desire and guilt. The lanky, white-haired Uncle Ben completes the classic triangle, his threatening manner laced with compliments and dubious encouragement.

In *Glengarry Glen Ross* (1992), Foley's noirish version of David Mamet's Pulitzer Prize–winning play, real estate salesmen are presented as an abrasive, desperate breed. Mamet has a special gift for drawing realistic portraits out of harsh yet funny lowlifers. A good deal of the salesmen's time is spent socializing with clients while waiting for new leads and new buyers. The movie's dramatic tension derives from the rancorous dialogue, rather than from the melodramatic plot about a theft and the subsequent police investigation.

The film maintains the play's unity of time, with the narrative spanning roughly twenty-four hours. Although Foley moves the action from the play's claustrophobic office interiors to a telephone booth or a Chinese restaurant, the sets and lighting remain deliberately stylized, befitting Mamet's dialogue which is more effective on stage than on screen. Even so, Mamet's use of the values of his native Chicago and of his experience in a real-estate office makes the film's postmodern minimalism uniquely American.

Mamet created a new character for the film, big boss Blake (Alec Baldwin), whose motto is "ABC—Always Be Closing." Baldwin's wonderfully staged entrance sets the intense tone for the entire picture. The main characters are Shelley Levene (Jack Lemmon), the alternately desperate and deceiving salesman, and the shrewd, self-confident Ricky Roma (Al Pacino). Conning the viewers into complicity, Mamet forces them to experience the anger felt by a humiliated buyer like James Lingk (Jonathan Pryce). Mamet's hellish vision of the business world as both immoral and amoral touches deep chords. Unlike Arthur Miller's preachy and moralistic *Death of a Salesman*, *Glengarry Glen Ross* reflects the 1990s zeitgeist and its unsanctimonious tone.

THE CON ARTIST—DAVID MAMET

David Mamet's spare, gritty work as a writer and filmmaker is inspired by the rhythms of British playwright Harold Pinter and by the harsh realities of Chicago. Like Pinter, he pares down his oneupmanship tales in the name of precision and austerity. Mamet's obscenely poetic plays (*American Buffalo*, *Glengarry Glen Ross*) reveal him to be a master of intensely muscular wordplay. His work shows fascination with con men, probably the only artists he respects, because they are smarter than anyone else. His heroes are petty criminals with a bizarre penchant for feverish yet eloquent outbursts of temper and words. Mamet expresses a paranoid view of reality and deep despair about human nature.

Set in a cluttered junk shop, *American Buffalo* (the 1977 play that put Mamet on the map and was made into a 1996 movie by Michael Corrente) is a character study of three small-time crooks who plan to burglarize a collector of a valuable American Buffalo coin. Through gutter dialogue laced with profanity, the men reveal their idiosyncrasies, inadequacies, and failures. In the end, unable to agree upon a plan, the inept thieves call the thing off. The play is an attack on the American business ethos, with the hoodlums standing in for the corporate class; Mamet does not distinguish between the lumpenproletariat and stockbrokers or corporate lawyers. For him, the essence of American business is its betrayals and compromises.

Mamet's first scripts were for the noir remake *The Postman Always Rings Twice* (1981), adapted from James Cain's novel, and for Sidney Lumet's court drama, *The Verdict* (1982). Arguably, his most exciting screenplays, *Wag the Dog* (with Hilary Henkin, directed by Barry Levinson) and *Glengarry Glen Ross*, have succeeded because other directors have staged them. Mamet made his directorial debut in *House of Games* (1987), a slick study of deceit, followed by *Things Change* (1988), *Homicide* (1991), *Oleanna* (1994), and *The Spanish Prisoner* (1998), his most accomplished and commercial film. The specific locale of his movies may vary, but they always center on themes of loyalty and always exhibit a noir sensibility.

With an eavesdropper's ear for everyday speech that can turn mundane conversations into poetry, Mamet relies on verbal acrobatics at the expense of plot. "If it's solely serving the interest of plot, I'm not interested," he said. "As a consequence, I go overboard the other way."[25] Mamet has traced his acute awareness of language and rhythm to his father, an amateur semanticist. His flair for exact expression, compelling silences, and terse dialogue underscores how little is really communicated when people exchange half-digested scraps of information.

Mamet's problems as a filmmaker stem from the nature of his writing rather than from his directing; his films are more evasive than his plays. Still a product of the theater, Mamet is not attuned to the possibilities of the camera; every aspect of his films is dominated by language. His arch speeches are more effective on stage than on screen, where close-ups, intercutting and editing break up verbal monologues whose emotional impact largely depends on continuity. Mamet's minimalism, like that of Jarmusch, suggests snobbish knowingness and disdain for conventional stories and fully developed characters. His hermetic narratives take the form of elaborate, elegant puzzles that are never made entirely clear. Like his characters, Mamet is a con artist, afraid that once cynicism is stripped away, the audience will be able to detect the implausibility of his plots.

Glengarry Glen Ross represents Mamet's vision of a uniquely American hell. In portraying the real estate world as cruel yet funny, Mamet critiques as well as celebrates the aggressive American business ethos, its desperation, lies, and gimmickry. Like a magician, Mamet tricks his audience into at once deploring and enjoying the greed and venality of his con men. His method is to pile on improbabilities in a matter-of-fact style, with minimum narrative and emotionalism. The strategy is to seduce the audience, bring it into hip complicity with his games.

Both fascinating and inept, *House of Games* is a conceptual movie about poker skills and con artists. In this deviously comic melodrama, the players don't withdraw. The script proceeds with twists and reversals, building like a poker game in which the stakes get higher and higher. Mamet is obsessed with insidiously addictive games in which the pot accumulates, tensions mount, and tempers shorten.

A psychoanalyst, Margaret Ford (Lindsay Crouse), has just written a best-seller, *Driven*, based on her studies of obsessive behavior. "You need joy," says a colleague to the needy Margaret, as if she were prescribing medication. Through her compulsive gambler-patient, who's suicidal, Margaret decides to investigate the world of crooked gamblers and swindlers, possibly for a new book. She does that with Mike (Joe Mantegna), a smooth talker whose cool and anger she finds charming—he is an invaluable source of information, a perceptive reader of character.

House of Games is devoid of any joy on the part of the actors. Pauline Kael noted that through his cool distance, Mamet gives the audience the blueprint rather than the plot or the feelings that go with it.[26] A control freak, Mamet dominates the actors; the flat performances are a stylistic statement. By turns comic, scary, and bizarre, the dialogue is spoken in an intensely monotonous, self-conscious manner, and the harsh lighting emphasizes the deliberately artificial and theatrical nature of the film. Although the movie was shot on location, in Seattle, there are no identifiable places; the physicality of the space is almost irrelevant to its characters.

In *Homicide*, Mamet's simplistic morality play, Bobby Gold (Joe Mantegna), an exemplary Jewish detective, defines himself in terms of his work—he is a tough cop. When Bobby stumbles onto the shooting of an elderly shopkeeper in the Jewish ghetto, his boss assigns him to investigate it. Removed from an important case to handle a minor one, he's offended. "I'm 'his people'?" Bobby tells his boss. "I thought I was your people." Clearly, Bobby's reference group is his gentile fellow cops; his partner is Irish.

The victim's relatives pull strings at City Hall to keep Bobby on the case, hoping that a Jew will take it more seriously. Utterly assimilated, Bobby resents their efforts to define him by his religion. At first, Bobby thinks that they are hysterical, that they lack any ground for their suspicion the crime was motivated by racial hatred, but then he comes across evidence that validates their claim. Gradually, Bobby's resentment yields to curiosity about his own Jewish roots, and in due course his value system shifts, leading him to betray everything he has believed in. The film ends with Bobby's loss of professionalism and a conversion that's psychologically unconvincing.

Mamet teaches a truism of urban survival, showing, as John Sayles did in *City of Hope* and John Guare did in *Six Degrees of Separation* (directed as a movie by Fred Schepisi in 1993), that in the big city everyone is related to everyone else and yet everyone is alone. Mamet's examination of Bobby's tormented identity is sincere, but he turns earnest, making Bobby and the other Jewish characters self-righteous. The film's sloppy, contrived plotting and its pat resolution may explain why it failed commercially.

In *The Spanish Prisoner*, a movie that revisits the turf of *House of Games* and *Homicide*, Mamet creates another controlled situation, although the style is closer to psychological realism than either the schematic *House of Games* or the preachy *Homicide*. "Who in this world is what they seem?" the secretary Susan Ricci (Rebecca Pidgeon) says. "You never know who anybody is." Indeed, the characters change identities often, reinforcing a smooth buildup of paranoia, the feeling that nothing is what it appears to be and that no one can be trusted.

The protagonist, Joe Ross (Campbell Scott), is a brilliant, self-made scientist-inventor who places a high value on integrity and respect. Though uneasy among the rich and famous, he is eager to join their ranks. Mamet never reveals Joe's invention—it's called "the process," an item that will earn billions for his parent company. Asked by his boss, Klein (Ben Gazzara), to make a presentation to the investors at a Caribbean island resort, Joe feels that his invention is being exploited without his receiving proper compensation. A mysterious businessman, Jimmy Dell (Steve Martin), shows up at the resort and addresses Joe in a way that tests his values; when they return to New York, the two strike up a friendship.

In theme, *The Spanish Prisoner* borrows from Mamet's radio drama, *The Water Engine*, a Depression-era fable about a naive inventor who designs an automobile water engine, only to have it stolen from him by corrupt industrialists. As expected, Mamet builds an intricately shaky puzzle. The movie, whose title derives from the name of "the oldest confidence game on the books," is set in a predetermined world, full of fatalism and coincidences, in which each participant is suspect. Over the years, Mamet's technical skills have improved: *The Spanish Prisoner* is his most entertaining charade. He keeps the settings simple, breeding mistrust in every encounter. As Joe gets more isolated, he sinks deeper and deeper into fear. It's Jimmy's smooth, cool manner that reflects Mamet's notion of how the world works.

In Mamet's previous movies, the actors were misguided: In *House of Games*, Mamet cast his first wife, Lindsay Crouse, in a dislikable role; in *The Spanish Prisoner*, he similarly cast his current wife, Rebecca Pidgeon, as a duplicious secretary who claims to be Joe's friend. Mamet demands that actors recite their dialogue with distancing emotional rhythms, which makes it sound stiff. If *The Spanish Prisoner* is more involving than Mamet's other puzzles, it's because the central actors (Scott and Martin) play their roles straight.

PROMISING AND DISAPPOINTING NEO-NOIR

Neo-noir in the 1990s is loaded with the excesses of overeager directors, playing with noir's ominous shadows and tough-guy poses to make their own contributions. A noir mystery about two half-brothers who get entangled in mistaken identity, *Suture* (1993), the debut feature of the San Francisco filmmakers Scott McGehee and David Siegel, has little to say but says it with panache. Vincent Towers (Michael Harris), the primary suspect in the murder of his wealthy father, plants evidence on his half-brother, Clay Arlington (Dennis Haysbert), by staging a car explosion in which Clay is the intended victim. Vincent switches identities with Clay, who miraculously survives, although he's left disfigured and amnesiac. Clay is presumed by everyone to be Vincent, the killer.

A sympathetic plastic surgeon, Renee Descartes (Mel Harris), reconstructs Clay's face from photographs, and a psychoanalyst, Max Shinoda (Sab Shimono), who narrates the film in flashbacks, restores his memory. A reworking of Hitchcock's *The Wrong Man*, the tale positions Clay as the falsely accused everyman who must prove his innocence. Meant to be a meditation on the representation of race and class, *Suture* concerns the issue of how a different exterior functions in a cultural environment that's opaque, or, in McGehee's words, "how a social group and a culture work?"

The story begins with the psychiatrist's calm, authoritative voice talking about the nature of identity. Looking down from above, the camera captures a startling image: A black man, dressed in white, stands on one side of a white shower curtain; a white man, dressed in black, stands on the other. The flashback leads full circle back to this point. When the long-lost half-brothers meet at their father's funeral, Clay comments on how much they look alike; in reality, Clay is tall and well built, whereas Vincent is pale and slight. Vincent concurs: "Our physical similarity is disarming, isn't it?" *Suture*'s main joke is that everyone acts as if Clay and Vincent are identical twins, but it's a purely visual joke, since the filmmakers fail to imbue it with any thematic weight.

For inspiration, the filmmakers drew from disparate stylistic and literary sources: paranoid thrillers, Japanese art films (Hiroshi Teshiga-hara's *Face of Another*), and American black-and-white films of the 1950s. From these works, they culled elements of fear and paranoia and plot devices like amnesia, plastic surgery, and doubles, taking these issues to logical extremes. The notion of twins is complicated by the characters' apparent inability to distinguish between black and white. "It's a suspension of disbelief," Siegel said, "but it's also breaking the fourth wall, an alienating effect that makes the whole process of cinema ultra-real, because you get to experience something outside of the narrative itself."[27]

Nominally, this stylishly elegant tale is about racial biases, but, in actuality, the clever, visually striking surface is the most important element, reflecting the directors' strong interest in art history and design. McGehee and Siegel shot the film in black and white in wide-screen, with Greg Gardiner's photography using gradations of blacks, silvers, and grays. Said McGehee: "Black and white is used in indies in guerrilla, 16mm gritty style. We wanted a pristine, studio look as much as we could get on our budget."[28]

Intriguing as the premise is, it serves the film as long as it's lightly treated, as when the plastic surgeon falls for Clay as Vincent or when the psychiatrist displays giant Rorschach blobs on his office walls as if they were decorative art, helping Clay sort out disturbing dreams about hypodermic needles turning into a car. But the film falls apart when it threatens to take itself seriously.

Mark Malone conceived *Bulletproof Heart* (1994, a.k.a. *Killer*), a movie about a nihilistic hit man, after reading Albert Camus's books and some articles about organized crime that said mobsters have stopped hiring psychopaths to do their killing because they have found them too unmanageable and unpleasant; the men who arrange mob killings now seek out nihilists instead. Aware of the comic possibilities in the premise, Malone and the writer Gordon Melbourne proceeded to make a moody piece of neo-noir fatalism.

Mick (Anthony LaPaglia), the cool hero, is the ultimate pro who supplies services for big bucks. But he's grown numb, incapable of any emotion. When first seen with a call girl, he's more intrigued by the violent potential of their encounter than by steamy sex. The prostitute is a gratuity from Mick's boss, George (Peter Boyle), for his latest assignment. Mick is assigned an unusual duty: killing Fiona (Mimi Rogers), a femme fatale inflicted with a mysteriously incurable disease. Predictably, as soon as Mick meets his enigmatic victim, who's willing to die, he falls for her. However, Mick is not a standard fall guy; his love for Fiona turns out to be a transformative redemptive act.

The unity of the action, set over the course of one night in New York, adds to the tightly controlled tension. Since most scenes are indoors, the film is appropriately claustrophobic. The story falters in its mid-section, a picnic in a cemetery, but it regains its vitality, and the tragic closure is emotionally satisfying. Noir yarns have portrayed many acts of killing, but seldom have they conveyed so precisely the feelings of a hit man and his victim seconds before the execution. It's in these scenes, and in the exploration of trust, that *Bulletproof Heart* achieves distinction.

Melbourne's script is deftly constructed, showing facility with fluent and bright dialogue. Avoiding noir's melodramatic clichés, Malone strikes the right balance between the theatrical and the cinematic. Just when the dialogue becomes static and the ambiance stagnant, he moves his camera or cuts the action. The specific manner in which flashbacks are inserted recalls *Reservoir Dogs*, and an all-night session that tests the manhood of three men recalls powerful scenes and poignant acting in Cassavetes's work.

In Dominic Sena's *Kalifornia* (1994), Brian Kessler (David Duchovny), a yuppie writer who is researching serial killers, persuades his girlfriend, the photographer Carrie (Michelle Forbes), to join him on a road trip through famous crime scenes. To split the expenses, Brian suggests that they recruit another couple, which turns out to be a serial killer, Early Grayce (Brad Pitt), a sociopathic felon, and his imbecilic girlfriend, Adele (Juliette Lewis). "Early beats me," Adele tells the horrified Carrie, "but only when I deserve it." Carrie immediately spots Early as trouble (earlier, he is seen killing his landlord), but Brian accuses her of being a snob. To prove his point, he bonds with Early and begins to assume his worst characteristics. Ironically, Early has a better-defined sense of self than Brian.

Kalifornia escalates toward a *Straw Dogs*-like confrontation, where the refined, educated types discover that under the "right" circumstances all humans are capable of violent brutality. The plot resembles that of *Cape Fear* but lacks the rich thematic structure and the dense texture of Scorsese's film or the original 1962 classic. The film is marred by an inconsistent point of view: Shot from Carrie's perspective, the film is disrupted by Brian's voiceover narration. It is burdened by heavy-handed religious symbolism—the villain's name is Early Grayce—and the yuppie couple's final crisis is set at Ground Zero, surrounded by mocking replicas of a nuclear family. The working-class characters are caricatures—liberals' nightmares of white trash—and the educated couple comes across as pretentious; Adele is the only sympathetic character.

Released by Gramercy, after winning the top award at the Montreal Festival, *Kalifornia* was dismissed by critics and failed at the box office, a fate met also by Gramercy's other noir that year, Peter Medak's *Romeo Is Bleeding* (1994). Like most of today's hip filmmakers, the writer Hilary Henkin perceives noir as a visual style, not a sensibility. *Romeo Is Bleeding* has all the familiar trappings—inky photography, hard-boiled ironies—but the arch script panders to the audience's sense of know-ingness, shuffling the clichés even more than the Coens'. Jack (Gary Oldman), a corrupt cop in the mold of *Bad Lieutenant*, works both sides of the law. Amoral, he tips off the mob as to the location of witnesses he's supposed to protect and lies to his wife (Annabelle Sciorra) about his mistress (Juliette Lewis) and to both of them about the other women in his life. Motivated by lust and greed, Jack is baffled when a mob boss (Roy Scheider) orders him to murder the seductively wild Russian hit woman Mona Demarkov (Lena Olin).

Directed with excessive stylistic tricks, *Romeo Is Bleeding* was aesthetically offensive to most critics and to the few viewers who saw it. From the ridiculous voice-over narration to the incomprehensible plot contortions, it is hermetic, with no link to the real world. All the cues derive from genre conventions, which the film misunderstands and lacerates. Olin gives an over-the-top performance as the alternately shrewd and bestial mob woman, and a scene in which she escapes a car while wounded is not just campy but preposterous. Movieish to the point of extinction, *Romeo Is Bleeding* is all hollow decorative set pieces and no substance.

CONCLUSION

The noir sensibility has permeated a large number of 1990s indies, whether or not their narratives fall thematically within noir's conventional territory. Darkly comic styles with noirish elements have become the norm in the new crime films, as is evident in Peter Berg's *Very Bad Things* and Sam Raimi's terrific studio-made film, *A Simple Plan* (both in 1998). Noir's limitless elasticity is also reflected in a new subgenre, the noir vampire.

In most Hollywood movies, vampires are demonic, bloodsucking freaks, played by the likes of Christopher Lee for frills and thrills. In the late 1970s, a number of movies, such as Stan Dragoti's *Love at First Bite* (1979), spoofed the genre, with the aging matinee idol George Hamilton cast as a mischievous Count Dracula in New York. In contrast, indie movies have reversed the formula and have used vampires as metaphors of anxiety for the art house crowd.[29]

Dismissed by most critics, *Vampire's Kiss* (1989) sets its story in a realistic context. Peter Loew (Nicolas Cage), a literary agent who keeps a photo of Kafka behind his desk, spends his nights prowling the discos, looking for love; like most men, he suffers from a fear of commitment. Failing to find happiness, he complains to his analyst, Dr. Glaser (Elizabeth Ashley), and in one session quite hysterically recites the alphabet in an apoplectic manner. One night he picks up Rachel (Jennifer Beals), and after she bites his neck in passion, he becomes convinced that she has turned him into her slave. Peter is an intelligent urban swinger who is deeply horrified by what's happening to him, yet he can't stop himself; he becomes crazy.

Using a style that's as darkly comic as its bizarre premise, Joseph Minion (who scripted Scorsese's noirish comedy *After Hours*) and the director, Robert Bierman, leave it ambiguous as to whether Peter has become a vampire or is just imagining the whole thing. Whether taken as a straight horror story or as a psychoerotic nightmare, *Vampire's Kiss* mixes fable and satire in startling manner. The movie works out the Nosferatu legend realistically—the more tragic Peter's situation is, the funnier it becomes. In the end, the thirsty Peter is seen walking around SoHo with blood on his jaws from the previous night. Bierman imbues the film with pervasive anxiety and ambiguity, never falling into the traps of low farce or routine horror.

Made in 1995, both *Nadja* and *The Addiction* are languid dream puzzles set in the netherworld of downtown Manhattan. Both feature young female vampires who speak in a punkish existential tone, and both are shot in black and white. In *Nadja*, Michael Almereyda's blend of the serious and frivolous recalls David Lynch, who served as the film's executive producer and who also appears in a cameo. Vampires stalk downtown New York in a stunningly executed film that mixes black-and-white 35mm photography and Pixelvision. Almereyda paints a portrait of a dysfunctional vampire family, not unlike the one in Kathryn Bigelow's *Near Dark*. Like Bigelow, Almereyda decorates scenes of vampire-hunting with pop psychology. "As you get older, you begin to realize that family is all that matters," says Jim.

The vast majority of vampire movies are retreads, but some innovative takes continue to appear. *Nadja*, at once an update of Bram Stoker's novel and a satire of it, proves there is still room for variation in the vampire concept. Andy Klein pointed out that in subject matter *Nadja* is Corman, in style New York underground.[30] Peter Fonda as a vampire killer represents the former, and Hal Hartley's veterans Elina Lowensohn and Martin Donovan the latter. The tone is set by the physically imposing, self-possessed modern vampire (played by Lowenshon), who is the main focus. But after creating an intriguing setup of vampires in nocturnal Manhattan, the narrative gets diffuse, cutting among too many characters that are much less intriguing.

Almereyda, who pioneered the use of the toy Pixelvision video camera in *Another Girl, Another Planet*, reprises its use here in scenes that relate the vampire's state of mind. The grainy, impressionistic images contrast vividly with Jim Denault's cinematography. The opening montage is shot with a Fisher-Price PXL 2000 camera, the out-of-production "toy" video camera favored by experimental filmmakers. In *Nadja*, the PXL footage presents the point of view of Nadja, Dracula's daughter. As she picks up her latest victim at a nightclub, Nadja is psychically informed that her father is finally dead. Dr. Van Helsing (Peter Fonda, playing the vampire hunter as a long-haired 1960s burnout) is being held for the Count's murder. While his nephew, Jim (Donovan), bails him out, Jim's wife, Lucy (Galaxy Craze), has a chance meeting with

Nadja, who transforms her into the undead. Jim and Van Helsing track Lucy to Nadja's apartment, where she has recently moved her brother, Edgar (Jared Harris), and his nurse, Cassandra (Suzy Amis).

All the characters are from two families; Cassandra is Van Helsing's daughter. *Nadja* moves into a dreamy insular world, where the generations-old struggle between the Draculas and the Van Helsings unfolds. Despite its dramatic problems, *Nadja* maintains its appeal through its peculiar atmosphere, impressive style, variegated sound, and campy dialogue. "He was tired, lost," Van Helsing says about Dracula's death. "He was like Elvis in the end, surrounded by zombies."

In *The Addiction*, a darkly humorous noir made with hard-edged spirit, Abel Ferrara converts the notion of vampire into a modern psychological horror story. The film succeeds in its visual aspirations but is undermined by its intellectual pretensions, straining in its attempt to link vampirism, the Holocaust, and Kierkegaardian philosophy. Kathleen (Lili Taylor), a NYU philosophy student about to receive her doctorate, is watching a slide presentation of the My Lai massacre, a horror she regards a collective rather than a personal responsibility. One evening, walking to her East Village basement apartment, a woman in an elegant evening dress (Annabella Sciorra) greets her in a friendly manner, then swiftly pushes her down into a dark staircase and bites her neck. After a sickness diagnosed as anemia, Kathleen becomes a vampire with a hunger for blood. Her new state alters her view of life, and she realizes that evil is the most addictive drug.

Reflecting Ferrara's obsession with redemption, *The Addiction* acknowledges the capacity for evil, urging viewers to take full responsibility, or there will be no way of arresting evil's diffusion from generation to generation. Shot in high-contrast black and white, this supernatural thriller delivers the gory entertainment associated with Ferrara. But, like *Nadja*, it's the campy dialogue (unintentional here) that lingers in the mind, as when Christopher Walken's tough vampire advises Kathleen, "Eternity is a long time; get used to it."

7

Comedy and Satire

Tackling Taboos

NEXT TO NOIR, comedy is the genre that most excites new indie directors. As in other genres, indie comedy (and satire) has built upon the work of influential directors: Robert Altman, George Lucas, and Barry Levinson. Seminal films, such as Altman's *M.A.S.H.*, Lucas's *American Graffiti*, and Levinson's *Diner*, all discussed in this chapter, have left a particularly strong mark on indie comedies of the past two decades.

Indie comedies have differed radically from those produced by Hollywood. Mainstream comedies of the 1980s were largely defined by Ivan Reitman, who has shown keen instincts for commercially viable material. After scoring box-office hits as the coproducer of *National Lampoon's Animal House* (1978) and the director of *Meatballs* (1979), Reitman launched a spectacular Hollywood career, capped by the whimsical blockbuster, *Ghostbusters* (1984). But, with the exception of *Dave* (1993), Reitman's other highly profitable comedies, *Twins* (1988) and *Kindergarten Cop* (1990), both starring Arnold Schwarzenegger, employed broad, infantile humor. When Reitman made *Legal Eagles* (1986), critics praised his foray into "adult comedy"; yet the film was still a teenage comedy in sensibility, albeit one populated by adult characters (played by Debra Winger and Robert Redford).

American comedies of recent years have been mechanical retreads of old formulas, as evidenced in the retro work of Nora Ephron (*Sleepless in Seattle, Michael, You've Got Mail*, the last a shallow remake of *The Shop Around the Corner*). Filmmakers seem unable to recognize that it's hard to make screwball comedy in the 1990s, when the social norms and manners that gave rise to those cinematic conventions no longer exist.

Romantic comedy took a turn in 1998, with *There's Something About Mary*, by the creators of *Dumb and Dumber*, Pete Farrelly and Bobby Farrelly. Filled with gross-out bathroom gags and overtly sexual humor, this comedy is cloaked in politically incorrect jokes about zippers, dogs, and hair gel. The Farrellys turned the genre on its ear, moving it away from the predictable, well-mannered yuppie romantic comedies of the past decade (*While You Were Sleeping*, *Forget Paris*, *One Fine Day*) into a much raunchier territory.[1]

There's Something About Mary cut across all demographics, reaching beyond the typical Jim Carrey audience of teenage boys. The key to the film's success is its universal story of love lost and found, and a central female character (Cameron Diaz) who's bright and appealing enough to make four men vie for her. The Farrellys felt that the studios have given up on adult comedies and that romantic comedies have become too stale. They have arguably both brutalized and energized the genre, displaying taste for crasser but also more poignant material.

But *There's Something About Mary* is the exception to the norm, and a deep gap still prevails between Hollywood and indie comedies. The function of non-studio comedy fare is to challenge the standard formulas by subverting audiences' expectations.[2] Hence, for a satirist like Alexander Payne (*Citizen Ruth*, *Election*), what gives indie comedies distinctive accent is their "flawed, unlikable" characters. This is not an easy goal to achieve as the twin "enemies" of indie comedies are broad television sitcoms and big-budget, hyperactive "dumb" movies, exemplified by the work of Jim Carrey. Both types have threatened to squeeze the more character-driven indies out of the market.

Most American comedies are so broad that they are about nothing—consider two of Carrey's films, *Ace Ventura* and its sequel. A comic working inside the studio system, Carrey has tried to do darker, less mainstream fare, like *Cable Guy*, which was not a box-office success by studio standards. "Carrey was violating his sacrosanct position in comedy," said Kevin Smith. "What he did with that movie was very ballsy, but ballsy isn't what the studios want."[3] Indeed, anxious to reclaim his box-office stature, Carrey chose for his next comedy the safer *Liar, Liar* (1997), and the public responded with the expected enthusiasm.

The distinct sensibility that permeated American comedy of the 1970s, in the work of Woody Allen, Mike Nichols, and Paul Mazursky, no longer exists. Woody Allen has retained his strength as an inventive comedy director (*Zelig*, *The Purple Rose of Cairo*, *Bullets Over Broadway*), but he has lost his broad base and now works as a niche filmmaker supported by a small audience.[4]

The work of gifted indie directors has tapped into the zeitgeist, armed with topicality and a point of view that defy the mass-marketing approach—Christopher Guest's style of mockumentary and improvisation, Kevin Smith's verbal gyrations among the randy twentysomethings, David O. Russell's neo–Woody Allen, neurosis-tinged comedies, Alexander Payne's political satire. Trying to sell *Spanking the Monkey* to the studios, Russell thought that they would quickly buy a movie that, after all, was about incest, but he underestimated the skittishness that topic would engender.

Payne's sharply observed satire, *Citizen Ruth*, sank quickly at the box office, despite Laura Dern's star power and Miramax's marketing clout. The cult status of *This Is Spinal Tap*, in which Christopher Guest also starred, didn't help his charming mockumentary *Waiting for Guffman*, which enjoyed a limited run in specialized venues. "What I do is just naturally a tough sell," acknowledged Smith. "The studios don't know what to do with my stuff." *Chasing Amy*, which depicts the stormy love between two comic book artists, with the twist that he's straight and she's a lesbian, is a sexually charged movie whose tonal shifts from light comedy to mature drama are deliberately designed to confound expectations.

Payne hopes that the studios will return to the character-based comedies of the 1970s. More optimistic than other directors of his generation, he says: "The Coens and Scorsese are studio filmmakers in the classic sense, so it's kind of hard to totally trash the studios." Guest, however, claims that successfully pitching cutting-edge comedies to the studios is now harder than it's ever been, because of the conglomerate nature of the studios. For him, the studios "are seduced by expensive projects" to the point where "it's a disgrace to make a movie for two million."[5]

Unlike dramatic realism and noir, in which young directors have drawn on the seminal work of Cassavetes and Scorsese, in the area of comedy there is no single major figure. With a number of significant satires to his credits, Altman has influenced the new indie wave, not so much thematically as stylistically. Equally important is Altman's model in maintaining an independent spirit in what can be described as a truly maverick and erratic career. Altman's film oeuvre is so rich and diverse that he could have been placed in any number of chapters. If he is profiled here, it's because two of his main disciples, Alan Rudolph and Tim Robbins, made comedies and satires.

THE ALTMAN EFFECT

The epitome of a nonconformist filmmaker, Altman has refused to play by the rules.[6] As Leo Braudy has observed, Altman built his work on attempts to reconcile basic contradictions in Hollywood: genre versus art film, popular versus serious director. Drawing on the energy of classic genres, Altman has brought an astutely ironic, irreverent gaze to bear on traditional American values. From the beginning, his approach has been freewheeling, nonlinear, and genre-deconstructive. Unlike other directors, Altman has never been a storyteller; he is more interested in mood and ambiance than in plot. An auteur whose multilayered, innovative films show a fondness for loose, incongruous style, Altman has rejected the well-made Hollywood movie in favor of a commitment to new ways of presenting stories.

After Altman's debut, *The Delinquents* (1957), an exploitation movie about juvenile crime, a full decade elapsed before he returned to features with *Countdown* (1968). Since then, he has directed inventive films that revisited and revised popular genres: the war movie (*M.A.S.H.*), the detective thriller (*The Long Goodbye*), the Western (*McCabe and Mrs. Miller*), love on the run (*Thieves Like Us*). Altman was influenced by vérité documentarians, Godard's street style, and Cassavetes's low-budget resourcefulness. The zoom was key to his innovative style, an unusual melding of fiction and documentary that gave his films an unprecedented freshness and sense of life. He would stage a master shot packed with people and then reach through the crowd with the zoom for close-ups. Warren Beatty has observed that "Altman had the talent to make the background come into the foreground and the foreground go into the background."[7]

Altman asserted himself as a front-rank director with *M.A.S.H.* (1970), an iconoclastic black comedy, which won the Palme d'Or at Cannes and an Oscar for Best Screenplay and which is still his biggest commercial hit. Displaying what became Altman's distinctive style of overlapping sounds and images, *M.A.S.H.* was less about combat than about the American way of practicing war. Altman looked away from carnage in favor of a nasty depiction of camp life during war. After the film's huge success, Altman was flooded by studio offers for big-budget productions, but he typically chose *Brewster McCloud* (1970), a modest, whimsical allegory, opening up a career-long chasm between the stubbornly individualistic director and the Hollywood establishment. *Mc-Cabe and Mrs. Miller* (1971), *Images* (1972), and *Thieves Like Us* (1974) garnered critical praise but were of limited marketability and failed at the box office.

For the second—but not last—time in his career, Altman came back from the cold with *Nashville* (1975), the fullest realization of his talent, an inventive mosaic of the American experience composed of twenty-four characters. The film was named Best Picture and Altman Best Director by the New York Film Critics Circle. *Nashville* featured a multilayered narrative, a large ensemble of gifted actors, breezy speed, witty music, and overlapping dialogue. The feel of time and space, stretching to contain the actions of two dozen figures, sharing equal time and moving in random turmoil and coincidence, was highly original.[8]

Having regained Hollywood's trust, Altman quickly squandered it on *Buffalo Bill and the Indians* (1976), *Three Women* (1977), and *A Wedding* (1978), varied, experimental works that again failed to win audiences. *Quintet* (1979), about a future ice age, and *Popeye* (1980), a big-budget comic strip, pleased neither critics nor audiences. In the 1980s, Altman ran into hard times with his reliance on theatrical material that seemed pedestrian after his 1970s work. Still, small-scale films, such as *Come Back to the 5 & Dime Jimmy Dean, Jimmy Dean*, *Streamers*, and *Fool for Love*, set the tone for an indie movement that targeted more discerning viewers. By the 1980s, the Hollywood establishment had written off Altman as unpredictable and uncommercial. Moving to Paris, he worked on *Secret Honor* (1984), a monologue about Richard Nixon. The cable miniseries *Tanner '88* (1988), a political satire, gained a favorable response, as did *Vincent and Theo* (1990), a meditation about Van Gogh, which was a return to form but didn't find its audience.

In 1992, Altman surprised Hollywood yet again with *The Player*, a black comedy about the industry, his first commercial and critical success since *Nashville*. The film was enriched by cameo appearances from numerous celebrities, including Bruce Willis and Julia Roberts. Heralded as Altman's comeback, *The Player* made Hollywood the butt of the joke. His droll, sinuously explorative camera style was evident in a showy eight-minute opening that conveyed vividly the ambiance on a studio lot. Thematically, it was a return to Altman's America as a place of frauds and dreamers, but the satire was not offensive enough, the target too easy. Even so, with a typical Altmanian irony, *The Player* earned major Oscar nominations and brought him renewed attention.

Altman has always struggled to get his movies made his own way, but his disenchantment with the studios and their obsessive concern with marketing led to a break. Following what he calls his "third come-back," Altman still refuses to conform to the conventions of traditional cinema: "Hollywood doesn't want to make the same pictures I do, and I'm too old to change."[9] *Short Cuts* (1993), based on Raymond Carver's stories, is a lengthy, complex film that interweaves two dozen charac-ters in a portrait of contemporary Los Angeles. The lack of faithfulness to the source material was a subject of contention, but the movie caught the hazy, slippery looseness of Los Angeles, specifically its casual vio-lence and childishness. As in *Nashville*, the cuts, the pans, and the look-ing sideways were interesting, though Altman's innate cynicism about people curdled the film.[10]

Altman's career has been devoted to the exploration of a variety of genres, a diversity of points of views, and a wide range of settings.[11] In his efforts to democratize American movies, he has resisted Holly-wood's formulas and has paid attention to the distinctive voices of women and blacks in such movies as *Three Women*, *Kansas City*, and, most recently, *Cookie's Fortune* (1999), an eccentric comedy dominated by women (played by Patricia Neal, Glenn Close, Julianne Moore, and Liv Tyler) that introduced the issue of race in the most casual and natu-ral manner.

For Altman, the medium is the message, which translates into his disorienting spectators by defying ordinary film syntax. Altman's sig-nature is specifically American, both in the turfs and in the styles used. His best work (*M.A.S.H.*, *McCabe and Mrs. Miller*, *Nashville*) deals with the tension between individualism and community, specifically with how Americans handle racism and violence—in other words, the cor-ruption of the American Dream—while remaining decent Americans. His films negotiate the viewers' attachment to—and detachment from—American culture, inviting them to engage in a debate about the link between the past and the present of America as the promised land.

Along with directing, Altman has functioned as a producer, most notably for his protegé, Alan Rudolph, in *Mrs. Parker and the Vicious Cir-cle* (1994), *Afterglow* (1997), and other films. The spirit of Altman's work is expressed in Rudolph's films as well as in Tim Robbins's first direc-torial effort, *Bob Roberts* (1992).

THE ROMANTIC—ALAN RUDOLPH

Alan Rudolph began his career as an assistant to Altman on *The Long Goodbye, California Split,* and *Nashville.* He later carved a path of his own with *Welcome to L.A.* (1977), which Altman produced, and *Remember My Name* (1979). Like his mentor, Rudolph operates well with tight budgets, and a repertory of actors, some of whom— Keith Carradine, Genevieve Bujold, Geraldine Chaplin—have also worked for Altman.

Rudolph has displayed an undeniably singular romantic vision: In his films, nothing is ever ordinary. Best known for his offbeat romantic comedies, Rudolph, like Altman, is an iconoclastic filmmaker who revels in subverting traditional genres. His work is marked by oddly eccentric moods, oblique entrances, elliptic passages, and archetypal characters. A director with a sophisticated visual sense, Rudolph makes movies for the intellectual art house crowd. His style is fanciful, whimsical, and occasionally frivolous. Pauline Kael has observed that it's often hard to distinguish in a Rudolph picture the intentional humor from the unintentional flightiness.[12]

Rudolph's films are never box-office successes (his audiences have been small), but they don't cost much, either. The only exception is the ambitious *Mrs. Parker and the Vicious Circle,* a big-party movie about the legendary literary wits of New York's Algonquin Round Table and Rudolph's most expensive ($7 million) film. The producer, Altman, managed with great difficulty to raise the funds, but the picture lost a bundle.[13]

It took seven years and four movies for Rudolph to find his style in *Choose Me* (1983), a giddy movie that is still the crown of his achievements. Structured as a lyrical fantasy, the film's characters wander in and out of a bar called Eve's Lounge, obsessively looking for love. The protagonist (Keith Carradine), a lunatic who radiates danger, turns out to be saner than anyone else. All the characters are at least vaguely amnesiac, and, as Kael noted, they are given dialogue that's "overintellectualized in a hammy way." But the movie's loose, choreographic flow and swoony camera fit its romantic ambiance and compensate for the weaknesses.

American audiences have not embraced adult fairy tales in the way European audiences have. The chic, subtle and bizarre *Choose Me* is a variation on Schnitzler's classic, *La Ronde,* set in an empty downtown Los Angeles where, except for a few prostitutes, people have vanished.[14] A deceptively fragile movie, *Choose Me* owes a lot to Altman's artful heedlessness: The fable about oddball lovers whose madnesses and illusions interlock is both subversive and upbeat. Rudolph's finest accomplishment as a moody romantic melodrama, *Choose Me* also boasts sinuously lurid visuals and a jazzy score.

Rudolph later made *Trouble in Mind* (1986), in which the situations are similar to those in *Choose Me*, except that the mixed-up lovers have been replaced by mixed-up gangsters and what was comic is now fatalistic.[15] In *Made in Heaven* (1987), Rudolph envisions a colorful world full of the dreaminess, romanticism, and tangled destinies that have marked his other films.

Choose Me was followed by a number of films set in the literary world, such as *The Moderns* (1988), about Paris's 1920s artistic milieu, and its companion piece, *Mrs. Parker and the Vicious Circle*, a fascinating but shallow look at the acerbic, self-destructive writer and her legendary cohorts. Like most of Rudolph's films, *Mrs. Parker* doesn't go anywhere dramatically, but it sustains a frivolous party atmosphere in its depiction of the literati as they booze, wisecrack, and engage in romantic affairs and infantile conduct.

Rudolph has used old literary conceits—the twins in *Equinox* (both played by Matthew Modine)—but his sensibility is decidedly modern. As a study in the duality of identity, *Equinox* centers on twin brothers Fred and Henry. Separated at birth, one grows up an orphan, the other is adopted; one becomes bad, the other good. Each exists as a half of a dark/light schematic but is beckoned by the other, yearning to meet the doppelganger he doesn't know is alive.

An ensemble piece about criss-crossing destinies that's socially-aware in its concern for the moral decay of urban society, *Equinox* suffers from a low-key tone and incoherent texture. Not exactly a romantic fable, it's more of a noirish fairy tale with rich imagery and subtle humor. The metaphor of life's randomness flashes through windows in the form of a neon lottery sign. The currents of human interaction that fascinate Rudolph are expressed in self-consciously noirish elements. Rudolph plays with the conventions of a thriller and the themes of good and evil to comment on the romantic loss and emptiness of modern life.[16]

Over the years, Rudolph has developed a control of rhythm and mood—a musical way of storytelling—that is most evident in *Afterglow* (1997), a romantic comedy that dissects the delicate imbalances of two sexually barren marriages. While lacking the more accessible appeal of *Choose Me*, *Afterglow* employs the same narrative structure, revolving around four lost souls whose paths cross while they wander in and out of a Montreal hotel.

A corporate executive, Jeffrey Byron (Jonny Lee Miller) is convinced that "everything's working well on many levels." In contrast, his frustrated wife, Marianne (Lara Flynn Boyle), believes that "nothing is working," least of all her desire to become a mother, a wish denied by Jeffrey. While Marianne carefully tracks her fertility cycle, Jeffrey tracks the stock market. Across town, Lucky "Fix-it" Mann (Nick Nolte), an amorous repair contractor, experiences marital problems with his long-time spouse, Phyllis (Julie Christie), a former B-movie actress, who spends her time watching her lousy pictures. Lucky still hurts over the fact that he is not the biological father of their teenage daughter, who has run away.

Rudolph does a masterful job of treating the tale like a jigsaw puzzle whose patterns gradually become clear. Rudolph's narratives are as shapely and graceful as their art decor, and *Afterglow* is no exception. The quartet is thrown off balance when Lucky arrives at the Byrons' hyperstylized apartment for repairs and Marianne becomes instantly infatuated with him. It takes no time for Jeffrey to meet and fall for the older, sophisticated Phyllis. The film cross-cuts between the two newly formed couples, and eventually they all meet at the Ritz Hotel.

Almost any definition of the word "afterglow" applies to the title, be it "a reflection of past splendor" or "a glow remaining where a light has disappeared." Rudolph favors the older couple (who are his age) with a more sympathetic and multishaded portrayal. Fluid mise-en-scène and leisurely pacing (Rudolph's hallmarks as director) make *Afterglow* serious and comic, frivolous and meaningful, giddy and lyrical. Like *Choose Me*, the movie displays a choreographic fluency, with Toyomichi Kurita's caressing camera matching Rudolph's romanticism like a silk glove.

THE POLITICAL SATIRIST—TIM ROBBINS

Tim Robbins's multiple talents as actor, writer, and director have prompted Altman to compare him to the young Orson Welles. The comparison is not warranted at this phase of his career, but it signals an alert acting and directing talent. Robbins made an impressive debut with *Bob Roberts*, a political satire about a right-wing Pennsylvania businessman-cum-folk-singer-politician. The timing—the film hit the theaters just weeks before the 1992 presidential elections—could not have been better.

Studying closely the work of his mentor, Robbins modeled *Bob Roberts* on *Nashville*, as a musical mosaic-satire. Like *Nashville*, in which the songs were improvised by the actors, the score for *Bob Roberts* was composed by Robbins and his brother David; their lyrics contain the film's shrewdest lines. Robbins also borrowed Altman's frequent cinematographer, Jean Lepine, to give the film a fitting look. Also like his mentor, Robbins chose a first-rate ensemble for cameo roles: Susan Sarandon as a TV anchorwoman; James Spader, Fred Ward, and Pamela Reed as newspeople; Alan Rickman as the campaign manager. The greatest casting coup was getting the novelist Gore Vidal to play Roberts's nemesis, the liberal incumbent Brickley Paiste.

Structured as a mockumentary, Robbins's film is *This Is Spinal Tap* (Rob Reiner's mockumentary about a rock group) for the political arena, with flashes of Altman's TV series *Tanner '88* thrown in. The idea of a singer turned politician can be traced back to 1950s Hollywood movies, such as *A Face in the Crowd* and *Wild in the Streets*. Robbins may have also been inspired by D. A. Pennebaker's documentary on Bob Dylan, *Don't Look Back*.

Playing the title role with dead eyes and a reptilian leer, Robbins appears both sweet and Machiavellian, recalling his delicious rendition of Griffin Mill, the murderous studio executive in Altman's *The Player*. Roberts rejects the ideals that his hippie parents have chosen for him, instead opting to become a right-wing folksinger, businessman, and politician. He runs a mean-spirited campaign; his associates are accused of channeling funds intended for the homeless into private enterprise. The news media, whose bubbleheaded telecasters' happy-talk approach to the news helps Roberts's rise to power, come under severe criticism in the movie.

A self-styled "rebel conservative" with oily, fabricated charisma, Roberts is a candidate who is not "one of those liberals who makes you feel guilty about what's wrong in society." "Why can't you get ahead?" Roberts asks, "Why has your American dream been relegated to the ashcan of history?" Nonetheless, when Roberts is slated to appear on a *Saturday Night Live*–type program, *Cutting Edge Live*, the production assistant is so appalled by the "yuppie fascist" that she literally pulls the plug on him.

Robbins shot *Bob Roberts* in November, at the time of an election in Pennsylvania to fill a vacant U.S. Senate seat, in which the Democratic Senator Harris Wofford won an unexpected victory over the Republican candidate, Richard Thornburgh, former U.S. attorney general. Those results buoyed Robbins's conviction that the satire was timely, a reflection of a growing discontent with right-wing politics. Hoping that people had had enough with conservative politics, he claimed, "Once they start seeing past the sound bite to what these people really feel, they'll start voting with their minds again."[17]

The son of the folksinger Gil Robbins (of the Highwaymen), Robbins worked for years on his ideas before writing this inspired bit of political chicanery—"I wanted to think of it before somebody did it for real," he said. He directed a short version of his movie as a sketch on *Saturday Night Live*, which received a positive response. But it took years to make the film. Eventually, the relevant satirical message and Robbins's clout as an actor persuaded Working Title to invest $4 million in the project.

As a filmmaker and actor, Robbins is concerned about the "Hollywoodization of Washington," an hypothesis central to his polemic. Indeed, there are striking parallels between Bob Roberts's candidacy and the real presidential race: Bill Clinton made the cover of *Rolling Stone* magazine, just like Roberts, and George Bush ballyhooed traditional values, also like Roberts. Said Robbins: "There are givens in any campaign, especially from the GOP. Their strategy has been based on diversion: smoke screens divert attention from the record."[18]

Though set in October 1990, during the Gulf War, Bob Roberts makes no explicit references to this context. To find out what's on the agenda of the sneaky demagogue, one has to look at the titles of his albums: "The Freewheeling Bob Roberts," "The Times Are Changing Back," and "Bob on Bob," all parodies of famous Bob Dylan albums. The movie's treatment of the material is light and subtle enough to send conflicting signals to viewers of any persuasion: Democratic and Republican viewers could find supporting evidence for their views of "what's wrong with America" and "who's guilty."

As a mockumentary, the film is filled with piercing barbs at the current state of American politics. For two reels, Robbins achieves a balance of humor and poignancy, but in the final one, the plot spirals out of control with a Reichstag-like scam and heavyhanded speeches. Not cutting deep enough, *Bob Roberts* lacks the more cynical, biting approach of Michael Ritchie's *The Candidate* (1972), in which Robert Redford plays an idealist who is talked into running for U.S. Senate and in the process learns the immoral operations of the American political machine. *Bob Roberts* assumes that the public already knows what it takes to run elections and, winking at like-minded viewers, the movie makes them feel superior to those on-screen. A moderate commercial success, the picture was probably seen by those who already agreed with its politics.

HIGH CAMP—PAUL BARTEL AND CHRISTOPHER GUEST

Like Tim Robbins, Paul Bartel has sustained a parallel career as a director and an actor, playing pudgy, prissy characters in his films as well as in those of his colleagues (*Eat My Dust!* [1976], *Chopping Malls* [1986], *Desire and Hell at Sunset Motel* [1992]). As a director, Bartel exhibits a satirical talent with a bent toward the offbeat and outrageous, but without John Waters's gross-outs. Bartel's campy style borders on the lewd and the perverse, although a naive sweetness still resides in his comedies.

In the 1960s, Bartel wrote and directed an eerie, funny comedy on paranoia, *Secret Cinema*, about a fragile young woman who believes that unknown persons are shooting a movie of her private life. He then made *Naughty Nurse*, *Private Parts*, and exploitation films like *Death Race 2000* and *Cannonball*. Bartel's best-known movie, *Eating Raoul* (1982), about sex, murder, and cannibalism, paved the way for many future rude satires. The movie is purposely directed in a flat, plain manner; the low-key tone is one of its chief droll points. As a spoof, *Eating Raoul* is slight and thinly textured, a thirty-minute episode of a soap stretched to a feature length. Even so, with the help of the downtown press, *Eating Raoul* became a long-running cult favorite.

Paul and Mary Bland (Bartel and Mary Woronov), a self-deluding couple, are convinced that they are superior to everybody else. Paul is a prissy mannerist, and Mary seems quiet, but her quietness conceals sexual longings. The Blands live in a Los Angeles apartment house inhabited by swingers, where every elevator ride threatens to become an adventure. Paul can quit his job in a cheap liquor store, Mary can leave her job as a hospital dietician, and together, they could open a gourmet restaurant with a name like Chez Bland.

In *Eating Raoul*, Bartel, Woronov, and Richard Blackburn, who collaborated on the script, create a comedy form that's between put-down and send-up, one that contains accidental jokes. Mary is in the kitchen when a drunk swinger, looking for an orgy down the hall, breaks in and attempts to rape her. Paul hits the intruder with a cast-iron skillet and kills him. Perceiving themselves practical, they empty the fellow's wallet and put him in the garbage compactor.

This first murder opens up a whole new world to the Blands. Having lost his job, Paul is now desperate for money. Mary's attempt to obtain a bank loan is denied when she turns down the credit manager (Buck Henry), who's fascinated with her breasts. With ads in the underground press, the Blands lure swingers to their apartment, kill them with a skillet, rob them, and dispose of the remains in the compactor. Their conscience is clean because, as Paul rationalizes, the victims are "horrible, sex-crazed perverts that nobody will miss anyway." Their progress is temporarily interrupted when Raoul (Robert Beltran), a Chicano locksmith with a desire for Mary, attempts to cut himself in on their racket.

Bartel's follow-up satire, *Scenes from the Class Struggle in Beverly Hills* (1989), reveals what goes on behind close doors in the mansions of the country's most affluent community. The heroine is Clare Lipkin (Jacqueline Bisset), a newly widowed matron who's busy planning both her husband's funeral and her return to TV, where she was once the star of a second-rank sitcom. Her Mexican cook, Rosa (Edith Diaz), who's the film's conscience, is treated shabbily by her employer. Among Rosa's responsibilities is taking care of Clare's eccentric guests: Dr. Mo Van de Kamp (Bartel), her portly "thinologist"; Lisabeth (Mary Woronov), a recent divorcée whose house is being fumigated; Lisabeth's brother Peter (Ed Begley Jr.), an ungifted playwright; and Peter's new black wife, To-bel (Arnetia Walker), the reason for Lisabeth's divorce from her husband, Howard (Wallace Shawn).

Principal movers of the plot are Clare's houseboy, Frank (Ray Sharkey), a fast-talking gigolo, and Lisabeth's naive houseboy, Juan (Robert Beltran), who dreams of becoming a transgressor—"crossing-over like Ruben Blades"—and belonging to Beverly Hills's elite. Frank has given up on such dreams; having been "on the other side," he realizes there isn't any difference. Out of boredom, Frank bets Juan that, if the latter can seduce Clare before Frank can seduce Lisabeth, Frank will give him $5,000 to pay off his gambling debts.

Like *Eating Raoul*, this farce, written by Bruce Wagner and based on Bartel's idea, switches from one set piece to the next. The movie's funny lines are delivered with the kind of self-consciousness that diffuses the rudeness. Asked about news stories that expose his clinic, the doctor says, "When you get a bunch of rich fat people who are determined to get thin at any cost, some of them are going to die. It's a rule of thumb." With the assist of Alex Tavoularis's witty production design, some images stand out, including that of Lisabeth's mansion being fumigated—covered with a pink cloth, the house looks as if it had been wrapped by Christo.

A major satire appeared in 1984: *This Is Spinal Tap*, directed by Rob Reiner who made an admirably precise parody of a rock documentary. Reiner played a director, Marti Di Bergi, who chronicles the latest American tour of an aging British rock group, a working definition of the word "has-been." This collaborative satire was improvised by Reiner and his cast, which includes cameos of many familiar faces: Michael McKean, Christopher Guest, Harry Shearer, Tony Hendra, June Chadwick. *This Is Spinal Tap* was so successful that in the 1990s the fictitious group reunited for a series of live concerts and a TV special, further blurring the lines between satire and reportage.

Guest contributed to the script of *This Is Spinal Tap*, in which he also starred as lead guitarist Nigel Tufnela, of the faux heavy metal band Spinal Tap. A veteran of TV, Guest performed and wrote material for various entertainment programs (including a 1976 Lili Tomlin special) and was a member of the *Saturday Night Live* cast. *This Is Spinal Tap* has become the standard against which all mockumentaries are evaluated. A few years before *The Player*, Guest satirized Hollywood—and the nightmares faced by film school graduates—in *The Big Picture* (1989), in which Martin Short plays a greasy, small-time agent who woos a modest, eager-to-please graduate (Kevin Bacon) and in the process turns his personal and professional lives into hell.

In 1996, Guest directed and cowrote *Waiting for Guffman* (with Second City's Eugene Levy). He starred in the film as Corky St. Clair, the creative force behind "Red, White, and Blaine," a musical pageant celebrating the glorious history of Blaine, "a little town with a big heart in the heart of the country." The small-town amateurs in *Waiting for Guff-man* cultivate their belief that their trifling musical tribute will go to Broadway. Like the fictional Spinal Tap, the troupe is clumsy in a charming way, echoing what Guest calls "a larger idea" than just this group of little people. The film "is not about offending hicks in the sticks, but seeing how it's human nature to want to be a star."[19]

Like *This is Spinal Tap*, *Waiting for Guffman* is an improvised mocku-mentary based on a loose script. "There would simply be no discussion with studios about this movie," Guest recalled. "People have been under the misperception that, because *Spinal Tap* was a cult hit, it opened doors. It didn't. The climate has changed: If you brought the *Spinal Tap* idea to studios today, they'd say, 'Where's the three-act script?'"[20]

A sly, gleeful comedy, *Waiting for Guffman* pokes fun at American musicals, amateur theatricals, and, above all, the culture of celebrity—the universal wish to be famous. Blaine is about to commemorate the 150th anniversary of its accidental founding, when an unscrupulous guide convinced a group of travelers that they'd arrived in California. Determined to produce an event that will become the standard by which sesquicentennials are judged, the town invites a crew to record the behind-the-scenes doings, from choosing the cast to the inevitable crisis of having to replace a player. Collaborating with Guest on the music and lyrics are *Spinal Tap* veterans Michael McKean and Harry Shearer, who wrote two of the numbers, "Nothing Ever Happens in Blaine" and "Nothing Ever Happens on Mars."

Ron and Sheila Albertson (Fred Willard and Catherine O'Hara) are travel agents who have never left town, but they have done enough local theater to merit the label "The Lunts of Blaine." The newcomers include Dr. Alan Pearl (Eugene Levy), the tone-deaf den-tist who claims to have an ancestor who was in the Yiddish theater, and Libby Mae Brown (Parker Posey), the Dairy Queen counter girl who courts Corky with a version of "Teacher's Pet." Sporting a goatee, bowl haircut, and puzzled look, Corky is the drama teacher who made audiences "feel the heat" in his stage version of *Backdraft*. Corky has the passion and vision to override all skeptics, like the music teacher Lloyd Miller (Bob Balaban). Corky anxiously expects the arrival of Mr. Guffman, a powerful New York producer, who, of course, never shows up.

INDIE COMEDIES OF THE 1990s

A new cycle of serio–youth comedies began in 1989-1990 with *sex, lies, and videotape*, the work of Hal Hartley, Richard Linklater, and Gregg Araki.[21] This cycle followed the publication of Douglas Coupland's 1991 novel, which coined the label "Gen-X" for the culture of the post–baby boom generation, born between 1962 and 1974. A catch-phrase, the label was immediately embraced by the media, though it was loathed by those to whom it purportedly applied. Even so, young filmmakers began making quirky films, specifically aimed at the scruffy core of the twentysomething market, that focused on brooding, disillu-sioned youths absorbed in edgy relationships and turbulent romances. As a sociocultural phenomenon, the concept of Gen-X has influenced both indies and Hollywood. Hollywood made Tim Burton's *Edward Scissorhands* (1990) and *Benny & Joon* (1993), both starring Johnny Depp, who became the quintessential actor of his generation, appearing in John Waters's *Cry Baby* as well as in more mainstream movies. Ben Stiller's *Reality Bites* (1994) enjoyed effective marketing campaign but, despite the hoopla and the stars, didn't catch fire at the box office.

Arguably, no single Gen-X movie has captured the zeitgeist in the same way that earlier movies have: *Rebel Without a Cause* (1955) with James Dean, *The Graduate* (1967) with Dustin Hoffman, *Saturday Night Fever* (1977) with John Travolta, and *Fast Times at Ridgemont High* (1982), which conveyed teen anxieties in the new mall culture. As heavy media consumers, young audiences made hits out of 1980s Hollywood ado-lescent fantasies, such as *Ferris Bueller's Day Off*, *Risky Business*, *The Breakfast Club*, *Sixteen Candles*, and *Pretty in Pink*, movies that featured the brat pack: Molly Ringwald, Demi Moore, Rob Lowe, Andrew Mc-Carthy, Emilio Estevez, and Ally Sheedy. In contrast,Gen-X flaunted its own cohort of cool performers: Eric Stoltz, Ethan Hawke, Winona Ryder, and Uma Thurman.

Defenders of the label claim that this one is essentially no different from previous labels generated for the convenience of the media, such as, in the 1950s, the Beat Generation, or, in the 1980s, the Me Generation. In actuality, Gen-Xers are more diverse, both demographically and cul-turally, than their screen image suggests, but it's always easier for Hol-lywood to use stereotypes. In film after film, Gen-Xers are depicted as overeducated and underemployed, cynical and disillusioned, media savvy and yet media-suspicious. They've been raised on junk sitcoms and trashy rock bands, and they hang out in coffee shops and bars, wear thrift-store threads, and smoke Marlboro Lights.

Michael Lehmann's *Heathers* (1989), which premiered in Sundance the same year as *sex, lies, and videotape*, heralded the Gen-X cycle. The filmmaker's caustic vision transforms a film about teen-age suicide into a dark farce whose tone is giddy but whose intent is serious. Daniel Waters wrote the script over two years while working as a videostore manager. The idea was born out of his "warped fantasies" about high-school girls and his column in the school paper, "Troubled Waters," which included cynical ramblings of the kind that set *Heathers* apart. Waters had the "weird hobby" of reading *Seventeen* magazine the way other kids would read comic books. "I've always loved books about angsty young girls who would write in their diaries and complain about life." Reading Simone de Beauvoir's *The Second Sex*, Waters was "amazed" by her observations about women's self-hatred. He thought that the way girls maintain their own oppression—hating fat girls more than guys do—was "great stuff" for a movie.

Films about suicide have tended to give it a noble feel, but Waters wanted "to take suicide off the menu of people's brains."[22] It never occurred to him that a film satirizing suicide might prove controversial, but many Hollywood agents were alarmed by it. Helmer Lehmann encountered similar touchiness even after New World Pictures agreed to invest $3 million. The mother of one teen actress who auditioned charged that the script was "satanic" and the filmmakers the "voice of evil."

Open-minded viewers, however, were provoked by scenes in which a teacher earnestly counsels a student: "Whether or not to kill yourself is one of the most important decisions a teenager has to make." "There are people who thought it a glib, cynical, socially irresponsible view of high school," Lehmann said. But the filmmakers held that their treatment of the issue was responsible, that "teenagers don't have any problem with it; it's always adults who are shocked."[23] Fearing their movie might be deemed pretentious in the way it addresses the malaise affecting youth, they decided to undercut the high-mindedness with laughs. Perceiving school as a cruel environment and adolescence as a time of "being angry and cynical," they expected viewers right out of school to be entertained by their satire.

The slang in *Heathers* was made up, since the writer believed that duplicating actual teen-age slang would invite obsolescence for the film. Most films about teenagers are based on dialogue recorded in cafeterias, but, by the time the movie gets made, the slang is out of date. For his film, Waters invented a new lingo, exemplified by Veronica's speech to her oblivious parents: "Great pate, but I have to motor if I want to be ready for that funeral."

In *Heathers*, the popular high-school beauties are a cross between the angst-ridden teenagers of John Hughes and those of David Lynch. With its teenage cast and school setting, *Heathers* ran the risk of being mistaken for yet another adolescent romp, but its satire was audaciously twisted. A Middle-American high school is dominated by a callow clique, The Heathers, named after three perfectly groomed girls who share the same name. As the name of choice, Heather signifies power, popularity, and license to make mischief. The trio (Shannen Doherty, Kim Walker, and Lisanne Falk) cruise the cafeteria with a fourth reluctant member, Veronica (Winona Ryder), in tow. Veronica, who scribbles diary entries about her friends' exploits, has misgivings about their conduct. She doesn't like their predilection for dirty tricks, but she goes along with them, taunting some classmates, flirting, and complimenting others on their clothes.

Defying etiquette, Veronica falls for a motorcyclist outcast, J.D. (Christian Slater). Alienated by her mates' casual cruelty and selfish vanity, Veronica wishes them dead, and the Mephistophelian J.D. finds original ways to fulfill her darkest wishes. As the body count at Westerburgh High grows, J.D. and his accomplice disguise the murders as suicides. The filmmakers succeed in exposing the hypocrisy of kids and parents in their hollow, media-conditioned responses to tragedy.

The gun-toting J.D. goads Veronica into playing out her resentments. When the wicked Heather Chandler pushes Veronica too far, J.D. suggests slipping her a drink laced with kitchen cleaner and encourages Veronica to forge a "proper" suicide message that says, "People think just because you're beautiful and popular, life is easy and fun. No one understood that I had feelings too." Veronica's use of the word "myriad" impresses her teachers. For their part, exhilarated by their murderous prank, Veronica and J.D. raise the ante. The next "suicides" are a pair of lame-brained football players. J.D., who likes planting props at the scene of the crime, leaves a bottle of mineral water, because in Ohio this item signifies homosexuality.

Buoyant style and energy turn *Heathers* into a mean-spirited sitcom, with its originality extending beyond the limits of ordinary school romp into the realm of the perverse—as one character says, "The extreme always seems to make an impression." As long as Lehmann and Waters have the temerity to sustain the bracingly nasty tone, *Heathers* is good fun. But the jaundiced vision of adolescence isn't as cynical as it appears, and the film loses its nerve when it demands that Veronica wake up to her crimes. At the end, Veronica is reestablished as a "nice" girl in a turnabout that isn't convincing and undermines the film's sardonic style.

Political satires and farces have never been popular in American films, a fact reaffirmed by the failure of *Citizen Ruth* (1996), for which Alexander Payne chose the controversial issue of abortion. Payne was inspired by the twists and turns in the life of Norma McCorvey, the Roe in *Roe v. Wade,* a victim of manipulation by spin artists on both sides of the conflict. The model for his film is Preston Sturges's small-town folly, *Hail the Conquering Hero* (1943), with its gallery of American eccentrics, but *Citizen Ruth* lacks a sharp point of view, which turns the satire into a series of gigs.

Ruth Stoops (Laura Dern), a glue-sniffing, unemployed derelict, finds out that she's pregnant for the fifth time. The impatient judge, tired of seeing her in court, is willing to drop the charge if she agrees to an abortion. Soon, however, Ruth's case comes to the attention of a pro-life organization, headed by Gail and Norm Stoney (Mary Kay Place and Kurtwood Smith), who live by religious platitudes. They take Ruth into their home with promises of unconditional care, but when she attacks their son for disrupting her sniffing, they send her off with another member of the group.

Payne and his cowriter, Jim Taylor, kept hearing complaints from studio executives about their "unsympathetic protagonist," which was "like making movies under Communism, because the studios impose a certain ideology you must follow, especially in comedy."[24] Payne was not against making accessible comedies, provided they reflected the anger he felt inside. Realizing that his "heroine" is a "pure trailer-trash loser, incapable of gaining control of her life, a weasel going from adventure to adventure," he knew that the trick was to make audiences care about her. Payne achieves that by giving Ruth recognizable human feelings without ennobling her and by depicting the pro-choice activists as even more despicable. "I'm not delivering a message either for or against abortion here, because the comedy is elsewhere—it's directed at people's endless ability to be fanatical and selfish," said Payne, which may explain why some critics labeled him a misanthrope.

Payne satirizes the pro-life advocates (their smarmy leader is played by Burt Reynolds, and Mary Kay Place's character is "squeaky-clean"), directing barbs at their deception and manipulation. For the sake of a more even approach, Payne spreads the nastiness around: Ruth "is rescued" from her Christian saviors by pro-choice activists, headed by stern lesbians (Swoosie Kurtz and Kelly Preston) and a Vietnam vet biker. As *Citizen Ruth* progresses, the focus moves from abortion to women's right to make a choice. Activists on both sides are painted as opportunists; neither camp wants Ruth to make her own decision, and both use her to "send a message," a phrase that becomes a running gag. If the cartoon feminists are painted more negatively than the Christians, it's because their manipulation is more hypocritical; at least the pro-lifers don't pretend to be interested in empowering Ruth. Clearly, given the choice, Ruth will go back to sniffing and drinking. *Citizen Ruth* begins as a brazen comedy, but, like *Heathers*, it ends up with a shaky, compromising coda that negates its audacious satirical intent.

COMING-OF-AGE COMEDIES

One of the perennial themes in American films, both comedies and dramas, is the painful transition from childhood to adulthood. Reflecting broader societal concerns, numerous movies have dealt with the rites of passage that mark, if not always facilitate, the progression from one phase to another.

Non-Western societies rely on specific rites of passage, based on tribal belonging. The in-group is defined by the exclusion of others, encouraging chauvinistic and often xenophobic attitudes of adolescents. But modern, pluralistic societies offer only vague guidance for dealing with the problems faced by youngsters, which leads them to rely heavily on their peers for support and to strong feelings of "us" versus "them." When social needs, once met by tribal rituals, are no longer fulfilled, youth initiations provide a context that would otherwise be lacking. Some teenagers manage the transition successfully, whereas others don't. When coming of age occurs, as in American society, in competitive contexts devoid of stable value systems, the process is bound to be filled with uncertainties and ambiguities.

Modern society gives little formal recognition to the physiological changes children undergo at puberty. Boys are teased when their voice changes or when they start shaving. Status changes from childhood to adulthood are usually marked by minor events rather than a single dramatic ceremony. Graduation from high school is a necessary step to maturity but it is not considered a definitive rite of passage. A driver's license and the twenty-first birthday are legal indications of adulthood, but they are not marked by ceremony.

In the American cinema, coming of age is depicted in comedies or serio-comedies, known in the industry as dramedies. Usually, these movies revolve around a bunch of high schoolers or twentysomething students who make disaffected comments about life's passing them by. They are mostly male characters looking for action—something to do—but it's the banter that counts. In most films, it's the guys who are low-spirited and conflicted, feelings that are reflected in their attitudes toward women. Screen guys are either committed to the wrong woman, unable to commit to the right one, or still pondering their options.

If *Mean Streets* is the quintessential crime and male-bonding movie for its generation, *American Graffiti* (released in the same year, 1973) is a milestone for the coming-of-age genre. Although he directed it in an impersonal style, George Lucas achieved startling success and cultural influence with *American Graffiti*, singlehandedly establishing the 1960s as a proper subject for cinematic nostalgia. Produced on a low budget of $750,000, *American Graffiti* became one of the most profitable American pictures ever. The film launched a whole cycle of rock-and-roll movies, demonstrating the commercial potential of rock-and-roll oldies soundtracks. It also served as source for TV spinoffs, endorsed youthful complacencies as legitimate values, and marked the debut of many fine actors.

Meant to evoke "what we once had and lost," *American Graffiti* is nominally set in 1962, but its icons are from the late 1950s: The cars are a Studebaker, a '58 Chevy, and a '58 Edsel; the songs are "Rock Round the Clock," Del Shannon's "Runaway," and the music of the Platters. The movie's idols are Connie Stevens and Sandra Dee for the girls, and Elvis Presley and James Dean for the boys. The drag race in *American Graffiti* lacks the consequential effects it had in *Rebel Without a Cause,* but it's likely that the youngsters have learned about racing from the James Dean movie.

Situating the narrative in a specific place and time, Lucas gives it a sociogeographic center (Mel's Drive-In) and a special look (red and blue neon). The film's action is confined to one long summer night, during which the adolescence of four boys comes to a dramatic end. Television has already established itself as the mainstay of American culture, but the dominant medium is still radio. As a mythic hero, disk jockey Wolfman Jack unites all of the kids. Although he is mostly unseen, his presence is felt through his popular show; he seems to interact with each listener separately. As the boys' unofficial leader, Wolfman arranges for a telephone interview between Curt and his object of desire, helping him to fulfill his dream. Cementing the episodic structure, the music unifies the characters' diverse paths, suggesting that all the kids, no matter their whereabouts, are listening to the same station.

Modesto is a town that changes personality; the alternation of day and night sequences captures its variable quality. During the day, Main Street consists of a strip of used-car lots, small shops, and greasy spoons. Haskell Wexler's dazzling cinematography makes the town look much more glamorous at night, with flashy neon signs and an endless parade of cars. Car cruising takes the form of a modern dance, in which the relations among cars shift and reform either by logic or by chance. Interaction takes place through the windows, but it's a rich communication of provocations, flirtations, and insults. A convenient shield, the car's window is the only window to the outside world. As the film's real star, the car provides emotional security and physical protection, serving as a metaphor for American society in the 1960s, as complacent, naive, and isolationist in foreign policy.

The central foursome represents recognizable types: the attractive and pleasant Steve (Ron Howard) is the class president. Curt (Richard Dreyfuss) is the bright, inquisitive intellectual who wins a college scholarship. Terry the Toad (Charlie Martin Smith) is the guy who follows and as a reward gets to use Steve's car. A bit older, John Milner (Paul LeMat) is the immature simpleton who's still obsessed with James Dean. Facing a turning point, each adolescent needs to decide whether to go to college. Curt has serious doubts about leaving Modesto, but for Steve, it's a "turkey town," a notion reinforced by the radio station's manager, who describes it as "not exactly the hub of the universe." Even so, Curt's departure for college is seen as a decision that carries a high price: the loss of intimate friendships never again to be experienced.

The fate of the quartet as adults, which is printed onscreen at the film's end, is shocking, because it violates the predominantly nostalgic mood. Thrown off balance by the transition from the fantasy of a dream to the reality of a newsreel, viewers are told that John is later killed by a drunk driver, Terry is reported missing in action in Vietnam, Steve becomes an insurance agent in Modesto, and Curt becomes a successful writer who goes to Canada to avoid the draft. Focusing on the boys, *American Graffiti* takes a decidedly male point of view; the girls exist mostly as romantic interests and lack individual personalities. If the movie had been made a few years later, it would have had to include stronger female parts. David Thomson has noted that boredom and malice have been erased from *American Graffiti*, along with misery and ecstasy—all the real, untidy ingredients of adolescent experience. For him, it's indicative of Lucas's bland, wholesome ideology that so many TV series sprang from the film with relatively little dilution.[25]

Like *American Graffiti*, Barry Levinson's *Diner* is an evocative coming-of-age tale, whose characters belong to the director's generation. Unlike *American Graffiti*, *Diner* is an autobiographical film made by an insider who gets the texture right, without nostalgia. Set in Baltimore, the film captures the mood of 1959 with authentic minutiae. Centering on young men who can't communicate with women, it provides a look at the sex battle just before the sexual revolution. As Pauline Kael has observed, *Diner* shows the sexual dynamics in the last period of American history when people could laugh (albeit uneasily) at the gulf between men and women, before the gulf became a public issue to be discussed. The movie isn't so much about sex as about the quest for sex, the obsession with making out.[26]

A critical success that suffered from studio indifference, *Diner* later gained a cult following thanks to its disarming quality and its sharp writing. With a growing positive word of mouth, through television showings and video rentals, *Diner* entered the collective consciousness and became a breakout kind of American art movie. Showing true fondness for actors, Levinson brought sympathy and verve to a slice-of-life movie that is full of interesting characters. Like Lucas, Levinson helped to discover new talent: Mickey Rourke, Kevin Bacon, Daniel Stern, Steve Guttenberg, Ellen Barkin.

Inspired by Fellini's *I Vitelloni*, *Diner* revolves around six men in their twenties who have been buddies since high school. Although moving in different directions, they still cling to their late night sessions at the Fells Point Diner, which is like a comedy club, with the boys as storytellers, taking off from each other. Levinson doesn't write like Neil Simon—his natural conversation is composed of overlapping jokes that are funny without punch lines. He shows a sensitive ear for nuanced dialogue with a lyrical intensity that lifts the lines right out of the situation and transcends it.

The boys go out on dates but then quickly dash back to the diner, where they always have plenty to talk about. When the boys are out with girls, they're nervous, constricted, insecure; they can't be the same with women as they are with one another. At the diner, where conversations roll on all night, they're so relaxed that they even sound bright and witty. Shrevie (Daniel Stern) has nothing to say to his wife, Beth (Ellen Barkin), a crass, ordinary, yet sensitive girl. Shrevie, who works in a store selling TV sets and refrigerators, asks her not to play his records because she gets them mixed up. The records represent his sacred private world, and it's slipping away from him. Shrevie's outbursts leave Beth emotionally devastated.

Eddie (Steve Guttenberg) lives for football and the Baltimore Colts. He's scheduled to get married on New Year's Eve, but only if his fiancee passes a football-trivia test. Eddie wants to make sure they'll be able to communicate after they're married. The bride's football exam, with her father judging the fairness of the scoring, is a piece of loony Americana that echoes Demme's TV games in *Melvin and Howard*.

The most charismatic guy is Boogie (Mickey Rourke), a gambler who's in trouble with his bookie. Boogie works in a beauty parlor but spends most of his time at the diner. He shows tenderness toward women, though he has no connection with them except sex. Loyal to his friends, Fenwick (Kevin Bacon) is a smart if self-destructive dropout who plays reckless jokes that get him arrested. When alone, he watches the College Bowl TV quiz show, beating all the contestants. Fenwick is so infantile that he goes out with a much younger girl. His father won't bail him out of jail; it's the others who take care of him and shield him.

Levinson doesn't pretend to know everything about his characters, and he avoids summing them up. Contrary to most Hollywood youth movies, *Diner* is so richly detailed that even the parents, who were left out of *American Graffiti*, are as multilayered as their kids. Levinson has influenced many indie directors through his emphasis on dialogue rather than plot, characterization rather than visual style. Unlike Lucas, who's always been enamored with toys, comic books, and special effects, as evidenced in the *Star Wars* and the Indiana Jones series, Levinson is a "sociological" director, a storyteller with fresh perspective and a good ear, but one with less impressive visual perception.

Several coming-of-age indies were inspired by Lucas and Levinson, although the influence mainfested itself in the 1990s rather than 1980s.

WALKING AND TALKING

No one should complain about dialogue-driven films, the missing element from mainstream Hollywood, assuming, of course, that the characters are not self-absorbed and that the themes of their banter go beyond their libidos. Louis Malle's brilliantly engaging *My Dinner With Andre* (1981) demonstrated what could be done with talk. The film is about two men (Andre Gregory and Wallace Shawn) who converse about a limitless range of issues: freedom, selling out—and food. Like the film's sensual food, the philosophical banter made viewers want to have red wine, quail—and smart talk. In the mid-1990s, several tyro directors embarked on what could be described as confessional serio-comedies about love, courtship, and romance, movies that favored talk over action, emotion over irony. The new trend showed the compulsion of young filmmakers to bare their souls, their willingness to take a risk with self-indulgent narcissism.[27]

Bodies, Rest & Motion (1993), Michael Steinberg's first solo feature (after codirecting *The Waterdance*) concerns a quartet of late-twentysomethings suspended between teeny-boppers and baby boomers in the malls of recession-ridden America. Plotless, the film is all anemic chat among its four characters. A bored salesman, Nick (Tim Roth), and his girlfriend, a waitress named Beth (Bridget Fonda), are unsure about their relationship, while Nick's former girl, now Beth's best friend (Phoebe Cates), and their house painter (Eric Stoltz) dispense common sense. The staccato dialogue is meant to echo the restless uncertainty of the characters. Some scenes are acutely observed, but there are no real insights into the characters' states of mind.

The Boston-based filmmaker Brad Anderson's *The Darien Gap* (1996) is one of the smartest, most iconoclastic of the Gen-X pictures. A personal film of postcollegiate entropy and emotional blockage, it speaks with as strong a voice as Levinson's. In outline, the narrative sounds like a compendium of clichés about the slacker generation. It centers on a penniless hero, Lyn Vaus (played by an actor of the same name), a layabout with a command of language and vague notion of making a documentary on his generation.

Lyn, who finds artistic release in recording his buddies talking about their problems and lack of prospects, plans to go to Patagonia, at the tip of South America, in search of a giant sloth that might be his animal world counterpart. The problem is how to get through the Darien Gap, an eighty-mile Panamian swamp that interrupts the road. Lyn shows up regularly in Boston's hip place, where he meets Polly Joy (Sandi Carroll), a vivacious fashion designer, who "interferes" with his ambitions. Polly, who doesn't mind paying for Lyn's drinks, is intrigued by the challenge of reforming Lyn, for whom the idea of commitment is like being in a mental institution.

What compromises *The Darien Gap* is Lyn's dwelling on past family problems—he is still bruised by his parents' divorce twenty years ago. Using a time-jumping scheme, Anderson records the couple's relationship, showing home movies of Lyn's idyllic Connecticut childhood before the divorce, his problems with his distant father, and a sampling of local Boston bands.

Despite the title, Ted Demme's *Beautiful Girls* is about immature guys preparing for their ten-year high school reunion. The young men know it's time to face adulthood but are clueless as to how to go about it. The film follows them as they work their way through various crises, the catalyst being Willie (Timothy Hutton), a struggling pianist who retreats to Knight's Ridge, a New England town buried in snow.

The returning prodigal son, who has been living in New York playing piano in bar lounges, has an uncommitted romance with Tracy (Annabeth Gish), whom he describes as "a solid 7 ½ on a scale of 1 to 10) in body, looks, and personality." Willie is torn between the romance with his lawyer girlfriend and his attraction to Marty (Natalie Portman), a precocious thirteen-year-old girl who lives next door. Age difference aside, Willie and Marty are well matched—"Romeo and Juliet, the dyslexic version," as she says. The irony, of course, is that they can't be together. Willie needs to decide whether he can settle for someone who's not perfect, whether to give up piano, and whether to wait another five years until Marty comes of age.

A snowplow driver, Tommy (Matt Dillon), a former jock who is disappointed in the way his life has turned out, breaks the heart of his patient girl, Sharon (Mira Sorvino), by fooling around with the married Darian (Lauren Holly), his high school flame. Tommy needs to end the affair and commit himself to one woman. Another suspended adolescent is the loutish Paul (Michael Rapaport), who talks endlessly about the supermodels and pinups on his wall. He, too, needs to recognize his limitations and accept his relationship with Jan (Martha Plimpton), a waitress.

John Powers has observed that American pop culture specializes in two kinds of small towns: Mid-American Babylons like *Twin Peaks*, where Mom's apple pie is wriggling with worms, and sitcom pipe dreams, aglow with decency.[28] Despite its brawls and infidelities, Knight's Ridge is of the second kind. Demme shows affection for small-town rituals: ice-fishing huts, intimate cafes where waitresses know customers by name, bars where people sing Neil Diamond tunes. But Demme also knows that such towns can paralyze men like Willie, keeping them in a state of perpetual adolescence.

Written by Scott Rosenberg, whose script for *Things to Do in Denver When You're Dead* was full of fake macho bravado, *Beautiful Girls* celebrates the crude poetry of male bonding while keeping the women in the background, waiting. Wildly immature, the men must learn to stop idealizing "beautiful girls" and commit themselves to the real women around them. To grow up, they need outside help, which is provided by Andrea (Uma Thurman), a beautiful visitor from Chicago, who can talk sports and drink whiskey just like the boys.

Reflecting a distinctly male sensibility, the film is full of women who are narrowly conceived: the adulterous Darian is bitchy and selfish, the weepy Sharon is dubbed "one of the good ones," Jan and Tracy are kind, Marty is a Lolita who quotes Shakespeare, and Andrea represents the ultimate desirable woman: gorgeous and smart like a guy. The quintet serves as adornment to a threadbare tale of men's bafflement in the face of woman. The only glimpse of how the women view the men is offered by Rosie O'Donnell, who delivers a show-stopping monologue about males' fantasies about female anatomy.

An ensemble piece about ennui-ridden slackers at loose ends, Steve Chbosky's *The Four Corners of Nowhere* is yet another film that aims to provide an authentic portrait of Gen-X values. With some satirical humor, Chbosky explains the aimlessness of his generation, caught between the 1960s hippies and the 1980s yuppies.[29] A low-budget, collectivist effort, the movie was shot in twenty-three days on the Ann Arbor campus of the University of Michigan. Recalling *American Graffiti*'s Wolfman Jack, and acting like Greek chorus, is a campus radio deejay who uses his program to rail at the 1960s as "nothing more than a bad movie with a great soundtrack," taking potshots at those of his generation who subscribe to political correctness.

Duncan (Mark McClain Wilson), a pensive, withdrawn student, is picked up hitchhiking by Toad (Eric Vesbit), a drug-loving 1960s throwback. Arriving in Ann Arbor, they invade the household of Toad's sister, Jenny (Amy Raasch), an aspiring singer who lives with a yuppie law student Calvin (Aaron Williams) and works at the local café. Jenny imposes her self-centeredness on her customers with touchy-feely environment songs. There's also Hank (David Wilcox), an artist who suffers from a creative block. Duncan and Jenny are a bland, uninspiring pair: He's a relatively inert personality who fancies himself a modern Rimbaud.

Noah Baumbach's precocious style and attractive cast are most suited for *Kicking and Screaming* (1996), his uncompromising take on guys who just can't let go of college and get on with their lives, an issue also addressed in *Beautiful Girls* and *Swingers*. Mixing the neurotic drive of Woody Allen with the urbane cleverness of Whit Stillman, *Kicking and Screaming* strikes a cheerful note. Chris Eigeman provides the link to Stillman's work, having appeared in *Metropolitan*, *Barcelona*, and *The Last Days of Disco*. Though familiar, *Kicking and Screaming* benefits from the director's keen recollection of what it's like to be smart, promising and adrift.

Making his debut at age 25, the Brooklyn-born director (whose mother is the film critic Georgia Brown) previously worked as a messenger at the *New Yorker*. Written with dexterity (and financed for $1.3 million), this satire examines the impact of changing times and shifting notions of work and friendship on bright, hopelessly neurotic youngsters.

Kicking and Screaming is a comedy of manners about four college graduates and the crowded knot of girlfriends, housemates, and assorted hangers-on who make up their surrogate extended family in a university town. Once again, the film revisits the alienating aftermath of college. When we first meet them at their graduation party, the quartet doesn't seem to have a clue about life after college; it clings with

pathos to what's familiar and comfy—the past. The graduates face uncertainty because of changes in their goals and in the times. As always,
the most poignant remarks are made by women. Though well-spoken
and erudite, the foursome not only talk alike but behave as if they were
still in school. It takes time to distinguish Grover (Josh Hamilton) from
Max (Chris Eigeman), Skippy (Jason Wiles), and Otis (Carlos Jacott), because they resemble one another physically. As in *The Darien Gap*, the father figure is prominent, but here Grover's father (Elliott Gould) is as
open and friendly as his son is self-absorbed.

Baumbach doesn't try to work up sympathy for his characters, who
spend their time at a local bar, presided over by Chet (Eric Stoltz), a
permanent student who epitomizes the protracted limbo of self-in-
flicted misery; only Otis finds a job, at a video store. Most of the time,
they worry about the future, obsess over the past, and trade wisecracks.
Kicking and Screaming is punctuated with flashbacks of Grover's longing memories of Jane (Olivia d'Abo), a radiant woman he let go, and on-
screen announcements like "Spring Break." The other women are
Miami (Parker Posey), who has outgrown Skippy, and a vivacious adolescent (Cara Buono). All three women are more grown up than the
men, which is the film's main point. Critics who dismissed the film
drew unfavorable comparisons with Kevin Smith's *Clerks* and the TV
series "Friends."

With its movie references and self-analytical dialogue, Baumbach's
follow-up, *Mr. Jealousy* (1997), a romantic comedy about an emotional
klutz consumed by jealousy over his girlfriend's ex-boyfriend, was imitative of Woody Allen. Technically more accomplished than Baumbach's first feature, it displays the same insider's tone: from the spoken
opening credits, through the use of Georges Delerue's music for Truffaut's *Jules and Jim*, to a voiceover narration that intones, "This is the
story of Lester and Ramona," to a lead character who takes his date to
see Renoir's *Rules of the Game*. Populated by people with too much spare
time and not enough to do, it is a knowingly referential movie.

Lester (Eric Stoltz), a former CNN producer and sometime substitute teacher, has drifted through life as a professional wannabe. He just
can't seem to make the right decisions, for example, whether to attend
Iowa University's writing program. Through friends, he's met the up-
front Ramona (Annabella Sciorra). Lester suffers from an uncontrollable jealousy—not so much over Ramona's twenty-six previous
boyfriends (echoing *Clerks*'s monologue about thirty-seven blow jobs)

as over her recent boyfriend, the arrogant best-selling author Dashiell (Eigeman). Consumed by suspicions, he joins Dashiell's therapy
group to discover whether the writer still loves her. The plot is clever,
but there are dull scenes—those with Dashiell's shrink (played by
Peter Bogdanovich)—and the overly long movie is also uncertain of its
ending.

The Pompatus of Love (1996), cowritten by Jon Cryer, Adam Oliensis
and Richard Schenkman, who also directed, is yet another movie about
a male quartet suffering through painful transition to maturity and
adulthood. "Some people call me the space cowboy," Steve Miller sings
in "The Joker," and it's the song's line about the "pompatus of love"
that serves as the film's title and inspiration. Four New Yorkers share
their innermost thoughts and engage in an endless journey into adult
angst, focusing specifically on the inscrutability of women. They seem
fated to remain young. In the manner of *Diner*, Schenkman uses quick
cuts between characters, allowing them to tell the same story and finish
one another's sentences.

At the center are the bonding rituals of Mark (Jon Cryer), Josh
(Adrian Pasdar), Phil (Adam Oliensis), and Runyon (Tim Guinee): vis-
iting a topless bar, meeting a playwright (Roscoe Lee Browne) who's
also pursuing younger women. Not much happens, except for Runyon's meeting with a TV producer in Los Angeles. Mark strives to be the
"evolved human" he writes about in his feel-good books. As in *Beautiful Girls* and *Kicking and Screaming*, the women (played by Kristen Scott
Thomas, Paige Turco, Jennifer Tilly, and Mia Sara) are far more intriguing than the men.

The Pallbearer (1997) follows David Schwimmer (of TV's *Friends*) as
an awkward twentysomething who officiates at the funeral of a school
acquaintance he doesn't even remember. It's a movie about "excruciating embarrassment, loneliness, loss and longing—a sad comedy, decidedly not hip, ironic, or detached as Tarantino's work." There's a large
measure of autobiography in *The Pallbearer*. Reeves, like his hero, once
officiated as a pallbearer at the funeral of a stranger, though he didn't
sleep with the dead man's mother. *The Pallbearer* was inspired by bitter
personal experience, but it was workshopped and then substantially
rewritten.

The most commercially successful film of the cycle was *Swingers*
(1996), a diverting comedy that recalls *Diner* and other classic hang-

ing-out movies. Directed with flair by Doug Liman and wittily writ-ten by Jon Favreau, *Swingers* is a coming-of-age comedy about unem-ployed showbiz types. It depicts the tribal rituals of singlehood and romantic success in the 1990s, the pleasures and terrors of life after dark: how to approach a girl at the right moment, how not to be too tentative or too aggressive, how not to call too soon after getting a girl's phone number.

Mike (Favreau) a newly landed actor in Hollywood, is still aching for the girl he left behind. Trent (Vince Vaughn), his smooth-operator friend, is a Dean Martin type. The pair, along with their faux-hipster buddies, roam the scene, toss back drinks, and sniff skirts. Occasionally, Trent steels his nerve and talks to the local talent, but not Mike, a forlorn comic who mostly pouts. Mike's friends try to help him overcome his romantic longing and his addiction to his answering machine and video games.

Manohla Dargis has perceptively pointed out that *Swingers* is im-plicitly homoerotic. As usual, what counts aren't the girls but the boys, their sweet-clumsy ways in which they make love to one an-other without ever shedding their clothes.[30] Liman covers parties and back-alley lounges, staging satirical allusions to *Reservoir Dogs*, *Good-Fellas*, and *Saturday Night Fever*, capturing, as Owen Gleiberman has noted, something hilariously touching—a new wistful attitude among macho cruisers.[31]

Swingers, said director Liman, was "the first film to address the pol-itics of answering machine and how it is now part of the dating cul-ture." Answering machines also feature prominently in Nicole Holofcener's *Walking and Talking* and Hal Salwen's *Denise Calls Up*, a ro-mantic comedy about New York yuppies who are always on the tele-phone. Said Holofcener, "Answering machines are a huge part of your life, especially when you're dating and you're living alone in New York."

Liman, who made *Swingers* for $250,000 and then sold it for $5 mil-lion to Miramax, consciously put his friends and their lingo onscreen: "We have a certain lingo that we use, which only means something to us, but it is infectious. When other people hear it, they start using it too." Holofcener also admitted that the lovelorn heroine in *Walking and Talking* is based on herself. "I do take my own life—but I leave out plenty—anything that makes me look too horrible. Amelia is somewhat pathetic, needy. If I can get a beautiful actress like Catherine Keener to play me and make people laugh, then I don't feel embarrassed about what is personal." Set in the West Village, *Walking and Talking* idealizes New York as a cozy little village with no violence and no harassment on the street.

CONCLUSION

Alan Taylor's *Palookaville* owes its existence to Levinson's classic, *Diner*, as well as to the film that inspired *Diner*, Fellini's masterpiece, *I Vitelloni* (1953). The three New Jersey layabouts in *Palookaville* make the loose-ends Los Angeles guys in *Swingers* seem motivated by comparison. The movie is about the serio-comic adventures and hapless doings of would-be romantics and would-be toughs who botch everything they do. Scripted by David Epstein and based on Italo Calvino's short stories, *Palookaville* is inspired more by Italian than by American pictures. The filmmakers credit Mario Monicelli's heist movie, *Big Deal on Madonna Street* (about a grand pawn shop heist that goes awry), and Rachel Portman's music recalls Nino Rota's scores for Fellini's movies. But the most immediate inspiration comes from *I Vitelloni*, which deals with a bunch of guys who have hung around the neighborhood for too long.

The film's novelty is the stronger female presence. The women have more sense than the "self-unemployed" men, who are always looking for a way out of their mundane lives. "Boys don't always grow up," says the acerbic hooker June (Frances McDormand). "They age, they put on weight, they lose hair, they grow lumps and warts, they have regrets, lose their tempers and they blame women, but they do not automatically grow up and become men."

Rejected by his wife, Sid (William Forsythe), the loneliest of the trio, lives with his dogs in an apartment he's about to get evicted from. By chance he meets Enid (Bridgit Ryan), who works in a thrift store. Jerry (Adam Trese) is married to Betty (Lisa Gay Hamilton), who supports the family, and they have a baby, but Jerry is the actual boy. Russ (Vincent Gallo), the self-styled leader, lives with his bullying mother, his sister, and his brother-in-law, a surly cop. Russ is not adult enough to acknowledge his involvement with a teenage girl who lives across the alley; he sneaks through the bedroom window when she signals that the coast is clear. Russ also gets thrown out of June's house whenever a paying customer appears.

Palookaville begins with a heist of a jewelry store that goes disastrously wrong, leading the guys to discuss whether they are cut out for a criminal career. "Don't think of it that way," says Russ. "It's just a momentary shift in lifestyles." Taylor's compassionate humanism is reflected in his sweet-natured heroes, New Jersey bozos who can't help but be good samaritans. The unemployed factory workers, who break into a doughnut shop after mistaking it for a jewelry store, talk endlessly about their respective love interests.

Basically bumbling clowns who are not craving to score big, they are naive, antimacho boys in a way that deviates from the typical American male characterization. Hence, instead of using machine guns, they plan to use orange plastic toy pistols. As preparation for the robbery of an armored car carrying cash from a local supermarket, they rent an obscure 1950 movie, *Armored Car Robbery*. Their outlandish scheme involves tinkering with the vehicle's overheated radiator at a particular location and then attacking the truck with their toys.

Each character is a comically eccentric sad sack: Russ is an inept ladies' man; Sid is a dog lover whose attempts at running a taxi service for the elderly fail when customers refuse to sit next to his stinking animals; dreamy Jerry is a reluctant tag-along whose wife Betty works in the supermarket that uses the armored car service. During the initial caper, the boys chisel their way through a brick wall and find themselves in a bakery; unfazed, Jerry puts some pastries under his coat as a surprise for Betty.

The drab, working-class world these inept thieves inhabit feels more like a small Italian town in the 1950s than a decaying New Jersey industrial city, which may explain why the movie failed commercially. This dislocation derives from the source material: Calvino's stories were more relevant in war-ravaged Italy. As Stephen Holden has noted, *Palookaville* ends on a sweetly ironic note, the staple of European caper films, with its old-time movie nostalgia and goofy fun intact.

8

Drama

Challenging Stereotypes

AMERICAN MOVIES RARELY debate the political problems of the day. This may stem from a mistrust of power and authority, which has been a pervasive strand in American life. Uncomfortable with politics, Americans like to think of themselves as being outside or above politics—which is why politicians continue to play their outsidedness.[1] The only "political movies" that continue to be made are those about big, powerful corporations covering up conspiracies, because the American public likes the notion of heroic individuals pitted against cruel and impersonal forces.

Indeed, some ideas about society and politics have remained permanent in American films. Prominent among these is the value of individualism: Film after film suggests that any problem, political or economic, can be resolved by a charismatic individual.[2] American films tell viewers that ordinary people can make a difference by rising up to challenges and fighting the system effectively. But "ordinary" in Hollywood terms means casting a role with attractive and powerful stars like Jane Fonda, Robert Redford, or Tom Cruise.

Action in American movies is always individual, seldom collective. Bad individuals and greedy corporations are blamed, but not the system as a whole. The message of the few socially conscious films made is limited, because they locate problems in individuals, not in the society at large. Movies seldom question the system itself, seldom raise issues that are not resolvable. At best, they point to a need for an occasional action to regulate or to correct what's essentially a well-functioning structure. And since there's always a heroic individual to take care of problems, most movies are reassuring rather that provocative—all viewers have to do is sit and watch passively.

Moreover, mainstream movies are uneasy with displaying any extreme ideology, which means that their narratives are centrist, presenting issues within accepted parameters. Hollywood films steer clear of taking a specific stand because they don't want to offend any segment of their potential audience. Psychologist Krin Gabbard has observed that, if anything, American films tend to the right, because the right is in favor of maintaining the status quo: "Filmmakers are nervous about undermining the status quo. They want people to walk out of the theaters feeling their lives are O.K., and that has to do with nuclear family and capitalist economy."[3]

For most people, political movies concern political parties and affiliations: right versus left, Republican versus Democrat. What they fail to realize is that every action and relationship has a political dimension if "political" is defined in terms of power and influence. The exclusion of ideology reduces all motives to self-interest and trivializes politics. American movies have supported the status quo through narrowing the political spectrum, insisting that the political process works. Movies that lean to the left are often perceived as radical simply for raising relevant issues (e.g., nuclear power, racism, greed, and corruption).[4]

American movies are liberal in intent, but not in effect. They reinforce faith in the system, endorsing rather than criticizing it. The cautious nature of American films is a direct result of Hollywood's blind commitment to entertainment. Obsessed with the box-office, the ultimate measure of success, filmmakers aim to please audiences, who expect to be entertained because movies have trained them to do so. Accustomed to shallow TV fare, viewers grow impatient with subtle movies of ideas, favoring action over talk, slick and mindless entertainment over disturbing provocation.

The studios' primary responsibility is to make money for their shareholders, which results in every picture's being weighed as a "moneymaking machine." American movies are profit-driven ventures that rely on the investment of banks and insurance companies, institutions that are inherently conservative. Moreover, as director Phil Alden Robinson (*Field of Dreams*) observed, "the studios are guided by foreign sales, and domestic politics is a very tough sell. The stuff that translates well is big action and star-driven movies."[5] Demographics also play a role, as screenwriter Frank Pierson (*Dog Day Afternoon*) explained: "The studios' principal interest is gratifying an audience that is defined by

14-to-24-year-old males, who are by nature the least political of animals."[6]

"To open movies wide," said John Sayles, "you're talking about 'elements,' which must be some kind of genre or plot or stars that people are dying to see." But the heavy reliance on movie stars necessarily tones down American movies. Stars radically alter a film's message: Imagine *All the President's Men* without Robert Redford and Dustin Hoffman, *Reds* or *Bulworth* without Warren Beatty, *Saving Private Ryan* without Tom Hanks. A close-up of Jane Fonda's face, instead of a long shot of a nuclear reactor in *The China Syndrome*, distorts filmgoers' perception of the issue. By focusing on one person, films individualize everything, losing sight of the broader sociopolitical context.

The collapse of the studio system has made it easier for independent filmmakers to make overtly political movies. Yet avoidance of political movies is one of the anomalies of contemporary indie cinema. John Sayles and Spike Lee may be the only major independents to make overtly political films, and left-leaning at that. Like their Hollywood counterparts, indie filmmakers elude probing issues, which explains the paucity of films about racial strife, class disparity, sexual harassment, and other social ills.

Indie cinema has not been an "engaged" art form, to borrow Jean-Paul Sartre's concept, indie directors don't see their primary role as bearing witness to contemporary life. Like Hollywood filmmakers, they are afraid that dealing with burning issues would mean sending "messages," and American audiences have proved time and again their reluctance to embrace serious movies, even if they concern worthy issues such as slavery. Hence, the lukewarm reception accorded Steven Spielberg's *Amistad* (1997) and the failure of Jonathan Demme's *Beloved* (1998).

Quite disappointingly, most issue-oriented indies have dealt with one institution: the family. In a critical piece, Mary C. Henderson reproached American dramatists for their narrow dramatic focus: "The world is too large a place, too teeming with the stuff of drama, and the table too small a human zone for playwrights to continue to rely on such a restrictive dramatic device."[7] Henderson finds it alarming that the playwrights' world has shrunk to the size of a tabletop, the claustrophobic milieu of the American family. Henderson's comments on the theater can easily be applied to films, both Hollywood and indie: The American family remains the center of our national concern.

GROWING UP AND THE FAMILY

Most coming-of-age movies tend to be comedies and revolve around boys. However, a number of poignant coming-of-age dramas concern female adolescents. A memoir of growing up in Las Vegas in the early 1950s, *Desert Bloom* (1986) is an earnest film developed at the Sundance Institute, the kind of virtuous fare in which public television has specialized. Although made by a man, Eugene Corr, a Bay Area documentarian, the movie feels like an authentic chronicle of a girl's maturation. The thirteen-year-old Rose (Annabeth Gish) lives with her kid sisters, her affectionate mom, Lily (JoBeth Williams), and her troubled stepfather, Jack (Jon Voight). When her Aunt Starr (Ellen Barkin), a good-time girl, moves in to establish residence for divorce, she becomes Rose's mentor.

The movie is set in the Nevada desert, circa 1950, during the government testing of the A-Bomb. Corr shows a satirical eye for the innocence of the "American bomb culture," the excitement generated by the tests. At a promotional event, girls vie for the title of Miss A-Bomb, and a radio announcer, hyping a casino, says, "You don't have to wait for the A-bomb to catch the show!" At the climax, mothers wake up their children to watch the blast, as a mushroom cloud, basked in purple light, rises over the desert.

The adult world is represented by Jack, a war hero who suffers from emotionally draining flashbacks to earlier battles. An alcoholic, as well as a rabid anti-Communist and anti-Semite, Jack is portrayed as a limited man, a paranoiac whose experience has left him mean and violent. Early on, Jack prevents Rose from going to a party, accusing her of breaking his radio. When Rose tells him he is being unfair, he slaps her, which forces her to wear sunglasses to cover her bruises. As David Denby has pointed out, Jack's rejection forces Rose to come to terms with adult anger at its most cruel and unreasonable.[8] The filmmakers don't try to understand Jack: A borderline clinical case, he's a mystery even when he finally shows some sensitivity to Rose.

The film's female characters are weak and submissive. Aunt Starr sits around painting her toenails; she's a sexy woman who's as desperate as she is kind. Winsome mom is patient until she, too, loses her temper. Strong and adaptable, Rose passes her youth in the shadow of the bomb, but Corr intimates that she will emerge stronger because of her childhood's uncertainties and cruelties. The opening scene, in which

Rose has her eyes examined, introduces vision as a recurrent motif. As David Edelstein has noted, the glasses are at first a badge of pride, then a means of taking in too much and a cover for bruises, and in the climax, a way for the stepfather to prove he cares.[9]

The film is framed by the narration of its grown up protagonist. The title is ironic, alluding to the bomb as well as to the young heroine—both are a desert bloom. Rose says in her narration that she loves the wild flowers that grow in the hardest places. In this picture, the bomb is used as a symbol of hope: When the bomb goes off, it rises in the sky like a rose amidst cactuses. With its depiction of shattered dreams and self-delusions, the film is a family drama in the vein of O'Neill or Tennessee Williams. But despite symbolic richness, *Desert Bloom* is not cinematic enough; most of the film is set within the house, which makes it constricted.

One of the most controversial indies of the 1980s was Tim Hunter's *River's Edge* (1987), based on an actual incident in Northern California. The film addresses the alienation and moral vacancy among American kids growing up in a drug-oriented, valueless culture. *River's Edge* has the disturbing quality of a collective fear—the cherished, eagerly awaited adolescence is presented as confusing and vacuous. Unlike most 1980s teenage sex comedies, this film doesn't glamorize youth, instead depicting it as a bleak, aimless coming of age, a time of boredom, stupor, and waste.[10]

The narrative begins at the river, here not the peaceful, pastoral place where small-town movie heroes usually flee to relax. Muddy, gray, and ominous, the river is the scene of a crime. Tim (Joshua Miller), a young boy, stands on a bridge, slowly dropping his sister's doll into the water. Across the bridge, another crime has taken place: Samson, nicknamed John (Daniel Roebeck), stares calmly at the nude body of his girlfriend, Jamie, whom he has murdered on a whim. A link is immediately established between Jamie and the drowned doll: Which act is meaner; which has left more impact on its perpetrator?

The scene soon becomes a touristic sight: The discovery of a dead body is not a shocking experience. Like *Stand by Me*, the film shows the fascination of seeing a dead body for the first time. John takes his friends to see Jamie's body, and they all stand transfixed by the sight, but no one moves or suggests calling the police. No one shows an emotional reaction, not even outrage. John doesn't apologize; he coolly explains that Jamie "upset" him.

Layne (Crispin Glover), a high-strung, self-proclaimed leader, believes in protecting the group's spirit at all costs. Perceiving loyalty as a sacred value, Layne is convinced that it's the group's duty to cover up the murder. He reasons that since Jamie is already dead, nothing can be done about it, but John is alive and needs their help. Layne would use any argument to persuade his mates of the need for loyalty. "Why do you suppose the Russians are gearing up to take us over?" he charges, expressing general disgust with weak Americans.

Contrasted with Layne is Matt (Keanu Reeves), who finally goes to the police. Except for this act, Matt is no different from the others: he smokes dope, skips school, and even "steals" Layne's girl. Director Hunter was intrigued by the moral paradox inherent in a situation in which the bad guy stands for loyalty and the good one is a stool pigeon who betrays his friends. Matt is only slightly more sympathetic than the others. When the police ask why it took him so long to report the crime, all he says is, "I don't know." "How do you feel about it?" the cop inquires. "Nothing," Matt says with disturbing honesty. A classmate, Clarissa (Ione Skye) is also unable to filter her feelings. "I cried when that guy died in *Brian's Song* [a TV movie]," she says. "You'd figure I'd at least be able to cry for someone I hung around with." Times have changed, and TV melodramas seem to exert greater effect on their viewers than reality itself.

Matt's twelve-year-old brother, Tim, is desperate to join Matt's group. The film draws a parallel between Tim, who "kills" his sister's doll, and John, who murders his girl. Judging by their motivation—or reaction—there is no significant difference. A parallel is also established between John and the psychotic Feck (Dennis Hopper), who keeps an inflatable doll in his house as a reminder of the girl he had killed. Ironically, the only adult to possess any humanity is Feck, a crazed loner who shows regret and at least feels something; John is incapable of any feeling. "Did you love her?" asks Feck, only to be outraged by John's nonchalance: "She was O.K."

In most teenage films, the group is cohesive, but here, friendships are not based on any intimate interaction or substance. What *River's Edge* does share with other youth films is its attitude toward adult figures, who are presented as irresponsible and indifferent. The kids are left to their own devices, with no role models from the adult world. Matt's father has disappeared, and his mother now lives with a brutish lover who is hated by the kids. Though engaged in nursing, a service profession, the mother cares more about her dope than her children. The family doesn't spend a single evening together; home is a place to be when there's nothing else to do. The 1960s hippie generation is also ridiculed; its representative schoolteacher tries to excite his apathetic students with stories of activism—"We took to the streets and made a difference"—but he's perceived by them as a caricature.

When Miramax slipped *Kids* (1995) into Sundance as an unannounced midnight screening, it immediately became the talk of the festival, and the most controversial film that year. Produced by Gus Van Sant, the movie marks the directorial debut of the noted photographer Larry Clarke. The clandestine screening, combined with Clarke's penchant for lurid subject matter, created a sensation. In its bold, candid approach to sex and drugs, *Kids* dwarfs most of Hollywood's youth movies and crosses the existing boundaries. For his bleak account of youth Clarke cast actual teenagers, not Hollywood actors, bringing a greater sense of horror and authenticity.

Set on a hot summer day, *Kids* is structured as a fast-paced twenty-four-hour chronicle of Manhattan kids who hang out on the streets looking for kicks, smoking pot, and guzzling booze. These kids are perpetually libidinous, and violence is an integral part of their lives: Gay baiting and black bashing are day-to-day occurrences. The opening scene observes Telly (Leon Fitzpatrick), a horny fourteen-year-old teenager, taking a naive blonde (Sarah Hendersen) to bed. As soon as the sex is over, the cocky kid hits the streets to boast to his buddies of his conquest. Telly's monologue about his obsession with virgins and his plan to score another conquest that night is unsettling precisely because it is so believable. In the afternoon, the kids head for a local pool for skinny-dipping and more sexual pranks. They finally crash at a friend's apartment, where they get high and drunk again, and another virgin is victimized by the careless seducer.

In an ultrafrank session, the girls discuss in vivid detail their favorite sexual positions. Jennie (Chloe Sevigny) admits to her friends that she has lost her virginity to Telly, the only guy she has ever slept with. With AIDS as constant threat, it's shocking when Jennie, the least promiscuous girl, is diagnosed as HIV-positive, after a one-time experience.

Raw and basically plotless, *Kids*'s graphic depiction of sex makes for an upsetting film, which is able to sustain a sense of horror and at the same time holds a voyeuristic fascination. It's one thing to read about teenage sex in *Time* magazine; it's another to see it on-screen. The middle-aged Clarke captures the values, speech, and sexual urges of his teenage characters. His intuitive understanding of angst—and libido— is no doubt helped by the fresh screenplay, written by the nineteen-year-old Harmony Korine.

The cinematographer, Eric Edwards, who has worked with Van Sant, uses a restlessly mobile camera to give the picture an improvisational feel; the cinema verité style is uncompromising. *Kids* achieves a remarkable feat: It is a polished film that feels like a documentary. Nonetheless, in its nonjudgmental view of its characters, *Kids* walks a fine line between a cautionary tale about unsafe sex and its undeniably voyeuristic and exploitative elements. *Kids* was picked up for $3 million by Miramax, whose aggressive marketing propelled the film to $7 million in box-office grosses. After Sundance's preview, two minutes were trimmed from the opening seduction scene, but the film still garnered an NC-17 rating. *Kids* never became the controversial "event" movie that Miramax hoped for, even after the Disney-owned company had to create a new label to release the film.

A starker, funnier and more poignant film than *Kids*, Todd Solondz's *Welcome to the Dollhouse* (1995), which premiered at Toronto and won the top prize at Sundance the following year, offers a sharply observed portrait of an adolescent's struggle to survive junior high. Though lacking the sensationalistic—and prurient—elements of *Kids*, *Welcome to the Dollhouse*, in its attention to detail and deliciously wicked humor, established itself as an instant classic about growing pains.

Dawn Wiener (Heather Matarazzo) is the middle child of a Jewish family in a Jersey suburb. Life is one continuous challenge for the unattractive, slump-shouldered misfit, who wears thick glasses and tacky clothes. As a seventh grader at Benjamin Franklin Junior High, she is tortured by the boys and girls who dub her "Wiener-dog." The first scene, set in the lunchroom, immediately suggests how reviled Dawn is. "Are you a lesbian?" asks a classmate, and before Dawn even has chance to respond, the whole group bursts out screaming, "Lesbo, lesbo."

Home doesn't provide much comfort, either. Her little sister, Missy, a ballerina dressed in a pink tutu, is clearly mom's favorite, and her older brother, Mark, a computer whiz and band leader, totally ignores her. Solondz challenges a sacred family value that is seldom questioned on-screen—that parents are expected to but might not always love their children equally. He also portrays sibling rivalry with uncharacteristic directness; late at night, Dawn saws the heads off her sister's dolls.

The narrative unfolds as a catalogue of mishaps—an unjust punishment at school, a denial of a favorite chocolate cake at dinner. Yet there's humor in even the most excruciating moments, as in a scene where Brandon (Brendan Sexton), the school's bad boy, threatens to rape Dawn, but the harassment is over when he realizes she has to be home at 4:30 and there's not enough time to execute his plan. Every creepy incident encountered by children in their transition to the more clearly defined high-school phase is conveyed with accuracy. Solondz refuses to sentimentalize his character or to pander to the audience. Dawn is not a Cinderella or an "ugly duckling" type, who, in the Hollywood tradition, removes her glasses and suddenly blossoms into a beautiful girl. Putting into effect the notion that deprivation is relative, Solondz shows how Dawn can be just as foul-mouthed as her tormenting peers: She turns against a sensitive boy who's tried to befriend her because he's a "faggot."

Solondz's look at the miseries of childhood is scathing and undoubtedly personal, but it contains a measure of universal truth. Assuredly directed, the film compensates for occasional lapses into melodrama (Missy's kidnap and Dawn's search for her in New York). Ideally cast, Heather Matarazzo has the look of a lonely girl desperate to be loved but also the resilient attitude of a survivor.

Solondz wrote *Welcome to the Dollhouse* after suffering through a miserable directorial debut, *Fear, Anxiety, and Depression* (released by Goldwyn in 1989), which, by his own admission, was misconceived. He told the *Los Angeles Times*:

> I wrote it six years ago, to redeem myself from the horror of what I'd
> been through, partially fueled by the success of *The Wonder Years*,
> which didn't speak to anything real in my experience. I hadn't seen an

English-language film that dealt with this material in an honest way that captured that period of life. Children are usually looked at as either cute or demonic, everything but what they really are—human beings.[11]

Solondz added, "What excites me and moves me are things that make me laugh and are poignant at the same time, where it's funny but touches something that hurts. As adults, we know what's truly a matter of life and death, but a child feels like the stakes are always high."

After the failure of his first film, Solondz switched to teaching English as a second language. Encroaching layoffs at school, and a call from his lawyer asking if he was still interested in directing, led to *Welcome to the Dollhouse*. Its world premiere in Toronto sparked a bidding war, which was won by Sony Classics. The film went on to become one of the year's most profitable indies, grossing close to $5 million.

Solondz continued to explore family life in middle-class America in *Happiness* (1998), a controversial film that premiered out of competition in Cannes, where it won the International Critics Award. It's based on the same strategy as *Welcome to the Dollhouse*, summed up by Solondz as "I am moved by what I find funny, and vice versa." The difference between the two movies is that the newer film had a "much more experienced production team and the lack of doubt that it was going to be finished."[12] Some of the most significant figures in independent cinema—Christine Vachon and Good Machine's Ted Hope—were involved. Good Machine self-released the movie when October, under pressure from its parent company, Universal, decided not to distribute it.

Drawing on his own upbringing, Solondz returns in *Happiness* to the fertile turf of American suburbia, sculpting a placid surface beneath which bizarre desires and anxieties are lurking. "We live in a country in which alienation is more acutely felt than anywhere else in the world," Solondz explained. "The family unity is not as tight as it is in Europe or certainly in the rest of the world."[13] Maintaining that "it is the daily fabric of your life that defines what your life is about, not Thanksgiving or Christmas," Solondz made a personal movie about desire, about people trying to reach out and connect.

The idea of structuring the film around three sisters—which recalls Chekhov as well as Woody Allen's *Hannah and Her Sisters*—was contrived to thread the different story lines together. Joy (Jane Adams) says she's getting better every day, but Mr. Right has not appeared yet. The married sister, Trish (Cynthia Stevensen), despairs that Joy will never "have it all," as she does. The third sister, Helen (Lara Flynn Boyle), is a best-selling author who has slipped into an angst that can be relieved only by kinky sex. Their parents are an aging couple falling apart: Mother ponders divorce while father longs for death, and the men in the sisters' lives are just as troubled.

One could argue, as Solondz does, that "a movie like *Happiness* can only come out of a society with a repressive culture, and yet there's nothing in the movie that isn't in the tabloids or talk shows."[14] The difference is that talk shows always have a moralistic voice, though that voice is always undercut by the exploitational treatment of the participants through close-ups, which create a titillating, freak-show atmosphere. Though deeply troubled, the characters in *Happiness* are not freaks: "I'm very invested emotionally in these characters, and at the same time, I have a kind of ironic detachment that enables me to laugh."

Also reflecting the zeitgeist of cynical portraits of dysfunctional families is Ang Lee's *The Ice Storm* (1997), based on Ron Moody's novel and adapted for the screen by Good Machine's James Schamus. Set in 1973, in upper-middle-class New Canaan, Connecticut, it depicts adulterous parents and jaded teenagers. Ben Hood (Kevin Kline), a commuter living in New Canaan, has achieved everything: a beautiful house, a seemingly happy marriage, two precocious kids, and even an affair with his next-door neighbor, Janey Carver (Sigourney Weaver). But a moral vacuum dominates New Canaan, just as it does the rest of the country. The pall of the Watergate scandal is in the background, with Nixon continually proclaiming his innocence on TV. The residents of New Canaan have achieved the American Dream, but the suburbs are infiltrated with late-1960s liberal notions of free love and sexual revolution. "Key parties," a form of wife swapping in which couples are randomly paired by drawing car keys from a bowl, are one sterile way in which the New Canaanites revel in their "hipness."

Entrapped in an unfulfilling marriage, Elena Hood (Joan Allen) is a product of a repressed generation, conditioned to become the loyal wife-mother. Elena is aware of the changing attitudes about women, but she is clueless as to what to do about it. There's no real communication in the Hood home; dinner conversations are truncated and awkward. Even Ben's affair with Janey feels halfhearted, a product of habit and the charm of secrecy rather than attraction. When Ben complains about his life, Janey coolly says, "You're boring me, Ben. I'm not your wife," then gets up and leaves him in mid-tryst.

The children follow in their parents' footsteps, emulating their aimless, disenchanted lives. The elder, Paul (Tobey Maguire), seems less damaged by changes in his parents' world, but his sexual frustrations and insecurities mirror those of his father, even as they are typical of boys his age. Pubescent Wendy Hood (Christina Ricci) is bewildered by her body's biological changes, but she is smart enough to know that she can manipulate boys with her body as she flirts with two of the Carver brothers.

The Ice Storm begins as a gentle satire that gradually changes into a serious drama about the inevitably tragic results of irresponsible behavior. Lee's earlier work (see Chapter 9) always featured a strong paternal character, but in *The Ice Storm*, the adults are just as confused and lost as their children. Without a moral center, the movie drifts along until it reaches its predictably sad conclusion. The tonal shift, as Andy Klein has noted, is a calculated device to lend the work more resonance, but it achieves the opposite effect, turning the movie into a more conventional family melodrama.[15]

With a budget of $16 million, *The Ice Storm* didn't fulfill commercial expectations. Nor did the similarly themed *The Myth of Fingerprints*, which was released the same year. Written and directed by Bart Freundlich, this solid drama revolves around a dysfunctional New England WASP family over the course of a Thanksgiving weekend. As Todd McCarthy said in his review, with middle-brow seriousness, *The Myth of Fingerprints* operates within a narrow emotional range that provides little surprise or excitement. Essentially high-toned television fare, it relies on the familiar theatrical format of a splintered family reuniting for a holiday gathering that inevitably results in the accentuation of frustrations and resentments and the unveiling of skeletons in closets and details of past unsavory actions.[16]

Just when it seemed that the American screen was exclusively preoccupied with dramas about dysfunctional families, a well-crafted "dramedy," *Big Night* (1996), swept writing awards in festivals and pleased the indie public. A lyrical love poem to food and family, the film reflects the belief of its protagonist, Primo, that "to eat good food is to be close to God." Like *Babette's Feast*, *Like Water for Chocolate*, and *Eat, Drink, Man, Woman*, *Big Night* cashes in, as Kenneth Turan observed, on the overlap between audiences for sophisticated indies and those for good restaurants.[17] The actor Stanley Tucci cowrote the script with his cousin, Joseph Tropiano, and codirected the film with Campbell Scott, who also plays a small part.

Determined to make it big in America, Secondo (Tucci) and his older brother, Primo (Tony Shalhoub), have emigrated from Italy. Set in the 1950s on the Jersey shore, *Big Night* centers on the Paradise restaurant, located amid Eisenhower-era philistines, who insist on spaghetti and meatballs and don't understand, as Primo says, that "sometimes spaghetti wants to be alone." Indeed, Primo's culinary genius, a great asset, turns out to be an impediment, for he is a perfectionist who refuses to lower his standards. Primo is continually shocked by American eating habits—"She's a criminal," he says, about a woman who orders spaghetti and risotto. Primo would like to believe that, "if you give people time, they will learn," but Secondo knows time is running out. Eager for a quicker, more conventional success, he has to battle his brother and the impatient bankers determined to foreclose on the Paradise. Stiff competition comes from a thriving neighboring restaurant, Pascal's Italian Grotto, the ultimate 1950s Italian restaurant, bathed in red lights like a bordello, with a glamorous hostess (Isabella Rossellini) and celebrity photos on the walls.

The volatile, contentious relationship between the brothers reflects an ear for the unintentionally poetic musings of people struggling with a foreign language. Though Primo hates his rival Pascal ("The man should be in prison for the food he serves"), Secondo envies his success. When Pascal offers help by convincing the celebrated musician Louis Prima to dine at the Paradise, Secondo accepts, and preparations for the big night begin. Of course, as in *Waiting for Guffman*, the eagerly awaited celeb never arrives. Warmhearted and bittersweet, the plot is simple, but the characterization is deft. With an understanding of the virtue of taking time in building mood, *Big Night* avoids the overindulgent performances that often damage movies directed by actors, such as John Turturro and Sean Penn.

RELIGIOUS AND SPIRITUAL REDEMPTION

"The Rapture is coming," reads the promotional tag line for *The Rapture* (1991), a film that deals with the apocalypse and other evangelical Christian tenets. The writer-director Michael Tolkin centers on a telephone operator (Mimi Rogers), who leads a wild, vacuous sex life. Tired of reckless sexual encounters, she suddenly converts to fundamentalist Christianity, reaching out to God and becoming "born again." The idea for *The Rapture* originated after Tolkin watched hours of "Christian TV," which made him sympathetic toward the fundamentalists' cause. "Their diagnosis seemed correct," he said, "but I disagreed with their prescription. Americans are obsessed with redemption—they are very scared."[18]

The film was conceived as a reaction to 1980s movies, which Tolkin believed, were turning audiences into a mass. "At the end of *Shampoo*, Warren Beatty is left alone and you identify with him. Compare that to *Rocky* and *Indiana Jones*, or *E.T.*, in which the audience is a violent mass, united against some scapegoat. Movies have become a 'lynch mob.'" Tolkin contrasts the new simplistic pictures to those that touched him as a kid, movies that "left you with your identity, with insight into yourself."[19]

Tolkin's indie, about a lost woman who finds temporary comfort through the discovery of God, stirred up controversy at the Telluride Festival, where it premiered. Tolkin made an audaciously disturbing movie, both pious and pitiless, that combined an unabashed avowal of the existence of God and a blood-curdling horror movie. Critics who supported the film saw it as a triumph of suspenseful storytelling, a personal revery.

The Rapture begins in a room full of telephone operators, each boxed in a little cubicle where she dispenses names and numbers. The protocol is boring, the faces attentive and vacuous, the voices hushed and affectless. A telephone worker, Sharon, cruises Los Angeles's airport and bars with her European partner, Vic, picking up couples for sex. The orgy scenes project the atmosphere of hard-core porn, without the hard-core content. One of Sharon's pickups, a youth named Randy, confesses that he has killed a man for money and she becomes awed by his capacity for evil.

At work, Sharon overhears some coworkers muttering about strange signs and coincidences related to the end of the world, the Apocalypse, and the Four Horsemen. She becomes consumed by her discovery and decides to forsake her hedonism. Randy, embracing her faith out of love for her, marries her, and they have a daughter. Leading a straight life, they rapturously await the end of time. Widowed by a hideous tragedy—Randy is shot in a mass killing—Sharon takes her daughter to the desert and waits for God. The critic Richard Alleva has suggested that *The Rapture* turns cruel in the way Flannery O'Connor stories do, punishing the characters for being shallow.[20]

In the last twenty minutes, the film breaks free and takes on a primitive force that recalls an *Outer Limits* or *Twilight Zone* episode. When God fails to keep his word, Sharon kills her daughter, then tries to kill herself. She speeds down the highway and gets arrested and put in jail, where she declares she no longer loves God. At this moment, the trumpet roars, and the Four Horsemen rise on a TV screen, interrupting a football game. Sharon, like *Shampoo*'s hero, is ambiguously left alone.

In the *Los Angeles Weekly*, Michael Ventura criticized Tolkin' staging and lighting, which invest every scene with "significance." Moreover, *The Rapture* suffers from trying to play it both ways: Sharon is deluded, yet the supernatural events she believes in begin to take shape in a twisted ending. Tolkin's offbeat thriller crosses into heretofore taboo spiritual territory, with viewers lauding or denouncing the picture for often contradictory reasons: Some nonbelievers thought it was pro-Christian, whereas born-again Christians found it offensive and blasphemous. Still others were upset that Christianity was portrayed as a cult, a New Age philosophy.

Fine Line marketed the picture as an intellectual-religious horror film, a *Close Encounters of the Religious Kind*, as its president, Ira Deutschman, noted. Deutschman explained that as many Christians have applauded *The Rapture* as have condemned it:

> The people who seem to care about the film the least are people who don't even think about religion and God, who just find discussion of those issues to be incredibly boring. Whereas anybody who has any thoughts of it whatsoever, on any end of the spectrum, who has any spirituality in their lives at all, appears to either love it or hate it in wildly unpredictable fashion.[21]

Deutschman thought there was "no reason" to court controversy because "it may serve to muddle the message of the film even further." It was easy for people to understand what the controversy was about with Scorsese's *The Last Temptation of Christ*, but *The Rapture* simply proved confusing. Dividing the critical establishment, *The Rapture* never became the controversial movie it was meant to be and, after a brief run, sank at the box office.

∎

The search for religious or spiritual redemption is also the subject of two major 1990s indies: *Dead Man Walking* and *The Apostle*. Tim Robbins made a quantum leap forward with *Dead Man Walking* (1995), a drama that explores the intimate relationship between a devout nun and a Death Row convict. A chamber piece for two, superbly acted by Susan Sarandon and Sean Penn, *Dead Man Walking* is marked by dense texture and rich characterization. Inspired by actual events and figures in Sister Helen Prejean's book, Robbins's movie defies the conventions of the Hollywood crime melodrama as well as those of the TV Movie of the Week.

Set in the St. Thomas Housing Project, the tale begins with a correspondence between Sister Helen Prejean (Sarandon), a pious but down-to-earth nun who lives amidst her poor constituency, and Matthew Poncelet (Penn), a convicted killer awaiting execution. Honoring his request, Sister Helen visits the convict in jail and agrees to become his spiritual adviser during his last days—a daring act never before attempted by a woman. With these parameters established and the countdown under way, a peculiar bond emerges between the courageous nun who's deeply disturbed by Poncelet's anguish and the criminal, who refuses to deal with his offense, a brutal murder of two innocent sweethearts. During the crucial week that frames the film, the two undergo emotional journeys that both parallel and complement each other. Fighting for Poncelet's life and soul, Sister Helen must overcome her own fears. Poncelet's path is even more rugged; he has to conquer his fear of death as well as come to grips with his sins and ask for forgiveness.

It's a measure of Robbins's intelligent treatment of tough material that, although the narrative unfolds in intimate interactions, the protagonists are not isolated from their surroundings. One of Sister Helen's challenges is to confront the rage of the victims' families, who are seeking retribution for their loss. In a riveting scene, she visits the murdered girl's parents, attentively listening to their *cri du coeur*. The couple assumes she's on their side, but when they realize she is making an effort to be fair to all the parties involved, they ask her to leave.

This scene illuminates Robbins's balanced, uncompromising approach, which refuses to judge any of the characters and gives all of them a chance to present their case with dignity and respect. Robbins's greatest achievement is in shaping an open-ended film without humanizing the killer. It's decidedly not the story of a wrongly accused murderer or of a "criminal with a heart." The events are seen through the nun's probing eyes, but the film presents multiple perspectives, allowing the audience a measure of freedom in interpreting the emotions that beset the characters.

Brief flashbacks of the rapes and murders are inserted with increasing frequency in the last reel, generating suspense as to which specific crimes Poncelet committed the night he and his buddy (who got life imprisonment because he was represented by a better lawyer) were partying in the woods. The manner in which the flashbacks are implanted—brief, partial snippets—also deviates from the more conventional use of lengthy images. Considering the stasis of the central situation—the nun and convict are divided by a partition—the film is highly absorbing. The lenser Roger Deakins gives the story a realistically unadorned look, which relies on tight closeups of Sarandon and Penn. Carefully etched, both performances build up to an emotionally satisfying denouement. Not since *I Want to Live!* Has there been a big-screen drama with such attention to the technicalities of execution, and Robbins surpasses the 1958 film with a chilling portrait of what it means to take a human life.

A labor of love reaching fruition after thirteen years, Robert Duvall's *The Apostle* (1997) is a sharply observed exploration of a preacher who embarks on a redemption odyssey after committing a crime. Financed, produced, written, and acted by Duvall, the film represents an indie triumph on every level.

A devout Pentecostal preacher from New Boston, Texas, Eulis "Sonny" Dewey (Duvall) lives a seemingly happy life with his wife Jessie (Farrah Fawcett) and his two children. In an early sequence, driving around with his mother, he stops his car at a road accident and converts with intense preaching a badly wounded driver just minutes before he dies. However, forced to face a series of adversities, he finds that his stable world is crumbling. Jessie is cheating on him with a younger minister, Horace (Tod Allen), and, manipulating the bylaws, she wrests control of the church from him. Losing his family and his congregation, Sonny descends into an uncontrollable rage and strikes Horace with a bat. When Horace falls into coma, Sonny flees town. In a wonderful image that conveys Sonny's deep confusion, he circles his car at a crossroad, not knowing which direction to turn. Boarding a bus for Louisiana and shedding traces of his past, Sonny chooses a new name, E.F., and baptizes himself as "The Apostle."

Landing in the predominantly black town of Bayou Boutte, Louisiana, E.F. befriends the Reverend Blackwell (John Beasley), a retired preacher with a bad heart. With a zealous passion that borders on obsessive self-righteousness, he persuades Blackwell to start up a new church. E. F. agrees to work as a garage mechanic for the local radio station owner, Elmo (Rick Dial), in exchange for free airtime to preach. Soon the Apostle marshals the entire community in an effort to renovate a rundown pastoral church. Burying the frustration of not being around when his mom dies, aggravated by the sorrow of Horace's death, the Apostle commits himself to his calling: He preaches on the radio, takes to the streets, gathers supporters on a revamped school bus. The Apostle's march toward salvation, however, is halted when his estranged wife discovers his whereabouts and informs the police.

Thematically, *The Apostle* recalls Peter Weir's *Witness*, in which a city cop (played by Harrison Ford) on the lam begins a new life in a rural Amish community. But the similarities are only on the surface, for the Apostle's psycho-moral journey is deeper, more disturbing, and less romantic. The film is deftly structured, and every scene leads to the next, each elaborating on the central theme of redemption. As a writer, Duvall never allows the viewers to think that he knows everything about the preacher, and he doesn't violate the character by summing him up; every encounter discloses another dimension of the Apostle's personality.

Duvall also reveals masterly touch as a director, achieving fluid storytelling with brilliant mise-en-scène. In a scene suffused with the threat of imminent violence, Sonny confronts his wife and begs her not to leave; then, contrary to expectations, he walks out quietly. In a later scene, when a racist troublemaker (Billy Bob Thornton) arrives on a bulldozer to destroy the church, the Apostle places his Bible on the ground and dissuades him with a sermon.

It's hard to imagine anyone but Duvall in the title role, which bears slight resemblance to his Oscar-winning turn in *Tender Mercies* (a film about the redemption of a country singer), but here Duvall renders an even more modulated performance. Sweeping all the major Spirit Awards, including Best Picture and Best Director, *The Apostle* proved to be one of the year's most commercially successful indies, with $22 million in grosses. *The Apostle* reached as substantial an audience as had been reached by Billy Bob Thornton's *Sling Blade* a year earlier.

Sling Blade (1996), which marks Thornton's directorial and solo writing debuts, is a Southern Gothic parable about good and evil. In *One False Move*, cowritten by Thornton and Tom Epperson, Thornton played a killer on the run (see Chapter 11). Here, he plays Karl Childers, a mildly retarded man who has been incarcerated for twenty-five years for slaying his mother and her lover. In an eerie prologue, the childlike Karl is seen by the asylum's window, wearing a weird half-smile on his face while staring straight ahead. Next to him stands a chatty inmate (J. T. Walsh), who talks of his sex crimes. Two high school girls prepare to interview Karl before his release. In a long, uninterrupted, darkly lit monologue, Karl recounts the murders he committed with a sling blade.

Uncomfortable rejoining society, Karl returns to the asylum at the end of his first free day; it's the only place he knows. But later, the head of the institution arranges for him a job and shelter in a nearby fix-it shop. Though hunched over and speaking in a monotone growl, Karl is met with kindness. He strikes up a friendship with a fatherless boy, Frank Wheatley (Lucas Black), whose widowed mother, Linda (Natalie Canerday), invites him to move into their garage. As Karl becomes part of the family, tensions arise between him and Linda's lover, Doyle (Dwight Yoakam). Sober, Doyle is a tyrant who tortures Frank; drunk, he is dangerously violent. Vaughan (John Ritter), Linda's gay boss at the local store, warns Karl that Doyle is a monster. Concerned with Linda and Frank's well-being, Vaughan is contrasted with the intolerant, quick-tempered Doyle.

Sling Blade centers on the friendship between Karl and Frank. Karl's life is presented as a quest for inner peace; Karl needs to demonstrate his capacity for goodness. In a role reversal that defies age, it's Frank who treats Karl as his little brother. The characters form an eccentric family: a kind, single mother; a lonely son; an abusive lover; a discreet gay man; and a mysterious killer, whose calm yet firm visibility forces others to acknowledge him. The simple yet harsh Karl recalls the brutish but naive character of Lenny in Steinbeck's *Of Mice and Men*. A slow-speaking, slow-moving man, with grotesque features and gestures, he wears an impenetrable gaze and uses a sparse, monotonous voice; his thick backwater growl rarely varies in pitch and volume.

Karl's horrific action is attributed to his father's (Robert Duvall) religious fanaticism and his abusive upbringing, seen in flashbacks to his childhood. *Sling Blade* highlights the noirish theme of the dark power of the past, but despite the dreariness and the dark visuals, the film shows some hope and even humor.[22] True to form, the story leads toward an inevitable tragedy in which justice is restored. The ending, in which Karl is brought full circle to the asylum, raises an interesting question. Opting for a more humanistic resolution, Thornton avoids dealing with the issue of how effective institutionalizing the mentally challenged is as a corrective measure.

CHALLENGING STEREOTYPES

Physical Stigmas: Disability and Obesity

When *The Waterdance* (1992) came out, inevitable comparisons were made with Hollywood movies about paraplegics: William Wyler's *The Best Years of Our Lives* (1947) and Fred Zinnemann's *The Men* (1950) with Marlon Brando, both of which concern war heroes. Set in a California rehab center, the new movie echoes these painfully earnest dramas, yet there is something fresh. Codirected by Neal Jimenez and Michael Steinberg, the film's protagonists are ordinary men who happen to be in wheelchairs. Uplifting and touching, the film is decidedly not in the manner of the TV Movie of the Week.

Jimenez, who wrote the disturbing movie *River's Edge*, based the script on his own experience. Paralyzed from the waist down, Jimenez tells the story of his recovery with astonishing humor. His alter ego is Joel Garcia (Eric Stoltz), a young novelist with a broken neck, who shares quarters with Bloss (William Forsythe), a racist biker, and Raymond (Wesley Snipes), a streetwise black man. "Every man got to find his place," says Raymond, announcing the movie's main theme: finding peace with oneself and with the world. Exploring the camaraderie that emerges among the men, the movie is coherent, attentive to detail, and unsentimental. With a wicked, down-to-earth humor, *The Waterdance* is at once funny and sad.

The first image is particularly arresting: a close-up of Joel's head, immobilized in a traction device called a halo. And a sex scene between Joel and his girlfriend, Anna (Helen Hunt), who's married to another man, is sensual and honest, pushing the movie to a new level of realism that a movie like *The Men* could never have achieved in 1950 because of censorship.

The entire cast is impressive, particularly Stoltz as a writer of ironic temperament. Snipes and Forsythe also give sorrowful performances that reflect the state of a shattered American masculinity. As a blustering fantasist, Snipes is extraordinarily moving, and the gravel-voiced Forsythe, playing a racist who's good at puncturing other people's illusions while protecting his own, suggests that adversity can make a man smarter. These two men fight endlessly and violently, until they realize they need each other for survival.

Jimenez originally developed his script about a hospital for paraplegics at Warners, which predictably let it go. It was then rescued by the independent producer Gail Anne Hurd (*Aliens*), who brought the script to RCA/Columbia Home Video (now Columbia/TriStar), a major training ground for young directors at the time. RCA/Columbia financed the $2.3 million movie, which Goldwyn distributed after its premiere at Sundance, where it won the screenwriting award.

James Mangold, the director of *Heavy* (1995), fits the description of an indie outsider like a glove. He wears dark clothes and boasts a New York address and a brooding intensity to match. After a frustrating time in Hollywood, Mangold found in New York's independent film world "a good, healthy, anti-Hollywood sentiment," where he could make movies "free of certain Hollywood aesthetic."[23]

Not surprisingly, the low-budget *Heavy* also concerns an outsider: a bald, overweight pizza cook named Victor (Pruitt Taylor Vince), who still lives with his domineering mother. When a young woman, Callie (Liv Tyler), takes a waitress job at the tavern, her effect on Victor and all the others is unmistakable. A stunning woman unaware of her beauty— her arrogant boyfriend is partly responsible for her low self-esteem— Callie is trying to figure out what to do with her life. Dolly (Shelley Winters), the tavern's proprietor, takes to Callie immediately, and so does her shy, homely son, who develops an unrequited passion for her, observing her with fascination as she changes into her uniform. But Callie triggers jealousy in Delores (Deborah Harry), a sultry bartender who's worked for years for Dolly and her late husband and is now aging none too gracefully.

The sad, sexually frustrated Victor, who hates making the pizzas that help keep him overweight, feels secure in being doted on by his mother. Blinded by her love for him, Dolly is aware that Victor has replaced her husband, but she's unaware of her crippling effects on him.

When Callie suggests that Victor enroll in a culinary institute, Dolly can't understand why they should pay money to teach Victor what he already knows.

In his observation of a dreary upstate New York town, Mangold avoids melodramatic condescension, resisting the temptation to turn the roadhouse into a metaphor for hopelessness. Nothing is predictable about the movie, which presents the marginal lives of its "little people" without pathos or hysteria.[24] Told from a detached perspective, *Heavy* dignifies the emotions of its characters by refusing to violate the ordinariness of their experience.

Mangold's compassionate look at Victor's inner life is a stinging rebuke to the judgmental portrayals of overweight characters in American films. Fat people are usually seen as riotous goofballs, amiable sidekicks, or pitiable losers; a case in point is Anne Bancroft's *Fatso* and practically every film Dom DeLuise, John Candy, and Chris Farley have made. Mangold paints a precise portrait of a loner, without a trace of condescension. *Heavy* is a subtle, restrained, but emotionally charged film that runs against the grain of both indie and mainstream cinema.

A personal film, *Heavy* was inspired by Mangold's trajectory in Hollywood, whose high point was a one-year contract at Disney that earned him a shared writing credit on the animated feature *Oliver and Company*. "My generation had this myth in our heads that you could get in bed with the studios and they would bring you up like a minor league baseball prospect," Mangold said. "I was twenty-one when I got this deal at Disney—and this mythical 'Steven Spielberg in a cubbyhole at Universal' was in my head."[25]

Mangold's Hollywood chapter came close to ending his career altogether. "Living in Hollywood after the Disney deal, I felt invisible. I had gone from being this hot prospect to being transparent. I gained twenty pounds. I would sit in my house making these elaborate breakfasts for myself, trying to get started writing a masterpiece to prove these fuckers wrong."[26] But Mangold channeled his frustration into a perceptive exploration of invisibility—Victor is described in the film as "a big ox nobody notices." Mangold's concept of Victor was also fueled by an encounter he had with an overweight boy in a Melrose Avenue comic bookstore. The boy wore a T-shirt that said "Fuck You" in iron-on letters on both sides, and he had a baseball hat that had on it a felt fist with the middle finger raised. Obviously, he was seething with rage. After this incident, Mangold began writing "like a maniac." "I imagined he would normally walk down the street and passers-by would see this fat kid and would look away. With this shirt and hat, he was preventing anyone from dismissing him with their eyeballs, before he could give them a good sock in the teeth. His experience must have been this continuous rejection of strangers' eyeballs looking askance."

Mangold's thoughts mushroomed into a skeleton of a script, which was later developed at Columbia, under the sponsorship of Milos Forman and Richard Miller (who became *Heavy*'s producer). Mangold's goal was to make a silent movie, entirely built of images—"a film that would be useless to blind people"—in which all the important ideas were exchanged between characters through gestures and glances. Mangold is grateful to Milos Forman, who would not let him punch the movie up, recognizing its unique texture of fragile glances. Michael Barrow's alert camera gives the film a harsh look, with restrained, lyrical compositions that capture, as Terrence Rafferty has noted, both the romantic aspirations and the isolation of the characters.

Throughout Mangold brings remarkable powers of observation: Victor's quandary gives way to a larger consideration of the inevitability of change, conveying the illusion of security bred by the comforting routines of everyday life. The downbeat ending also defies Hollywood conventions: Callie is not going to seek refuge in Victor's big arms, and Victor is not going to kill himself in despair. "I just didn't want to give Victor 'the girl,' or a lottery ticket, or some easy solution," explained Mangold. "I thought I had a satisfying ending—just not a deliriously blissful ending. There had to be a certain level of realism or the film would be a sham."[27]

Heavy was acclaimed at every festival it played, winning a special jury prize at Sundance. The film quickly sold around the world, but not in the United States, where it took more than a year to get theatrical distribution. It wasn't until the 1995 Toronto Festival that CFP stepped forward, although Miramax had already made a deal to do Mangold's next movie, *Copland*, a cop drama with Sylvester Stallone and Robert De Niro. After Cannes, *Heavy* was trimmed from 115 to 103 minutes, but, according to Mangold, it's not the running time that viewers found challenging; it's the deliberate rhythm. "Americans are so used to fast-paced movies that they don't tolerate any indulgence; they perceive it as arrogance."[28]

Mental Disability

John McNaughton's *Henry: Portrait of a Serial Killer* (1991) is imbued with suspense and graphic violence, combining a clinical approach with a quasi-documentary technique that results in genuinely disturbing horror. This intelligent look at a murderer is profoundly upsetting, more for the questions it raises than for the mutilated bodies it shows. The fictionalized story is inspired by Henry Lee Lucas, a Texan drifter on Death Row who confessed to numerous murders but who then recanted and said he had killed only his mother. From these facts, McNaughton and his cowriter, Richard Fire, construct the life of Henry, an ex-convict and killer who lives with a former prison friend named Otis and Otis's sister, Becky.

Henry was made in 1988 for a video company that expected a mainstream horror film. A theatrical release fell through because of an X rating, and the movie kicked around for years. It was only after its successful screening at Telluride that *Henry* was rescued by Greycat, a small, courageous company, which released it unrated.

McNaughton, who has worked in advertising in Chicago, shows strong command of the camera and of his narrative. As Henry (played by Michael Rooker with astonishing calm and control) drives along the road, the film flashes back to quick graphic visions of his victims: a woman sawed in half, another killed, with a broken bottle still sticking out of her eye. McNaughton takes the audience into the sordid, claustrophobic life of a killer without ever explaining his psyche. When Henry teaches his friend Otis (Tom Towles) to kill, Otis is as excited as a child with a new toy. Becky (Tracy Arnold), a former topless dancer, is the film's only innocent character. A woman with a golden heart, Becky sympathizes with Henry's killing of his abusive mother, because she, too, has been abused by her parent (in her case, her father).

The film doesn't try to understand Henry's motives, but McNaughton's observations are always precise. When Henry and Otis videotape and then play their murder of a family, McNaughton implicates his audience in the killers' position as they coolly watch themselves on television. But if McNaughton leads the audience into the lower depths of social pathology, he never addresses it from a position of moral authority. As Andrew Sarris has suggested, the director's formal and thematic achievement resides in imprisoning the audience in gruesome behavior without ever aestheticizing evil.[29]

Using a similarly chilly, nonjudgmental strategy, Lodge Kerrigan's drama, *Clean, Shaven* (1994), examines the collapse of a schizophrenic. The comma in the title is a break in the flow, a deliberate imperfection. Kerrigan's goal is to challenge public stereotypes of mental illness as seen in movies and TV. "I was tired of seeing mentally ill people being props, going around shooting people, or just waiting for that little bit of love' to be able to overcome their incapacity."[30] *Clean, Shaven* is also a stark riposte to recent Hollywood movies that depict the mentally ill as fonts of simple wisdom.

Kerrigan, an NYU film school graduate, shot his film on weekends over a two-year period—"Whenever I got some money, I'd go out and shoot." The final budget was well under $1 million. Framed as a mystery about a child killer searching for his young girl, *Clean, Shaven* is based on a fragmented narrative. The unsettling portrait illustrates the mental state of Peter Winter (Peter Greene), although not much is known about him. Hastening his breakdown, as he travels in a car with windows pasted over with tabloid newspapers, are hallucinations and the grating scanning of radio channels.

A blistering piece of cinematic inventiveness, *Clean, Shaven* operates in the realm of empty, eerie spaces. Few films have succeeded so convincingly in putting the audience inside a schizophrenic's head, allowing it the experience of being battered by a jumble of uncontrollable impulses. What makes the film even more disturbing is that it adopts the formula of an innocent man hunted by a relentless cop, although it never allows the audience the comforting certainty that Peter is innocent. Kerrigan refuses to compromise in order to make things more soothing for the viewers.

The heightened tension comes from the film's narrow focus on Peter's distorted view—his vision deliberately excludes other people. The most gruesome violence is inflicted by Peter on himself. He gouges his own body to remove what he imagines are a receiver in his scalp and a transmitter under his fingernails, which he believes were implanted while he was in the hospital. Kerrigan shows impressive conceptual and directorial skills. Peter's thought processes, captured by unpredictable editing, convey the constant threat of terrible violence; every minor event might push him over the edge. The soundtrack reverberates with conversational snippets and unrecognizable sounds that continuously rupture the movie. These devices prompt a discomfort Peter shares with the audience, with his memories intruding in the most frightening ways.[31]

Once Peter moves past the silent scenes and begins to communicate with other characters, *Clean, Shaven* loses its eerie mystery and assumes a more ordinary shape. The text contains only two other characters: an investigator who's on Peter's trail and Peter's mother, who seems to bring out the worst in him. Like *Sling Blade*, the movie doesn't interpret much, suggesting (perhaps too simplistically) that the mother may be the reason for Peter's problems.

Insulated Domesticity

It took Todd Haynes four years after *Poison* to get funding for his next feature, *Safe* (1995), an emotionally devastating portrait of insulated domesticity. The film's protagonist is Carol White (Julianne Moore), a San Fernando housewife who develops peculiar health problems. Carol's immune system is compromised by an "environmental illness," an all-encompassing allergy to chemicals that has baffled the medical establishment and has gained the label "20th-century disease." Helpless, she turns to a self-help organization, which leads her to greater isolation from the real outside world.

A seductive entry into Carol's bourgeois milieu opens the film, with the camera tracking a hill populated with houses that get increasingly larger and derivatively similar in their design. This sequence was influenced by Haynes's childhood in Encino, where architecture was "frightening—fake Tudor, fake country manor." Haynes also looked at films that depict Los Angeles as a futuristic city, where every trace of nature has been superseded by humans. For Haynes, Los Angeles is like an airport, "because you never breathe real air, you're never in any real place. You're in a transitional, carpeted hum zone."[32]

Conventional cinematic cues that usually tell viewers how to respond are avoided. *Safe* breaks the Hollywood mold by not using close-ups and other audience-controlling devices. The film minimizes manipulation, letting the viewers make up their own minds through their own subjective perceptions. Haynes refuses to judge his characters or to subject them to the ridicule to which a mainstream movie would resort. Indeed, the film's subtlety was mistaken by some viewers as endorsement of dubious fads, as if it were promoting New Age philosophies and places like Wrenwood, the "Wellness Center." In actuality, *Safe* is critical of New Age therapies, perceiving them as a trap no better than the mindless materialism that defines Carol's bourgeois lifestyle. The chilling conclusion shows how Carol's self-imposed exile is carried to an extreme. Standing in front of a mirror, with a blank expression on her face, Carol says repeatedly, "I like you."

Haynes's challenge was to overcome the gap between himself and Carol, who could have become an easy target for criticism for her bourgeois class and her lack of self-knowledge. The same even-handed approach was taken with the New Age characters, as Haynes said, "I wanted to challenge my own innate criticism of their worlds. I had no interest in condemning them or placing myself above them." At the same time, Haynes didn't want Carol to become too attractive, or to be the larger-than-life character she would have been in a more conventional Hollywood movie.

Haynes dissects Carol's identity, her incessant need to be affirmed and reaffirmed by society. He wants Carol to evoke the vulnerable, fractured nature of modern identities, an issue American films rarely address. Identity formation, and how it is manipulated by larger social forces, is subtlely explored. Like many other women, Carol never masters the ability to break out. "L.A. and Wrenwood both have isolation built into them, but both are telling you you're not alone, and if you do these things, you'll be affirmed as part of the group."[33] *Safe* shows the cost of "joining a group or giving up things in ourselves that can never be harnessed." While refusing to indulge in a sappy style, *Safe* belongs to the tradition of "the woman's film," drawing on the melodramas of Douglas Sirk and Fassbinder. Haynes uses the melodramatic format to place limits on his narrative: "Carol is somebody enclosed in certain systems, whether it's L.A. or another system."

The irony and the measured rhythms of *Safe* are exquisite, yet austere, and they are conveyed through the anesthetic suburban spaces through which Carol moves: grand "living" rooms, cavernous car parks, clotted freeways, spotless spas. From the first scene, featuring her husband's selfish "lovemaking," to which Carol dutifully submits, Haynes chronicles Carol's increasing loss of control in her desperate efforts to conform: the *Bride of Frankenstein* perm she receives, the fruit diet embraced on a friend's recommendation. As *Safe*'s silence is disrupted by technological sounds—vacuum cleaner, television, radio station call-ins—Carol's identity undergoes shutdown. "Who am I?" she wonders with quiet desperation.

Carol fits the outline of Haynes's earlier protagonists, who were mostly victims. Shaped by her environment, paddled by patriarchs, she belongs to his series of plastic dolls. Is Carol herself the problem, a humorless Stepford wife, honed by aerobic drill instruction, looking like an emaciated replicant, a luminous pod, never breaking a sweat?[34] Shot by Alex Nepomniaschy in wide angle that reduces all human activity to miniaturized doll movements, *Safe*, like Haynes's *Poison*, is steeped in paranoia and malaise.

Safe plays on the "comfort and resolve" (Haynes's words) of the TV Movie of the Week, quietly subverting the rhetoric of the recovery guru Peter Dunning, a "chemically sensitive person with AIDS," to whom Carol turns for help at the Wrenwood retreat. In one subtle scene, Carol, looking more haggard than ever—supposedly she is "adjusting" to Wrenwood—is approached by Peter, who's concerned over her reluctance to join in group-think. Eager to fit in, Carol admits she's "still just learning the words." Peter responds, "Words are just the way we get to what's true," turning what she's said into an essentialist statement. For Haynes, "words show you how truth is unobtainable, because you can never articulate it."[35]

By insisting on pride (which equals self-blame), Dunning allows his patients to fall, while his "therapeutic success" allows him—like the image of his majestic villa high on a hillside—to ascend. Haynes wanted to examine the New Age philosophies of Louise Hay, the self-help author of *You Can Heal Your Life*, which led to an upsurge in similar treatments among gay men with AIDS. "What is it about these philosophies that make the sufferer of incurable illnesses feel more at peace? Why do we choose culpability over chaos?"[36] It's a tribute to *Safe*'s complexity and subtlety that it doesn't provide answers to these absorbing questions.

Misogyny

Haynes's *Poison*, which won the 1991 grand prize at Sundance, took the indie world by storm (see Chapter 12). Neil LaBute's *In the Company of Men* (1997) didn't win Sundance's jury award (it received the Film-makers' Trophy), but it was easily the most provocative entry that year. This dark comedy probes yuppie angst as it manifests itself in the workplace and in the interpersonal arena. It's a dissection of the white male psyche effected through the relationship of two thirtysomething executives: the handsome and arrogant Chad (Aaron Eckhart) and his friend from college and now his superior at work, Howard (Matt Malloy).

Appropriately enough, the tale begins in the men's room, when Chad examines Howard's bruised ear, a product of a fight with his girlfriend. Touching a nerve, Chad ignites Howard by describing him as "a victim of an unprovoked assault" perpetrated by women, a gender he utterly despises. En route to a six-week business trip at a branch office in an unnamed city, they share their frustrations—the tough corporate culture, expectations for promotions that have not materialized, the cruel mating game that has left them both rejected.

As a therapeutic measure for their bruised, insecure egos, Chad proposes a scheme: They should find an appealing woman who's susceptible enough to be lured and dated by both of them. The plan is to dash this woman's hopes so that she will lose control and, as Chad says, "suddenly call her mom and start wearing makeup again." Then, when the "business" is over, they'll go back to normal, "like nothing happened," able to laugh about their adventure for years to come.

At work, Chad spots Christine (Stacy Edwards), a beautiful typist who's hearing impaired although she can speak. Having been out of the mating race for years, she seems the "ideal" prey, vulnerable to a fault. Christine goes on separate dates with both men, but it's clear she's attracted to Chad. Soon, both men begin to show some feelings and even declare love for her. What ensues is a mean-spirited cat-and-mouse game of one-upmanship that eventually escalates into psychological warfare. What begins as a frat-boy prank escalates into a lethal power game. It's a tribute to LaBute's taut control that only at the very end are the motivations of each man revealed.

Despite the horrible contest, the sharply poignant dialogue is amusing. LaBute sustains the misogynistic banter, making an edgy movie in which speech is action. His script doesn't turn schematic, the way the futile *Swimming with Sharks*, which it superficially recalls, does. There are, however, a few bad scenes, such as the one in which Chad asks a black intern to take off his underwear and show that he has the balls for the job.

Visual style is simple—frontal, medium-range shots and a camera that doesn't move—but it doesn't matter, for the film is deftly written and superbly acted. In a career-making performance, Eckhart embodies a 1990s yuppie, nastily cocky and ruthlessly ambitious. He is ably supported by Edwards as a woman who's just a means to an end, a pawn easily captured and then tossed aside in the duel for corporate ascension.

As Ray Pride has suggested, *In the Company of Men* is a black satire about the male ego run amok. It offers a moral take on the corrupt aspects of the corporate world: how men treat themselves. Chad and Howard become the ego and the id of one person. LaBute's control of the symmetric scenario and pacing is impressive; he attacks his subject with a playwright's vigor. LaBute was influenced by the British playwright Harold Pinter and the very American writer David Mamet. The film's distancing strategies were inspired, according to LaBute, by Stanley Kubrick, a brilliant filmmaker known for his cold exposés.

Funding for the film was as unconventional as its narrative. After a freak car accident, LaBute's friends Toby Graff and Mark Heart unexpectedly came into a sum of money—"I went right for the jugular like an ambulance chaser," recalled LaBute. "'As long as you're going to be all right, can I have your money?' They both acquiesced."[37] Working with limited means became a trick, making every economic decision look artistic. The film was shot in eleven days, for $25,000, with LaBute saving money by using simple master shots and framing the tale narrowly on its three characters. LaBute got a kick out of the way his movie was marketed—"the feel-bad hit of the summer."[38] *In the Company of Men* opened in August, as counterprogramming. Sony Pictures Classics invested money in postproduction and scored with a hit that generated $3 million, way above indies' average performance.

Your Friends & Neighbors (1998), LaBute's follow-up, continues his darkly comic exploration of misogyny as it defines the relationships of endlessly loquacious urbanites. This contemporary (im)morality tale suffers from the relentless misogyny and unpleasantness of its male characters and from the static quality of the staging, which approximates a theatrical mode, lacking narrative momentum or dramatic excitement. As he showed in his first film, LaBute has a penchant for sharp dialogue and deft characterization but is less concerned with plot mechanics and visual mise-en-scène. In LaBute's universe, biting words, not actions, are the ultimate weapons. The source of inspiration for LaBute's work continues to be David Mamet, here, the play *Sexual Perversity in Chicago*. Like Mamet's, LaBute's approach is precise and detached. In his direction, LaBute also follows Mamet, placing his characters close to the camera without much depth of field.

Though doubling his ensemble to a sextet, *Your Friends & Neighbors* is as narrowly focused thematically as *In the Company of Men*, but here the battlefield is the bedroom, rather than the boardroom. The power games played by the characters in the new movie are motivated by sexual politics. In its cynically bitter tone, *Your Friends & Neighbors* bears a thematic resemblance to Mike Nichols's *Carnal Knowledge*. LaBute's modern males recall the misogynist, impotent men played by Jack Nicholson and Art Garfunkel in that 1971 picture.

In the precredit sequence, a handsome man named Cary (Jason Patric), sweaty from exercise, says dramatically, "I think you're a great lay." It turns out Cary is talking to his tape recorder, rehearsing lines that in no time will be used on a variety of desirable women. LaBute's incisive perspective is evident in the very first sequence, a montage of couples in bed. The married Jerry (Ben Stiller) and Terri (Catherine Keener) are making love, but Terri is tired of his endless talk—"I don't need the narration," she angrily tells him. "This is not a travelogue." Cut to another married couple, Mary (Amy Brenneman) and Barry (Aaron Eckhart), who experience sexual problems. Barry later confides, "The best lay I ever had is myself. My wife is great, but she is not me."

Jerry, a theater instructor, seems the most balanced of the men, but appearances deceive. When Jerry initiates an extramarital affair with Mary, he sets in motion a chain of events that affect all the other characters. The narrative centers on the intricate maneuvers of upscale urbanites: deceit and betrayal of love and friendship. In due course, Terri falls for another woman, Cheri (Nastassja Kinski), who works in an art gallery, and, in a senseless, incoherent ending, Mary finds herself in Cary's arms.

Schematically constructed to represent a cross-section of urban society, the characters are divided into an equal number of males and females. Of the women, one is a masochist, another is a married bisexual, and a third is a lesbian. The men, too, are archetypes: Jerry is an adulterer who keeps secrets because he's never honest with himself, Barry epitomizes the inadequacies of a man who's lost control of his life, and Cary is the sexually potent male for whom women are toys to be played with.

Some of the interactions are sharply observed with dark humor, but sheer cynicism wins out, giving the impression that LaBute set out to shock his viewers. The whole film is overly studied and calculated, including the symmetrical overture and finale. The film begins with a series of bedroom scenes and ends with a series of mirrored bedroom scenes. LaBute goes for emotionally distancing effects, as is evident in a repetitive cycle of gallery scenes wherein all the characters engage in identical introductory dialogue. Unfolding as a series of theatrical tableaux, the film lacks dramatic or cinematic momentum.

CONCLUSION

Tony Kaye's *American History X* (1998) provides an instructive example of the simplistic approach taken by movies in the all-too-rare cases when they tackle social issues, here racism. Well intentioned if unconvincing, the writer David McKenna's cautionary tale centers on Derek Vineyard (Edward Norton), a skinhead neo-Nazi whose body is covered with tattoos, including a swastika on his chest. Derek is presented as an intelligent former honors English student, whose life has been shaped by a personal tragedy and a neo-Nazi guru who uses propaganda to convert insecure, frustrated kids into racists. A budding neo-Nazi who idolizes Derek, his younger brother Danny (Edward Furlong) has written a report celebrating *Mein Kampf*. The black school principal instructs Danny in a personal tutorial (which he calls American History X), assigning him a paper about his brother's influence on their family. The narrative switches back and forth between past (in black and white) and present (in color), with Danny's narration commenting on the action.

A vicious killing of a black teenager who has tried to steal his car sends Derek to prison. After three years, Derek returns a totally reformed person: He lets his hair grow, encourages his mom to watch her health, and urges his worshipful brother to give up smoking and skinhead ideology. Derek is presented as a thoughtful fellow who's worked through his rage and has come to recognize the errors of his ways. Nonetheless, Derek's conversions seem more dramatically convenient than psychologically coherent. The script is full of one-dimensional explanations for radical changes in behavior: Derek's rage, for example, is explained by the murder of his racist father.

David Ansen has pointed out that the material is charged enough without piling on hysterical melodrama and stylized violence (shot in slow motion to religious music). The movie sacrifices reportage for showoff filmmaking, a possible result of Kaye's background in commercials. Kaye stages an attack on a Korean grocery and scenes of sexual violence in a jazzy way: When a black boy is killed in a public place, the scene is empty, because to do it otherwise would mess up a cool shot.[39]

9

Cinema of Diversity

THE PAST TWO decades have seen the beginnings of a multicultural cinema, defined by filmmakers of diverse racial backgrounds: Latino, African American, Asian-American, and even Native American. Minority directors, like women, have found it easier to break into the independent cinema than the mainstream. It's the richly textured work of these directors that justifies indie cinema's claim to multiculturalism in both ideology and practice.

HISPANIC CINEMA

Of the 1,384 films distributed by the major studios during the past decade, 2.2 percent (thirty films) were directed by Latinos, 4.2 percent by blacks, 1.2 percent by Asians, and none by Native Americans. Although there are currently 23 million Latinos in the United States (roughly 8 percent of the population), in the 1990s Latinos accounted for only 1 percent of characters in prime-time TV entertainment programs. Opportunities on the big screen are only slightly better: Latinos characters amounted to 2.5 percent of all characters in film, according to studies conducted in 1992 and 1995.[1]

In theatrical productions, minority casting continues to be low according to Victor Contreras, an American Film Television Radio Association (AFTRA) board member, and the kinds of roles available are limited: "The vast majority of roles Hispanics are cast in are either as victims—poor and downtrodden and helpless—or they're the perpetrators, the criminals." When good Hispanic roles do surface, they tend to be filled with white actors. In *The House of the Spirits* (1994), based on the Argentinean Isabel Allende's best-selling novel, for example, the lead roles were played by Jeremy Irons, Meryl Streep, and Glenn Close.

American movies have depicted Hispanics in stereotypical ways, mostly as simpletons, ne'er-do-wells, drug dealers, and murderers. Javier Garcia Berumen's survey, *The Chicano/Hispanic Image in American Film*, found that Latinos were invariably portrayed as lazy, dimwitted, oversexed, and criminal. Hollywood's conventional wisdom is myopic, based on ignorance and on a misreading of the facts. This cultural divide raises the question of how to move beyond the limiting definitions of Latino films and allow Latino directors to make quality fare.

In recent years, a number of Latino Film Festivals have sprung up to address this problem. Celebrating the Latino experience in all its variety, these festivals show works that explore the rich Hispanic experience, a heritage that has never found its way into textbooks or popular culture. The first Los Angeles International Latino Film Festival was held in 1997 under the leadership of the actor Edward James Olmos: "The studios are in it for the money, not cultural diversity, and right now they don't see any big moneymakers."[2] This, despite the fact that Latinos have become the fastest-growing ethnic block of moviegoers in the nation.

When Hollywood tackles Hispanic-themed movies, the results can be disastrous. In the Disney-made *Bound for Honor* (1993), the director Taylor Hackford aims at creating a Hispanic street epic but winds up with an oddly diffuse movie. The film purports to track the changing codes of alliance in Los Angeles barrio life, using the Latino half-brothers Paco (Benjamin Bratt) and Cruz (Jesse Boreo) and their half-Anglo cousin Miklo (Damian Chapa) as a triangle. But the characters are stereotypes: Paco is the directionless loco who becomes a narc after a family tragedy; Cruz is the promising artist who turns to drugs after the tragedy; Miklo is the hothead whose desire to prove dedication to his turf sends him to prison. The movie spins out digressions, losing sight of its central characters. Ross Thomas's script centers on the dull character of Miklo and his struggle for prison supremacy. Racial issues are treated in a confusing way, without nuance, and the movie's population is claustrophobically small: No girlfriends or neighborhood denizens other than gang members. Gang life in East Los Angeles is complex enough to warrant a more interesting and accurate film than Hackford's earnest, overlong drama, whose original title was *Blood in, Blood Out*.

According to Moctesuma Esparza (who produced *Selena*), part of the reason the studios have made so few Latin-themed films is the paucity of Latino executives at the top echelons who have greenlighting power. A further challenge is luring Latino audiences to see these movies. Unlike black audiences, which have shown great loyalty to urban films, Latinos do not go to see a movie just because it's about a Latino subject.[3]

DOING HISTORY JUSTICE—THE SEARCH FOR HEROES

The problem is not that Latino-themed movies have been directed by white filmmakers such as Hackford but the specific approach taken by mainstream white filmmakers. A case in point is Robert Young, a white director who has dedicated most of his career to a more honest and realistic portrayal of Latinos on screen. Born in 1925, Young is sometimes called a father figure in the indie cinema. Though a generation older than most of the filmmakers discussed in this book, he has produced his best work over the past twenty years, at once contributing to and benefiting from the new indie resurgence.

Young began his career as a documentarian, making his first feature, *Secrets of the Reef*, in 1957. This was followed by a series of prize-winning *White Paper* documentaries for NBC. Young was fired for directing *Cortile Cascino*, about poverty in a Sicilian slum, which the network decided not to telecast because it was "too real for the American public to handle." Serving as cowriter, coproducer, and cinematographer, Young then collaborated on Michael Roemer's *Nothing but a Man* (1964), a groundbreaking indie made for $230,000. Together they made a lean, unpretentious drama about a black Alabama laborer who needs to adjust to earning a livelihood, supporting a family, and maintaining his dignity.

Young moved from documentaries to features with *Alambrista!* (*The Illegal*), winner of the 1978 Caméra d'Or at Cannes. The film offers a vivid view of illegal farm laborers through its touching, insightful tale of Roberto, a Mexican boy (Domingo Ambriz) who illegally crosses the border seeking work to support his family. *Alambrista!* is a small, gentle, unsentimental film, which follows Roberto as he discovers that California is decidedly not the land of opportunity. The cinema verité (handheld camera, expressive close-ups) shifts smoothly from the lyrical to the more nightmarish tones.[4]

Young captures Roberto's status as an outsider, chronicling his futile pilgrimage from Mexico and the events that inevitably force him to return home. Speaking no English, Roberto gets an extensive education. Joe (Trinidad Silva) gives him a lesson in how to march into a café, cross his legs like a gringo, order a gringo's breakfast ("what you really want is tortillas and beans, but here you order ham-eggs-coffee"), and flirt with the waitress. Married in Mexico, with his mother nearby, Roberto hasn't fully detached himself from a society of women, but he now must adjust to the company of men.

Young followed up with *The Ballad of Gregorio Cortez* (1983), based on a true story of racial injustice. It was first shown on PBS as part of the *American Playhouse* series. In 1901, Gregorio (Edward James Olmos) killed a sheriff in Gonzales, Texas, while being interrogated. Gregorio was pursued for eleven days by a 600-man posse of Texas Rangers. His trial revealed that an interpreter had inadvertently distorted the sheriff's inquiry, which was perceived by Gregorio as a threat. He was sentenced to fifty years behind bars but served twelve before being freed on the governor's pardon.

For Young, the tale's poignancy derives from the fact that, despite Gregorio's rich heritage, he was forced by the alien Anglo culture to become an immigrant and to speak a language that needs translation. Young, however, wanted to convey a broader meaning that would transcend the particular incident.[5] Through a carefully balanced treatment, he wished to chronicle the prevalent racism but also, as he said, "a system of law that makes us better people than we might be."

The intentionally simple style was designed to create an intimate portrait of Gregorio as an innocent civilian—a young husband and father—who is hunted, captured, and subjected to unfair trial. While the film's sincerity is beyond doubt, the tone is pedagogic, the characters solemn, and the drama too muted. *The Ballad of Gregorio Cortez* tells a potentially stirring story in a plain style that lacks verisimilitude, despite its authentic setting (the trial was filmed in the court where Gregorio was indicted). What's missing is a spark, an immediacy that might have made the characters—here played passively—recognizably human rather than figures in a well-meaning pageant.

Isaac Artenstein's *Break of Dawn* (1988) also pays tribute to a misunderstood hero, Pedro J. Gonzalez, a star in the Latino community. Based in San Diego, Artenstein first made a documentary about Gonzalez, then decided to treat the story as a feature. One of the century's more remarkable characters, Gonzales was, over the course of his life, Pancho Villa's telegrapher, an illegal alien, the singing host of a celebrated radio show, the victim of a bogus rape charge, an inmate at San Quentin before the "rapee" recanted, and a border radio star for thirty years. When the movie was made, Gonzalez, age 96, was living with his wife of seventy years in Lodi, California.

The film describes racism of the most blatant kind. When politicians railed against Mexican migrants for stealing American jobs, the United States reportedly deported numerous people in a fury of hateful retaliation. Gonzalez's radio show rallied the Spanish-language audience, creating a political force. When Gonzales protested the deportation policy, the power structure fought back. Starring the Mexican actor Oscar Chavez as Gonzalez, the film is simplistic, but it displays charm and has affecting music from Chavez.

Ramon Menendez's *Stand and Deliver* (1987) belongs as well to the genre of earnest, uplifting Latino films. Edward James Olmos gave a tour-de-force, Oscar-nominated performance as the tough math teacher, Jaime Escalante, who inspired his East Los Angeles students to take an Advanced Placement calculus test. The film is based on the actual experiences of Escalante, a businessman turned school teacher, who is willing to go the extra mile for inner-city students most adults would rather stay away from, let alone teach. Set in 1982, the movie follows Escalante as he pushes his students to prepare for an especially difficult college calculus exam. Only 2 percent of all high school students nationwide pass this test, and the notion of having this group even attempt it is understandably daunting.

Nonetheless, Escalante is unwavering in his efforts to gain the trust of his students. Using unorthodox teaching methods and setting extraordinarily high standards, Escalante develops individual relationships with each student. By the end of the film, however, the formula of an unorthodox teacher and lovable-though-troubled kids struggling for success against odds yields predictable results. The film's only loose, unanticipated element is the kids' disappointment at the Educational Testing Service's suspicions about the unanimous results.

At present, there are only three Latino filmmakers who direct with a distinct ethnic sensibility and with whom the studios feel comfortable: Gregory Nava, Robert Rodriguez (*El Mariacchi*, *From Dusk Till Dawn*), and Luis Valdez (*La Bamba*).

UNABASHED MELODRAMATIST—GREGORY NAVA

The dominant theme of Robert Young's earlier movies, the plight of illegal aliens in the United States, has also been an abiding concern for Gregory Nava, a filmmaker of Mexican-Basque heritage. It's a subject Nava feels hasn't been addressed in appropriate depth in American movies. *La Bamba*, a commercially successful film about the Latino roots of the early rock 'n' roll star Ritchie Valens, was effective on a musical level, but its depiction of the Latino reality was "less than accurate," according to Nava.[6] "Have you heard of Sierra Madre? How about the Camino Real? This was Mexico before some shifty land-grabbers came along and cooked up a little war. Latinos in California have been experiencing 140 years of occupation."

Nava's debut feature, *The Confessions of Aman*, written in 1973 but not released until 1977, was made in Spain for the "nonbudget" of $20,000, using props and costumes left over from Samuel Bronson's epic, *El Cid*. A neo-Bressonian medieval romance, *Confessions of Aman* tells the tragic love affair of a young philosophy tutor and a lord's wife. Like Bresson, Nava is less interested in the affair than in the moral choices the protagonists are forced to make. The film is observed from a distance, a detached perspective that Nava abandoned as his career progressed.

Though little seen, *Confessions of Aman* helped Nava make his next low-budget feature, *El Norte* (1984), which pleased most critics and enjoyed decent box office after its premiere at Telluride. Despite an elaborate story and greater immediacy than *Confessions of Aman*, narratively, *El Norte* is far more conventional. It displays Nava's strengths—and weaknesses—as a filmmaker, his penchant for overwrought narratives and schmaltzy soap operas. Nava's films, like his later *Mi Familia*, have enough subplots and sentiments to qualify them as TV miniseries. Nava would like to bring to the screen the magical realism of such novels as *El Señor Presidente* and Gabriel Garcia Marquez's *One Hundred Years of Solitude*, but he lacks the requisite vision and technical skills. His attraction to melodrama and "big emotions" guarantees that his movies are never boring but also ensures their dismissal by the more cerebral critics and audiences.

With the somber gentleness of a fairy tale like "Hansel and Gretel" transplanted to 1980s Central America, *El Norte* is a bittersweet fable of two Guatemalan Indians, brother and sister, Enrique and Rosa, who are

forced to flee their village after their father is murdered for antigovern-
ment activities and their mother imprisoned. Brainwashed by photographs in glossy American magazines like *Good Housekeeping*, the siblings believe that every American house has flush toilets and TV sets
and that no American is too poor to have his own car. As Hoberman has
observed, the journey from the Guatemalan highlands to Los Angeles is
less a journey from a poor country to a rich one than an epic trip from
one century to another.[7]

Until its arbitrary—and arguably unnecessary—tragic ending, *El
Norte* is effective at satirizing America as a land of opportunity. Life in
dreamland California is everything Enrique and Rosa had imagined it
would be. Bright, good-looking, and eager to succeed, Enrique (David
Villalplando) works his way up from busboy to a waiter's assistant in
an elegant Beverly Hills restaurant. Baffled by automatic washing machines, Rosa (Zaide Silvia Gutierrez) finds a decently paying job as a
cleaning woman for a rich but sympathetic white woman. The film's
poignancy resides not in the tragedy faced by the siblings but in the
ease and eagerness with which they adopt the gringos' world. The
white, neon-lit, plastic-like society embodied by Los Angeles so en-
chants them that they devastatingly deny their roots.

Demonstrating injustice in a vivid yet personal way, *El Norte*
doesn't patronize its "little people"—it doesn't contemplate the in-
equality suffered by poor peasants exploited in a capitalistic society.
Nor does the film use those violations as a dramatic convenience to
raise the audience's awareness. Nava's attention to dramatic detail
doesn't allow much time for editorializing about good and evil. More
specific in satirizing American culture than in exploring Latin American
political unrest, *El Norte* is not as overtly political as might be expected.

El Norte, however, suffers from a weak opening—an exposé of
Guatemala's reign of terror that mixes corny National Geographic visuals, sanctimonious postures, clumsily directed scenes of violence, and
a fussy soundtrack with persistent flute-windchime-birdcaw clamor.[8]
The picture becomes more assured as the siblings travel north, and once
the scene shifts to Mexico, the Tijuana passages are truly powerful.

Breaking with the modest look of indies at the time, *El Norte* falls
into another trap, that of crude filmmaking. Nava adores the picturesque landscape, which enhances the dramatic impact of the journey,
but his fondness for dreams and apparitions is both simplistic and dis-
tracting. Ultimately, as Hoberman noted, *El Norte* ranks higher for its

good intentions than for effective execution. It's arty without being artful, concerned without being politically lucid. Even so, if the film remains compelling for two hours and twenty minutes, it's because of its deft characterization and acting rather than its social insight or aesthetic coherence.

Nava's second feature, the studio-made *Time of Destiny* (1988), was a major disappointment, a soap opera about a World War II tragedy that haunts two close friends and fellow soldiers (poorly played by William Hurt and Timothy Hutton). Made on a larger canvas, with a bigger budget and Hispanic stars (Jimmy Smits, Esai Morales, Edward James Olmos), *My Family* (1995) became Nava's breakthrough film. Presenting Latinos in a positive light, this chronicle of a large family living in East Los Angeles is structured as a series of painful intergenerational clashes juxtaposed against the indomitable endurance of blood ties. One generation after another, the Sanchez clan struggles against the social limits foisted on them by their elders; the only constant factor is the racist surroundings.

"When you can't look to authority for protection," Nava has said, "you find other ways to protect yourself, and this is one of the reasons gang activity has become so prevalent. Gangs are an old part of Chicano culture, but unfortunately they're growing increasingly virulent. In the 1950s, the streets were safe for children and old people, and there were boundaries the gangs respected. But nowadays there are security bars on the windows, a sad reflection on Latino life in L.A."[9] The contribution *My Family* makes to the depiction of barrio life is that, "instead of putting gangs at the center of Latino culture, which the media have done, the family is at the center." The gangs, the Catholic Church, immigration problems, and music orbit around the family, but for Nava, the film tells a universal story about a family that happens to be Latino. With all the difference between Latino and Anglo families, Nava wants to show that "we all have more in common than we realized. The family is one of those things."

Through all the battles and violence, the characters never abandon the shelter provided by the family. "Because Latino culture in L.A. has been poor and oppressed, these people have always looked to their families for protection and strength," Nava said of his film, cowritten with his wife and partner, Anna Thomas. But the movie is not particularly hopeful: "Following this family through three generations, it doesn't get less oppressed. People do move up and you see change, but you also see the development of a permanent under-class."

Told from the point of view of Paco Sanchez (Edward James Olmos), who plays a writer, the story begins in rural Mexico early in the century and follows his parents as they immigrate to California, carving out a life for themselves in a less than hospitable environment. Early in the film, Mexican workers are shown building various parts of the city. For Nava, this has become a permanent aspect in America: "Latinos are still doing the jobs nobody else wants to do—they're still washing dishes and digging ditches."[10]

An exhibition by the Chicana artist Patssi Valdez prompted Nava to invite her to collaborate with the art director Barry Robison in shaping the movie's visual look. Valdez's paintings became a reference point, with domestic scenes rendered in bold colors. Robison carried around color photocopies of her paintings, because Nava wanted a literal rendition. "Valdez's colors are vivid, there's a cartoonish quality—hence, every room in the house is painted a different color." "The safe way to do this film would have been in warm sepia tones with everything muted, but Nava went in the opposite direction," Robison said of the director's attempt at magical realism. For the 1920s, they used earth colors, referring to the folk art of Michoacan; the 1950s segment, influenced by the work of Diego Rivera and Frida Kahlo, is dominated by pastel; the 1980s are entirely congruent with Valdez's style.

Nominally, the central figure is Chucho (Morales), a brooding "bad" boy who gets killed in the course of the action. But in actuality, the chief character is the house, a living organism that expands, contracts, and takes on different characters as time goes by. As the tale progresses and the family expands, the house grows, too. By the time the story jumps to the 1980s, the colors have become intensely dark, and the house has begun to sag because there's been so much living in it.

New Line did an astonishing marketing for *My Family*, which after its premiere at Sundance scored with both Latino and art house audiences, reaching $11.1 million on some 400 screens. Showing that he was ready to undertake a big studio movie, provided that it dealt with Latino culture, Nava then directed *Selena* (Warners, 1997), an exuberantly colorful if simplistic biopicture of the late popular Mexican singer. *Selena* set a record for another nonfilmic reason: Its star, Jennifer Lopez, was paid $1 million, making her the highest-paid Latina in Hollywood's history. Nava followed the commercially viable *Selena* with *Why*

Do Fools Fall in Love (Warners, 1998), a disappointingly cartoonish biopicture of the tangled romantic life of the rock star Frankie Lymon, who died in 1968.

While *Selena* was still in theaters, a promising Latino helmer, Miguel Arteta, burst onto the indie scene with *Star Maps* (1997), a melodrama about the destruction a villainous patriarch brings upon his family. A macho bully, Pepe (Efrain Figuera) has driven his wife insane—she spends her time in bed staring vacantly at her TV screen and conversing with the late Mexican comedian Cantinflas. Pepe's eldest son is a fat, lewd child who enjoys dressing up as a masked wrestler. In contrast, his daughter is ultrasensitive and insecure, always on the verge of hysteria. Carlos (Douglas Spain), the youngest son and the hero of the story, is forced by his father to become a hustler. Pepe justifies his pimping by saying, "Life is hard, nobody gives you anything for nothing." The innocent, good-natured Carlos clings against all odds to the belief that his hustling is temporary, something he'll do until his acting career takes off.

Representing an uneasy balance of Latino and art house fare, *Star Maps*'s story is told with crude, lurid simplicity only occasionally touched by lyricism. Arteta creates a dense texture of oppression (Pepe's malevolence knows no limits), encouraging the audiences' sympathy for Carlos, but the film is unrefined and lacking in dramatic or emotional subtlety. Terrence Rafferty has observed that the film could have worked as a parody of overbearing patriarchy, but Arteta chose instead a conventional approach to the story of a father selling his son, attaching no symbolic meaning. It's the kind of squalid family melodrama that's more at home on sleazy talk shows like *Jerry Springer* than on the big screen.[11] Still, using the obvious whore metaphor, Hollywood serves as a backdrop for some astute observations on race, class, sexuality, and family. Almost every character in the film is engaged in a transaction, cutting deals of one type or another, including a rich white matron who promises to advance Pedro's career in exchange for sexual favors.

Born in Puerto Rico to Peruvian and Spanish parents, Arteta complains that, "because I am Latino, people tend to expect me to make one of two types of films: either a gang-banging, drug-dealing hustling film with one-dimensional characters, or a film that deals strictly in positive images of Latinos."[12] He resents Hollywood for not showing a more diverse Latino culture: "You see Latinos as gardeners or busboys or maids and these kids stand on the corners of Sunset Boulevard waving their maps seductively, trying to sell bits of dreams." Observing these youngsters on Sunset, Arteta found them to be a great metaphor for the culture clash in Los Angeles.

If the ideas for a screenplay came easy to Arteta, financing the movie proved a nightmare, as his story has nine characters and more than forty locations. "On top of that," Arteta recalled, "it's about a father prostituting his own son—and with Latinos! We showed the script to a few people in the industry, and they thought we were crazy." Arteta and his producer, Matthew Greenfield, decided to hunt for investors outside the mainstream. The Los Angeles film patron Scott King committed $50,000, but by the time the shoot wrapped, twenty-nine days later, the budget had blossomed into "a healthy six figures." Postproduction was completed the day before *Star Maps* world premiered at Sundance, where it was picked up by Fox Searchlight for $2.5 million. The film first opened in New York and Los Angeles, then went wider in cities with large Latino populations such as San Antonio, San Diego, Phoenix, Dallas, and San Francisco, eventually reaching 100 screens. However, at $600,000, the box-office outcome was a major disappointment.

ASIAN-AMERICAN CINEMA

Like other ethnic groups, Asians and Asian-Americans have endured unfavorable treatment in American movies, which have not shown three-dimensional Asian characters. A distinction should be made between Asian and Asian-American movies.[13] There are a few of the former, an outgrowth of the long history of American military involvement in Asia. The United States has been at war with various Asian nations since 1941, reinforcing the perception of Asians as the enemy. Hollywood films have promoted the belief that people with darker skin are of less value as human beings, with Japanese soldiers in World War II movies stereotypically depicted as short, nearsighted, and sadistically violent.

Among the earliest Asian film stars was Anna May Wong, who usually played characters of mystery and sexuality, as in *Shanghai Express*. The familiar madonna-whore dichotomy was translated into

Asian terms, making women either lotus blossoms or dragon ladies. If the Asian female was feminine to the point of caricature, her male equivalent was emasculated in American movies. Roles associated with Asian men have been feminine, showing them as cooks or house-boys. Over the years, Asian men have gone from being laboring coolies to technical coolies: the white lab coat, pocket calculator and business suit were the dominant images in the 1980s. Asian males are acceptable in film if they are children. Significantly, the only sympathetic nonwhite in *Indiana Jones and the Temple of Doom* is a Chinese boy.

The most popular on-screen Asian has been Charlie Chan, who, though cleverer than his adversaries, was nonthreatening to whites. Servile, nonsexual, and ingratiating, Chan was preferable only to a character like Fu Manchu, who was evil. Chan was a middle-aged man who spoke lines straight out of a fortune cookie; that he was usually played by white actors in yellowface was a great irony. Then Bruce Lee leaped into American pictures, demonstrating his box-office appeal in martial arts movies. Attractive and powerful, he spurred progress toward creating a more positive image of Asians, although it took him years to get the role of the sidekick Kato in *The Green Hornet* series. Unfortunately, Lee died young, in 1973, right after completing the popular movie *Enter the Dragon*.

Michael Cimino's sleazy actioner, *Year of the Dragon* (1985), about gang warfare in New York's Chinatown, was typical 1980s fare in terms of its portrait of Asian-Americans. A major reason for the consistent neglect and unfair treatment of Asians is that, unlike other groups, there have been no Asian-American filmmakers to deal candidly with issues specific to their background. Which explains the warm reception accorded Wayne Wang when he came out of nowhere.

GENTLE SATIRIST—WAYNE WANG

The pioneering director Wayne Wang, who was born in Hong Kong and educated at California's College of Arts and Crafts, established himself in the 1980s with incisive portraits of Chinese-American life, all of which focus on the ambiguous notion of home. As a tribute to a lifestyle and tradition, Wang's movies display a buoyant subtext of ethnic variety: His immigrants are upbeat and cheerful, if not totally adjusted to their American surroundings.

As a filmmaker, Wang is calm, generous, and kind. Like Nava's, Wang's films have a family focus, but unlike Nava, Wang seldom accentuates the melodrama in his films—in the writing or in the mise-en-scène. There are few dramatic confrontations, just subtle hints and wistful regrets, and human miseries are gently presented and gently accepted as integral parts of life.[14] In contrast to Sayles's characters, Wang's are trying to make sense of their lives without being crushed by the big, powerful forces enveloping them.

"Because of the complete avoidance in talking about China, and having grown up in a British colony, and my parents being very pro-American, I grew up with no sense of identification with a country," Wang told *Film Comment*. "My father would say, 'In America the oranges are bigger.' The dream, the myth was so powerful. I was already half-American even before I ever set foot here." Wang wanted to integrate into American society, although he didn't understand the language or the humor. In the 1970s, Wang was totally unaware of racism—"I had thought in America everybody treated everybody equally." This proved to be an advantage, since he didn't know what to be afraid of.[15]

"In terms of wanting to be American," Wang explained, "I've gone through cycles. First, I wanted to be completely American, even to the point that I was almost a drug addict. That was around 1972, when I went back to Hong Kong and realized I didn't fit there. Then I came back and went through an all-Chinese period. There was a lot of political movement in all the minority communities, and I went back to working in San Francisco's Chinatown and became all Chinese. Then I came out of that cycle and said, 'Well, I'm not really that Chinese, so maybe I'm a mix.'"[16]

The director's first name was inspired by John Wayne, after his parents saw the Western *Red River*. Wang studied photography and film in the United States before landing several assignments in his homeland, including the Chinese scenes in Robert Clouse's thriller *The Golden Needles* (1974). He then took over a popular Hong Kong TV series, *Below the Lion Rock*, a kind of *All in the Family* soap opera. In 1975, Wang codirected (with Richard R. Schmidt) his first American feature, the atmospheric San Francisco–based comedy-drama *A Man, a Woman, and a Killer*.

Seven years later, with grants from the American Film Institute and the National Endowment for the Arts, Wang made his solo directorial debut, the quirky comedy *Chan Is Missing*. Scraping together a meager $22,000 budget for a ten-day shoot, Wang made the film a model for efficient regional filmmaking. "A lot of stuff was donated, and nobody got a cent," Wayne recalled, "but everybody owned an equal share and got paid more in the end than they would've up front."[17] Making what became the first indie with an all–Asian-American cast and crew, Wang opened up possibilities for multicultural cinema before the term even existed.

Set in Chinatown, *Chan Is Missing* shows a previously unrevealed view of modern Chinese-American culture. A hip, Zen-inspired detective story, cowritten by Wang, Isaac Cronin, and Terrel Seltzer, the film dissects some prevalent stereotypes about Asians. On the surface, it's a thriller, a light shaggy-dog, Rosebud-like inquiry into the whereabouts of Chan Hung, a mysterious Taiwanese wheeler-dealer who has absconded with the savings of two Chinese-American cabbies, Jo (Wood Moy) and his hip nephew Steve (Marc Hayashi), who are hoping to get their own taxi medallion. The search for the elusive Chan, known as Hi-Hi for the crackers he carries in his pocket, provides an intimate perspective on Chinatown through a witty compendium of urban lore.

Wang shows a gift for sustaining the tempo of a heavy stream of words, as well a as deft touch with characterization. The dialogue varies from campy Charlie Chan references to dry semiological lectures on Chinatown slang. *Chan Is Missing* has all the attributes of an intriguing Chinese puzzle, where meaning is found not in what is known but in what is unknown. The movie's modest nature belies its sophisticated ambitions: As a treasure trove of cultural illuminations, it could have been made only by an insider. The movie evokes Charlie Chan and other Asian stereotypes in order to contest them. Under the guise of a detective story, the film takes the audience on a guided tour of San Francisco's Chinese-American community, where Wang explores issues of assimilation and identity and the political schism between Taiwan and China.

Each character tells a different story about Chan, and the emergent portrait is full of contradictions and anticlimaxes. However, like *Citizen Kane*, the riddle, not the solution, is the point. Chan becomes an offscreen symbol of the complexity of the Chinese-American experience. As David Ansen has pointed out: "Irony is Wang's mode, droll digressions his manner, cross-cultural cacophony his delight."[18] The streetsmart Steve talks in idioms that disdain the new rhetoric—"That identity shit is old news." A cook in a Samurai Night Fever T-shirt sings "Fry Me to the Moon" as he stir-fries. A Chinese rendition of the popular song "Rock Around the Clock" blasts from car radios.

Wang's most inventive creation is an earnest female academic, who discourses on how people of Chinese descent loath coming directly to the point. To prove her thesis, she deconstructs the cross-cultural linguistic misunderstandings in the aftermath of a traffic accident. In his zest to challenge viewers' stereotypes of Chinese-Americans, Wayne pokes fun at the Chinese as well as at the American side of the hyphen. Jo describes how whenever a tourist gets into his cab, he (Jo) starts counting, "1,000, 2,000 . . . " and before he reaches 4,000, the passenger asks for a good Chinese restaurant.

Assorted thriller conventions—the Other Woman, threatening phone calls, newspaper photos that fail to provide a lead—are blended together. "If this were a TV mystery," muses Jo in his narration, "an important clue would pop up at this time and clarify everything." The important clue is not forthcoming, yet much is revealed: struggles between Taiwanese immigrants and former mainlanders, capitalists and Communists. The message, as David Denby suggested, is clear: Nothing in Chinatown is simple; it's only for white Americans that people simply exist as "Chinese."[19]

When Chan disappears with their loot, the two cabbies crack self-mocking jokes about Charlie Chan and rake the community for traces of a man who has meant different things to different people. Indeed, the more they find out about Chan, the less they know. Chan's estranged wife, a haughty, Americanized lawyer, dismisses Chan as a hopeless case, "too Chinese." There are reports that Chan has returned to Taiwan to settle a large estate and that he may have important ties to China. Chan seems to have played a part in a scuffle between rival political factions during a New Year's parade, when marchers sympathetic to Taipe locked flags with marchers sympathetic to Peking. Jo studies a newspaper photograph, looking for *Blow-up* clues, only to realize that the photograph is of another scuffle. There are also suggestions that Chan, who committed a minor traffic violation the day he disappeared, is connected with an argument between two elderly Chinese in which one fellow shot the other in a fit of temper.

The search for Chan and the Chinatown revealed are not part of Philip Marlowe's shadowy world. It's an ordinary place, with middle-class apartments, a center for the elderly, street markets. A witty movie made with assured technique and humor, *Chan Is Missing* pays tribute to film noir: It employs a narrator and darkly shadowed black and white cinematography, with an alert camera following the characters in and out of apartments, restaurants, clubs, and offices.[20]

Chan is Missing borrows from Welles's *The Third Man* and *Citizen Kane*, with its missing protagonist and the problem of reconstructing his life. In the process, Jo becomes more interested in discovering who the chameleonlike immigrant is than in getting his money back. Hence, when the money is unexpectedly returned by Chan's daughter, it's an anticlimax. Chan is never found, but he serves as a perfect metaphor for the mysteries of the Chinese-American community. David Denby has noted that for some artists, the lack of a clear identity might be debilitating or tragic, but for Wang, the untidiness of Chinese-American life is part of its diversity and glory.

Everything in the film is used to illustrate its underlying concerns: identity, assimilation, sociolinguistics, and what the academic, describing Chan's argument with a cop, defines as "cross-cultural misunderstandings." An appreciation of a way of life that few Americans know anything about, the closing shots, dazzling in their simplicity, offer an empty Chinatown, devoid of people. This visual closure serves as a reminder of what Jo and Steve have learned—that what is not seen and what cannot be proven are just as important as what is seen and proven.

A word-of-mouth success, *Chan Is Missing* led to a number of Wayne-helmed films about Chinese-American culture. Centering again on San Francisco's Chinese-American community, *Dim Sum: A Little Bit of Heart* (1985) examines family relationships while dealing with the erosion of traditional values. Playfully celebrating Asian cuisine, every scene displays food. With dialogue in both English and Cantonese, the film achieves a measure of authenticity.

Dim Sum is casually constructed, with no single event more important than any other. The film's main characters are Mrs. Tam (Kim Chew), an aging, Chinese-born mother, and Geraldine (played by Kim's real-life daughter, Lauren Chew), the last of Mrs. Tam's American-born daughters to marry and leave home. Mrs. Tam, a Jewish mother by temperament, says she wants to see Geraldine married, but whenever Geraldine tries to make the break, she begins to fret about her loneliness. When the widowed mother is told by a fortune teller she's nearing death, she decides to go "home" to China to pay her last respects. She also decides to become an American citizen, although she prefers to answer the immigration officer's questions in Cantonese. While the mother's away, Geraldine and Uncle Tam (Victor Wong) make a hash of authentic Chinese cuisine and go to McDonald's for a Big Mac.

Like *Chan Is Missing*, *Dim Sum* is composed of anticlimaxes, but here they seem too soft and inconsequential. Simple and direct, Wang's style achieves its impact through the rhythmic editing of disparate images. Gentle but poignant, swinging between laughter and tears, *Dim Sum* displays the vitality of Capra and the graceful stillness of Ozu. David Thomson has observed that Wang's families, like Ozu's, sit and talk about their concerns, but their problems continue to persist, like the ritualistic pleasure involved in preparing and eating their meals.[21] References to Ozu suggest that perhaps Wang and the screenwriter, Terrel Seltzer, were aiming at making a version of *Tokyo Story*, but *Dim Sum* lacks the humor that is so refreshing in *Chan Is Missing*.

In *Chan Is Missing*, Wang's fondness for vacant rooms and streets generates meaning, but the vacant spaces that *Dim Sum*'s characters leave behind have less emotional impact. Unlike *Chan Is Missing*, the movie is made up of subsidiary events, without the support of a strong central story. All the characters are seen in candid moments, but whether it's the family's Chinese New Year celebration or Uncle Tam brushing his false teeth, these moments don't add up. Uncle Tam talks sadly of the Chinese food that will no longer be made as traditions are lost, but the film never defines that sense of loss.

Wang cemented his status as an indie director of Chinese-American tales with *Eat a Little Bowl of Soup* (1989), another small, modest work about the arranged marriage of a Chinese couple and how they deal with their interfering families. His next picture, *Life Is Cheap . . . but Toilet Paper Is Expensive* (1990), is a bizarre story about a courier sent to Hong Kong to deliver a metal briefcase that has been handcuffed to his wrist. Upon his arrival, he's unable to deliver the mysterious package and decides to visit the city's sights instead. When some uncharacteristically violent scenes threatened to earn the picture an X rating, Wang decided to release it unrated, which guaranteed that the visual concept would remain intact, but no one saw the film.

The Joy Luck Club (1993), Wang's first and, to date, only studio picture (Touchstone), also deals with intergenerational conflict and cultural assimilation. The movie is considered a breakthrough for its portrayal of Asians in mainstream cinema. Wang adapted Amy Tan's best-selling novel and made a warm, heartfelt woman's picture about the generation gap between Chinese mothers and their American-born daughters. The movie probes the perennial issue of mothers' high expectations for their daughters and their inevitable disappointment when the latter end up just as victimized as the mothers had been in China.

Wang's next three pictures were independently made. He scored a commercial success with *Smoke* (1995), based on a short story by the novelist Paul Auster that originally appeared as a Christmas Day op-ed piece in the *New York Times*. Employing film as an extension of literature, *Smoke*, a deceptively quiet film, celebrates the art of storytelling—and the art of kindness. The five major characters act benevolently in their need to establish meaningful links with one another. An unexpected act of kindness is always the beginning of a story, which comments on the teller's life. Set in Brooklyn's Park Slope, where Auster lives, *Smoke* is about the joy of neighborhood life, about people taking care of one another. Gentle but not soft, *Smoke* was greeted enthusiastically by critics, partly because it was released in the summer amid a cycle of violent, Tarantino-like movies.

A freewheeling offshoot of *Smoke*, *Blue in the Face* (1995), codirected by Wang and Auster, is a series of improvised scenes about Brooklyn that includes some witty Lou Reed recollections, Roseanne in her fishwife routine, and an embarrassing striptease by the actress Mel Gorham. Uneven, nostalgic, and self-congratulatory, the movie exhibits some charm.

Almost coming full circle, Wang returned to Hong Kong to shoot his latest film, *Chinese Box* (1998), an ambiguous love poem to the international city just as it was changing political hands, reverting to Chinese control after 156 years of British rule. Strong on ambience and nuance but hampered by a loose, amorphous narrative (cowritten by Jean-Claude Carriere, Paul Theroux, and Wang), the film concerns a bizarre, disintegrating romance between a dying British journalist (Jeremy Irons) and a beautiful bar hostess (Gong Li), a mainland refugee.

In the 1990s, just as Wang was moving away from the Asian-American tradition that had defined his earlier work, another young Asian director was beginning to leave his mark on indie cinema—Ang Lee.

CROSS-CULTURAL SATIRIST—ANG LEE

Committed to a more accurate representation of the Asian heritage in American films, the Taiwanese-born director Ang Lee has made comedies whose international success is a tribute to the universality of their themes: sexual politics and the need of children to escape the control of their parents. Like Wang's, Lee's style is articulate but self-effacing; he finds humor in painfully ordinary situations. When people ask Lee, "Do you consider yourself an American or a Chinese director?" his answer is, "I'm a New York filmmaker. Whether I'm doing an American movie or a Chinese film, whether I shoot in Taiwan or China, I will always have a New York point of view. I was very conscious of whether I was Chinese or American for a while, but then, what the hell, I'm myself. Let me be an individual filmmaker and try to do the best I can."[22]

In Taiwan, Lee was encouraged by his parents, who were scholars, to pursue an American education in the hope that he, too, would become a scholar. His father was dismayed when Lee chose film instead; the choice was considered disgraceful: "It wasn't until I won the Berlin Festival Award that he [Lee's father] finally thought it was OK." Lee says he was inspired by the movies of Billy Wilder, Frank Capra, and Woody Allen. His student films at NYU, including his award-winning thesis, *Fine Line*, brought him recognition but no break. Struggling for fifteen years in what he calls "development hell," Lee was supported by his wife, a microbiologist. Hollywood didn't quite know what to do with him. Producers considered his complex scripts to be of limited appeal, but Lee insists that he never experienced racism—"producers simply weren't interested in my stuff."[23]

In 1990, Lee's script for *The Wedding Banquet* won a Taiwan state film competition, but the Central Motion Picture Corporation, which is backed with government funds, balked at financing "a gay movie." It did, however, greenlight another film, *Pushing Hands*, which became Lee's first feature. In *Pushing Hands*, the widowed Mr. Chu, a former Tai-Chi master, arrives in America from Beijing to live with his son's family. Lee explores cross-cultural and generational conflicts, issues that would become the backbone of his work. In what might be called a *Father Knows Best* trilogy, all featuring the wonderful actor Sihung Lung, *Pushing Hands* was the first in a series of tales about a parent who confronts a rapidly changing world.

Shot in Westchester, *Pushing Hands* lacks the technical sheen of Lee's subsequent films, but it shares their warmth and wisdom. The film begins on a quiet day in suburban Westchester, as Mr. Chu goes about his solitary rituals, exercising, preparing food, watching Chinese videos. But Chu's presence makes it impossible for his daughter-in-law, Martha (Deb Snyder), a writer, to work. "No metal in the microwave!" she lashes out, thrusting earphones at him. It's a painful predicament for his loving son, Alex (Bo Z. Wang), who's caught between his wife and his father. A gentle man, Mr. Chu has to face the cruel reality that, unlike the Chinese, Americans have no respect for the elderly. The title refers to a Tai-Chi exercise, designed to help one keep one's balance while destroying the opponent's. In the end, Mr. Chu regains his balance and takes control of his life, independent of his son's.

The sharply observed *The Wedding Banquet* (1993), Lee's best film, is a madcap comedy about a marriage of convenience between a gay Taiwanese-American and a Chinese woman in need of American citizenship. The movie examines the primacy of the individual within a culture that worships authority and rewards conformity, a society in which tradition carries the weight of generations. Tapping the resources of his homeland and adopted country, Lee's film conveys with humor his ambivalence about that heritage. While the protagonist finds his freedom and happiness in the United States, tradition is imposed on him by his parents in the guise of a wedding banquet— the "Red Monster," in Lee's words, "an all-red, noisy event, giving people splitting headache."

Wei Tung (Winston Chao), a successful businessman, has hidden his homosexuality from his Taiwanese parents, who are desperate to have grandchildren. His yuppie lover, Simon (Mitchell Lichtenstein), suggests a marriage of convenience to Wai Wai (May Chin), a struggling artist who'll do anything to get a green card. When Wei's parents unexpectedly arrive from Taiwan, they lament the impersonal civil service ceremony. Finally, Wei Tung gives in to their demands for a more lavish and traditional wedding.

With pointed humor, Lee describes traditional weddings as being all about food and the "torture" of the bride and groom. "As a ceremony, it's very flamboyant, and emotion plays very high. It's more for the parents than for your own self. It's very absurd, very insincere, and very expensive." *The Wedding Banquet* is a personal film: Lee's parents were upset when he opted for a real-life version of the marriage-bureau scene—"my mother burst out crying." Years later, Lee agreed to have a "wedding banquet" to celebrate his marriage to filmmaking. The film's titular sequence was cast with friends and people recruited through ads in a Chinese-language newspaper. Many came because they just wanted to see May Chin, a famous pop star in Taiwan. Lee didn't have to direct the bit players because they already knew the conventions. The extras got a free lunch but were told not to eat anything on the tables; the food contained a poisonous preservative to make it shine.

The idea for *Wedding Banquet* originated in an anecdote recounted by Neil Peng, Lee's writing partner. A mutual gay friend from a Taiwanese military training camp had been deceiving his family while living with a Caucasian boyfriend in Washington, D.C. They had been lovers for eight years, but the parents didn't know about it. Fascinated by the "white lies," Lee realized the situation was ripe for a satire of banquets. The actual case inspired Lee to conceive of an arranged marriage and then wonder, "What if something were to go on under the blankets?" The sex scene between the drunk bride and groom that takes place during their honeymoon has been criticized as unrealistic, given the man's homosexuality. But Lee defends it: "They're drunk, they're confused by the ceremony. Cross-sex sexuality is not that impossible." For Lee, "the real point is that he stays gay. It should be read as a mishap."[24]

When Wai Wai seduces her inebriated husband, she announces, "I'm liberating you." Her statement has been misinterpreted, as if it applied to sexuality, but for Lee it was a political joke: "She's from China, and the scene's very red, and it's like he's going back to the motherland. That's one of the Chinese slogans aimed at Taiwan: 'Someday, we'll liberate you.'"[25]

Lee satirizes a political situation; Taiwan and China are farcically reunited through a fake marriage. A lot of people go to China to invest, and a lot of illegal immigrants in Taiwan are from China. The current movement toward Taiwanese independence has affected Lee's own identity. "I'm not a native Taiwanese because my parents are from China. If they go independent, who am I? Am I Chinese or Taiwanese? And China after the Communist revolution is not the China I had in mind from what I was taught by my parents. It's something else; it's a grand illusion. And then I stay here as a minority in America for fifteen years." Like Wayne Wang in the 1980s, it's "all mixed up" for Lee in the 1990s.

Sympathetic toward the parental point of view, Lee constructed the mother (Ah-Leh Gua) as the strongest character, for whom "the whole establishment of her existence is the family. She's the one who really manipulates; the father's just playing his part to maintain his self-image to the mother. It's a very typical Chinese family. The mother seems submissive, but she gets what she wants the way she wants it."[26]

The Wedding Banquet represented a major achievement for a country where homosexuality has rarely been publicly acknowledged (it was the first Chinese film to show two men kissing). While pleased by the positive response, Lee still hoped to provoke the audience: "I love stirring things up rather than sticking to the Chinese ideal, which is to appeal for calm." Lee humorously probes Chinese society's hypocritical attitudes: "Sex is erotic and is how families come into being, but Chinese families will never talk about it." Lee tried to create an authentic picture of a loving, healthy gay relationship, while also drawing on his relationship with his parents. He understood on a very personal level "the need for Wei Tung to be free of this political burden of being the first-born."

Produced on a skeletal budget of $750,000 and financed by Taiwan's Central Motion Picture Corporation, *The Wedding Banquet* grossed more than $4 million domestically, which qualifies it as the highest-grossing Taiwanese film in history. On the basis of its cost-to-earnings ratio (with global grosses of $30 million), *The Wedding Banquet* was the most profitable film of 1993, beating even the blockbuster *Jurassic Park*.

On the heels of *The Wedding Banquet*'s success, Lee returned to Taipei to film *Eat, Drink, Man, Woman*, a Chinese-language film whose structure recalls Woody Allen's *Hannah and Her Sisters*. The title derives from a Confucian teaching, according to which "sex and food are the basic drives of human behavior. If you throw away all the bullshit, that's what life's about."[27] Self-discovery and self-actualization, Lee's recurrent thematic motifs, are also at the center of *Eat, Drink, Man, Woman*, with the focus again on the family. This time, it's a Taiwanese cook and his three unmarried daughters who seek liberation. The film presents a greater breaking away from convention and tradition than does *The Wedding Banquet*. However, the food in the film is more colorful than the characters, which are contained in what is essentially a soap opera. Critics were quick to point out the resemblance between Lee's film and the Mexican erotic hit *Like Water for Chocolate*, which was released the year before.

Eat, Drink, Man, Woman became the final film in Lee's trilogy about traditional families experiencing friction caused by the growing Western influence over the younger generation. The three films complement each other. *Pushing Hands* and *The Wedding Banquet* explore father-son relationships, and the offspring's lifestyle upsets the parents, whereas *Eat, Drink* looks at father-daughters relationships, and it is the parent's rigidity that disappoints the children. All three movies are characterized by warm humor and charged interactions within the family, but while *Pushing Hands* and *The Wedding Banquet* follow a linear story line, *Eat, Drink, Man, Woman* boasts a more complex structure.

An ensemble piece featuring Sihung Lung, a regular in Lee's films, the Hong Kong–based Sylvia Chang, and the stalwart Taiwanese actress Ah Lea Gua, the narrative consists of four interlinked stories about a family that has lost its ability to communicate. The father, a cook in Taipei's Grand Hotel, and his daughters gather each Sunday for a sumptuous meal. At each dinner, however, the family members become progressively more distanced from one another. The father simply can't relate to the varying shadings of Western attitudes adopted by his off-springs.

Lee's continuing concern with the conflict between the older generation's traditional values and the younger generation's Westernized attitudes hits home for many Chinese families. "In Chinese culture, you must submit to your parents," Lee explains. "They are the ones who give you life. For thousands of years, the Chinese have built a society on this arrangement. Now they're facing a transition. A younger generation wants to find Western-style individual freedom, but the concept of filial piety still haunts from behind."[28]

Using food as a metaphor for primal human bonding, the movie opens with a dazzling montage of Mr. Chu preparing a lavish meal; he slices, spices, dices, steams, and sizzles with utmost elegance and precision. The irony is that he has lost his sense of taste—a metaphor for the erosion of tradition. The Sunday dinners are no fun for the widower or for his daughters, who have so many problems they barely touch the food. Jia-Jen (Kuei-Mei Yang), the eldest, is a schoolteacher ridiculed by her pupils for being an old maid. Jia-Jing (Yu-Wen Wang), the youngest, works in an American-type fast-food restaurant. The middle one,

Jia-Chien (Chien-Lien Wu), is an airline executive and a frustrated chef herself. Failing to perceive the meals as a symbol for love, they see them as a form of torture, which adds to their already complicated entanglements. The spinster pines for a lost love but begins to moon over the new gym teacher; Jia-Jing takes a lover who reads Dostoyevsky and rides a motorcycle; and Jia-Chien continues to engage in affairs that go nowhere.

Romantically, too, the father does better than his daughters. Cooking has taught him to blend calculation and improvisation. Old Chu investigates recipes for food that are designed to stimulate the sexual function. The moral is simple: Feed the body artfully and the soul will take care of itself. Like the cuisine it celebrates, *Eat, Drink, Man, Woman* is tart, sweet, and subtle. In an introduction to the published script, cowritten by Lee, Hui-Ling Wang, and James Schamus, Schamus recalls Lee's complaint that the psychology of the characters wasn't Chinese enough. Schamus proceeded to deliberately make the scenes as Jewish as possible, after which Lee said: "Ah, ha, very Chinese!" Which shows again the universal appeal of Lee's work.

In recent years, Lee, like Wayne Wang, has expanded the range of his work beyond Asian or Asian-American themes. He directed a popular film adaptation of Jane Austen's *Sense and Sensibility* (1995), which was nominated for the Best Picture Oscar, and the WASPish family drama *The Ice Storm* (1997), which had its world premiere at Cannes (see Chapter 8).

JEWISH-AMERICAN HUMOR—ALBERT BROOKS

The paucity of Jewish-themed movies made by Jewish directors in the new indie cinema may be a result of the fact that Jewish humor has become integrated into the mainstream through the work of such prominent filmmakers and writers as Mel Brooks, Woody Allen, Paul Mazursky, and Neil Simon. Of the younger generation of Jewish filmmakers, the most interesting figure is Albert Brooks, whose movies are studio financed but still manage to display a feisty, independent spirit. The best of Brooks's bitingly personal satires revolve around one dominant character: the Jewish yuppie.

A most incisive screen comedian, Brooks imbues his satires with acidic humor and criticism. The son of the radio comedian Harry Einstein (better known as Parkya Karkus), he grew up with the burden of a name like Albert Einstein—and a morbid outlook as well. "My father died when I was young," Brooks recalled. "It made a very strong impression on me. I got to see the end of life before I saw the beginning."[29] Brooks made some shorts for the first season of *Saturday Night Live*, including the parody, *A Star Is Bought* (1976), a catalogue of radio styles in which he played most of the roles. As an actor, Brooks has appeared in other directors' films: as Goldie Hawn's husband in *Private Benjamin*, as the talented but luckless TV journalist in *Broadcast News*, and, most recently, as an obnoxious Wall Street raider in Soderbergh's *Out of Sight*.

However, Brooks is truly inspired when he delivers his own sarcastic material, as in *Real Life* (1979), *Modern Romance* (1981), and *Lost in America* (1985). Brooks has played variations on the same character in most of his films—the smart, fast-talking, indefatigable climber who's always defeated by one force or another. His screen persona is that of a friendly but aggressive educated man who has obsessively dedicated himself to a single idea and in the process has become blind to other interests. Exhaustingly intelligent yet deeply foolish underneath, Brooks's men are pathetically sincere. His best comedies can be described as studies in humiliation and defeat, farces of insecurity and desperation. No wonder mainstream success has eluded Brooks—his characters are too egotistical and overbearing.[30]

Like most sharp comics, Brooks is a loquacious monologuist, at once self-critical and self-glorifying. His early movies are like one-man shows, in which his persona is both embraced and lacerated. Brooks is more maniacally self-indulgent than his equally control-freak peers, Woody Allen and Steve Martin. However, refusing to pander to the audience, Brooks has dissociated himself from other, softer comics-turned-filmmakers, such as Marty Feldman or Gene Wilder.

In *Real Life*, Brooks plays a comedian turned cinema verité director who sets out to record a "typical" American family and in the process succeeds in destroying what he's studying. The movie is so deft at showing how filmmaking distorts the very reality it purports to record that it's hard to watch family documentaries any more without thinking of *Real Life*. A satire aimed at revealing the truth about TV's "slice-of-life" nonfictional fare, the movie was inspired by the PBS series *An American Family*, illustrating the absurdity of TV's reality-mongers, from PBS's cinema verité to CBS's Charles Kuralt. Brooks scores off the pretensions of "realism" and the stuffiness of scientific techniques in sampling the "typical" family.

The typical family in *Real Life* are the Yeagers (Charles Grodin and Frances Lee McCain), residents of Phoenix, Arizona. Brooks records their daily activities as well as his own as a director: *Real Life* is a fictional movie about a real-life comic recording the "real life" of fictional characters. With false reassurance, Brooks guarantees Mrs. Yeager, on her way to see a gynecologist, that "I won't film anything that'll embarrass you. I couldn't use it anyway; I'm locked into a PG." Of course, everything goes wrong, and the gynecologist is infuriated, not so much because of the invasion of his patient's privacy, but because he has already had a terrible experience with a *60 Minutes* exposé of "baby slave auctions."

Real Life follows the adventures of the film crew as it proceeds in a cinema verité and deadpan manner to pester the Yeagers and invade their privacy mercilessly. Brooks films the family from odd, unflattering angles, never allowing them a peaceful moment. It never occurs to the fanatic director that he is warping reality. Assisted by a crew that wears its cameras over its heads, he captures the veterinarian Dr. Yeager as he inadvertently kills a horse on the operating table. When the family falls into a deep depression, Brooks shows up in a clown outfit that only makes matters worse. A proponent of spontaneous, unrehearsed reality, he fails to see that his presence is pushing the family into a nervous breakdown.

Brooks stubbornly claims that show business has a perfect right to be everywhere. But, finally, an exasperated studio chief (a disembodied phone voice, played by the real-life studio executive Jennings Lang) shuts down the project, sternly reminding Brooks that reality, like any other commodity, needs the right packaging to be sold. By the end, the Yeagers cling precariously to sanity.

The writing is inspired, with a wonderful opening sequence in which Brooks announces his project to a cross-section of Phoenix citizens, shamelessly flattering the banality of their lives, playing them the way Merv Griffin orchestrates his Vegas patrons. Brooks explains at the beginning of his film that his idea is to "depict day-to-day living in contemporary America and at the same time hold a motion picture audience spellbound." Rationalizing later why the project has strayed so far from the original plan, he says: "There's no law that says we can't start real and end fake." Brooks reveals a sophisticated ear for the doubletalk of Hollywood self-promoters in an insider's movie for audiences hip to the cliches of the media.[31] Satirizing his own profession, Brooks is the type who fools everyone else with fake sincerity—"I'm a shallow guy," he tells Mrs. Yeager as she begins to show interest in him.

Brooks shows good comic insights, but his exposure of showbiz fakery is a series of routines. In this movie, he's still a stand-up comedian, whose relentless bursts of energy are extended riffs. Ultimately, *Real Life* feels like a thirty-minute gag stretched to a feature-length movie. Brooks's performance doesn't help much: He's like an aggressive emcee who doesn't know when to turn the show over to his guests. If *Real Life* is not as successful as it should be, it's due to Brooks's overwhelming ego; in future films, Brooks would give the other characters more space to maneuver.

Modern Romance (1981), Brooks's second film, reworks the formula of boy-loses-girl-boy-wins-girl. Brooks plays a neurotic film editor, obsessively devoted to Mary Harvard (Kathryn Harrold) but unable to build a normal relationship. Full of theories about what relationships should be, he hardly looks at the girl he first kicks out, then furiously pursues. Alternately irritating and hilarious, the film brims with injokes about filmmaking.

Brooks's chef d'oeuvre, *Lost in America* (1985), is a sharply observed satire about disillusioned yuppies who take to the road in an ill-fated attempt to "find themselves." More open and generous than his previous films, and with an hero who's less obnoxious, the movie became Brooks's first commercial success. David Howard, a thirtysomething yuppie at a big Los Angeles ad agency, anticipates his promotion to vice president after eight years of hard work. He and his wife Linda (Julie Hagerty) have purchased a new house and plan to buy a Mercedes sedan. They are among the new corporate narcissists who define their lives by conspicuous consumption. Each extravagant purchase leads to a bigger one, but there's always something wrong: the new car costs more than $40,000, but it doesn't have leather seats.

Instead of receiving his promotion, David is offered a new account and immediate transfer to New York. Since his whole life has been building up to that promotion, David's failure is perceived as a repudiation of his entire life. Disgusted and enraged David quits his job, and puts pressure on his wife to quit hers too. After the initial shock, David gets inspired. He suggests that they sell their possessions and buy a mobile home and wander wherever the impulse takes them—"It's just like *Easy Rider*, only now it's our turn." That 1969 movie made a lasting impression on him as the ultimate image of freedom; David and Linda leave Los Angeles in their new Winnebago to the tune of "Born to Be Wild." David embraces his new capacity as a self-proclaimed social dropout with his customary bravado.

Lost in America was the first inspired comedy in a cycle of films about yuppies' mid-life crises. "Nothing's changing anymore. We've just stopped," Linda says, not realizing that their options are just going to get bleaker. The adaptable Linda starts out as a tower of strength but crumbles at a Vegas dice table, where she loses the family's worshiped nest egg with hysterical abandon. In the film's most hilarious scene, David makes a stab at persuading the casino owner (Garry Marshall) that his generosity to them would be good for the image of the place.

Nominally a road movie, *Lost in America* is basically an antitravel movie, a yuppie anthem, as Andrew Sarris has noted, alongside Bruce Springsteen's blue-collar ballad "Born in the U.S."[32] The cross-country odyssey becomes an abbreviated, object-lesson voyage into America's landscape of the 1980s. *Lost in America* is still Brooks's most darkly comic movie, with the humor inherent in the dismal progression of disasters, but it's also his most forgiving. Nothing works— David is unqualified for anything but his old ad job and his subsequent one as a school crossing guard. At the end, he and Linda crawl back to society, begging for mercy. The movie dissects yuppie materialism mercilessly and then mercifully acknowledges the realities of life in 1980s America.

Defending Your Life (1991), which Warners distributed, also boasts an independent spirit. It belongs to the life-after-death genre (*Here Comes Mr. Jordan, Heaven Can Wait*), but, whereas most filmmakers treat this subject whimsically, Brooks turns earnest. Brooks plays a Los Angeles yuppie, Daniel Miller, who crashes his new BMW convertible and dies. The movie is set in purgatory, Judgment City, which looks like the San Fernando Valley, with its manicured lawns, wraparound glass miniskyscrapers, and smiling people who greet everyone with "Have a nice day."

Daniel is put on trial. The defense attorney (Rip Torn) and the prosecutor (Lee Grant) examine scenes from his life projected on-screen. Not surprisingly, they are mostly scenes of defeat, in which Daniel allowed himself to be shamed by a bully or failed to invest in a company that later became profitable. In short, Daniel's life was dominated by fear. If he can prove now that he has conquered fear, he will go on to a higher form of existence, in which humans use a larger portion of their brains. But if he is found guilty of cowardice, he'll be sent back to Earth. A new romance with a fearless person (Meryl Streep) is meant to test whether Daniel has the courage to date or will be held back by fear.

The production, with crowds in hospital robes walking in the sterile corridors, is visually impressive. However, neither a satire nor a morality tale, *Defending Your Life* is more like a long, earnest therapy session whose lesson, "Seize the day," is not complex enough for a full-length comedy. Brooks never specifies what's wrong with being sent back to Earth and why that is a failure.

For people who believe that a son can never go home again, *Mother* (1996), cowritten by Brooks and Monica Johnson, came as a surprise. A sci-fi writer, John Henderson (Brooks), realizes after two divorces that if he doesn't straighten out his relationship with his mother, Beatrice (Debbie Reynolds), he'll never have a stable relationships with a woman. He moves back home, trying to figure out what went wrong and hoping to find answers that will make him happier. But as soon as he moves back, he upsets his entire family. John can't conceal his jealousy of his younger, more successful brother (Rob Morrow), and he's shocked to find out that his mother has a boyfriend and that a mother doesn't hide in a closet when her children grow older. Beatrice pretends she's helpless, but she's independent and strong and actually likes her new world and privacy.

One of the few films, independent or studio, to deal with a mother-son relationship in a comic yet realistic way, *Mother* was prompted by Brooks's feeling that, "American movies show two kinds of mothers. The first kind thinks that every single thing their children do is perfect and their children are God's gift to the world. And then there's the other kind. My movie is about the other kind."[33] *Mother* raises some intriguing questions: Did John (and by implication, all children) move out of their families and go on to adulthood too soon? Do children really understand their mothers? The script also conveys children's universal fear of winding up exactly like their mothers. It's a tribute to the film's success that at the end, all three characters are awakened to a new awareness and a new life: Mother and sons are forced to reexamine the real meaning of family.

NATIVE AMERICAN—CHRIS EYRE

Until the 1990s, there were few indigenous films about the Native American experience. In general, Native Americans received less attention by the media than did other disenfranchised groups. Under the guise of benevolence, some white filmmakers did make movies about Native Americans. However, if Kevin Costner had wished to alter the public perception of Native Americans with his Oscar-winning *Dances With Wolves* (1990), he would have set the story in the present, not in the nineteenth century. The issue is not only the manner in which Native American culture is presented, but the context in which it's embedded. *Dances With Wolves* reinforces the idea that the genocide of American Indians was a "sad inevitability."

In *Fantasies of the Master*, a collection of essays on the cultural representation of Native Americans, Ward Churchill documents the treatment of the Indians' genocide in literature and films.[34] Three stereotypes are discussed: "Creature of Another Time," the most prevalent image, which portrays Indians with flowing headdresses and galloping ponies; "Defined by Eurocentric Values," in which Indians are presented without any specific cultural grounding; and "Seen One, Seen Them All," which is based on the assumption that there are no distinctions among Indian cultures. Over the years, Hollywood has created a nonexistent hybrid Indian culture that appropriates disparate groups and defines its values from a strictly European-American perspective.

The category of "Defined by Eurocentric Values" led to the depiction of Native American culture as homogenous, with no acknowledgment of reality. In a cycle of 1970s films, *A Man Called Horse, Soldier Blue*, and *Little Big Man*, Hollywood imposed its Eurocentric values through the device of a white male's voiceover narration. Movies have played an important part in the obliteration of Native American identity, as Cylena Simonds observed: "American inigenous people have been reduced in terms of cultural identity through movie treatments, TV programming and literature to a point where the general public perceives them as extinct.[35]

Against this context came *Smoke Signals* (1998), made by Native American filmmakers Chris Eyre and Sherman Alexie, the latter a prolific writer who was raised on the Coeur d'Alene Indian Reservation. The film premiered at Sundance, where it won the Audience Award and the Filmmakers Trophy. "This is a new voice from our oldest culture, and it's about time," said Miramax's Harvey Weinstein, who released *Smoke Signals*. "It gives an insight into people we've never really understood. We needed them to tell us a story, and we needed to hear it in their words."[36]

Based on Alexie's story, "Lone Ranger and Tonto Fistfight in Heaven," *Smoke Signals* concerns two young Native Americans, Victor (Adam Beach) and Thomas (Evan Adams), who travel from Idaho to Arizona to pick up the ashes of Victor's father. Along the way, the movie sends up Indian stereotypes (the stoic Indian warrior face), while grappling with what Alexie described as "our dysfunctions," namely, parental abandonment and alcoholism. Originally, *Smoke Signals* was called "This Is What It Means to Say Phoenix, Arizona." But Scott Rosenfelt, whose company financed the picture, knew that a distributor would change the title to something less mellifluous, because "mellifluous doesn't play." Centering on absentee fathers and wandering sons, *Smoke Signals* is about the kinds of endemic dislocations that Indian audiences can relate to.

Unlike earnest and preachy films about Native Americans, *Smoke Signals* presents an affectionate portrait of friendship and rapprochement. On the eve of July 4, 1976, a couple on Idaho Coeur d'Alene Reservation celebrate the bicentennial, but the party ends in a tragic fire in which they lose their lives. Thomas Builds-the-Fire, their baby boy, is thrown out a window and is caught by Arnold Joseph, who raises him along with his own son, Victor. The story cuts back and forth between the present and 1988, when Victor and Thomas were twelve and Victor's alcoholic father (Gary Farmer) left his wife (Tantoo Cardinal) and their son at their trailer home.

Victor goes to Arizona to settle his father's affairs and bring back his ashes, but he can't afford to go without the financial help of Thomas, who insists on going along. Over the years, the two have grown into different kinds of men: Victor is proud and cynical, whereas Thomas is a bright and resourceful raconteur of outrageous tales. Victor has been bitter about his father's drinking and abandonment, but in Phoenix he learns some truths about his father from a kind woman (Irene Bedard) who looked after him before he died. Structured as a journey, *Smoke Signals* is basically a coming-of-age story that emphasizes the need for reconciliation between father and son, and between past and present.

When a group of people has been oppressed, it is not unusual for the oppressors to "ennoble" them, which explains the notion of the Indian as "the noble savage" in American culture. However, with their newly gained power, the filmmakers expect to fight white hostility with new weapons: their movies and books. For Alexie, *Smoke Signals* is "our *Great Train Robbery*, a seminal Native American big bang." Based on the notion that Indians are "fundamentally different and don't want to change that," the movie is about "self-love."[37]

Alexie was influenced by all those historical romance novels about Indian warriors ravaging virginal white schoolteachers. If Indians were depicted as blue-eyed, it's because half-breeds were perceived as sexier then full-blooded Indians. Indians in novels always perform "animalistic" acts, inspiring white women to commit acts of primitive ecstasy. In the movies, Indians were always accompanied by ominous music. The only mainstream films to portray contemporary Indians were the *Billy Jack* films, an attempt to cash in on the exploitation fare that had proved successful with black viewers. Indians cheered as Billy Jack fought for every single Indian, conveniently ignoring the fact that the actor Tom Laughlin was not Indian. Such luminary white actors as Charles Bronson, Burt Reynolds, Burt Lancaster, and Charlton Heston had already portrayed Indians.

When it came to the movies, Indians learned to be happy with less, as Alexie observed: "We didn't mind that cinematic Indians never had jobs, were deadly serious, and were rarely played by Indian actors." Cinematic Indians were supposed to climb mountains or wade into streams and sing songs. Indians became so passive to the possibility of dissent and so accepting of their lowered expectations, that they canonized a film like *Powwow Highway* (1989).[38] But times have changed and when Alexie rewatched *Powwow Highway* for the first time in years, he reportedly cringed in shame and embarrassment over its blatant stereotyping, such as the scene in which the protagonists wade into a stream and sing to the moon.

The commercial success of *Smoke Signals*, which grossed $7 million, has already had enormous effect. "Every dusty Indian screenplay that's been sitting on a shelf for fifteen years is offered to us for development," Alexie said. "Every loincloth movie in Hollywood has been resurrected." However, Alexie is committed to creating a new image, "a native character with a career, a teacher, a lawyer." For him, moral responsibility is at stake: "There are boys and girls who are going to see themselves on screen, who are going to know that Chris and I directed and wrote it, who are going to know that all the actors in it were Indians playing Indians, and it's going to hand them dreams.[39]

CONCLUSION

The latest addition to multicultural cinema is *Three Seasons*, Toni Bui's impressive directorial debut, which won three awards at the 1999 Sundance Festival: the Grand Jury Prize, the Audience, and the Cinematography Award. With a powerfully poetic vision, Bui, who cowrote the script with his brother, has made a visually sweeping movie about contemporary life in Vietnam. Interweaving four stories into a striking pictorial tapestry, *Three Seasons* contrasts traditionalism with modernity in a country caught in the chaotic throes of transition. Traffic jams, a billboard advertising Coca Cola, American hotels, and other Western cultural icons define the rapidly changing milieu.

The film's protagonists are ordinary people living almost as strangers in their own land: a young girl hired to aid a reclusive spiritual master; a cyclo driver who becomes obsessed with a proud prostitute; a young boy hustling lighters and cheap watches; and an American Vietnam vet searching for the daughter he has never met. *Three Seasons* is a drama of alienated people who are struggling to find place and meaning in a country once torn apart by war and now battling to regain its soul. Intensely lyrical, with the deliberate pacing and detailed mise-en-scène that recall European film masters (Bui's favorite director is Andrei Tarkovsky), *Three Seasons* is beautifully shot by Lisa Rinzler, who previously shot such seminal indies as the Hughes brothers' *Menace II Society* and Steve Buscemi's *Trees Lounge*.

Bui, who is a graduate of Los Angeles's Loyola Marymount University, previously directed the short *Yellow Lotus*, which won awards in international festivals. The first American film to be entirely shot in the Socialist Republic of Vietnam since the war, *Three Seasons* boasts a remarkable Vietnamese cast and an emotionally evocative performance by indie icon Harvey Keitel, who's also the film's executive producer.

10

Female/Feminist Sensibility

ALTHOUGH HOLLYWOOD IS still dominated by men, women are more visible in the film industry today than ever before. With all the progress made, however, the independent milieu remains more hospitable to female filmmakers than mainstream Hollywood is. The Sundance Film Festival has been particularly friendly to first-time women directors. Of the 238 features shown in the dramatic competition from 1985 to 1999, about 20 percent were directed by women, a larger proportion than woman-helmed movies in any given year in Hollywood's history.

But women continue to lag significantly behind their male counterparts in holding key creative positions. A study of the top 100 grossing movies of 1997, 1992, and 1987 found that while the number of female producers and writers increased significantly over the last decade, the number of female directors, cinematographers, and editors remained stagnant.[1] Only 5 percent of the top 100 films released in 1997 were directed by women—up from 3 percent in 1987. On average, men outnumbered women eight to one per film in behind-the-scenes roles.

There are subtle and pervasive biases that make it difficult for women to succeed in Hollywood. Hence, the highest percentage of women directors worked on musicals and serio-comedies, and the lowest on action or horror movies. As movie budgets increase, studio heads (who are mostly men) tend to go with producers and directors (also mostly men) whose work they know, which, of course, perpetuates the status quo.

The significant issue, however, is not the number of women filmmakers, but the nature of their creative expression. Is there a distinctly female sensibility in indie narratives written and directed by women? Are new meanings established? Do women-directed indies address their audiences in different ways? In other words, what is the contribution of Joyce Chopra, Penelope Spheeris, Susan Seidelman, Allison Anders, Lizzie Borden, Mira Nair, and Nancy Savoca to the new independent cinema? What is distinctive about the work of women from different races and subcultures?

One cannot assume that women directors necessarily make feminist or even enlightened films; consider Barbra Streisand's latest retro work as a director, *The Mirror Has Two Faces*. If this chapter focuses on feature debuts, it's because first films, like first novels, tend to be more personal in their reflection of filmmakers' inner emotional experiences. It takes greater talent and tough-mindedness to make personal films about relationships—to put a personal sensibility on the screen—than to shoot formulaic, action-oriented pictures. Hence, women uninterested in genre films experience a harder time in Hollywood as well as indiewood.

Women have always participated more actively outside mainstream cinema. Since the 1930s, there has been a periodic call for a women's countercinema that would rewrite the patriarchal properties of Hollywood's language. Whether overtly feminist or not, women directors have shown the need to rupture Hollywood's typically closed, homogeneous forms of representation. The interventions of Mary Ellen Bute's abstract films of the 1930s, Maya Deren's avant-garde work of the 1940s, and Shirley Clarke's realistic films of the 1950s and 1960s, have been particularly important to the new indies.

Laura Mulvey has called Maya Deren the mother of the American avant-garde, crediting *Meshes of the Afternoon* (1943) with inaugurating the American experimental film. With a new paradigm for underground cinema, this film launched Deren's career as a filmmaker with strong interests in myth and ethnography. Deren stressed the poetic, dreamlike quality of film, its ability through framing and editing to displace a "normal" sense of time and place and to express the tension between interiority and exteriority. Shot in black and white, *Meshes of the Afternoon* employs innovative techniques to evoke women's conflicting impulses of fear and desire.

Deren may have been the first woman to point out that Hollywood movies are big on budget but small on artistry. "I made my pictures for what Hollywood spends on lipstick," she once observed. As Lauren Rabinowitz has pointed out, Deren led the radical formalist movement as an oppositional force with a new set of economic and aesthetic standards that rebelled against a patriarchal society in which women were denied a voice.[2]

Though Deren's concern with formal control over imagery set precedents for experimental filmmaking, her work ultimately proved less influential than that of Shirley Clarke. Clarke applied cinema verité to her first, independently produced feature, *The Connection* (1961), which was shot in black and white on a minuscule budget. Adapted from Jack Gelber's Living Theater drama about heroin junkies, this controversial film was banned for a year because of its "foul" language. Though it is now acclaimed as a trailblazer for alternative cinema, at the time, most critics deemed *The Connection* crude and offensive.

Clarke's follow-up, *The Cool World* (1963), a startling, verité-infused drama about a street gang, was shot on location in Harlem with a non-professional cast. This time, the critical response was more positive, although some still complained about deficiencies of structure and technique.[3] Controversy again erupted over Clarke's *Portrait of Jason* (1967), a feature-length, single-camera interview with a black male prostitute, which was labeled "repulsive" by conservative reviewers. However, the film was appreciated in Europe where it won festival prizes—Ingmar Bergman called it "one of the most fascinating films I've ever seen."

Unlike Deren, Clarke saw the limitations of experimental cinema and the limited scope of exploring female subjectivity and sexual desire. Instead, she displaced her sense of marginalization onto an urban cinema of alienation, centering on outcasts and misfits, as personified by African Americans, homosexuals, and drug addicts. Out of the antagonism between documentary and fictional narratives, Clarke activated a cinema of protest that went beyond the language of the feminized.[4]

Clarke was drawn to the rhetoric of social relevancy through the work of Robert Flaherty and Italian neorealism, which synthesized poetic and documentary techniques. The French New Wave and cinema verité, each striving for relevancy and realism, highly influenced her work. The New Wave advocated low-budget, freewheeling personal films, and cinema verité, then associated with Jean Rouch and Chris Marker, propagated the use of new, portable equipment and synchronized sound, which helped capture reality much more spontaneously. Clarke explored the political premises of cinema verité, positing self-reflexive forms as a means to radicalize audience experience of social issues. Challenging the filmmaker's gaze as objective reality, she showed how the production of images is inevitably intertwined with the production of meaning.

While Deren and Clarke were developing their ideas in New York, Dorothy Arzner and Ida Lupino were the only women directors in Hollywood. That the entire contribution of women to mainstream cinema from the 1930s to the 1960s could be summed up in terms of two sustained, though not terribly long, careers is truly depressing.[5] For decades, male-centered narratives have featured women in front of the cameras as love interests, objects of desire, and sexual threats—in other words, "negligible roles," to use the words of critic Marjorie Rosen.[6]

The first major wave of feminism, at the turn of the century, coincided with the invention of movies. The second wave, in the late 1960s and 1970s, produced an impressive body of critical and theoretical work and some distinguished alternative filmmaking. However, as Robin Wood has observed, feminism had no radical impact on mainstream film production either on the economic and power structures of a patriarchal industry, or on the thematic and aesthetic structures of the films themselves.[7]

Indeed, in Hollywood there is no women's movement, only individual women directors. The prevalent notion of women's equality, rather than women's liberation, is narrow as it denies a transformative dynamic to women's struggles. It implicitly sets men's achievements as the standards to which women should aspire and against which their progress is measured.[8] Hence, the problem is perceived as women's catching up to the men, rather than a problem for both men and women to resolve by changing the socioeconomic condition of their lives, from micro- to more macrointeractions.

TRADITION VERSUS MODERNITY—JOAN MICKLIN SILVER

In the 1970s, a number of women played prominent roles in the emergence of a new feminist independent cinema. Joan Micklin Silver collaborated with James Bridges on the screenplay of Limbo (1972), a drama about women whose husbands were captured or missing in Vietnam. Striking out on her own, she began in shorts before making her directorial debut with Hester Street (1975), a modestly shot black-and-white film set on the Lower East Side of New York circa 1896.

Adapted from Abraham Cahan's story, the movie centers on the assimilation of a Russian-Jewish immigrant to the New World.

Jake (Steven Keats) has been working in a sweatshop for three years
when his wife, Gitl (Carol Kane), and their son join him in New York. In
her absence, Jake has fallen for Mamie (Dorrie Kavanaugh), a down-to-
earth dresser who works at a dancing academy, the social center for
greenhorn Jews trying to become more American. Jake wants to detach
himself from Gitl, a pious waif in drab clothes and Orthodox wig who
speaks only Yiddish. Shy, passive, and superstitious, she evokes a culture in which he was never respected or accepted. Clearly, director Silver sides with Gitl, the movie's emotional center, whereas Jake is portrayed as a fool, abandoning a sensitive woman for Mamie, whose crass
gaiety—and large bosom—represent freedom to him.

The film is nostalgic for what Jewish immigrants have lost by becoming Americanized, but it doesn't address what they have gained.[9]
Condescending to Jake, who stands for vulgar American materialism,
Hester Street fails to demonstrate what the newly obtained freedom
meant to semiliterate Jews like Jake, who grew up in a tradition that values learning above all. Jake escapes not only Russian persecution but
the oppression of his own culture. Part of the film's commercial appeal,
as Pauline Kael noted, stems from its class putdown. If Gitl's docility
seems sweet and refined, it's only because Silver idealizes her. After
years of dejection, Gitl learns English and slowly comes into her own.
As in a fairy tale, at the end the timid Gitl, betrayed and humiliated, gets
a better man and a measure of financial independence.

The amiable ensemble struggles with their accents and shallow
roles. The shyster lawyer, hired by Jake to help him get a divorce, is a
cartoon, and so is the yenta (Doris Roberts), who mutters, while lacing
Gitl into a corset, "If you want to be an American, you gotta hurt." Bernstein (Mel Howard), the scholar-boarder who sleeps in the kitchen, is
also a type, a kind of hippie scholar. The movie identifies with Bernstein's commonsensical wisdom and sarcasm—his old-fashioned attitudes and suspicion of the New World blended neatly with the late
1960s counterculture, still felt in the 1970s, when the movie was released.

Small and anecdotal, *Hester Street* lacks plot or in-depth characterization.[10] But Silver filters the folkloristic material through the feminist
attitudes of the 1970s. Her directorial touch is unassured, and her dialogue is blunt and repetitive, but the restrained style makes for a likable

movie in which scenes are underwritten and underdramatized. The black-and-white cinematography and the simple characterization recall Hollywood's naive movies about the Big City. As a commentary on the Jewish-American experience—materialism versus spiritualism—the film assumes the shape of a pedagogic fable.

Silver's modest follow-up, *Between the Lines* (1977), served more as a showcase for talented performers than a critical view of the underground press, where it is set, or a compelling study of disenchantment among 1960s radicals, a topic addressed much more effectively in John Sayles's *Return of the Secaucus Seven* several years later. The movie explores the conflicts between writers' vanity and their public-spiritedness, the interplay of careerism and carnality. Drawing on his own journalistic experience, the screenwriter, Fred Barron, constructs for the film an editorial staff that's too likable and too uniform in age, taste, and outlook. The movie's major merit is a terrific cast that includes Jeff Goldblum, John Hurt, and Lindsay Crouse, all of whom would leave their mark on the emergent indie cinema.

Silver returned to the theme of *Hester Street*, the clash between tradition and modernity, in *Crossing Delancey* (1988), adapted by Susan Sandler from her play. Amy Irving plays a self-reliant New Yorker whose grandmother arranges for her to meet an eligible bachelor through a marriage broker—much to her chagrin. Once again, a light tone compensates for lack of a point of view and flawed technique. What's missing from Silver's work—and the reason she hasn't become a major director—are personal style and distinctive vision that would prompt an inside rather than an outside look at her subjects.

FEMALE FRIENDSHIP—CLAUDIA WEILL

The same year that *Between the Lines* was released also saw Claudia Weill's *Girlfriends*, a sympathetic look at a young, unattractive woman who tries to make it as a photographer in New York. The screenplay was written by Vicki Polon, based on Katherine Mansfield's story "Bliss." Prior to her feature debut, Weill produced a number of documentaries, including the acclaimed *Joyce at 34*, and directed the Oscar-nominated documentary *The Other Half of the Sky: A China Memoir* (1975), a chronicle of the first women's delegation to China, led by Shirley MacLaine.

Girlfriends, which began as a short at the American Film Institute, was the first indie to be backed by grants (totaling $80,000) from government and city councils. Bringing the feature to the screen, however, was a long, arduous task. Shooting lasted six weeks, but postproduction stretched out for more than a year. When the funding from the National Endowment for the Arts and the New York State Council on the Arts ran out, Weill was forced to interrupt her work and scrape up completion money from private backers.

The protagonists of *Girlfriends*, Susan Weisblatt (Melanie Mayron) and Anne Munroe (Anita Skinner), are college graduates who share a walk-up apartment on the Upper West Side of New York. They are constructed as types: Susan is Jewish (*Fiddler on the Roof*–like music plays when she's on-screen), and Anne Munroe is gentile (her music is neo-Baroque). Their friendship is put to the test when Anne, an ambitious but not very talented poet, opts for marriage, and Susan is left alone. Susan works with an urbane rabbi (Eli Wallach) on bar mitzvahs and weddings, but at heart she is an artist yearning for recognition. Desperately needing affection and companionship, Susan has to overcome her fears of herself and of a permanent relationship.

Girlfriends could have easily degenerated into soap opera, but Weill keeps the slice-of-life film simple and realistic, with charm and humor evident under the quiet desperation. As a study of loneliness (it's implied that New York is filled with girls living unfulfilled lives), the film draws on Mayron's strong performance. With her halo of frizzled hair and her intelligently expressive face, Mayron registers a problematic life with hesitant, repressed gestures.

Male friendships, with their robust macho romanticism, have often been celebrated in American films. A spate of male buddy movies was produced in the 1970s as a backlash against the women's movement. According to Molly Haskell, the emotional intensity of these films exists between the men; feminism gave filmmakers the freedom to drop the token women from their narrative altogether.[11] Weill reacted against those buddy films, which ignored or downgraded women. Simplistic in their notion of friendship, most of these films revolve around "two men with beautiful faces and the adventures they have together," but for Weill, "what's more interesting is what's not said, what people want from each other."[12]

A woman's intimacy with a man is such a cherished experience that society tends to disregard friendship among women. Hence, female friendship has been largely ignored by Hollywood, giving the erroneous impression that it hardly exists. The more prevalent stereotype is of women going at each other or competing for men. However, with divorce rates on the rise and marriage an increasingly fragile institution, a search for new bonds began, and friendship between women gained new interest as a subject for films.[13] With the emergence of the women's movement, social attitudes began changing. "Today, it's considered bad form to break a date with a woman if a man calls," observed Weill in 1977. "Not long ago, the man always came first."[14]

In the late 1970s, a cycle of Hollywood films exalted female friendship: *Julia*, *The Turning Point*, and *An Unmarried Woman* were all released within a year. Most of these pictures centered on a pair of women friends, usually opposites in personality. Fred Zinnemann's *Julia* depicts Lillian Hellman's (Jane Fonda) idealized friendship with the heroic Julia (Vanessa Redgrave) as a mythic figure who may or may not have existed. At the center of *The Turning Point*, also directed by a man (Herbert Ross), is the rivalry between two friends who have chosen radically different lives: One (Anne Bancroft) has pursued a dance career with dedication, while the other (Shirley MacLaine) has chosen a life as a wife and mother. In neither picture is the friendship convincingly or richly detailed, and neither film opened the door to new cinematic subject matter.

Weill, on the other hand, aimed to show that "female friendship is as fragile, delicate, supportive, complex, nourishing, painful and difficult as a love affair," because, at the end of the day, "you share meals, you go to the movies together, and you see friends together."[15] Her film doesn't suggest that friendship with another woman is better than friendship with a man, only that it's different: "With two women, you know how a person is going to respond, there's a kind of bonding with identical things shared."

Loosely inspired by Weill's experience with her roommate at Radcliffe College, both characters in *Girlfriends* draw on her life—"I have been Susan and I have been Anne." Despite the title, however, *Girlfriends* is better at depicting Susan's commitment to work than at dissecting her friendships. Less defined than Susan, the WASPy Anne is used as the Other, a counterpoint to Susan's values and choices. By marrying young, bearing a child, and giving up her career, Anne follows a traditional woman's role. Eventually, the two women are brought together on a deeper level of friendship, on the day Susan achieves professional success with her first exhibition in a SoHo gallery. In the final sequence, they even sneer at the man (Bob Balaban's prim, insidious jerk) who broke up their friendship.

Girlfriends brought the label "feminist filmmaker" to Weill, but she felt neither limited nor pressured by it: "It's extremely chauvinistic to assume that because you are a woman you have to make films about women or relationships. Feminism is a point of view you can use on any subject, even a big entertainment film."[16] Weill was gratified that both male and female viewers enjoyed her candid view of friendship. *Girlfriends* drew positive comments from men, including one who confided in Weill, "When my best friend got married, I felt lost."

OLD FORMATS, NEW SENSIBILITY—SUSAN SEIDELMAN

Though bad-mouthed by critics and currently in artistic decline, Susan Seidelman's importance to the indie cinema of the 1980s is beyond dispute. Seidelman's perspective is revisionist but not polemically feminist; her work is mildly original without being truly risky. Even when her films display sexual hostility between the sexes, Seidelman doesn't glamorize women at the expense of men. In fact, her strongest affinity is with desperate, aggressive women who never stop hustling.

Seidelman's best satires, *Smithereens* and *Desperately Seeking Susan*, examine contemporary issues of fame and self-fulfillment, personal identity and social relationships. One of the first filmmakers to put the hip "downtown" sensibility on the screen, she showed the good and bad of the East Village down-and-out bohemia. Seidelman shares with Jonathan Demme a fondness for kitsch (in furniture, fashion, and attitude) and an instinct for off-center casting, but she lacks Demme's vision and narrative skills.

On the strength of her early shorts, *And You Act Like One Too, Deficit* and *Yours Truly,* and *Andrea G. Stern,* which showed a satirical flair, Seidelman was able to raise $80,000 for *Smithereens* (1982), a tale of a hustler whose ambition is to manage a punk rock band. Wren (Susan Berman) is a village groupie who wants fame but lacks discernible talent for anything. Cowritten by men, Ron Nyswaner and Peter Asking, the movie provides a view of bohemia at low ebb, the world of bummed-out youngsters who work at marginal jobs and steal to get by.

Smithereens is a cautionary tale about ragamuffin punks immersed in media and addicted to TV sets that are never off. Products of a demoralized era, they are drawn to the rock-club scene by its promise of a potentially exciting life.[17]

When first seen, Wren is putting up photographs of herself in the subway. "Who Is This Girl?" says the caption above the picture, signaling that Wren lacks an identity. The nineteen-year-old Wren escapes from New Jersey, vowing never to return. She wants to be part of the rock world, but she can't play an instrument or sing. She wants to be famous but lacks talent or strong personality, and hence is relegated to a groupie. Energetic yet inept, she continually talks about her "plans" but eventually drifts toward prostitution.

The movie stays within its confined milieu, tracking its heroine through dimly lit corridors and graffiti-covered lots, giving it a rough, squalid look. The realistic details—cramped Avenue B streets, empty refrigerators with only a single pizza slice—are expressively shot by the cinematographer, Chirine El Khadem. The camera zeroes in on Wren's long legs in plastic boots under a miniskirt because she's always on the run. Wren barges into a noisy club, where she lays siege to a musician and gets thrown out. Desperate to score, she strikes out because she's too eager. Brassy and indefatigable, cocky and calculating, Wren is essentially a loser.

Wren links up with Paul (Brad Rinn), an innocent Montana boy who lives in a van in the docks, but she refuses to move to New Hampshire with him and later dumps him for Eric, a rock musician. But the handsome Eric (played by the New Wave guitarist Richard Hell) proves indifferent; when he takes her home, he falls asleep. Wren hustles wildly, trying to latch on to Eric, but in the end, she's struggling just to keep a roof over her head.

A dislikable character, repeatedly humiliated, Wren is thrown out of her apartment and gets water dumped on her head. It's unclear whether she is rejected for her ineptness and shallowness or whether she is a victim of her own doing. *Smithereens* shows the downtown club scene as a demeaning symbol of a wasteland. For the critic Stanley Kauffmann, Wren is the product of hype—"disc-jockey, discotheque, *National Enquirer*, TV-commercial, carbonic-gas-injected hype"—everything hateful in pop culture.

The first American indie to be shown in competition in Cannes, *Smithereens* enjoyed a successful run in the United States and in Europe.

The film is important in another way—it prefigures Seidelman's more fully realized follow-up, the farcical *Desperately Seeking Susan* (1985). If there was a "forced" hiatus after *Smithereens*, however, it's because the projects Seidelman was offered were dopey teenage comedies. She decided to bide her time until *Desperately Seeking Susan*, a comedy about an identity mix-up between a New Jersey housewife and a downtown New York rocker, came along. Financed by Orion at $5 million, the movie was overlaid with antibourgeois attitudes, which paid off commercially.

The movie's appeal derives largely from its varied cast, which includes a rock star (Madonna), an up-and-coming actress (Rosanna Arquette), actors from recent hot indies (John Lurie and Richard Edson from *Stranger Than Paradise*, Anne Carlisle from *Liquid Sky*), and gifted stage actors (Laurie Metcalf, Mark Blum, Robert Joy, and the comedian Steven Wright). In addition, a taxi driver is played by Rockets Red Glare, Sid Vicious's former bodyguard, and a jail matron by Shirley Stoler (*Seven Beauties*).

The plot's complications rely on an ancient device—amnesia, a gimmick imposed on a stylish East Village comedy, underscoring the discrepancy between the film's punk postures and its use of old formulas. As David Ansen pointed out, the collision of contrary styles in a New Wave fairy tale was partly inspired by the French cult film *Diva* (1982), and partly by *The Prince and the Pauper* and *Alice in Wonderland*.[18]

Roberta (Arquette), a bored housewife married to Gary, a hot-tub entrepreneur, escapes her routine by reading personal ads and following the adventures of a man who's "desperately seeking Susan." Roberta's insatiable curiosity leads to Susan (Madonna), a voluptuous gold-digger wanted for a mysterious death in Atlantic City and tailed by a mobster for the precious Egyptian earrings in her possession. While spying on Susan, Roberta gets bopped on the head—when she wakes up, she believes she's Susan.

Orion tried to interfere with the casting, recommending "a perfect blonde" for Madonna's part. But Seidelman wanted "a dark, spicy blonde," perceiving Susan as a woman who "floats through the funkiness in which she lives as if she were a princess." The whole movie was conceived as a party—"Girls Just Want to Have Fun"—and no party would be complete without party favors and astonishing props such as pink, shell-encrusted phones.

After *Desperately Seeking Susan*, Seidelman had bigger budgets at her disposal—and pressure to match. The studios wanted her to remake the comedy over and over again, but, instead, she chose *Making Mr. Right* (1987), a satire about a public relations expert. On the surface, it's a feminist version of *Frankenstein*: Frankie (Ann Magnuson) is hired to socialize an android astronaut called Ulysses (John Malkovich), and, over the objections of his inventor, she does such good a job of humanizing him that she falls for him.

Like *Desperately Seeking Susan*, *Making Mr. Right* relies on the notion of mistaken identity—a robot who develops a heart—but this outing lacks charm. As cowritten by Floyd Byars and Laurie Frank, the movie is supposed to provide commentary on modern relationships: Real men are so repulsive that women prefer androids who are sweet and open about their feelings. The male characters are priggish, self-centered, and sexually inept. The film's message is kneejerk feminist at its most cynical, suggesting that men are so inadequate they have to be manufactured by women. The android's wide-eyed amazement—a boy in the body of a grown man (with a big penis)—makes him desirable. Seidelman repeats Mel Brooks's use of the monster in *Young Frankenstein*, but, unfortunately, without the obscenities and Madeline Kahn's high-pitched thrills.

Though obvious, *Making Mr. Right* offers some incidental pleasures. The Miami atmosphere, a mixture of Jewish and Cubano (Se Habla Yiddish, a store sign reads), is a corrective to *Miami Vice*'s stylish glaze. The opening scene, which shows a pressured Frankie shaving her legs while driving to work, presents a comic view of modern working women. John Malkovich, an offbeat casting choice, plays both the prissy scientist who constructs the android in his own image and the android itself. As the hapless inventor Dr. Peters, who hates and fears women, Malkovich talks in a droning, pedantic voice. As the android Ulysses, he walks in a stiff-kneed Frankenstein stagger, his mouth frozen in a dumb grin. During sex, Ulysses gets so excited that his head turns around backward and his body short-circuits and falls apart. However, having an intelligent woman as Frankie fall for an android strains the film's credibility, particularly as Malkovich doesn't register the wild sexuality to pull it off.

Making Mr. Right began a downward trend for Seidelman, who went on to make a succession of inept and innocuous movies such as *Cookie* (1989), a comedy about a mob hood (Peter Falk) and his wacky daughter (Emily Lloyd), and *She-Devil* (1989), which concerns the vengeance wreaked by a fat, dumpy housewife (Roseanne Barr) on her attractive rival (Meryl Streep), an author of cheap romantic novels. The movie was meant to be an ironic tale of liberation, but the casting was lopsided and served feminism only in theory.

Blaming Hollywood for sucking her vision, Seidelman simply stopped working for a number of years. She rebounded in 1994 with the short *The Dutch Master*, an erotic tale whose protagonist, like most of Seidelman's females, seeks a fantasy life that's more exciting than what her reality offers. This Oscar-nominated short allowed her to regain the artistic freedom she had lost. Having tasted both indies and Hollywood, Seidelman says her fondest memories are still of *Smithereens*, because it was entirely free of compromise.

DECONSTRUCTING PROSTITUTION—LIZZIE BORDEN

A contemporary of Seidelman, Lizzie Borden has shaped a polemic feminist cinema concerned with the cultural representation of women. Borden's political engagement might have begun with the decision to change her name at age 11 from Linda to Lizzie. Borden moved away from the mainstream after graduating from Wellesley College and relocating to New York, where she painted and wrote reviews for *Art Forum*. She decided to become a filmmaker after attending a Godard retrospective and taught herself film craft by experimenting with rented equipment. By day, she edited films for Richard Serra, and on weekends, she worked on *Born in Flames*, a $40,000 self-financed film, which took five years to finish.

The militantly feminist *Born in Flames* (1983) is set in New York ten years after a socialist revolution. The white women leaders are dupes, leftist journalists who talk a good line, but have been coopted by the government. Wordy but gutless, they argue that social change takes time. Reacting to their mealy-mouthed stasis, black women take matters into their own hands. Some form a women's antiviolence street brigade, others organize a women's army, and still others, pushed by joblessness and racism, buy arms. The women want to take over the mass media, which they believe to be the first step in a guerrilla war.

When Borden asked women if they would ever resort to using violence, their answer was no. She then posed the question: "What if women did use violence? What if, through a socialist revolution, the hopes of women for an egalitarian system were raised? What if we came so close to getting it and then the government began putting women's needs on the back burner? . . . What if our second-class status—the fact that we're always put down—what if we couldn't escape the violence, the rape, getting kicked out of the job market—what would we do then?"[19] These questions became the premise of her film.

Most of the characters in the film were drawn from real-life personalities Borden has encountered. With the exception of the character acted by Jeanne Satterfield, a woman apprehended by the government for buying arms, the other roles were not played by professionals. It was important that each woman preserve her own profile and speak in her own voice. Unfortunately, situated in an unspecified future that seems remarkably like the present, *Born in Flames* is neither a fantasy nor an allegory. It begins with several women, few of whom even know each other, going about their business in a casual way. As the story progresses, the characters remain murky. The one rebel, Adelaide, who might function as repository of goals, is killed off in prison, long before the climax. Even so, despite its structural and political problems, for a first feature, the film had an ersatz documentary style—grainy texture, hand-held camera, abrupt editing—that was impressive.[20]

Borden created a greater stir in 1987 with her second film, *Working Girls*, which premiered at Sundance. The film provides an incisive look at a well-appointed Manhattan brothel, whose prostitutes are a far cry from Hollywood call girls. In Hollywood movies, prostitutes are usually stalked by psychopaths and get killed in the last reel, if not before. In contrast, the women working in the film's immaculately clean bordello are educated; none has been lured away from home, none is hooked on drugs. Most are there because the pay is good and the hours flexible enough to accommodate other interests.

Cowritten by Borden and Sandra Kay, *Working Girls* covers a day in the life of Molly (Louise Smith), a Yale art history graduate who hopes to become a photographer. Molly has a stable relationship with her black female lover (who doesn't know about her "job") and the latter's small daughter. The women are at ease in their work, because there's something else going on in their lives: Dawn (Amanda Goodwin) is a beautiful woman who studies for a law degree; April (Jane Peters), who's forty-three and deals cocaine on the side, seems to be there mostly to prove to herself she still has the right stuff. The place is run by a madam (Ellen McElduff) who shows appreciation for promptness, cleanliness—and the buck.

Although fictional, *Working Girls* looks and sounds as authentic as a documentary. Photographed by Judy Irola in a self-effacing manner, the film is as straightforward as the protagonists perfunctorily go about their business. The camera attends to the girls' duties without cuing any specific emotional responses, observing them as they service customers, giving them their money's worth and occasionally attempting to build a camaraderie with some of them.

Prostitution is seen by Borden as grubby and exhausting, but also as a demonstration of power. For one thing, men's bodies are exposed and vulnerable, whereas women have the ability to conceal. Facing the risk of condoning prostitution while still wanting to be considered a feminist, Borden claimed that "sex is a natural resource for women that, as long as society remains as it is, might as well be exploited." Contesting the prevalent stereotypes, Borden sets out to demystify what prostitutes do. In most bordellos, the sexual activity takes only minutes out of the half-hour session; the rest of the time is devoted to making the men comfortable, soothing their egos. The movie is intentionally unerotic—at most, a man's stomach is shown as he's being jerked off.

As preparation for making the film, Borden visited a number of bordellos to learn the different rituals: what kind of safety measures women use, how they act with police protection, how they treat dangerous clients. For most women, prostitution is not about sex but a means to accomplish other goals—put themselves through college, get a green card, place their kid in a private school. Some work for a short period, then stop, and nobody even knows about it. Borden encountered a new breed of prostitutes, women from the fashion industry and Wall Street. "The more I saw, the more I realized it didn't fit the stereotypes I'd seen in movies, where degradation or victimization tends to dominate," she said.[21] Missing in these films was the humor that enables women to handle their daily routines. The project took its specific shape when Borden met well-educated women from Yale and Columbia, who contrasted sharply with street prostitutes.

Borden opted for a nonjudgmental, nonsensationalistic look. What the audience sees in the course of one long day is insightful, banal, tedious, infuriating—everything but erotic. There's businesslike nudity upstairs in the bedrooms and a number of sexual encounters, but it would be difficult to find anything remotely sexy in them. "If you re-

move the moral judgment," Borden explained, "the movie is deroman-
ticized, capturing the boredom and routine of such experiences. The romance of prostitution has to do with the 'bad girl'—either on the lowest level, the street, or the highest call-girl-with-furs level."[22] What fascinated Borden was the rituals—the hygiene of the hotel-like
atmosphere, the codified movements, and, above all, the camaraderie
among the women.

Borden initially set the film in an antiseptic brothel on the Upper
East Side, where she observed working girls. But, later, in the name of
flexibility, she turned her downtown Manhattan home into a movie set.
Casting was difficult, especially for the male roles. Most of the men are
played by nonprofessionals. Borden located one Chinese client though
Screw magazine, because she could not find a Chinese male over age 35
who would take his clothes off. Men in the film were treated the way
men usually treat a prostitute—the more clothes they took off, the more
they got paid. When the actresses first came to rehearse, they looked
like street hookers, but Borden forced them go to a real "house" and
apply for a job. They came back amazed—the prostitutes they met reminded them of their college roommates. The experience changed entirely their conception of their parts.

Though some still consider prostitution a humiliating, exploitative
profession, for Borden, the film was feminist, "because it shows prostitution from a woman's point of view." "As long as prostitution exists,
women have to take control of it and of the images," Borden said. "We
all wish prostitution didn't exist. But as long as there is such an economic differential in this culture between what men and women earn,
a woman has the right to choose. If she decides to rent her body rather
than do a demeaning 40-hour-week, she should not automatically be
seen as a 'fallen woman.'"[23]

For Borden, prostitution was less an isolated phenomenon than a
mirror of other exploitative, male-dominated jobs. "Prostitution is
perhaps the lowest form of selling yourself in our culture, but within
capitalism, one is always selling an aspect of oneself. Who can decide
whether renting your body is worse than renting your brain?" In this
view, prostitution is like other service-oriented jobs—waitress, hostess, secretary—that depend on looking good and making men feel
comfortable. *Working Girls* is less a tract on female oppression than a
matter of-fact demystification of prostitution, which is presented as a
kind of acting. Depicting prostitution as labor, the film desanctifies

and objectifies sex, refusing to fulfill audience expectations of the sordidness of brothel life.

Borden's examination of prostitution and brothels is linked thematically if not stylistically to another original exploration of what's typically a men's domain, the porn movie theater, in Bette Gordon's *Variety*.

DECONSTRUCTING SEXUAL DESIRE—BETTE GORDON

Bette Gordon's interest in how sexual difference is constructed and how the gaze is split in films—men look, women are looked at—motivated her to direct *Variety* (1984), a film that uses pornography as a site of feminist exploration of sexual desire.[24] Feminists have avoided dealing with sexual fantasy, because pleasure in mainstream films is promoted by and dependent on the objectification of the female body. Challenging the notion of sexuality as a fixed identity, Gordon constructs a protagonist, Christine, who works in a porn movie theater as a ticket-seller.

Obsessed with watching one male client, Christine gradually succumbs to her curiosity and begins to follow him, which leads her to the Fulton Fish Market, Yankee Stadium, and the Staten Island Ferry. Significantly, the traditional roles of male as voyeur and woman as object are reversed, positing the woman as voyeur. Working inside a booth, Christine watches and listens to the activities of Forty-second Street, letting the images and sounds affect her in a way that blurs actuality from fantasy. She begins to construct elaborate fantasies about the man she follows, fictions that parallel her description of the movies she watches in the theater. The ticket booth is a central image, a transitional place between the theater and the streets, one that provides Christine with a vantage point of viewing men and their sexual desires.

In *Variety*, porn films become extreme examples of mainstream Hollywood—both employ voyeurism to exploit women as objects of male fantasy. However, rather than making a movie that uses explicit sex to explore these issues, Gordon raises the question of how cinema produces certain prescribed sexualities and marginalizes others. She assumes that because pornography doesn't tie women's sexuality to reproduction or domesticity it offers other possibilities for women. If Gordon is not interested in creating alternative feminist erotica, it's because "alternative" suggests marginality—the "other place," outside of culture, where women have already been.

Christine's boyfriend, an investigative reporter, is researching an article about the Fulton Fish Market. He talks about his work and, as usual, she listens. However, when she begins to speak, describing her fantasies, he shows discomforts—men become anxious when women express their desires. He becomes mute, as her speech takes over, hence reversing the dominance of male speech. Since speaking of fantasies is taboo in American culture, and the language of desire is male, Christine's articulation of sexual fantasy represents a new, radical activity. *Variety* suggests that women, even in patriarchal culture, could become active agents in the subjective way in which they utilize cultural symbols.

The audience never sees the porn movies; they only hear Christine's description. The focus on her reactions raises the question of credibility and subjectivity. Christine has no sex in the movie—she only talks about it. At first, she describes what she sees, but then she begins to describe what she wants to see, based on her desire. Following the anonymous client into a porn bookstore, Christine finds herself in a typically male space. Reversing the dominant cultural pattern, Christine becomes a viewer of male activities; a baseball game and a porn store are considered to be men's domain.

Later in the film, Christine follows the man to a New Jersey motel and searches through his suitcase—the most sexual act in the movie. But all she finds are shaving cream, a shirt, an address book, and a porn magazine. She returns to work and watches films, but now she imagines her own fantasies—how the man enters the motel room and approaches her as she sits on the bed. He gets closer, she looks, he looks— all shown in slow motion. Finally, Christine calls him to confess. She says, "I've been watching you," but we don't hear his side of the conversation. They agree to meet at the corner of Fulton and South Streets, and the final scene shows the dark corner in the rain. Christine doesn't show up and neither does he. The enigma is never explained, seductively suggesting an unfulfilled desire. Gordon's point becomes clear: Porn offers fantasy and desire for a promised, but seldom found, gratification.

PUSHING THE ENVELOPE—KATHRYN BIGELOW

Kathryn Bigelow and Susan Seidelman began their careers at the same time, yet their sensibilities could not be farther apart. If Seidelman's narratives are old-fashioned, relying on such conceits as amnesia and mistaken identity, Bigelow's texts are postmodern, marked by a flair for black humor and a cool, horrifying beauty. Bigelow has used B-movie plots to tackle more serious themes, such as political apathy and urban alienation. Like her favorite filmmakers, Oliver Stone and Scorsese, she favors films with edge and complexity that are not "comforting or pacifying."[25]

With unassailable artistic chops, Bigelow has devoted her career to a gender (and genre) busting study of film art and screen violence. Endowed with unique vision and bravura technical skills to match, she could have become a provocative filmmaker were it not for her crippling ambition to make it with the Hollywood boys' club as an action director and for her insensitivity to matters of narrative logic.

Bigelow's concern for the perfect image in terms of tone, color, and composition may stem from her painterly background. A member of New York's art world, her work has been shown at the prestigious Whitney Museum. Bigelow first discovered the possibilities of film as a "social tool" when she worked with the radical Art and Language Group. Switching from canvas to celluloid, Bigelow attended Columbia, where she made an impressive short, Set Up (1978), about a back-alley fight.

In 1982, Bigelow cowrote and codirected (with Monty Montgomery) The Loveless, a nihilistic meditation on 1950s biker movies. Featuring Willem Dafoe in his first screen role, it's the story of a biker band invading a theme park in rural Georgia. But the film owes more to Kenneth Anger's cult movie Scorpio Rising than to the Marlon Brando vehicle The Wild One. The Loveless is notable for its use of color and for its visual edge. The film's evocation of tough-guy glamour, however, is stilted; it regards the past with no detachment or wit. Janet Maslin panned the movie as "a pathetic and slavish homage to the 1950s," motivated by an unmistakable longing for that era, a nostalgia reflected in "silly, lifeless posturing."[26]

The bikers' leader, Vance (Dafoe), spends a lot of time playing with his jacket; the closest he comes to showing any emotion is when another character commits suicide. Ultimately, The Loveless shows more concern for fashion than for narrative—the gang is dressed in white T-shirts and black leather, but it doesn't project much menace. Along with the colors and the era's music (Robert Gordon, as one of the gang members, also provided songs), Bigelow seems to have unintentionally incorporated the 1950's blatant sexism. Although the gang's blonde tough (Tina L'Hotsky) talks as nastily as the men, she is basically a moll. The heroine, a pretty local girl named Telena (Marin Kanter), is also an incoherent creature who first sneers at Vance, then goes to bed with him.

Despite the movie's mostly dismissive reviews, the director Walter Hill was sufficiently impressed to give Bigelow a development deal. Five years later, she came up with *Near Dark*, a poetic horror film about a gang of vampires roaming the Midwestern plains. As Hoberman noted, nothing about *The Loveless* prepared for the supple glitter of *Near Dark*, an Americanized version of the European vampire myth.[27] The barroom violence in *The Loveless* is expanded and elaborated on in *Near Dark*'s horrifying mass murder.

Borrowing from classic outlaw-on-the-lam sagas, the hero is Caleb (Adrian Pasdar), a handsome Oklahoma farm boy who encounters the winsome Mae (Jenny Wright) standing by the road suggestively licking an ice cream cone. Caleb offers her a ride—and his life changes. Kidnapped by her undead family, a ragtag, rowdy bunch in a stolen Winnebago, he gradually becomes one of their kind. Captivated by Mae's charm, Caleb acquires a taste for fresh blood, but he is reluctant to adopt the violent ways—he can't bear the idea of killing. In the image of a wistful Mae giving blood from her arm to the starving Caleb, Bigelow reached lyrical tones. It's a sexual surrender that leads to complications but implies no moral judgment.

Bigelow, who cowrote the script with Eric Red, gives *Near Dark* an eerie pacing and enriches the dialogue with wry asides. The message— the sanctity and unity of the family—is no different from other films of the late 1980s, such as *Fatal Attraction*. The vampires are essentially a model family: mother, father, an older brother, and a little boy. Jesse (Lance Henriksen) is the patriarch, and the leather-clad Severin (Bill Paxton) is the gang leader. Following genre conventions, they live by night; sunlight causes them to burst into flames. However, quite shrewdly, the word "vampire" is never mentioned in the text.

Some reviewers compared *Near Dark* to *The Lost Boys* (also released in 1987), which pandered to the trendiness it purported to satirize. Taking a different approach, Bigelow combines thrills, dark eroticism, and humor, striking a strange balance between the other-worldly tone of

Adam Greenberg's stylishly chilling photography, Tangerine Dream's tense score, and the characters' realistic conduct. Odd as they are, the characters are played straight, and the film justifies their violence in a rational matter: They rob and kill because they need the blood to survive. In a well-choreographed scene, the gang gleefully wipes out the inhabitants of a redneck bar, while the song "Fever" (by The Cramps) plays on the jukebox. Humor is not neglected, either: Severin complains of the scruffy Hell's Angel whose neck he's about to bite: "I hate 'em when they ain't been shaved."

Near Dark was the first horror film to be given a Museum of Modern Art Cineprobe since George Romero's *Night of the Living Dead*, in 1968. Despite rave reviews, the movie was not commercial, although it became a cult hit on video. Still, the movie caught the eyes of Edward Pressman and Oliver Stone, who decided to produce whatever project Bigelow wanted to do next.

Like Seidelman, after *Near Dark*, Bigelow received numerous scripts for high-school comedies. "That seemed to be the only avenue for women directors at the time," Bigelow told *Vogue*. "So, in response, I tried to define a path that was antithetical to that. I was trying to make it very clear that I wanted to do something else."[28] Bigelow was determined to shatter gender stereotypes, to push the envelope of women's filmmaking. In an age when women directors were still expected to make "women's films"—small, modest, sensitive—she proceeded with flamboyant pictures such as the cop movie *Blue Steel* (1990) and the action-thriller *Point Break* (1991).

Women directors have rarely been given the chance to explore psychosis from a woman's point of view, which is what Bigelow set out to do in *Blue Steel*. A New York policewoman, Megan Turner (Jamie Lee Curtis), becomes the object of an obsession of a psychotic stalker (Ron Silver). Bloody and absurd, *Blue Steel* inadvertently became a visual exercise in erotic violence, turning uniforms and guns into fetishism. Despite its strong female protagonist and its art-world decorations, the movie was tiresomely familiar. Labeling *Blue Steel* a *Dirty Harriet* movie, David Denby wrote: "I can't see that much has been gained now that a woman is free to make the same rotten movie as a man."[29] Bigelow chose the kind of narrative done with greater skill by Don Siegel in *Dirty Harry* and by the star of these movies, Clint Eastwood. Concluded Denby: "*Blue Steel* proves definitely that testosterone-crazed movie violence is by no means the sole province of male directors."

As if to prove the validity of Denby's point, Bigelow followed with *Point Break*, a visually delirious but intellectually vapid thriller about a band of Zen-spouting surfers. As with *Blue Steel*, Bigelow imposed technical virtuosity on a routine story, the peculiar complicity between a law officer (Keanu Reeves) and a seductive criminal (Patrick Swayze). *Point Break* reaffirmed Bigelow's talent as a director of fast-paced, high-adrenaline actioners, burdened with absurd narratives.

Bigelow's most recent studio movie, *Strange Days* (1995), is a futuristic noir about apocalyptic Los Angeles during the last two nights of the century. Painting America as a society whose primary responses to anarchy are voyeurism and escapism, this morality tale concerns the redemption of Lenny Nero (Ralph Fiennes), a black-market dealer in "playback," a technical device that permits one person to feel another person's experience (witnessing murder, committing rape). Caught in murder, race riots, and partying, Lenny, "the Santa Claus of the subconscious," undergoes a moral crisis and is forced to sort through the squalor of secondhand experiences, a failed romance with a rock singer, and his true feelings for Mace (Angela Bassett), the only person of integrity in an otherwise corrupt world.

In her effort to capture the millennium's hallucinatory mood, Bigelow stages the finale as a huge dazzling riot inspired by Woodstock, Altamont, and Lollapalooza all in one. But the eruption of color, sound, and motion—the panorama of orchestrated chaos—didn't fool discerning critics and viewers, who noted again the great divide between a simplistic plot and technical sophistication.

THE DOCUMENTARY ROUTE

Not surprisingly, a number of women directors have begun their careers in documentaries. It's easier to break into the film industry, both mainstream and indie, via documentaries than through feature films.

Penelope Spheeris is uniquely equipped to examine suburban alienation. Her childhood was spent on the road with her father, who worked as a carnival strongman. After the family settled in Orange County, Spheeris's father was murdered, and her mother, an alcoholic, married nine times. Tragedy continued to dog Spheeris. The father of her daughter Anna died of a drug overdose when Anna was a child. Spheeris's films demonstrate her penchant for dealing with outsiders in a way that invites interest, but without the romantic skew of Hollywood pictures. Spheeris evinces compassion for disadvantaged youth, along with a genuine understanding of their anger.

In 1980, Spheeris made the first of her anthropological surveys of disaffected teen punks, *The Decline of Western Civilization*. For her, "one of the greatest contributions of punks was going against the lifestyles of the rich and famous, in contrast to heavy metal which buys into the rock-star trip." Two reasonably effective sequels followed: *The Decline of Western Civilization Part II: The Metal Years* (1988) and *The Decline of Western Civilization Part III* (1998).

Spheeris made two moody features about youth angst and alienation. The first, *Suburbia* (a.k.a. *The Wild Side*, 1983), is a drama about angry kids who cut their hair (in lieu of growing it long) and live in abandoned, rat-infested crash pads. The film concerns the clash between a group of punkers and their enraged neighbors. Some humor is submerged within a conventional morality tale about punkers who are blamed for a murder they didn't commit. The film tries to make a statement while wallowing in random violence and maudlin sentiment. Framed by the death of two children, *Suburbia* is a heavy-handed, intentionally repellent film about how America destroys its youth. Sympathizing with the rejected children, Spheeris puts the blame for their mischief on society's adult members.

The Boys Next Door (1985) stars Maxwell Caldwell and Charlie Sheen as alienated teens who go on a killing spree. Tired of being jeered at and ignored, the duo use murder to express their rage over not being loved, but Spheeris doesn't use their violence as a turnon. A movie about inarticulate despair, *The Boys Next Door* attempts to do more than other teenage movies, though Spheeris's portrait of hopelessness lacks fresh insights into the boys' motivations. As in most of her work, blame for the youth's problems is attributed to society's decadent values and to careless, inattentive families.

SEXUAL AWAKENING—JOYCE CHOPRA

Like Spheeris, Joyce Chopra did her early work in documentaries: *A Happy Mother's Day, Medal of Honor Rag*, a Vietnam play that she produced for television, and *Joyce at 34*, shot during an on-camera pregnancy. Chopra made her feature debut with *Smooth Talk* (1986), a disturbing tale of sexual awakening based on Joyce Carol Oates's story "Where Are You Going, Where Have You Been?" The film deals with the painful transition and the muddle of emotions that separates girl- hood from adulthood. Oates's story was written in 1966, but the movie (cowritten by Chopra and Tom Cole) is set at the time of filming, amid the emerging shopping mall subculture.

At fifteen, Connie Wyatt (Laura Dern) displays both naivete and flirtatiousness, irritating shallowness as well as poignant vulnerability. Spending the summer lazing around her house, Connie finds the mo- notony of her life oppressive. She can't bear talking to her overly con- cerned mother (Mary Kay Place) or to her pathetic older sister, June (Elizabeth Berridge), who won't stop nagging her. Connie leads a dou- ble life: At home, she is gawky and lazy, but with her friends she's spir- ited and lively. Connie really comes to life at the mall; her forays with her mates exhibit giddy-girlish high jinks.

Connie is an insecure adolescent on the verge of becoming a sexual woman. With an almost perpetual nervous smile on her face, she begins to realize her sexual power over men. Chopra keeps Connie front and center, showing her misery and her confusion, her lust and her an- guish—above all, her curiosity and excitement about sex. Connie's dreams of having boys look at her come true when she meets a glib se- ducer, A. Friend (Treat Williams) at a drive-in. "A. Friend," as he intro- duces himself, isn't eighteen, as he tells Connie, but closer to thirty.

A psychopath, who hangs out with the kids in town, A. Friend (or Arnold) terrorizes her until she agrees to go for a ride with him. When Connie begs him not to talk dirty to her, she represents every girl who knows she has gone too far but can't stop it. In what is one of the longest, most startling seduction scenes in American film, Connie walks to the seducer's car with the dreamy fatalism of a sleepwalker. The emotional effect of the scene derives from the vagueness of the man's identity as well as from his reading of Connie's burgeoning fears and desires.[30]

Almost to the end, Chopra and Cole are faithful to the spirit of the story, although they have altered the narrative balance. Oates skips through the sketchy background of an empty-headed, pleasure-seeking teenager, but in the film Connie is endowed with more emotional shel- ter. As Andrew Sarris has noted, Oates looks down on her yearning pro- tagonist; the bulk of the story consists of a verbose seduction of a girl by an older guy with a menacing style of smooth talk. The movie's first part is so convincing that the shift in tone at the climax comes as a shock. At the last minute, *Smooth Talk* takes a benevolent turn that leaves the audience baffled. Although Oates publically embraced the entire movie, the new ending is a betrayal. The tacked-on happy coda—the stoical resignation and reconciliation between Connie and her family—drains the narrative of its sense of horror.

Despite these deficiencies, *Smooth Talk* renders a precise definition of a very particular American existence: the lower-middle-class family, headed by an easygoing, distant father (Levon Helm) and an overconcerned mother. The family interludes, like the mall scenes, are perceptively written and acted. Chopra's loose style, however, lets some crucial scenes wander in a tempo that some critics found draggy.

Smooth Talk is remembered mostly for the performance of Laura Dern, then eighteen, who brought a sense of danger to the tough role of the sexually voyaging siren. Dern's sexuality and intelligence stood in sharp contrast to those of Molly Ringwald, the other popular teen actress at the time, who also made coming-of-age movies (*Sixteen Candles*, *Pretty in Pink*). Dern went on to become a quintessential figure of the new indie cinema, starring in such movies as *Blue Velvet*, *Wild at Heart*, *Citizen Ruth*, and, perhaps most interesting of all, *Rambling Rose*, directed by Martha Coolidge.

FEMALE CAMARADERIE—MARTHA COOLIDGE

When Martha Coolidge first read the screenplay for *Rambling Rose*, she felt an instinctive urge to make the picture. Adapted from Calder Willingham's novel, the script had bounced around Hollywood for two decades. Coolidge immediately thought of Laura Dern for the role of Rose, the teenager servant, and of Laura's real-life mother, Diane Ladd, for Mother, the household matron. Coolidge's documentaries, *David On David Off* (1972) and *Old Fashioned Woman* (1973), about her family, showed compassion for ordinary life and attention to detail, qualities that she brought to *Rambling Rose*. At that time, Coolidge was associated with movies like *Valley Girl* (1983) and *Real Genius* (1985), teen comedies that had become her calling card, and all the offers she was receiving involved more youth comedies. With *Rambling Rose*, Coolidge finally broke out of the "teen ghetto."

It's 1971, and Buddy Hillyer (John Heard) drives back to his home-town in Georgia, recalling his youth. When Buddy was thirteen, he had a crush on a sweet but wild woman named Rose. "In deep Dixieland, the month of Octobah is almost summry," he says in a voiceover narra-tion, before the central story shifts to its Depression setting. Rose, a warmhearted, ignorant girl, moves in with the Hillyers, an upper-mid-dle-class family, and wreaks havoc. A rather promiscuous girl, she has been sent to work at the Hillyers' after being pursued by too many men at home. She looks both innocent and provocative; her blond ringlets peek out from under her hat as her long, shapely legs move restlessly beneath a flowered dress.

Rose becomes as infatuated with Mr. Hillyer (Robert Duvall) as Buddy is with her. Coolidge plays the scenes between the two men and Rose for both comedy and poignancy; their delicacy reflect her direc-tion at its best. In their first encounter, Rose stops washing dishes and throws herself onto Mr. Hillyer's lap, begging to be kissed, while Buddy observes through the kitchen door. Initially, Hillyer is tempted but he quickly comes to his senses: "A man is supposed to be a fool about this, but not women. What are you, a nincompoop?"

Later that night, the distraught Rose goes to Buddy's room for in-nocent comfort and arouses his sexual curiosity. Lying next to the eager Buddy (Lukas Haas), Rose says, "You're just a child and wouldn't un-derstand what kind of thing can stir a girl up." Treated with both comic Southern Gothic and erotic audacity, this scene was hailed as a sexual breakthrough in American films. What begins as an intimate conversa-tion turns into an awkwardly heated sexual experience in which Rose allows herself to be caressed by the boy to the point of reaching orgasm. As Andrew Sarris observed, "It's not so much what's shown explicitly as what's accepted matter-of-factly as normal adolescent behavior."[31]

When Rose marches off to town to find a man, Hillyer and Buddy watch from their car, impressed with the speed of her success. Before long, various men are fighting over her in the front yard. Is Rose a scoundrel? A disreputable heroine? Unsure, Hillyer thinks she ought to leave the house, but Mother protects her, and ultimately the film sides with her. Mother says, "This girl doesn't want sex, she wants love." Ac-tually, Rose wants both. With moral weight, Mother stands firm against both doctor and husband, refusing to allow them to solve Rose's "nymphomania" with a hysterectomy. The movie features an antiestab-lishment stance in the figure of Dr. Martinson (Kevin Conway), who represents the villainous medical authority in his suggestion of abortion.

Even when Rose tries to seduce Mr. Hillyer, Mother shows compassion for her. The film puts the audience in Hillyer's position, as he tries to figure out what to do about Rose and, at the same time, comes to terms with his wife's enlightened concerns. Mother is a modern heroine: responsible, open-minded, and educated, working on a master's thesis at Columbia University. In her scenes with Rose, she exemplifies a newly discovered female camaraderie.

Seen though the eyes of an adolescent, *Rambling Rose* is an uncommon coming-of-age tale that raises universal questions about the mysteries of sex and love. Coolidge finds a fresh angle to frame the story, while keeping firm control over the changing emotional tone. The film is structured as one long flashback from Buddy's point of view, as he turns to his past to retrieve honor and dignity. Coolidge's films usually lack psychological depth, but *Rambling Rose* is an exception. Here, the depiction of human decency is not preachy, and her feminist concerns are in tune with Willingham's frankness about the frustrations shared by both men and women. Arguably, only a woman filmmaker could see the female point of view as clearly and sympathetically as the male's, fully embracing the notion that even the most promiscuous women are looking for love rather than sex.

Cashing in on the relative success of Seidelman, Bigelow, Chopra, and others, a new generation of women directors came of age in the 1990s. Exciting, often innovative films were released in the early years of this decade by Nancy Savoca, Allison Anders, Mira Nair, and Stacy Cochran, all graduates of film schools. Most of these women enjoyed spectacular beginnings and, unfortunately, just as spectacular declines.

A VIEW FROM THE KITCHEN—NANCY SAVOCA

The surprise winner of the 1989 Sundance Grand Jury Prize was a low-budget film called *True Love*, an exuberantly raucous portrait of an Italian-American wedding. Its director, Nancy Savoca, was then an unknown quantity to most filmgoers. Cowritten by Savoca and her husband, Richard Guay, the film has a perceptive eye for humorously realistic settings and down-to-earth characterizations—so much so that some viewers didn't realize they were watching a feature movie. *True Love* boasts a semidocumentary quality and an "obscure" cast of thespians who don't look like actors.

Since then, with three pictures to her credit, Savoca has carved a well-defined niche for herself in the indie world. Savoca's movies benefit from a fresh perspective—her heroines are "natural" and unglamorous, drawn from her outsider's status as a woman. "If there's feminism in my films," Savoca said, "it's a feminism that asks questions and doesn't define. We should be asking questions rather than laying down the rules of what a woman should or shouldn't do. It's all about choice."[32] Savoca's work has evolved from the light social satire of *True Love* to melodrama in *Dogfight* to an unsuccessful attempt at magical realism in *Household Saints*. Her movies are demanding, but not entirely rewarding—they tend to be dreary and bland. Only *True Love* found its audience; *Dogfight* and *Household Saints* were failures.

The heroine of *True Love* is a young bride who is planning the wedding she had dreamed about her whole life. Savoca portrays the rites and travails and all the minor details that go into orchestrating a wedding extravaganza—the squabbles over tuxedos, food, rings. But more than anything else, she dwells on the gulf between the sexes. A Bronx native herself, Savoca conveys the sexual segregation of her own childhood: Women in her films convene in the kitchen.

True Love was made as a counterpoint to such Hollywood movies as *Moonstruck* (1987), a romantic comedy starring Cher and Nicolas Cage as mismatched lovebirds in an Italian-American community. Savoca steers clear of *Moonstruck*'s charming but phony treatment of the material. Her movie is closer to the Italian-American humor in Scorsese's *Mean Streets* and Jonathan Demme's *Married to the Mob*, which were also attentive to the characters' flamboyance. Never condescending, *True Love* shows affection for the specifically ethnic neighborhood and a good ear for the local language of both genders. One of Savoca's poignant observations is that the bride and her friends talk the same way as the men, but they are much tougher than the men are.

Like his friends, Michael, the groom, never finishes a sentence without a certain indispensable, all-purpose modifier. Michael and his buddies cap off the bachelor party by driving to Atlantic City. They drink themselves sick, then mournfully discuss how to arrange the newlyweds' "Mediterranean" furniture suite. For her part, the bride gets advice from her aunts, who wish her well, but also instruct her how to order her husband to "take gas"—stick his head in the oven—just in case.

Donna (Annabella Sciorra) and Michael (Ron Eldard) want to get married, but they don't realize what exactly marriage entails. Michael represents a mix of contradictions; he's a sweet, decent fellow beneath all the bluster. It's hard for Michael to get a grip on marital responsibilities, to realize that he can't go out with his friends after the wedding. Savoca works a strain of pathos into her comedy, showing a nervous, inexperienced couple in danger of being buried beneath—"I just don't wanna end up hating my life," Michael says.

In her second film, *Dogfight* (1991), Savoca also explores sexual politics, this time focusing on an unattractive girl—a type rarely seen in mainstream films. Questioning society's standards of beauty, *Dogfight* is about an exceedingly cruel set-up (hence the title), an old Marine ritual in which each participant contributes money to a pot and the winner is the man who shows up with the ugliest date. This "dogfight" takes place in San Francisco, the night before a bunch of marines is shipped out to Vietnam. Reflecting the naivete of the early 1960s, the film is a tender examination of the evolving romance between Eddie Birdplace (River Phoenix) and his "date," Rose Fenney (Lili Taylor). Savoca fleshes out Rose's experience of the events as she struggles to salvage her dignity. Both Rose and Eddie are seen as victims of societal conceptions of femininity and masculinity.

Savoca plays for laughs the scenes in which Eddie and his pals search for their "dog." There's a lovely scene early on in which Rose gets ready for the date, putting on her nicest dress and discreet makeup, while Eddie tries to trick her into smearing lipstick over her face. Savoca also puts her signature as a woman director on the sex scene, which is presented with characteristic attention to detail. The scene lingers on such prosaic issues as when and where you get undressed on your first date, issues that Hollywood movies never bother with.

Savoca orchestrates a radical shift in the audience's perception of the heroine. Rose begins as an ugly, gullible, duped woman facing heartbreaking cruelty. But by the end of the film, she's perceived as beautiful, and not in the fake manner of the Australian Cinderella tale *Muriel's Wedding*, in which a fat girl (Tony Collette) is transformed into a winning beauty. In *Dogfight*, it is Rose's gracious personality that emerges triumphant.

Despite good elements, Savoca misdirects the film with the kind of pathos that encourages viewers to feel sorry for its characters, first for Rose, then for Eddie. The performances of both Lili Taylor and River Phoenix are exceptional, but the movie would have worked better if it had been cast with a truly unattractive woman; Taylor is too appealing for the part. Savoca overidealizes Rose, making her a spiritual woman with pacifist philosophy and liberal politics. In forgiving Eddie, Rose relieves him of the last traces of his marine machismo and misdirected rage.

Although released by Warners, *Dogfight* was basically an independent film. The film met with unfavorable reviews and even poorer commercial success. The same fate would befall Savoca's next feature, *Household Saints*, her most ambitious film to date, a tragicomic exploration of three generations of Italian-American women as they struggle with the conflicting demands of the Catholic Church on their sexuality and spirituality.

Based on three intertwined tales, the film begins with the grandmother, Carmela (Judith Malina), a jealous, superstitious woman, praying for vengeance on her daughter-in-law Catherine (Tracy Ullman). Perfectly average, Catherine was won as a bride by Carmella's son Joseph (Vincent D'Onofrio) in a pinochle game. Raised Catholic, their teenage daughter, Teresa (Lili Taylor), begins to experience fervent visions, which are interpreted as psychotic experiences. Is Teresa mad, or is she a saint in delirious pursuit of a union with Christ? "We've gotten to a point in our society," said Savoca, "where things that have to do with God and spirituality are taboo, and we treat spiritual matters very much like mental illness."[33]

Attracted to the magic realism of Francine Rose's book, Savoca frames her movie as a folkloristic tale. "When you hear family tales, you don't question whether it happened or not," Savoca said. "You accept it as a certain kind of reality that's different."[34] In all of her films, Savoca looks for the extraordinary in the ordinary (e.g., the Jesus miracle in *Household Saints*). The author of the book upon which the film is based told Savoca that Jesus should be "the Vanilla Ice of Jesuses," because Teresa is a teenage girl in love. Savoca wanted "someone who would make your heart stop if you were fourteen," so she cast the pop star Sebastien Roche as Jesus.

Savoca's singular perspective is defined by her womanhood. Unlike Kathryn Bigelow, she makes movies that could not be mistaken for those directed by men. The scene in *Household Saints* in which Teresa loses her virginity and then hears the angels singing recalls a similar sequence in *Dogfight*. Loss of virginity is a subject rarely addressed in films, and when it is portrayed, as in Bertolucci's *Stealing Beauty*, it's an epiphany that rarely approximates the awkward and painful experience it is for many women.

The exploration of the Italian-American heritage is also done from a distinctly female perspective, complementing the films of Coppola, Scorsese, and other Italian-American directors, which have ignored women or allotted them peripheral roles. Savoca observed: "As much as it's frustrating for me to watch Italian-American movies made by men, in which there are no women of consequence, there's a very segregated social situation with working-class Italian-Americans. What I love about Scorsese's movies, *GoodFellas*, *Mean Streets*, is that I see where those guys go when they leave. When the door closes behind them, it's a Scorsese movie, but when the door closes and we're still in the kitchen, then it's mine."[35]

Coming of age in the 1970s, an era of antiheroes in American film, Savoca developed an interest in flawed characters like those played by Gena Rowlands in *A Woman Under the Influence* and Al Pacino in *Dog Day Afternoon*. Savoca's philosophy is rather simple—she wants to see on-screen women like herself, women she can recognize. Refusing to romanticize women, she is intrigued by the opportunity to explore real characters—she believes that to idealize women is akin to "cheating." Stylistically unassuming but thematically substantial, Savoca's work contrasts with the overhyped work of Allison Anders.

THE SEARCH FOR THE MISSING MALE—ALLISON ANDERS

If Allison Anders's screen work had been as interesting as her provocative offscreen persona, she would have become the most prominent contemporary woman director. Unfortunately, it is not. With all the attention surrounding her career and her winning of a MacArthur Foundation Genius Award, Anders remains an uneven filmmaker, with only one satisfying film to her credit, *Gas Food Lodging*.

Anders professes no interest in what she dubs the "masculine

A modern, different kind of romantic triangle is at the center of Ang Lee's social satire *The Wedding Banquet* (1993), with Winston Chao playing a gay Asian in love with a white man (Mitchell Lichtenstein, *left*), but marrying a woman (May Chin) to facilitate her getting a green card. Courtesy of the Academy of Motion Picture Arts and Sciences.

Alienation is the central theme of Tim Hunter's controversial *River's Edge* (1987), featuring a group of young actors *(from left to right)* Keanu Reeves, Crispin Glover, Roxana Zal, Phil Brock, Josh Richman, Daniel Roebuck, and Ione Skye, shockingly numb when their friend is found strangled. Courtesy of the Academy of Motion Picture Arts and Sciences.

Whit Stillman brought the new milieu of society galas and Christmas debu-
tante soirées to the screen in his splendidly written debut, *Metropolitan* (1990).
Top: Audrey (Carolyn Farina) becomes enchanted with outsider Tom (Edward
Clements) at a dinner dance. *Bottom:* Cynthia (Isabel Gillies), Charlie (Taylor
Nichols), and Sally (Dylan Hundley) attend another upper-crust soirée at the
latter's Park Avenue mansion. Courtesy of the Academy of Motion Picture
Arts and Sciences.

Sexual awakening: Promiscuous Rose (Laura Dern) introduces teenager Buddy (Lukas Haas) to some of life's adult mysteries in Martha Coolidge's *Rambling Rose* (1991). Courtesy of the Academy of Motion Picture Arts and Sciences.

Allison Anders missed a unique opportunity to provide an inside view of her tough Echo Park Latinas, Angel Avilez *(seated at left on bench)* and Seidy Lopez, in *Mi Vida Loca* (*My Crazy Life*, 1994). Courtesy of the Academy of Motion Picture Arts and Sciences.

In the turbulent wedding that serves as the climax of *True Love* (1989), Nancy Savoca's comic portrait of a modern marriage, Donna (Annabella Sciorra) retreats in anger and frustration to the restroom in the midst of the festivities. Courtesy of the Academy of Motion Picture Arts and Sciences.

In *To Sleep With Anger* (1990), directed by Charles Burnett, arguably the most underrated black filmmaker, Gideon (Paul Butler, *left*) and Harry (Danny Glover) are former friends, reunited when Harry brings the superstitions of the old South to contemporary South Central Los Angeles. Courtesy of the Academy of Motion Picture Arts and Sciences.

At 21, Matty Rich directed and costarred with Lawrence Gilliard, Jr., and Mark Malone in *Straight Out of Brooklyn* (1991), a raw, angry drama about the impossibility of decent life in the Red Hook Projects for black youths, whose dream is to "crossover" to Manhattan and start a new life. Courtesy of the Academy of Motion Picture Arts and Sciences.

Revamping the old European vampire sagas as a modern American erotic thriller, Kathryn Bigelow made a stunning solo debut in *Near Dark* (1987), lyrically shot in the Southwest, with Adrian Pasdar and Jenny Wright as a romantic couple. Courtesy of the Academy of Motion Picture Arts and Sciences.

In the romantic comedy *She's Gotta Have It* (1986), Spike Lee put at the center a liberated woman who enjoyed having sex with three different men. Conservative males are the butt of the joke, as in this scene, in which Nola Darling (Tracy Camilla Johns) tries to convince one of her beaus, Jamie Overstreet (Redmond Hicks), to give their relationship another chance. Courtesy of the Academy of Motion Picture Arts and Sciences.

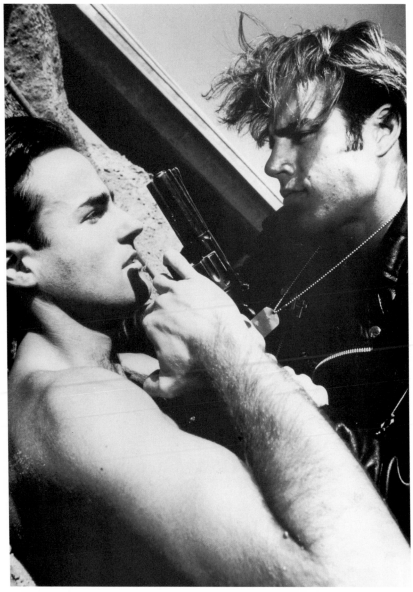

In Gregg Araki's most resonant work, the AIDS road movie *The Living End* (1992), a reckless hunk (Mike Dytri) forces a frustrated West Hollywood film critic (Craig Gilmore) to make love at a gun point. Courtesy of the Academy of Motion Picture Arts and Sciences.

Out in the wilderness—and in limbo—hunk Mike Dytri and beau Craig Gilmore are with no present or future in Araki's *The Living End* (1992). Courtesy of the Academy of Motion Picture Arts and Sciences.

Gay yuppies received a most positive treatment in *Longtime Companion* (1990), the first indie about the AIDS crisis and how it was met by the gay community, represented by TV actor Howard (Patrick Cassidy) reading on the phone to his lover the first story in the *New York Times* about the "strange new disease," as Willy (Campbell Scott) and Fuzzy (Stephen Caffrey) enjoy a walk on the Fire Island dunes shortly after meeting. Courtesy of the Academy of Motion Picture Arts and Sciences.

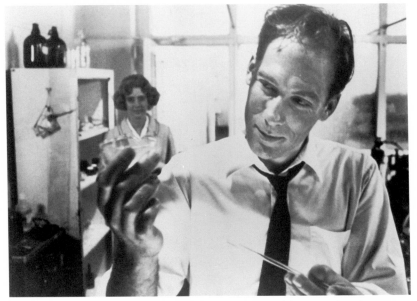

In "Horror," one of the three interlinked stories in Todd Haynes's poignant anthology *Poison* (1991), a doctor (Larry Maxwell) and his assistant (Susan Gayle Norman) conduct experiments. Courtesy of the Academy of Motion Picture Arts and Sciences.

In *Poison*'s most powerful segment, "Homo," a boy is about to be tortured and spit on as punishment for being gay. Courtesy of Zeitgeist Films.

Marc Levin's *Slam* (1998), the grand prize winner of the Sundance Film
Festival, was a different kind of black-themed drama, one that illuminated
anguish through street poetry, with real-life poets Saul Williams *(top)* and
Sonjah Sohn *(bottom)* writing and performing their own material. Courtesy
of the Academy of Motion Picture Arts and Sciences.

In the opening sequence of Allen and Albert Hughes's *Menace II Society* (1993), one of the most auspicious debuts in indie history, O-Dog (Larenz Tate, *left*) and Caine (Tyrin Turner) have a tragically violent confrontation with the owner of a Korean grocery which sets the tone for the entire film. Courtesy of the Academy of Motion Picture Arts and Sciences.

In his charming, offbeat comedy debut, *Clerks* (1994), Kevin Smith celebrated the aimless politics of Gen-X in a movie almost entirely shot at a convenience store, where his anti-heroes (Brian O'Halloran, *left,* and Jeff Anderson, *right*) simply engage in talk. Courtesy of Miramax Films.

Tarantino's striking feature debut, the ultraviolent crime-heist picture
Reservoir Dogs (1992), became a model for a whole generation of filmmakers.
Harvey Keitel *(right)* and Steve Buscemi *(on the floor)* face each other in what
became one of the most celebrated scenes in indies of the 1990s. Courtesy of
Quentin Tarantino and Miramax Films.

Tarantino's Oscar-winning *Pulp Fiction* (1994), one of the few indies to have crossed the $100 million mark at the box office, resurrected the career of John Travolta, who played a hit man, here dancing with his boss's wife (Uma Thurman), in a self-reflexive scene that commented on Travolta's early musical films. Courtesy of Quentin Tarantino and Miramax Films.

Driving in a bloodied car, hit men Vincent (John Travolta, *left*) and partner Jules (Samuel L. Jackson), representing the ultimate in cool, find time to chat about a whole range of issues, trivial as well as serious. Courtesy of Quentin Tarantino and Miramax Films.

model" of filmmaking and its limited vocabulary, with "three-act structure and certain kind of pacing, one that sets out with goals and resolves
things."[36] She is more intrigued by a movie like *The Hours and Times*,
which doesn't use a traditional model and instead creates a new narrative language, one of process. But theory and praxis don't cohere in Anders's case. She hasn't applied new models to her work, and her latest
film, the astoundingly inept *Grace of My Heart* (1996), is conventional in
the worst sense of the term.

Anders's work, however, is fiercely personal. Her first, codirected
feature, *Border Radio* (1988), about the punk scene in Los Angeles, was
done while she "partied and smoked and listened to Fairport Convention with a bunch of guys." Displaying grit, vitality, and honesty, *Gas
Food Lodging* (1992), the story of a single mother bringing up two
teenage daughters in a dusty New Mexico town, drew on Anders's experience as a single mother. For *Mi Vida Loca* (1995), she looked no further than her Echo Park neighborhood and its Hispanic girl gangs.

Anders works mostly by instinct in her preference for scripts about
working-class women. A cross between a 1960s earth mother and a
Hell's Angels biker, she sports long, untamed red hair and a floral tat-
too on her forearm with the names of her daughters, Tiffany and Devon,
both born out of wedlock. Anders's checkered background proved to be
an asset to her career, as she has said: "I've always had this way of turning what was shameful into this kind of boastfulness." Told that being
an unwed mother would ruin her life, she turned it into an opportunity:
"It was neat to see that my single parent background ended up being
why my career really kicked in."[37]

Born in Kentucky, Anders was abandoned by her father at the age
of five, sexually abused throughout childhood, and gang-raped at
twelve. Her stepfather's violent behavior escalated, and one night he
held a gun to her head. Anders is proud that her daughters are the first
generation in her family not to have been sexually abused. When Anders's favorite Beatle, Paul McCartney, was rumored to be dead, she re-
treated into a fantasy bond with him. During the "Paul Is Dead" hysteria, she claimed to have heard McCartney beckoning her to join him in
the grave. Trying to kill herself, she spiraled into a self-destructive cata-
tonia—"I just went nuts, I just went over the edge," she recalled.

At age 17, Anders dropped out of high school and headed back to
Kentucky to live with relatives. A meeting on a bus with an English
student took her to London, where she worked in a bar until she got

pregnant. When her beau didn't want her to have the baby, she returned to Los Angeles, getting by on waitressing and welfare. Anders enrolled in a junior college and later attended UCLA's film school, where she became intrigued with Wim Wenders: "I read a huge article about him, and I loved the things he said. I thought this is exactly what I want to do with film."[38] A fan letter to the German director culminated in her obtaining an internship to work on his movie *Paris, Texas*.

Border Radio, codirected by Kurt Voss, Anders, and Dean Lent, was a "no-budget" movie about the marginal lives of rock musicians. Shot in a gritty black and white, it reflects the insecurity in musicians' lives, their strenuous struggle to survive. Her solo directorial debut, *Gas Food Lodging*, represented the perfect meeting of artist and subject. "Putting a huge amount of autobiographical stuff into the script," she created a film whose strongest scene is one in which a young woman tells a British geologist about the traumatic experience of being gang-raped. Though the film touches on issues relevant to women, Anderson was careful not to make a stridently antimale film.

Adapted from Richard Peck's novel *Don't Look and It Won't Hurt*, *Gas Food Lodging* tells the story of Nora (Brooke Adams), a working-class mother who lives in a trailer with her two daughters. Trudi (Ione Skye) seems to be a tough, foul-mouthed tramp, but she's essentially a victimized girl. Shade (Fairuza Balk), her younger sister, who spends her time watching Mexican melodramas in a local moviehouse, dreams of reuniting her mother with the father Shade has never met. The film cuts deep into the dreary life and anxieties of single women; yet, for all the bleakness, the women are not devoid of humor, highly aware that life could be better.

With a tight focus on the women's relations with one another, the film depicts thankless jobs, trailer homes—and a yearning for something meaningful to happen. "I don't think anyone rescues anyone else in this film," Anders said. "The men change nothing for these women." Perceiving the movie as less about sex or love than about the search for intimacy, Anders claimed she "could have easily made this intimacy come from women." But she cannot: Impossible men are an issue for Anders, on-screen and off-, as she once confessed: "I don't feel safe with men a lot of the times because inevitably I'm going to be made to feel like I'm crazy."[39]

After the film, Anders received numerous letters from teenage mothers who wanted to connect with one of their own. "I fell in love with it," said Callie Khouri, *Thelma & Louise*'s scripter, who was a juror at Sundance, where Anders's film premiered. "I was jealous of it in the best possible sense." Blessed by the New York Film Critics Circle with a Best First Film Award, *Gas Food Lodging* is by far Anders's best film.

For her next picture, *Mi Vida Loca* (*My Crazy Life*), Anders turned to Latinas gangs. Like *Gas Food Lodging*, the movie concerns the plight of teenage girls who become welfare mothers, stuck with no future outside the barrio. Demonstrating her commitment to working-class women, Anders focuses on Echo Park Latinas, providing a fresh respite from the male-themed movies that have dominated the gang genre. Films about street gangs have been replete with clichés and stereotypes. Even the gritty ones dwell on macho, volatile men who stake out their territories in graffiti and blood, and women are seen mostly as sex objects.

Mi Vida Loca is about adolescent girls who seek solace in outlaw life in defiance of their poverty. The nonlinear narrative is divided into three interrelated chapters, which depict the barrio without sensationalism or condescension. The melodrama consists of long flashbacks, interwoven with a romantic interlude about a woman who falls in love with her prison pen pal. The first tale is about the animosity between two best friends, Mousie (Seidy Lopez) and Sad Girl (Angel Aviles), over their mutual boyfriend. The second, lighter story concerns the release of Giggles (Marlo Marron) from jail and her return to Echo Park. A more ironic tone resurfaces with the closing segment, which involves the disillusionment of Blue Eyes (Magali Alvarado) with the playboy she worships.

The mix of unknown professionals with actual homegirls pays off: It's almost impossible to distinguish the actors from the residents. Throughout, there's keen attention to textures, with a sumptuous camera recording background details. In all of her films, Anders has employed a heightened sense of color. Here, Blue Eyes wears a red dress that matches the bridge, and a closeup of Sad Girl's mouth reveals erotic lips that are as purple as petals.

Anders's intent was to show that the women don't need men. But they do. Sad Girl and Mousie have been best friends since childhood, but their friendship is strained when each becomes pregnant by Ernesto (Jacob Vargas), a sweet-tempered drug dealer who cares more for his painted truck than for either of them. Tough around the edges but soft at the center, *Mi Vida Loca* comes from Anders's heart rather than her head. One girl says, "Women don't use weapons to prove a point, they use weapons for love," but before the movie is over, a rival proves her wrong. The women live in a world where struggle is expressed in absolute terms of love or hate.

In its blend of ethnography and flawed storytelling, the movie wavers, revealing Anders's uncertainty over whether she was making a melodrama or a documentary. The episodic structure accentuates the film's problematic shifts in tone from romanticism to realism. And the use of multiple voiceovers is confusing, especially in the beginning, when the two main characters, Mousie and Sad Girl, narrate their stories. The logic of the narrative is flawed, as Holly Willis has pointed out, because the film doesn't convince us that the girls are irrevocably entrapped by their milieu.[40]

Mi Vida Loca received a lot of publicity as the first movie about Latinas. But, whereas her background as an unwed mother proved an asset for *Gas Food Lodging*, Anders brings no special understanding of her characters; a Latino filmmaker might have been more sensitive to the material. Though Anders talked to the barrio girls at length, her script lacks the intimacy and immediacy of *Gas Food Lodging*, made as it is from the outside. To her credit, Anders doesn't patronize the Latino community with another stereotypical portrait. "The last thing I wanted," Anders declared in a manifesto, "and certainly the last thing these kids needed was to be colonized by a white liberal, preaching a point of view that hands out easy solutions." Nonetheless, her treatment lacks a discernible point of view, which may stem from her confusing honorable sociology with mediocre filmmaking.

Anders's next feature, *Grace of My Heart*, began when Scorsese wanted to team her with his friend Ileana Douglas for a film he would produce. The story traces the career of a woman who yearns to be a singer but ends up as a Tin Pan Alley songwriter. Spanning the years from the 1950s through the psychedelic 1970s and covering too much thematic ground, the film falls into a predictable narrative rhythm: Every scene is followed by the song it inspired. The men represent narrowly conceived types, and the relationships are too schematic. Anders's message—that in the 1960s guys were either creeps or married men—is reductive and embarrassing. Instead of offering an in-depth look, Anders opts for a sprawling, old-fashioned melodrama in the vein of *A Star Is Born* and *The Way We Were*. As Richard Corliss has pointed out, a historian could quibble with the details, but the problem is not historical; it's dramatic.[41] The Anders touch—energy, color—is in limited supply, and what there is of it fails to compensate for the obvious approach to the material (a character intones, "Marriage is a bourgeois convention").

The critic Ella Taylor noted that *Grace of My Heart* is the first film in which Anders achieves a measure of distance from her central creative neurosis: the search for an absent male. At film's end, Denise is told: "Your talent has been meaningless to you." It's the first conscious evaluation of what has been the unconscious heart of Anders's work: "*Grace of My Heart* is the story of a woman for whom no amount of success can make up for the fact that the absent male is her first priority, only now she knows it. In its emotional essentials, the movie is the untidy story of Anders herself."[42]

EROTICA—MIRA NAIR

Mira Nair belongs to a rising generation of women who are not necessarily making "women's films" but who still reflect a female sensibility in their work. Indian-born and Harvard-educated, Nair is attracted to outsiders who live on the margins of society, yearning to establish a "home." Her debut, *Salaam Bombay*, which won the 1988 Cannes Caméra d'Or, is a powerful exposé of homeless children. For her second film, *Mississippi Masala*, Nair chose a spicy interracial romance in the Deep South. *The Perez Family* chronicles the entangled lives of Cuban immigrants as they try to forge new existence in Miami.

Nair grew up in a small town in the Indian state of Orissa, where she later worked as an actress. In 1976, she went to Harvard as an undergraduate and discovered filmmaking, which led her to make a number of documentaries dealing with Indian society. Her short *India Cabaret* (1985), a portrait of strippers in a Bombay nightclub, won international recognition. Galvanizing the critics, her next film, *Salaam Bombay!*, was a harrowing account of a young boy's life among Bombay's thieves, prostitutes, and drug dealers. Inspired by a host of classic children pictures, including Vittorio De Sica's *Shoeshine*, Hector Babenco's *Pixote*, and the early work of her compatriot Satyajit Ray, the film drew its intensity and its color from its locale, the slums of Bombay. Despite its documentary feel, *Salaam Bombay!* was a slicker and more poised film than Nair's next effort, *Mississippi Masala*.

Staying away from Hollywood, Nair travels the world to raise money for her films. *Mississippi Masala*, made for $7 million, was financed by British TV's Channel 4 and other sources. More original than *Salaam Bombay!*, the film introduced a new subject, the transplanted Indian population in the American South, thereby contributing to the relevant discussion of what is the meaning of home.

The story begins in Uganda, in 1972, when the monstrous Idi Amin expelled resident Indians from the country. Jay (Roshan Seth), a prominent lawyer in Uganda, his wife, Kinnu (Sharmila Tagore), and their daughter, Mina (Sarita Choudhury), are forced to leave. Jay is told by his black nationalist friend, "Africa is for Africans." His loss is visually accentuated by the lushness of the African countryside and the vibrancy of its colors—a staple of Nair's work. Eighteen years later, Jay and his family are trapped in a deadend roadside motel business in the Deep South. The Indian residents get along with their black neighbors, but from afar, looking down on them. The two communities are linked—both are dislocated, both cling to their past, both search for a future, and both are mistreated by white America. Yet the two groups are unaware of their similarities, seeing only their differences.

A furor erupts when Mina falls in love with Demetrius (Denzel Washington), a black man who runs a carpet-cleaning business. Their romance becomes the film's Romeo and Juliet centerpiece, overshadowing the more interesting social context. Indeed, Nair neglects the broader issues; there's no real sense of how the exiled Indians mix with each other or with the black community. Nair also lacks the skills to tell a hot-spiced romance (*masala* is an Indian word for a mix of hot spices); the film is marred by an awkward mise-en-scène.

When the affair is disclosed, it challenges the biases and prejudices of both the Indian and the black communities; until then, the Indians had coexisted in superficial harmony with the blacks. Nair, however, doesn't deal with an obvious irony: Many of the Indians grew up in Uganda and had no contact with India, but they still identify themselves as Indian. In Mississippi, they are exiles twice removed; and their exile from a homeland they never knew should link them to the black people. Yet a color-caste system is evident: Lighter-skinned than the blacks, the Indians abhor the notion of interracial romance. Jay's resentment of Demetrius goes back to a painful split from his best friend in Uganda. It takes one more visit to Africa for Jay to finally release himself from his inner exile.[43]

Unlike Spike Lee's *Jungle Fever*, which also deals with interracial romance, Nair's treatment is nonjudgmental, taking neither a moral stand nor accusing either group of racism. The soundtrack, a mixture of African, Indian, and blues music, reinforces the film's themes. Released at a time when national boundaries in Europe and other regions were falling apart and the definition of home was changing, *Mississippi Masala* was a timely movie about displacement, distorted memories, and frail identities. Nair seems to imply that, despite the racial separatism that exists, the United States is one of the few societies where different races can really coexist.

Search for a new home also informs Nair's *The Perez Family* (1995), a movie burdened with an unconvincing ensemble cast that is unable to elevate a serio-comic exploration of Cuban immigrants. For two decades, Juan Raul Perez (Alfred Molina) has endured hard prison life, dreaming about reuniting in Miami with his wife, Carmela (Anjelica Huston), and their daughter. When freedom materializes, Juan jumps on a boat, glancing rhapsodically across a glistening blue ocean that separates him from the promised land. On the boat, he meets Dottie Perez (Marisa Tomei), a spunky, free-spirited prostitute ("I'm like Cuba, used by many, conquered by no one"), who has already absorbed the icons of American pop culture: rock and roll, Elvis Presley, John Wayne.

The immigration authorities erroneously document Juan and Dottie as a married couple, since they share the same surname. On the other side of town, Carmela's anticipation about meeting her husband turns to disappointment on her mistaken belief that he has not come to Miami. The sprawling tale depicts how Juan and Carmela deal first with abandonment, then with the need to adjust to a new way of life. With half of the cast overacting and the other underacting, *The Perez Family* is a messy picture with no dramatic core. The tone changes from scene to scene, as does the quality of writing and acting. Nair tries to be poignant but misses the mark: The individual stories don't cohere into something larger and more meaningful. The movie also suffered commercially from unfavorable comparisons with Gregory Nava's similarly themed but more enjoyable *My Family*, then in release.

Nair's latest film, *Kama Sutra: A Tale of Love* (1997), demonstrates again her sharp eye for composition and color. On-location shooting, lushly lensed by Declan Quinn, gives the picture an exotic pull, but it also reaffirms Nair's insensitivity to narrative credibility. Princess Tara and her servant Maya grow up together, but as adults, Tara (Sarita Choudhury) keeps Maya (Indira Varma) in her place. In revenge for her humiliation, Maya seduces a local king, Jai, on the eve of his marriage to Tara. Branded a whore, Maya is forced to wander until she is rescued by a sculptor. After a brief affair, he lets her go, and she decides to become an artist by studying the Kama Sutra with the court's former courtesan.

The explicit sex was toned down by Trimark, which released the movie without an MPAA rating. With its spectacular locales, lavish costumes, lush score, and beautiful stars, *Kama Sutra* is sensual rather than erotic. Nair and her cowriter, Helena Kriel, overlay a feminist sensibility on what's basically melodramatic material. Disguised as a story of female empowerment, the film fails as a softcore fantasy as well as a melodrama about sexual politics in sixteenth-century India. The modern notion of empowerment through sex, combined with contrived plotting, erode the logic of the historic narrative.

WOMEN OF COLOR

Refreshing as it is to see black men given the opportunity to make indie (and mainstream) films, they have unfortunately eclipsed a complex body of work by black women, who have offered critical alternatives to the stereotypical portrayal of black women in Hollywood movies. The pioneering generation of black female filmmakers includes Kathleen Collins (*Losing Ground*, 1982), Ayoka Chinzera (*Alma's Rainbow*, 1992), and Camille Billop (*KKK Botique Ain't Just Rednecks*, 1993).[44] Collins died young in 1988, but her legacy continues in the work of Julie Dash, her student at City College.

Dash's first film, *Illusions*, was produced while she was a member of an artists group at UCLA. Shot in black and white, on a budget of $28,000, the thirty-four-minute film centers on a light-skinned, upwardly mobile woman who cleverly manipulates her hybrid status to gain foothold in Hollywood, circa 1942. *Illusions* was the first installment of a projected trilogy about the historical experience of African American women. Dash's highly acclaimed *Daughters of the Dust*, set in the nineteenth century, became the second part of a series whose third segment, *Bone, Ash, Rose*, will be set in 2050.

In *Daughters of the Dust* (1991), Dash defines an African American experience different from the violent, inner-city life usually shown in American films. African American women have been depicted conventionally in historical dramas (*The Color Purple*) and in TV series (*Roots*);

Dash counters this trend with a serious meditation on the identity crisis facing black women, who are questioning the price of assimilation: Is the damage done by voluntarily abandoning one's heritage greater than the damage imposed by others?[45] Dash, who is of Gullah heritage on her father's side, paints a portrait of a resilient community of women. Lacking a linear plot, her film recaptures a time, a place, and a sensibility by exploring experiences in a ritualistic way. A celebration of a now forgotten culture, the film conveys Dash's version of history through the personal journeys of half a dozen women. Showing the links in an intergenerational cultural chain, *Daughters of the Dust* is a family quilt that interweaves fragments of history.

At the center are Sea Island women, living off the coasts of South Carolina and Georgia, on the eve of their migration to the mainland. Some women are determined to make the trip and leave tradition behind, while others are intent on remaining and preserving their heritage. Dash's narrative lends equal weight to the varying views of Gullah women as they struggle over questions of heritage. Nana Peazant (Cora Lee Day), the old matriarch, wishes to adhere to the old beliefs and remain on the island with her talismans and artifacts. Opposing her is Haagar Peazant (Kaycee Moore), who denounces the "hoodoo mess" of tribal ways and looks forward to the land of opportunity. A former prostitute, Yellow Mary (Barbara-O), and a would-be mother, Eula Peazant (Alva Rogers), fall between these extremes, torn between the comfort of home and the lure of the new world.

Using the format of oral history, the women's conflicts are presented in beautiful imagery laced with narration in a Gullah dialect. As they move around in long white dresses, the women are in sharp contrast to the landscape's palette of orange, green, and brown. The alternating viewpoints, contained in a tale steeped in mysticism and melancholy, clarify both the recollection of slave ancestry and the progressive drive to the new world. Informative without being didactic, the picture has sensual style that captures the era. More impressionistic than factual, *Daughters of the Dust* provides a tapestry of vivid Gullah beliefs. Dash views her women as both individuals and symbols: Nana Peazant wears the figurative clock of tradition, Yellow Mary represents the indignities suffered by black women, and Eula Peazant stands for the bridge between the old and new world. But Dash never allows the symbolism to get in the way of the women's individuality and their distinctive traits.[46]

Like Dash, Leslie Harris is one of the few black women making features today. But if *Daughters of the Dust* is about past traditions, Harris's *Just Another Girl from the IRT* (1993) couldn't be more contemporary. This ragged, vastly uneven movie centers on a neglected screen heroine: a young African American woman. It's a timely report from a front largely ignored by mainstream and indie movies, most of which are male-oriented and about the inner city.

The chief character, a product of the hip-hop generation, is confrontational, and not very sympathetic. Chantel (Aryan Johnson) is an arrogant Brooklyn high school student who thinks she's smarter than everybody else; she tells off a haughty woman who shops in the deli where she works, her parents, and her boyfriend. Chantel challenges her Jewish teacher: "Why study the Holocaust? Why not study the death of young black men in the cities?," implying that Jews are keeping blacks in their place. The trials and travails of a teenage black girl are an interesting subject, but not in Harris's contradictory treatment. Chantel is supposed to be a good student, but she's never seen studying. She's meant to be sassy and energetic, but these qualities prove self-defeating. Aiming to become a doctor, Chantel perceives her pregnancy (by her smooth, hip boyfriend) as a trap, but she's unwilling to have an abortion. Crude and heavy-handed, *Just Another Girl* could have been a disturbing cautionary tale of teenage ignorance of life on the street and in the bedroom, but, apart from the street ambiance, there's not much reality on screen.

Even so, Harris's take on a girl's state of mind is fresh, and the film has several lively scenes, such as Chantel's interaction with her girlfriends, trading wisdom about birth control, and a scene in which she confounds a stolid suitor. Shot in a raw style, the film uses a quick rhythm and cutting to convey the restlessness of the city. However, the film mixes a pounding rap score (by Nikki D and Cee Asia) with every message in the inner-city book on poverty, public schools, teenage pregnancy. The jittery pacing and profane candor were designed to appeal to black teens, whom the movie failed to attract, probably because it was too critical of them.

Arguably the most talented of the recent African American directors is Darnell Martin, who made a quintessentially indie movie within the studio system. When Columbia agreed to produce *I Like It Like That*, Martin became the first African American woman to direct a movie at a major studio. She was also able to go home again—to Findlay and 167th Street in the heart of Bronx—to tell an authentic story about the maturation of a young couple, Lisette (Lauren Velez) and Chino (Jon Seda) Linares, amid the push and pull of their barrio families. Defying easy labels, *I Like It Like That* blends drama, comedy, and romance as it chronicles the emotional and sexual tug-of-war in an interracial marriage between a black woman and a Latino.

Inspiration for the movie came directly from the streets, the schoolyard (of Public School 64), and the building where Martin grew up. Its buoyancy reflects the director's firsthand familiarity with the milieu. Her characters emerge out of the behavior, talk, and music she saw and heard on her block. Martin shows a vivid ear for profane street language, with all its put-downs and sexual frankness.

Set on a hot summer night, against Bronx's vibrant street life, the film follows the Linareses after a citywide blackout. Though raising three children, the Linareses are themselves kids who need to learn how to become responsible to each other—and to themselves. A goofy macho, Chino proudly times his staying power in bed (eighty-nine minutes in the first scene), but he can't support his family from his earnings as a bicycle messenger; Lisette sarcastically labels him "The Layaway King." Running herself ragged, Lisette is trying to stave off creditors, raise boisterous kids, and keep from being overwhelmed by her husband. When Lisette threatens to get a job (to buy a new stereo), Chino impulsively joins in some neighborhood looting and is caught by the police. Chino's imprisonment forces Lisette to get a job with a record company. Her success and a tentative romance with her white boss threaten to tear the family apart.

I Like It Like That unfolds through the eyes of Lisette, whose role as wife and mother is challenged. Remarkably, Martin evokes the giddy but infuriating love of the Linareses without demeaning men. Her sympathy is clearly with Lisette's search for fulfillment, but she views Chino with compassion and humor. The story of a squabbling couple is old-fashioned, but Martin gives it a vibrant Afro-Caribbean lilt, placing it in a teeming multicultural neighborhood. Prior to making this feature, Martin had worked as assistant to Spike Lee, and she absorbed his gift for lively, energetic imagery. Martin keeps everything perking along with a bouncy style, rap, salsa, and colorful characters: women who desire independence, men who need to mature, a Latino transvestite yearning for a sex-change operation.[47]

Kasi Lemmons, *Eve's Bayou* (1997) is a family drama that mixes elements of Southern Gothic with the kinds of characters and tensions one finds in the work of Tennessee Williams. Focusing on a prosperous Creole family, Lemmons adds a significant panel to the growing portraiture of the African American experience. Set in Louisiana in 1962, this woman-dominated film sharply deviates from the wave of black inner-city films, establishing a more direct link with *Waiting to Exhale* and its black middle-class women. Assured mise-en-scène, great ensemble acting, and Amy Vincent's splendid on-location shooting make *Eve's Bayou* an accomplished first effort.

The Batiste clan is headed by a suave patriarch, Louis (Samuel L. Jackson), a doctor respected by his community and known for his ability "to fix things." Although married to the proud and gracious Roz (Lynn Whitfield), he is unable to control his weakness for other women, often his patients. During a party, Louis engages in an amorous escapade with a married woman in a barn, not realizing that he's being observed by his youngest daughter, Eve (Jurnee Smollett), who happens to be there by accident. Traumatized by the experience, Eve is reassured by her father that he still loves her mom, but, unable to forget the incident, she shares her secret with her older sister, Cisely.

A coming-of-age saga, *Eve's Bayou* begins with Eve's voiceover narration: "Memory is a selection of images. Some elusive, others printed indelibly on the brain. The summer I killed my father, I was ten years old." Though we know about Louis's death from the start, it's still shocking to observe the circumstances in which he is killed and the effects of his death on the family. The story is seen from the perspective of a perceptive girl, whose illusions of family unity and loyalty have been forever shattered. The film conveys how easily children are manipulated and corrupted by the adults they trust. Cisely fabricates another scenario of her dad's adultery, and there are intimations of incest in Cisely's relationship with her father.

Well versed in the traditions of the South, Lemmons blends the Gothic and the primal, bizarre voodoo rituals and Southern gentility, into a narrative that reflects the inner strains of a black family that, for once, is not oppressed or discriminated against. Significantly, there are no white characters. Lemmons etches half a dozen strong female characters: a precocious girl who pries open her family's secrets; an urbane, noble wife and mother who seems to "have it all," except her husband's fidelity; a superstitious young widow whose three husbands never survived her affections; and a voodoo visionary whom Eve consults in her struggle to save her family.

RETRO, SOFT, AND HARDCORE FEMINISM

The offscreen scandals that surrounded Jennifer Lynch's *Boxing Helena* (1993) were far more interesting than her film. It should have been a small movie that deserved to flop, but, after all, it was made by David Lynch's daughter. Initially, Madonna was cast as the woman with no arms. When she turned it down, another star, Kim Basinger, was quickly recruited. But Basinger changed her mind too, prompting an unprecedented Hollywood trial that ended in Basinger's paying a huge amount of money for commitment breaking. The persistent notoriety gave the movie name recognition, but it never became the provocative work Lynch intended it to be.

Lynch's grandmother had a replica of the Venus de Milo, and people would look at the statue—not as something flawed and broken, but as something beautiful. Using that as her guide, Jennifer wished to explore the kind of violence couples inflict on each other when they try to feel safer or to ensure that their lovers will never leave. In the film, a surgeon, Nick Cavanaugh (Julian Sands), can't get over his obsession with his contemptuous former flame, Helena (Sherilyn Fenn). When Helena is injured in a car accident, Nick takes her in, amputates her legs, and keeps her as a prisoner in his house. She continues to be hostile to him, and he amputates her arms.

A journey into the Lynchian realm of the grotesque and the bizarre, *Boxing Helena* could have been a deliciously demented film. Horror fans, however, were vastly disappointed because the film lacked gore, sex, or dark humor. The film also became the target of women's groups, which protested the violence against women. Lynch denied the charges of misogyny and pornography, claiming that the mutilation was meant as a metaphor: The character's self-esteem is her beauty, and a man is taking that away from her. All metaphors, *Boxing Helena* lacks authenticity or emotional power. The hype that accompanied the film made it impossible to see the twisted love story without prejudice. "This was just supposed to be a little low-budget movie," Jennifer said in her defense. In Britain, critics savaged her for accusing Britons—Sands is British—of being sexually inept. Other critics lambasted the ending as smacking of a typical tacked-on Hollywood cop-out. No doubt, *Boxing Helena* is neutralized by a denouement that turns the story into the surgeon's dream-fantasy.

The producer, Philippe Caland, wanted to focus on the violent and erotic elements of the story, but when interested directors wanted to turn it into a horror film, Jennifer became protective of her script: "I was in love with this story, and it wasn't about a guy hacking up some beautiful woman he wanted to screw." Although she never intended to direct—"film was Dad's thing and I had so much respect for what he did that I just considered it all his"—Jennifer got aboard "so that it wouldn't turn into some horrible misinterpreted gore-fest."[48] The fact that she was Lynch's daughter motivated some people to see the movie out of curiosity; the Lynch name was a welcome mat for the bizarre. Judging by the end result, however, nothing was gained by assigning a woman to the picture, which actually gave a bad name to indies and also demonstrated the power of hype. Prior to its world premiere at Sundance, *Boxing Helena* was the hottest ticket in the festival; two hours later, the movie was dead.

Tamra Davis's *Guncrazy* (1992), a loose remake of Joseph H. Lewis's classic noir, *Gun Crazy* (1949), is an intense contemplation of characters under pressure. Her film lacks the tragic sweep of Lewis's film or of Fritz Lang's *You Only Live Once* (1937) and Nicholas Ray's *They Live by Night* (1949). As Andrew Sarris noted, apart from the gun fever and the *amour fou*, Davis tells a different story (written by Matthew Bright), with a shift of point of view from the boy in the 1949 film to the girl (Drew Barrymore) in the remake.[49] The emotions in the original are clearer than in the new version, which emphasizes trailer-park pathology and sexual impotence (borrowed from *Bonnie and Clyde*).

In most movies, teenagers are played by older actors, which undercuts the credibility, but Barrymore undertook the role of Anita when she was sixteen. Portraying the emotional wreckage of a lost adolescence, Anita is emotionally numbed by her sordid existence as she clings to her awakened romantic feelings for Howard (James Le Gros), the pen-pal-convict who becomes her lover. The adventures of the gun-happy lovers are over almost before they have begun. Davis's postmodernist mode makes every killing seem like an unintended catastrophe, although some compassion comes from Anita's loyal friend, Joy (Ione Skye), and her parole-officer father, Kincaid (Michael Ironside).

Another retro item by a woman director was Katt Shea's *Poison Ivy* (1992), which came into being when New Line asked Shea and Andy Ruben, her writer-producer and former husband, to make a teenage *Fatal Attraction* on a $3 million budget. The team came back with a variant on *Fatal Attraction*, *The Hand That Rocks the Cradle*, and *The Stepfather* (and of course Pasolini's *Teorema*), in all of which the order of a middle-class family is interrupted by a depraved interloper. In Shea's film, the outsider is Ivy (Drew Barrymore), a Lolita-like teen seductress with a Kewpie doll mouth, strategically placed tattoo, and high heels, who lusts after Darryl (Tom Skerritt), the manager of a local TV station.

Boxing Helena, Guncrazy, and *Poison Ivy* are minor footnotes amid a host of far more exciting women-directed films, such as *My New Gun* (1992), in which the gifted director Stacy Cochran examines suburbia in a manner devoid the usually nasty, mean-spirited approach to the subject. Unlike the films of her downtown New York cohorts, *My New Gun* displays no irony or condescension; yet its quirkily laconic, minimalist perspective goes against expectations. Like Hartley's deadpan, elliptical tragicomedies, Cochran creates a world in which people try to make contact through long silences and cryptic half-sentences.

Before turning to features, Cochran used her savings to make two shorts about suburban lifestyle: *Cocktails at Six* (1987), about a suburban party seen from the point of view of a six-year-old, and *Another Damaging Day* (1990), a comedy about a teen struck by lightning while washing his car in the driveway. Barely a year after receiving a film degree from Columbia, Cochran made *My New Gun*, written for a screenwriting class. The black comedy relates a deceptively simple tale: what happens when a gun is brought into the lives of a suburban couple. Budgeted at $2.1 million, with financing from IRS and Columbia-TriStar HomeVideo, *My New Gun* was shot in less than a month in Teaneck, New Jersey, at a townhouse whose interiors were used for multiple purposes, doubling as the homes of both the doctor's family and their neighbors.

Debbie Bender (Diane Lane) and her husband, Gerald (Stephen Collins), are spending an evening with their friend Irwin. To mark their engagement, Irwin gives his teenage fiancée a diamond ring and a revolver engraved with her name. Debbie is at first horrified, but, a few days later, when Gerald presents Debbie with *her* gun, she calmly puts it in her drawer. The pompously boring Gerald buys the gun to protect them from what he describes as a "sick world out there." It's a purchase that reflects the banality and tediousness of their marriage. Terrified, Debbie wakes up one night screaming from a nightmare, and she's comforted by her eccentric neighbor Skippy (James LeGros), who hears her from across the street. Skippy lives with his mother (Tess Harper), a washed out country-Western singer who's trying to escape her sinister former husband (Bill Raymond). The narrative then depicts the peculiar circumstances under which Debbie learns how to use her gun.

Set in a place ridden with the mild-mannered angst of suburbia, *My New Gun* is quasi-autobiographical—Cochran grew up in Passaic, New Jersey. "There's a childlike quality to the story," said Cochran, who wrote for kids' magazines before attending Columbia. "The whole movie is built on ellipses, hopefulness combined with dread."[50] The pastel-toned sets contrast with the potential violence, and Debbie's outfits match the wallpaper of her tract house. While suburbanism is depicted as fostering boredom and paranoia, the movie is not a moralistic attack. For all its dreariness, suburbia is also a place where unexpected things happen, where people have neighborly relationships and try to take care of one another.

The opening cocktail scene establishes right away Cochrane's quirky touch. "It's a funny shot," Cochran said of the unbroken, high-crane shot looking in on Gerald and Debbie as they try to enjoy their back patio. "But is it a neighborhood distance, a voyeur's distance, or a threatening distance? I was trying to create some sort of paranoia about the perpetual chaos out there, but at the same time constantly undermine the need for paranoia."

Cochran portrays her protagonist—a housewife, a prevalent type in feminist films—differently from Seidelman. She doesn't rely on artificial devices—amnesia, mistaken identity—to transform Debbie's awareness. There's obviously more to Debbie than just being a housewife—she's a curious, ambitious woman determined to make a career out of her life. Cochran explained: "Whether it's guns or vacuums, there are assumptions you make when you see the products of a woman's life, and I wanted to undermine those assumptions."[51] Cochran achieved her goal not through speeches, but through the accumulation of visual detail.

Maggie Greenwald's *The Ballad of Little Jo* (1993) is an earnest drama about a woman who disguises herself as a man to survive hardship in the Old West. Inspired by a true story, the film is set in 1866, during the Gold Rush. Josephine Monaghan (Suzy Amis), a wealthy Easterner, is an outcast because she has had a child out of wedlock. Heading West, she continues to encounter contempt and sexual harassment, until she realizes that her only chance to attain freedom is as a man. She cuts her hair, scars her face, puts on trousers—and changes her name to Little Jo.

Jo begins a new life in a frontier mining outpost populated by fortune-seekers where she is accepted as a man. Before long, she learns how to mine, hunt, and manage a self-sufficient existence. Her life changes after she saves an Asian outcast, Tinman Wong (David Chung), from lynching. In a role reversal, he's assigned to cook and mend, while she is the breadwinner. However, once Wong discovers her identity, an affair ensues, and they secretly set up house. It's only at her funeral that Jo's identity is revealed—to the utmost shock of the town members.

Greenwald wanted to show that 1990s cross-dressing was not a new phenomenon, that women have been dressing up as men for centuries. Their motivations were varied: "Some did it because they were gay. Some wanted to go to war either because they believed in the cause, or because they wanted to fight beside their husbands. Some wanted to vote. Some wanted to earn decent wages. And some were just looking for adventure."[52] A feminist who always wanted to make a Western, Greenwald saw a golden opportunity in the material.

As Little Jo moves around, she encounters women who are forced to live out the limited roles society deems proper for them: Ruth, the frontier wife forced to put up with her husband's insensitivity; a Russian homesteader who dreams of a better life but who realizes the West is no place for a visionary woman; Mary, who marries the first man she finds passable; Elvira, a traveling whore who services men until an angry drunk carves her face with a knife. Looking at the women around her, Jo realizes that passing for a man isn't a bad idea after all.

Greenwald brings a contemporary feminist vision to the frontier saga genre, in which most films are about men and are told from a man's point of view. In the Old West, Greenwald explained, it was considered deviant for women to don men's clothing. If caught, women faced fines or expulsion from the county. The fear of being caught or jailed forces Jo to give herself a large scar on her face; the scar is her commitment, her refusal to go back.

Greenwald captures the harshness of the vast, uninhabited land and the indomitable spirit of one fearless woman. Nonetheless, her revisionist film is solemn, and important issues remain unexplored, such as Jo's maternal instincts for her illegitimate son (whom she never sees). Greenwald doesn't convey Jo's struggle to maintain her disguise—her fear of getting caught and her relationship with Chung are sketchily depicted. Greenwald is so committed to her feminist agenda that she leaves out the humor in the story; the sequence in which a young woman (Heather Graham) thinks she's found the ideal husband in Jo is full of droll possibilities. With all her efforts to demystify the Old West, Greenwald ends up mythologizing her heroine as a symbol of survival.

The search for modern protagonists has motivated women directors to investigate the past as well as the present. Unlike most of Hollywood's Gen-X movies, Daisy von Scherier Mayer's *Party Girl* (1995) was made by an insider. Mary (Parker Posey) may be considered a modern version of *Breakfast at Tiffany's* Holly Golightly: By day, she works as a library clerk; by night, she's queen of the club scene. A camp diva blessed with deadpan cool and funkiness, Mary is essentially a good girl whose "badness" is a pose. At heart, the movie is an earnest coming-of-age saga: When Mary finally breaks the ancient code of the Dewey Decimal System, it opens her life, and she experiences an epiphany. In a flash of inspiration, she arranges the record album collection of her deejay roommate.

Party Girl is meant to be a *Desperately Seeking Susan* for the 1990s, with the same hip downtown sensibility. Reflecting the zeitgeist, Mayer and her cowriter, Harry Brickmayer, depict Manhattan as a multicultural milieu: Mary is attracted to a Lebanese falafel vendor, Mustafa; her roommate, Leo, is Latino; her friend, Rene, is gay; the club is predominantly black. Slight and inconsequential, *Party Girl* offers a superficial portrait of New York nightlife, too cheerful and self-pleased to pursue any issue. Mayer shows no sense of comic pacing, imposing on the film a moralistic tone that sends Mary soul-searching for her responsible side.

Far more ambitious, Mary Harron's drama *I Shot Andy Warhol* (1996) explores the political and psychological contradictions of Valerie Solanas, the woman who shot Andy Warhol. Harron aimed to show that Solanas was a visionary whose tragedy stemmed from a lack of self-awareness; she possessed little understanding of her actions. Valerie defined herself as a lesbian, although her orientation was motivated less by sexual desire than by the fact that she was living in a male-dominated society. Her hatred for men was activated by society's view of women as weak-minded and intuitive. Valerie thwarted the media's attempts to categorize her as lesbian; she had slept with men and had lived with a man for a while.

Harron sympathized with Valerie's anger at being told what a woman should or should not do. When Harron worked at the BBC, she was surrounded by "boy geniuses" who were expected to go off and make movies, but she had to have "a lot more drive to prove myself."[53] Films about ambitious young women coming to the city to pursue their careers (*Dance, Girl, Dance, Stage Door, Breakfast at Tiffany's*), influenced Harron's perception of Valerie, along with intense psychological studies of demented minds like *Taxi Driver*. Though Harron credits *Taxi Driver* and its character, Travis Bickle, *I Shot Andy Warhol* is more of a variant of Scorsese's *King of Comedy*. Like Scorsese's protagonist (also played by De Niro), Valerie is an ambitious but untalented nobody obsessed with a celebrity (Andy Warhol) who rebuffs her.

Like Lee's *She's Gotta Have It*, the title has a B-movie ring, but the film turns out to be a conventional high-minded biopicture. The main action is interrupted by black-and-white sequences of Valerie looking straight into the camera and reciting passages from the SCUM (Society for Cutting Up Men) manifesto. The movie includes scenes from Valerie's college days, intended to dramatize her evolving "feminism," but most of the narrative is inherently undramatic. Since Valerie's pathology is full-blown from the start, the movie has nowhere to go dramatically; there's no suspense, since Valerie's act is known.

Furthermore, Valerie is not interesting enough to be the center of the movie; she should have been a secondary character. Harron and her coscreenwriter, Daniel Minahan, attempt to portray Valerie as a complex tragicomic figure, but she really is not. As Terrence Rafferty observed: "Valerie had her requisite fifteen minutes of fame twenty-five years ago, and it was more than she deserved."[54] What compensates for the dramatic shortcomings are the vivid production design and secondary characters that are more interesting than the leads. The re-creation of period decor and of the atmosphere at the Factory, with its Warhol crowd, is vivid. The artist (wittily played by Jared Harris), the bitchy luminary Ondine (Michael Imperioli), and the superstar transvestite Candy Darling (Stephen Dorff) are amusing, but they don't get sufficient screen time.

From her work in documentary TV (*The South Bank Show* programs on Warhol, Jackson Pollock) Harron learned that "you have to balance every person's account against what other characters say. Everyone has mixtures of good and bad about them in different proportions. The power relations with others, that is what's important to discover."[55] There was some pressure to make Valerie more sympathetic, but for Harron, the essence of the film is that she really wasn't.

Harron credits Minahan with encouraging her to make things up when it was necessary dramatically. Hence Minahan and Harron consolidated some characters without substantially altering the facts. Initially, they had Valerie get thrown out of her apartment or exchange sex for a place to sleep, but, in the end, they cut these scenes out. The biggest challenge, which the film doesn't meet, was to locate the catalyst that sent Valerie over the edge. Harron has no idea of why Valerie shot Warhol: "It wasn't until the editing that I acknowledged that I just don't know, and that I should leave it a mystery."[56]

EXPERIMENTAL FILMMAKERS

Beginning with Maya Deren and continuing with Shirley Clarke, a number of women directors have come to films from the field of dance. In her work as a choreographer, Yvonne Rainer pioneered a minimalist style, with limited movement and emotion, thereby divesting dance of convention and artifice. Searching for new means of expression, she experimented with the incorporation of film into her dances. Gradually drawn to filmmaking for its own sake, Rainer made her first feature, *Lives of Performers*, in 1972.

Rainer's films are collages of reality and fiction, thought-provoking blends of images and sounds that shun narrative cinema. Audiences are invited to participate in Brechtian-style exercises that are responses to timely sociopolitical issues. It's an approach that channels divergent topics into one text, while experimenting with the strengths and limitations of the medium. Rainer gives the impression of deciding anew in each scene the priorities of images and sounds.

In *Privilege* (1991), the issues are rape, racism, and menopause, with voices ranging from the disarmament advocate Helen Caldicott to the militant writer Eldridge Cleaver. Though *Privilege* has a more mainstream feel than Rainer's earlier work, it retains the quality of a personal rumination about life changes from a distinctly female perspective—the movie came directly from the challenges Rainer faced at the time. As she explained, "I've been dealing with my own menopause off and on for a couple of years, and there is a point where you realize you're more at the end of your life than at the beginning, and a sense of mortality that inevitably comes. But there's also a way of looking at your life as a set of accretions and achievements and completions rather than an ending."[57] Rainer's strategy is based on the violation of taboos: She eliminates sound, imposes voiceovers of a stiffly read script, and employs dialogue that runs counter to the images. Several actors play one character, and she lights them with a single spotlight, relays their images to a video monitor, or abandons them entirely, filling the frame with texture or moving the lens randomly around a room. The result is a deliberate disruption of Hollywood's glossy and unified style.

Silence is an important component of *Privilege*, a film that addresses "the silence that emanated from friends and family regarding the details of my middle age. Now that I did not appear to be looking for a man, the state of my desires seemed of no interest to anyone." In the film, Jenny is interviewed about the dreaded menopause, but she doesn't want to discuss it—"Keeping your dignity as you enter menopause is like fighting City Hall," she says. Jenny describes a near-rape that occurred when she was a dancer. Based on an incident in Rainer's life, the story underlines the links among gender, race, and victimization. Warnings about the effects of therapy are intercut with educational films in which patronizing male doctors discuss menopause and women talk about their reactions to middle age. Then Eldridge Cleaver engages in an inflammatory monologue about black-on-white rape, which Rainer included despite warnings that the material might fuel white paranoia.

As emotionally unsettling but not as challenging, *Murder and Murder* (1996), a logical follow-up to *Privilege*, is at once a soap opera, black comedy, love story, and political meditation. The movie contests popular misconceptions about lesbian sexuality, aging, and medical biases about cancer, critiquing them as artificial cultural constructions. Through slapstick humor, visual metaphors, and commentary, Rainer's formal discursive strategies are invoked and dismantled. Periodically, Rainer (who also underwent a mastectomy) herself punctures the narrative with inquiries into the politics of breast cancer.

Two white women, Mildred and Doris, are juxtaposed. Mildred is of the upper middle class, while Doris hails from a poor family and has raised her daughter alone. Mildred is a tenured professor; Doris didn't attend college and has never had a steady job. Mildred shops at Barney's; Doris plunders catalogues and thrift shops. Mildred has been a lesbian all her life; Doris is attracted to a woman for the first time. Told from Doris's perspective, the movie explores the pleasures, uncertainties, and ambiguities of late-life lesbianism in a culture obsessed with youth and heterosexual romance.

A generation younger than Rainer, Nina Menkes is an uncompromising filmmaker committed to a radical and personal cinema. A combination of feminist politics and aesthetic rigor links her work to Chantal Akerman's, particularly her precise composition and framing. Menkes's bleak portraits of women are based on her explorations of their reactions to narrowly defined roles in society. Thematic motifs and formal patterns recur in Menkes's films, all of which feature Tinka, Nina's sister, as protagonist. Menkes's work is manipulative in a subtle, mystical way. Like Maya Deren, Menkes uses cinema to create new forms and new spiritual experiences. Menkes's films are challenging in their unusually long takes and repetition of imagery. Viewers are asked to abandon preconceptions and expose themselves to images imbued with the power of consciousness altering.

Menkes's career began with a forty-minute film, *The Great Sadness of Zohara* (1983), which follows the spiritual journey of a woman named Zohara from the streets of Jerusalem to the markets of Morocco and back again. Inspired by the work of Gertrude Stein and Mary Daly, Menkes's first feature, *Magdalena Viraga*, is a discomfortingly complex film evoking a reality rarely depicted on-screen. Set in seedy hotel rooms and decaying dance halls in East Los Angeles, it's about an emotionally numb prostitute who is seeking acceptance in an oppressive world. The narrative revolves around the spiritual liberation of a prostitute who is wrongly accused of murder. Menkes described the film as a "descent into the home of the 'monstrous feminine,' a journey through the vortex of unadulterated female space."[58] Stylistically, the film is marked by longeurs and a rigorous visual design.

In *Queen of Diamonds*, set in Las Vegas's Par-a-Dice casino, the protagonist, Firdaus, is less victim and more onlooker. The film is punctuated by long takes and sparse dialogue, contrasted with Firdaus's expressive facial and body gestures. Some plot elements are suggested, but the emphasis remains on Fridaus's isolation. Within the casino, there's a cacophony of sounds and lights, of poker chips and cards flashing across green tables, but outside, the lights are bright, the sand is glaring white, and the sky is dark blue. Night scenes bring eeriness (a dead cat and Christ upside down on a cross) and beauty (three elephants move with an amazing grace). Said Menkes, "The difference between the two films is that in *Magdalena*, the oppressed woman recognizes what's going on, and she's really involved in battling against the oppressors, yet she desperately wants validation from them. *Queen of Diamonds* is light-years ahead of that. Firdaus has relinquished that desire; she's much less involved in that judgement. The self-hate is lifted."[59]

Menkes continued to explore alienation in *The Bloody Child*, her most powerful film to date. A meditation on violence, inspired by the real and infused with the surreal, it's loosely based on an actual incident in which a marine was arrested for murdering his wife and burying her in the Mojave Desert. The murder represents an intersection of different kinds of violence. On the most obvious level, it's a case of homicide, but implicit in the narrative is an indictment of the mass media and the military for perpetuating violence.

Bloody Child is at once an anatomy of a specific murder and a meditation on violence, gender, and power. In most American films, violence serves as a plot point and is related to external events, whereas Menkes is interested in the "inner condition" of violence, the constellations inside individuals that causes violence. Rather than assign the blame, she is looking at the trap that links the victim, the perpetrator, and the investigator. Subtitled *An Interior of Violence*, the film examines the echoes of the shock waves that crime sets off in the lives of all those involved. Like ripples in a pond, the murder impinges on everyone. A collective portrait of damage, Menkes described the film as a "vision of hell, because real evil goes unnamed and unrecognized."

Menkes repeats one unsettling image: an enraged marine captain (played by Tinka) shoving the murderer's face into the bloody remains of his victim. The sequence implicates the viewers, forcing them to feel the murderous rage. Menkes explained: "It's not that there's one moment of violence and then it's contained and resolved. There's no sense of closure. The violence of the murder is ricocheting around and has nowhere to go."[60]

Tinka serves as Nina's alter ego, allowing the director to explore her own psyche. The powerful alchemy with Tinka may explain the intensity of Menkes's films. Is it like Cassavetes's relationship with Gena Rowlands, in which the various roles Rowlands played in his movies could be seen as one character on a single trajectory? Is Tinka playing one evolving persona as she moves from one film to another?

Menkes finds mainstream narrative to be as predetermined as a codified language. She quotes Angela Carter, who believes that women will be lulled by the propaganda of romantic stereotypes until they have the courage to believe in the truth of their own experience. Menkes's fiercely personal oeuvre is marked by visual experimentation and feminist critique, along with intimate exploration of her own psyche. "My struggle as a woman and artist is to allow myself to be who I am," Menkes said. That sounds easy, but it's not: "A lot of women are struggling with the idea of themselves as subjects."[61]

Menkes holds that power means "to look in the mirror and say 'I have a wrinkle, therefore I am less valuable.' To not internalize it." She asserts: "Women are denigrated in our society, they're held in contempt, violence against women is rampant. As a woman, if you pick up on any of these vibrations, you will either become political, or you're going to believe there are some things not good about you."

Experimental filmmaker Kelly Reichardt described her 1995 debut, *River of Grass*, as "a road movie without the road, a love story without the love, a crime story without the crime." It's an accurate description, for Reichardt evokes the familiar lovers-on-the-run genre, only to stand it on its head with fresh meanings and droll humor. In the process, she confounds predictable formulas, forcing the audience to recognize the banality of her characters.

A lonely thirtysomething mother of three, Cozy (Lisa Bowman) lives in a drab suburb of Florida's Broward County with her police detective father and her dull husband. One Friday night, she dresses up and heads for the local bar, where she meets Lee (Larry Fessenden). Lee is an equally lonely layabout who grew up in a broken home and has been thrown out of the house he's shared with his mother and grandmother. Cozy and Lee could hardly be more ordinary; everything about them, starting with their looks, is average. Lacking the opportunity to live anything but a bleak existence, they somehow ignite within each other the possibility of a more adventurous life. Circumstances lead them to believe they could be killers, although they are clueless—they are stopped at a toll gate because they lack a quarter.

Cozy narrates the film in a deliberately flat and affectless voice, which accentuates the mysterious workings of fate. As in *My New Gun*, chance thrusts a gun in Cozy's hands. Nervously and hilariously, she grips her father's pistol with one hand and steers the car with the other. Elliptically Godardian, *River of Grass* offers a provocative meditation on female subjectivity, free will, and the failure of movie myths, or how real life defies reel life.[62]

CONCLUSION

Like their male counterparts, most women directors have been white. Since Julie Dash's breakthrough film, *Daughters of the Dust*, in 1991, only three black women, Leslie Harris, Darnell Martin, and Kasi Lemmons, have made films that received major theatrical release; of the three, only Lemmons's *Eve's Bayou* was commercially successful. According to Deidre Fribaum, the lack of films by black women in theatrical distribution derives from their failure to conform to the narrative conventions of both Hollywood and indie movies. Black women are unable to "fit in" or "negotiate," to use her words, what's still an overwhelmingly male business.

But Asian-American women have been even fewer than African Americans. This may explain why Kayo Hatta's feature debut, *Picture Bride* (1995), received such critical attention and was shown at both Sundance and Cannes. Set in 1918, it tells the story of Riyo (Youki Kudoh), a shy Japanese adolescent who travels to Hawaii for an arranged marriage with a middle-aged laborer, who has deceived her with a dated photograph of himself. Hatta, a UCLA graduate, was under pressure from Miramax to trim ten minutes and replace a classic score with a more upbeat Asian–Pacific Island score. With a historical prologue added, and love scenes reshot in Japan, the budget (raised from Japanese investors), doubled to $2.5 million, which the film's modest grosses could not recoup.

Unfortunately, the work of white female directors has not fared much better in the late 1990s. Of the twenty women profiled in this chapter, only a few are still making movies today. Lizzie Borden, Susan Seidelman, and Bette Gordon have not made a movie in years. Stacy Cochran moved to Hollywood and made an interesting picture, *Boys* (1995) with Winona Ryder, but Touchstone didn't believe in the movie and dumped it on the market.

Many of the women who had brilliant beginnings stumbled and rapidly declined in their subsequent outings. In the early 1990s, with the release of Martha Coolidge's *Rambling Rose*, Allison Ander's *Gas Food Lodging*, Stacy Cochran's *My New Gun*, and Nancy Savoca's *Household Saints*, it seemed as if women had finally made their mark on the indie milieu. But, alas, this was not to be the case. Arguably, one of the most skillful women working today is Katherine Bigelow, who began with interesting indies, then proceeded with bigger-budgeted, more technically accomplished pictures. Nonetheless, even Bigelow has not made a film since *Strange Days*, which was a commercial failure, four years ago.

The second (and third) picture is harder to get going than the first for all filmmakers, but particularly for women, even if their first one was promising. The intervals between first and second features are much wider for women than for men. Two of the more visible women, Anders and Savoca, had new movies in the 1999 Sundance Film Festival, *Sugar Town* (codirected by Kurt Voss) and *The 24 Hour Woman*. Both movies were weak, failing to show any indication of progress by their directors.

An experimental filmmaker like Kelly Reichardt (*River of Grass*) can only hope for limited showing of her work. The only way to see this no-budget, no-star movie in today's competitive market is in festivals and in the art-house circuit, hoping that a risk-loving distributor—in this case Strand—will pick it up.

Robin Wood has observed that, to be admitted to Hollywood, feminism had to repress its politics. The pervasive antifeminism in the 1980s resulted in the reinstatement of traditional role models, putting assertive women in their place. Men continue to resist women in positions of power. The aversion is always to power that is visible and concrete, hence the paucity of women directors and producers. But there is less objection to women behind the cameras, writers or editors. The question of what possibilities exist for a distinctly female or feminist discourse in the indie film world, which is also male dominated, is interesting but unanswerable. Feminist critics have argued that the language of cinema—the organization of gaze, both within the film and among the spectators—was developed by patriarchy in order to perpetuate the status quo and therefore should be rejected. But how does one go about changing that, in Hollywood and indiewood? Only time will tell.

I I

The New African American Cinema

UNTIL THE 1990s, most of Hollywood's black-themed movies were directed by white filmmakers. There were a few exceptions, such as *The Learning Tree* (1969), which was produced, directed, and written by Gordon Parks. Based on his semiautobiographical novel, the film presents the initiation of a black adolescent into love, death, injustice, and racial hatred. Parks became, according to *Newsweek*, "the first black man in the history of American cinema to direct a major Hollywood production." But it took another two decades for black filmmakers to create their own cinema.

At first, to leave their mark, black directors had to create their own opportunities. When Spike Lee experienced difficulties at finding work after graduating from NYU, he proceeded on his own with *She's Gotta Have It* (1986). In the same year, Robert Townsend, a West Coast actor who got tired of being typecast, directed and starred in his own vehicle, *Hollywood Shuffle*. The turning point in the history of the new independent black cinema was *She's Gotta Have It*, but the beginning of the cycle dates back to the 1970s and the work of Charles Burnett.

INDIE PIONEER—CHARLES BURNETT

The first black director to leave his mark on the new indie cinema was the visionary Charles Burnett. To this day, however, Burnett has not received the recognition he deserves, possibly because of the low-key, understated style of his work. Burnett made his feature debut in 1973 with *Killer of Sheep*, but it took four years before the film was shown publicly. *Killer of Sheep* is one of two films by black filmmakers (the other is *The Learning Tree*) to be recognized by the Library of Congress National Film Registry Act.

"Nobody is making movies like Burnett," observed Michael Tolkin, who likened Burnett's approach to Rossellini's neorealism, without Rossellini's romanticism. "The people in his films live maybe ten miles from Century City, but it could be the moon." Burnett may have been the first director to draw his inspiration from the black neighborhoods of Los Angeles. Burnett has criticized Hollywood for suppressing creativity through its eternal concern with the bottom line, which results in an inevitable split between the director's vision and box-office reality. "People would in the most helpful way ask me why I didn't make something more commercial," he recalled. "But I just knew that what I was doing was a different ball game. It's not the same market. If you don't realize those differences, you go crazy."[1]

Burnett claims that the studios' efforts to project the image of liberal institutions is false. In actuality, not many people of color are involved in the decision-making process. Women also are not represented at the top, because there's a lot of hostility toward them in the business. Burnett believes that "if you get women filmmakers, you would get a different perspective," and the same applies to black filmmakers who have "distinctive stories" to tell, "new dimensions" to show.

For Burnett, most studio films perpetuate racism because they are not interested in depicting life realistically. Films create stereotypes about black people since they appear mostly in action-packed dramas about crime and drugs. Mainstream producers don't even try to get black directors to do films with black themes. This means that it's up to black directors to shake things up. Concerned with the studios' control over the collective representation of blacks, Burnett claims that "only a black director can lend 'something special' to a black theme."

Burnett began his career with three low-budget indies: *Killer of Sheep*, *My Brother's Wedding* (made in 1983 but released later), and *To Sleep With Anger* (1990). In terms of style, *My Brother's Wedding* falls between the gritty simplicity of *Killer of Sheep* and the more elegant and technically accomplished *To Sleep With Anger*.

Constituting virtually a one-man crew, Burnett shot *Killer of Sheep* over weekends for a whole year. The film, which was shown at the Whitney Museum in 1978 and at the Toronto festival in 1981, draws strength from its sharp observations of one poverty-row black family.

Stan (Henry Sanders), a remote, rather depressed man, works in a slaughterhouse (hence the title) but dreams of a better job, although his possibilities are limited. Stan's wife is bored and sexually frustrated, and his two children walk around aimlessly.

The movie offers glimpses of Stan's monotonous life, which are punctuated by cuts to the slaughterhouse. Burnett said that he tried "to recreate a situation without reducing life to a simple plot." Nonetheless, photographed in a spare black and white, the film is too studied, giving the impression that Stan's estrangement is further accentuated by the director's own detachment. The dialogue is spoken with either insufficient or excessive emphasis by the amateur actors. Burnett shows a keen eye for life's tiny moments, but the picture is arid and barren. The more mainstream critics complained about the film's inability to imbue the observed events with broader meanings.

In *My Brother's Wedding*, which Burnett coproduced, wrote, directed, photographed and edited, the goal was to change the image of Watts (South Central Los Angeles), long before the 1992 riots. For Burnett, Watts was not an urban jungle but a place where people lead ordinary lives, built around work, family, and friendship. Portraying Watts as both Anywhere USA and a specific locale, Burnett shows the area's many facets as a battleground with guns in the streets, good china on the table, and the blues wafting through the trees.[2]

An embittered youth, Pierce Monday (Everett Silas), is entrapped between two worlds: the "safe" comfort and middle-class existence of his lawyer brother, Wendell, who is about to marry an attorney, and the hell-bent world of his buddy, the ex-con Soldier Richards. Like the uncle in Burnett's later film, *To Sleep With Anger*, Soldier is a troublemaker, a symbol of rebellion against the things that both repel and attract Pierce. For Burnett, neither man is a satisfying role model: Wendell is smug, while Soldier is a near-psychopath.

The story includes attempted murders, chases, fights, and violent deaths. Burnett reduces horror to a sudden eruption of violence in the lives of ordinary people who are concerned with making a living and getting through the day. As in *To Sleep With Anger*, he encloses his tale in biblical invocations and ironic suggestions of redemption and damnation. Burnett's script is strong, but the pace is deliberate and the acting amateurish. As Michael Wilmington observed, what makes the film special is the way Burnett lingers on details, breaking off climaxes and entering the action halfway through with unexpected touches.

Burnett's brand of humor and his original mix of drama and irony are evident in his best film, *To Sleep With Anger*. Also set in South Central, it concerns the problems of a black middle-class family headed by Gideon (Paul Butler), a retired man who raises chickens, and his wife Suzie (Mary Alice), who teaches midwifery. The placidity of their lives is interrupted by the arrival of Harry (Danny Glover), a man who grew up with Gideon and Suzie in the Deep South. A strange interloper who disrupts the lives of a tightly knit family, Harry appears on their doorstep with a winning smile, claiming he's on his way to San Francisco. Gideon and Suzie ask him to move in and make himself at home, which he does comfortably.

Harry can be both charming and rude. While Gideon and Suzie are at church, he goes through their house like a burglar, looking into drawers, reading old letters. He believes in spells, and when Sunny accidentally brushes his shoes with a broom, he behaves as if the boy had aimed a gun at him. At a reunion of old Southern friends living in Los Angeles, Harry insults the matronly Hattie, a former girlfriend who's now a born-again Christian, by making references to the "house" her mother ran. Hattie warns the family that Harry is evil: "Everybody associated with him winds up with pennies over his eyes." There are hints that Harry had something to do with the murder of a black man, a murder that was made to look like a lynching in order to shift the blame on whites. Wherever he goes, Harry spreads mistrust and discord: a couple splits up, and Gideon falls mysteriously ill.

Harry is a demon, the soul of the Southern black sharecropper, who comes to haunt gentle folks who fondly remember the past in terms of food, music, and farming. Densely written by Burnett and played by Glover with seductive ease, Harry is by turns naive, threatening, sophisticated—and lost.

At first, as Vincent Canby has noted, *To Sleep With Anger* seems to take place in an idealized black middle-class landscape, not unlike the one depicted on TV's *Cosby Show*. But gradually the film becomes a more complex, unpredictable comedy of substance, keeping the audience in suspense about the next change in tone.[3] Though small in scope, *To Sleep With Anger* contains big comic scenes and a clamorous ending, two among many other virtues that somehow didn't help the film find its audience, black or white.

CREATING OPPORTUNITIES—ROBERT TOWNSEND

A comic with the Second City troupe in Chicago, Robert Townsend found himself stuck in unsatisfying movie roles. Having appeared in *A Soldier's Story* and *Streets of Fire*, he had established himself as a decent supporting actor. Townsend might have remained in that category indefinitely had he not had the audacity to challenge his fate. Raising $100,000, some from a cash advance against credit cards, he cowrote (with Keenen Ivory Wayans) and directed *Hollywood Shuffle* (1986), which is based on his encounters on the job hunt. The format, a series of daydreams and digressions, is very thin. As a satire of black stereotyping, *Hollywood Shuffle* ridicules the whole industry—rude white producers, directors of black films, TV critics like Ebert and Siskel. The humor derives from Townsend's anger and frustration over the grotesque "choices" forced on black actors.

Townsend plays Bobby Taylor, a black actor who's auditioning for a sleazy pimp role in a blaxploitation picture. Bobby's heart isn't in it, and he's not the type, but there are no decent roles available to him. In auditions, white filmmakers ask the actors to be "more black, more street." No matter how "black" they are, the players are never black enough (although light-skinned blacks don't stand a chance). In a dream sequence, the NAACP pickets Bobby's house because he has "betrayed" his people and taken the pimp's role: Idealistic black actors are forced to become a new kind of Uncle Tom, caricaturing themselves for the profit of white producers.

Despite his hopes of landing a lead role, Bobby is distressed by what is happening to him psychologically. Could the leading black TV actor of the day really be the winged star of *There's a Bat in My House*, a TV show that asks, "Can a black bat from Detroit find happiness with a white suburban family? He's half bat, half soul brother— but together he adds up to big laughs!" Dismayed, Bobby withdraws into a fantasy world that includes dreams of omnipotence and scenes of humiliation. He imagines a black movie culture, from *Rambo* to *King Lear*, with himself playing all of the heroes. In one reverie, Bobby plays a black Superman, flying over the city; in another, he sees an acting school for blacks staffed with white teachers instructing their students how to speak, how to stand, and how to swagger. In an earlier sequence, actors are asked to swagger like Eddie Murphy—to be Murphyesque or Murphonic.

The principal complaint, demonstrated in a scene in which Bobby practices the line "You done messed with the wrong dude, baby," is that the roles available to blacks are severely limited. The closing credits list a group of "Zombie Pimps" and one of "Eddie Murphy Types," with the same cast reappearing over and over in similar capacities. As Bobby watches classically trained actors turn up at casting calls to read lines like "Why you be gotta pull a knife on me?," he despairs, but when he lands a starring role as a hoodlum, he feels even worse.

In the funniest sequence, Townsend and Jimmy Woodard, in caps and jackets, play movie critics on a TV show called *Sneakin' in the Movies*. Borrowing from Eddie Murphy's character Rahiem Abdul Mohammed on *Saturday Night Live*, they use either profane or pretentious words like "effervescence" and rely on a wider range of gestures than the usual thumbs up or down to express their opinions of films like *Amadeus* and *Dirty Harry*. At show's end, they are thrown out of the theater by an angry usher.

Townsend shot some of the movie on bits of stock donated by directors he had worked with; many scenes had to be done in a single take. Unevenly written, *Hollywood Shuffle* is a collection of skits interspersed with earnest domestic passages. Townsend's two missteps include tacking on an earnest ending and sugarcoating the parts played by women, thus making his movie conventional. Bobby lives at home with his mother, grandmother, and kid brother, and he's respectful and courtly with his chaste girlfriend. It's the women who keep Bobby from losing sight of his real values. Even so, *Hollywood Shuffle* is a satire with enough comic breeze to override its deficiencies. What the film lacks in structure it makes up for in likable humor. Ragged and movieish as it is, *Hollywood Shuffle* is funny and even poignant—which cannot be said about Townsend's subsequent films as a director, *The Five Heartbeats* (1991), *Blankman* (1993), and *B.A.P.S* (1996).

THE TURNING POINT—SPIKE LEE

Spike Lee assumes his position as dean of the African American directors by virtue of his talent, productivity (thirteen features in thirteen years), and attitude—call it chutzpah. Early on, Lee's dedication to the making and marketing of his movies was noteworthy—he hawked hats and T-shirts, showing up at theaters to hype the opening day. Lee's showmanship is without peer in the indie world. A media celeb with a knack for controversy, he has increased the visibility not just of his but of all African American films. Moving back and forth between Hollywood and the indies, Lee continues to serve as a role model for a young generation of black filmmakers.

Confronting directly the racial problems that beset American society, Lee makes purposefully didactic films that call for consciousness awakening. In a film he made while at NYU, *Joe's Bed-Stuy Barber Shop: We Cut Heads*, a sleeping character is hailed with the line "Wake up! The black man has been asleep for 400 years." In the climax of the musical *School Daze*, warring factions greet sunrise with the cry "Wake up!" In Lee's chef d'oeuvre, *Do the Right Thing*, the same refrain introduces both the film and the character Mookie (played by Lee).[4]

From his very first film, Lee projected the impression of a filmmaker who possesses not only a strong point of view but also the determination to get movies made his own way. Of Lee's films, only three or four movies, including *Girl 6* and *Get on the Bus*, are independent; the rest are studio made. Bursting onto the indie scene in 1986 Lee immediately established himself as a filmmaker of note. He won acclaim for his debut, *She's Gotta Have It*, a stylish black-and-white comedy whose sharp, witty direction impressed both critics and audiences. Lee's portrayal of the streetwise hustler Mars (with his trademark litany "Please, baby, please, baby, please, baby, please baby") proved to be a compelling element as well.

Distressed that so little of the vibrant black life he had experienced as a boy has been portrayed onscreen, Lee was determined to dedicate his work exclusively to the African American experience. Black people are usually portrayed in stereotypically offensive roles. *She's Gotta Have It*, which Lee produced, wrote, directed, edited, and acted in, gave him a chance to show a slice of black urban life in which white characters don't even exist.

Lee has criticized Woody Allen for not casting black actors in his movies (a situation that finally changed in the 1996 film *Deconstructing Harry*). Nonetheless, there are several similarities between Allen and Lee. *She's Gotta Have It* has been compared to Allen's early work for its humor and its loving treatment of New York (in Lee's other pictures, the city is not portrayed so lovingly). Lee also resembles Allen in the comic energy he brings to his acting, although the roles he has played, Mars in *She's Gotta Have It* and the pizza delivery boy in *Do the Right Thing*, are far from Allen's neurotic, self-absorbed characters. There's another, rather unfortunate similarity between the two filmmakers. Allen's films of the 1990s have each grossed less than $14 million, despite the director's exalted status among critics. Similarly, in his recent work, Lee has become a niche director. The difference is that Allen has a realistic idea of his audience size and budgets his films so that they at least break even, whereas Lee has not reduced his budgets and his films have been losing money.

The title of *She's Gotta Have It* may have been inspired by Frank Tashlin's camp comedy *The Girl Can't Help It*, starring Jayne Mansfield. At the center of the film is the sexual life of a young black graphic designer, Nola Darling (Tracy Camilla Johns), who can be perceived as a precursor to the attractive black women in *Waiting to Exhale* (1995). Nolas has affairs with three men and ends up dismissing all of them. As a sex comedy, *She's Gotta Have It* stays close to Nola's bed: The film begins with her rising from under the bedcovers, and it ends with her diving under the covers. In a role reversal, Nola is as self-centered as most men are; unlike most men, however she doesn't attempt to hide from her lovers the existence of the others. Nola enjoys her power over men, but, apart from sex, she doesn't know what she wants from them. At the same time, she is intelligent enough to understand that her determination to be independent carries a price.

Lee constructs a strong woman who possesses the same right to sleep around as men. The men perceive Nola as alluring but "emotionally sick," because she can't choose one man. The film satirizes selfishness and sexual role playing among men; the ultimate joke is on the men who, hypocritically, are upset by Nola's freewheeling sexuality. In a most poignant sequence, Nola turns to the camera and ridicules their self-love and tired come-ons—a dozen men deliver silly pickup lines like "Baby, you need a man like me to hold you." When Lee's film was shown at a benefit for the Black Filmmaker Foundation, the women in the audience laughed louder than the men. During the discussion that followed, one man remarked how unusual it was to see "the shoe on the other foot." "That's primarily the reason I made the film," Lee replied, noting that it's the men who are the butt of the humor.[5]

Nola's lovers are each lacking in crucial ways. Jamie (Tommy Red-mond Hicks), the solid, sensitive type, loves her, but he's too possessive and jealous of the other men. A fashion model, the muscled Greer (John Canada Terrell) treats his body as if it were a work of art; he takes so long to fold his clothes before going to bed that Nola loses interest in sex. A little man on a bike, Mars, the third lover, is the smartest; he wears a satin baseball jacket and Air Jordan sneakers, which he refuses to remove in bed. Endlessly talking, Mars shows self-confidence while arguing his way into bed.

She's Gotta Have It is set in a world that runs parallel to but doesn't clash with the white world. For white audiences, it offered the oppor-tunity to see how the black middle class lives. For blacks, it was a chance to see themselves on screen for the first time—and to like what they saw. Lee's innovation, as Pauline Kael has pointed out, was to break the pattern of casting black actresses with light skin and WASPish features.[6] Lee doesn't deny the blackness of his characters, but once the racial milieu is established, the viewers aren't distanced by it.

Lee's financial limitations were used by him to an advantage: Made on a shoestring, for a mostly deferred budget of $175,000, the movie was shot on location in Brooklyn in twelve days. Visually, Lee combines a casual style with a disciplined approach. The film is loose and open ended, relying on characters who address the camera directly, little photo essays, cameo appearances, comic riffs—and one weak dance in-terlude set in Central Park, which is shot in color.

Kael has noted that, like Scorsese, Lee has a fresh style of filmmak-ing that is at once the subject of the movie and the joy of watching it. De-termined to make an accessible movie, Lee gives the film the structure and title of an exploitation flick, with all the standard ploys in the soft-core market: Nola Darling is a porn-picture name; she's courted by a leering lesbian; she consults a sex therapist, who tells her she's healthy; when she doesn't have a man around, she plays with herself. But *She's Gotta Have It* is so stylish that it transcends the material's weaknesses. As a witty comedy of manners, the tempo is fast, making for a sparking movie. Lee is ingenious about varying the pulse, and his exuberance compensates for the botched ending—Lee didn't know how to con-clude the film.

Nonetheless, the film contains some problems that would plague Lee's future pictures as well. He shows weaknesses in developing a tight narrative and in sustaining a consistent tone, in this case, a satiri-cal mood. In most of Lee's films, the subsidiary characters outshine the principals—here, Nola is more interesting when she's surrounded by men than when she's alone on-screen.

Lee expected the movie to spawn controversy, since it showed be-haviors and attitudes that blacks might not want to see. But the film cut across racial barriers, avoiding the "either-or" dilemma black artists often face. When he wrote the script, Lee had black audiences in mind, but *She's Gotta Have It* crossed over and appealed to white viewers as well. It's one of the most successful "no-budgeters," not just on the basis of its financial returns ($7.1 million domestically) but also by virtue of the career it launched. Lee used his early success to gain access to stu-dio money, with which he made thematically challenging and formally inventive films.

Indeed, following his "guerrilla filmmaking" debut, he made *School Daze* (1988), which was financed by Columbia with no interference, making Lee the first black director to be ever given complete artistic control. With an all-black ensemble, Lee's musical comedy addresses satirically class and color divisions within a black college where afflu-ent light-skinned "gammas" clash with the underclass dark-skinned "jigaboos." *School Daze* proved that a film about African Americans could succeed, redeeming a history of stereotypical images. Despite Co-lumbia's poor promotion and unenthusiastic critical reviews, the film grossed more than twice its cost.

Lee's chef d'oeuvre, *Do the Right Thing* (1989), enlarged upon his former efforts thematically and artistically. Based on racially motivated acts of violence, his polemically charged drama stirred controversy even before it was released. Praised for its energy and craftsmanship, *Do the Right Thing* presents a realistic look at one predominantly black block of Bedford-Stuyvesant, in Brooklyn. The interracial violence be-tween the black underclass and the Italian-American family that runs the local pizzeria climaxes with the killing of a black youth by a white cop and a fiery street riot. The mise-en-scène, music (by Lee's jazz bassist father), and dialogue are rich in allusions to African American culture. As in *School Daze*, Lee presents the divisions within the black community by showing photographs of both Malcolm X and Martin Luther King, Jr., ending the movie with seemingly opposing quotations from them.

THE WATERSHED YEARS

Lee set in motion an explosion of black directorial talent. In 1991, about fifteen films by black directors were released, more than in the preceding two decades. Matty Rich's *Straight Out of Brooklyn* opened two weeks before Lee's *Jungle Fever* and two months before John Singleton's *Boyz 'N' the Hood*, the movie that changed the definition of black-themed movies. The new black wave embraced a dozen directors, including John Singleton, Bill Duke (*House Party*), Carl Franklin (*One False Move*), Julie Dash (*Daughters of the Dust*), and Mario Van Peebles (*Posse, Panther*). But it was not just the quantity that was striking; it was also the quality, energy, and diversity.

Representing the most interesting development in American film of the 1990s, the black film movement was as significant as the New American Cinema of the 1960s. The new wave didn't occur overnight; Gordon Parks (*The Learning Tree*), Melvin Van Peebles (*The Watermelon Man*), and others have tried before to generate interest in black themes. However, what was exciting about the new cycle, beyond its magnitude was the fresh point of view. The new wave was headed by young directors, for the most part graduates of film schools: Singleton was twenty-five, Rich was only twenty-one. Through vigorous story telling, they provided an insider's view. Although some of the movies were messagey and socially conscious, they had a certain cool about them, a hip sense of style, a new kind of music. Collectively, these new movies declared the end of films dominated by the white perspective on black issues.

The new films stood in sharp opposition to the earlier blaxploitation films, such as *Shaft*, *Three the Hard Way*, and *Dolemite*. They may have been slick in style, but they were not emotionally vacuous. *Boyz 'N' the Hood* had its share of moralizing speeches about father-son relationships, but the immediacy of its message—the importance of a strong male authority figure for black teenagers in a violent-ridden community—was undeniable. Made in a country sharply polarized by race, these movies showed topical relevance, expressing anger at white society for neglecting the black community.

The new movies unraveled portraits of black lifestyles previously omitted from or misrepresented by the media. "Either they don't know it, or they won't show it," says a character in *Boyz 'N' the Hood* about media coverage of black life. Singleton depicted South Central, Spike Lee filmed in Brooklyn's Bedford-Stuyvesant, and Matty Rich showed Brooklyn's Red Hook. The locations may have been different, but the message was quite similar.

Boyz 'N' the Hood and the other films turned cold statistics on homicide within the black community into emotionally charged probing of black lifestyles. They offered a window into another world, informing white viewers about issues they hadn't know much about. The filmmakers didn't look away from "negative" characters when they erred and refused to sentimentalize them to facilitate emotional identification. While empathy was encouraged, pathos and self-pity were to be avoided at all costs.

The visibility of the new films and the public's curiosity about them benefited from recent demographic trends. The emergence of a black middle-class in the 1980s provided new characters for TV sitcoms (*The Cosby Show*), but also stressed the sharp inequalities that existed within the black community itself. *Jungle Fever* and *Do the Right Thing* showed "good" and "bad" characters, often within the same family. In *Jungle Fever*, Wesley Snipes plays a successful architect whose brother (Samuel L. Jackson) is a pitiable drug addict. In *Straight Out of Brooklyn*, a teenager is forced to turn against his alcoholic and abusive father.

The increasing number of African American films has encouraged black artists in every capacity to pursue their careers more aggressively. The pool of black players, male and female, has never been as impressive as it is at present, with Wesley Snipes, Samuel L. Jackson, Denzel Washington, Laurence Fishburn, Angela Bassett, and Halle Barry starring in both studio and indie films. Enjoying the media's attention and support, these performers finally began to receive the roles, recognition, and rewards they deserved.

COMEDIES AND SATIRES

Not all the new black-themed films were about inner-city crime or drugs. Mixing social issues and comedy, Charles Lane wrote, produced, directed, and starred in *Sidewalk Stories* (1989), an almost silent black-and-white film, a Chaplinesque fantasy about the plight of the homeless in America. Lane plays a homeless man struggling for survival in

Greenwich Village who finds himself caring for a toddler whose father has been stabbed by muggers.

Lane's next comedy, *True Identity* (1991), was a showcase for Lenny Henry, the British comedian who is a master of accents and mimicry. Henry plays a struggling black actor, Miles Pope, whose dream is to play Othello but whose experience has been limited to playing a raisin in a TV commercial. On a plane about to crash, Miles gets a confession from a businessman named Leland Carver (Frank Langella), who's actually the underworld boss Frank Luchino, long thought to be dead. But the plane doesn't crash, and Luchino puts out a contract on Miles.

Miles has to disguise himself, which he does by taking on a series of outrageous personalities. Henry is least interesting when he plays a sincere man, and most entertaining as a hit man, Frank LaMotta. In white-face, with false nose and wig, LaMotta is so convincing that he gets the contract to rub himself out. He also masquerades as James Brown's brother, dressed in a purple velvet tux, and plays Miles's best friend, Duane, a makeup man who provides Henry's disguises. The running gag is that the five-foot-five-inch Duane is obsessed with tall and hefty women.

True Identity was written by Andy Breckman, who expanded it from a Eddie Murphy routine for *Saturday Night Live*. In the sketch, a white-faced Murphy discovers how white people live when there are no black people around; everything in stores is free, there are cocktail parties on trains, and so on. As in *Hollywood Shufffle*, a white acting coach wants Miles to be more "Harlemesque." Although it takes a few stabs at racial stereotypes, *True Identity* is impaired by its disappointing direction.

In *House Party* (1990), the first feature by the Hudlin brothers (Reginald writes and directs; Warrington produces), black suburban teens try to throw a party without being hassled by their parents or the cops. Though slight, this comedy is more joyful and less cloying than its counterparts, 1960s white teen-party movies. Before *House Party*, there was a clear division: nice black kids were on TV, bad ones were in film. *House Party* was perhaps the first picture devoted to the innocent side of black suburbanites, who don't do drugs and are careful about sex. There are thugs, but they're harmless, and all the dangers are safely whisked away.

A buoyant comedy of teen-age manners, set in an idealized and sanitized society, *House Party* is about a sealed world, where avoiding an irate parent, sidetracking a bad report card, and getting to a party on time are always fraught with danger.[7] Unlike most teen-age movies, which attempt to impose an adult, moralizing view, *House Party* displays a light, witty touch, although eventually it too succumbs to the urge to offer lessons in responsibility. Overall, style is more important than plot: The Hudlins avoid "important" themes and weighty dialogue in favor of showing exuberant, spontaneous behavior.

The upbeat comedy was followed by an animated TV series, *Kid 'n Play*, and two sequels based on the characters created by Reginald, who later sold the franchise. The first *House Party* contained comic highlights and mishaps about a watchful father, vicious dogs, inept cops, and neighborhood bullies, all obstacles to Kid's attending Play's late-night jam. But the less imaginative sequel, *House Party 2* (1991), turned socially conscious and preached the virtues of education for black teenagers.

In Doug McHenry's uninspired follow-up, Kid is heading off to college—if he can just hold onto the money raised by the church for him. When Play loses his tuition money, Kid realizes that the only way to raise funds is to throw a house party. Burdened with a flimsy story and an educational message, the movie became bigger, louder and messier. Whereas the Hudlins were careful to anchor the story in a recognizable world, McHenry offers an unrealistic college life. The Hudlins managed to be sexy without dehumanizing women, but the new movie has Queen Latifah make speeches about women's autonomy and then treat women as bimbos. Kid 'n Play are funny, but it's Martin Lawrence who steals the picture as their friend Bilal.

Also lacking the genial goofiness and infectious good nature of the first films is the disjointed *House Party 3* (1994). Meant as the next step in the natural progression in the escapades of the hip-hop duo, it's about the engagement of Kid to the beautiful Veda (who replaces his former girlfriend, Sydney). Kid's anxieties about matrimony are meant to unify a vignettish comedy about his friendship with Play and his disapproving in-laws. The material for the series was always ephemeral, but *House Party 3* is too self-conscious about its humor and characters. The success of each party film has depended on the quality of its guests. Despite having talent drawn from hot clubs and TV shows—the comedians Bernice Mac, Michael Colyar, and Chris Tucker from HBO's *Def Comedy Jam*, the young rappers Immature, and a girl group called Sex as a Weapon, *House Party 3* doesn't fully utilize its varied cast. Pandering to the audience, the movie comes to life only in the last reel, when everybody shows up at Kid's bachelor party. Remarkably, despite the films' varying quality, the *House Party* series found its audience, and New Line scored a huge success with all three movies.

Bill Duke adapted *A Rage in Harlem* (1991), a caper comedy set in 1956, from Chester Himes's crime novel. Wonderful as the book is, it had failed to make it to the big screen earlier because of Hollywood's lack of conviction about the commercial viability of an all-black story. Believing that a black director was needed to maintain the book's integrity, the producer, Kerry Boyle, chose Duke because he was older than other candidates and the material called for maturity. Duke had made his debut with *The Killing Floor* (1984), about a man who risked his life to unionize a meat-packing plant.

Since John Toles-Bey and Bobby Crawford's screenplay is shallow, the characters are revealed entirely by the actors who play them. The movie stars Robin Givens as a sexy hustler with a trunkful of gold, pursued by a naive Bible-thumper, his street-smart brother, and other thugs. *A Rage in Harlem* was the first project featuring a black glamorous actress since Diana Ross's ill-fated *Mahogany*. Like the late Dorothy Dandridge, Givens has sex appeal and acting skills. The film's most entertaining moments are incidental to the central plot, but Duke compensates with an affectionate portrait of Harlem's vibrant street life, hustling and bustling with con artists.

Far more impressive was Joseph H. Vasquez's taut film, *Hangin' With the Homeboys* (1991), which showcased a finely tuned ear and superb comic timing. The film follows the (mis)adventures of four young men, two black and two Hispanic, on a typical Friday night as they cruise their Bronx neighborhood. Charting the same territory as other "cruising" pictures (*American Graffiti, Diner*), *Hangin' With the Homeboys* serves as an allegory about growing up and making choices. Even if the odds appear insurmountable, the film suggests, survival depends on taking charge of one's life. By the end of the film, it's clear who among the four will make something of his life and who will be left behind.

Night on the town turns into a series of comic disasters; every activity shimmers with danger and suspense. The quartet prowl the streets in search of excitement, before descending on Manhattan, where they frequent discos, pool halls, peep shows, and subway stations. Confused and perpetually broke, Willie (Doug E. Doug) blames every tiny setback in his life on racism. "You're doing this because I'm black!" he sputters in what becomes a humorous refrain. Tom (Mario Joyner), an unemployed actor with a job in telemarketing, exudes the kind of self-confidence that survives even after he smashes up his car, loses his girlfriend, and is arrested by the police for jumping a subway turnstile.

Johnny and Vinny, who are both Puerto Rican, are just as dissimilar. Johnny (John Leguizamo), who works as a grocery clerk, can't make up his mind whether to go to college. A depressive type, he combats self-pity by reminding himself of all the starving people in China. The most compelling character, Johnny has a secret crush on a sultry young woman, whom he later sees in a peep show. The most extroverted is Vinny (Nestor Serano), a gigolo who lives off women while passing himself off as Italian. His hostility toward women is reflected in his obsession with quick seduction. Vinny, whose real name is Fernando, stakes so much of his identity on his phony Italian image that when he is challenged by an Italian-American cop, he's utterly humiliated.

Hangin' With the Homeboys, whose screenplay was cited at the Sundance festival, failed to find an audience despite critical support. It was released at a time when the public seemed more intrigued by a cycle of inner-city dramas, or hood movies, as they became known. Three movies defined this cycle: *Boyz 'N' the Hood*, a studio movie, and *Straight Out of Brooklyn* and *Menace II Society*, both quintessential indies albeit in different ways.

HOOD MOVIES

John Singleton was the first director to successfully translate the swing and heat of hip-hop culture into cinematic language. Singleton's movies are studio financed, but he is responsible for making the quintessential *Boys 'N' the Hood* (1991), which launched a whole cycle of indies about inner-city life. *Boyz 'N' the Hood* received Oscar nominations for Best Original Screenplay and Best Director, making Singleton the first African American and the youngest person to ever be nominated for a directorial Oscar. Produced for a modest $6 million, the film grossed $57 million, an input-output ratio that made it the most profitable picture of the year.

Singleton was out of the University of Southern California's film school for only a month when Columbia made a bid to finance his semi-autobiographical story of young men coming of age in South Central. Singleton insisted on directing the film himself; he felt that too many bad films had been made about black people by white directors. He perceived a movie like Dennis Hopper's *Colors* (1988) as a misfire, because the filmmaker knew nothing about the culture of South Central. Marketed as a gang movie, *Colors* was actually a buddie movie about two white cops, played by Robert Duvall and Sean Penn.

The first all-black movie to be bankrolled by a major studio, *Boyz 'N' the Hood* deals with family disintegration and gang wars. A sharp portrait of violence and retribution, the film centers on the struggles of one family to provide its son with the necessary tools for survival. Having grown up in drug-ridden hoods, Singleton knew the environment firsthand; living in South Central has given him a perspective different from that of white directors.

Singleton has survived, but not without scars. As a filmmaker, he continues to search for inspiration and affirmation on the streets of his home turf. When Singleton was nine, his father took him to see *Star Wars* (Lucas and Spielberg were his idols), which he liked, but even then he knew that American movies didn't tell stories about his kind. Singleton has always been an outsider, whether being bused to white schools or mingling with white students at USC. As a student, Spike Lee became his role model; if it had not been for Lee, Singleton would not be making movies. Lee is the one filmmaker who made it big—and managed to stay black.

Amid gang war and hard-core rap, *Boyz 'N' the Hood* follows three boys from their preteen years to postadolescence. Singleton turns the sexual confession of Tre (Cuba Gooding Jr.) into a hyped-up fantasy; the scene in which older boys intimidate younger ones becomes a primal myth, both intense and pathetic. Doughboy, the 'hood's gun-toting enforcer, returns from prison with a sense of doom; he spends his time cruising the streets with a posse, ogling women, and sizing up rivals. Of the trio, only Tre has a father, Furious Styles (Laurence Fishburn), who steers him away from gang activities. Furious preaches black-pride sermons about discipline and dignity. But can the one-parent family survive the mean streets of South Central?

Full of the crackle of gunfire and the whirl of police helicopters, the film's soundtrack is a constant reminder of violence and police patrol. Demythologizing ghetto life, while advocating self-sufficiency, *Boyz 'N' the Hood* features another novelty: None of the women is a prostitute, servant, or welfare mother—all demeaning roles that black women have been assigned to play in Hollywood movies. The critic Armond

White has noted that the father's name, Furious Styles, suggests what drives Singleton's art: a sense of commitment and an interest in technical display. Singleton turns a typical coming-of-age drama into an expression of the contemporary social pressures that affect black men. Drawing a contrast between *Boyz 'N' the Hood* and the 1980s Brat Pack youth films, White has observed that black teens see life in terms of survival, whereas white kids perceive life in terms of fun. In fact, as I have noted, introducing fun into black films was the novel accomplishment of the *House Party* films.

THE AMATEUR—MATTY RICH

Matty Rich became the darling of the 1990 Sundance festival, and the youngest director to have a movie in the dramatic competition. While technically raw, *Straight Out of Brooklyn* generated excitement for its fresh voice and unsparing look at the disintegration of one black family. Set in the Red Hook housing projects in Brooklyn, it depicts kids growing up in a neighborhood infested with drugs and shootouts who can't escape the vicious cycle of violence.

To lift himself out of misery, Dennis (Lawrence Gilliard Jr.), an adolescent sick of impoverishment, plans with two homeboys, Kevin (Mark Malone) and Larry (played by Rich), to rob a local drug dealer and use the money to escape. Dennis and his girlfriend, Shirley, ponder their life against the glorious skyline of Manhattan. "They built New York by steppin' on the black man, steppin' on the black family!" says Dennis, expressing the director's grim credo. Trying to take a shortcut to fulfilling his yearnings, Dennis instead provokes his family's ruin. The family in the film stands as a microcosm for a ghetto society, in which frustrated men take out their anger on their dearest ones. Like *Boyz 'N' the Hood*, *Straight Out of Brooklyn* focuses on the efforts of one teenager to find a way out. But, unlike *Jungle Fever*, in which explosive racism and drug abuse serve as subtexts, in Rich's movie they are the text.

The characters are straight out of Rich's life. Dennis is modeled on a childhood friend, Lamont Logan, who was arrested for stealing a motorcycle and later died of kidney disease in a juvenile detention center. And Rich's abuse by his own father inspired the opening scene. In a drunken rage, Ray beats his long-suffering wife, while in an adjacent bedroom their terrified children lie in bed, listening to the argument. When Rich was eight, he lay in bed listening to "things crashing" in the next room as his father took out his frustration on his mother. "All I could hear," Rich recalled, "was knocking on the door and people shouting to open up. The police came in and took my father—and that was the last time I ever saw him."[8]

The couple in the movie, the spiritually broken father and the forgiving mother, are modeled on Rich's aunt and uncle. His uncle was killed at a bus stop in Red Hook on his way to the hospital to visit his cancer-ridden wife. For Rich it was a "double whammy": His uncle died in the ambulance, and his aunt in the hospital shortly thereafter. The film's climactic sequence shows the simultaneous deaths—in a hospital and on the streets—of Dennis's parents, events edited together in a quick, calibrated rhythm to suggest the hand of fate.

In Rich's vision, the essentials of the African American experience boil down to poverty and death. "I can show you the exact places in Red Hook where my friends died one by one," Rich told the *New York Times*. "They died because they wanted that rush-rush-quick-quick money, that whole American dream of 'I want it now.'" A blend of polemics and art, *Straight Out of Brooklyn* is dominated by the former. "I wasn't interested in film because I loved film," Rich said. "I was angry. I was upset that everybody around me got destroyed in the community. . . . Instead of sitting on a street corner and selling something, instead of killing somebody, which my friends did, I started to use my brain. That's the difference between me and the others."[9]

Black kids want to get "there"—"there" being Manhattan, visible from the projects like a glass-and-steel mirage. "That's the American Dream, that's what the kids want, to go straight out of Brooklyn. But the movie is about saying, 'You don't have to go over there to make it.'"[10] Rich thinks successful people should break the habit of leaving their neighborhoods. "I'm not saying to get angry with white society because we're already angry. I'm saying, pluck them out of your head and rebuild the community. Show young people self-respect and show them you don't have to go straight out of Brooklyn, or out of Watts, to make it. You don't have to live on Park Avenue to make it. You can stay at home."

Like Singleton, Rich knows first hand the inner city, and, like Singleton, he enjoyed family support that helped him escape a life of hopeless despair. At sixteen, Rich was already infected with "the filmmaking bug," but he had no money and had never held a camera. In Rich's case, ignorance of the movie business may have been a blessing, because he didn't realize that his dream was "virtually impossible to achieve." But Rich's movie is amateurish, suffering from lack of technique, with out-of-focus compositions, cluttered blocking with the actors' backs to the camera, and a restaurant scene in which the sounds of eating garble the dialogue. What is presented as rough-hewn and natural and as having a certain charm basically derived from Rich's total lack of skills.

For a first film, *Straight Out of Brooklyn* was all right, but Rich's amateurishness backfired when he undertook a bigger film. Changing pace and working with a larger budget on a studio film, Rich directed *The Inkwell*, a satire of the black bourgeoisie set in the summer of 1976. Messy and incoherent, *The Inkwell* tries to be at once a rowdy farce, a political tract, and a coming-of-age drama, but it is unsuccessful at all of them. As Stephen Holden has noted, forcing these disparate ingredients together through sheer emotionalism, Rich misdirects the cast to overact with hysterical intensity.[11] Rich and his writers caricature black conservatives to ludicrous extremes, but the project proves too much of a stretch for the director of *Straight Out of Brooklyn*.

THE PROS—ALLEN AND ALBERT HUGHES

If the charm of Rich's first film derived from its rawness, Allen and Albert Hughes's *Menace II Society* (1993) is arguably the most striking debut in black cinema, even more stunning than *Boyz 'N' the Hood*, to which it bears a thematic resemblance. Born in Detroit and raised in Pomona, California, the twins began making music videos at age 12, and they were only twenty when they made the film. The Hugheses use an extraordinary technique to make a tragic film about violence, loss, and death. Dramatizing the plight of an entire class of men, the story is told by directors who were the same age as their heroes, young enough to get deep inside their characters.

Tyger Williams wrote the script, which is based on a story he and the Hugheses developed together. While many of the events are true to life, they aren't necessarily drawn from Williams's life. Williams was a suburban child, but he believes most black males in America go through the same things, whether they are raised in Bel-Air or in Watts. Still, to guarantee authenticity, Williams and the Hugheses spent time in South Central, imbuing their script with the anger and frustration they found there.[12]

Despite the obvious comparisons to Boyz 'N' the Hood, Menace II Society may be closer to Scorsese's work. Williams watched carefully Taxi Driver, Raging Bull, and GoodFellas, as well as Oliver Stone's Platoon and Brian De Palma's Scarface, all vibrantly energetic films with gritty realism and effective use of voiceover narration. Working with the cinematographer Lisa Rinzler, the directors employ a visual style that is associated with Scorsese (and Sergio Leone), but the point of view is very much their own. Like Singleton, the Hugheses offer a despairing vision of family disintegration in the inner city, and, like him, they believe the way to survive is to stay close to the family. But the Hugheses provide a much fuller understanding of black nihilism than does Singleton. The film is a portrait of street brutality—the violence, motivated by petty revenge and uncontrollable rage, bursts out abruptly, as in Scorsese's movies.

Steeped in harsh social and emotional realism, Menace II Society shows how one adolescent, Caine, comes around to caring about living, even though it's too late. One of the most wrenching scenes is the one in which Caine visits his mentor, Pernell, who's in prison, and gets "permission" to date his girl (Jada Pinkett). To counterbalance the mayhem, the Hugheses turn preachy, and the only sentimental note is in Caine's relationship with his girlfriend. Fortunately, the Hugheses' instincts as filmmakers override their moralizing, and the film's overall impact is powerful. Shot with flair, the film exhibits a freeform style. The Hugheses are torn between the hopelessness of the present and the possibility of a better future. They're split between fatalism and optimism, a schism that expresses the attitudes of a whole black generation. The message is undeniably powerful: These black men belong to the first generation of Americans who are more afraid of life than of death.

Explaining the film's huge success, Albert said, "We tapped into a reality no one has seen before, and we tried to add cinematic style to it."[13] Indeed, Menace II Society appealed to both the hard core and the art crowd, grossing over $27 million. "We're independent-minded, although we can't stay independent as far as budgets go," said Allen Hughes, signaling their ambition to make studio movies. "We're talking to studios because we want a home and we want our films to get out to a wider audience. We want to make the type of films that make people say, 'I can't believe Hollywood made that film.'"

REVISITING HISTORY/REVISING GENRES

"We need some new voices out there, with something different to say about the African American experience besides young hip-hop kids toting guns and killing each other," declared Spike Lee in 1992. Indeed, some of the new black filmmakers realized that classic Hollywood genres can be reinvented by using a fresher, more explicit racial point of view.

To be sure, new movies continued to be made in the old-fashioned, borderline blaxploitation style. A prime example is Mario Van Peebles's *New Jack City* (Warners, 1991), a violent gangster thriller about the crack cocaine trade in Harlem masquerading as a moralistic melodrama. A cynical director, Van Peebles has technical style to burn, but his work is disappointingly flashy and senseless. The film's supposedly antidrug message is clouded by an overblown melodrama in which a white power structure doesn't care about poor blacks. A New York police detective hires two maverick ex-cops (Ice T and Judd Nelson) to bring down a druglord, Nino Brown (Wesley Snipes).

Van Peebles flaunts a baroque style and rapid cutting, odd camera angles, and a brashness that superficially recalls Spike Lee, without the latter's substance. *New Jack City* is basically an offshoot of Brian De Palma's *Scarface* (which inspired Snipes's character), of blaxploitation flicks like *Superfly*, and of the black-and-white cop films that became popular after *Lethal Weapon*. The film's language is atrocious: When Nino orders a rival killed, his gunman assures him that "he gonna be hanging with Elvis." Using sadism to generate excitement, the lurid action is accompanied with loud rap music.

Spike Lee himself undertook the filming of *Malcolm X* (1992), an ambitious epic about the assassinated militant leader, which was contentious from preproduction until its release. *Malcolm X* is not really revisionist, but it provides a distinctly black perspective on American history, mythologizing a controversial figure as an African American hero for our times. As a piece of filmmaking about a charismatic personality who lived during pivotal historical times, *Malcolm X* is superior to biopictures like *Gandhi*, which favors spiritual nobility and high-mindedness in lieu of dramatic excitement.

The magnitude of the subject matter, as a statement on race relations in America, and the immensity of the historical era, which spans four decades, from 1925 to 1964, are impressive. Malcolm's sharp mind, brilliant language, and humanity come to life, but Lee's treatment is reverential, glossing over Malcolm's attitude toward the Black Muslims and muting his assassination and the suspicion that the murder was encouraged or carried out by the FBI. For his part, Lee claimed that he was not interested in resolving the murder mystery or engaging in another conspiracy theory.

What was important to Lee was to show the relevance of Malcolm X for the current political scene, which motivated him to make the beginning and end of the film "contemporary." Like *Patton*, *Malcolm X* opens with the image of a huge American flag—only the flag is burning. This image is intercut with video footage of the Rodney King beatings and Malcolm's strong statements against the "murderous" white man. At the end of the film, a group of black kids stands up in a classroom and exclaims: "I'm Malcolm, I'm Malcolm."

REVISIONIST NOIR—CARL FRANKLIN

Carl Franklin's crime thriller *One False Move* (1992) mixes elements of the noir fatalism of *They Live by Night* with the drug-infused pathology of the TV series *Miami Vice*. Franklin tackles American anxieties—interracial love, guilt, and denial—that have been ignored in American movies, showing a mature understanding not only of his characters but also of the dichotomies of city and country, black and white, man and woman.

Unlike other neo-noir, *One False Move* is not just an exercise in style. It's about real behavior—reckoning with one's fate—and its consequences. The film deals with a perennial noir issue, the destructive grip of the past, the notion that one can try running from the past, but one can never escape it. Blending gritty realism with stylized noir, the cowriters, Tom Epperson and Billy Bob Thornton, have reinvented *High Noon*, with its inevitable showdown between good and evil. What makes this film unusual is that the "action" is entirely driven by its characters: Ray (Bill Paxton), a white-trash Southerner, and Fantasia (Cynda Williams), his former black girlfriend and, unbeknownst to him, the mother of his son.

The film evoked controversy because of its uncompromising take on violence. Resenting the flippant way in which violence is depicted in Hollywood movies as glamorous and exhilarating, Franklin begins the movie with a drug rubout and the brutal slaughter of seven people as seen through the eyes of one of its victims. After the murder, the three killers hit the road to sell the drugs. Franklin captures the sordid desperation and the anguished intimacy of people on the run. An encounter with a highway cop ends with another murder when Fantasia pulls the trigger. As the three killers head South to Fantasia's hometown, they are followed by two Los Angeles detectives, one black, one white.

David Denby has observed that Thornton and Epperson, who grew up in a small Arkansas town, know that in the South, whites and blacks aren't as distant as they are in the North.[14] In the South, whites and blacks coexist; interracial relations are an intricate tangle of attraction and fear. Franklin brings out these ambiguities and tensions, which continue to build up to the last scene. Structurally inventive, the narrative makes good use of its central organizing principle: the trio. Each of the film's trios is racially mixed: the three killers; the two cops from Los Angeles and their Southern colleague; Fantasia, Ray, and their little boy; and Fantasia, her brother, and her son. In each case, the trio is broken (often through death) so that a more balanced duo emerges at the end.

One False Move served notice that an exceptional filmmaker has arrived. In his previous films, Franklin has proved a good actor's director, having worked on the other side of the camera on TV's *A-Team* and on other shows. Franklin's measured pacing and James L. Carter's sharp cinematography give *One False Move* a bold look. With emotional honesty, Franklin shows a stronger interest in characterizations and minute pieces of behavior than in plot. Although the film works within the noir idiom, Franklin transcends the hopelessness of the genre. The gratifying resolution, in which a wounded Ray is forced to recognize his black child (the only survivor in the mayhem that has killed the child's mother), lifts the film's emotional level above ordinary despair and suggests that there is a chance of redemption.

Franklin's follow-up, an unusually creative studio film, *Devil in a Blue Dress* (Columbia, 1995), also captures the feeling of a genre and a bygone era, Los Angeles in 1948. Based on Walter Mosley's novel, the film blends the hard-boiled poetry of Raymond Chandler with the social realism of Richard Wright. The hero, Easy Rawlins (Denzel Washington), is a decorated World War II vet who is trying to carve out a decent existence for himself. Unemployed, with house payments to make, Rawlins accepts an offer to locate a woman who has mysteriously disappeared. This seemingly inconsequential job draws Rawlins deeper and deeper into a web of murder and corruption.

For Franklin, *Devil in a Blue Dress* is more about the false promises of the American Dream than just a murder mystery: "Los Angeles was a mecca for black people who came to work for the shipyards and the defense plants during the war years. The movie is about a veteran coming home with expectations of participating in the prosperous postwar economy, only to find out that some doors are closed to him." On another level, the film is about learning how tenuous middle-class life is, about a black man who overcomes his fears in segregated America. Rawlins makes a deal with the devil and has to do the dance, but he comes out at the end wiser. The physical locale is an important character in the film. Los Angeles is perceived by Franklin as "a Babylon, a get-rich-quick kind of town where anything goes." The movie is set against the backdrop of Central Avenue, the heart of the black community in the 1940s, by day the home of black businesses, by night a neon-lit array of nightclubs where Billie Holiday and Charlie "Bird" Parker performed. For a short period of time, it was a crossroads of cultures, where black and white people from uptown and country folk from the South socialized together.

DISTORTING/REVISITING BLACK HISTORY

Mario Van Peebles's independent film, *Posse* (1993), was a rousing hip-hop Western that flaunted its garish style at the expense of coherent narrative or sharp characterization. The motivation for making the film was no doubt honorable: *Posse* pays tribute to black frontierspeople, who had previously been ignored in Hollywood Westerns. In a narration that recalls the revisionist *Little Big Man*, Woody Strode tells the audience about a hidden history—the Wild West we don't know. But, except for featuring black performers in leading roles, *Posse* didn't break any new ground as a revisionist Western.

Van Peebles endows the tale of a racially integrated unit, battles with a corrupt cavalry and land-grabbing Ku Klux Klansmen with flamboyance, as if his goal were to outshine the style of Sergio Leone's and Clint Eastwood's spaghetti Westerns. The screenwriters, Sy Richardson and Dario Scardapane, employ familiar motifs with allusions to *The Magnificent Seven*, *High Noon*, *The Wild Bunch*, and other classic Westerns. Jesse wears an Eastwood poncho, a fierce squint, and a "Man With No Name" black hat. Imitative of baroque Westerns, the movie's MTV-style score mixes Michel Colombier, blues, and rap.[15]

Jesse Lee and the "Buffalo Soldiers," the black unit infantry that fought in the Spanish-American War, return to the West as outlaw deserters. They are hounded by a corrupt officer (Billy Zane), who later betrays them. Jesse becomes the reticent leader of the fugitives, who are all black except for one white soldier. The film's revenge story is clichéd: Jesse returns home to avenge the death of his preacher father and finds that Freemanville is besieged by a crooked white sheriff (Richard Jordan) and his black partner (Blair Underwood), who want to sell the town to the railroad.

The cast includes the blaxploitation cult figures Pam Grier and Isaac Hayes, as well as Robert Hooks, Paul Bartel, Nipsey Russell, and Mario's father, Melvin Van Peebles, as a wise patriarch. There are barroom brawls and desert treks, jailbreaks, bordello blowouts, and an updated character, a schoolmarm who has R-rated scenes in a boudoir. Van Peebles perceives the group as "an eclectic Robin Hood posse with a mission and a sense of values," but the two genres don't mix. When Jesse hits Freemanville and switches from posse head to a loner with a wounded past, the camaraderie is dropped. Attempting to be at once a neo-Western, a revisionist morality play, and a tribute to black cowboys, *Posse* is incoherent and anachronistic, with liberal speeches that reflect contemporary rather than historical attitudes.

Representing a simplified history of the Black Panther Party, Van Peebles's next film, *Panther*, tries to reconstruct the 1960s idealism and optimism that led to the party's formation. However, in his fictionalized narrative, Van Peebles does harm to the subject he intends to honor. *Panther* suffers from the same narrative and stylistic problems that had plagued Van Peebles's earlier movies. The Panthers have been so maligned in the past two decades that a movie about them requires a more serious and responsible treatment, of which Van Peebles is obviously incapable.

Working from a script by his father, Melvin, Van Peebles positions as narrator Judge (Kadeem Hardison), a Vietnam vet who is attending Berkeley on the GI bill. Judge wants to stay out of radical politics, but circumstances in the Oakland ghetto push him into the Panthers, then a handful of armed blacks standing firm against Oakland's racist police. Judge gets close to Huey Newton (Marcus Chong) and Bobby

Seale (Courtney B. Vance), and when Judge is approached by Oakland Police Department Detective Brimmer (Joe Don Baker) to inform on the Party, Newton encourages him to act as double agent. When Newton is thrown into jail, Judge has no way to allay the Panthers' suspicions that he may be an informant. The spy plot is designed to provide a center, but Judge's predicament isn't integrated into the story, and the other, equally problematic characters suffer from sketchy conception.

Van Peebles shows some of the party's dark side with occasional references to its condescension toward women. But, as Andy Klein has pointed out, no mention is made of the difference between the San Francisco Bay Area and the Los Angeles ghettos, and there is no reference to the race dynamics of the 1960s.[16] Stylistically, every scene is pitched at the same level, which creates monotony, and the frequent shifts between color and black and white feel arbitrary. Van Peeble's worst mistake is his choice of music, which takes liberties with chronology.

A fatuous potboiler, the film transforms an American tragedy—the rise and fall of Black Panthers—into kitsch. As a fictionalized account, *Panther* represents a gloss on history. Simplified, when it should be complex, sanitized when moral ambiguity doesn't suit its agenda, *Panther* glorifies the positive aspiration of the late 1960s Black Power movement, blaming the FBI for its relentless efforts to destroy the Black Panthers, a campaign led by FBI Director J. Edgar Hoover, who labeled the group Public Enemy No. 1.

Much more significant as history and film art was *Dead Presidents* (1995), the Hughes brothers' ambitious follow-up to *Menace II Society*. Released after Spike Lee's *Clockers* and Carl Franklin's *Devil in a Blue Dress*, *Dead Presidents* was the third significant African-American film to be released by a studio within the same month. Although the twins were the youngest of the directors, their film was the most unsettling of the three.

Set in the Bronx, the movie tells an epic story through one individual's experience. *Dead Presidents*, whose title is a slang term for paper money, concerns the devastating effects of the Vietnam War on a black marine. Spanning five years in the life of Anthony Curtis (Larenz Tate), the movie depicts a generation that has been shaped—and distorted—by the Vietnam War. Despite some violence, the commentary on American society is presented with restraint. The Bronx has become a symbol of urban despair, but when the tale begins, in 1968, it's still a vibrant multiracial area.

A high school senior with plans for the future, Anthony is a numbers runner for a pool hall owner, Kirby (Keith David), who lost a leg in Korea. Kirby and his own father were war vets, and now Anthony enlists in the marines, joined by his pals Skip (Chris Tucker) and Jose (Freddy Rodriguez). Socializing with mates like the psychotic Cleon, whose idea of souvenirs is severed heads, leaves a permanent mark on Anthony. "No bad habits," he later tells his mother about the experience, "except a little killing, for my country, of course." As other Vietnam movies have shown, the country does not treat the returning vets well. Drugs have become a force in the neighborhood, and there are no legitimate jobs. Anthony's experience affects his relationship with his girlfriend Juanita, who in his absence has given birth to his daughter. Since his goal is to survive, he grabs the first opportunity for change, even if it involves crime.

Though gloomy and despairing, *Dead Presidents* has no "convenient villains" and refuses to indulge in stereotypes. The whites in Anthony's world are not villains; even a pimp turns out be bright and provocative. The fault seems to reside with the bigger, impersonal forces of racism and political indifference. Racial issues hover—Skip says Vietnam "is not our war," and Anthony finds a pamphlet with a similar message on the battlefield. As in *Menace II Society*, by the time Anthony gets involved with Juanita's radical sister Delilah and begins to gain a new, more positive awareness, it's too late for him to survive.

WHITE PERSPECTIVES ON BLACK ISSUES

While most black-themed movies of the 1990s were directed by African Americans, some white filmmakers have rejected the argument that only blacks should tackle "black" topics. "If you deal with a subject in a responsible fashion," Anthony Drazan said, "then why should you be prevented from exploring it?" Drazan cites Mark Twain as an example of the many white artists who have shown fascination with and understanding of African American culture.[17] But theory is one thing and practice another, and Drazan's *Zebrahead* (1992) is a mixed bag, a film that uses fresh actors in a stale plot that echoes *Romeo and Juliet* (and *West Side Story*).

The romance between a Jewish boy, Zack (Michael Rapaport), and his black girlfriend, Nikki (N'Bushe Wright), alienates their classmates. Inspired by black culture, Zack finds emotional nourishment in it; in many ways, his love for Nikki is an extension of his love of black folklore. Zack takes Nikki to a party given by his white friends, and she accidentally overhears him indulging in a casual racist remark. This incident forces Zack to realize that his familiarity with black culture can't erase overnight his black friends' wounds of rage and prejudice.

Though *Zebrahead* contains no sex or nudity and has only one violent scene, Drazan feared that a love story about a white boy and a black girl might still be taboo. The film is based on Drazan's memories of growing up in a racially mixed Long Island neighborhood; the inspiration for Dee, Zack's best friend, comes from Drazan's black buddy. Drazan went to the NYU Film School with Spike Lee, but he refused to see *Jungle Fever*, which also dealt with interracial romance, because he didn't want to be affected by it. The first draft for *Zebrahead*, written in 1987, set the story in the 1970s, during Drazan's high school years, but later the story was made more contemporary. To tap into today's hip-hop consciousness, Drazan hung out at high schools and interviewed students.

Produced with the support of Oliver Stone, who received a presentation credit, *Zebrahead* got a big push from Sony's Triumph Releasing, which earmarked $2.8 million to promote the film, more than it cost to make ($2.5 million). The movie received a warm reception on the festival circuit, with one jab—a negative review in the *New York Times*. Despite the hope that it would appeal to the youth market, *Zebrahead* was a failure.

A much more commercially accessible film by a white director who explored black issues was Boaz Yakin's *Fresh* (1994), which revolves around a resourceful twelve-year old boy (Sean Nelson). Speed chess provides the central theme, functioning as bond between Fresh and his vagrant father, Sam (Samuel L. Jackson), an expert at the game. It also serves as a metaphor for the precarious existence of a boy who runs drugs for local dealers. Surprisingly, the film didn't generate controversy over its ambiguous morality, which positions a child as instigator of bloodshed and forces him to make the sort of decisions that no kid should have to make.

In the opening scene, Fresh shows up late for school, a result of his running late on his morning rounds as a drug courier. Living with eleven female cousins under the care of his aunt, Fresh keeps his own counsel as he delivers for the local heroin kingpin, Esteban (Giancarlo Esposito), and others. Adept at looking after himself, Fresh is estranged from his family. His mother is not around, and his sister Nichole (N'Bushe Wright) is a heroin addict drawn to the married Esteban.

Although forbidden to see his derelict father, Fresh surreptitiously meets with him in Washington Square for chess sessions. Like the black character in *Searching for Bobby Fisher*, Sam proves to be a tough taskmaster, lecturing Fresh about discipline and reproaching him for careless moves or lack of concentration. A believer in traditional values despite his dissolute lifestyle, Sam occupies an ambivalent place in his son's life.

Fresh features a new kind of screen protagonist, a teenager who is willing to do anything to escape his fate. But the film's use of social issues as an excuse for cheap thrills gets increasingly offensive. No matter how sympathetically Fresh is presented, he's still part of the problem that precipitates a cycle of death. In a shocking sequence, a pickup basketball game turns deadly as a crack dealer shoots an opponent. Like the boy in *A Bronx Tale*, Fresh, a witness to the crime, can't talk to the authorities if he wants to stay alive. As Fresh makes his way through the neighborhood, events out of his control come together in a terrifying manner. His shrewd plan for escape sets a trap that engulfs the drug dealers in a bloody battle over turf.

Fresh implies that his chess-playing skills enable Fresh to concoct an intricate plan, but, as the plan unfolds, the film abandons realism. Borderline exploitation, *Fresh* titillates, with authenticity sacrificed as one violent scene follows another. Kenneth Turan has dismissed the film for using social consciousness as a come on, a masquerade for commercial filmmaking that has more in common with Yakin's script for Clint Eastwood's actioner *The Rookie* than with *Boyz 'N' the Hood*.[18]

Yakin doesn't delve into the sources of the drug problems; he just assumes they exist. And his point of view remains vague, perhaps intentionally, so that the audience could make its own judgment. What makes *Fresh* effective, however, is its tragic view of a boy who has never experienced the joys of childhood. It is only at the very end that the stone-faced Fresh finally breaks down, the tears on his cheeks revealing sign of humanity.

Like Anthony Drazan, Marc Levin dispels the theory that white filmmakers can't provide an authentic view of African American issues.

Slam (1998), his powerful debut, defies easy categorization: Part gritty prison drama, part inner-city ghetto chronicle, it's a compassionate plea for a new direction for black men if they are to survive oppression in a white-dominated society. Levin, an accomplished documentarian who has previously explored troubled youth, street gangs, prison life, and the justice system, effectively blends narrative and nonfictional conventions. Based on firsthand information obtained by Levin while observing prison life and having in its cast several men who have served time in jail, *Slam* is imbued with raw intensity and a cinema verité style seldom seen in feature films.

Ray Joshua (Saul Williams), a product of a housing project in Washington, D.C., lives in a war zone known as "Dodge City" because of the ongoing gang warfare. He lives by his wits, making a meager existence through minor drug dealings. Endowed with a natural talent for language, Ray expresses himself through street poems. One summer night, while he is talking to Big Mike, his drug contact, Big Mike is gunned down. The police arrive, and Ray is busted for suspicion of murder as well as possession of pot. Thrown into jail, Ray faces a new danger that makes his life inside as risky as it was outside: Two rival gangs vie for his membership.

A public defender explains to Ray that, as a black ghetto male, he has three options: He can fight the charges, but if he loses (which is 99 percent sure), he'll get at least ten years; he can turn snitch and rat on his friends and walk free; or he can cop a plea to the pot charge and serve only two years. For practical reasons, Ray's lawyer recommends that he grab the third option.

On the cellblock, Ray befriends Hopha (Bonz Malone), a gang leader who first tries to persuade Ray to join his crew. But, later, Hopha understands Ray's refusal to participate and out of respect for his art gives him a pad of paper to pursue his writing. Some romantic interest is introduced in the figure of Lauren (Sonjah Sohn), a volunteer who runs a creative writing workshop and who encourages Ray to use his gift to voice the anguish of his lost generation. When funds for Lauren's program are cut and she leaves, it's clear that their relationship will continue.

When the rival gangs begin yet another fight in the yard, Ray unleashes his anger in a dazzling display of lyrics that leaves the men stunned. With Hopha's help, Ray returns to "Dodge City," only to realize that Big Mike is not dead but has lost his vision. It's the confrontation between the two men, with Hopha demanding retaliation and Ray insisting that revenge just perpetuates the vicious circle of killing, that conveys the film's message, carrying it way beyond the cautionary tales of *Boyz 'N' the Hood* and *Menace II Society*. Ray claims that gang warfare destroys the black community and doesn't achieve anything.

Slam also reveals the origin of street poetry as an art form and its psychopolitical functions. Levin gives his film a spontaneous, loose form that fits well its unstable milieu through the use of a restlessly mobile handheld camera and intimate close-ups of the protagonists. Deep moral conviction marks the fervent performances by the real-life poets Williams and Sohn, who wrote their own material.

BLACK CINEMA AT A CROSSROAD

Spike Lee's furious pace—thirteen films in thirteen years—has kept him at the forefront of the new black film wave. Until 1992, Lee's movies were profitable: *Do the Right Thing* cost $6.5 million and earned $28 million; *Jungle Fever* cost $14 million and made $33 million.[19] Those numbers ensured that the studios would keep financing his projects. *Malcolm X* represented the height of Lee's career, but the well-publicized battle with Warners over the $35 million budget was damaging. Most of Lee's films after *Malcolm X* have been commercial failures; the budgets were lower, but so were the grosses. *Crooklyn* (1994), a charming personal period piece with no stars, grossed $13.6 million. *Clockers* (1995) represented a move forward for Lee, but was released at a time when audiences were fed up with the black crime genre, and it grossed only $13 million.

No one expects Lee's films to be blockbusters. Other serious films by black filmmakers, such as Charles Burnett and Carl Franklin, have also fared poorly at the box office. But, ironically, Lee's signature, his fiercely personal vision, may be what's failing to attract young black viewers to his movies. Black viewers propelled movies like Martin Lawrence's *A Thin Line Between Love and Hate* to an impressive $35 million. *Dead Presidents, Friday, Higher Learning*, and *Set It Off* have all cast rappers or comedians in major roles and relied on hip-hop/R & B soundtracks to pull in audiences. Lee's use of trained actors and his jazzy and folkloristic scores make his films seem out of touch with young black audiences.

Lee's hot streak cooled when his deal with Universal ended, but the indie world benefited with a series of smaller, more personal films. *Get on the Bus* (1996), an independently financed film inspired by the Million Man March, cost only about $2 million and recouped its expense. *Girl 6* (also in 1996), featuring a splendid performance by Theresa Randall as a phone sex operator, was an artistic and commercial disappointment, but his next project, *4 Little Girls* (1997), was not.

An informative look at the four girls (Addie Mae Collins, Denise McNair, Cynthia Wesley, and Carole Robertson) who were murdered when a former Ku Klux Klan member blew up their Baptist church in 1963, *4 Little Girls* was nominated for the Best Documentary Oscar. Interweaving archival photos, newsreel footage, and home movies with present-day interviews, Lee lets the material tell the story. Commemorating one of the defining moments of the civil rights movement, the film strikes an admirable balance between the personal memories of witnesses and a more detached political analysis. Obviously, a major talent like Lee's can't be held back, as was evidenced with his latest feature, *He Got Game* (1998), an emotionally engaging father-son melodrama set in the sports world.

The gifted Charles Burnett struggled for five years after *To Sleep With Anger* to make *The Glass Shield* (1995), a film more explicitly steeped in racial politics than his previous efforts were. The film's sympathetic hero, J.J. (Michael Boatman), is an idealistic black cop put to the test in a racist precinct. The action begins with J.J., a new academy graduate, assigned to an all-white precinct, and an anonymous voice grunting, "Lucky you, you're about to make history." Looking for acceptance, J.J. wants to fit in, but nothing helps. Soon, the word "nigger" gets scrawled on a bathroom mirror. J.J. continues to smile, even when a cop refuses to recognize him as a fellow officer, and humiliatingly tells him to park in the rear.

In a harrowing scene, a detective pulls a gun on J.J. and shatters the rookie's trust that justice will prevail. J.J.'s only ally is a Jewish cop, Deborah (Lori Petty), who's biding her time on the force before going to law school. The association of a black man and a Jewish woman is a welcome addition to a genre that has stressed the disparity between genders and between races. The two outcasts join forces against institutional racism and injustice, when an innocent black man (Ice Cube) is framed for murder. In an attempt to increase the movie's commercial appeal, Miramax forced Burnett to reshoot the final scene, originally written to have J.J. fight with his girlfriend. In the new ending, J.J. just pushes her away and smashes his fist through her car window. Regardless, *The Glass Shield* didn't find an audience, and Burnett had to turn to television (the Disney Channel) for his next project, *Nightjohn* (1998), the story of a young, illiterate slave and her thrilling experience of acquiring basic human skills.

Oversupplied with stories of young men in violent hoods, audiences became eager to see different kinds of black images. Honoring Spike Lee's plea to expand the range of black films, the latest black cycle has tackled themes pertaining to the expanding class of the black bourgeoisie. This trend began on television, with *The Cosby Show* and other popular series about black middle-class mores. Once again, Hollywood lagged behind television in its concern with timely issues. But typically, as soon as the studios sensed the potential new business, they rushed a slate of movies into production, the most successful of which was *Waiting to Exhale*.

The huge crossover success of *Waiting to Exhale* (1995), based on Terry McMillan's best-selling novel, showed how ignored the black middle class, particularly its women, had been on the screen. Until the mid 1990s, black women were cast in limited roles in mainstream movies: Anna Deavere Smith as a White House aide in *The American President*, Whitney Houston in the trashy romance *The Bodyguard*. Forest Whitaker, an actor-turned director, made *Waiting to Exhale* in the vein of Douglas Sirk's glossy 1950s studio melodramas (*Written on the Wind*, *Imitation of Life*), with four heroines who are all beautiful career women: Savanna (Whitney Houston), Bernadine (Angela Bassett), Robin (Lela Rochon), and Gloria (Loretta Devine). *Waiting to Exhale* takes an old-fashioned soap-opera formula and refurbishes it for the glitzy age of talk shows and tabloids.

McMillan's and Ronald Bass's script serves up romantic fantasies while using the language of self-empowerment. However, as David Ansen has noted, despite the film's efforts to celebrate self-sufficiency, the women define their identities exclusively in relation to men.[20] When they are in one another's company, the women are spontaneous and interesting, even when they are talking about sexual frustrations. But the men in their lives are cardboard caricatures, unworthy of them. Even so, *Waiting to Exhale* must have appealed to viewers' primal instincts, for a scene in which the vengeful Bernadine sets the car of her rich husband on fire received rousing applause from the audience.

CONCLUSION: NEW VOICES IN BLACK INDIES

Reflecting the new demographics and zeitgeist, namely, the need for entertaining pictures that went beyond crime and drugs, a new
post–Spike Lee cohort of black filmmakers addressed different kinds of
issues and experiences.

With a comic view of street life, F. Gary Gray's *Friday* (1995) is about
two South Central homeboys who hang out together. Lacking plot, the
film is just a series of skits. But, as a ruder, more energetic version of the
hip hop *House Party* movies, *Friday* was embraced by black adolescents.
Boasting a front-porch philosophy about the way street life enters pop
culture, the comedy displayed an attitude that set it apart from other,
mostly preachy movies about the hood. Perhaps more importantly, *Friday* provided a voice for Gray, a new talented director, who proceeded
with another New Line production, *Set It Off* (1996), a "Girls 'N' the
Hood" actioner with social conscience, and with the studio-made ac-
tion-suspenser, *The Negotiator* (Warners, 1998).

Influenced by both *Thelma & Louise* and *Waiting to Exhale*, *Set It Off*
stood out among a cycle of female bonding and empowerment films, released in 1995–1996, including the ultraraw *Girls Town*, the dismal
MTV-like *Foxfire*, the special-effects ridden *The Craft*, and the shamelessly maudlin *The Spitfire Grill*. Scripted by Kate Lanier and Takashi
Bufford, *Set It Off* combines elements of the male-dominated, inner-city
genres with ideas drawn from women-oriented melodramas. The pre-
credits sequence centers on upwardly mobile Frankie (Vivica A. Fox), a
bank employee ambitious to move up the corporate ladder. In a heist
that goes awry, she gets fired, because she recognizes the black robber
and is therefore suspected of collusion with him. Having lost the one
thing that mattered to her, Frankie is primed for revenge.

The story provides each member of a central quartet with a distinct
motivation to engage in crime. Stony (Jada Pinkett) invests all of her
dreams in her kid brother, Stevie (Chaz Lamar Shepard), only to see him
shot by the police. Cleo (Latifah) is a hot-tempered lesbian, and Tisean
(Kimberly Elise) is a single mom whose baby is taken from her for "neglect" when she takes him to her janitorial job and he accidentally injures
himself. Out of desperation and the hopeless trap they're caught in,
they decide to rob a bank. The action and the money prove to be exhilarating and liberating and they go on to more robberies, culminating in
the death of three of the four.

Unlike *Thelma & Louise*, which uproots the protagonists from their milieu and is basically a road movie, *Set It Off* keeps the women in their hood, where they live a "normal" life, meaning they have to endure exploitative, low-paying jobs and insensitive men. The importance of the hood is conveyed when Cleo tells Stony, who's desperate to get out, "Where will I go? I belong here." Cleo's lesbian relationship is handled matter-of-factly, without any hustle or perceived victimization. With a keen eye for detailed characterizations and a flashy style (learned from making music videos), Gray gives the film an undeniable urgency, which helped make it one of the decade's most popular black indies.

Larenz Tate, who played the thoughtless, homicidal O-Dog in *Menace II Society*, and the innocent-turned-haunted Vietnam vet in *Dead Presidents*, became an important transitional figure in the new middle-class cinema, beginning with *love jones* (1997), in which he was cast as a handsome, sophisticated man. Setting the movie in Chicago's artistic milieu, the writer-director Theodore Witcher depicted, to use his words, "overeducated and underemployed" African Americans. His slick romance, which won the Sundance audience award, heralded something new in black films: the appearance of smart, educated urbanites who listen to jazz and read poetry. Nocturnal life centers at a trendy spot, the Sanctuary, where the characters engage in intellectual discussions about books, music, relationships, and the meaning of life.

What's unusual about the protagonists is that they don't conform to any stereotype. They are struggling, as middle-class Chicagoans, with the same problems faced by whites—how to combine romance and career, how to engage in honest relationships. Despite some racial references, the script with some changes could have been used for a white romantic comedy. New Line got credit for taking a chance with a black love story aimed at a mainstream audience, but contrary to expectations, the film didn't have crossover appeal. Despite the complaint that violent films about urban males represent only a narrow spectrum of the black experience and risk the reinforcement of existing stereotypes, black audiences have been more easily identified for such films than for middle-class movies. It's easier to induce audiences to see Ice Cube in a mediocre film like *The Player's Club* (1998) than to attract them to see *love jones*.

The black screwball comedy *Hav Plenty* (1998), faced even worse commercial results. Wittier and more deftly constructed than *love jones*, although not as polished, *Hav Plenty* depicts the fables and foibles of educated twentysomething blacks. Christopher Cherot made a debut as writer, director, editor and star of a bittersweet, modern-day love story that recalls early Woody Allen movies. Reversing the ploy of the similarly themed *She's Gotta Have It*, Cherot centers on an attractive male, Lee Plenty (Cherot), an always broke would-be novelist, who likes to shock people with his stories about being homeless. Waiting for the big break, Lee has been living on the streets and off friends. His best friend, the rich and successful Havilland Savage (Chenoa Maxwell), invites him to a quiet gathering at her family's home for New Year's Eve.

Like most screwball comedies, *Hav Plenty* introduces two appealing characters who seem to be opposites. Hav is a woman who has everything but love; Lee is a man who has nothing but love. Lee is passive; Hav is aggressive. Lee is energetically unambitious; Hav is always on the make. Lee is a dedicated celibate; Hav is engaged to be married. Much in the genre's tradition, everyone but Hav and Lee know that despite their differences they're destined to be together.

An intimate holiday turns into a chaotic weekend, full of surprises, with Lee as the desirable male for every woman: Hav's pretentious friend who lusts after his body; Hav's newlywed but uncertain sister, who won't object to a "friendly" kiss; Hav's old school pal, who wants to share secrets with Lee. Cherot is careful not to repeat the mistake of *love jones*, in which the lovers consummated their relationship too soon. He also knows that the trick of successful romantic comedy is to invent obstacles to an unavoidable union.

The Bronx-born Cherot quit the NYU film school just three classes shy of graduation, when his mother agreed to take out another mortgage on her house to finance his "$65,000 project." Miramax bought *Hav Plenty* for $1.2 million and gave Cherot a $2.5 million multipicture deal. At first, it bothered Cherot that *Hav Plenty* was called a "black romantic comedy," because, to him, "there are parts of it that aren't that humorous to watch." Summing up what is the credo of the latest wave of black filmmakers, Cherot said, "It will be my job to stand out from the lump people want to put all black filmmakers into. We all have very different styles, and I'd like to develop my own." All along, Cherot intended to make a movie that transcended the black movie genre—"A comedy about complex characters who just happen to be black."[21]

12

The New Gay and Lesbian Cinema

GAY DIRECTORS AND a gay sensibility are hardly new to American movies. According to David Thomson, a gay sensibility was so central to Hollywood that homosexual directors like George Cukor or Mitchell Leisen didn't have to promote it in their movies.[1] Still, the fact that Cukor, Leisen, and others were homosexuals was an open secret in Hollywood, and every effort was made to keep their sexual orientation out of the public eye.

Until the 1990s, Hollywood's official record on homosexuality was deplorable. To be sure, there were always gay characters in movies, even during the Production Code era, when "sex perversion," and everything else about sex, was forbidden. But, under the studio system, gays and lesbians suffered from stereotyping of the worst sort, as chronicled in Vito Russo's 1981 landmark book, *The Celluloid Closet*, and the 1996 documentary based on it. It was both appropriate and timely that *Celluloid Closet*, Rob Epstein and Jeffrey Friedman's chronicle of gays in Hollywood, would be made in a year that celebrated the centennial of movies. Insightful about what was permissible and forbidden in mainstream cinema, it's a deconstruction of sexual politics in American culture.

Surveying hundreds of movies, *Celluloid Closet* examines every gay type, from comic sissies to lesbian vampires, from pathetic queens to sadistic predators. As the narrator, Lily Tomlin, points out, "Homosexuality has been traditionally used by Hollywood to get easy laughs from straight audiences, and to inspire fear among gays by condemning their deviant lifestyle." Homosexuals have consistently suffered distortion, derision, and condescension. As a minority, they have experienced a systematic effort to devalue their subculture. American movies have depicted "fairies" as comic relief or, worse, as psychopathic villains, reinforcing ignorance and prejudice among what Christopher Isherwood once called "the heterosexual dictatorship."

Over the decades, the treatment of homosexuals has shifted from light and humorous in the silent era to nefarious and abominable in the

1950s to a more liberal depiction today. Epstein and Friedman had rich footage to work with, but the assembly of images is only one element of the film's density. The filmmakers decided not to be polemic, not to engage in a diatribe against Hollywood. Instead, witty commentary is offered by gay writers (e.g., Gore Vidal) and by straight directors and actors (William Wyler, Tony Curtis), who shed light on the context in which these films were made and on their meanings. Quentin Crisp notes, for example, that the stock character of sissie, perceived as one of "nature's mistakes," often flirted with transvestism, which was played for humor. Yet women in male drag were less threatening, as evidenced by Marlene Dietrich's wearing a man's suit and kissing a woman on the lips in *Morocco* and Greta Garbo's posing as a Swedish bachelor monarch in *Queen Christina*.

Under the studio system, the classification of films as "acceptable," "morally objectionable," or "condemned" meant that gay characters had to be shamefully degraded. To meet the requirements of the Production Code, gays were made to be pitiable or doomed (e.g., Tom Lee's role in *Tea and Sympathy* or Sal Mineo's in *Rebel Without a Cause*). In the 1950s, some movies portrayed tough lesbians behind bars (Hope Emerson as a leathery ward in *Caged*), or as sleek socialites (Lauren Bacall in *Young Man With a Horn*). The screenwriter Jay Presson Allen (*Cabaret*) interprets these films as warnings to women to get back to domesticity, back to the kitchen.

Although censors were determined to remove any explicit gay elements from movies, traces of homosexuality remained. Gore Vidal recounts how he introduced sexual tension in the relationship between Ben-Hur and Massala in *Ben-Hur*. The director William Wyler saw his point, but, aware of Charlton Heston's conservative politics, he asked Vidal not to tell his star. The scene in which Stephen Boyd looks straight into Heston's eyes while holding his hand takes on a whole new meaning with this understanding. Similarly, Tony Curtis describes how his erotic hot-tub scene with Lawrence Olivier was deleted from *Spartacus*.

RAISING AWARENESS—GAY DOCUMENTARIES

Diverse and positive images of gays were also missing from the field of documentary filmmaking. There were isolated examples, such as *The Queen* (1967), Frank Simon's look at male transvestites in a beauty contest, or Shirley Clarke's feature-length interview with a black male hustler, *A Portrait of Jason* (1967). But getting openly gay people to appear before the cameras was a problem and the difficulties in financing gay subject matter insurmountable.

The first work to reflect the Gay Liberation movement was *Some of Your Best Friends* (1971), by Ken Robinson of the University of Southern California, who in cinema verité form examined the origins of the movement in New York and Los Angeles by interviewing participants about their oppression. Six years passed before other filmmakers followed Robinson's initiative. The rising tide of antigay propaganda, spearheaded by Anita Bryant's Bible-thumping crusade, revitalized the gay movement. The efforts of socially conscious filmmakers resulted in two landmark works, *Gay USA* and *Word Is Out: Stories of Some of Our Lives*. Both films rely on the interview format, but their footage and method differ greatly.[2]

In 1975, the producer Peter Adair envisioned a short film about gay people to be used as teaching material in schools. After two frustrating years of searching for foundation support, he resorted to private investors. Adair joined forces with his sister Nancy, his assistant cameraman, Andrew Brown, a sound editor, Veronica Selver, and the filmmakers Lucy Massie Phoenix and Rob Epstein, and the Maripose Film Group came into existence. What began as a modest presentation of positive role models for gay people became a chronicle of the vast range of gay experience.

Committed to collectivist organization, the filmmakers decentralized the shooting and editing processes. They preinterviewed 200 persons, then jointly selected twenty-six women and men for the film. Choice of location and props—clothes—were made in consultation with the interviewees. To make the subjects feel at ease, a stationary camera was used, and, since the camera operator was also the interviewer, communication proceeded smoothly. Along with interviews, footage was assembled about the subjects' working and living situations. The Maripose Group spent more than a year editing fifty hours of footage down to two hours and fifteen minutes. Various cuts were screened for gay audiences and responses solicited, allowing the community to participate in determining the final cut.

Word Is Out is divided into three sections: "The Early Years," "Growing Up," and "From Now On." Subjects were carefully chosen to display diverse lifestyles; their interviews are broken up and used in more than one section. Frontal medium to close shots are employed, giving the impression of a portrait in which the subject directly addresses the camera and creating an intimate rapport between subject and viewer.

Interviewees included Elsa Gidlow, age 79, the eldest subject; two lesbian mothers, Pam Jackson and Rusty Millington; a drag queen, Tede Mathews; and a middle-aged couple, Harry Hay and John Burnside, seen picking berries in the country. Despite the ethnic and sexual diversity of the subjects, certain patterns emerge that assert middle-class values. The large number of stable couples in the film suggests the pattern of traditional matrimony; only one character speaks up for casual sex, which was then the norm for many gay men.

The final section, "From Now On," focuses on various dimensions of gay politics. Powell, of the National Gay Task Force, relates her "coming out" of a heterosexual marriage. Her assertion that "lesbians and gay men have a great deal to offer in terms of restructuring the world culture" is seconded by the feminist Sally Gearhart, who claims that all humans are born with bisexual potential but are made half-persons by society's strict gender programming.

The inclusion of stereotypical dykes such as Pat Bond and effeminate men like Roger Herkenrider suggests the complexity of role playing in gay life. There are also Donald Hackett, a black truck driver, and Linda Marco, both of whom were married before coming out (another pattern among the cast members). While the film's most intellectual arguments come from women, the strongest emotional moments involve men. One man confesses, "In high school, I thought I was just one of those people who could never love anybody. When I fell in love with Henry, it meant I was human."

Like *Word Is Out*, *Gay USA* is a collective production, made under the banner of Artists United for Gay Rights. However, unlike *Word Is Out*, it was filmed in one day, June 26, 1977, and was the product of one filmmaker, Arthur Bressan, who conceived the project and shaped its form. In the wake of the defeat, in Miami, of a gay rights initiative on June 7, 1977, Bressan joined a demonstration at San Francisco's City Hall. Bressan then formed camera crews in six cities (San Francisco, San Diego, New York, Chicago, Houston, and Los Angeles), using parades in those cities to document the emerging gay consciousness. By cutting from one city to another, the film gives the impression of a united coast-to-coast struggle against bigotry and oppression.

If *Word Is Out* explores private experiences, *Gay USA* captures a communal excitement. It was the first film to chronicle the intense anger and joy embodied in public expressions of freedom. Bressan amplifies the 1977 material with footage from the first Christopher Street Parade, in New York, in 1970, and from subsequent parades in other cities. Slides, stills, and footage of civil rights marches and Nazi parades are interpolated in the film.

In *Gay USA*, Bressan presents images from widely varied groups in society: lesbians, sympathetic straight families, drag queens, professionals, youths, former prisoners, dykes on bikes, blacks, school teachers, and antigay dissenters. Bressan's montage presents a dialectical opposition of sound and image, giving the work a spirited tone of debate. A proponent of repealing laws against gays is juxtaposed with an antiabortionist who supports Anita Bryant. A statement by a young gay Catholic who voices his protest against Church policies is followed by a fundamentalist who cites the Bible in condemning homosexuality as an "unnatural way of living."

"Dykes on Bikes" lead off the procession, followed by thousands of women sporting banners: "We are your teachers," "Gay, Alive, and Healthy," and "Remember the Witch Hunts." The film picks up momentum with the "Are You Gay?" sequence, in which a hand-held tracking camera cuts from response to response, from "I don't think I can classify myself" to "That's none of your business." The kaleidoscopic vision imparted by *Gay USA* combines frivolity and seriousness. Although Bressan's tone is positive, the inclusion of dissenting opinions enriches his work. Even in an environment where gays can openly pursue a "free" life, there still is intimidation and violence. Just days prior to the 1977 march in San Francisco, Robert Hillsborough was brutally stabbed on the street: Bressan dedicates *Gay USA* to him and closes it with a memorial ceremony at City Hall.

Bressan's ideological and aesthetic contrasts underline the differences within the gay community on various issues, including crossdressing. A parade float with blowups of Stalin, Hitler, Anita Bryant, a Ku Klux Klan member, and Idi Amin, is intercut with Nuremberg footage from Leni Riefenstahl's *Triumph of the Will*, as a young man notes that "in fascist societies, people are taught to dress and act alike." Bressan highlights the point that lack of individuality is the basis for racist and sexist stereotyping.

Word Is Out and *Gay USA* both reflect the politics of a rapidly growing gay minority, with each film presenting voices long denied access to
the media because of bigotry and oppression. Aired on public TV, and
seen mostly by gay viewers, ultimately these documentaries failed to
realize their potential as consciousness-raising tools to reach those outside the gay community.

GAY FILMS IN THE 1980s

By the early 1980s, there were still no indie films that dealt matter-of-
factly with the gay experience. "Hollywood films usually don't deal
with homosexuality," said Larry Kardish, the film curator of the Museum of Modern Art, in 1986. "When they do, the focus is on the subject
of homosexuality and the reactions to it rather than the gay characters
themselves." "Hollywood has treated homosexuality as the primary
dramatic point," confirmed Vitto Russo. "But the films usually are
about homosexuality, not about people and their stories."[3]

In 1986, two films by first-time directors heralded a new gay wave:
Donna Deitch's *Desert Hearts* and Bill Sherwood's *Parting Glances*. Both
were financed in large part within the gay community. In the past, the
typical industry version of a gay film had a story line "that attempted
to justify the gay lifestyle for straight audiences, rather than take it for
granted," said Ira Deutschman, citing *Making Love* (1982), a much pub-
licized studio effort, as the prototypical Hollywood gay film.[4]

What was different about the new gay films was that they presented homosexuality as a natural part of life and let their characters
and stories go on from there. In other words, they set out to tell stories
about characters that happen to be gay. A prime example is Stephen
Frears's *My Beautiful Laundrette* (1986), a vibrant British film, with its
straightforward handling of a love affair between a Pakistani and a
British punk. "I wanted the story to be about Asians, not about gays, so
the gay relationship had to seem perfectly natural," said the writer,
Hanif Kureshi. The novelty of *My Beautiful Laundrette* was the casual development of the gay affair, which happened but did not take over the
characters' lives.

Sherwood's and Deitch's films deal with homosexuality from different angles. The contemporary *Parting Glances* is about twenty-four

hours in the lives of a gay New York triangle. "I intended the film as an homage to New York and also to the gay community, which, in spite of the AIDS crisis, continues to be such a life force," said Sherwood.[5] *Parting Glances* tackles AIDS, an issue that could not be ignored in a film about gay life in the 1980s.

In contrast, *Desert Hearts*, set in the 1950s, concerns a love affair that grows out of two women's search for identity. Deitch was attracted to Jane Rule's novel *Desert of the Heart*, for the simple reason that no one had yet made a film about a romantic attachment between women for the commercial cinema. When such romantic relationships were explored, they usually ended in suicide or in a bisexual triangle. Even *Personal Best* (1982), a Hollywood film that deals with a character's coming to terms with her lesbianism, presents the process as traumatic. Feeling that times had changed and that there could be more frank discussion of sexuality, Deitch purchased the film rights to Rule's novel.

Both Sherwood and Deitch made their films "from scratch," outside the Hollywood system. Sherwood raised $40,000 from friends and an additional $250,000 from gay patrons. He opted to use first-time New York actors, none of whom were members of the Screen Actors Guild. Sherwood had no desire to work within the system, and he couldn't have cared less about being pegged a gay filmmaker. Once made, however, *Parting Glances* had no major difficulty finding a distribution. Within a week after Cinecom's Ira Deutschman saw the film, a distribution deal was set. What impressed Sherwood was that "Cinecom had no qualms about presenting the film as a gay film."

Deitch's struggle to raise the $1.5 million budget took nearly four years. Unlike Sherwood, Deitch wanted a name cast, but several actresses declined to read for the lead role "on the basis of the lesbian theme." Eventually, the part was played by Helen Shaver. At first, Deitch relied on private donors, but, later, she was forced to sell her house to cover completion costs. It is unlikely that Sherwood or Deitch would have been given the opportunity to direct if their movies had been made by the studios.

Parting Glances was not the first gay yuppie picture, but it represented a significant contrast to such inconsequential fare as *Making Love*, which presented a fake romantic portrait. *Parting Glances* was one of the first gay movies not to deal with coming out. The characters' sexual orientation have long been resolved when the story begins; as the youngest character, a Columbia freshman, says: "Your dick knows what it likes." Sherwood showed the audience a new world through the eyes of its own denizens, and unlike the masochistic and self-loathing *The Boys in the Band* (1970), *Parting Glances* is upbeat, despite its AIDS theme.

Fully rounded lives are shown through the breakup of a gay relationship. Structured as a romantic triangle, the script packs everything into twenty-four hours in the lives of Michael (Richard Ganoung), an editor, and his lover of six years, Robert (John Bolger), an official who works for an international health organization. Michael and Robert enjoy a comfortable lifestyle: They live in a nice apartment, listen to Brahms, go to dinner parties, have regular sex. But Michael is feeling a little too settled; something is missing from his life, and he's still tormented by his first love, Nick (Steve Buscemi), a rock singer who is dying of AIDS.

As the film opens, Robert is preparing to leave for a long stint in Africa, allowing Michael to reflect on their bond. This triggers flashbacks to Michael's love affair with Nick, who represents a wilder, more reckless past. Michael drops by at Nick's to cook, clean, and listen to his sardonic musings. He brings him a record of *Don Giovanni*, and Nick gets stuck on the part where Don Giovanni goes up in flames, refusing to repent. Similarly, in the film, Nick declines to renounce his past. Sherwood makes Nick the moral center, the suffering spirit of modern gay life, the proud, unrepentant person with AIDS.

A gay Everyman, Michael is poised between his former and his current lovers, between a thrilling, dangerous past and an unexciting, domesticated present. Complicating the issue is a potential new lover, Peter, who works in a record store. When Michael meets Peter, he sees a 1980s variation on his youth, except that Peter is apolitical and unformed, drifting from one party to another looking for adventure. Peter may be more comfortable with his sexuality, but he's also less interesting than Michael or Nick.

Sherwood attempted something ambitious in this film, as David Edelstein noted in his review: "Crafting sort of the State of the Union for the AIDS era, a look at where gay men have been, where they might be going, and the uneasy ground on which they stand."[6] Wishing to restore reality and dignity to gay lifestyles, which are usually depicted sensationalistically, Sherwood treats gays as ordinary people who, like their straight counterparts, work, argue, and reconcile. Sherwood broke new ground: For the first time, gay men could watch themselves on-screen and like what they saw. Rather than being hysterical or sentimental about AIDS, the film is elegiac: *Parting Glances*, like the later *Longtime Companion*, ends with a lament for a bygone, free-spirit past.

Sherwood said that he was motivated by the public's "astounding ignorance" of gay lifestyles: "One of the problems Hollywood has had dealing with this subject is that it's usually approached so gingerly."[7] He cited *Kiss of the Spider Woman*, in which it takes one hour for the characters (played by William Hurt and Raul Julia) to kiss, and then it's set up to shock the audience. "This is why I had the men kissing right from the start, to get it over with right away and allow us to get on with their interaction with other people and with what's going on in all their lives."

Indeed, the movie's opening scene is attention-grabbing: A sturdy, blue-eyed jogger bounds past a man who's reading a book, kicks him playfully in the butt and nuzzles his neck. A moment later, the two step into their apartment, and the jogger paws the reader. The reader wants no part of it, but the jogger gives him a lingering kiss, and the reader succumbs. The camera then follows them to the bedroom, where their sneakered feet entwine. In the next shot, the door of the shower opens and the couple stand in the steam, with the jogger's arms around the reader. The jogger and reader are Robert and Michael.

Sherwood wanted to strike a universal chord, to show that gay and straight men are not that different. A SoHo cocktail party gives him the opportunity to turn gay and straight stereotypes upside down. The only person cruising there is straight—he's caught in the bathroom with a German artist while the latter's husband fumes outside the door. And it's a gay man, Robert, who advises a female friend on how to maintain a difficult relationship.

Much more solemn than Sherwood's film, the lesbian romance *Desert Hearts* wears its liberal message on its sleeve. Set in 1959, it revolves around Vivian Bell (Helen Shaver), an English literature professor who arrives in Reno to divorce her husband. The tall, haughty Easterner descends from the train wearing a tailored gray suit, her blonde hair gathered beneath a matching gray hat. It's clear from the opening shot that it's a matter of time before Vivian's suit comes off and the hair comes down. Sure enough, at the end, Vivian lets her hair down and discovers sexual freedom. A proud, uptight woman, Vivian needs someone to liberate her, and this woman turns out to be Cay Rivvers (Patricia Charbonneau), a lesbian daredevil who works nights as a casino cashier. Wild and fearless, Cay makes her entrance driving backward at top speed down a narrow dirt road.

The whole narrative builds toward the women's meeting, and bonding. It doesn't happen right away: There are confidences traded while horseback riding, a long drive into the desert, an innocent kiss. When Vivian is asked to move out of her motel, she is angry and humiliated, but she's singlemindedly pursued by Cay. Tired of one-night stands, Cay is intrigued by Vivian. After several misunderstandings and soulful conversations, inhibitions fade, and heated sex follows.

To film a book that was published in the 1970s required major changes, but the screenwriter, Natalie Cooper, doesn't provide any dark corners or shadings to the characters. The well-groomed Vivian, the Eastern stiff, is severe, standoffish, and inhibited. She stays at a dude ranch, a comfortable hideaway where about-to-be-divorced women sit on the porch complaining about men. Vivian remains inside, reading with her glasses on, a spinster who doesn't know her own nature. Cay is her opposite: younger, prettier, a free spirit. By day, Cay throws pottery in a studio-shack on the ranch, which is owned by Frances, the hard-drinking mistress of her late father. Frances loves Cay as if she were her daughter, but she can't approve of her intensely independent lifestyle. When Frances begins to fear she might lose Cay, she turns nasty and mean.

Unlike *Parting Glances*, *Desert Hearts* is concerned solely with the issue of coming out. One waits impatiently to see if Vivian will bed Cay, as if this decision were sufficient to sustain a whole drama. Men aren't an issue, because they are hardly present; Vivian's husband-professor remains safely off-screen.[8] Cay, who's defiantly open about her sexuality, attacks Vivian's defenses, but it's not clear whether she's attracted to Vivian for her brain, her success, or the thrill of the chase. With so narrow a focus, the material cries out for comedy, but the movie is earnest and the dialogue stiff. Scenes in the ranch are so dry that one wishes for the nasty humor of George Cukor's *The Women*, which is also set in a Reno divorce ranch. Directed by Deitch in an impersonal style, the film follows Vivian's denial through every hesitation, prompting David Denby to describe *Desert Hearts* as symptomatic of the hygienic American attitude toward sex.

THE BEGINNING OF QUEER CINEMA—GUS VAN SANT

The undisputed leader of the new queer cinema is the Portland-based director Gus Van Sant, an iconoclast who has provided a fresh, distinctive voice in American movies. Unlike Tarantino and other young directors, Van Sant has a style that is too deviously personal to be imitable. His explorations of society's Skid Row have yielded several potent films: *Mala Noche* (1987), *Drugtsore Cowboy* (1989), *My Own Private Idaho* (1991). With relatively small budgets, Van Sant's movies are about the lives of people who inhabit the seamy underground. Van Sant makes wildly subjective pictures that celebrates outsiders: illegal immigrants, male hustlers, drugstore cowboys. But despite their bleak circumstances, his films display nihilistic humor.

Van Sant's depiction of drug addicts and male prostitutes reveals their humanity without exploiting their tawdriness. His eccentric point of view provides an intimate look at down-and-out characters, on the fringes of society, whom he neither romanticizes nor pities. It's as if his camera "were looking through a peephole, dropping in on the secret lives of people."[9] Although drawn to realistic issues, Van Sant treats them playfully; the critic J. Hoberman singles out "the unabashed beatnik quality to his worldview."[10] Van Sant's attraction to street people and to their sordid milieu is based on his belief that they are more interesting, that there's more drama in their lives than in those of bourgeois characters.

Van Sant's expressive imagery is based on odd rhythms and a jagged camera style. Coming to filmmaking by way of painting (he studied at Rhode Island's Art Institute), he is more concerned than other directors with the use of images to tell stories. He favors images shot at odd angles: the grille of a car with clouds overhead, the edge of a pack of gum, the printing on the top of a light bulb. These idiosyncratic shots yield powerful moments that prevent his narratives from being too smooth.[11]

An unsettling sensibility has prevailed in Van Sant's work since the twenty-minute short *The Happy Organ* (made in collaboration with a high school classmate), about two siblings who go on a tragic weekend trip, and *Alice in Hollywood*, a never released, low-budget screwball comedy about a teenage girl who goes to Hollywood to become a star and winds up a street urchin.

Van Sant rose from obscurity in 1986 with the self-financed *Mala Noche*, which follows the doomed infatuation of Walt (Tim Streeter), a clerk in a Skid Row liquor store, with a Mexican immigrant (played by a Native American, Doug Cooeyate), who barely understands a word of English. The source material is a novella written by Walt Curtis, a Portland street poet. Van Sant kept the manuscript, which was "sexually explicit like a dirty book," under his bed for years. It was shot on cutrate stock with a meager $25,000 budget from savings built up during years of working at an ad agency. An admirer of Andy Warhol's underground movies, Van Sant cast local Portland actors in the leads. The mix of the Pacific Northwestern locale and Van Sant's nihilistic sensibility marked the arrival of an exciting talent.

Pauline Kael singled out the film's "authentic grungy beauty," its "wonderfully fluid, grainy look," which she found expressive, with an improvised feel that reminded her of Jean Genet's short film *Un Chant d'Amour*.[12] *Mala Noche* received scant attention until it won the Los Angeles Film Critics Award for Best Independent Film and went on to become a staple of the festival and art house circuits. *Mala Noche* still remains a model of romantic film grunge for young indie filmmakers.

Van Sant's follow-up, *Drugstore Cowboy*, chronicles the (mis)adventures of bumbling petty criminals. Lyrically shot, it was funny and nonchalant but, by Van Sant standards, a tad conventional and straightforward. Based on an unpublished novel by James Fogle, an inmate at Washington State Penitentiary, the film journal depicts the exploits of Bob (Matt Dillon), a drug addict and dealer who supports his habit by stealing pharmaceuticals.

Efforts to find Hollywood backing for the project were thwarted by Van Sant's nonjudgmental depiction of drugs (it was the era of Nancy Reagan's "Just Say No," hollow, sloganeering prescription for a drug-free America). Since the script was rich with procedural details of how to obtain and use drugs, producers feared that the movie would promote drug use. Of course, for Van Sant, the film was an antidrug story, "like an antiwar film that has a lot of killing."[13] The only concessions he made were to set the film in 1971, thereby eliminating the specter of AIDS and crack, and to make the lead character, Bob, more sympathetic. A newly formed company, Avenue Pictures, which favored unorthodox films, came to the rescue with the necessary $5 million. The bigger budget enabled Van Sant to work with professional actors, and to cast the novelist William S. Burroughs as a junkie priest.

An absurdist comedy that is more funny than sordid, *Drugstore Cowboy* provides an inside view of the drug world and its druggies, who are proud of their aimless existence. The film delineates perceptively a quartet that functions as one outlaw family: Bob (Dillon), his wife Diane (Kelly Lynch), younger member Rick (James Le Gros) and his girlfriend Nadine (Heather Graham). The foursome see themselves as romantic figures—contemporary Bonnies and Clydes—though their robberies are generally a shambles. Their lives are totally devoted to getting high—all their activities are subsumed under their goal to stay high. In a methadone program, the shamelessly unrepentant Bob explains to the social worker that people who use drugs are trying to "relieve the pressures of the everyday life, like having to tie their shoes."

For Pauline Kael, Van Sant's films are "an antidote to wholesomeness," yet manage to achieve a controlled style out of the random and the careless.[13] With Kael's active support, the National Society of Film Critics named *Drugstore Cowboy* Best Picture and Best Screenplay of 1989. Van Sant became the surprise winner over such promising talents as Spike Lee and Steve Soderbergh, who that year had made their breakthrough films, *Do the Right Thing* and *sex, lies, and videotape*, respectively.

After the success of *Drugstore Cowboy*, the studios courted Van Sant with lucrative offers, but he resisted the mainstream lure and was rewarded with critical and popular acclaim for his next film, *My Own Private Idaho*. A retelling of Shakespeare's *Henry IV*, set among street hustlers, the film was by turns nonchalant, touching, and angry, graced with unexpected images and narrative hairpins. Having teenage hustlers lapse into Shakespearean verse didn't always work, but it suited the story. More problematic for mainstream viewers was the film's veering off the narrative track, making it resemble a pileup of open parentheses within parentheses that never got satisfactorily closed.[14]

At the center of the story is Mike Waters (River Phoenix), a narcoleptic hustler, who is searching for the mother who abandoned him when he was a child. Mike falls in love with Scott Favor (Keanu Reeves), a fellow hustler, who stands to inherit a fortune from his father, Portland's paraplegic mayor. Scott looks upon Bob Pigeon (William Richert), a cocaine-dealing braggart—and the film's Falstaff—as his "true father." As the Prince Hal figure, Scott intends to renounce his carefree streetlife and repudiate his friends when his father dies.

For his modern, Skid Row reworking of Shakespeare, Van Sant was inspired by Orson Welles' 1966 film *Chimes at Midnight*, which is based on Shakespeare's *Henry IV*, with Welles in the Falstaff role. But *My Own Private Idaho* reads like an expanded version of Van Sant's earlier films, elevating their issues to a more poetic and universal level. Once again, he courted controversy in his treatment of the homoerotic exploits of male hustlers. Characteristically, however, he ignored warnings that male prostitution and homosexuality were taboos in a social climate marked by hysteria over the AIDS epidemic.

THE AIDS FACTOR: DOCUMENTARIES AND FEATURES

Robert Epstein's two Oscar-winning films, *The Times of Harvey Milk* (1984) and *Common Threads: Stories From the Quilt* (1989), the latter co-directed by Jeffrey Friedman, helped prepare the background for feature movies about AIDS. *The Times of Harvey Milk* chronicles the life, rise to political power and murder of Harvey Milk, one of the country's first openly gay elected officials. Milk's story parallels the story of the modern gay rights movement, specifically the heady times of the 1970s in what's probably the most organized gay community in the world, San Francisco's Castro district. As a mobilizing symbol, the gay community couldn't have asked for a more potent representative than Milk.

With elements of both tragedy and nostalgia for a unique period in gay history, Milk's story is told chronologically. Unsuccessful in his first attempt to win a City Supervisor seat, Milk eventually won after the city underwent redistricting. His campaign and his triumphant victory are related by a former campaign aide, who tells of Milk's kindness, generosity, and insistence on a diverse campaign staff. The footage of his victory shows Milk and his supporters reacting with both disbelief and unmitigated joy.

The tragedy that follows is foreshadowed as we learn of Dan White, the fellow San Francisco Supervisor who murdered Milk and Mayor George Moscone in 1978. Despite White's confession and overwhelming evidence of intent, he was given a sentence of only seven years. As a result, San Francisco's gay community was catapulted into a state of grief and rage that produced riots at City Hall. The scene of the candle-light march held for Milk after his murder is especially poignant. *The Times of Harvey Milk* is at once a piece of history and a tribute to an endearing figure in the gay rights movement.

A documentary about the AIDS Memorial Quilt, *Common Threads* tells the stories of five people who have died from AIDS or are in varying stages of HIV progression. The film describes the impact of their illness on their lives and on those of their loved ones. The individual stories of gay men, an African American intravenous drug user, and a twelve-year-old hemophiliac are interwoven with historical footage that marks the progress of the AIDS epidemic—photographs, newsprint, videos and radio clips. This patchwork style highlights the similarities and differences among the individual histories, and provides an effective metaphor for the film's subject, the AIDS quilt.

Common Threads popularizes the issue of AIDS through real lives and painful experiences. Statistics on AIDS's human toll are presented, but instead of being asked to consider those statistics, which are overwhelming, viewers are presented with actual people. The film describes the size of the epidemic, recording its scope and its effects on both the personal and the collective levels. This crystallizes in the final scene, in which the camera slowly pulls back to reveal the entire AIDS quilt on display in Washington, D.C. That each of the thousands of panels represents a life as unique as the five just witnessed is heartbreaking.

For years, Hollywood denied the possibility of a viable dramatic entertainment about AIDS, even though the epidemic was everywhere. A subject once considered untouchable "suddenly" surfaced in a number of diverse and compelling projects: HBO's adaptation of Randy Shilts's *And the Band Played On;* Jonathan Demme's *Philadelphia*, the first major Hollywood movie about AIDS; a French film, *Savage Nights;* and even an AIDS musical, John Greyson's *Zero Patience*. Unlike earlier works, such as the TV-made melodramas *The Ryan White Story* and *An Early Frost*, which treated AIDS as a tragic tale of courage and nobility, the new efforts viewed the epidemic in a larger, more realistic context.[15]

The question faced by filmmakers was how to respond to the devastating AIDS crisis. Too much "drama" and emotion might seem an indulgence, an intrusion on feelings of grief. On the other hand, too calm and lucid a response might be perceived as dignified but not entirely honest. A movie about AIDS can easily slip into sensationalism and obviousness. Not surprisingly, many filmmakers took the middle road, aiming to humanize a tragedy that initially evoked fear and hostility.

Norman Rene's *Longtime Companion* (1990) carried the burden of being the first theatrical movie to deal directly with AIDS. As such, it had the task of placing the AIDS crisis on the national agenda. But it also meant that the film was gentler and more uplifting than it needed to be. *Longtime Companion* was not, however, the first fictional work on AIDS. It followed Larry Kramer's angry play *The Normal Heart* and William Hoffman's *As Is*, both structured as family melodramas.

In *Longtime Companion*, gay friends and lovers suffer an attack on their fundamental values and, finally, on their very existence. The movie implies that AIDS seeps into everyday life, changing love, work, and play. Specifically, in Craig Lucas's screenplay, AIDS is seen through the suffering of one particular group: upwardly mobile white gay men who have well-paying jobs, wear designer clothes, shop at Bloomingdale's, and spend summers on Fire Island. The men are all handsome, and, until the advent of AIDS, their lives are joyous. The film chronicles the terrible events that overtake eight friends between 1981, when they first become aware of the "strange" virus, and 1989, when loved ones are memorialized and buried. *Longtime Companion* ends as it begins, emphasizing the toll AIDS has taken within the gay community and the need to face the catastrophe with heroic dignity.

All the characters are sympathetic, particularly the central figure, David (Bruce Davison), a rich, middle-aged man who doesn't have to work for a living. With his smooth, reassuring manner, David is a pillar of strength. When his friends begin to get sick, he shifts from living for trivia and gossip to being a compassionate caregiver. David is a stabilizing father figure to all the other men: his lover, Sean (Mark Lamos), a successful soap opera writer; Fuzzy (Stephen Caffrey), a showbiz lawyer; sweet-tempered John (Dermot Mulroney); John's friend Willy (Campbell Scott), a gym instructor who takes up with Fuzzy; Howard (Patrick Cassidy), an actor who appears as a gay character on Sean's soap; and Howard's live-in lover, Paul (John Dossett). The only female character is Lisa (Mary Louise Parker), who hangs out with the men as friend and confidante.

Longtime Companion is at its most urgent when it's specific. The most memorable passages are those in which David cares for his disintegrating lover, whose mind progressively weakens. At first, in an attempt to fool Sean's producer, David writes his scripts as well as instructions on how to communicate them. But the befuddled Sean garbles the instructions, and the conversations disintegrate in scenes that are as painful as they are funny. When hope vanishes, David gently urges Sean with the unforgettable credo "Just let go. Relax. Nothing bad is going to happen. Let go." Nursing Sean to the very end, David is a solacing angel, easing his lover toward death.

The story is structured as a fable about an extended family in which the parent figures (David and Sean) die, leaving the children bereft and alone. Attempting to recreate a casual chronicle, *Longtime Companion* implies that this is a typical group of New York homosexuals. In the *New York Times* Vincent Canby accused the film of being parochial and self-absorbed—"It's as if the rest of America didn't exist. This self-absorption makes the movie so tough to take, so depressing."[16] The film's racial homogeneity is undeniable. In one brief scene a Hispanic with AIDS gets a mercy call, and the only black in the film is a male nurse who attends a dying white man. But is Canby's accusation fair? Canby himself concedes that "a movie doesn't have to mention everything going on in the world to convince the audience of its awareness." Is it valid to expect every black-themed film to embrace the entire spectrum of black lifestyles?

In his astute review, Andrew Sarris discussed the problem of creating individualized characters in the context of a collective statement. *Longtime Companion* is undeniably ambitious and conscientious about depicting the AIDS catastrophe, but is it fair, Sarris asked, to apply rigorous aesthetic standards to movies about AIDS? For Sarris, the film views gay subculture from the inside, but he felt that the dialogue was so knowing, the laughter so confidentially unexplained, that nongay audiences would feel excluded from the conversation.[17]

When first encountered, in Manhattan and on Fire Island, the men are part of a community riding high. In 1981, when the *New York Times* first reports on a rare form of cancer found among homosexuals, they respond with jokes, shrugging off the story with disbelief. Even as things begin to worsen, there's no new consciousness or activism. The group continues to get together and engage in cooking, chatting, and lovemaking. Following the group over the next eight years, the movie chronicles how men devoted to pleasure and friendship shed their high spirits to take up new responsibilities, caring for one another unto death. Bafflement gives way to uneasy coping and finally to mournful accommodation. The change is realistically gradual. At the finale, with

half of the members dead, a surviving couple vows to become politically active.

The filmmakers intended to show how people make the best of an
inconceivable situation; their goal was to console and inspire. Yet the
movie is not flawless. Produced by *American Playhouse*, it has the re-
straining good taste that has marked this outfit's other productions.
Nostalgia and self-protection imply that everything in gay life was
lovely before the curse; the promiscuity of the Fire Island scene is
flaunted as a pre-AIDS Paradise Lost. *Longtime Companion* is a tad too
tame and earnest in showing how a hedonistic community becomes a
therapeutic one. The film implies that AIDS improves everyone's character: No one panics, no one deserts his sick lover, no one gives way to
despair.

THE NEW QUEER CINEMA

In an attempt to be inclusive, mainstream Hollywood has always held
to a naive belief in America as the melting pot. The strategy that followed ignored gender, racial, and sexual distinctions in search of a common, unifying cultural denominator that would be acceptable to all and
offensive to none. As a result, until the late 1980s, moviegoers seeking
gay or lesbian fare had limited options, mostly avant-garde and experimental film.

But the climate has changed. "It would be difficult to be like
George Cukor in the 1990s," said Gregg Araki, "if only because
there's a sense that the issues have become so charged that you have
to take a stand one way or another."[18] Explaining the new sensibility,
Araki described a "new generation of queers who feel that being gay
is a very big part of their identity and are much more vocal and much
more expressive about it." Gay and lesbian audiences began to express more aggressively their discontent with how they were shown
in pictures, and to demand fairer treatment, but Hollywood did not
care—or dare.

That attitude changed in the early 1990s, when an independent film
movement polemically known as "queer cinema" began to coalesce.
The watershed years of the queer film wave were, like those of the
black film cycle, 1991–1992, which saw the release of Todd Haynes's
Poison, Gus Van Sant's *My Own Private Idaho*, Jennie Livingston's *Paris*

Is Burning, all in 1991, and Tom Kalin's *Swoon,* Christopher Munch's *The Hours and Times,* Gregg Araki's *The Living End,* all in 1992.

A more pronounced gay visibility finally hit Hollywood in the mid-1990s, when new voices began challenging old stigmas and fought for more realistic representation. The more mainstream cinema responded with comedies like *Three of Hearts* and *Threesome* and Jonathan Demme's AIDS drama, *Philadelphia,* all in 1993. The queer cycle reached its maturity at the 1994 Sundance Festival, when the director Rose Troche and her cast stormed Park City with *Go Fish,* their edgy lesbian romantic comedy. Industry suits suddenly began to think about gay and lesbian spending power.

As soon as the possibilities seemed lucrative, suggesting there was money to be made out of gay product, the "new" market began to garner an unprecedented response from producers. "The reason there's a higher degree of attention now is because distributors have shown a profit," said Mark Finch of Frameline, a distribution company specializing in gay fare. Strand Releasing is another gay-friendly distributor, with a catalogue that includes Lino Brocka's *Macho Dancer* and works by Araki and other gay directors. "It's just like any trend," notes Strand's copresident, Marcus Hu. At a particular moment, the new films heralded the arrival of Queer Cinema.

The new gay film market did not appear overnight. It was gradually and steadily built by dedicated filmmakers, festival programmers, and savvy distributors. A number of factors have contributed to the solidifying of the gay market[19]:

- *The role of critics.* Critical attention, which initially came through the independent press, spread to more mainstream media. In the 1980s, papers like the *Village Voice, Los Angeles Weekly, Los Angeles Reader,* performed a crucial role, as key critics, gay and straight, consistently reported on the gay film scene.
- *Unique marketing strategies.* The director Nicole Conn self-distributed her film *Claire of the Moon,* using a grassroots marketing campaign before turning the movie over to Strand for wider distribution. Strand has developed its own strategies to serve its audiences. As Hu said, "We have tried very hard to link our company with films that are fun, and we market them like exploitation horror films. We don't spend money on publicity, but go for

word of mouth." The word-of-mouth tactic has been successful thanks to the solid infrastructure of explicitly gay networks and media outlets.

- *Gay magazines.* The explosion of interest in gay films was paralleled by a similar expansion in the publishing industry, with the inauguration of numerous gay magazines (joining the well-established *Advocate*), such as *Out, OutWeek, Genre, Ten Percent.* Gay cable shows and online gay bulletin boards constitute a powerful information network that weaves in and around the mainstream networks.
- *Gay and lesbian film festivals.* The impact of gay film festivals on the burgeoning queer cinema is immeasurable. For a decade or so, gay films began their lives—literally—at festivals. By the 1980s, almost every major city had a gay film festival, often screening movies that were unlikely to break beyond the festival circuit. The festivals deserve credit for serving as makeshift distributors—there's nothing as powerful as the word of mouth generated at such festivals. Filmmakers whose careers received a boost from such forums include Gus Van Sant, whose *Mala Noche* first gained attention at some 1987 festivals, and Jennie Livingston, whose *Paris Is Burning* was a festival hit in 1991.

The first gay film festival took place in San Francisco in 1977, when a few local filmmakers posted placards around the Castro district announcing a free showing of their films. They were amazed when hundreds of patrons showed up. Thus began what would become the San Francisco Lesbian and Gay International Film Festival. Two decades later, the San Francisco event is not only the oldest but also the largest gay festival in the country. Recent editions have unspooled in three venues, the Castro, Victoria, and Roxie, presenting close to 200 titles from such farflung locales as Cuba, Serbia, and China.

The old gender stratification began to decline within the gay artistic world. "It's harder and harder to identify films as either lesbian or gay," said the San Francisco Gay Festival's codirector, Jennifer Morris. "Both creative personnel and on-screen characters are no longer exclusively 'one or the other.'" In the early days of the Los Angeles gay festival, now called Outfest, founder Larry Horne had to persuade Hollywood executives that films would not be stigmatized or made more difficult to market if they first appeared at the festival. Resistance declined when distributors realized that the gay market was not to be taken lightly.

- *New organizational networks.* The development of new channels for exhibiting and distributing specialized films has had a major impact. In 1991, Strand was so confident of the gay market that it began producing gay features, such as Araki's *Totally Fu***d Up*, the AIDS comedy-drama *Grief*, and the more risqué and experimental *Frisk*.

- *The gay presence in the film industry.* In the 1990s, midlevel management within the major studios began to be populated with lesbians and gay executives. While they work within a system that is dependent on commercial market considerations, it's encouraging to see gay executives promoting gay causes within the mainstream power structure.

- *The AIDS factor.* AIDS, the lethal transformer of gay life, has influenced every aspect of American culture. AIDS has generated as much anger as sadness, revealed through veiled and not so veiled references to politically correct values that sparked new offensives against homosexuality. However, there is no denying that many gay and lesbian filmmakers have been energized by the ongoing debate. The new gay directors have stretched the boundaries of traditional cinema, rolling the stylistic dice, challenging viewers' expectations with innovative narratives and styles. The British director Derek Jarman (*Edward II*) and the American Gus Van Sant (*Mala Noche, My Own Private Idaho*) have served as role models for young gay directors.

The new gay films have varied in style and sensibility. To assign *Swoon* and *The Living End* to the same category requires a certain bias, but it's tempting to generalize about their similar motivations and effects. Several films have centered on social outcasts or fugitives from the law, individuals propelled toward a tragic fate by a hostile world and their own obsessive desires. Gregg Araki's *The Living End* can be perceived as a gay version of *Bonnie and Clyde* and *Gun Crazy*. The two male protagonists wrestle with hypocrisy, mortality, and redemption, issues that mainstream cinema has not probed with honesty. "Gay content in film is usually in the independent sector," said Jennie Livingston, whose documentary *Paris Is Burning* is about black and Latino drag queens. "Before and after the Hays Code, gay subject matter was not permissible except as an index of freakishness, which you still see in films today."[20]

In 1991 alone, four major films (*JFK*, *Basic Instinct*, *The Prince of Tides*, and *The Silence of the Lambs*) came under fire for their one-sided, distorted portrayal of gay characters. Hollywood's well-intentioned but flaccid efforts to be sensitive about gay issues, from *Personal Best* and *Making Love* in 1982 to *Philadelphia* in 1993, have only reinforced the idea that gay filmmakers must create their own cinema. The fact that *Philadelphia* was written by a gay writer, Ron Nysmayer, obviously didn't matter much, judging by the film's broad and clinical approach. For a director like Rose Troche, *Philadelphia* is not really a gay film but "a tidy representation of gays, a safe film that straights could embrace because everyone knows Tom Hanks is straight. There's no way that film would've done what it did if they'd cast a gay man in the lead."[21]

Still, the commercial success of *Philadelphia* in Middle America made it easier for adventurous gay films to thrive in the marketplace. "The studios have realized these films can make money," said Troche, "but their attempts to cash in on the market have been pathetic."[22] *Three of Hearts* is fairly typical—it's always a threesome of one man and two women where heterosexual desire has the final word. With their "implied disclaimer on homosexuality," they leave people like Troche "feeling used."

"I don't think *The Living End* or *Swoon* or *The Hours and Times* are 'spokesperson' films," said Kalin, "but the whole issue raises questions about being a spokesperson, about a community, about the debate over presenting 'positive images,' what's the inside and outside of queer?" Some gay movies have crossed over, appealing to wider audiences, but despite their relative commercial success, compared to mainstream Hollywood movies, both their budgets and their profits have been minuscule. The crop of gay and lesbian indies came out of a Hollywood tradition, even if their strategy was to fracture the very foundations of that tradition. The new films were counterreactions, playing off Hollywood constructions and genres. Perhaps the most profound change effected by queer cinema was noted by Todd Haynes: "At least Hollywood is discovering that money isn't homophobic."[23]

ENFANT TERRIBLE I—TODD HAYNES

Gus Van Sant's *Mala Noche* may have recalled Jean Genet's *Un Chant d'Amour*, but it's not a coincidence that the French *enfant terrible* inspired another gifted director, Todd Haynes, who has arguably made the most provocative movie on the AIDS crisis to date, *Poison* (1991). One of *Poison's* stories, "Homo," makes an explicit link to Genet's fictional reminiscences of his days in reform school and prison.

The iconoclastic *Poison* is akin to two Haynes shorts, *Dottie Gets Spanked* and *Assassins*, a film about the French poet Rimbaud. Both of these gay-themed movies are "messy," according to Haynes, because they deal with things he felt passionately about, "deviant" characters and acts of transgression. Haynes's second feature, *Safe* (1995), (see Chapter 8), is more aligned with his short *Superstar*; both are "conceptual projects" about people in whom he didn't have "an initial investment," and who were approached from the outside.

The audacity of Haynes's forty-three-minute film *Superstar: The Karen Carpenter Story* derives from its inspired casting concept: the late, anorexic singer, her brother, Richard, and their overbearing parents, are portrayed as Barbie-type dolls. But Haynes never cleared the rights for the Carpenters' music, and Richard blocked the film's theatrical release. Nonetheless, *Superstar* went on to become an outlaw film, circulating on bootlegged videos and making Haynes an underground figure even before *Poison* won the top prize at Sundance in 1991.

Denounced by one of the country's most outspoken conservatives, the Reverend Donald E. Wildmon, *Poison* was attacked for containing "explicit porno scenes of homosexuals involved in anal sex." Although he never actually saw the film, Wildmon was infuriated by the support the film received from the National Endowment for the Arts, a $25,000 postproduction grant. But the embattled NEA chairman, John E. Frohnmayer, defended the film as a responsible work of art, claiming that "the central theme is that violence breeds violence, lust breeds destruction. It is clearly not a pornographic film."

Although one section of *Poison* deals with homosexual obsession, the film's overall tone is neither pornographic nor explicit. *Poison* is a socially conscious art movie, the kind government agencies should subsidize. But for many, the fact that *Poison* portrays homosexuals sympathetically was enough to condemn the NEA support. Almost every major newspaper and TV program, from the *CBS Evening News* to *Entertainment Tonight*, covered the fuss; when *Poison* opened to well-deserved critical praise, it was already infamous. The NEA attack pushed an avant-garde artist into the spotlight.[24] Like Genet, whose release from a life prison sentence was achieved with the help of Jean-Paul Sartre and Simone de Beauvoir, Haynes was catapulted from outlaw director to celebrated filmmaker by the NEA controversy.

Soaked in paranoia, *Poison* opens with a provocative statement, "The entire world is dying of panicky fright," and subjective shots of police breaking into a besieged apartment. The theme is deviance and the pain and isolation that deviance generates. The title refers to society's practice of penalizing deviants by stigmatizing them. Pushing the boundaries of narrative cinema, *Poison* both parodies and challenges the conventions of classic Hollywood. Composed of three interwoven stories, the anthology derives its cumulative power from its disorienting juxtapositions of themes and relationships. As Hoberman pointed out, the bodily fluids (blood, pus, saliva) that leak from the various characters, and the relentless equation of love and death, serve to bind the three texts in a tight web of cross-references.[25] Everything amplifies everything else: The stories seem like three aspects of a single biography.

The film is most inventive in the black-and-white "Horror" sequence, which mocks the genre's cheap look and stilted dialogue. In this spoof, a mad scientist, Dr. Thomas Graves, distills the "mysteries of the sex drive" in a bubbling teacup, then accidentally drinks his concoction and turns into a contagious leper whose kiss can kill. "Leper Sex Killer on the Loose," a tabloid headline screams, while Dr. Nancy Olson, the sweet scientist who loves Tom, contemplates his "change of heart." Although Haynes never mentions AIDS, the allusions to the lethal virus are obvious and the message clear—Nancy's naive dreams give way to knowledge that love equals death.

The theme of "Horror" is echoed in the other stories. In "Homo," the most controversial segment, a prisoner, John Broom (Scott Renderer), becomes obsessed with a fellow inmate, Jack Bolton (James Lyons). Haynes constructs a prison whose blue-shadowed filth and claustrophobia contrast sharply with flashbacks to a reform school set in a lush countryside, where Broom first glimpses his object of desire. A powerful scene in "Homo" shows school boys relentlessly spitting into Bolton's mouth. "Homo" is more about mental than sexual brutality: A homosexual rape is discreetly shot, emphasizing the emotional rather than the physical violence. The film's third section, "Hero," is a fake documentary in which reporters investigate the disappearance of a little boy. The boy's mother claims that, to save her from savage beatings, he shot her husband and then fled through an open window.

Poison intercuts a triptych of visually divergent episodes, each set in a world "dying of panicky fright," but stylistically the entire film displays bravura technical skills. A parody of black-and-white movies, "Horror" is shot in the slightly exaggerated noir vein, with skewed angles and dark shadows. "Hero" employs TV-like banal camera setups and talking heads. "Homo" is shot in a soft romantic style that suggests 1950s Hollywood melodramas by Douglas Sirk and Nicholas Ray. Washed in blue light and populated by blue-clad convicts who remove their shirts and touch their scars tenderly, the prison scenes are deliberately shot like a gay fantasy. The reformatory scenes of sexual initiation or degradation take place in a courtyard with exotic flowers and are splashed with sunlight.

Critics who felt that *Poison* was too academic based their argument on the film's self-consciousness and symbolic subtext. The movie gives the boy, an angel of light, the name of Beacon; the diseased scientist is called Graves; and there are symbolic doors and windows and quotations from Genet. The dedicated scientist who turns into a monster is like Dr. Jekyll, and the little boy who kills his father and flies away is like Peter Pan. All three characters are linked to death: The scientist plunges to death from one window, the little boy soars away through another, and the convict remains locked away, which is also a form of death.[26]

ENFANT TERRIBLE II—GREGG ARAKI

Younger than Van Sant and older than Haynes, Gregg Araki is as rooted in Los Angeles as Van Sant is in the Northwest and Haynes is in New York. A determinedly noncalling-card director, Araki claims he "just never wanted to be Steven Spielberg." Instead, he cites Hollywood screwball comedies, alternative music, and Jean-Luc Godard as major influences on his work, particularly Godard—Araki's movies offer American parallels to the French *Breathless* and *Band of Outsiders*, both directed by Godard. Araki's work concerns one major issue: being young and doomed in wasteland America, epitomized by Los Angeles, an alienating city filled with 7–Elevens, minimalls, and parking lots. The youths in Araki's films are on the road from nowhere to nowhere, but he doesn't neglect humor in depicting their alienation and self-absorption.

Self-advertised as irreverent and irresponsible, Araki's movies are responsible by default. Violence and its flip side, apathy, define his America. In his movies, violence assumes a double role: It's a symbol of gay oppression but also a symbol of gay liberation. The tone of Araki's films vacillates among the romantic, the disenchanted, and the prankish. Characters in his films clutter their apartments with inflatable dinosaurs, squeaky rubber asses, and plastic fish that jump to clapping hands. There's a disturbing note in Araki's enjoyment of bloody excess, a childishness that goes with the plastic dinosaurs.[27] But there's also a willingness to take risks and to experiment, not so much with ideas as with styles.

At heart, Araki is a surrealist, enamored of the aesthetics of the extreme. His penchant for whimsy helps him avoid solemnity, but it also cheapens his intelligence. As Ella Taylor noted, Araki doesn't yet have the intellectual chops or assurance to deliver a complex argument about America's youth, but his bitingly raw dialogue and sharp camera rhythms offer compensations that turn his pictures into energetic cinematic experiences.[28]

Araki's first feature, *Three Bewildered People in the Night* (1987), which he wrote, produced, directed, shot, and edited, cost $5,000, less than the lunch budget of a Hollywood executive. The script, Araki said, would never get through USC's film school, because "they teach specific structural rules on screenwriting, but I like long, angsty passages where characters are ecstatic about how miserable they are. They like production values. I shot with a Bolex, on 4X stock using available light, without synch sound." Araki shoots on location, without permits or lighting, and the scene takes "as long as it takes to drive there, do it, and drive back."

A soul-searching drama about a trio struggling with their sexuality, the movie dissects the dissolution of a heterosexual relationship and the tentative beginning of a gay one. Alicia (Darcy Marta) is a video artist who likes to confess in front of a camera and then watch her confessions. She lives with Craig (John Lacques), a journalist who wishes to go back to acting but spends most of his time with Alicia's best friend,

David (Mark Howell), a gay performance artist; a black patch on his eye suggests John Ford or Fritz Lang. Shot in grainy black and white, the film is set mostly at night, with the trio wandering around coffeeshops, galleries, and empty streets. *Three Bewildered People* is dominated by countless phone calls and revelatory conversations, with references to Godard and Jarmusch.

The Long Weekend (a.k.a. *O' Despair*), Araki's second feature, is aesthetically similar to the first, a low-budgeter shot in black and white. Centering again on "fucked-up people," it was made with a light parodic touch, combined with sympathy for the malaise of youth culture. Some young marginals, gay and straight, gather at the apartment of a depressed friend and spend the weekend trying to figure out their confused identities and troubled relationships.

It was *The Living End* (1992), self-described as "my most desperate movie," that put Araki on the movie map. By turns quirky, depressing, and invigorating, this road movie about two HIV-positive runaways is Araki's most bleakly romantic film, a tale of impossible love in the face of death. Its hero, Jon (Craig Gilmore), is a cynical film critic with a West Hollywood haircut and Snoopy slippers—"just a bummed-out, HIV-infected homo minding my own business," he says. Jon complains to his friend Darcy (Darcy Marta) about the disruptions he faces while writing an essay on the death of cinema; Andre Bazin's "What Is Cinema" hits the trash can in the first scene.

Things change when Luke (Mike Dytri), a hunky psychotic killer, explodes into Jon's life. A loose cannon with an appetite for instant pleasure, the muscled Luke seduces Jon in a matter of seconds and then lands both of them in enough trouble to set up a fugitive road movie. With nothing to lose, they hit the road in search of what might be their last chance at fun. Running away from both AIDS and the police, they live on fries and Jack Daniels.

Armed with an uncle's Gold Card and a gun stolen from dykes, Luke carries off a sulky but excited Jon on a clueless journey to nowhere—nowhere being an all-too-real Los Angeles of supermarkets, gas stations, and fast-food joints. "We got nothing to lose," Luke says. "We're totally free." Freedom in this case means knocking off club-wielding gay bashers and a cop, shooting up a recalcitrant auto teller, and periodically threatening Jon with a gun to the mouth. In the closing scenes, Jon develops a fever and a slight cough, the first AIDS symptoms, indicating the terror of what's still to come. "It's living inside me,"

Luke says, as he slits his wrist. "But I can't see it. This just looks like regular old boring blood to me."

Though Araki is not HIV-positive, making *The Living End* was a kind of "cathartic experience," reflecting "a certain attitude among gay people." Bashing homophobes and blowing off a policeman's head in the film was a kind of wish fulfillment. For Araki, the major "benefit" of AIDS has been this "real sense of urgency."[29] *The Living End* opens with a "Choose Death" bumper sticker and a man spray-painting "Fuck the World" on a wall. "Being gay in the 1990s is not just a matter of what you do when you have sex," Araki said. "It has to do with your outlook, your place in society; homophobia is so prevalent, it becomes ingrained in your personality on all levels. It really informs my films." At the same time, Araki allowed that "my outlook is not exactly embraced by the gay community. I am in no way a spokesman for gay people in the 1990s."

Araki would rather have his audience enraged than sympathetic or understanding. *The Living End* is dedicated to "the hundreds of thousands who've died and the hundreds of thousands more who will die because of a big white house full of Republican fuckheads." Unlike *Longtime Companion*, there's no inspiration, no grace under pressure, no Fire Island gays lamenting their dying lovers, no sudden conversions to activism. There are only two HIV positives, losing it in waves of paranoia and panicky euphoria in wasteland America. As Ella Taylor wrote: "Dignity is low priority in a film that panders to nobody, makes no excuses for its sexuality, refuses to turn its characters into noble martyrs, and takes flying pot shots at the myth of straight normality whenever the opportunity presents itself."[30]

It took three months to shoot *The Living End*, a $20,000 project and Araki's most expensive film to date. Describing the experience of working with a "big" budget, he said, "Before, we were just winging it with three people. When you have fifty, you can't just go into a coffeeshop and start filming. I just don't like to deal with all those people, you have to feed them all the time. That's the biggest problem: keeping them fed."[31]

With each film, Araki tries to push harder, never thinking about the audience for his movies. "If people like them, that's great, and if they don't, I'm not going to kill myself over it, which is why I get criticized for being self-indulgent."[32] Lack of audiences, however, became a real problem with Araki's next feature, *Totally F***ed Up* (1994).

Delving again into the troubled world of gay teenagers, Araki targets gay bashing and institutionalized homophobia. Angered by the disproportionately high suicide rates among gay teens, Araki speaks his mind without being preachy. Once again, he evokes desolate images of nocturnal Los Angeles, described by one character as "the alienation capital of the world." It's a city of looming billboards, deserted parking lots, all-night coffee shops in which disaffected youth hang out, like the characters in Linklater's SubUrbia.

This film began a new strategy for Araki, one that favors large ensembles of diverse characters. Andy (James Duval), a lonely, appealing youth, doesn't believe love exists—until he meets the handsome and more experienced Ian (Alan Boyce). His pals, the aspiring filmmaker Steven (Gilbert Luna) and his lover, Deric (Lance May), are going though a crisis in their relationship. When Steven strays, he blames it on a guy who seduced him with a bootleg Nine Inch Nails tape. Reflecting the zeitgeist, the gay characters are indistinguishable from the other teenagers, a fact reinforced by the predominantly straight cast. Along with interviews taped by Steven's camcorder, Araki punctuates the film with quotes from Godard.[33]

Responding to criticism of the lack of racial diversity in his films, Araki has said: "The essential problem is they're gay in a homophobic society. It's not like their racial differences cause a problem." In fact, Araki finds "ethnic bonding" in a cliquish way to be backward: "I don't like blacks who hang out with blacks because those are the only people that relate to them. That's racism in a bad way."[34] For him, it's the characters' predicaments, not their race, that make his movies universal. Except for Nowhere, his films have featured mostly white characters, a reflection of Araki's own experience: "I live in a place where anything goes, you could be gay, of color, whatever, just mind your own business."

KILLERS AND LOVERS

Tom Kalin's radical perspective in Swoon (1992) establishes a link with other new queer films, Poison, The Living End, and The Hours and Times (discussed later), all of which are revisionist in their own way. Kalin revisits the infamous case of the real-life killers Leopold and Loeb against the context of rampant homophobia. Prior to undertaking the project, Kalin and his cowriter, Hilton Als, asked themselves whether "the world really needs another film about Leopold and Loeb." After all, the "thrill killers" have been the subject of Hitchcock's *Rope* (1950) and Richard Fleischer's *Compulsion* (1958). But realizing there hasn't been a film about "the disturbing, romantic, unconscious elements" of the story provided the extra persuasion needed.[35]

Taking a different track from Hitchcock or Fleischer, who viewed the killers from the outside, *Swoon* pulls the viewers inside the killers' minds, reveling in their passion. While not minimizing their horrific crime, the movie is concerned more with the surrounding homophobia, past and present. Kalin exposes the era's prejudices and their effects on the present, although the polemical satire is less convincing than the period details. *Swoon* doesn't want the viewers to sympathize with murderers, but like *Poison* and like Araki's movies, it forces the audience to face a society that brands all deviance as homicidal.[36]

In 1924, against the backdrop of underworld Chicago, two precocious students, Nathan Leopold Jr. (Craig Chester) and Richard Loeb (Daniel Schecter), kidnapped and murdered a thirteen-year-old boy. When a haphazard trail of evidence was discovered, their arrogant confession caused a media uproar that focused on their youth, their Jewishness, and their homosexuality. What concerns Kalin is the killers' "otherness"—their being "geniuses," "Jews," and "queers"— and the way society framed their crime as a direct outcome of their deviance. For Kalin, the couple are as much victims as they are victimizers.

In the 1990s, what was once considered the "crime of the century" has largely faded from public consciousness, except for those who grew up near Chicago, like Kalin's grandmother, who had a Leopold and Loeb scrapbook. Kalin's father was a social worker in the state parole department, and Kalin himself had a pen pal who was a penitentiary inmate. This friendship opened him up to the topic. For Kalin, the real, untold story is in the public's eagerness to see homosexuality as the cause of criminal behavior. In the trial, this attack was waged by "alienists" (early expert witnesses on mental competence), who testified that failure to separate from the mother precludes a heterosexual choice in adulthood. For Kalin, "the fault wasn't in Leopold's object choice, but in the fact that he lived in a time when he couldn't negotiate a relationship with a man."[37]

The film's moral stance is audacious; it asks the audience to empathize with the propagators of an abhorrent crime. Both killers were prodigiously intelligent—at age eighteen, Loeb was the youngest graduate ever of the University of Michigan. They killed, as Michael Wilmington noted, for kicks, for aesthetics, and to seal their bond as two imaginary Nietzschean Übermenschen.[38] Challenging the notion that they were driven to murder by "inversion," Kalin rejects *Rope*'s Nietzschean rationale, but he doesn't dig deep enough into the idea that perhaps class, not homosexuality, might have been the real problem.

Loeb is seen through Leopold's rapt vision—as an Adonis. Kalin strips the relationship to its primal sadomasochistic core: "Dickie" Loeb is a narcissistic stud who gets off on crime, and "Babe" Leopold is the infatuated admirer, enslaved to the confident, amoral Loeb. In the end, only Clarence Darrow's courtroom eloquence saved their lives. Loeb was later killed in prison in a shower brawl, and Leopold went through rehabilitation and served as a missionary in Puerto Rico.

Centering on a doomed couple, united by lust, whose idyll is cut short by the outside world, the elegant black-and-white *Swoon* is made in the noir tradition of films on deviant couples (*Gun Crazy*, *The Honeymoon Killers*, *Bonnie and Clyde*, and *Badlands*). The film blends real and mockumentary footage with eerily inventive images by the cinematographer Ellen Kuras: a ring exchange in a cavernous cityscape, horrific woods that backdrop the murder, a campy theatrical with flapper transvestites, and the sudden, surreal appearance of the lovers' bed in the courtroom. As a dark poem of love and madness, *Swoon* is powerful; as social polemic, it's strained. Ironically, the imagined scenes—the murder, the lovemaking—seem real, and the documentary footage and trial recreation are too campy, an impression strengthened by the declamatory style used by the actors.

Reinterpreting the lives of celebs and cultural history is also the prime motivation behind Christopher Munch's *The Hours and Times* (1992), a meditation on the friendship between John Lennon and Beatles manager Brian Epstein. Exquisitely written and performed, the film is fraught with erotic tension between an urbane, longing Epstein and a sexually ambivalent Lennon. One of the most interesting films at the 1991 Sundance Festival, *The Hours and Times* won a special jury prize for artistic excellence.

Structured as a fictional account of what might have happened in April 1963, when Lennon and Epstein spent a weekend in Barcelona, the trip is the only factual element; the rest of the film is an evocative reflection on the meaning of friendship between two vastly different men. Epstein (David Angus) was an educated, upper-middle-class Jew from London; Lennon (Ian Hart) was a curious, working-class youth from Liverpool. Epstein was the entrepreneur; Lennon had the genius. Six years his senior, Epstein was a sophisticated gay man; Lennon a rough, unrefined youth.

From the opening scene, one senses Lennon's admiration for Epstein and the latter's hopeless yearning to develop a meaningful bond with the younger man. Intense dialogue defines the tension-charged scenes, building up to an emotionally gripping climax in which they begin to engage in sexual intercourse, but Lennon can't go through with it. But the movie is by no means a tale of seduction; it's Lennon who asks questions about intercourse, and it's he who encourages Epstein to jump into the tub with him. The Hours and Times suggests curiosity, flirtatiousness, and willingness to experiment with a unique friendship. "I only came here to get away with you," Lennon says in earnest. "We could have gone to the North Pole for all I care."

Like Swoon, the film is elegantly shot in black and white. In its long, static shots, Munch's minimalist style recalls Jarmusch's early work. The first image, a blank white screen, gradually dissolves into brief shots of Gaudi's famed buildings in Barcelona. For long stretches, the camera zeroes in on Epstein's face, staring at Lennon with wistful longing. To alleviate the compressed intensity, Munch employs some melodramatic devices and secondary characters, such as a sexy stewardess who shows up in their hotel, with a jealous Epstein offended by Lennon's attraction to her. And, in a rare outdoor scene, they meet a Spanish businessman whom Lennon invites to their hotel.

In his sensitive treatment of a tenuous relationship, Munch shows the shifting balances and imbalances, the steps and countersteps that are expressed in words and gestures. Considering that it deals with celebrities, The Hours and Times avoids trivializing them and lacks any intimations of gossip or sleaze. Munch deals with particular personalities, but his spare, precise, essaylike film illuminates the constraints of any friendship—gay or straight—and the sad realization of friendship's limitations.

THE NEW LESBIAN FILMS

By the early 1990s, no American movie with a lesbian theme had been widely released since *Desert Heart*. That Hollywood continued to bleach out lesbian elements in its mainstream fare was evident in Whoopi Goldberg's lesbian scene in *The Color Purple*, and in the lack of sexual tension between the female friends in *Fried Green Tomatoes*. *Basic Instinct*'s murderous bisexual, played by Sharon Stone as a male fantasy, was ardently protested by gay activists. In *Internal Affairs*, the lesbian cop partner was just a variation on the male prototype, existing to offer support for the lead heterosexual.[39]

Into this barren context came Nicole Conn's lesbian love story, *Claire of the Moon* (1993), a movie more noteworthy for its production and release strategies than for its artistic merits or its contribution to genuine lesbian cinema. The setting is a writer's retreat on the beautiful Oregon coast that is run by a sultry lesbian, who mischievously books into the same cottage the elegant Noel Benedict (Karen Trumbo), a respected therapist and writer, and Claire Jabrowski (Trisha Todd), a successful satirist.

Conn uses the familiar premise of two mismatched personalities coming together. Claire is a free-spirited, chain-smoking blonde in tight jeans who enjoys the thrill of anonymous heterosexual sex, while the turtlenecked Noel still pines for her lost lover. When Noel expresses her lesbianism in a group meeting, she begins to command Claire's attention. Unlike Noel, Claire has hard time believing that men and women "speak a different language" and therefore can never be as close as two women. Avoiding deeper issues of sexuality and identity, Conn conveniently charts a predictable evolution of sexual attraction.

The movie strains for sophistication and wit, but its language is starch. The central figures are smart, but their company is not. Conn compensates for a drab script with erotic imagery: A lengthy buildup and titillating foreplay on a dance floor finally leads to consummation. Many women reportedly went to see *Claire of the Moon* because its sex scenes were steamy by the standards of mainstream cinema.

Almost diametrically opposed to Conn's tale is Rose Troche's *Go Fish* (1994), a fresh romantic comedy about contemporary lesbian lifestyles in a Chicago community. A girl-meets-girl movie with a light-hearted look at five hip lesbians, *Go Fish* became one of the most commercially successful lesbian films ever, grossing $2,421,833. Bold and innovative, *Go Fish* proved to be a breakthrough film for lesbian cinema in the same way that Spike Lee's sex comedy, *She's Gotta Have It*, was for African American directors. Refreshingly, *Go Fish* is not about coming out, nor is it burdened with the stiff, sanctimonious tone of *Claire of the Moon*. Instead, its point of departure is that women can—and do—have emotionally fulfilling lives in exclusive lesbian communities without being stigmatized by the surrounding society.

The comedy begins with Kia (T. Wendy McMillan), a black professor, speculating with her students about who might be lesbian in America. Kia, who is romantically involved with Evy (Migdalia Melendez), an Hispanic divorcée, would like Max (Guinevere Turner), her younger roommate, to meet a girl, and she sets her up with Ely (V. S. Brodie), a former student who's in the process of terminating a long-distance relationship. The story builds up to a hilarious date between Ely and Max, with their friends insisting on getting all the "dirt"—the before, during, and after. By cross-cutting between Max's and Ely's households, *Go Fish* conveys the folklore women share when there are no men around—a sort of contemporary lesbian version of Gregory La Cava's *Stage Door*, though a far cry from George Cukor's *The Women*, two Hollywood classics dominated by women.

Intimate in scale, *Go Fish* is charged with fierce intelligence about ordinary lesbians—their hopes, anxieties, romances. Troche's "healthy" approach is especially evident in her handling of her characters' sexuality. Sex in the 1990s is treated naturally, without condescension. In the most political scene, Daria, who committed a "sin" and slept with a man, is abducted by militant lesbians and subjected to a collective investigation that touches on the meaning of lesbian identity in the 1990s. A light self-mockery enhances the film's offbeat mood. With montages and dissolves, set to a swift tempo, the film judiciously intercuts the various glances—lusty, duplicitous, suspicious—exchanged by the women. *Go Fish* may have been the first film in which women look unabashedly and unapologetically like lesbians—not lipstick lesbians but women who wear no makeup, short hair, baggy pants, and unadorned T-shirts.

To subvert the prevalent clichés about lesbians, Troche demystifies sexual orientation, showing that, while they might appear strange to outsiders, "lesbians do live completely and normally ordinary lives." Troche contests the stereotypes of lesbians as essentially "straight" women, "passable" by heterosexual standards. Other debunked clichés are the notions that lesbians hate men and that lesbians always go after straight women, who in the course of the narrative discover their lesbianism. Aware that *Go Fish* might not speak to every lesbian, Troche presents a portrait "specific to a particular urban lesbian."[40] Offering an alternate lifestyle, Troche depicts women who have "healthy relationships and aren't obsessed with their place in the straight world."

Far more naive and technically raw than *Go Fish* is Maria Maggenti's *The Incredibly True Adventures of Two Girls in Love* (1995), a romantic fable celebrating the sacredness of first love. The surface is rather conventional, detailing the growing attraction between two high school seniors who stick together against all odds. Nonetheless, the overtly lesbian milieu, as well as the characters' young age, set the film apart from other lesbian stories.

Randy (Laurel Holloman), a rebellious tomboy who lives with her lesbian aunt and her aunt's lover in a working-class community, keeps a boring part-time job at her aunt's gas station. Her life changes radically when she spots Evie (Nicole Parker), a black classmate who is one of the school's most popular girls. Evie drives into the gas station to have her posh Ranger Rover checked, a few meaningful looks are exchanged—and Randy falls in love. But the experience is foreign to Evie, who's still involved with a boy.

Unlike most Hollywood fables, in which romance is depicted as glamorous and abstract, *Incredibly True Adventures* takes a simple and concrete view of the central attachment. To explore teenagers' sexuality, Maggenti employs a more nuanced language, one of tenderness and pain. Randy's and Evie's dates are recorded in dead-on, serio-comic manner, with all the awkwardness and unbearable intensity of teenage love—holding hands, the first kiss. Not much is made of the interracial dimension—race is not an issue for the girls or for their friends. Prejudice against lesbians, however, is very much at the forefront, as in a restaurant scene where Evie's straight friends desert her one by one.

Maggenti has etched two portraits of women whose sexual identities are fluid enough to change, showing a sensitive ear to the lingo spoken by teenagers when they're in love. Cluttering up the landscape, however, are subsidiary characters who are narrowly conceived— Evie's stuffy mother, a severe career woman, and a voluptuous woman who provides fake comic relief. Unpolished production values call attention to the director's lack of skills in camera placement, pacing, and framing.

Like Troche, Maggenti aims to portray lesbians in a positive but re-alistic light. "All I wanted to do was make a movie about falling in love," she said. "But I couldn't do it with a boy-girl story, because that's not my experience." *Incredibly True Adventures* is dedicated to Maggenti's first love. The sweet, innocent treatment of youths flirting and wooing each other with poetry hits universal tones, except in this film it concerns lesbians. "I didn't make a niche-market film," Maggenti contended. "It wasn't about 'Let's make a lesbian film and a bunch of lesbians will go see it.' I wanted to make a film about an authentic human experience, which happens to be with women of the same sex. When you live your life, it feels as normal as anything else."[41]

Handling sexual issues presented no problem for the tyro director, whose major challenge was "to get this film made for under $60,000, do it on 16-millimeter, and do half of my shots in one take." However, the roles did present a challenge for the lead actresses, Laurel Holloman and Nicole Parker, neither of whom is lesbian. Holloman, who plays the tomboy Randy, and Parker, as the more feminine Evie, educated them-selves by attending lesbian activities. The absence of men in the crew helped the actresses. "When you have a woman director or writer, then a woman producer will be drawn to the film, and from there other women gravitate to it," Maggenti explained. Holloman found this use-ful: "A lot of girls on the crew were like my character, so I could just look around and pick up lingo from one and behavior from another, and it made it easy to stay in character." The all-female crew freed the ac-tresses from men's gaze and made them less self-conscious.

It was only a matter of time before a woman of color made a mod-ern lesbian film. Picking up Troche's torch, Cheryl Dunye filmed *The Watermelon Woman* (1997), which revolves around a black lesbian film-maker who conducts research about the life of a 1930s actress known as "The Watermelon Woman." Poking fun at various sacred cows in Amer-ican culture, the film deconstructs the power of narrative and the own-ership of history. Like Dunye's shorts (e.g., *The Potluck and the Passion*), the film has an elliptical and circular narrative. Dunye borrows the for-mat from Jim McBride's *David Holtzman's Diary*, particularly the end-ing, when viewers realize they have been watching a fake documentary.

The director was inspired by Melvin Van Peebles's *The Watermelon Man*, about an Archie Bunker type who wakes up black one day and finds his whole life changed. Dunye was preparing a course on African American women in film when she read about Mable Hampton, Ma

Rainey, and other artists who existed on the fringe of the Harlem Renaissance and of early Hollywood. Her lead figure, Cheryl, is a constructed character who is based partly on Dunye's life. For this film, Dunye worked for the first time with a lenser, Michelle Crenshaw. Coming from the video world, where she wore twelve different hats, she found it hard to let go of duty. As she explained: "There's a certain look I get shooting by myself, a certain comfort and feel, but here, there were twenty crew people in the room."[42] Dunye was forced to give up the control and intimacy of video for the sake of better technical values.

Unexpectedly, the reaction to the film from certain members of the African American community was virulent. A *Washington Times* article noted the anger among black conservatives: "How can the NEA blaspheme the black community with this gay stuff?" someone asked, referring to a $31,500 grant Dunye received to complete the film. For Dunye, the accusation was ridiculous; she says that the humor in her film allows "everyone a space to enter," regardless of their history.

With *The Incredibly True Adventures of Two Girls in Love* and the sensitive coming-out drama *All Over Me* (1997), both of which showed at Sundance, the producer Dolly Hall asserted her central position in films documenting lesbian lifestyles in all their varied manifestations. *High Art* (1998), which Hall produced and Lisa Cholodenko directed, is set in New York's art world among a triangle of fascinating women. Cholodenko depicts with unwavering veracity the breakup of one longtime relationship just as another, unexpected one begins. The film's central axiom is that chance encounters can lead to the most momentous changes in a person's life. An intricate meditation on love, careerism, and self-sacrifice, Cholodenko's script, which won the Sundance's Waldo Salt Screenwriting Award, revolves around two women whose paths cross and whose lives change as a result of a chance meeting.

Syd (Radha Mitchell), an ambitious editor-in-training at *Frame*, an art photography magazine, is romantically involved with James (Gabriel Mann), but, clearly, something is missing from their relationship. Taking a bath one day, she notices a leak from the ceiling and goes upstairs to complain about it. Entering as an outsider, Syd observes her neighbor, Lucy Berliner (Ally Sheedy), and her friends as they go about their routines—booze, drugs, music. A once-celebrated photographer, Lucy has decided to retire in mid-career. Living with her heroin-addicted girlfriend, Greta (Patricia Clarkson), a former actress who appeared in Fassbinder's films, Lucy plays host to hard-living party kids who are stoned more often than sober. The two lived in Berlin for a while, but Greta has relocated to New York in order for Lucy to pursue her calling.

A tentative friendship soon evolves into a passionate affair, though initially, Syd and Lucy come across as opposites. Much younger, Syd strives to achieve recognition in an industry driven by hype. In contrast, Lucy is a disaffected photography prodigy who has seen it all. However, vulnerable to Syd's infatuation and her offer to let Lucy shoot the next cover of *Frame*, Lucy struggles with her present reality. Depicting the women's step-by-step friendship and transformation, *High Art* contains one of the most candidly photographed sex scenes in American films, showing the awkwardness and heat when an older experienced woman makes love to a young and insecure one.

The culture of "heroin chic" is also painstakingly dissected. The complex bond—and the inevitable conflict—among the three women embodies irony and risk. In a marvelously staged scene that is almost too painful to watch, Lucy, who has cleaned up her act, gives in to pressure from Greta to do heroin again. This silent sequence reflects the ambivalent emotions lovers feel as they must choose between protecting themselves and getting into risky situations just to prove their commitment to their companions. Impressive as Cholodenko's direction is, the film's emotional impact largely depends on its three actresses. In a major comeback, Sheedy shakes up her old screen image and emerges as a mature, disciplined actress. As her German lover, Clarkson excels in portraying an aging, disenchanted actress who is desperately clinging to Lucy and to drugs. The ravishingly beautiful Mitchell also registers strongly in her touching scenes with Sheedy.

WHAT'S A GAY FILM, ANYWAY?

In the late 1990s, a growing debate persists over the issue of what constitutes a gay or lesbian movie. Rose Troche holds that the question is unanswerable yet. A film written, directed, and edited by a lesbian will probably be a lesbian film but that's not always true. Troche's commitment is not necessarily to lesbian film, but to "films with strong female characters that women can identify with."[43] For her, it's not a matter of content; it's a matter of sensibility. But how does one define gay sensibility? Can this sensibility cross over to the mainstream?

Creating crossover audiences for distinctly gay fare is an alluring proposition. For Strand's Marcus Hu, it signals a reduced need to designate films by their director's or protagonist's sexual orientation. It also signals an increase in the opportunities afforded gay filmmakers to reach a wider public. For some, this crossing over is a natural, inevitable process; Hollywood has always appropriated subcultures. Frameline's Nancy Fishman says that the mainstreaming of gay culture is advantageous educationally; the more crossover there is, the more the general public becomes aware of gay-themed issues. And then there are those who wish to abolish altogether the gay label. "I long for the day," said Tom Kalin, "when gay subject matter doesn't need to be bracketed by saying it's a gay film. If a gay film means there is an up-front representation of a gay person, I could claim for gay history the show *Bewitched*."[44]

However, shifting genres and broadening story lines do not necessarily represent positive developments, as the stylish, utterly frivolous *Bound* (1996) shows. The only twist the writers-directors Larry and Andy Wachowski bring to *Bound*, their clichéd crime thriller, is that the crime partners are women who become lovers. Corky (Gina Gershon), a butch femme out of jail, gets involved with her neighbor Violet (Jennifer Tilly), whose boyfriend, Caesar (Joe Pantoliano), is a mob accountant. When Caesar is entrusted with mob money, Violet and Corky scheme to abscond with it. Of course, things go awry, and the two are forced to improvise a way out. Told from Corky's libidinous point of view, the film drips with cheap eroticism, fancy Coen brothers camera tricks, and graphic Tarantino-like violence, but it has little, if anything, to do with lesbian cinema.

The real issue is not so much explicit gay content as gay sensibility, the "gay look"—how gays and lesbians perceive and dissect Hollywood movies, how they read films against the grain, looking for meanings not just in the text but in the subtext. In the documentary *The Celluloid Closet*, the writer Paul Rudnick (*Jeffrey*) deconstructs the campy gym scene in *Gentlemen Prefer Blondes*, where Jane Russell is surrounded by gorgeous men but is totally ignored by them. Gay men have always interpreted the scene as camp, whether or not it was originally intended as such by the filmmaker, Howard Hawks.

REREADING FILM HISTORY—MARC RAPPAPORT

A distinctly gay sensibility characterized the 1970s work of John Waters, and it is also the signature, twenty years later, of the films of Marc Rappaport, a pop sociologist who has made fictional film biographies his specialized genre. Rappaport's meditations on life, art, and Hollywood have defied the conventions of public TV's earnest docudramas as well as those of Hollywood's more conventional biopictures. His work represents a shrewd blend of fiction, biography, and cultural analysis, as he looks with detached cynicism at movies. Rappaport's perceptive explorations regard pop culture as an embattled field open to deconstruction and to multiple, contradictory readings.

In the late 1980s, Rappaport came down with chronic fatigue syndrome. Since going on location became impossible for him, he had "to reinvent" himself. Making fictional biographies became the solution. Rappaport discovered the world of videotape, which made it possible to make movies much less expensively. Influenced by Godard's *Histoire(s) du Cinéma*, a personal film-essay-like history told from a specific perspective, Rappaport reexamines American film with a critical theory that "puts everything up for grabs." This strategy resulted in two fascinating film meditations, *Rock Hudson's Home Videos* (1992) and *From the Journals of Jean Seberg* (1995).

In the savvy compilation *Rock Hudson's Home Movies*, the actor Eric Farr poses beside cutouts of Rock Hudson and supplies the late actor's inner voice. "Who can look at my movies the same way ever again?" the fictional Rock says. Hudson's films come under a caustic gaze that dissects the latent content of his screen persona. Rappaport's central assertion is that the star's hidden homosexuality was an open secret and that his romantic, leading-man image always had a sly, knowing side to it. "It's not like it wasn't up there on the screen, if you watched carefully," Rock says. Showing the actor's split personality—"Dr. Macho Jekyll and Mr. Homo Hyde"—Rappaport uses Hudson's own words, culled from various biographies, to construct the persona of a celebrity liberated by death.

Innocent-seeming situations and relationships between Hudson and his leading ladies are revisited with new interpretations that expose their repressive conventions. "I haven't any wife," Hudson's hero explains to Elizabeth Taylor in *Giant*. "I live with my sister." And when

Doris Day asks why he can't marry, he replies that "it's the kind of thing a man doesn't discuss with a nice woman." In *Written on the Wind*, a sultry Dorothy Malone eyes Hudson knowingly, then says, "There's only so much a woman can do, and no more."

Rappaport begins with Hudson's infatuation with the actor Jon Hall (*Hurricane*), followed by his Douglas Sirk melodramas and the comedies with Doris Day and Tony Randall. Says the fictional Rock of Randall, "Such a preening, prissy, neurotic nerd, my sexuality is never called into question." Scenes in Hudson's movies show him engaged in stereotypically gay behavior in order to fool Doris Day into thinking he is no lady-killer—"doing my shy homo routine to get Doris to seduce me." Several characters played by Hudson were devoted to their mothers and showed interest in recipes and cooking.

Rappaport surveys Hudson from his big-screen Don Juan image to his AIDS patient real life in the 1980s. He starts with the knowledge of a lie—the heterosexual image Hudson embodied in 1950s movies—and proceeds to deconstruct their farcical plots. As the critic Armond White observed, Rappaport undermines their premises through inference, implication, and innuendo that make his cleverly selected clips more than hagiography.[45] A remarkable sequence of interrupted kisses between Hudson and his leading ladies (Lauren Bacall, Doris Day, Cyd Charisse, Angie Dickinson, Dorothy Malone) shows Hudson's face registering disgust.

Rappaport's homage represents an exchange between the cultural heritage that defines the fabric of American dreams and a postmodern consciousness that feels compelled to deride them. Farr's narration maintains the distance between the charade that created a "heterosexual" idol and the truth about a successful actor forced to deny his true self. The result is a more objective inspection, imbued with ambivalence toward an embarrassed artist.[46] Indeed, it's no longer possible to watch *Pillow Talk*, or any Hudson film, as just a simple, entertaining comedy, without bringing to it knowledge of his homosexuality; audiences will never be that innocent again.

When Rappaport cast Mary Beth Hurt as Jean Seberg in *From the Journals of Jean Seberg*, he didn't know that she was born in Seberg's own town, Marshmallows, Iowa. He then learned that Seberg was Hurt's babysitter and that their families were friends. In close-cropped hair and a T-shirt similar to the one Seberg made famous in *Breathless*, Hurt narrates the film in an effort to explore the meaning of the star's life. A girl with an accent as flat as her town's fields (and with acting ability to match), Seberg was plucked out of a pool of 18,000 hopefuls and groomed for stardom. Whether it was luck or coincidence, Seberg appeared in some interesting films: *Saint Joan, Bonjour Tristesse, Breathless*. But Seberg never caught up to her stardom, which she herself perceived as unwarranted.

"It's called show business," says Hurt in her narration. "It's not called show art," as she identifies Hollywood as a treacherous place for its front-line practitioners, the actors. As numerous beautiful stars have been degraded on-screen by their filmmaker-husbands, Rappaport throws into the mix Jane Fonda and Vanessa Redgrave, contemporaries of Seberg who, like her, began in bimbo parts in films directed by their spouses. All three actresses became political activists; Fonda and Redgrave survived, while Seberg did not. Seberg's career curse began with Otto Preminger's *Saint Joan*, which has developed an afterlife among film cognoscenti. While shooting the climactic burning-at-the-stake scene, the actress caught fire, and the notoriously sadistic director was apparently thrilled with the cinema verité accident.

Hudson's life derailed with his death of AIDS at age fifty-nine; Seberg's ended with her suicide at age forty. In fairly convincing fashion, Rappaport finds premonitions of both tragic endings early in their lives. Seberg's support of the Black Panthers made her prey to investigations by J. Edgar Hoover (the FBI director had a vendetta against the Panthers), which at least partly caused her downward spiral and her suicide in a car parked on a street in Paris.

The Mexican novelist Carlos Fuentes, who wrote *Diana: The Goddess Who Hunts Alone*, a fictionalized account of his affair with Seberg, thinks Rappaport's films are more illuminating than documentaries: "Fiction is closer to life, because it realizes that life is full of paradoxes. This is a work of imagination about a ghost. A dead woman is speaking, and how do you speak from the grave?"[47] Rejecting the notion of "sacrosanct biography," Rappaport is unapologetic about putting personal thoughts into the narration. Asked where he had found Seberg's journals, he wittily said, "The same place where Charles Dickens found David Copperfield's." For him, biography is not about fact but is "a collection of what you found, or didn't find out, and how you put together what you found out." Rappaport allows that viewers may question his interpretation of the events, but they can't question his "evidence"—the film clips themselves.

NEW DIRECTIONS

Some of the brilliant directors who began their careers with gay-themed movies have moved on to other themes or have expanded their range in different directions. Todd Haynes's follow-ups to *Poison* were the deconstructive woman's drama *Safe* (see Chapter 8) and the innovative musical *Velvet Goldmine* (1998). Gus Van Sant failed with his screen adaptation of Tom Robbins's 1970s novel, *Even Cowgirls Get the Blues* (1993), then rebounded with the black comedy *To Die For* (1995) and the Oscar-winning *Good Will Hunting* (1997), which became Miramax's most popular film to date.

A mean-spirited comedy, told in a mock-tabloid fashion, *To Die For* traces the rise and fall of Suzanne Stone (Nicole Kidman), an ambitious small-town girl obsessed with becoming a TV star. Unhappily married to a dim restauranteur, Larry Maretto (Matt Dillon), she sleeps with a network exec (George Segal) and gets promoted to the weather spot at her local station. Feeling entrapped by her husband's desire for children, Suzanne involves some innocent teenagers in a scheme to kill him. Whether priming for the camera or pondering reality ("Everything is part of a big master plan"), Suzanne shows herself to be sly, flirtatious, and amoral. Her TV-age narcissistic philosophy is simple: "What's the point of doing anything worthwhile if no one is watching?" As John Powers has noted, Suzanne is a peculiarly American monster who can transform anything, even murder, into what she calls "a learning experience."[48]

As a send-up of media madness, the film disappointed Van Sant's devotees, who expected something fresher and wilder than yet another spoof of tabloid culture. As Powers observed, "For all its hilarious moments, the picture feels slightly desperate, as if the filmmakers were trying to fatten up a satire that's not outrageous enough to compete with pictures like *Natural Born Killers*, let alone the reality of Kato Kaelin, John Wayne Bobbitt, and all those lunatic statues of Michael Jackson."

True to his instincts, however, Van Sant shows sympathy for the alienated teenagers, finding something beautiful in the forlorn isolation of the pudgy Lydia (Alison Folland) and in Jimmy's (Joachim Phoenix) reckless love for Suzanne, which he explains by references to the zombies in *The Night of the Living Dead*. Despite their indifferent parents and a trashy culture, Van Sant's working-class youths still have the capacity to feel—in contrast to Araki's in *The Doom Generation* and *Nowhere*.

Who would have thought that Araki, the guerrilla filmmaker who made small, modest pictures, could work on a grand visual scale, given the proper budget? *The Doom Generation* (1995) and *Nowhere* (1997) are visually dazzling apocalyptic journeys into the unknown—America's netherlands. While the technical level is new, both movies continue to explore a quintessential Araki issue: the nihilism of alienated youth. Both works contain the ingredients of hot midnight movies (which they never became): steamy sex, macabre violence, absurdist humor, boisterous music, and flamboyant art design.

Depicting a society that has lost its moral center, *Doom Generation* reflects the subculture of the "Lollapalooza Generation," cool American youngsters who grew up on MTV, junk food, and chaos. Its central trio consists of the spoiled Amy Blue (Rose McGowan), her sweet, suburban boyfriend Jordan White (James Duval), and a mysterious drifter, Xavier Red (Johnathon Schaech). After blowing off the head of a QuickieMart clerk, they embark on an outlandish journey that gets darker and darker. What unites these freefloating souls is their refusal to be defined by sexual orientation—or any conventional morality; their changing relationships know no rules or boundaries. Araki's nonjudgmental treatment reinforces the thesis that his youngsters are more amoral than immoral.

A product of dull middle-class suburbia, Jordan is naively romantic. As his princess, Amy is a modern Lolita with a touch of Bonnie Parker. Xavier is driven by insatiable libido; if he can't get laid, voyeuristic masturbation will do. Violence comes naturally to him—it's a running joke that whenever they stop for fries and drinks, someone ends up getting killed, each time in a more ghastly way, as when amputated arms fly through the air. Although *Doom Generation* is Araki's first film not specifically situated in a gay milieu, its homoerotic imagery is unmistakable. Araki's road comedy is hallucinatory and psychedelic in a style that recalls *Natural Born Killers*, but, unlike Oliver Stone's obvious satire, Araki's is more ambiguous. Shying away from moralizing, he refuses to tidy things up in the last reel.

Nowhere, the final installment of Araki's "Teen Apocalypse" trilogy (which began with *Totally F***ed Up*), is also a vibrantly colorful, wildly nihilistic poem to America's libidinous youth. Style and contents are inseparable here. Thematically, the picture has nothing new to offer, but visually it shows Araki's growing fascination with surrealism. *Nowhere* is like a fast-forwarded, hallucinatory *Beverly Hills 90210*. Spanning one zany day, the film surveys the emotional and sexual turmoil experienced by a multiracial, pansexual clique of adolescents. Situating his yarn in John Hughes' teen-angst turf (*Sixteen Candles*, *The Breakfast Club*), Araki's teenagers are hurtling through pubescent insecurity, a quest for true love, and the highs of sexual discovery. James Duval, the center of Araki's "Teen Apocalypse" trilogy, plays "Everyteen" Dark Smith, a youngster obsessed with "the End of the World" and finding love before it's too late. He loves Mel (Rachel True), who can't commit to one person—or gender—and who is attracted to an acid-tongued girl named Lucifer.

Araki conveys the extremities of youth, the notion that everything is accentuated, a matter of life and death. The tone shifts from rapturous exultation to melancholy and despair; yet, for all the careening action, *Nowhere* never loses sight of its central issue—alienation. At heart, Araki has always been a surrealist, and now that he has financial backing—and the technical skills to match—he lets his imagination run wild. Araki's universe has increasingly become anarchic, with no stable identities or fixed sexual orientations. As always, the point of reference is mainstream culture, as defined by TV shows like *Melrose Place*. Steeped in hip visual and aural codes, *Nowhere* is Araki's tribute to an ever-changing pop culture, equally informed by Annie Leibovitz's photos of John Lennon and Yoko Ono and the violent fury of comic strips. However, since he has lost his core gay audience, it's impossible to predict Araki's future as a filmmaker.

Also moving in a new direction is Christopher Munch, whose *Color of a Brisk and Leaping Day* (1996) was an eloquent tribute to the obsession of one man to revive the defunct Yosemite Valley Railroad. At the end of World War II, a Chinese-American man, John Lee (Peter Alexander), who works at repairing trolley cars, breaks with his family over his singleminded determination to revive service on the YVR, a seventy-eight-mile line that is scheduled to be scrapped. He secures backing from a financier to run the railroad for a year, a heroic mission that is inevitably doomed due to the rising popularity of cars. Lee's Chinese grandfather, who came over to lay track, provides a personal tie to railway history. Forced to carry the banner alone, Lee is consumed with passion to realize his dream. With a minimalist, undernourished script, stilted dialogue, and ambiguous sexuality, Munch exalts but doesn't illuminate Lee's fervor. Lavishly shot in black and white by Rob Sweeney, in a style that suggests Ansel Adams's photographs, the movie fails to register the excitement that must have informed its protagonist's zeal.

THE NEW GAY IMAGES

For more than a decade, independent movies were far ahead of the mainstream in dealing with gay characters However, in the late 1990s, Hollywood finally began to take notice of the new gay lifestyles, which resulted in movies that propagated a revised gay image. Gays are no longer portrayed as "tortured perverts" or "diseased victims," and films have moved away from "swishy queen humor" (*The Adventures of Priscilla, Queen of the Desert, The Birdcage*) to more substantive dramas.

At present, gays are more likely to be cast as "charming, lovable, playful, emotionally accessible, vulnerable, and unapologetic."[49] Fox's *The Object of My Affection*, Lifetime's *Labor of Love*, and last year's popular comedies, *My Best Friend's Wedding*, and *In and Out*, all feature gay characters who are handsome, masculine—and center stage. A new gay "type" has emerged—the best friend next door, likely to be played by the British actor Rupert Everett. Despite the changes, these films have been criticized, specifically for their refusal to recognize gay parenthood and for their avoidance of detailing the sexual lives of their gay characters. In *The Deep End of the Ocean*, Whoopi Goldberg plays an openly lesbian detective, but she is not given any private or sexual life.

To be sure, there are still missteps and reactionary moves. The critic Larry Kramer argues that Hollywood still dilutes the diverse images of gay men. A case in point is Greg Kinnear's gay man in *As Good As It Gets*, which Kramer labels a "total joke, a total victim," and Kevin Kline's "one-dimensional cartoon" in *In and Out*. By and large, however, it seems that mainstream America is finally realizing that "family units are no longer defined by blood ties, marriage, or heterosexuality." Family is no longer an "obscene" word for gay men, per Ron Nyswaner (who scripted *Philadelphia*), but even Nyswaner looks forward to a time when gay characters are the lead, "and nothing with the 'h' word is mentioned throughout the entire movie."[50]

The mid- to late 1990s also saw new trends in indie filmmaking, including a decline in AIDS dramas and a corresponding rise in serio-comedies about the subject.

Richard Glatzer's *Grief* (1994), a modest AIDS comedy-drama, was based on Glatzer's personal experience as producer of *Divorce Court*. Jo (played by Jackie Beat, known as Kent Fuher), a producer of a TV show called *Love Court*, runs his office like a tyrannical earth mother, a stance that is needed in view of the sexual games that go on there. Mark (Craig Chester), one of the show's writers, commemorates the first anniversary of his lover's death (the film is dedicated to Glatzer's lover, who died of AIDS), but both he and his college friend Jeremy are attracted to the sexually ambiguous Bill (a miscast Alexis Arquette), who might get back with his girlfriend. Despite the rich emotional and comic possibilities, *Grief* is a bit dull and its dialogue strained. Jo's heterosexual assistant (Ileana Douglas) brings some humor, but the movie fails to wring more laughter from the *Love Court* plots, summarized in shorthand (e.g., "circus lesbians"). Still, Glatzer's humanistic message—that these coworkers function as an intimate group—comes across.

Christopher Ashley's *Jeffrey* (1995) tested the grounds for a gay screwball comedy about AIDS, in which the characters' sexuality is a given—outfront, unapologetic, and exuberant. According to the screenwriter Paul Rudnick, the studios were apprehensive—"a comedy about AIDS, no thank you"—and offers failed to materialize.[51] The title character (Steven Weber) is an aspiring, cheerfully oversexed actor, who decides to put his sex life on hold because "sex wasn't meant to be safe or negotiated or fatal." AIDS has forced him to believe that emotional contact carries with it the heartbreak of losing someone. But as soon as Jeffrey makes his celibate vow, he meets Steve (Michael T. Weiss), a hunk who's HIV-positive. What's a handsome boy to do?

There's plenty of kissing within the film's first minutes, reflecting the guiding philosophy of *Parting Glances*. "We wanted to get it out of the way," said Rudnick, "so that the audience would realize that *Jeffrey* is not about some kind of shocking revelation. People have been so programmed to expect gay film to be about soap opera and nobility in hospital rooms. *Jeffrey* is not about that." The subjects of homosexuality and AIDS are treated in a hip, campy style.

Composed of vignettes, *Jeffrey* explores the "adventures" of droll gay men: Sterling (Patrick Stewart), a wise-cracking interior decorator, and his boyfriend Darius (Bryan Batt), a dancer in the Broadway musical *Cats*. Other characters are just as eccentric: a proud Mafia princess (Olympia Dukakis) who's the mother of a "preoperative transsexual lesbian," and a bullying, double-talking evangelist (Sigourney Weaver).

Famous actors—Weber (*Wings*), Stewart (*Star Trek: The Next Generation*), Weaver (the *Alien* movies), Dukakis (*Moonstruck*)—were cast to minimize the commercial risk and to enhance the movie's appeal, but despite decent reviews, the movie didn't cross over.

Also failing to cross over was *Love! Valour! Compassion!* (1997), based on Terrence McNally's play about gay life in the AIDS era. Although sharply written, the movie barely overcame the material's theatrical sensibility and Joe Mantello's static direction. McNally's forte, as is evident in his other screen adaptations (*The Ritz* and *Frankie and Johnny*, neither an exciting movie) is writing witty dialogue that reflects the unique lifestyles of his protagonists. As in *Longtime Companion*, all the characters are gay men, and the humor is pertinent to their subculture. McNally contents himself with examining white, upper-middle-class men, structuring his work around three long weekends—Memorial Day, the Fourth of July, and Labor Day—as eight men gather in a country house to share painfully candid moments, dominated by their fear of AIDS.

Most of the characters are coupled: The host, Gregory (Stephen Bogardus), an aging dancer, lives with his younger, blind lover Bobby (Justin Kirk), and John (John Clover), a nasty, hateful Briton, arrives with his flame, a Hispanic hunk, Ramon (Randy Becker). Longtime companions Arthur (John Benjamin Hickey) and Perry (Stephen Spinella), an accountant and lawyer, represent the "straight" yuppies. Presiding over the group with sharp tongue is musical buff Buzz (Jason Alexander), a chubby HIV-positive scared of dying alone. Tensions are provided by two outsiders, Ramon and Bobby, whose sexual encounter forces their partners to reassess their relationships. In its good moments, *Love! Valour! Compassion!* recalls the hilarious exchanges in a Noel Coward comedy, the achingly intimate revelations in a Chekhov play, the wistful playfulness in a Sondheim musical. In its bad ones, such as the sequence in which men disclose in first-person narration their eventual deaths, the film betrays its theatrical roots.

CONCLUSION: NEW VOICES IN GAY CINEMA

Borrowing conventions from classic Hollywood cinema and applying them to specifically gay locales has characterized gay films of the late 1990s. After a whole decade in which the most impressive gay films dealt with AIDS and other serious issues, a new cohort of filmmakers seems committed to expanding the range of gay films with light comedies, satires, and farces.

Tony Vitale's *Kiss Me Guido* (1997), a farce in the mode of *Desperately Seeking Susan*, plays gay and Italian-American stereotypes against one another. The opening scene sets up the great divide between the two subcultures, represented by sexy pizza-parlor worker Frankie (ex-model Nick Scotti), and a gay stage director, Warren (Anthony Barrile). They end up as roommates, as a result of a misunderstanding; Frankie naively believes that "GWM" in a *Village Voice* ad means "Guy with Money." The whole point of this rather schematic film was to show that gays and straights can be friends.

Sexual orientation has become such a determining factor in American life that it's rare to see nonjudgmental films in which gays, lesbians, and heteros coexist in the same universe. P. J. Castellaneta's *Relax, It's Just Sex* (1998) is such a film, a romantic comedy about the various dimensions of sex: as physical pleasure, as expression of love, as avenue to new life, but also as transmitter of AIDS. For structure, Castellaneta draws on Arthur Schnitzler's classic *La Ronde*. Addressing the camera directly, each person begins to tell a story that involves another, a strategy that allows the action to switch among multiple locales and to link all of the characters in a close-knit web.

In the first scene, a solemn voiceover depicts a "lipstick" lesbian couple and a "gym" gay couple, demonstrating a friendly, nonthreatening embrace. This is controverted in the next scene, which shows protagonist Vincey engaged in steamy anal and oral sex. A transition leads to the fag hag Tara (Jennifer Tilly), a gossipy mother hen who's busy preparing a Friday dinner party for her friends. The evening's joyous mood is interrupted by the news that one of the friends is HIV-positive and by a provocative assertion from a black artist that AIDS is just a conspiracy. Not neglecting the women, there's the white Megan and her black lover Sarina, a long-enduring couple that breaks up when Megan confesses to an affair with Sarina's male cousin. Waiting in the wings is Robin, who offers Sarina the kind of love she has never had with Megan.

Changing the tone from the comic to the serious, the central sequence involves a gay-bashing attack on Vincey and his retaliation, when he rapes his attacker in front of his utterly shocked comrades. Vincey's act splits the group sharply, but reconciliation is achieved in the name of friendship, a value that's beautifully celebrated in the coda.

Also pointing to a new direction is Tommy O'Haver's *Billy's Hollywood Screen Kiss* (1998), a light romantic comedy about a self-absorbed gay photographer (Sean P. Hayes) who arrives in Los Angeles in search for love and success. For his project, Billy chooses to recreate famous movie love scenes with drag queens; a drag group lipsyncs old songs as bridges among the film's sequences. Billy is frustrated by his career and his love life (he shares a Hispanic lover with another man) until he meets Gabriel (Brad Rowe), a handsome waiter who is conflicted about his sexual identity. Utterly transfixed, Billy begins an obsessive pursuit.

Heralding a new age in gay cinema, the lead in Billy's *Hollywood Screen Kiss* is meant to be Everyman, as O'Haver said, "I wanted people to forget that this is a gay man—it could be anyone."[52] As a love story, the movie takes the prototype of 1950s women's melodramas and applies it to gay men in the 1990s. No big issues to tackle, no self-loathing, just a regular guy looking for love—just as Sandra Dee and Doris Day did in the 1950s. Thematically, O'Haver is inspired by William Wyler's *The Heiress*, in which the audience couldn't tell whether or not Montgomery Clift really loved the unattractive heroine until the very end. There's one difference, though: Billy does get his Hollywood screen kiss at the end from a mysterious stranger. O'Haver shot his film in CinemaScope, with musical numbers, wild parties, and dream sequences soaked in the bold colors of pink and red. At once a witty homage to screen romance and a celebration of an ever-present gay sensibility, *Billy's Hollywood Screen Kiss* lives up to its subtitle, *A Tommy O'Haver Trifle*.

Jim Fall's *Trick* (1999), an appealing gay date movie, is similar but superior to *Billy's Hollywood Screen Kiss*. This emotionally true film belongs to a new cycle (it's premature to call it a genre) of gay movies that are not about social issues but deal with universal situations (dating, first love) relevant to everyone, regardless of sexual orientation. In structure, scriptwriter Jason Schafer's romantic tale recalls classic screwball comedies, detailing the (mis)adventures of a newly formed couple during one long, frustrating night. The premise is quite simple: Two boys, infatuated with each other, are desperate to find a place to consummate their passion.

Gabriel (Christian Campbell) is a young musical composer whose romantic life leaves a lot to be desired. Like many aspiring artists, he keeps a day job, but whenever possible he rehearses his play over the phone with his best friend, Katherine, who is a struggling actress. After hearing a song from Gab's musical, his friend Perry feels that something is missing—it's too bland, too cautious—which Perry believes reflect's Gab's barren life. Taking action, Gab heads out to the local gay bar, where he is struck by the sight of a gorgeous go-go boy, Mark (John Paul Pitoc). Enraptured, but not courageous enough to approach Mark, Gab leaves, but as fate would have it, he encounters Mark at the subway station. It feels like the perfect one-night stand, except they have no place to go.

Following generic conventions, the filmmakers pile up barriers so that Gab and Mark will not consummate their burning desire. Obstacles are presented by the insensitive Katherine who's in Gab's apartment printing out her résumé, and Gab's roommate's refusal to leave their flat because he's having sex with a new flame. In one of the film's most poignant scenes, Gab and Mark find themselves in an empty public restroom, where they can kiss. But, alas, it doesn't feel right. The story progresses toward its upbeat, emotionally satisfying denouement, in which a smiling Gab walks down the street with Mark's phone number in his hand. It's a scene that felicitously recalls Giulietta Masina's walk at the end of *Nights of Cabiria* and Holly Hunter's in *Living Out Loud*.

The wedding film, a staple of American comedies, has returned in the form of stories about gay men who wish but are unable to get married legally. Brian Sloan's *I Think I Do* (1998) is a screwball comedy of manners with a current, more complex sexual politics. Sloan thought that "it would be really fun to take the wedding film premise and all its stock characters and plug in more modern situations—not just by having the gay couple be the focus, but also by treating the wedding movie in a different way."[53] The novelty is that the narrative is just as concerned with the friends in the seats as with the couple at the altar. True to the screwball format, the tale unfolds during one tumultuous weekend when all hell breaks loose. Making a shift in gay films away from activist queer cinema toward a lighter fare, *I Think I Do* is based on the assumption that comedy is still one of the most subversive genres.

Don Roos, the gifted filmmaker of *The Opposite of Sex* (1998), has built a reputation as a screenwriter specializing in female characters (*Love Field*, *Boys on the Side*). The openly gay Roos unflinchingly throws himself into political incorrectness. "I can tolerate a lot of ugly behavior," Roos said, recalling how he learned early on to use a quick wit in dealing with adversity because he couldn't beat anybody up as a kid. "He doesn't have negative issues with women," noted Lisa Kudrow, who appears in *The Opposite of Sex*. "He doesn't play the gender roles."[54]

The film's (anti)heroine, Dedee (Christina Ricci), is a preternaturally tough adolescent who runs away from home and insinuates herself into the life of her gay half-brother, Bill (Martin Donovan), and his lover, Matt (Ivan Sergei). As the acid-tongued narrator and teen fatale, Ricci sports a blond bob, pouty red lips and deep cleavage. From the start, Bill's pals recognize Dedee as a threat, but he remains clueless until the nymphette has seduced Matt, becomes visibly pregnant, run away with Bill's savings, and jeopardized his teaching job. All the characters are trapped in emotional binds, which provide prime pickings for the conniving Dedee. Rather than writing a morality tale, Roos opts for a dark comedy with an honest take on sex. *The Opposite of Sex* serves up murder, unwanted pregnancy, and other problems—all undercut by Dedee's offensive asides. Dedee's voiceover narration puts an ironic spin on serious themes. "If you think I'm just plucky and scrappy and all I need is love, you're in over your head. I don't have a heart of gold, and I don't grow one later," she tells the audience irreverently.

"I am certainly not one of those angry queer filmmakers directing a movie about hustling on Santa Monica Boulevard," Roos told *Premiere*.[55] "I don't have a particularly grim worldview." Roos describes himself as a "bridge" filmmaker who crosses the divide between gays and straights: "I want to make sure that we are all living in the same world." *The Opposite of Sex* gives each character—straight or gay, repressed or promiscuous—an epiphany about sex. Roos is a rude Woody Allen for the 1990s, without the fake bravado of David O. Russell, whose work is also inspired by Allen. *The Opposite of Sex* ends with a homage to *Annie Hall*, with Roos as the gay Woody Allen. Representing a new, inclusive front among indies, Roos is not interested "in being everybody's cup of tea," because that would make his writing "awfully watered down." *The Opposite of Sex* covers broad enough bases to give audiences of diverse orientations something to relate to, which explains its commercial success.

Conclusion: Independent Film Now

INDEPENDENT FILM CONTINUES to be a hot media topic, as evidenced by *Entertainment Weekly*'s indie film supplement and the *New York Times* Sunday magazine's "Two Hollywoods" issue, both of which appeared in November 1997. The buzz word in Hollywood of the 1990s is "independent": Gifted first-time filmmakers are courted by distributed, fêted by mainstream critics, and invited to direct bigger-budget studio movies. Clearly, indies are no flavor of the month; they're here to stay.

Around the globe, too, American indies have become more visible. In the 1998 Cannes Film Festival, four indies but no studio movies competed for the Palme d'Or: Hal Hartley's *Henry Fool*, Todd Haynes' *Velvet Goldmine*, John Turturro's *Illuminata*, and Lodge Kerrigan's *Claire Dolan*. Two of these were singled out by the jury: *Velvet Goldmine* for artistic achievement and *Henry Fool* for writing. In the same year, two of the highlights of the Directors' Fortnight in Cannes were *High Art* and *Slam*, which snagged the Caméra d'Or.

While there's no doubt that independent films have arrived, questions persist about how much they have changed, in what direction, and to what effect. Prominence has brought significant changes in the indies' structure and operation. Risks are involved in the independents' newfound affluence: Critics warn that the deeper pockets of some distributors are causing indie filmmakers to make the same bland movies—and inflationary mistakes—as the majors. Observers are concerned about the extent to which American indies represent a true alternative to the mainstream, the extent to which they challenge the status quo.

As I have shown, it's easier to determine what the American independent cinema is not than what it is. Most American indies of the past decade have steered clear of the avant-garde, the experimental, and the underground. True art films tend to challenge assumptions and shake

494

up established views, but most indies have functioned as soothing entertainment, reaffirming rather than questioning basic values. At the same time, if it's hard to define the narrative or aesthetic edge in indies today, it's because independent cinema is not a unified phenomenon. It never was. "It's diversity, by definition," says Sundance's codirector Geoffrey Gilmore. "It's not a simplistic ideological vision—American ideology is confused, and it shows up in the film."[1] But diversity and confusion do not denote the same thing, and both concepts can be applied to Hollywood as well.

Movies have always conjured an aura of power, glamour, and mystique, but in the 1990s, a moviemaking career has become more alluring than ever before. "The change from when I was in film school in the 1980s is monstrous," observed David O. Russell (*Flirting with Disaster*).[2] "In the 1990s, kids can tell their parents they want to go to film school and their parents will happily pay for it, imagining—like law school or medical school—there is a guaranteed career on the other side." In 1980, 35 percent of all first-time studio directors were film-school graduates. By 1997, the percentage had jumped to 80. That year, *M* magazine ran a cover story featuring Martin Scorsese, an NYU alumnus, and labeling a film degree the MBA of the 1990s.

In the 1990s, hype dominates both Hollywood and indiewood. Year after year, there are success stories of young directors coming "out of nowhere" with an original film. A filmmaker like Robert Rodriguez, with his $7,000 *El Mariachi*, can achieve today a much higher and faster profile—including the benefits of an influential agent and a studio deal—than he could have a decade ago. The quintessential 1990s American auteur is Tarantino, who has made personal yet commercially entertaining movies. Tarantino's artistic expression is fully bound up with the celebrity machine. A showman quickly cashing in on an image, he celebrated his meteoric rise as Hollywood's latest artistic genius with promotion on talk shows and guest-hosting on Saturday Night Live.[3]

The frenzy created by Tarantino's appearance at the British National Film Theatre (NFT) for an on-stage interview was beyond parallel. For a seating capacity of 450, there were no fewer than 3,000 applications. The British adulation of Tarantino was not confined to the NFT, but was also evident at bookstores where he signed his screenplays. "There was complete hysteria, no one could recall a similar response to a guest celebrity in recent years, including Robert Redford and Warren Beatty," said Brian Robinson, NFT's spokesman.[4] "Tarantino touches a nerve of popular taste in this country. Directors don't get mobbed often, but Tarantino's broken the mold—he's become almost like a rock star."

It's easier and cheaper to make indies today than ever before. Financing is available from a variety of sources: presales, limited partnerships, personal loans, and private investors. Low-budget movies such as *Laws of Gravity, El Mariachi, Clerks,* and *In the Company of Men,* have made a virtue out of their limitations, surmounting financial deficiencies with great ingenuity. As no-budget features, they have inspired young filmmakers to use models that didn't exist in the past.

One thing is beyond doubt: Indie film production has reached outstanding proportions. The number of submissions to the 1998 Sundance Film Festival has doubled since the early 1990s; over 500 films were submitted for the 16 slots in the dramatic competition alone. Slamdance's executive director, Peter Baxter, reported that submissions to the 1999 festival reached an unprecedented number of 1,716 films (500 more than the year before).

This huge volume may explain the phenomenon of "festival explosion." Almost every big city in the United States has its own film festival. Along with the prestigious, acquisition-heavy festivals like Sundance and Toronto there are regional festivals that showcase local work and provide launches for specialty films before their theatrical release. Even a town like Nantucket has a film festival, one guided by a mission to promote the screenwriter (rather than the director) within the filmmaking process.

Nowadays, fledgling filmmakers, faced with rejection from competitive festivals, have choices. They can enter the Reject Filmfest, a Philadelphia event whose primary entry requirement is that pictures have been rejected by every other festival to which they have been submitted.[5] Denied entry into the 1997 Philadelphia film Festival, D. Mason Bendewald and Don Argott took matters into their hands and began a new forum, the Reject, whose 1998 edition screened 100 features and shorts. Bendewald is not worried about lack of interest from distributors, claiming that his chief interest is in "just getting films shown." But Reject is not above rejection itself. Being competitive inevitably means that some submissions will be excluded, and there is a good possibility that those rejectees will go on to create their own venue.

With all the criticism that it attracts, Sundance is still the leader of the pack. Sundance has worked outside the system to change the system. Robert Redford insists that the festival became a market "in spite of itself."[6] And while he professes mixed feelings about his operation, he holds that at its core, Sundance hasn't changed—it's still about the films.

Others, however, see Sundance as a place where hopeful filmmakers seek the "big break," using their films as calling cards, audition pieces for mainstream Hollywood. David Denby has described the 1999 Sundance festival as a "mix of naivete and sophistication, purity and salesmanship."[7] For Denby, the festival represents a peculiar combination of trends: "On the one hand, Sundance is devoted to low-budget and independently made movies; on the other, it has become, after Cannes, the most important film market in the world, a place crawling with publicists, agents, producers, distributors, all whirling about in an ecstasy of advanced communication."

Fluctuations in the nature and quality of indie production are reflected in Sundance's dramatic competition. While 1988 was one of the worst years in its history, with *Heat and Sunlight* winning the grand jury prize, the following year was one of the best. Sundance's strongest editions are always remembered for one or two films: *sex, lies, and videotape* and *True Love* in 1989, *Reservoir Dogs* and *The Hours and Times* in 1992, *Clerks* and *Go Fish* in 1994, *In the Company of Men* in 1997. The 1998 festival was abundant in quality and variety, with compelling films like π, *Slam*, and *High Art*, which were distinguished not so much by style as by poignant narratives that were about something other than moviemaking or violence.

Over the years, Sundance has helped to create a mainstream independent cinema. "One of the festival's objectives was to build a platform for independents, help legitimate it for theatrical release," says programmer Geoffrey Gilmore.[8] The terrain of the festival is an in-between space that's "not entirely outside commercial determination, but not directly commodified." Hence Sundance's role as the chief gatekeeper for American film culture. For Gilmore, independent film still has its roots in storytelling, in regional work about people the studios deem unworthy of attention. But artistic creativity seems to be in decline. Now independent film is judged by its commercial success, not by its aesthetic daring or narrative quality. The synergy between the film's release and the other ancillary products has become more critical, with the potential for toy lines being more important than whether or not a story is memorable.

The Independent Feature Film Market (IFFM) has also changed in the two decades of its operation. As Sony Classics' Michael Barker observed: "In the early years, the prime reasons buyers like Sony went to the Market was to find a specific film to buy—now that's only a small part of it. A major part of it is discussing talent that will be important for us in the future."[9] Indeed, Sony Classics and other distributors (e.g., October and Fine Line) have expanded their activities to include production, not just picking up movies made by other companies.

The director Mark Rappaport concurs that the IFFM did not use to be the kind of feeding frenzy it is now:

> People didn't have to take their badges off so nobody would recognize them. American companies didn't attend then—they just didn't take it seriously. But people also did not expect to have their careers made or broken as a result of the IFFM in those days. It's very different now, like "I've got to get discovered. I've got to get Miramax to pick this film up and make my career." Independent film was not this thing that everybody either wanted to be part of or escape from.[10]

HOLLYWOOD AND INDIES

As always, the key to understanding indies is Hollywood. Commercial cinema is so pervasive in the American movie consciousness that even when filmmakers develop alternative forms Hollywood's dominant cinema is implicit in those alternatives.[11] Indeed, Scott Siegel, *Suture's* codirector, holds that it's almost impossible "to be an American director and not be a *Hollywood* director. You need validation to some degree by that system."

The demise of the studio system and the fragmentation of Hollywood has made independent cinema a viable mode of filmmaking. Hollywood's devotion to mass-produced, mass-marketed films has allowed alternatives to be created outside the studio system. In the late 1990s, the studios don't just want home runs, they want grand slams—anything less than $100 million is not interesting to them. As the studios make bigger—and fewer—blockbusters, they create greater opportunities for niche movies. Hollywood has ignored the gay/black/female/left sectors, leaving them to the indies because of Hollywood's commitment to dominant values (defined by white middle-class men) and its fear of alienating any segment of the potential public.

In an article entitled "The End of the Middle," Neal Gabler argues that "in the beginning of cinema, there were essentially no high or low ends, just one large, gratifying middle, where you could find the comedies of Frank Capra, Warner Brothers gangster dramas, Fred Astaire–Ginger Rogers musicals, and the westerns of John Ford."[12] But movie attendance took a nosedive as a result of television, suburbanization, and other factors. For Gabler, the turning point was the release of Spielberg's *Jaws* in 1975, a movie that helped "tip the American aesthetic to one that is sensation-driven." *Jaws* changed dramatically the ways American moviegoers experience film because of the media attention and ancillary products associated with it, a phenomenon that has grown common today. Gabler sums up the relationship between the indie and the blockbuster in the following way: "The independents have relieved their filmmakers of the obligation to reach a large audience, and the studios have relieved theirs of the obligation to make intelligently crafted pictures." Unless this changes, he warns, "the movies will be providing half of something for each, but not a satisfying whole for all."

The growth of the independent sector was a direct response to changes within and without the studios. Management changes rocked the studios in an unprecedented way, and new corporations took over. The growing global market demanded a less sophisticated kind of film. Gone were the days when movies like *The Godfather*, *The Conversation*, and *Chinatown* could be made in Hollywood. Instead, *Rocky*, *Rambo*, and the *Beverly Hills Cop* series became the models of filmmaking. The blandness of the studio films was partly responsible for the growth of the independents, but the unbelievable success of some of the independent movies was also a factor, said Michael Tolkin, who scripted *The Player*. The studios had no reason to make other kinds of films because blockbusters helped boost the box-office take from $3 billion in 1981 to $5 billion in 1989 and over $6 billion in 1999.

The change in Hollywood is evident in the career of the director Paul Schrader, who came to Hollywood in the late 1960s, when the industry was at its most open to new ideas. Slightly older than the other filmmakers discussed in this book, Schrader has cultivated a reputation of an outsider in his screenplays (*Taxi Driver*, *Raging Bull*) as well as movies he directed (*American Gigolo, Light Sleeper, Affliction*). Most of Schrader's characters are loners who operate on the margins of society, lost and confused men, given to violent behavior. Schrader's dark, fiercely personal films were clearly a touchstone for independent films of the 1990s.

Because studios are not interested in Schrader's kind of projects, he must go to independent sources for finance. Schrader's recent films have all been financed by foreign money in Japan, France, and England. His latest—and best—film, *Affliction* (1998), is an adaptation of Russell Banks's novel about male violence as it passes from one generation to the next with superlative performances by Nick Nolte and James Coburn. Schrader says he is incapable of following the Hollywood formula. "Audiences regard the arts as essentially trivial and decorative," he told the *Los Angeles Times*. "When audiences don't demand much from artists, that doesn't mean they quit working. It means they start talking to themselves. The result is self-referential filmmaking, a kind of in-joke art."[13]

Every year, Hollywood "redeems" itself with several respectable and only one or two great movies. In 1998, an exceptionally good year for Hollywood, *Saving Private Ryan, The Truman Show, Bulworth, He Got Game*, and *Rushmore* qualified as great or near-great films. In 1992, the best year for indies in the past decade, only one studio movie stood out: Clint Eastwood's revisionist Western, *Unforgiven*. Written in the 1970s, *Unforgiven* might as well have been an independent. It was made at Warners, because the star-director was powerful enough to get his way.[14] The year's other memorable movies—*The Player, Howards End, One False Move, Laws of Gravity, Gas Food Lodging, Bob Roberts, The Crying Game*, and *Reservoir Dogs*—were all independents.

Since the stakes are high, the studios seem content to glide along, waiting for indies to make a splash, whereupon they scoop up new hot talent, such as Soderbergh, the Coen brothers, and most recently Andy and Larry Wachowski (*The Matrix*). In 1992, it looked as if Miramax might go into business with Paramount (they coreleased *Bob Roberts*), hoping that studio distribution clout plus independent production might create a niche-oriented operation along the lines of certain publishing houses. But the arrangement turned out to be a single-film deal. After *Bob Roberts*, Harvey Weinstein realized that "we're in two different businesses: The studios are in the movie business; we're in the film business."[15]

Companies like Miramax and Fine Line are not happy about the studios' trampling on their turf. "If I were the head of Universal, with their overhead, I would get my own house in order," said Weinstein. For Fine Line's former president, Ira Deutschman, "whenever the studios try to get into the quality-film business, they muck it up for everybody. They create a situation where you can't make money on those movies, because everybody gets paid too much."[16] A case in point is the $10 million acquisition fee Castle Rock paid for Sundance's audience favorite, *The Spitfire Grill*, a movie that grossed only $14 million.

THE MAINSTREAMING OF INDIES

The concept that best describes independents in the 1990s is that of institutionalization. Indies now form an industry that runs not so much against Hollywood as parallel to Hollywood. American culture has two legitimate film industries, mainstream and independent, each grounded in its own organizational structure. While audiences overlap for some Hollywood and indie fare, the core audience for each type of film is different too.

Occasionally, there are thematic similarities between the two industries, although indies often play the upper hand. The reunion genre arguably began with John Sayles's *Return of the Secaucus Seven* (1980), a much better film than Lawrence Kasdan's glossy, all-star package, *The Big Chill* (1983). Indies were also the first to tackle capital punishment in Tim Robbins's *Dead Man Walking* (1995). Less than a year later, Hollywood came up with *Last Dance*, a shallow view of the issue, which prompted the critic David Ansen to entitle his *Newsweek* review "Dead Gal Walking."[17] Bruce Beresford's *Last Dance* features a deglamorized Sharon Stone as Cindy Liggett, a convict who killed two youngsters while committing a burglary. On death row for twelve years, she has only one more chance to escape execution—a young attorney, Rick Hayes (Rob Morrow), who's also wasted his life. Rick's superiors count on his incompetence, but after meeting Cindy, he's transformed. Ron Koslow's formulaic script then conveniently and safely shifts the point of view from Cindy to the redemption saga of a lawyer.

A decade ago, the idea that industry forces such as the Creative Artists Agency (CAA) or Twentieth Century-Fox would embrace fringe players was unthinkable. But CAA now represents indie cinema's guru

David Lynch, and Fox established a division, Fox Searchlight, to produce artistic movies. The heavyweights' foray into the indie sector continues in full force. The big agencies now have officers who specialize in indies. The William Morris Agency recently restructured its independent film division, which has its own logo and is autonomous, with the goal of boosting the agency's status in the independent world.

Indies also have their own Oscars—the Spirit Awards. Over the years, the Spirit Awards have grown from a small communal affair to a well-publicized event, televised on cable and attended by Hollywood's elite. The Spirit nominations are not just a kudo to caress filmmakers who work without the studio safety net. Good pictures do not always find their audiences, and one cannot trust that excellence will win out. Spirit nominations and awards can mean the difference between a career launch and a home movie.

A funny, violent noir action film such as *Pulp Fiction* didn't need the 1995 Spirit Award to avoid getting lost, but a Best Supporting Actress nomination for Mare Winningham in *Georgia* put the Spirit where it should be—celebrating difficult fare that fights for commercial viability in a mainstream marketplace. The Spirit Awards have provided both prophecy and moral support: *Blood Simple*, the Coen brothers' debut, won the Spirit Award before *Barton Fink* swept the Cannes awards six years later. *Drugstore Cowboy* put Gus Van Sant on the map long before his Oscar-winning blockbuster *Good Will Hunting* came out.

In 1983, when John Sayles's *Lianna* was released, Richard Corliss wrote in *Time* magazine, "Handicapped by budgets as low as $50,000, struggling with unknown actors and make-do shooting schedules, independents demand the viewer's rooting interest to see them over the rough spots and through the inevitable langueurs."[18] For Corliss, the one thing independents were dependent on was adventurous audiences. At present, however, the range of indies is extremely wide and only a small proportion, the truly bold, require risk-taking viewers. The rest—that is, the majority—have gotten closer to the mainstream.

In the past, it was not hip to be in little independent movies; it was a signal that an actor's career was in trouble. But in the 1990s, acting in indies doesn't mean having to say you're sorry. Take Bruce Willis, one of the few Hollywood stars to command $20 million for his mainstream movies (*Armageddon*). In 1998, Willis made a little, quirky film, *Breakfast of Champions*, an adaptation of Kurt Vonnegut's novel. Willis's company, Rational Packaging, bought the book rights and raised independent financing for the $12 million film. "The film is kind of outside Holly-wood," Willis told the *Los Angeles Times*, stressing the gallows humor and oddball sensibility that define his character, a wealthy Midwestern car dealer who is losing his mind. Willis explained, "Every once in a while, I've got to satisfy myself. I can count on one hand, and not use my thumb, the number of films in the last couple of years that I looked forward to going to work every day [on]."[19]

Big stars—John Wayne, Clint Eastwood, Mel Gibson—have tried before to exercise control over their careers, but usually did so by di-recting studio films. Willis, however, like Robert Duvall (*The Apostle*) before him, avoided the studio interference altogether. Owning the film's negative, he enjoys the kind of creative control he has not had in his Hollywood pictures. Willis, who had previously appeared in char-acter roles in other indies (e.g., *Pulp Fiction*), is not the only major star to appear in indies. John Travolta, whose career was resurrected by *Pulp Fiction*, appears in indies (*White Man's Burden, She's So Lovely*) as well as studio movies (*Phenomenon, Primary Colors, A Civil Action*). Nicolas Cage and Nick Nolte also commute regularly between the two indus-tries.

By and large, though, indies, like Hollywood, have their own hier-archies of acting and directorial talent. A dozen players dominate the field, going from one project to another, often making as many as three films a year. Among them are John Turturro, Eric Stoltz, Steve Buscemi, and William H. Macy. Lili Taylor is the indies' preeminent dramatic ac-tress in the 1990s. Taylor appeared in three features that competed at Sundance in 1996, including *I Shot Andy Warhol*. The following year, Parker Posey held the record with three films at Sundance, where she won particularly strong accolades for *The House of Yes*.

Major Hollywood stars, like Julia Roberts, Demi Moore, and Goldie Hawn, rarely work in indies, unless it's a Woody Allen film. Allen may be the only major filmmaker to mix actors from both worlds. "Actors who want interesting careers have to make hard choices," said Julianne Moore, because for their work in indies they get paid union scale—about $1,500 a week.[20] Moore has moved back and forth between the indie and commercial worlds, appearing in some challenging movies, *Vanya on 42nd Street* and *Safe*, for which she earned critical praise. After playing a paleontologist in Spielberg's *The Lost World*, Moore was seen bottomless in *Short Cuts* and topless in *Boogie Nights*, in a role that Paul Thomas Anderson wrote specifically for her.

When David Putnam was head of Columbia, he tried to create an ethos where turning a film with a potential $3 million net into a film with a $6 million net would be seen as a triumph. Putnam believed that "people create their careers in this industry out of their perceived successes at the box office." Needless to say, Putnam failed.

In the 1980s, *Liquid Sky, Eating Raoul, El Norte, Stranger Than Paradise, Blood Simple*, and *Desperately Seeking Susan* showed that films can be independent and still make money—not a lot of money, but enough to remove the stigma from the word "independent"—and recoup their cost. In the 1980s, said indie producer Christine Vachon (*Velvet Goldmine, Happiness*), "when you were working on *Parting Glances* or *Stranger Than Paradise*, you were just lucky to be where it was happening. You worked 16 or 17 hours a day, but there was a passion that trickled down. You cared about the movie and the director's vision." But in the 1990s, the definition of success has changed, as Vachon has observed: "Back then, we used to think a film was a success if it grossed over $1 million. Now, it's not even a success if it grosses over 5 or 10 million."[21]

Indeed, John Horn has recently suggested "to retire the conventional wisdom on the differences between the independent film community and the big studio machines."[22] While indies have typically been seen as "brassy innovators," and the studios as the "fortresses of corporate mediocrity," a role reversal is now taking place. The major studios are willing to invest in "edgy little films," allowing creative control to the filmmaker, whereas indies are becoming more concerned with "each and every detail." The reason for this is monetary. The typical indie-type film costs the equivalent of "pocket change" to Warners, Disney, or Paramount, but as independent outfits start producing movies that cost several million dollars, their executives become more frugal.

Reflecting these changes, indies are now no longer content with a modest profit, but instead want the next *Full Monty* or *The English Patient*. Ironically, earning studio-level grosses has become a near necessity in the new economics of independent films, which now requires a significant infrastructure to accommodate increased demand (Miramax now has 300 employees). "The risk is that you become your antithesis," said Fox Searchlight's Tony Safford. The switch in indie philosophy has brought "corporate worries—fear of embarrassing public relations and boycotts by intolerant activists." Some fear that this new environment will lead to a chilling of the creative environment associated with indie filmmaking.

For Vachon too, indies have become "more of an industry."[23] It's almost impossible to get financial backing for a small film without stars. "You really need to have some good stock to get a role," Lili Taylor told the *New York Times*, "Everybody wants someone who can bring a little bit more money to the table. It's all distribution, and the distributor is saying you don't have a name."[24] The trend of using name casts is part of a broader transformation of the indie industry. "It is virtually impossible to get movies financed unless you have some kind of star attached." confirms William Morris agent Cassian Elwes.[25]

> If you can do a movie with unknowns for less than $1 million, you might be able to get the financing. Otherwise you need stars. That's because the straight to video business is virtually gone, and to make money, you either have to sell the picture directly to Pay TV or release it theatrically, and you can't get either of those achieved without a star. HBO won't buy it unless there are at least two or three stars involved.

Hence, for many, "independent film" in the 1990s has become a euphemism for a small-studio production. As Paul Schrader explained, "The middle has dropped out. With a few exceptions, there's no place for a $20 to $30 million movie anymore." Hollywood has dropped the ball by leaving social issues to the independents. The movies that studios traditionally made for their prestige value have fallen to the independents, which of course are not so independent."[26] The gap between indies and studio films has gotten more extreme—a $40,000 experimental feature and a $40 million New Line film may have only one thing in common: Kodak film stock. Even so, a middle ground has grown up, populated with indie filmmakers who speak a language educated moviegoers can understand. It is to this middle ground that most independents aspire.

Robert Redford also feels progress has been made toward the goal of breaking down the distinction between independent and studio movies. For him, an independent film is "not necessarily a bunch of people running around SoHo dressed in black making a movie for $25,000. It's simply a film that stays free as long as possible to be what it wants to be. In an ideal world, there won't be a distinction between types of movies, just a broader menu."[27]

Critics are divided over what constitute indies' most important functions in the 1990s. Some hold that indies should continue to create an alternative environment for young filmmakers with new visions, while others feel that indies' major contribution is to cultivate talent for mainstream Hollywood.

CONTEXTS AND TRENDS

Perhaps the greatest achievement of indies in the 1980s was to defy Reaganism, an ideology reflected in mainstream movies that embraced Reagan's politics and celebrated the values associated with his administration: materialism, opposition to big government, straight, white machismo, simplistic notions of right and wrong, and an idealized version of America as superpower. When Reagan assumed power, expensive movie cartoons that favored spectacle over storytelling (*Superman*), as well as simplistic gung-ho movies like *Rambo* and *Top Gun*, were made. The Don Simpson and Jerry Bruckheimer pictures (*Flashdance*, *Top Gun*, *Days of Thunder*) were a perfect expression of Reaganism. As the writer-director Robert Towne put it:

> So much of the 1970s was about revealing the disparity between what the country said it was and what the filmmakers perceived it to be. When the 1980s came along, we entered a world of steroided out superheroes. Sly Stallone, Arnold Schwarzenegger, even Bruce Willis would refight the Vietnam War, and win. A country that in L. B. Johnson's words had truly become a helpless giant needed a fantasy where it was as strong as Arnold, as invulnerable as Robocop.[28]

The Reagan administration attacked public funding for the arts, which was designed to support ethnic minority, blue-collar, and regional artists. The attack affected the independents. During the Reagan-Bush era, American indies attempted to combat Republican triumphalism with nostalgia for rural simplicity. As Terrence Rafferty noted: In high-minded movies, the golden haze on the meadow was darkened by clouds of corporate greed. Since nobody goes to Hollywood movies to see losers or working-class people, the portrayal of these characters was left for low-budget indies.[29]

There's no doubt that the range of indies is much wider than that of Hollywood movies. However, if a large proportion of indies seem immature, it's a result of their being made by young directors, recent graduates of film school, who know a lot about movies but little about real life. How else to explain the disproportionately large number of coming-of-age movies? In all of these films, the values and anxieties of the younger generation are explored by directors who are themselves twentysomething. "A sizable portion of directors are first-timers in their 20s who display the tentativeness and anomie that go with that age," noted Kenneth Turan. "Their films seem fearful of feeling too much, of engaging the viewer on an intellectual level."[30]

The cool cynicism and emotional blankness in most of the Coen brothers' movies before *Fargo* led to vacant, violent movies that were basically exercises in style. At the same time, gifted American independents, such as Gus Van Sant, Richard Linklater, and Gregg Araki explored alienation and anomie in American culture in truly original ways. Unfortunately, they had scores of untalented imitators, and audiences got tired of vicariously experiencing shallow, self-indulgent work. Sundance's Geoffrey Gilmore has complained about some of the twentysomething filmmakers "who want to ride a trend and conquer the world with an arrogance and lack of sophistication."[31]

Charged with sex and violence, the imagery of 1990s indies is urban and multiracial rather than rural and white. The new films flaunt a hip, comically absurd sensibility defined by brutality and nihilism. In the past, indie movies were noted for their candid portrayal of sex, promising the public more than they could find in mainstream fare. But in the 1990s, a wave of neoviolent movies (*Reservoir Dogs*, *Bad Lieutenant*) replaced sex with violence, providing their audience with the same kind of cathartic release. In the gay milieu, sex and violence cohabited (*Poison*, *The Living End*, *Swoon*), and, for a short time, women directors (*Guncrazy*, *My New Gun*, *Mi Vida Loca*) also incorporated violence into their work, albeit in different ways.

In the 1990s, in the wake of *Reservoir Dogs* and *Pulp Fiction*, no self-respecting independent could resist making a movie without stylized violence, soaked with irony. The mixture of bloody violence and nihilistic comedy has made its mark on national cinemas around the world. Crime films (comedies and dramas) about hit men and con men (or former con men) have dominated American screens in *After Dark*,

My Sweet, American Heart, House of Games, and, most recently, in *Buffalo 66* and *The Spanish Prisoner.* Filmmakers like David Mamet, whose work is mostly in the noir vein, cash in on viewers' guilty pleasures and fondness for con men so long as they are not their victims.

In the mid 1990s, however, young indie directors embarked on confessional, candid comedy-dramas about courtship and love, evidenced in Doug Liman's *Swingers,* Matt Reeves's *The Pallbearers,* and Nicole Holofcener's *Walking and Talking.* Driven by a compulsion to bare souls, they made movies that risked being self-indulgent and narcissistic. Parading their personal experiences on the screen, they made films that favored talk over action, emotion over irony.[32] But the late 1990s saw the decline of Gen-X, as evident in *Good Will Hunting* (1997), an uncynical, un–Gen-X movie with a middlebrow, therapeutic sensibility, whose hero (Matt Damon) is a bristling working-class genius with a chip on his shoulder.

Indie trends in the late 1990s run in the direction of self-conscious irony, deep cynicism, and moral nihilism. Explorations of troubling material—the dark side of human nature—are motivated by an eagerness to shock viewers. This trend prevails in all the arts, but it's in film that it is most noticeable and most celebrated, threatening to take over the intellectual soul of the medium.[33] Glib satires like Solondz's *Welcome to the Dollhouse* and *Happiness,* urban bleak shows like *I Shot Andy Warhol,* (im)moral exposés like Neil LaBute's *In the Company of Men* and *Your Friends & Neighbors,* and the exploitative *Very Bad Things,* which makes a comedy out of grotesque murder, are examples of this trend.

Numerous indies have deconstructed dysfunctional families until the very terms became a cliché. Some of the more interesting films, such as *Spanking the Monkey* and *Citizen Ruth,* had a point of view (the former) or were funny (the latter), but others, such as *The House of Yes,* were so thrilled with their depiction of perversity that they forgot to ask to what extent their texts had any merit beyond shock value. There are no taboos anymore in American society, which might explain the declining value of filmmakers like David Lynch and John Waters. In 1998 alone, the once-unspoken of subject of pedophilia was treated in *Happiness,* the new version of *Lolita,* and the Danish film *The Celebration.* "The trouble is neither the presence nor the success of these films," critic Kenneth Turan noted. "It's what we've been missing as a result. Grim films take precedence over upbeat films that have the unfashionable temerity to have a sunnier outlook on life."[34]

DISTRIBUTION IN TODAY'S MARKET

The development of ancillary markets like cable, home video, and foreign television and theatrical sales, has taken some of the risk out of indie financing. A low-budget feature can lose money in theatrical distribution and still break even in other markets particularly if a name cast is attached to it. But easier ways to get financing don't solve the problem of continuity of work. It's always difficult at the end of every film to get the money for the next one. "It's not [difficult] just for me," said indie veteran Alan Rudolph. "It's for everyone trying something original. Having to define yourself from scratch each time—you get no continuity."[35]

Practitioners agree that the issue plaguing indies in the 1990s is the difficulty of getting viable theatrical distribution. Often, audiences have no chance to become aware of indies because of poor distribution; after all, viewers can't see indies if they're not available. "The real discussion is distribution," reaffirmed Rudolph, "How do you get it out to be seen? I've never had a good release, and now that the corporate world has taken over almost every distribution company, it's a matter of tolerance." Directors really have to make the kind of film that the distributors think they can make money on. According to Rudolph, "the trouble is, a lot of these distribution companies try to attract off-center films. But once they get them, it's as if they're embarrassed by them. So they try and make them seem regular, deny the very essence and qualities they were attracted to." Rudolph quoted his mentor, Robert Altman: "Why do people pay so much money to see something they've already seen?" For Rudolph, the answer is simple: "It's because they're being told in invisible ways to conform. It's the whole teaching of culture, to control, to conform. It's as if anything different is too weird."[36]

In the past, makers of small independent films got their widest exposure on video. Today, however, getting into video stores also presents a challenge. Most of Rudolph's films are not available on video because they were not distributed by a major company. The notion that a film can enjoy a "second life" on video is a fallacy, because video distribution is just as difficult as theatrical distribution. Blockbuster Video, which is more powerful than any theater chain, lives up to its name; it is obsessed with volume. Echoing Jon Jost's motto, Rudolph holds that in American culture, "the emphasis is on big, fast, wide, but never deep."

In the late 1980s, some of the indies' major financial sources collapsed. Orion, New World, Vestron, De Laurentiis, and Avenue all went out of business, signaling that it took deep pockets to stay in the business. But the long-term effect was to create niche audiences for nonstudio fare that in turn provided a regular market for independent distributors. Indeed, in the topsy-turvy independent arena, there's always a new crop of outlets. "The glass is always half full in this business," said CAA agent John Ptak. "If you don't accept that, and if you don't focus on the goal as opposed to the problems, then maybe you shouldn't be in the independent business."[37]

For New Line's former marketing chief, Mitch Goldman, "there are grounds for optimism. The new megaplexes are creating an opportunity for specialized films to be distributed in places they might not have been seen in before." Along with the rapidly expanding plexes, there are the new foreign territories. John Ptak is concerned not just with distribution within the United States, which represents 40 percent of the worldwide market, but also with what happens to a title when it goes through the revenue streams around the world: "When people look at this country, they see nothing but growth; they see 26,000 screens servicing 285 million people. You look at Europe, and you have 365 million people serviced by only 16,000 screens." Banque Paribas's consultant, Michael Mendelsohn, concurred: "The only way for American companies to stay alive is to have a more sophisticated worldwide view. The minute I get beyond a certain financial level, that movie absolutely has to be of interest to the entire universe."[38]

The two front-running distributors, New Line Cinema and Miramax, are now successful mini-major studios with strong financial backing, vigorous leadership and aggressive marketing. Both companies have long moved beyond acquisitions into production. Miramax has come to prominence in the 1990s with the British imports *Scandal* and *The Cook, the Thief, His Wife, and Her Lover*, several Oscar winners for the Best Foreign Picture, *Cinema Paradiso*, *Il Postino*, and *Life Is Beautiful*, and Best Picture Oscars for *The English Patient* and *Shakespeare in Love*.

Unlike Miramax, New Line has made its name not with highbrow, but with middlebrow and populist fare, such as *Teenage Mutant Ninja Turtles* and the *Nightmare on Elm Street* series. New Line falls right behind the major studios in market share, occasionally even outpacing them. It boasts more distribution clout than other indies, and is able to start a movie small and expand it if it takes off without extra pressure.

In 1990, New Line established an art division, Fine Line, under the leadership of Ira Deutschman. "Many American filmmakers are caught in a real trap," Deutschman said. "The only way to make movies is to play by the rules. A lot of filmmakers can't. We can give them the chance to do what they do best."

As to the danger that the studios will "corporatize" the independents, that Disney will transform Miramax and that Warners (and before that Turner) will change New Line, Mitch Goldman noted: "Disney has not had that much effect on Miramax. Quite the contrary: If it weren't for Disney, they might not be around today. In terms of audiences and new directors, Miramax has done a fantastic job of stretching the edge of that envelope. Ted Turner has had virtually no impact on anything that New Line has produced."[39] In the case of Fox Searchlight, chief Lindsay Law observed, "I say, 'if the name Fox gets in your way, then just forget the name is there. Don't be afraid to embarrass us, don't be afraid to make something daring."[40]

October Films scored a big coup at the 1996 Cannes festival with Mike Leigh's Palme d'Or winner, *Secrets & Lies*, and Lars Von Trier's Grand Jury Prize winner, *Breaking the Waves*. The Cannes success underscored the rapid expansion of a small, vibrant company that has made its name by careful handling of specialized products. Industry observers believed that October was shaping up to be Miramax's main competitor in the acquisitions market thanks to newly boosted credit lines and equity. October has carved a unique place for itself in the niche-driven distribution. The successful firm has released Mike Leigh's *Life Is Sweet*, Claude Sautet's *Un Coeur en Hiver*, Victor Nunez's 1993 Sundance Grand Prize winner, *Ruby in Paradise*, Altman's *Cookie's Fortune*, and this year's Sundance Grand Prize winner, *Three Seasons*. "We're one of a handful of companies who know what we're doing," said cofounder Bingham Ray. "There are basically five viable companies that work consistently. Although we're one of them, we're also the youngest, the hardest working and the truest in spirit in terms of what constitutes an independent sensibility."

The new kid on the block is Artisan Entertainment. In 1997, Bill Block, Mark Curcio, and Amir Malin took over a beleaguered video and film distributor, Live Entertainment, and changed its name to Artisan in an effort to turn it into a preeminent independent. By making quick decisions about greenlighting films, they wish to forge a reputation as the ministudio where "passion projects" get made. They are highly aware that, as a new company, they have to prove themselves: "Right now, we will spit blood for every one of our films, because success in this town breeds success."[41] That attitude has helped Artisan sign big names like Roman Polanski on *The Ninth Gate*, a $30–million thriller starring Johnny Depp, and make some high-profile acquisitions with π and Ken Loach's *My Name Is Joe*.

Artisan seeks to fill the niche markets that open up as once-smaller studios begin to make bigger-budget pictures. "They're poised to launch into orbit," said Brad Krevoy. "They're in the right place at the right time to basically take over the indie slot that Orion, New Line, and Miramax once occupied."[42] With a film library of 2,600 titles that includes *Basic Instinct* and *Terminator 2*, Artisan is determined to shed Live's unenviable image as the company that used to be the last door at the end of the hallway. Unlike Miramax, Artisan is not going to do thirty films a year, because it doesn't want to lose sight of its films. The company plans to acquire eight to ten films annually, but even its genre items are promised to have the Artisan brand identification.

After 1997, the much ballyhooed "year of the indies," when Miramax's *The English Patient* won the Best Picture Oscar, 1998 proved to be quieter and gentler.[43] There was too much product and screens were dominated by major releases—screen shortage has been an ongoing problem for indies. In this overcrowded market, the term "critic driven" holds importance for indies. Unless there's a positive critical response, a specialized release is likely to run aground before word of mouth can generate a stir.

Fall used to be the traditional season in which small art films found favor, laying the groundwork for the upcoming awards season. But in the 1990s, indie distributors have all exploited the summer doldrums with savvy counterprogramming to the big Hollywood productions. Fox Searchlight released Bertolucci's *Stealing Beauty* in the midst of the summer's blockbusters, reflecting a conscious decision to offer an alternative. In the same month, July 1996, viewers could see *Lone Star*, *Welcome to the Dollhouse*, and *I Shot Andy Warhol*, all of which performed well.

In summer 1998, the siphoning off of grown-up filmgoers by adult-oriented studio pictures (*The Truman Show*, *Out of Sight*, *Saving Private Ryan*), left art-house fare languishing in a glutted marketplace. There were three times as many summer releases in 1998 as in 1997. Despite the relative success of *Smoke Signals*, *The Opposite of Sex*, and *Next Stop Wonderland*, indie distributors didn't produce a single breakout hit that topped $10 million in domestic box-office, which raises again the definition of "success" in the indie world.

One explanation for the summer's disappointing grosses is the increasingly competitive battle for the specialty market. A glut of indie releases—combined with the shortage of screens—and a huge rise in marketing costs prevent even strong indies from performing as they might have done a few years ago. Can "small" interesting films like π or *High Art* compete against studio films with massive media campaigns? According to Fox Searchlight's Lindsay Law, the crucial variable is "how much money you have to spend to open up these movies. You can't take a nice film, open it in New York, which you used to be able to do 10 years ago on $100,000, and plunk it down in a theater and let it catch on. Even the die-hard art-house theaters play a film of ours for two or three weeks, and then we are out of there."[44] Companies pull slow-starters from theaters before giving them a chance to find their legs, to build word of mouth. Said Law, "Summer is ripe for our audience; what's hard is grabbing attention in the press. With the media focusing on studio event films, it is harder to promote smaller releases, especially those that lack an obvious hook."

There is also the issue of indies' changing audiences. According to Sony Classics' Michael Barker, "audiences are becoming more selective, which means movies have to be edgier."[45] "There are companies that have resources to provide proper marketing and distribution," said Law. "The audience has definitely demonstrated a taste to see movies that are not the norm. It is no longer an art-house versus a mainstream audience. The people going to see *Twister* are also seeing *Dead Man Walking*.[46]

Consensus holds that more opportunities exist in Hollywood today than ever before, that the industry is "basically color-blind and gender-blind," as Alan Rudolph observed. "If they can make money, they don't care. That's what's great about it." And there is something to be said for chaos, as Rudolph noted:, "The more chaos enters the system, the less predictable it gets, the better chance the audience will get served with some quality." For Rudolph, there are more encouraging than discouraging signs: "It's what people are choosing to do with their success.

That's where you have to really respect the true independent. Everybody's corruptible on one level. It's hard to turn down a million dollars when you're broke."[47]

The American independent cinema is no doubt influenced by the socioeconomic contexts in which it operates. Some critics bemoan the movement of indie filmmakers into the mainstream, the loss to Hollywood of talents like Spike Lee or Soderbergh. However, with all the criticisms against indies, their collective achievement still stands out, particularly when contrasted with Hollywood's formulas, remakes, sequels and spin-offs.

No economic or industrial force will stop enterprising filmmakers from pursuing their dreams. Each and every year, there is a new cohort of gifted directors eager to fill the space vacated by the more established indie filmmakers. If film art is driven by the need and passion of some individuals to be creative and express new visions, one should expect the continuous renewal of the American independent cinema by artists who are likely to be outsiders. Hence the title of this book.

Appendix I

Major Indie Movies by Title (1977–1998)

PICTURE	DISTRIBUTOR	YEAR	BOX-OFFICE
The Addiction	October	1995	307,308
Affliction	Lions Gate	1998	
After Dark, My Sweet	Avenue	1990	1,300,000
Afterglow	Sony Classics	1997	2,537,428
After Hours	Warner	1985	
Alambrista!		1978	
Alan and Naomi	Triton	1992	259,311
Albino Alligator	Miramax	1997	
All Over Me	Fine Line	1997	287,000
All the Vermeers in New York	Strand	1992	142,721
Amateur	Sony Classics	1995	856,108
American Buffalo	Goldwyn	1995	643,129
American Heart	Triton	1992	384,048
American History X	New Line	1998	6,286,313
Amongst Friends	Fine Line	1993	265,000
Angelo, My Love	Cinecom	1983	1,350,000
Angels and Insects	Goldwyn	1996	3,411,301
Angus	New Line	1995	4,821,759
Another Day in Paradise	Trimark	1998	906,154
The Apostle	October	1997	22,000,000
At Close Range	Orion	1986	
Babyfever	Rainbow	1994	269,904
Bad Lieutenant	Aries	1992	2,000,022
B.A.P.S	New Line	1997	7,246,735
Barcelona	Fine Line	1994	7,200,277
Barfly	Cannon	1987	1,380,000
Bar Girls	Orion Classics	1995	573,953
The Basketball Diaries	Fine Line	1995	2,133,288
Basquiat	Miramax	1996	3,011,195
The Beans of Egypt, Maine	IRS	1994	73,056
Beautiful Girls	Miramax	1996	
Before Sunrise	Sony/Castle Rock	1995	5,381,891

PICTURE	DISTRIBUTOR	YEAR	BOX-OFFICE
Before the Rain	Gramercy	1994	763,847
Belly	Artisan	1998	9,449,688
Between the Lines	Midwest Film	1977	
Beyond Therapy	New World	1987	
Big Night	Goldwyn	1996	12,005,955
The Big Squeeze	First Look	1996	
Billy's Hollywood Screen Kiss	Trimark	1998	2,100,430
Blessing	Star Valley	1995	11,860
Blood and Wine	Fox Searchlight	1997	1,094,668
Blood Simple	Circle	1985	3,275,045
The Bloody Child	Self-Distributed	1996	20,000
Blue in the Face	Miramax	1995	1,275,999
Blue Steel	Vestron	1990	
Blue Velvet	D. D. Laurentiis	1986	10,000,000
Bob Roberts	Miramax	1992	4,479,470
Bodies, Rest & Motion	Fine Line	1993	700,000
Boogie Nights	New Line	1997	26,410,771
Born in Flames	First Run	1983	
Bound	Gramercy	1996	3,811,206
Box of Moonlight	Trimark	1997	795,128
The Boys Next Door	New World	1985	
Bright Angel	Hemdale	1991	158,243
A Bronx Tale	Savoy	1993	17,287,898
Brother From Another Planet	Cinecom	1984	3,700,000
The Brothers McMullen	Fox Searchlight	1995	10,402,068
Buffalo 66	Lions Gate	1998	2,380,606
Bulletproof Heart	Republic	1994	377,108
The Celluloid Closet	Sony Classics	1995	1,366,746
Chain of Desire		1992	205,008
Chameleon Street	Northern Arts	1991	
Chan Is Missing		1982	1,000,000
Chasing Amy	Miramax	1997	12,000,000
Chinese Box	Trimark	1998	2,272,923
Choose Me	Island Alive	1984	
City of Industry	Metromedia	1997	1,554,338
Claire of the Moon	Strand	1992	687,859
Clay Pigeons	Gramercy	1998	1,793,359
Clerks	Miramax	1994	3,144,431
Clockers	Universal	1995	13,070,156
The Clockwatchers	Artistic License	1998	228,473
Coldblooded	IRS	1995	20,000

PICTURE	DISTRIBUTOR	YEAR	BOX-OFFICE
Colors	Orion	1988	46,616,067
Combination Platter	Arrow	1993	65,558
Come Back to the 5 & Dime, Jimmy Dean, Jimmy Dean	Cinecom	1982	2,000,000
Crimes of the Heart	D.D. Laurentiis	1986	10,000,000
The Crossing Guard	Miramax	1995	832,910
Crossover Dreams	Miramax	1985	
The Crow	Miramax	1994	50,693,129
Cube	Trimark	1998	314,484
Dancer, Texas, Pop. 81	Columbia	1998	
Dangerous Ground	New Line	1997	5,303,931
A Dangerous Woman	Gramercy	1993	1,497,222
Daughters of the Dust	Kino	1991	1,642,436
The Daytrippers	CFP	1997	2,099,677
Dazed and Confused	Gramercy	1993	7,993,039
The Dead	Vestron	1987	1,653,210
Dead Man	Miramax	1996	1,079,233
Dead Man Walking	Gramercy	1995	39,311,306
Defending Your Life	Warner	1991	16,371,128
The Delta	Strand	1997	90,000
Denise Calls Up	Sony Classics	1996	169,115
Desert Bloom	Columbia	1986	
Desert Hearts	Goldwyn	1986	3,500,000
Desire and Hell at Sunset Motel	Two Moon	1992	2,708
Desperately Seeking Susan	Orion	1985	
Devil in a Blue Dress	TriStar	1995	16,078,364
Different for Girls	First Look	1997	334,958
Dim Sum: A Little Bit of Heart	Orion Classic	1984	
Diner	MGM/UA	1982	23,200,000
Dirty Dancing	Vestron	1987	
Dogfight	Warner	1991	394,631
Don Juan DeMarco	New Line	1994	22,150,451
The Doom Generation	Trimark	1995	284,785
Down by Law		1986	
Down in the Delta	Miramax	1998	5,190,697
Dream Lover	Gramercy	1994	256,264
Dream With the Fishes	Sony Classics	1997	543,000
Drugstore Cowboy	Avenue	1989	4,457,027
Earth Girls Are Easy	Vestron	1989	1,845,909
Eat, Drink, Man, Woman	Goldwyn	1995	7,294,403
Eating	Rainbow	1990	4,000,000

PICTURE	DISTRIBUTOR	YEAR	BOX-OFFICE
Eating Raoul		1982	4,700,000
El Mariachi	Columbia	1992	2,040,000
El Norte	Island Alive/Cinecom	1984	2,200,000
Equinox	IRS	1992	198,488
Eraserhead	Libra	1977	3,000,000
Everything's Relative	Tara	1996	100,123
Eve's Bayou	Trimark	1997	14,000,000
Extremities	Atlantic	1986	5,100,000
Eye of God	Castle Hill	1997	60,000
Fargo	Gramercy	1996	24,547,526
Fear of a Black Hat	Goldwyn	1993	233,824
Federal Hill	Trimark	1994	514,775
Feeling Minnesota	New Line	1996	3,124,117
Female Perversions	October	1997	967,203
54	Miramax	1998	16,757,163
First Love, Last Rites	Strand	1998	
The Five Heartbeats	Twentieth Century-Fox	1991	8,750,400
Flash of Green		1985	
Flirt	CFP	1995	261,984
Four Rooms	Miramax	1995	4,257,354
Freeway	Roxie	1996	232,109
Fresh	Miramax	1994	8,094,616
Friday	New Line	1995	27,467,564
Frisk	Strand	1995	76,420
From Dusk Till Dawn	Miramax	1996	25,800,000
The Funeral	October	1996	1,232,648
Gal Young 'Un		1979	
Gas Food Lodging	IRS	1992	1,342,613
Georgia	Miramax	1995	1,120,906
Get on the Bus	Columbia	1996	5,751,690
The Gingerbread Man	Polygram	1998	1,677,131
Girlfriends		1978	
Girl 6	Fox Searchlight	1996	4,855,000
Girls Town	October	1996	509,958
The Glass Shield	Miramax	1995	3,313,633
Gods and Monsters	Lions Gate	1998	5,541,853
Go Fish	Goldwyn	1994	2,421,833
Going All the Way	Gramercy	1997	113,000
Grace of My Heart	Gramercy	1996	660,313
Gray's Anatomy	Northern Arts	1996	

PICTURE	DISTRIBUTOR	YEAR	BOX-OFFICE
Gridlock'd	Gramercy	1997	5,573,929
Grief	Strand	1994	99,890
The Grifters	Miramax	1990	5,100,000
Gummo	Fine Line	1997	116,799
Guncrazy	Man Ray Associates	1992	114,516
Guy	Gramercy	1997	
Hairspray	New Line	1988	3,200,000
Handle With Care (Citizen's Band)	Paramount	1977	
Hangin' With the Homeboys	New Line	1991	532,000
Happiness	Good Machine	1998	2,982,011
Hav Plenty	Miramax	1998	2,337,637
Heartbreakers	Orion	1985	
Heart Condition	New Line	1990	2,000,000
Heartland	Levitt-Picman	1979	1,400,000
Heathers	New World	1989	1,100,000
Heavy	CFP	1996	986,128
Henry Fool	Sony Classics	1998	1,385,002
Henry: Portrait of a Serial Killer	Greycat	1990	
Hester Street		1975	
High Art	October	1998	1,936,997
Higher Learning	Columbia	1995	38,290,723
Hollywood Shuffle	Goldwyn	1986	
Homage	Arrow	1996	2,601
Homicide	Triumph	1991	2,971,661
Hoosiers	Orion	1986	
The Hours and Times	Good Machine	1992	
Household Saints	Fine Line	1993	
House of Games	Orion Classics	1987	
The House of Yes	Miramax	1997	626,000
House Party	New Line	1990	26,400,000
House Party 2	New Line	1991	19,438,638
House Party 3	New Line	1994	19,281,235
The Hudsucker Proxy	Fox	1994	2,816,518
Hurlyburly	Fine Line	1998	2,000,000
Hurricane Streets	MGM	1998	
The Ice Storm	Fox Searchlight	1997	8,038,061
I Like It Like That	Columbia	1994	
Illtown	Shooting Gallery	1998	
The Impostors	Fox Searchlight	1998	2,194,929
Incredibly True Adventures of Two Girls in Love	Fine Line	1995	1,970,000

PICTURE	DISTRIBUTOR	YEAR	BOX-OFFICE
The Indian Runner	MGM	1991	191,125
Infinity	First Look	1996	192,788
The Inkwell	Touchstone	1994	8,880,705
Inside Monkey Zetterland	IRS	1992	32,133
In the Company of Men	Sony Classics	1997	2,990,135
In the Soup	Triton	1992	256,000
I Shot Andy Warhol	Orion	1996	1,862,295
It's My Party	MGM	1996	622,503
Jeffrey	Orion Classics	1995	3,487,767
Johns	First Look	1997	
The Joy Luck Club	Buena Vista	1993	32,901,136
Juice	Paramount	1992	20,146,880
Just Another Girl on the IRT	Miramax	1993	479,000
Kafka	Miramax	1991	1,059,071
Kalifornia	Gramercy	1993	2,395,231
Kama Sutra	Trimark	1997	4,140,071
Kansas City	Fine Line	1996	1,356,329
Keys to Tulsa	Gramercy	1997	57,561
Kicked in the Head	October	1997	116,775
Kicking and Screaming	Trimark	1995	718,490
Kids	Miramax	1995	7,412,216
Killer: Journal of a Murderer	Legacy	1996	82,029
Killer of Sheep		1978	
Killing Zoe	October	1994	418,953
King of New York	New Line	1990	1,150,000
King of the Hill	Gramercy	1993	1,214,231
Kiss Me Guido	Paramount	1997	1,920,000
Kiss of the Spider Woman	Island	1985	4,152,390
The Last Days of Disco	Gramercy	1998	3,024,198
The Last Good Time	Goldwyn	1995	65,081
Last Night at the Alamo		1984	
The Last Seduction	October	1994	3,779,257
Last Summer in the Hamptons	Rainbow	1995	801,984
The Last Supper	Sony Releasing	1995	442,965
The Last Time I Committed Suicide	Roxie	1997	460,000
Late Bloomers	Strand	1996	
Laws of Gravity	RKO	1992	117,480
Leaving Las Vegas	UA	1995	31,968,347
Light Sleeper	Live	1992	1,050,861
Liquid Sky	Cinevista	1983	1,164,204

PICTURE	DISTRIBUTOR	YEAR	BOX-OFFICE
Little Odessa	Fine Line	1995	1,095,885
Live Nude Girls	IRS	1995	23,808
The Living End	October	1992	692,585
Living in Oblivion	Sony Classics	1996	1,148,752
Living Out Loud	New Line	1998	12,626,134
Livin' Large	Goldwyn	1991	5,467,959
Lone Star	Sony Classics	1996	13,095,312
Longtime Companion	Goldwyn	1990	4,600,000
The Long Walk Home	Miramax	1990	1,700,000
Looking for Richard	Fox Searchlight	1996	1,408,575
Lost Highway	October	1997	3,935,314
Lost in America	Warner	1985	4,300,000
Love and Death in Long Island	Lions Gate	1998	2,581,014
Love Crimes	Miramax	1992	2,287,928
Love Field	Orion	1992	1,014,726
love jones	New Line	1997	12,500,000
Love Streams	Canon	1984	
Love! Valor! Compassion!	Fine Line	1997	2,940,000
The Low Life	Cabin Fever/CFP	1996	40,850
Making Mr. Right		1987	
Mala Noche		1987	
Mallrats	Gramercy	1995	2,119,688
A Man in Uniform	IRS	1994	93,623
Man of the Year	Seventh Art	1996	203,891
The Man Who Loved Women		1985	
Manny and Lo	Sony Classics	1996	502,447
Map of the Human Heart	Miramax	1993	2,806,881
Marvin's Room	Miramax	1996	
Matewan	Cinecom	1987	1,000,000
Menace II Society	New Line	1993	27,912,072
Men With Guns	Sony Classics	1998	956,145
Meteor Man	MGM/UA	1993	8,016,708
Metropolitan	New Line	1990	1,350,000
A Midnight Clear	Interstar	1992	1,526,697
Mighty Aphrodite	Miramax	1995	6,401,297
Miller's Crossing	Twentieth Century-Fox	1990	
Mindwalk	Triton	1991	774,048
Mississippi Masala	Goldwyn	1992	7,308,786
Mistress	Rainbow/Tribeca	1992	1,102,469
Mi Vida Loca	Sony Classics	1994	3,269,420

PICTURE	DISTRIBUTOR	YEAR	BOX-OFFICE
Mo' Better Blues	Universal	1990	16,153,593
Modern Romance	Columbia	1981	
The Moderns	Alive	1988	1,000,000
Monument Avenue	Lions Gate	1998	
Moonlight and Valentino	Gramercy	1995	2,484,226
Most Wanted	New Line	1997	6,391,946
Mother Night	Fine Line	1996	392,362
Motorama	Two Moon	1993	10,535
Mr. Jealousy	Lions Gate	1998	
The Music of Chance	IRS	1993	259,400
My Dinner With Andre	New Yorker	1981	1,900,000
My Family	New Line	1995	11,100,000
My Own Private Idaho	Fine Line	1991	6,500,000
Mystery Train	Orion Classics	1989	
Mystic Pizza	Goldwyn	1988	6,574,328
The Myth of Fingerprints	Sony Classics	1997	539,123
Nadja	October	1995	430,000
Naked in New York	Fine Line	1994	1,038,959
Near Dark	D. D. Laurentis	1987	
New Jack City	Warner	1991	47,624,353
New Jersey Drive	Gramercy	1995	3,570,000
Next Stop Wonderland	Miramax	1998	3,395,581
Night on Earth	Fine Line	1992	2,015,810
1918	Cinecom	1985	
Nobody's Fool	Island	1986	
Notes from Underground	Northern Arts	1995	
Nowhere	Fine Line	1997	176,000
The Object of Beauty	Avenue	1991	2,302,456
Once Upon a Time. . . . When We Were Colored	Legacy	1996	2,296,954
One False Move	IRS	1992	1,543,112
One Tough Cop	Stratosphere	1998	1,313,607
The Opposite of Sex	Sony Classics	1998	6,376,184
The Pallbearer	Miramax	1996	5,682,631
Palookaville	Orion	1996	333,758
Panther	Gramercy	1995	6,834,525
Paris Is Burning	Miramax	1991	3,800,000
Parting Glances	Cinecom	1986	
Party Girl	First Look	1995	472,370
Pastime (a.k.a. One Cup of Coffee)	Miramax	1991	267,265
Pecker	Fine Line	1998	2,281,761

PICTURE	DISTRIBUTOR	YEAR	BOX-OFFICE
The Perez Family	Goldwyn	1995	2,832,826
Permanent Midnight	Artisan	1998	1,171,001
π	Artisan	1998	3,200,000
Picture Bride	Miramax	1995	940,446
Pink Flamingos	Saliva/New Line	1972	1,900,000
Platoon	Orion	1986	137,963,328
The Player	Fine Line	1992	21,706,101
Pleasantville	New Line	1998	
Poison	Zeitgeist	1991	1,000,000
Polish Wedding	Fox Searchlight	1998	632,588
Polyester	New Line	1981	1,120,00
Posse	Gramercy	1993	8,555,000
Postcards from America	Strand	1995	84,436
A Price above Rubies	Miramax	1998	1,130,732
Privilege	Zeitgeist	1990	
Public Access	Panorama	1995	
Pulp Fiction	Miramax	1994	107,928,762
Pump Up the Volume	New Line	1990	4,000,000
A Rage in Harlem	Miramax	1990	
Rambling Rose	New Line	1991	6,254,095
Ready to Wear	Miramax	1994	6,113,186
Reckless	MGM/UA	1984	
Reckless	Goldwyn	1995	116,993
Red Rock West	Roxie	1994	1,995,845
Reefer Madness	New Line	1970	1,443,000
Reservoir Dogs	Miramax	1992	2,837,029
Return of the Secaucus Seven		1980	
Rhythm Thief	Strand	1995	22,596
River's Edge	Hemdale/Island	1986	1,700,000
Romeo Is Bleeding	Gramercy	1993	3,275,585
Roosters	IRS	1996	13,354
Rounders	Miramax	1998	22,921,898
Ruby in Paradise	October	1993	1,001,437
Safe	Sony Classics	1995	465,498
Salaam Bombay!	Cinecom	1988	2,000,000
Salvador	Hemdale	1986	
Schizopolis	Northern Arts	1997	
Search and Destroy	October	1995	390,000
The Search for One-Eyed Jimmy	Northern Arts	1996	71,314
Selena	Warner	1997	35,450,113
Serial Mom	Savoy	1994	7,881,335

PICTURE	DISTRIBUTOR	YEAR	BOX-OFFICE
Set It Off	New Line	1996	36,049,108
sex, lies, and videotape	Miramax	1989	24,741,667
S.F.W.	Gramercy	1995	63,649
She's Gotta Have It	Island	1986	7,100,000
She's So Lovely	Miramax	1997	9,000,000
She's the One	Fox Searchlight	1996	9,538,948
Short Cuts	New Line	1993	6,015,877
Sidewalk Stories	Island	1989	
Silent Tongue	Trimark	1994	61,274
Simple Men	Fine Line	1992	141,554
Slacker	Orion	1991	1,228,108
Slam	Trimark	1998	1,009,819
Sleep with Me	MGM/UA	1994	161,410
Sliding Doors	Miramax	1998	11,911,200
Sling Blade	Miramax	1996	
The Slums of Beverly Hills	Fox Searchlight	1998	5,500,000
Smithereens		1982	
Smoke	Miramax	1995	8,349,430
Smoke Signals	Miramax	1998	6,888,442
Smooth Talk	Spectra	1986	
A Soldier's Daughter Never Cries	October	1998	1,799,537
Something Wild	Orion	1986	
South Central	Warner	1992	
The Spanish Prisoner	Sony Classics	1998	10,272,230
Spanking the Monkey	Fine Line	1994	1,359,736
The Spitfire Grill	Sony	1996	12,700,000
Stand and Deliver	Warner	1988	13,700,000
Star Maps	Fox Searchlight	1997	659,440
Steal Big, Steal Little	Savoy	1995	3,150,170
Steel	Warner	1997	1,734,074
Stonewall	Strand	1996	708,047
Straight Out of Brooklyn	Goldwyn	1991	2,712,000
Stranger Than Paradise	Goldwyn	1984	
Streetwalkin'	Concorde	1985	
SubUrbia	Sony Classics	1996	727,571
Suicide Kings	Artisan	1998	1,730,156
Sunday	CFP	1997	444,823
The Sure Thing	Embassy	1985	7,859,349
Suture	Goldwyn	1993	102,780
Sweet Nothing	Warner	1996	102,350
Swimming With Sharks	Trimark	1995	376,928

PICTURE	DISTRIBUTOR	YEAR	BOX-OFFICE
Swingers	Miramax	1996	4,625,879
Swoon	Fine Line	1992	340,000
Sydney (a.k.a. The Hard Eight)	Goldwyn	1997	
Things to Do in Denver When You're Dead	Miramax	1996	600,252
The Thin Line Between Love and Hate	New Line	1996	34,564,385
This World, Then the Fireworks	Orion Classics	1997	51,000
Three of Hearts	New Line	1993	5,500,000
Threesome	Tri-Star	1994	7,800,000
The Times of Harvey Milk		1984	
To Die For	Columbia	1995	21,234,690
Torch Song Trilogy	New Line	1988	2,500,000
To Sleep With Anger	Goldwyn	1990	1,161,000
Totally F***ed Up	Strand	1993	101,071
Traveller	October	1997	537,581
Trees Lounge	Orion Classics	1996	619,522
Trick	Fine Line	1999	
The Trigger Effect	Gramercy		3,622,979
The Trip to Bountiful	Island	1985	
True Identity	Buena Vista	1991	4,693,236
True Love	MGM	1989	
Trust	Fine Line	1991	650,000
Twilight of the Golds	CFP (Avalanche)	1997	21,000
Twin Peaks: Fire Walk with Me	New Line	1992	4,160,851
Two Girls and a Guy	Fox Searchlight	1998	2,057,193
Ulee's Gold	Orion	1997	9,163,425
The Unbelievable Truth	Fine Line	1990	
Underneath	Gramercy	1994	536,023
Unforgettable	MGM	1996	2,821,671
Unhook the Stars	Miramax	1996	
The Usual Suspects	Gramercy	1995	23,331,117
Valley Girl	Atlantic	1983	4,000,000
Vampire's Kiss	Hemdale	1989	
Velvet Goldmine	Miramax	1998	1,053,788
Very Bad Things	Polygram	1998	9,735,745
Vincent and Theo	Hemdale	1990	1,000,000
Wag the Dog	New Line	1997	
Waiting for Guffman	Sony Classics	1997	2,880,945
Waiting for the Moon	Skouras	1987	
Walking and Talking	Miramax	1996	1,297,265

PICTURE	DISTRIBUTOR	YEAR	BOX-OFFICE
The Walking Dead	Savoy	1995	6,014,341
The Waterdance	Goldwyn	1992	1,500,000
The Wedding Banquet	Goldwyn	1993	6,933,459
Welcome to the Dollhouse	Sony Classics	1996	4,770,514
What Happened Was	Goldwyn	1994	325,000
Where the Day Takes You	New Line	1992	390,152
White Man's Burden	Gramercy	1995	3,734,515
The Whole Wide World	Sony Classics	1996	305,559
Wigstock	Goldwyn	1995	688,512
Wild at Heart	Goldwyn	1990	
Wilde	Sony Classics	1998	2,412,001
Without Air	Phaedra Cinema	1997	
A Woman Under the Influence	Faces International	1974	6,117,812
Working Girls	Miramax	1987	
Year of the Horse	October	1997	260,791
The Young Poisoner's Handbook	CFP	1996	580,640
Your Friends & Neighbors	Gramercy	1998	4,714,658
Zebrahead	Triumph	1992	1,557,000

Appendix 2

Major Indie Movies by Year (1977–1998)

1977

PICTURE	DIRECTOR	CAST
Alambrista!	Robert M. Young	Domingo Ambriz, Trinidad Silva
Between the Lines	Joan M. Silver	Jeff Goldblum, John Heard
Desperate Living	John Waters	Divine
Eraserhead	David Lynch	John Pance, Charlotte Stewart
Welcome to L.A.	Alan Rudolph	Keith Carradine, Geraldine Chaplin

1978

PICTURE	DIRECTOR	CAST
Girlfriends	Claudia Weill	Melanie Mayron, Anita Skinner
Killer of Sheep	Charles Burnett	Henry Sanders, Kaytee Moore
The Whole Shootin' Match	Eagle Pennell	Sonny Carl Davis, Louis Perryman

1979

PICTURE	DIRECTOR	CAST
Gal Young 'Un	Victor Nunez	Dana Preu, David Peck
Heartland	Richard Pearce	Rip Torn, Conchata Ferrel
Northern Lights	John Hanson, Rob Nilsson	Robert Behling, Susan Lynch
Remember My Name	Alan Rudolph	Geraldine Chaplin, Anthony Perkins

1980

PICTURE	DIRECTOR	CAST
Return of the Secaucus Seven	John Sayles	Mark Arnott, Gordon Clapp

1981

PICTURE	DIRECTOR	CAST
Modern Romance	Albert Brooks	Albert Brooks, Kathryn Harrold
My Dinner With Andre	Louis Malle	Andre Gregory, Wallace Shawn
Polyester	John Waters	Divine, Tab Hunter

1982

PICTURE	DIRECTOR	CAST
Chan Is Missing	Wayne Wang	Wood Moy, Marc Hayashi
The Chosen	Jeremy Paul Kagan	Maximillian Schell, Rod Steiger

PICTURE	DIRECTOR	CAST
Come Back to the 5 & Dime, Jimmy Dean, Jimmy Dean	Robert Altman	Cher, Sandy Dennis
Eating Raoul	Paul Bartel	Paul Bartel, Mary Woronov
Smithereens	Susan Seidelman	Susan Berman, Brad Rinn

1983

PICTURE	DIRECTOR	CAST
Angelo, My Love	Robert Duvall	Angelo Evans, Michael Evans
Born in Flames	Lizzie Borden	Jeanne Satterfield, Adele Bertel
Breathless	Jim McBride	Richard Gere, Valerie Kaprinski
Lianna	John Sayles	Linda Griffiths, Jane Hallaren
Liquid Sky	Slava Tsukerman	Anne Carlisle, Paula E. Sheppard
Love Letters	Amy Jones	Jamie Lee Curtis, James Keach
My Brother's Wedding	Charles Burnett	Everett Silas, Jessie Holmes
Streamers	Robert Altman	Matthew Modine, Michael Wright
Valley Girl	Martha Coolidge	Nicolas Cage, Deborah Foreman

1984

PICTURE	DIRECTOR	CAST
Brother From Another Planet	John Sayles	Joe Morton, David Strathairn
Choose Me	Alan Rudolph	Keith Carradine, Lesley Ann Warren
Dim Sum: A Little Bit of Heart	Wayne Wang	Laureen Chew, Kim Chew
El Norte	Gregory Nava	David Villapando
Last Night at the Alamo	Eagle Pennell	Sonny Davis, Lou Perry
Love Streams	John Cassavetes	John Cassavetes, Gena Rowlands
Reckless	James Foley	Aidan Quinn, Daryl Hannah
Secret Honor	Robert Altman	Philip Baker Hall
Songwriter	Alan Rudolph	Willie Nelson, Kris Kristofferson
Stranger Than Paradise	Jim Jarmusch	John Lurie, Richard Edson
Variety	Bette Gordon	

1985

PICTURE	DIRECTOR	CAST
After Hours	Martin Scorsese	Rosanna Arquette, Griffin Dunne
Blood Simple	Joel Coen	Frances McDormand, John Getz
The Boys Next Door	Penelope Spheeris	Maxwell Caulfield, Charlie Sheen
Crossover Dreams	Leon Ichasi	Ruben Blades, Shawn Elliott
Desperately Seeking Susan	Susan Seidelman	Rosanna Arquette, Madonna
Flash of Green	Victor Nunez	Ed Harris, Blair Brown
Kiss of the Spider Woman	Hector Babenco	William Hurt, Raul Julia
Lost in America	Albert Brooks	Albert Brooks, Julie Hagerty
The Man Who Loved Women	Yvonne Rainer	
The Sure Thing	Rob Reiner	John Cusack, Daphne Zuniga
The Trip to Bountiful	Peter Masterson	Geraldine Page, John Heard

1986

PICTURE	DIRECTOR	CAST
At Close Range	James Foley	Sean Penn, Christopher Walken
Blue Velvet	David Lynch	Kyle MacLachlan, Laura Dern

Crimes of the Heart	Bruce Beresford	Diane Keaton, Jessica Lange, Sissy Spacek
Desert Bloom	Eugene Corr	Annabeth Gish, Jon Voight
Desert Hearts	Donna Deitch	Helen Shaver, Patricia Charbonneau
Down by Law	Jim Jarmusch	John Lurie, Tom Waits
Extremities	Robert M. Young	Farrah Fawcett, James Russo
Hard Choices	Rick King	Margaret Klenck, Gary McCleary
Heavy	James Mangold	Pruitt Taylor Vince, Liv Tyler
Hollywood Shuffle	Robert Townsend	Robert Townsend, Anne Marie Johnson
Hoosiers	David Anspaugh	Gene Hackman, Dennis Hopper
Nobody's Fool	Evelyn Purcell	Rosanna Arquette, Eric Roberts
Parting Glances	Bill Sherwood	John Bolger, Richard Ganoung
Peggy Sue Got Married	Francis F. Coppola	Kathleen Turner, Nicolas Cage
Platoon	Oliver Stone	Charlie Sheen, Willem Dafoe
River's Edge	Tim Hunter	Keanu Reeves, Crispin Glover
Salvador	Oliver Stone	James Woods, James Belushi
She's Gotta Have It	Spike Lee	Tracy Camilla Johns
Sid and Nancy	Alex Cox	Gary Oldman, Chloe Webb
Smooth Talk	Joyce Chopra	Laura Dern, Treat Williams
Something Wild	Jonathan Demme	Melanie Griffith, Jeff Daniels
True Stories	David Byrne	David Byrne, John Goodman

1987

PICTURE	DIRECTOR	CAST
Beyond Therapy	Robert Altman	Julie Haggerty, Jeff Goldblum
Dirty Dancing	Emile Ardolino	Jennifer Grey, Patrick Swayze
The Loveless	Kathryn Bigelow, Monty Montgomery	Willem Dafoe, Dan Ferguson
Making Mr. Right	Susan Seidelman	Ann Magnuson, John Malkovich
Matewan	John Sayles	Chris Cooper, Mary McDonnell
Near Dark	Kathryn Bigelow	Adrian Pasdar, Jenny Wright
Rachel River	Sandy Smolan	Zeljko Ivanek, Pamela Reed
Waiting for the Moon	Jill Goodmilow	Linda Hunt, Linda Bassett
Working Girls	Lizzie Borden	Louise Smith, Ellen McElduff

1988

PICTURE	DIRECTOR	CAST
The Chocolate War	Keith Gordon	John Glover, Adam Baldwin
Colors	Dennis Hopper	Sean Penn, Robert Duvall
Hairspray	John Waters	Ricki Lake, Divine
Miles from Home	Gary Sinise	Richard Gere, Kevin Anderson
The Moderns	Alan Rudolph	Keith Carradine, Linda Fiorentino
Mystic Pizza	Donald Petrie	Lili Taylor, Julia Roberts
Salaam Bombay!	Mira Nair	Shafiq Syed

1989

PICTURE	DIRECTOR	CAST
84 Charlie Mopic	Patrick Duncan	Jonathan Emerson, Nicholas Cascone

Drugstore Cowboy	Gus Van Sant	Matt Dillon, Kelly Lynch
Earth Girls Are Easy	Julien Temple	Geena David, Jeff Goldblum
Mystery Train	Jim Jarmusch	Screamin' Jay Hawkins, Cinque Lee
Say Anything	Cameron Crowe	John Cusack, Ione Skye
sex, lies, and videotape	Steven Soderbergh	Peter Gallagher, Andie MacDowell
Sidewalk Stories	Charles Lane	Charles Lane, Nicole Alysia
True Love	Nancy Savoca	Annabella Sciorra, Ron Eldard
Vampire's Kiss	Robert Biberman	Nicolas Cage, Maria Conchita Alonso

1990

PICTURE	DIRECTOR	CAST
After Dark, My Sweet	James Foley	Jason Patrick, Rachel Ward
Blue Steel	Kathryn Bigelow	Jamie Lee Curtis, Ron Silver
The Grifters	Stephen Frears	Anjelica Huston, John Cusack
Heart Condition	James D. Perriott	Bob Hoskins, Denzel Washington
Henry: Portrait of a Serial Killer	John McNaughton	Michael Rooker, Tracy Arnold
House Party	Reginald Hudlin	Christopher Reid, Robin Harris
King of New York	Abel Ferrara	Christopher Walken, Wesley Snipes
The Lemon Sisters	Joyce Chopra	Diane Keaton, Carol Kane
Longtime Companion	Norman Rene	Bruce Davison, Campbell Scott
The Long Walk Home	Richard Pearce	Whoopi Goldberg, Sissy Spacek
Metropolitan	Whit Stillman	Christopher Eigeman, Carolyn Farina
Miller's Crossing	Joel Coen	Albert Finney, Gabriel Byrne
Mo' Better Blues	Spike Lee	Denzel Washington, Spike Lee
Privilege	Yvonne Rainer	
Pump Up the Volume	Allan Moyle	Christian Slater, Ellen Greene
A Rage in Harlem	Bill Duke	Forest Whitaker, Gregory Hines
To Sleep With Anger	Charles Burnett	Danny Glover, Paul Butler
Vincent and Theo	Robert Altman	Tim Roth, Paul Rhys
The Unbelievable Truth	Hal Hartley	Adrienne Shelly, Robert Burke
Wild at Heart	David Lynch	Nicolas Cage, Laura Dern

1991

PICTURE	DIRECTOR	CAST
Boyz 'N' the Hood	John Singleton	Larry Fishburne, Cuba Gooding Jr.
Bright Angel	Michael Fields	Dermot Mulroney, Lili Taylor
Cadence	Martin Sheen	Charlie Sheen, Larry Fishburne
Chameleon Street	Wendell B. Harris	Wendell B. Harris, Angela Leslie
Daughters of the Dust	Julie Dash	Cora Lee Day, Alva Rodgers
Dogfight	Nancy Savoca	Lili Taylor, River Phoenix
The Five Heartbeats	Robert Townsend	Robert Townsend, Michael Wright
Hangin' With the Homeboys	Joseph P. Vasquez	Doug E. Doug, John Leguizamo
Homicide	David Mamet	Joe Mantegna, William H. Macy
House Party 2	Doug McHenry, Christopher Martin	Christopher Reid, George Jackson
The Indian Runner	Sean Penn	David Morse, Viggo Mortensen
Kafka	Steven Soderbergh	Jeremy Irons, Joel Grey

Livin' Large	Michael Schultz	T. C. Carson
Mindwalk	Bernt Capra	Liv Ullmann, Sam Waterston
Mistress	Barry Primus	Robert Wuhl, Martin Landau
My Own Private Idaho	Gus Van Sant	River Phoenix, Keanu Reeves
New Jack City	Mario Van Peebles	Wesley Snipes, Ice T.
The Object of Beauty	Michael Lindsay-Hogg	John Malkovich, Andie MacDowell
Paris Is Burning	Jennie Livingston	
Pastime (a.k.a. One Cup of Coffee)	Robin B. Armstrong	William Rus, Glenn Plummer
Poison	Todd Haynes	Edith Meeks, Larry Maxwell
Rambling Rose	Martha Coolidge	Laura Dern, Diane Ladd
Slacker	Richard Linklater	
Straight Out of Brooklyn	Matty Rich	George T. Odom, Ann D. Sanders
Trust	Hal Hartley	Adrienne Shelly, Martin Donovan

1992

PICTURE	DIRECTOR	CAST
Alan and Naomi	Sterling VanWagenen	Lukas Haas, Vanessa Zaoui
All the Vermeers in the World	Jon Jost	Emmanuelle Chaulet, Stephen Lack
American Heart	Martin Bell	Jeff Bridges, Edward Furlong
Bad Lieutenant	Abel Ferrara	Harvey Keitel, Frankie Thorn
Bob Roberts	Tim Robbins	Tim Robbins, Gore Vidal
Chain of Desire	Temistocles Lopez	Malcolm McDowell, Linda Fiorentino
Claire of the Moon	Nicole Conn	Trisha Todd, Karen Trumbo
Desire and Hell at Sunset Motel	Allen Castle	Sherilyn Fenn, Whip Hubley
El Mariachi	Robert Rodriguez	Carlos Gallardo, Consuelo Gomez
Equinox	Alan Rudolph	Matthew Modine, Lara Flynn Boyle
Guncrazy	Tamra Davis	Drew Barrymore, James LeGros
The Hours and Times	Christopher Munch	Ian Hart, David Angus
Inside Monkey Zetterland	Jefery Levy	Steve Antin, Katherine Helmond
In the Soup	Alexander Rockwell	Steve Buscemi, Seymour Cassel
Laws of Gravity	Nick Gomez	Peter Greene, Adam Trese
Light Sleeper	Paul Schrader	Susan Sarandon, Willem Dafoe
The Living End	Gregg Araki	Mike Dytri, Graig Gilmore
Love Crimes	Lizzie Borden	Sean Young, Patrick Bergin
Love Field	Jonathan Kaplan	Michele Pfeiffer, Dennis Haysbert
A Midnight Clear	Keith Gordon	Peter Berg, Kevin Dillon
Mississippi Masala	Mira Nair	Denzel Washington, Sarita Choudhury
Night on Earth	Jim Jarmusch	Winona Ryder, Gena Rowlands
One False Move	Carl Franklin	Bill Paxton, Cynda Williams
The Player	Robert Altman	Tim Robbins, Greta Scacchi
Reservoir Dogs	Quentin Tarantino	Harvey Keitel, Tim Roth
Simple Men	Hal Hartley	Robert Burke, William Sage
South Central	Steve Anderson	Glenn Plummer, Byron Keith Minns
Swoon	Tom Kalin	Daniel Schlochet, Craig Chester
Twin Peaks: Fire Walk With Me	David Lynch	Sheryl Lee, Kyle MacLachlan
The Waterdance	Neal Jimenez, Michael Steinberg	Eric Stoltz, Wesley Snipes, William Forsythe

Where the Day Takes You	Marc Rocco	Dermot Mulroney, Sean Austin
Zebrahead	Anthony Drazan	Michael Rapaport, N'Bushe Wright

1993

PICTURE	DIRECTOR	CAST
Amongst Friends	Rob Weiss	Joseph Lindsay
Bodies, Rest & Motion	Michael Steinberg	Phoebe Cates, Bridget Fonda
Combination Platter	Tony Chan	Jeff Law, Colleen O'Brien
A Dangerous Woman	Stephen Gylenhaal	Debra Winger, Barbara Hershey
Dazed and Confused	Richard Linklater	Jason London, Wiley Higgins
Fear of a Black Hat	Rusty Cundieff	Larry B. Scott, Mark Christopher
Fun	Rafal Zielinski	Alicia Witt, Renee Humphrey
Household Saints	Nancy Savoca	Lili Taylor, Vincent D'Onofrio
The Joy Luck Club	Wayne Wang	Kieu Chinh, Trai Chin
Just Another Girl on the IRT	Lesley Harris	Ariyan Johnson, Kevin Thigpen
Kalifornia	Dominic Sena	Brad Pitt, Juliette Lewis
King of the Hill	Steven Soderbergh	Jesse Bradford, Jeroen Krabbe
Menace II Society	Allen Hughes, Albert Hughes	Tyrin Turner, Larentz Tate
The Music of Chance	Philip Haas	James Spader, Mandy Patinkin
Posse	Mario Van Peebles	Mario Van Peebles, Charles Lane
Romeo Is Bleeding	Peter Medak	Gary Oldman, Lena Olin
Ruby in Paradise	Victor Nunez	Ashley Judd
Short Cuts	Robert Altman	Julianne Moore, Matthew Modine
Suture	Scott McGehe, David Siegel	Dennis Haysbert, Mel Harris
Three of Hearts	Yurek Bogayevicz	William Baldwin, Kelly Lynch
Totally F***ed Up	Gregg Araki	James Duvall, Roko Belic
The Wedding Banquet	Ang Lee	Winston Chao, May Chin

1994

PICTURE	DIRECTOR	CAST
Barcelona	Whit Stillman	Taylor Nichols, Chris Eigeman
The Beans of Egypt, Maine	Jennifer Warren	Martha Plimpton, Kelly Lynch
Before the Rain	Milcho Manchevski	Katrin Cartlidge, Rade Serbedzija
Bulletproof Heart	Mark Malone	Anthony LaPaglia, Mimi Rogers
Bullets Over Broadway	Woody Allen	John Cusack, Dianne Wiest
Clerks	Kevin Smith	Brian O'Halloran, Jeff Anderson
Dream Lover	Nicholas Kazan	James Spader, Madchen Amick
Federal Hill	Michael Corrente	Nicholas Turturro, Anthony DeSando
Fresh	Boaz Yakin	Sean Nelson, Samuel L. Jackson
Grief	Richard Glatzer	Alexis Arquette, Craig Chester
Go Fish	Rose Troche	V. S. Brodie, Guinevere Turner
House Party 3	Eric Meza	Christopher Reid, Christopher Martin
The Hudsucker Proxy	Joel Coen	Tim Robbins, Jennifer Jason Leigh
I Like It Like That	Darnell Martin	Lauren Velez, Jon Seda
The Inkwell	Matty Rich	Larenz Tate, Joe Morton

Killing Zoe	Roger Avary	Eric Stoltz, Julie Delpy
The Last Seduction	John Dahl	Linda Fiorentino, Peter Berg
A Man in a Uniform	David Wellington	Tom McCamus, Brigitte Bako
Mi Vida Loca (My Crazy Life)	Allison Anders	Angels Avilez, Seidy Lopez
Naked in New York	Dan Algrant	Eric Stoltz, Mary-Louise Parker
The New Age	Michael Tolkin	Peter Weller, Judy David
Pulp Fiction	Quentin Tarantino	John Travolta, Samuel L. Jackson
Ready to Wear	Robert Altman	Lili Taylor, Julia Roberts
Red Rock West	John Dahl	Nicolas Cage, Dennis Hopper
Silent Tongue	Sam Shepard	Richard Harris, Alan Bates
Spanking the Monkey	David O. Russell	Jeremy Davies, Alberta Watson
Threesome	Andrew Fleming	Lara Flynn Boyle, Stephen Baldwin
Underneath	Steven Soderbergh	Peter Gallagher, Alison Elliott
What Happened Was . . .	Tom Noonan	Tom Noonan, Karen Silas

1995

PICTURE	DIRECTOR	CAST
The Addiction	Abel Ferrara	Lili Taylor Christopher Walken
Amateur	Hal Hartley	Isabelle Huppert, Martin Donovan
American Buffalo	Michael Corrente	Dustin Hoffman, Dennis Franz
Angus	Patrick Read Johnson	Charlie Talbert, George C. Scott
Bar Girls	Marita Giovanni	Nancy Allison Wolfe
The Basketball Diaries	Scott Kalvert	Leonardo DiCaprio, Mark Wahlberg
Before Sunrise	Richard Linklater	Ethan Hawke, Julie Delpy
Blessing	Paul Zehrer	Melora Griffin, Carlin Glynn
Blue in the Face	Wayne Wang, Paul Auster	Harvey Keitel, Lou Reed
The Brothers McMullen	Edward Burns	Edward Burns, Mike McGlone
The Celluloid Closet	Bob Epstein, Jeffrey Friedman	Lily Tomlin
Clockers	Spike Lee	Harvey Keitel, John Turturro
Coldblooded	Wallace Wolodarsky	Jason Priestley, Peter Riegert
The Crossing Guard	Sean Penn	Jack Nicholson, Anjelica Huston
Dead Man Walking	Tim Robbins	Sean Penn, Susan Sarandon
Devil in a Blue Dress	Carl Franklin	Denzel Washington, Jennifer Beals
Don Juan DeMarco	Jeremy Leven	Marlon Brando, Johnny Depp
The Doom Generation	Gregg Araki	Rose McGowan, James Duvall
Eat Drink Man Woman	Ang Lee	Sihung Lung, Kuei-Mei Yang
Flirt	Hal Hartley	Bill Sage, Parker Posey
Four Rooms	Allison Anders	Madonna
	Alexander Rockwell	Jennifer Beals
	Robert Rodriguez	Antonio Banderas
	Quentin Tarantino	Bruce Willis
Georgia	Ulu Grosbard	Jennifer Jason Leigh, Mare Winningham
The Glass Shield	Charles Burnett	Michael Boatman, Lori Petty
Higher Learning	John Singleton	Omar Epps, Laurence Fishburne
The Incredibly True Adventures of Two Girls in Love	Maria Maggenti	Laurel Holloman, Nicole Parker
Jeffrey	Christopher Ashley	Steven Weber, Patrick Stewart

Kicking and Screaming	Noah Baumbach	Josh Hamilton, Eric Stoltz
Kids	Larry Clark	Leo Fitzpatrick, Justin Pierce
The Last Good Time	Bob Balaban	Armin Mueller-Stahl, Olivia d'Abo
Last Summer in the Hamptons	Henry Jaglom	Viveca Lindfors, Victoria Foyt
The Last Supper	Stacy Title	Cameron Diaz, Ron Eldard
Little Odessa	James Gray	Tim Roth, Edward Furlong
Living in Oblivion	Tom DiCillo	Steve Buscemi Catherine Keener
Mallrats	Kevin Smith	Shannen Doherty, Jason Lee
Mighty Aphrodite	Woody Allen	Mira Sorvino, Woody Allen
Moonlight and Valentino	David Anspaugh	Elizabeth Perkins Whoopi Goldberg
My Family	Gregory Nava	Jimmy Smits, Esai Morales
Nadja	Michael Almereyda	Elina Lowensohn, Peter Fonda
New Jersey Drive	Nick Gomez	Sharron Corley, Gabriel Cassus
Notes from Underground	Gary Walkow	Henry Czerny, Sheryl Lee
Party Girl	Daisy von Scherler Mayer	Parker Posey, Omar Townsend
The Perez Family	Mira Nair	Alfred Molina, Marisa Tomei
Picture Bride	Kayo Hatta	Youki Kudoh, Akira Takayama
Safe	Todd Haynes	Julianne Moore, James Le Gros
Search and Destroy	David Salle	Griffin Dunne, Illeana Douglas
S.F.W.	Jefery Levy	Stephen Dorff, Reese Witherspoon
Smoke	Wayne Wang	Harvey Keitel, William Hurt
Swimming with Sharks	George Huang	Kevin Spacey, Frank Whaley
The Usual Suspects	Bryan Singer	Kevin Spacey, Gabriel Byrne
White Man's Burden	Desmond Nakano	John Travolta, Harry Belafonte
Wigstock: The Movie	Barry Sills	Alexis Arquette, Jackie Beat

1996

PICTURE	DIRECTOR	CAST
Angels and Insects	Philip Haas	Kristin Scott Thomas, Mark Rylance
Basquiat	Julian Schnabel	Jeffrey Wright, David Bowie
Big Night	Stanley Tucci, Campbell Scott	Stanley Tucci, Tony Shalhoub
The Bloody Child	Nina Menkes	Tinka Menkes
Bound	Larry Wachowski Andy Wachowski	Gina Gershon, Jennifer Tilly
Boys	Stacy Cochran	Winona Ryder, Lukas Haas
Dead Man	Jim Jarmusch	Johnny Depp, Gary Farmer
Denise Calls Up	Hal Salwen	Liev Schreiber, Caroleen Feeney
The English Patient	Anthony Minghella	Ralph Fiennes, Kristin Scott Thomas
Everyone Says I Love You	Woody Allen	Alan Alda, Goldie Hawn
Everything's Relative	Sharon Pollack	Monica Bell, Olivia Nephron
Fargo	Joel Coen	Frances McDormand, William H. Macy
Feeling Minnesota	Steven Baigelman	Keanu Reeves, Vincent D'Onofrio
Freeway	Matthew Bright	Reese Witherspoon, Kiefer Sutherland
From Dusk Till Dawn	Robert Rodriguez	George Clooney, Harvey Keitel
Get on the Bus	Spike Lee	Ossie Davis, Charles S. Dutton
Girl 6	Spike Lee	Theresa Randle, Isaiah Washington

PICTURE	DIRECTOR	CAST
Girls Town	Jim McKay	Lili Taylor, Bruklin Harris
Grace of My Heart	Allison Anders	Illeanna Douglas, John Turturro
The Grass Harp	Charles Matthau	Piper Laurie, Sissy Spacek
Gray's Anatomy	Steven Soderbergh	Spalding Gray
Homage	Ross Kagan Marks	Sheryl Lee, Blythe Danner
I Shot Andy Warhol	Mary Harron	Lili Taylor, Jared Harris
Imaginary Crimes	Anthony Drazan	Harvey Keitel, Fairuza Balk
Infinity	Matthew Broderick	Matthew Broderick, Patricia Arquette
It's My Party	Randal Kleiser	Eric Roberts, Gregory Harrison
Kansas City	Robert Altman	Miranda Richardson, Jennifer Jason Leigh
Killer: Journal of a Murderer	Tim Metcalfe	James Woods, Robert Sean Leonard
Late Bloomers	Julia Dyer, Gretchen Dyer	Connie Nelson, Dee Hennigan
Lone Star	John Sayles	Kris Kristofferson, Chris Cooper
Looking for Richard	Al Pacino	Al Pacino, Winona Ryder
The Low Life	George Hickenlooper	Rory Cochran, Kyra Sedwick
Man of the Year	Dirk Shafer	Dirk Shafer
Manny and Lo	Lisa Krueger	Scarlett Johansson, Aleksa Palladino
Marvin's Room	Jerry Zaks	Diane Keaton, Meryl Streep
Mother Night	Keith Gordon	Nick Nolte, Sheryl Lee
Once Upon a Time . . . When We Were Colored	Tim Reid	Al Freeman Jr., Phylicia Rashad
The Search for One-Eyed Jimmy	Sam Henry Kass	John Turturro, Samuel L. Jackson
Set It Off	Gary Gray	Jada Pinkett, Queen Latifah
She's the One	Edward Burns	Edward Burns, Jennifer Aniston
Stonewall	Nigel Finch	Frederick Weller, Guillermo Diaz
SubUrbia	Richard Linklater	Giovanni Ribisi, Steve Zahn
Sweet Nothing	Gary Winick	Michael Imperioli, Mira Sorvino
Swingers	Doug Liman	Jon Favreau, Vince Vaughn
Things to Do in Denver When You're Dead	Gary Fleder	Andy Garcia, Christopher Walken
The Thin Line Between Love and Hate	Martin Lawrence	Martin Lawrence, Lynn Whitfield
Trees Lounge	Steve Buscemi	Steve Buscemi, Chloe Sevigny
Unforgettable	John Dahl	Ray Liotta, Linda Fiorentino
Unhook the Stars	Nick Cassavetes	Gena Rowlands, Marisa Tomei
Walking and Talking	Nicole Holofcener	Catherine Keener, Anne Heche
Welcome to the Dollhouse	Todd Solondz	Heather Matarazzo, Brendan Sexton Jr.

1997

PICTURE	DIRECTOR	CAST
Afterglow	Alan Rudolph	Julie Christie, Nick Nolte
Albino Alligator	Kevin Spacey	Matt Dillon, Faye Dunaway
All Over Me	Alex Sichel	Allison Folland, Tara Subkoff
Boogie Nights	Paul Thomas Anderson	Julianne Moore, Burt Reynolds
Box of Moonlight	Tom DiCillo	John Turturro, Sam Rockwell

A Brother's Kiss	Seth Zvi Rosenfeld	Nick Chinlund, Michael Rayner
Chasing Amy	Kevin Smith	Ben Affleck, Joey Lauren Adams
The Daytrippers	Greg Mottola	Hope Davis, Parker Posey
Deconstructing Harry	Woody Allen	Woody Allen, Judy Davis
The Delta	Ira Sachs	Shayne Gray, Thang Chan
Dream With the Fishes	Finn Taylor	David Arquette, Cathy Moriarty
Eve's Bayou	Kasi Lemmons	Jurnee Smolett, Samuel L. Jackson
Eye of God	Tim Nelson Blake	Martha Plimpton
Female Perversions	Susan Streitfeld	Tilda Swinton, Amy Madigan
Going All the Way	Mark Pellington	Jeremy Davies, Ben Affleck
Gridlock'd	Vondie Curtis-Hall	Tupac Shakur, Tim Roth
Gummo	Harmony Korine	Jacob Reynolds, Nick Sutton
The House of Yes	Mark Walters	Parker Posey, Josh Hamilton
In the Company of Men	Neil LaBute	Aaron Eckhart, Stacy Edwards
Johns	Scott Silver	Lukas Haas, David Arquette
Kiss Me Guido	Tony Vitale	Nick Scotti, Anthony Barrile
The Last Time I Committed Suicide	Stephen Kay	Thomas Jane, Keanu Reeves
Lost Highway	David Lynch	Bill Pullman, Patricia Arquette
love jones	Theodore Witcher	Larentz Tate, Nia Long
Love! Valor! Compassion!	Joe Mantello	Jason Alexander, John Glover
The Myth of Fingerprints	Bart Freundlich	Blythe Danner, Roy Scheider
Nowhere	Gregg Araki	James Duvall, Rachel True
Schizopolis	Steven Soderbergh	Steven Soderbergh, Betsy Brantley
Selena	Gregory Nava	Jennifer Lopez
Star Maps	Miguel Arteta	Douglas Spain, Efrain Figueroa
Sunday	Jonathan Nossiter	David Suchet, Lisa Harrow
Sydney	Paul Thomas Anderson	Philip Baker Hall, Gwyneth Paltrow
This World, Then the Fireworks	Michael Oblowitz	Billy Zane, Gina Gershon
Twilight of the Golds	Ross Marks	Jennifer Beals, Faye Dunaway
Ulee's Gold	Victor Nunez	Peter Fonda, Patricia Richardson
Wag the Dog	Barry Levinson	Dustin Hoffman, Robert De Niro
Waiting for Guffman	Christopher Guest	Christopher Guest, Parker Posey

1998

PICTURE	DIRECTOR	CAST
54	Mark Christopher	Ryan Philippe, Salma Hayek
American History X	Tony Kaye	Edward Norton, Edward Furlong
Belly	Hope Williams	Nas, DMX
Billy's Hollywood Screen Kiss	Tommy O'Haver	Sean P. Hayes, Brad Rowe
Buffalo 66	Vincent Gallo	Vincent Gallo, Christina Ricci
Celebrity	Woody Allen	Judy Davis, Kenneth Branagh
Chinese Box	Wayne Wang	Jeremy Irons, Gong Li
Clay Pigeons	David Dobkin	Vince Vaughn, Janeane Garofalo
The Clockwatchers	Jill Sprecher	Toni Collette, Parker Posey
Down in the Delta	Maya Angelou	Alfre Woodard, Wesley Snipes
The Gingerbread Man	Robert Altman	Kenneth Branagh, Embeth Davidtz
Gods and Monsters	Bill Condon	Ian McKellen, Brandon Fraser
Happiness	Todd Solondz	Jane Adams, Dylan Baker

Hav Plenty	Chris Cherot	Chris Cherot, Chenoa Maxwell
Henry Fool	Hal Hartley	James Urbaniak, Thomas Jay Ryan
High Art	Lisa Cholodenko	Ally Sheedy, Radha Mitchell
Hurlyburly	Anthony Drazan	Sean Penn, Kevin Spacey
Hurricane Streets	Morgan J. Freeman	Brendan Sexton III, Shawn Elliott
The Impostors	Stanley Tucci	Stanley Tucci, Oliver Platt
The Last Days of Disco	Whit Stillman	Chris Eigeman, Kate Beckinsale
Living Out Loud	Richard LaGravenese	Holly Hunter, Danny DeVito
Love and Death on Long Island	Richard Kwietniowski	John Hurt, Jason Priestly
Monument Avenue	Ted Demme	Denis Leary, Ian Hart
Next Stop Wonderland	Brad Anderson	Hope Davis, Alan Gelfant
The Opposite of Sex	Don Roos	Christina Ricci, Martin Donovan
Pecker	John Waters	Edward Furlong, Christina Ricci
π	Darren Aronofsky	Sean Gullette, Pamela Hart
Slam	Marc Levin	Saul Williams, Sonjah Sohn
The Slums of Beverly Hills	Tamara Jenkins	Natasha Lyonne, Alan Arkin
Smoke Signals	Chris Eyre	Adam Beach, Evan Adams
The Spanish Prisoner	David Mamet	Campbell Scott, Steve Martin
Suicide Kings	Peter O'Fallon	Christopher Walken, Denis Leary
Two Girls and a Guy	James Toback	Robert Downey Jr., Heather Graham
Velvet Goldmine	Todd Haynes	Jonathan Rhys-Mayer, Ewan McGregor
Your Friends & Neighbors	Neil LaBute	Aaron Eckhart, Ben Stiller

Notes

NOTES TO THE INTRODUCTION

1. Joshua Mooney, *Hollywood Reporter*, Special Independents Issue, August 1994.

2. Ibid.

3. Roger Ebert, *Chicago Sun-Times*, April 13, 1987.

4. James Mangold, *Filmmaker*, Spring 1996.

5. David Denby, *New York*, April 7, 1986.

6. *Hollywood Reporter*, Special Independents Issue, August 1996.

7. Ibid.

8. Ibid.

9. The following discussion draws on Jim Moran and Holly Willis, *Filmmaker*, Spring 1998.

10. Jonathan Culler, *The Pursuit of Signs: Semiotics, Literature, Deconstruction* (1981).

11. Phillip Robert Kolker, *The Altering Eye: Contemporary International Cinema* (1983).

12. Leo Braudy, *The World in a Frame* (1976).

13. Oscar Wilde's quote appears in his *De Profundis and Other Writings*.

14. Harold Bloom, *The Anxiety of Influence* (1973).

15. Robin Wood, *Hollywood from Vietnam to Reagan* (1986).

NOTES TO CHAPTER I

1. Quoted in *Los Angeles Weekly*, July 25, 1997.

2. Quoted in Christine Spines, *Premiere*, July 1996.

3. The differences between Tarantino's and Scorsese's sensibilities are explored in Chapter 3.

4. Peter McAlevey, *New York Times*, Sunday Magazine, December 6, 1992.

5. Ibid.

6. Bernard Weintraub, *New York Times*, August 3, 1995.

7. Susan Stover, *Filmmaker*, Fall 1998.

8. Profile of John Pierson, *New Yorker*, 1995.

9. Ibid.

10. The following section draws on Janet Maslin, *New York Times*, December 13, 1992.

11. Susan Sontag, *New York Times*, Sunday Magazine, February 25, 1996.

12. Quoted in Maslin, *New York Times*, December 13, 1992.

13. Quoted in Kenneth Turan, *Los Angeles Times*, January 24, 1992.

14. Maslin, *New York Times*, December 13, 1992.

15. Ibid.

16. Ibid.

17. Quoted in Colin Brown, *Moving Pictures*, May 1994.

18. Rex Weiner, *Daily Variety*, January 24, 1997.

19. Ibid.

20. Doris Toumarkin, *Hollywood Reporter*, Special Independents Issue, August 1993.

21. Ibid.

22. Monica Roman, *Daily Variety*, March 5, 1997.

23. *Premiere*, July 1987.

24. *Time*, February 3, 1986.

25. *Wall Street Journal*, March 25, 1994.

26. Quoted in ibid.

27. Fred Pampel, *American Demographics*, March 1994.

28. Aljean Harmetz, *New York Times*, April 6, 1987.

29. Len Klady, *Daily Variety*, November 29, 1993.

30. Elaine Dutka, *Los Angeles Times*, October 26, 1996.

31. Christine Ogan, *Journal of Communication*, Fall 1990.

32. Len Klady, *Daily Variety*, January 26, 1998.

33. Quoted in Maslin, *New York Times*, December 13, 1992.

34. Michael Cieply, *Los Angeles Times*, March 15, 1988.

35. Viva Hardigg, *U.S. News and World Report*, March 21, 1994.

36. Torene Svitill, *American Film*, August 1990.

37. Caryn James, *New York Times*, May 19, 1988.

38. Jamie Diamond, *American Film*, July 1989.

39. Quoted in *Los Angeles Times*, December 18, 1994.

40. Michael Cieply, *Los Angeles Times*, March 15, 1988.

41. Walter Kirn, *New York Times*, Sunday Magazine, November 16, 1997.

42. Anne Thompson, *Los Angeles Weekly*, February 12, 1993.

43. Claudia Eller and Alan Citron, *Los Angeles Times*, January 31, 1994.

44. Quoted in Maslin, *New York Times*, December 13, 1992.

45. Caryn James, *New York Times*, January 25, 1994.

46. David Ansen, *Newsweek*, February 10, 1992.

47. Robert Koehler, *Daily Variety*, January 15, 1997.

48. Len Klady, *Daily Variety*, January 26, 1998.

49. Doris Toumarkine, *Hollywood Reporter*, Special Independents Issue, August 1994.
50. Adam Pincus, *Filmmaker*, Summer 1997.
51. *Broadcasting and Cable Yearbook*, 1997.
52. *Daily Variety*, July 24, 1997.
53. Richard Natale, *Los Angeles Times*, March 24, 1995.
54. Richard Corliss, *Time*, April 21, 1997.
55. Quoted in *New York Times*, Sunday Magazine, November 27, 1997.
56. Corliss, *Time*, April 21, 1997.

NOTES TO CHAPTER 2

1. My discussion of innovation draws on Howard Becker, *Art Worlds* (1982).
2. John Sayles, *Index on Censorship*, November–December 1995.
3. My discussion of modernism is based on Robert B. Ray, *A Certain Tendency of the Hollywood Cinema* (1985).
4. Louis Menand, *New York Review of Books*, March 23, 1995.
5. My summary of postmodernism in film relies on John Hill's essay in John Hill and Pamela Church Gibson (eds.), *The Oxford Guide to Film Studies* (1998).
6. See David Harvey, *The Condition of Postmodernity* (1989); Annette Kuhn (ed), *Alien Zone: Cultural Theory and Contemporary Science Fiction Cinema* (1990); Tania Modleski, *Feminism Without Women: Culture and Criticism in a "Postfeminist" Age* (1991).
7. Dominic Strinati, *An Introduction to Theories of Popular Culture* (1995).
8. Fredric Jameson, *Postmodernism: Of the Cultural Logic of Late Capitalism* (1991).
9. Strinati, *An Introduction to Theories of Popular Culture* (1995).
10. Manohla Dargis, *Village Voice*, January 22, 1991.
11. Jon Jost, *Film Comment*, March–April, 1992.
12. The following analysis draws on Peter Lunenfeld's essay on Jon Jost, *Film Quarterly*, Summer 1992.
13. J. Hoberman, *Village Voice*, October 24, 1977.
14. Michael Wilmington, *Los Angeles Times*, May 1, 1992.
15. Andy Klein, *Los Angeles Reader*, May 4, 1992.
16. Lunenfeld, *Film Quarterly*, Summer 1992.
17. Ibid.
18. Nicholas Nicastro, *New York Observer*, August 27, 1990.
19. *Current Biography*, 1986.
20. David Denby, *New York*, January 14, 1985.
21. *Toronto Globe and Mail*, September 19, 1986.
22. *Esquire*, September 1986.

23. *Chicago Tribune*, September 25, 1986.
24. J. Hoberman, *Village Voice*, October 24, 1977.
25. Pauline Kael, *New Yorker*, October 27, 1980.
26. Terrence Rafferty, *New Yorker*, March 10, 1997.
27. Ibid.
28. Richard Corliss, *Time*, March 3, 1997.
29. Tom Crow, *Los Angeles Village View*, April 8, 1994.
30. Ibid.
31. Ephraim Katz, *Film Encyclopedia* (1994).
32. Patrick Goldstein, *Los Angeles Times*, February 25, 1988.
33. Crow, *Los Angeles Village View*, April 8, 1994.
34. Janet Maslin, *New York Times*, October 15, 1977.
35. Goldstein, *Los Angeles Times*, February 25, 1988.
36. Ibid.
37. Crow, *Los Angeles Village View*, April 8, 1994.
38. Christine Spines, *Premiere*, July 1996.
39. David Denby, *New York*, February 15, 1993.
40. David Thomson, *A Biographical Dictionary of Film* (1994).
41. Spines, *Premiere*, July 1996.
42. John Sayles, *Index on Censorship*, November–December 1995.
43. Spines, *Premiere*, July 1996.
44. Richard Corliss, *Time*, March 14, 1983.
45. Michael Wilmington, *Los Angeles Times*, December 20, 1992.
46. Spines, *Premiere*, July 1996.
47. Denby, *New York*, February 15, 1993.
48. Anthony Lane, *New Yorker*, July 8, 1996.
49. Paul Malcolm, *Los Angeles Weekly*, July 3, 1998.
50. Aljean Harmetz, *New York Times*, July 23, 1989.
51. Janet Maslin, *New York Times*, October 22, 1989.
52. David Ansen, *Newsweek*, February 3, 1992.
53. John Powers, *Vogue*, June 1995.
54. Malcolm, *Los Angeles Weekly*, July 3, 1998.
55. Ibid.
56. Jeff Gordinier, *Entertainment Weekly*, November/December 1997.
57. Malcolm, *Los Angeles Weekly*, July 3, 1998.

NOTES TO CHAPTER 3

1. David Thomson, *A Biographical Dictionary of Film* (1994).
2. Dave Kehr, *Chicago Reader*, February 1989.
3. Raymond Carney, *American Dreaming: The Films of John Cassavetes and the American Experience* (1985).

4. J. Hoberman, *Premiere*, October 1991.
5. Carney, *American Dreaming* (1985).
6. *Current Biography*, 1969.
7. Paula Span, *Washington Post*, August 21, 1991.
8. Steve Murray, *Atlanta Constitution*, March 8, 1993.
9. Span, *Washington Post*, August 21, 1991.
10. David Denby, *New York*, October 4, 1994.
11. The discussion of women's screen images in Scorsese's work draws on Marion Weiss, *Martin Scorsese* (1987).
12. Timothy Corrigan in Jon Lewis (ed.), *The New American Cinema* (1998).
13. See Phoebe Hoban's profile, *New York*, February 1, 1993.
14. David Denby, *New York*, November 18, 1996.
15. Quoted in Hoban, *New York*, February 1, 1993.
16. Denby, *New York*, November 18, 1996.
17. John Powers, *Vogue*, October 1994.
18. Peter McAlevey, *New York Times*, Sunday Magazine, December 6, 1992.
19. Amy Taubin, *Sight and Sound*, December 1992.
20. David Denby, *New York*, October 3, 1994.
21. Quoted in Peter Biskind, *Premiere*, October 1995.
22. Barry Graham, *Phoenix New Times*, January 8, 1998.
23. David Denby, *New York*, October 3, 1994.
24. Powers, *Vogue*, October 1994.
25. Ellen Paul, *New York Times*, August 23, 1993.
26. Malcolm Johnson, *Hartford Courant*, December 4, 1992.
27. Peter Brunette, *Washington Post*, April 23, 1995.
28. Amy Taubin, *Village Voice*, September 10, 1996.
29. Ibid.
30. Production Notes, *Desperado* (1995).
31. Terrence Rafferty, *New Yorker*, February 3, 1996.
32. Todd McCarthy, *Daily Variety*, January 25, 1996.
33. Manohla Dargis, *Los Angeles Weekly*, October 17, 1997.
34. Sarah Lyall, *New York Times*, July 13, 1993.
35. Quoted in Jessica Seigel, *Chicago Tribune*, February 4, 1994.
36. Peter Rainer, *Los Angeles Times*, August 11, 1993.
37. Wolf Schneider, *Los Angeles Weekly*, August 7, 1995.
38. J. Hoberman, *Premiere*, September 1994.
39. Production Notes, *Killing Zoe* (1994).
40. Peter Rainer, *Los Angeles Weekly*, August 26, 1994.
41. Manohla Dargis, *Los Angeles Weekly*, August 18, 1995.
42. David Denby, *New York*, August 28, 1995.
43. Quoted in *Premiere*, July 1995.

NOTES TO CHAPTER 4

1. Other movies set in the country and/or dealing with country music were *Urban Cowboy, Honeysuckle Rose,* and *Hard Country* (all in 1980), and *Tender Mercies* (1983).

2. Jack Kroll, *Newsweek,* November 11, 1985.

3. Janet Maslin, *New York Times,* December 21, 1986.

4. David Ansen, *Newsweek,* July 14, 1991.

5. David Edelstein, *Village Voice,* August 23, 1988.

6. J. Hoberman, *Premiere,* September 1988.

7. Edelstein, *Village Voice,* August 23, 1988.

8. Michael Sragow, *Rolling Stone,* March 19, 1981.

9. Production Notes, *Melvin and Howard.*

10. Christopher Lasch, *The Culture of Narcissism* (1979), p. 2.

11. Tom McDonough, *American Film,* October 1986.

12. Production Notes, *True Stories.*

13. J. Hoberman, *Village Voice,* October 14, 1986.

14. Production Notes, *True Stories.*

15. David Denby, *New York,* January 25, 1988.

16. Terrence Rafferty, *New Yorker,* June 17, 1996.

17. Terry Christensen, *Reel Politics: American Political Movies from "Birth of a Nation" to "Platoon"* (1987), p. 166.

18. J. Hoberman, *Village Voice,* January 26, 1988.

19. Stephen Holden, *New York Times,* April 12, 1995.

20. Susan McHenry, *Ms.,* May 1985.

21. Vincent Canby, *New York Times,* September 24, 1979.

22. Production Notes, *Ruby in Paradise.*

23. Vincent Canby, *New York Times,* July 15, 1984.

24. Robert Horton, *Film Comment,* 1991.

25. J. Hoberman, *Premiere,* June 1991.

26. Horton, *Film Comment,* 1991.

27. Geoff Pevere, *Toronto Globe,* September 10, 1993.

28. David Denby, *New York,* October 4, 1993.

29. Peter Rainer, *Los Angeles Times,* September 24, 1993.

30. David Denby, *New York,* February 6, 1995.

31. Ibid.

32. Susan King, *Los Angeles Times,* March 26, 1998.

33. Pat Aufderheide, *Independent Film and Video Monthly,* January–February 1998.

34. Renee Graham, *Boston Globe,* August 16, 1998.

NOTES TO CHAPTER 5

1. J. Hoberman, *Village Voice*, April 15, 1981.
2. *Filmmaker*, Fall 1996.
3. Lawrence Van Gelder, *New York Times*, October 21, 1984.
4. Pauline Kael, *New Yorker*, November 12, 1984.
5. Janet Maslin, *New York Times*, January 18, 1985.
6. *Current Biography*, 1990.
7. David Denby, *New York*, September 27, 1989.
8. Pauline Kael, *New Yorker*, October 20, 1986.
9. My analysis draws on Graham Fuller, *Interview*, September 1992.
10. Ibid.
11. Andrew Sarris, *New York Observer*, November 20, 1992.
12. Steve Weinstein, *Los Angeles Times*, August 11, 1991.
13. John Harkness, *Now*, September 10, 1992.
14. Ibid.
15. Quoted in Weinstein, *Los Angeles Times*, August 11, 1991.
16. Ibid.
17. Hal Hinson, *Washington Post*, August 15, 1991.
18. Production Notes, *Simple Men*.
19. Fuller, *Interview*, September 1992.
20. Andrew Sarris, *New York Observer*, August 27, 1990.
21. *Filmmaker*, Spring 1998.
22. Beth Kleid, *Los Angeles Times*, August 10, 1998.
23. David Gritten, *Los Angeles Times*, September 8, 1993.
24. *Filmmaker*, Spring 1998.
25. J. Hoberman, *Premiere*, 1992.
26. Chris Smith, *New York*, April 29, 1996.
27. Ibid.
28. Ellen Pall, *New York Times*, July 10, 1994.
29. Richard Corliss, *Time*, June 9, 1997.
30. My discussion of Smith's background is based on a profile in *Details*, 1994.
31. Ibid.
32. Robert Koehler, *Daily Variety*, February 25, 1997.
33. Production Notes, *Clerks*.
34. Susan King, *Los Angeles Times*, April 24, 1997.
35. Corliss, *Time*, June 9, 1997.
36. Peter Rainer, *Los Angeles New Times*, April 10, 1997.
37. Manohla Dargis, *Los Angeles Weekly*, April 11, 1997.
38. Corliss, *Time*, June 9, 1997.
39. Bernard Weintraub, *New York Times*, August 3, 1995.

40. Ibid.

41. John Powers, *Vogue*, September 1997.

NOTES TO CHAPTER 6

1. Paul Schrader, *Film Comment*, Spring 1972.

2. J. P. Telotte, *Voices in the Dark: The Narrative Patterns of Film Noir* (1988), p. 10.

3. Ephraim Katz, *The Film Encyclopedia* (1994), p. 452.

4. Vincent Canby, *New York Times*, 1984.

5. Telotte, *Voices in the Dark* (1989), pp. 17–21.

6. Kenneth Turan, *Los Angeles Times*, April 21, 1995.

7. Bruce Crowther, *Film Noir: Reflections in a Dark Mirror* (1990).

8. Geoffrey O'Brien, *New York Review*, August 15, 1991; Jon Tuska, *Dark Cinema: American Film Noir in Cultural Perspective* (1984).

9. David Denby, *New York*, January 21, 1985.

10. Todd McCarthy, *Daily Variety*, January 29, 1994.

11. Peter Rainer, *Los Angeles Times*, March 13, 1994.

12. John Powers, *New York*, March 18, 1994.

13. David Denby, *New York*, January 21, 1985.

14. David Denby, *New York*, September 24, 1990.

15. Production Notes, *Barton Fink*.

16. Stanley Kauffmann, *New Republic*, September 30, 1991.

17. Powers, *New York*, March 18, 1994.

18. John Powers, *Vogue*, March 1996.

19. Richard Schickel, *Time*, November 14, 1994.

20. David Handelman, *Vogue*, March 1996.

21. Ibid.

22. Schickel, *Time*, November 14, 1994.

23. J. Hoberman, *Premiere*, December 1994.

24. David Denby, *New York*, August 25, 1990.

25. Mark Zweigler, *After Dark*, August 1976.

26. Pauline Kael, *New Yorker*, November 14, 1988.

27. Patrick McGavin, *Chicago Tribune*, July 10, 1994.

28. Ibid.

29. Owen Gleiberman, *Entertainment Weekly*, August 23, 1995.

30. Andy Klein, *Los Angeles Reader*, August 25, 1995.

NOTES TO CHAPTER 7

1. Judith I. Brennan, *Los Angeles Times*, August 1, 1998.

2. Robert Koehler, *Daily Variety*, February 25, 1997.

3. Ibid.

4. Woody Allen's commercial comedies of the past decade have grossed around $10 to $14 million and some of his most recent ones, such as *Celebrity* (1998) much less than that.

5. Koehler, *Daily Variety*, February 25, 1997.

6. Altman's profile is based on Ephraim Katz, *The Film Encyclopedia* (1994), *Hollywood Reporter*, Special Independent Issue, August 1993; and other sources.

7. Peter Biskind, *Easy Riders, Raging Bulls* (1998), p. 104.

8. David Thomson, *A Biographical Dictionary of Film* (1994).

9. Jan Stuart, *Los Angeles Times*, February 12, 1998.

10. Thomson, *A Biographical Dictionary of Film* (1994).

11. See Helene Keyssar, *Robert Altman's America* (1991).

12. Pauline Kael, *New Yorker*, December 24, 1984.

13. Joshua Mooney, *Hollywood Reporter*, Special Independents Issue, August 1994.

14. Vincent Canby, *New York Times*, January 13, 1985.

15. Pauline Kael, *New Yorker*, April 7, 1986.

16. Michael Wilmington, *Los Angeles Times*, June 16, 1993.

17. Harry Kloman, *New York Times*, September 1, 1992.

18. Rita Kempley, *Washington Post*, August 21, 1991.

19. Koehler, *Daily Variety*, February 25, 1997.

20. Ibid.

21. The discussion of Gen-X relies on Patrick Goldstein, *Los Angeles Times*, April 24, 1994.

22. *New York Times*, March 26, 1989.

23. Ibid.

24. Koehler, *Daily Variety*, February 25, 1997.

25. Thomson, *A Biographical Dictionary of Film* (1994).

26. The following analysis of *Diner* draws on Pauline Kael's essay, *New Yorker*, April 5, 1982.

27. Geoffrey McNab, *Guardian*, January 3, 1997.

28. John Powers, *Vogue*, March 1996.

29. Todd McCarthy, *Daily Variety*, February 6, 1995.

30. Manohla Dargis, *Los Angeles Weekly*, September 10, 1996.

31. Owen Gleiberman, *Entertainment Weekly*, September 8, 1996.

NOTES TO CHAPTER 8

1. John Clark, *Los Angeles Times*, July 7, 1996.

2. See Terry Christensen, *Reel Politics: American Political Movies from "Birth of a Nation" to "Platoon"* (1987).

3. Clark, *Los Angeles Times*, July 7, 1996.

4. Peter Roffman and Jim Purdy, *The Hollywood Social Problem Film* (1981).

5. Clark, *Los Angeles Times*, July 7, 1996.

6. Ibid.

7. Mary C. Henderson, *New York Times*, August 30, 1987.

8. David Denby, *New York*, April 28, 1986.

9. David Edelstein, *Village Voice*, April 29, 1986.

10. The following discussion is based on my book, *Small-Town America in Film: The Decline and Fall of Community* (1991).

11. Kenneth Turan, *Los Angeles Times*, January 25, 1996.

12. Scott McCauley, *Filmmaker*, Fall 1998.

13. Production Notes, *Happiness*.

14. McCauley, *Filmmaker*, Fall 1998.

15. Andy Klein, *Los Angeles Reader*, October 15, 1997.

16. Todd McCarthy, *Daily Variety*, January 1997.

17. Kenneth Turan, *Los Angeles Times*, September 20, 1996.

18. Chris Willman, *Los Angeles Times*, September 15, 1991.

19. Ibid.

20. Richard Alleva, *Commonwealth*, March 13, 1992.

21. Willman, *Los Angeles Times*, September 15, 1991.

22. Robert Abele, *Los Angeles New Times*, November 26, 1996.

23. *Filmmaker*, Fall 1996.

24. Terrence Rafferty, *New Yorker*, June 17, 1996.

25. Max Alexander, *Variety Weekly*, February 27, 1995.

26. *Filmmaker*, Fall 1996.

27. Ibid.

28. Alexander, *Variety Weekly*, February 27, 1995.

29. Andrew Sarris, *New York Observer*, March 30, 1990.

30. *Premiere*, March 1994.

31. Chris Chang, *Film Comment*, May–June 1994.

32. David Sterritt, *Christian Science Monitor*, July 25, 1995.

33. Ibid.

34. Chuck Stephens, *Film Comment*, July–August 1995.

35. Production Notes, *Safe*.

36. Stephens, *Film Comment*, July–August 1995.

37. Ray Pride, *Filmmaker*, Summer 1997.

38. John Clark, *Los Angeles Times*, August 3, 1997.

39. David Ansen, *Newsweek*, October 26, 1998.

NOTES TO CHAPTER 9

1. Wolf Schneider, *Los Angeles Weekly*, June 23, 1995.

2. Eric Gutierrez, *Los Angeles Times*, June 28, 1998.

3. Amy Wallace, *Los Angeles Times*, June 28, 1998.
4. J. Hoberman, *Village Voice*, September 24, 1979.
5. Chris Chase, *New York Times*, October 14, 1983.
6. Production Notes, *My Family*.
7. J. Hoberman, *Village Voice*, January 17, 1984.
8. Ibid.
9. Production Notes, *My Family*.
10. Kristine McKenna, *Los Angeles Times*, April 15, 1995.
11. Terrence Rafferty, *New Yorker*, July 20, 1997.
12. Hazel-Dawn Humpert, *Filmmaker*, Summer 1997.
13. The following discussion draws on David Huang, *New York Times*, August 1, 1985.
14. David Thomson, *A Biographical Dictionary of Film* (1994).
15. David Thomson, *Film Comment*, 1985.
16. Ibid.
17. Tony Chiu, *New York Times*, May 30, 1982.
18. David Ansen, *Newsweek*, June 21, 1982.
19. David Denby, *New York*, April 7, 1982.
20. Vincent Canby, *New York Times*, April 24, 1982.
21. Thomson, *A Biographical Dictionary of Film* (1994).
22. Nancy Blaine, *Los Angeles Village View*, August 13, 1993.
23. Ibid.
24. Production Notes, *The Wedding Banquet*.
25. Ibid.
26. Blaine, *Los Angeles Village View*, August 13, 1993.
27. Production Notes, *Eat, Drink, Man, Woman*.
28. Blaine, *Los Angeles Village View*, August 13, 1993.
29. Production Notes, *Real Life*.
30. David Denby, *New York*, February 25, 1985.
31. Jack Kroll, *Newsweek*, March 7, 1979.
32. Andrew Sarris, *Village Voice*, December 1985.
33. Production Notes, *Mother*.
34. Ward Churchill, *Fantasies of the Master Race: Literature, Cinema, and the Colonization of American Indians* (1992).
35. Cylena Simonds, *After Image*, January 21, 1994.
36. John Clark, *Los Angeles Times*, June 28, 1998.
37. Production Notes, *Smoke Signals*.
38. Clark, *Los Angeles Times*, June 28, 1998.
39. Ibid.

NOTES TO CHAPTER 10

1. Robert Welkos, *Los Angeles Times*, July 17, 1998.
2. My discussion of Maya Deren and Shirley Clarke draws on Lauren Rabinowitz, *Points of Resistance* (1991).
3. Bosley Crowther, *New York Times*, April 21, 1964.
4. Rabinowitz, *Points of Resistance: Women, Power, and Politics in the New York Avant-Garde Cinema, 1943–1971* (1991).
5. For a discussion of Arzner's career as a woman director, see Claire Johnston, *The Work of Dorothy Arzner: Towards a Feminist Cinema* (London: British Film Institute, 1975).
6. Marjorie Rosen, *Popcorn Venus: Women, Movies, and the American Dream* (1973).
7. Robin Wood, *Hollywood from Vietnam to Reagan* (1986).
8. Ibid.
9. My discussion draws on Pauline Kael, *New Yorker*, November 25, 1975.
10. Walter Goodman, *New York Times*, November 2, 1975.
11. Molly Haskell, *From Reverence to Rape: The Treatment of Women in the Movies* (1987).
12. Judy Klemesrud, *New York Times*, August 4, 1978.
13. Barbara Quart, *Women Directors: The Emergence of a New Cinema* (1988).
14. Cecilia Starr, *New York Times*, August 6, 1978.
15. Ibid.
16. Klemesrud, *New York Times*, August 4, 1978.
17. David Denby, *New York*, January 17, 1983.
18. David Ansen, *Newsweek*, April 8, 1985.
19. Production Notes, *Born in Flames*.
20. Marcia Pally, *Village Voice*, November 15, 1983.
21. Katherine Dieckmann, *Village Voice*, March 10, 1987.
22. Annette Insdorf, *Los Angeles Times*, April 7, 1987.
23. Ibid.
24. My analysis draws heavily on Bette Gordon's essay in Patricia Erens (ed.), *Issues in Feminist Film Criticism* (1990).
25. John Powers, *Vogue*, October 1995.
26. Janet Maslin, *New York Times*, January 20, 1984.
27. J. Hoberman, *Village Voice*, April 24, 1988.
28. Powers, *Vogue*, October 1995.
29. David Denby, *New York*, March 26, 1990.
30. Andrew Sarris, *Village Voice*, March 4, 1986.
31. Andrew Sarris, *New York Observer*, September 24, 1991.
32. Nancy Blaine, *Los Angeles Village View*, October 8, 1993.
33. Production Notes, *Household Saints*.

34. Blaine, *Los Angeles Village View*, October 8, 1993.
35. Ibid.
36. Manohla Dargis, *Village Voice*, August 18, 1992.
37. Laurie H. Benenson, *New York Times*, July 26, 1992.
38. Ibid.
39. Alex Demyanenko, *Los Angeles Village View*, August 14, 1992.
40. Holly Willis, *Los Angeles Reader*, July 22, 1994.
41. Richard Corliss, *Time*, September 19, 1996.
42. Ella Taylor, *Los Angeles Weekly*, September 17, 1996.
43. Peter Rainer, *Los Angeles Times*, February 14, 1992.
44. John Williams, *Black Scholar*, Spring 1995.
45. Tom Crow, *Los Angeles Village View*, March 6, 1992.
46. Ibid.
47. John Powers, *Vogue*, September 1994.
48. Production Notes, *Boxing Helena*.
49. Andrew Sarris, *New York Observer*, January 20, 1993.
50. Devon Jackson, *Village Voice*, November 17, 1992.
51. Ibid.
52. John Petrakis, *Chicago Tribune*, September 6, 1993.
53. *Filmmaker*, Spring 1996.
54. Terrence Rafferty, *New Yorker*, May 19, 1996.
55. *Filmmaker*, Spring 1996.
56. Ibid.
57. Chiori Santiago, *San Francisco Chronicle*, June 1991.
58. Gloria Ohland, *Los Angeles Weekly*, June 16, 1989.
59. Sean Smith, *Los Angeles Village View*, May 2, 1996.
60. Eric Freedman, *Filmmaker*, Spring 1996.
61. Smith, *Los Angeles Village View*, May 2, 1996.
62. Amy Taubin, *Village Voice*, August 8, 1995.

NOTES TO CHAPTER 11

1. Charles Burnett and Charles Lane, *American Film*, August 1991.
2. Michael Wilmington, *Los Angeles Times*, April 26, 1991.
3. Vincent Canby, *New York Times*, October 5, 1990.
4. Ephraim Katz, *The Film Encyclopedia* (1994).
5. Larry Rohter, *New York Times*, August 10, 1986.
6. Pauline Kael, *New Yorker*, October 6, 1986.
7. Vincent Canby, *New York Times*, March 9, 1990.
8. Richard Bernstein, *New York Times*, May 28, 1991.
9. Ibid.
10. Ibid.

11. Stephen Holden, *New York Times*, April 22, 1994.

12. Robin Rauzi, *Los Angeles Times*, June 3, 1993.

13. Anne Bregman, *Los Angeles Times*, October 3, 1995.

14. David Denby, *New York*, July 27, 1992.

15. Michael Wilmington, *Los Angeles Times*, May 14, 1993.

16. Andy Klein, *Los Angeles Reader*, October 1995.

17. Patrick Goldstein, *Los Angeles Times*, October 25, 1992.

18. Kenneth Turan, *Los Angeles Times*, August 31, 1994.

19. N'Gai Croal, *Newsweek*, April 22, 1996.

20. David Ansen, *Newsweek*, January 8, 1996.

21. *Premiere*, July 1998.

NOTES TO CHAPTER 12

1. David Thomson, *A Biographical Dictionary of Film* (1994).

2. The following discussion draws on Lee Atwell's analysis in *Film Quarterly*, Fall 1979.

3. Clarke Taylor, *Chicago Tribune*, March 12, 1986.

4. Ibid.

5. Production Notes, *Parting Glances*.

6. David Edelstein, *Village Voice*, Feruary 25, 1986.

7. Production Notes, *Parting Glances*.

8. Vincent Canby, *New York Times*, April 4, 1986.

9. Thomas J. Meyer, *New York Times Sunday Magazine*, September 15, 1991.

10. J. Hoberman, *Village Voice*, October 10, 1989.

11. *Current Biography*, 1992.

12. Pauline Kael, *New Yorker*, October 30, 1989.

13. Ibid.

14. Terrence Rafferty, *New Yorker*, October 7, 1991.

15. Richard Natale, *Los Angeles Weekly*, August 16, 1993.

16. Vincent Canby, *New York Times*, May 11, 1990.

17. Andrew Sarris, *New York Observer*, May 15, 1990.

18. John Anderson, *Los Angeles Times*, August 23, 1992.

19. The following discussion is based on thematic panels in various festivals dealing with the new gay and lesbian cinema of the 1990s.

20. Anderson, *Los Angeles Times*, August 23, 1992.

21. Kristine McKenna, *Los Angeles Times*, July 10, 1994.

22. Ibid.

23. Anderson, *Los Angeles Times*, August 23, 1992.

24. This background is provided in Caryn James, *New York Times*, April 14, 1991.

25. J. Hoberman, *Premiere*, February 1991.
26. Michael Wilmington, *Los Angeles Times*, May 17, 1991.
27. Ella Taylor, *Los Angeles Weekly*, August 21, 1992.
28. Ibid.
29. Lawrence Chua, *Bomb*, Fall 1992.
30. Taylor, *Los Angeles Weekly*, August 21, 1992.
31. Chua, *Bomb*, Fall 1992.
32. Ibid.
33. Kevin Thomas, *Los Angeles Times*, November 2, 1994.
34. Chua, *Bomb*, Fall 1992..
35. Jennine Lanquette, *Premiere*, 1992.
36. Michael Wilmington, *Los Angeles Times*, September 25, 1992.
37. Lanquette, *Premiere*, 1992.
38. Wilmington, *Los Angeles Times*, September 25, 1992.
39. Anne Thompson, *Los Angeles Weekly*, September 24, 1992.
40. Kristine McKenna, *Los Angeles Times*, July 10, 1994.
41. Chris Riemenschneider, *Los Angeles Times*, June 25, 1995.
42. Jennifer Taylor, *Filmmaker*, Summer 1996.
43. McKenna, *Los Angeles Times*, July 10, 1994.
44. Lanquette, *Premiere*, 1992.
45. Armond White, *Film Comment*, July–August, 1996.
46. Ibid.
47. Jean Nathan, *New York Times*, February 25, 1996.
48. John Powers, *Vogue*, September 1995.
49. Cliff Rothman, *Los Angeles Times*, April 19, 1998.
50. Ibid.
51. Patrick Pacheko, *Los Angeles Times*, July 30, 1995.
52. Production Notes, *Billy's Hollywood Screen Kiss*.
53. Filmmaker, Fall 1998.
54. Tom Roston, *Premiere*, June 1997.
55. Ibid.

NOTES TO THE CONCLUSION

1. Pat Aufderheide, *Independent Film and Video Monthly*, January–February, 1998.
2. Chris Smith, *New York*, April 29, 1996.
3. Timothy Corrigan in Jon Lewis (ed.), *The New American Cinema* (1998).
4. David Gritten, *Los Angeles Times*, February 4, 1995.
5. Daniel Lorber, *Daily Variety*, August 6, 1998.
6. Walter Kirn, *New York Times*, Sunday Magazine, November 16, 1997.

7. *New Yorker*, February 2, 1999.

8. Aufderheide, *Independent Film and Video Monthly*, January–February, 1998.

9. *Filmmaker*, Spring 1998.

10. Ibid.

11. Scott MacDonald, *A Critical Cinema: Interviews with Independent Film-makers* (1988).

12. *New York Times*, Sunday Magazine, November 16, 1997.

13. Richard Natale, *Los Angeles Times*, December 2, 1998.

14. Peter Biskind, *Premiere*, April 1993.

15. Quoted in the 1992 catalogue of the Los Angeles/American Film Institute Film Festival.

16. Biskind, *Premiere*, April 1993.

17. David Ansen, *Newsweek*, May 6, 1996.

18. *Time*, March 14, 1983.

19. Amy Wallace, *Los Angeles Times*, October 19, 1998.

20. *New York Times*, Sunday Magazine, November 27, 1997.

21. John Clark, *Los Angeles Times*, September 5, 1998.

22. *Premiere*, October 1998

23. Susan Strover, *Filmmaker*, Fall 1998.

24. *New York Times*, Sunday Magazine, November 27, 1997.

25. *Hollywood Reporter*, Special Independents Issue, August 1996.

26. Natale, *Los Angeles Times*, December 2, 1998.

27. *New York Times*, Sunday Magazine, November 27, 1997.

28. Peter Biskind, *Easy Riders, Raging Bulls* (1998).

29. Terrence Rafferty, *New Yorker*, June 17, 1996.

30. Quoted in Emanuel Levy, *Daily Variety*, January 15, 1998.

31. Aufderheide, *Independent Film and Video Monthly*, January–February 1998.

32. Geoffrey McNab, *Guardian*, January 3, 1997.

33. Kenneth Turan, *Los Angeles Times*, November 22, 1998.

34. Ibid.

35. Joshua Mooney, *Hollywood Reporter*, Special Independents Issue, August 1994.

36. Ibid.

37. *Hollywood Reporter*, Special Independent Issue, August 1996.

38. Ibid.

39. Ibid.

40. Ibid.

41. Amy Wallace, *Los Angeles Times*, July 27, 1998.

42. Ibid.

43. Stephen Gaydos, *Filmmaker*, Fall 1998.

44. *Hollywood Reporter*, August 1996.
45. Quoted in *Daily Variety*, July 24, 1997.
46. *Hollywood Reporter*, August 1996.
47. Mooney, Hollywood Reporter, August 1994.

Select Bibliography

This bibliography contains a selected list of articles and books used. It excludes the hundreds of film reviews that were consulted and used in the text. The publication and date of these reviews appear in the Notes section for each chapter.

Acker, Ally. *Reel Women: Pioneers of the Cinema, 1896 to the Present.* New York: Continuum, 1991.

Anderson, John. "Out There Struggling." *Los Angeles Times,* August 23, 1992.

Anderson, Phil. "Prairie Film Companion." *American Film,* November 1982.

Ansen, David. "A Grab Bag of Gothic Styles." *Newsweek,* February 3, 1992.

———. "Up Where the Air Is Clear." *Newsweek,* February 10, 1992.

———. "The Talent Bazaar." *Newsweek,* February 15, 1993.

Atwell, Lee. "Word Is Out and Gay U.S.A." *Film Quarterly,* 1979.

Aufderheide, Pat. "Man of the Hour: Sundance's Geoff Gilmore." *Independent Film and Video Monthly,* January–February 1998.

Barr, William R. "Brakhage: Artistic Development in Two Childbirth Films." *Film Quarterly,* 1976.

Barsam, Richard M. *Non-Fiction Film: A Critical History.* Bloomington: Indiana University Press, 1992.

Bart, Peter. "Why the Studios Find Oscar Nominations a Non-Event." *Daily Variety,* February 18, 1997.

Barthes, Roland. *Elements of Semiology.* London: Jonathan Cape, 1967.

———. *Mythologies.* New York: Hill and Wang, 1972.

Becker, Howard. *Art Worlds.* Berkeley: University of California Press, 1982.

Bellafonte, Gina. "Generation X-Cellent." *Time,* February 27, 1995.

Bennett, Leslie. "The New Realism in Portraying Homosexuals." *New York Times,* February 21, 1982.

Berger, Arthur Asa. *Media Analysis Techniques.* Beverly Hills: Sage, 1982.

Berger, Warren. "Film Channels." *New York Times,* November 5, 1995.

Bernstein, Richard. "The Film and the Dream: A Brooklyn Story." *New York Times,* May 28, 1991.

Berube, Allan. *Coming Out under Fire: The History of Gay Men and Women in World War II.* New York: Free Press, 1990.

Biskind, Peter. *Seeing Is Believing*. New York: Pantheon, 1983.

———. "Dead Zone." *Premiere*, April 1993.

———. *Easy Riders, Raging Bulls*. New York: Simon and Schuster, 1998.

"Black Filmmakers Special Report." *Daily Variety*, October 8, 1993.

Blaine, Nancy. "East by Northeast." *Los Angeles Village View*, August 13, l993.

———. "Saints, Sinners, Savoca." *Los Angeles Village View*, October 8, 1993.

Bloom, Harold. *The Anxiety of Influence*. New York: Oxford University Press, 1973.

Bordwell, David, and Kristin Thompson. *Film Art*. New York: Knopf, l986.

Bosworth, Patricia. "How Could I Forget What I Am? Gordon Parks."*New York Times*, August 17, 1969.

Braudy, Leo. *The World in a Frame*. New York: Doubleday, 1976.

———. *Native Informant: Essays on Film, Fiction, and Popular Culture*. New York: Oxford University Press, 1997.

Braudy, Leo, and Marshall Cohen (eds.). *Film Theory and Criticism*. 5th ed. New York: Oxford University Press, 1999.

Braxton, Greg. "Rediscovering Pioneers of Black Film." *Los Angeles Times*, October 11, 1998.

Breitbart, Eric. "Four New York Independents." *American Film*, May 1985.

Brennan, Judith I. "The New Comedy." *Los Angeles Times*, August 1, 1998.

Broadcasting and Cable Yearbook 1997. New Brunswick, N.J.: R. R. Bowker, 1997

Bronwen, Hruska. "Susan Seidelman." *Los Angeles Times*, March 6, 1994.

Bruckner, D. J. R. "Film: Spike Lee's 'She's Gotta Have It.'" *New York Times*, August 8, 1986.

Cagin, Seth, and Philip Dray. *Hollywood Films of the Seventies*, New York: Harper and Row, 1984.

Canby, Vincent. "Films for Viewers Who Think for Themselves." *New York Times*, September 7, 1986.

———. "Rejoice! Right Now It's Independents Day." *New York Times*, October 8, 1989.

———. "Gross Encounters in Comical 'House Party.'" *New York Times*, March 9, 1990.

Carey, James W. (ed.). *Media, Myths, and Narratives: Television and the Press*. Calif.: Sage, 1988.

Carney, Raymond. *American Dreaming: The Films of John Cassavetes and the American Experience*. Berkeley: University of California Press, 1985.

Carson, L. M. Kit. "New Kids on the Lot." *Esquire*, September 1992.

Cerone, Daniel. "Independent Film Makers, Marketers Confront Box-Office Crisis." *Los Angeles Times*. September 15, 1989.

———. "The Honeymoon Is Just Beginning for 'True Love' Director." *Los Angeles Times*, November 21, 1989.

Chin, Daryl. "Multiculturalism and Its Masks: The Art of Identity Politics." *Performance Arts Journal*, 14 (1992).

Christensen, Terry. *Reel Politics: American Political Movies from "Birth of a Nation" to "Platoon."* New York: Blackwell, 1987.

Chua, Lawrence. "I Love My Dead Gay Son." *Village Voice*, December 5, 1989.

Churchill, Ward. *Fantasies of the Master Race: Literature, Cinema, and the Colonization of American Indians.* Monroe, Me.: Common Courage Press, 1992.

Cieply, Michael. "Some Independents Face Leaner Diets." *Los Angeles Times*, October 23, 1987.

———. "Film School Boom Proves Fast but Still Rocky Road to Big Time." *Los Angeles Times*, March 15, 1988.

———. "Film Schools Face Effects of Success." *Los Angeles Times*, March 16, 1988.

Clark, John. "Penelope Spheris." *Premiere*, March 1992.

———. "No Reservations." *Los Angeles Times*, June 28, 1998.

———. "Christine Vachon." *Los Angeles Times*, September 5, 1998.

"Class Reunion." *Filmmaker*, 1998.

Cohn, Lawrence. "Poetic Justice." *Premiere*, July 1994.

Coker, Cheo Hodari. "Can a Real 'Love' Conquer?" *Los Angeles Times*, March 20, 1997.

Conley, Tom. "State of Film Noir." *Theatre Journal* (1987).

Corrigan, Timothy. *A Cinema without Walls: Movies and Culture after Vietnam.* New Brunswick, N.J.: Rutgers University Press, 1991.

Corliss, Richard. "Backing into the Future." *Time*, February 3, 1986.

———. "One Dumb Summer." *Time*, June 30, 1997.

———. "The Three Faces of Evil." *Time*, October 20, 1997.

Costikyan, Barbara. "Longtime Companion." *New York Times*, May 21, 1990.

Crouch, Stanley. "Artistry in Any Color." *Los Angeles Times*, October 22, 1995.

Crowther, Bruce. *Film Noir: Reflections in a Dark Mirror.* New York: Ungar, 1990.

Culler, Jonathan. *Pursuit of Signs: Semiotics, Literature, Deconstruction.* Ithaca, N.Y.: Cornell University Press, 1981.

Damico, James. "Film Noir: A Modest Proposal." *Film Reader* 3 (February 1978).

Dargis, Manohla. "Giving Directions." *Village Voice*, August 18, 1992.

———. "Allison Anders." *Los Angeles Weekly*, July 22, 1994.

———. "You Can't Get a Line Reading on Tears." *Los Angeles Weekly*, April 18, 1997.

Daily Variety, Special Annual Independent Issues, 1993–99.

Dempsey, John. "Indie Channel Adds to Lineup." *Daily Variety*, February 21, 1996.

Denby, David. "Lost in America." *New York*, February 25, 1985.

———. "Flesh and Fantasy." *New York*, September 29, 1986.

Denby, David. "Let Us Now Praise Famous Moguls." *Premiere*, May 1989.
———. "Mr. Vice Guy—American Me." *New York*, March 23, 1992.
———. "Curls of Smoke." *New York*, June 19, 1995.
———. "Coming of Age in Park City." *New Yorker*, February 8, 1999.
Diamond, Jamie. "Film School Confidential." *American Film*, July–August 1989.
Diawara, Manthia. "Cinema Studies, the Strong Thought and Black Film." *Wide Angle*, July–October 1991.
Dieckmann, Katherine. "Let's Hear It for the Girl." *Village Voice*, April 19, 1988.
Doane, Mary Ann, Patricia Mellencamp, and Linda Williams (eds.). *Revisions: Essays in Feminist Film Criticism*. Frederick, Md.: University Publications of America, 1984.
———. *The Desire to Desire*. Bloomington: Indiana University Press, 1987.
———. "Feminism Failed." *New York Times* Sunday Magazine, June 26, 1988.
Dortch, Shannon, "Going to the Movies." *American Demographics*, December 1996.
Dunning, Jennifer. "Making Films before Fame Knocks." *New York Times*, September 1, 1994.
Dutka, Elaine. "Boom Time for Indies Nears Glut." *Los Angeles Times*, October 26, 1996.
Dyer, Richard. *Now You See It: Studies on Lesbian and Gay Film*. New York: Routledge, 1990.
Easton, Nina J. "Good News/Bad News of the New Black Cinema." *Los Angeles Times*, June 16, 1991.
———. "The Invisible Women." *Los Angeles Times*, September 29, 1991.
Economist, February 26, 1994.
Eisenbach, Helen. "Up from Oblivion: Tom DiCillo." *New York*, July 28, 1997.
Erens, Patricia (ed.). *Sexual Strategem: The World of Women in Film*. New York: Horizon Press, 1979.
———. *Issues in Feminist Film Criticism*. Bloomington: Indiana University Press, 1990.
Evans, Greg. "Spate of New Pix Tests Limits of Friendship." *Variety Weekly*, December 18, 1995.
Fiedler, Leslie. *Love and Death in the American Novel*, New York: Dell, 1969.
———. *The Return of the Vanishing American*. London: Paladin, 1972.
Fishman, Nancy. "Genre Focus: Gay and Lesbian." *Moving Pictures*, May 18, 1994.
Fox, David J. "They Found Out How Tough a Sell AIDS Really Is." *Los Angeles Times*, May 13, 1990.
———. "Can Hollywood Do the Right Thing?" *Los Angeles Times*, July 16, 1991.
——— "Summer: Independents' Day?" *Los Angeles Times*, April 13, 1994.
Freedman, Alix M. "Lights! Camera! Big Investment Action!" *Wall Street Journal*, April 18, 1986.

Friedberg, Anne, "An Interview with Lizzie Borden." *Women and Performance,* Winter 1984.

Friedman, Lester D. (ed.). *Unspeakable Images: Ethnicity and the American Cinema.* Urbana: University of Illinois Press, 1991.

Frolick, Billy. "Hey, That Wasn't in the Script!" *Los Angeles Times,* November 10, 1996.

———. *What I Really Want to Do Is Direct: Seven Film School Graduates Go to Hollywood.* New York: Dutton, 1996.

Frost, Dan. "Marketing the Movies: Tweaking the Story." *American Demographics,* March 1994.

Geier, Thom. "Indie Meltdown: Press and Product Get Blame." *Hollywood Reporter,* September 10, 1998.

Gledhill, Christine. "Recent Developments in Feminist Criticism." in Gerald Mast and Marshall Cohen (eds.). *Film Theory and Criticism: Introductory Readings.* 3d ed. New York: Oxford University Press, 1985.

Goldstein, Patrick "Director John Waters Teases 'Hairspray.'" *Los Angeles Times,* February 25, 1988.

———. "His New 'Hood Is Hollywood." *Los Angeles Times,* July 7, 1991.

———. "A Horse of Different Colors." *Los Angeles Times,* October 25, 1992.

———. "When X Doesn't Mark the Spot." *Los Angeles Times,* April 24, 1994.

———. "A Story That Hits Close to Down Home: Sling Blade." *Los Angeles Times,* November 24, 1996.

Goldstein, Richard. "The Gay New Wave." *Village Voice,* December 5, 1989.

Gombrich, E. H. *Art and Illusion.* Princeton: Princeton University Press, 1961.

Gorov, Lynda. "Cinema 101: Inside the USC Film School Where Future Movie Moguls Are Made." *Chicago Tribune,* June 7, 1992.

Gramsci, Antonio. *Prison Letters.* New York: Pluto Press. 1996.

Grant, Lee. "Where Are the Woman Directors?" *Los Angeles Times,* June 20, 1980.

Greenspun, Roger. "Frame of Reference at N.Y.U." *New York Times,* October 16, 1969.

Grimes, William. "So, You Wanna Be a Director?" *New York Times,* January 17, 1993.

Gubernick, Lisa. "We Don't Want to Be Walt Disney." *Forbes,* October 16, 1989.

Guerrero, Ed. *Framing Blackness: The New African American in Film.* Philadelphia: Temple University Press, 1993.

———. "A Circus of Dreams and Lies: The Black Film Wave at Middle Age." In Jon Lewis (ed.). *The New American Cinema.* Durham, N.C.: Duke University Press, 1998.

Gutierrez, Eric. *Los Angeles Times,* June 28, 1998.

Hall, John. *The Sociology of Literature.* New York: Longman, 1979.

Hardig, Viva. "Full House at Film School." *U.S. News and World Report,* March 21, 1994.

Hardy, Ernest. "Hustling: Miguel Arteta." *Los Angeles Weekly*, July 25, 1997.

Harmetz, Aljean. "Independent Films Making It Big." *New York Times*, April 6, 1987.

———. "Independent Films Get Better but Go Begging." *New York Times*, February 1, 1989.

———. "Sex, Lies, Truth, and Consequences." *New York Times*, July 23, 1989.

———. "Now Showing: Survival of the Fittest." *New York Times*, October 22, 1989.

Harvey, David. *The Condition of Postmodernity: An Enquiry into the Origins of Cultural Change*. Oxford, England: Blackwell, 1989.

Harvey, Dennis. "The San Francisco Gay Fest." *Daily Variety*, May 31, 1996.

Haskell, Molly. *From Reverence to Rape: The Treatment of Women in the Movies*. 2d ed. Chicago: University of Chicago Press, 1987.

Hill, John, and Pamela Church Gibson (eds.). *The Oxford Guide to Film Studies*. New York: Oxford University Press, 1998.

Hindes, Andrew "Arthouse Pix Flunk Out of College." *Daily Variety*, August 23, 1996.

———. "The Magic Number: Daily Variety Special Issue on Indie Finance." *Daily Variety*, February 28, 1997.

Hirschberg, Lynn. "The Actresses." *New York Times* Sunday Magazine, November 16, 1997.

Hoberman, J. "Return to Normalcy: Blue Velvet." *Village Voice*, September 23, 1986.

———. "The Children of David Lynch." *Premiere*, February 1991.

———. "Two Wild and Crazy Films." *Premiere*, June 1991.

———. "Cassavetes and Leigh: Poets of the Ordinary." *Premiere*, October 1991.

———. "Return to New York." *Premiere*, May 1992.

———. "Back on the Wild Side." *Premiere*, August 1992.

———. "Woolf in Potter's Clothing." *Premiere*, July 1993.

———. "Have Camera, Will Travel." *Premiere*, July 1994.

———. *Vulgar Modernism: Writings on Movies and Other Media*. Philadelphia: Temple University Press, 1991.

Hollywood Reporter, Special Independents Issues, 1993–99.

Honeycutt, Kirk. "Martha Coolidge." *Los Angeles Times*, September 15, 1991.

hooks, bell. "The Oppositional Gaze." In bell hooks, *Black Looks: Race and Representation*. Boston: South End Press, 1992.

Hornblower, Margot. "Great Expectations: Gen-X." *Time*, June 9, 1997.

Horton, Andrew S. (ed.). *Comedy/Cinema/Theory*. Berkeley: University of California Press, 1991.

Horton, Robert. "Stranger Than Texas: Slacker." *Film Comment*, May–June 1991.

Hruska, Bronwen. "James Gross: At 26, Who Knows What a Break Is?" *Los Angeles Times*, June, 4, 1995.

Hwang, David. "Are Movies Ready for Real Orientals?" *New York Times*, August 1, 1985.

"Indie Movie Maven Picks the Pix: Profile of John Pierson." *New Yorker*, 1994.

Jackson, Devon. "Under the Gun." *Village Voice*, November 17, 1992.

James, Caryn. "Hollywood Sends Talent Scouts to Film School." *New York Times*, May 19, 1988.

———. "A Dance of Sex and Love, through a Lens Darkly." *New York Times*, August 4, 1989.

———. "Politics Nurtures Poison." *New York Times*, April 14, 1991.

———. "Rambling Rose." *New York Times*, September 20, 1991.

James, Clive. "Hit Men: Bogdanovich." *New Yorker*, July 7, 1997.

James, David E. *Allegories of Cinema: American Film in the Sixties*. Princeton: Princeton University Press, 1989.

Jameson, Fredric. *Postmodernism: Of the Cultural Logic of Late Capitalism*. London: Verso, 1991.

Johnson, Tom. "Double-Edged Diploma." *American Film*, July 1991.

Johnston Claire (ed.). *Notes on Women's Cinema*. London: Society for Education in Film and Television, 1973.

———. "Women's Cinema as Counter-Cinema." In Bill Nichols (ed.), *Movies and Methods*. Berkeley: University of California Press, 1976.

Kael, Pauline. *For Keeps*. New York: Dutton, 1994.

Kaplan, Ann E. *Women in Film Noir*. London: British Film Institute, 1980.

———. *Women and Film: Both Sides of the Camera*. New York: Methuen, 1983.

Karini, A. M. *Toward a Definition of American Film Noir*. New York: Arno, 1976.

Kasindorf, Jeanie. "Lesbian Chic." *New York*, May 10, 1993.

Katz, Ephraim. *The Film Encyclopedia*. New York: Harper, 1994.

Keyssar, Helene. *Robert Altman's America*. New York: Oxford University Press, 1991.

Kim, Jane Bryan. "Alternative Fare Finds Solace Midstream." *Advertising Age*, March 15, 1993.

King, Susan. "Expecting the Unexpected: Linklater." *Los Angeles Times*, March 26, 1998.

———. "Race Movies: Separate and Unequalled." *Los Angeles Times*, June 28, 1998.

Kirn, Walter. "Robert Redford Has This Problem." *New York Times* Sunday Magazine, November 16, 1997.

Klady, Leonard. "Stunted Growth of Core Audience Frustrates Filmers." *Variety Weekly*, November 29, 1993.

———. "Dub and Dubber: U.S. Wary of Foreign Pics." *Daily Variety*, November 5, 1997.

———. "Dorothy Victorious—Slamdance 1998." *Daily Variety*, January 26, 1998.

Koehler, Robert. "In Your Face, Slamdance: Stepchild That Won't Go Away." *Daily Variety*, January 15, 1997.

———. "Comedy of the Subversive." *Daily Variety*, February 25, 1997.

Kolker, Phillip Robert. *The Altering Eye: Contemporary International Cinema*. New York: Oxford University Press, 1983.

———. *A Cinema of Loneliness*. New York: Oxford University Press, 1988.

Kornbluth, Jesse. "The Little Studio That Could." *New York*, April 6, 1987.

Kroll, Jack. "On the Werewolf Circuit." *Newsweek*, September 11, 1978.

Krutnik, Frank. *In a Lonely Street: Film Noir, Genre and Masculinity*. New York: Routledge, 1991.

Kuhn, Annette. *Women's Pictures: Feminism and Cinema*. Boston: Routledge and Kegan Paul, 1982.

———. *Alien Zone: Cultural Theory and Contemporary Science Fiction Cinema*. London: Verso, 1990.

Kuryla, Mary, and Holly Willis. "Brisky Business." *Moving Pictures*, May 13, 1994.

Lacher, Irene. "Guiding the Future of Film." *Los Angeles Times*, December 18, 1994.

Lasch, Christopher. *The Culture of Narcissism: American Life in an Age of Diminishing Expectations*. New York: Warner, 1979.

Leland, John, and Lynda Wright. "Black to the Future," *Newsweek*, May 27, 1991.

Leong, Russell (ed.). *Moving the Image: Independent Asian Pacific American Media Arts*. Seattle: University of Washington Press, 1991.

Letofsky, Irv. "Dawn Profiles Latino Radio Personality." *Los Angeles Times*, April 11, 1990.

Levi-Strauss, Claude. *Structural Anthropology*. New York: Doubleday, 1967.

———. *The View from Afar*. New York: Blackwell, 1985.

Levy, Emanuel. *And the Winner Is: The History and Politics of the Oscar Award*. New York: Ungar, 1987; new expanded ed., 1990.

———. *John Wayne: Prophet of the American Way of Life*. Metuchen, N.J.: Scarecrow, 1988.

———. *Small Town America in Film: The Decline and Fall of Community*. New York: Continuum, 1991.

Lewis, Jon (ed.). *The New American Cinema*. Durham, N.C.: Duke University Press, 1998.

Linfield, Susie. A 'False Move' That Paid Off." *New York Times*, August 9, 1992.

Lippard, Lucy. *Mixed Blessings: New Art in a Multicultural America*. New York: New Press, 1990.

———. *Partial Recall: Photographs of Native North Americans*. New York: New Press, 1992.

Lorber, Daniel. "Indie Rejects Welcome." *Daily Variety*, August 6, 1998.

Lyons, Donald. "Star City Shrapnel." *Film Comment*, September–October 1992.

McCarthy, Todd. "Redford Keeping Sundance Small." *Daily Variety*, January 25, 1993.

———. "Sundance Glow No Promise of Box Office Sizzle." *Daily Variety*, August 17, 1993.

———. "Tix Selling Briskly for Sundance Fest." *Daily Variety*, December 3, 1993.

———. "Growing Sundance Still Far Away from H'wood." *Daily Variety*, February 4, 1994.

———. "Sundance Fest Followup: Where Are They Now?" *Daily Variety*, January 17, 1995.

McConnell, Frank. *Storytelling and Mythmaking*. New York: Oxford University Press, 1973.

McConville, Jim. "IFC on the Move." *Broadcasting and Cable*, February 26, 1997.

McCreadie, Marsha. "Stacy Cochran." *New York Times*, October 25, 1992.

McDonough, Tom. "Making Sense of David Byrne." *American Film*, October 1986.

McKenna, Kristine. "Crossover Hopes: Can 'Fish' and 'Priscilla' Find the Mainstream?" *Los Angeles Times*, July 10, 1994.

———. "Getting to the Heart of One Family's Life." *Los Angeles Times*, April 15, 1995.

McNab, Geoffrey. "Reservoir Puppies." *The Guardian*, January 3, 1997.

MacDonald, Scott. *A Critical Cinema: Interviews with Independent Filmmakers*. Berkeley: University of California Press, 1988.

Maltby, Richard. *Harmless Entertainment*. Metuchen, N.J.: Scarecrow, 1983.

Marton, Andrew M. "Up, Up, and Away." *Premiere*, October 1990.

Maslin, Janet. "Lately the Lens Frames Moral Issues." *New York Times*, October 22, 1989.

———. "Is a Cinematic New Wave Cresting? *New York Times*, December 13, 1992.

Mast, Gerald, Marshall Cohen, and Leo Braudy (eds.). *Film Theory and Criticism*. 4th ed. New York: Oxford University Press, 1992.

Mehler, Mark. "The Film School's Credo: 'Get It Done.'" *Daily Variety*, October 22, 1990.

Mellen, Joan. *Women and Their Sexuality in the Movies*. New York: Horizon, 1973.

———. *The Big Bad Wolves: Masculinity in the American Film*. New York: Pantheon, 1977.

———. "The Return of Women to Seventies Films." *Quarterly Review of Film Studies* (Fall 1978).

Metz, Christian. *Film Language: A Semiotics of Cinema*. New York: Oxford University Press, 1974.

Michaelson, Judith. "TV Adjusts Its Mirror." *Los Angeles Times*, September 22, 1991.

Mims, Sergio Alejandro. "A New Life: Independent Black Filmmaking during the 1980s." *Black Camera*. 1990.

Modleski, Tania. *Feminism without Women: Culture and Criticism in a "Postfeminist" Age*. London: Routledge, 1991.

Monaco, James. *American Film Now*. New York: New American Library, 1981.

Moore, Darrell. "White Men Can't Program: The Contradictions of Multiculturalism." *Afterimage*, Summer 1992.

Moser, James D. (ed.). *International Motion Picture Almanac, 1997*. New York: Quigley, 1997.

Mulvey, Laura. "Visual Pleasure and Narrative Cinema." In Gerald Mast, Marshall Cohen, and Leo Braudy (eds.). 4th ed. *Film Theory and Criticism*. New York: Oxford University Press, 1992.

Murphy, A. D. "Summer Pattern Is Now a Trend." *Daily Variety*, July 7, 1981.

———. "Film B.O. Sets a July-Mid." *Daily Variety*, August 19, 1981.

Napier-Pearce, Jennifer. "How Certain Films Find a Groove." *Los Angeles Times*, August 18, 1998.

Natale, Richard. "Low-Budget 'Move' Stands Out." *Daily Variety*, June 19, 1992.

———. "AIDS as Metaphor: Four Politically Astute Films about the Epidemic." *Los Angeles Weekly*, August 16, 1993.

———. "Independent Spirit Still Taking Shape." *Los Angeles Times*, March 24, 1995.

———. "Independent Films Showing Main Stream Muscle." *Los Angeles Times*, August 26, 1995.

———. "Gaysploitation Films Find a Nice Profitable Niche." *Los Angeles Times*, December 10, 1995.

———. "Looking for Clout in Hollywood." *Los Angeles Times*, June 14, 1998.

"The New Hollywood: Inside the World of Independent Films." *Entertainment Weekly*, Special Issue, November–December 1997.

Nicastro, Nicholas. "Sweet Smell of Success." *Film Comment*, September–October 1992.

Nichols, Bill (ed.). *Movies and Methods*. Berkeley: University of California Press, 1976.

———. *Ideology and Image*. Bloomington: Indiana University Press, 1981.

Nimmo, Dan, and James E. Combs. *Subliminal Politics: Myths and Mythmakers in America*. Englewood Cliffs, N.J.: Prentice-Hall, 1980.

Nochimson, Martha P. *The Passion of David Lynch: Wild at Heart in Hollywood*. Austin: University of Texas Press, 1997.

O'Brien, Geoffrey. "The Return of Film Noir." *New York Review of Books*, August 15, 1991.

O'Connor, Thomas. "John Hughes: His Movies Speak to Teenagers." *New York Times*, March 9, 1986.

Ogan, Christine. "The Audience for Foreign Film in the United States." *Journal of Communication* (Autumn 1990).

Ohland, Gloria. "Nina Menkes." *Los Angeles Weekly*, June 16, 1989.

Ottoson, Robert. *A Reference Guide to the American Film Noir*. Metuchen, N.J.: Scarecrow, 1981.

Pacheko, Patrick. "The Sound of Two Men Kissing." *Los Angeles Times*, July 30, 1995.

Pally, Marcia. "Is There Revolution after the Revolution?" *Village Voice*, November 15, 1983.

Pampel, Fred. "Marketing the Movies: Smaller and Less Violent." *American Demographics*, March 1994.

Perifirio, Robert G. "No Way Out: Existential Motifs in the Film Noir." *Sight and Sound*, Autumn 1976.

Petrakis, John. "Her Own Man: Maggie Greenwald." *Chicago Tribune*, September 6, 1993.

Pierson, John. *Spike, Mike, Slackers and Dykes: A Guided Tour across a Decade of American Independent Cinema*. New York: Hyperion/Miramax, 1995.

Pincus, Adam. "Executive Decision." *Filmmaker*, Summer 1997.

Place, J. A., and L. S. Peterson, "Some Visual Motifs of Film Noir." In Bill Nichols (ed.), *Movies and Methods*. Berkeley: University of California Press, 1976.

Powers, John. "Bleak Chic." *American Film*, March 1987.

———. "The Director Wore Black—Kathryn Bigelow." *Vogue*, October 1995.

Pribram, E. Deidre. "Straight outta Money: Institutional Power and Independent Film Funding." *Afterimage*, Summer 1993.

Pristin, Terry. "I'm Never Afraid of Competition—Sam Goldwyn." *Los Angeles Times*, October 28, 1993.

Propp, Vladimir. *Morphology of the Folktale*. Austin: University of Texas Press, 1973.

Pryor, Kelli. "Allison Anders." *Entertainment Weekly*. July 22, 1994.

Quart, Barbara. "Friendship in Some Recent American Films." *Film Criticism*, Winter 1982.

———. *Women Directors: The Emergence of a New Cinema*. New York: Praeger, 1988.

Quart, Leonard, and Albert Auster. *American Film and Society since 1945*. New York: Praeger, 1988.

Quinn, Michelle. "Gay Film Fest at 10," *Los Angeles Times*, July 9, 1992.

Rabinowitz, Lauren. *Points of Resistance: Women, Power, and Politics in the New York Avant-Garde Cinema, 1943–1971*. Urbana: University of Illinois Press, 1991.

Radway, Janice. *Reading the Romance: Women, Patriarchy and Popular Culture*. Chapel Hill: University of North Carolina Press, 1984.

Rauzi, Robin. "Brother from Another Suburb." *Los Angeles Times*, June 3, 1993.

Ray, Robert B. *A Certain Tendency of the Hollywood Cinema*. Princeton: Princeton University Press, 1985.

"Rebel Yells: Independents Symposium." *Premiere*, October 1998.

Rich, Ruby. "Art House Killers." *Sight and Sound*, December 1992.

———. "In the Name of Feminist Film Criticism." In Patricia Erens (ed.), *Issues in Feminist Film Criticism*. Bloomington: Indiana University Press, 1990.

Riemenschneider, Chris. "Just Another Girl-Gets-Girl Story." *Los Angeles Times*, June 25, 1995.

Roberts, Jerry. "A Slow Fade for Foreign Pix." *Daily Variety*, January 6, 1998.

Rodman, Howard A. "In the Shadow of the Factory: Independent Filmmaking in a Company Town." *Village Voice*, December 6, 1988.

Roffman, Peter, and Jim Purdy. *The Hollywood Social Problem Film*. Bloomington: Indiana University Press, 1981.

Rohter, Larry. "Spike Lee Makes His Movie." *New York Times*, August 10, 1986.

Roman, Monica. "Indies Make Mark at Mart." *Daily Variety*, September 15, 1997.

———. "IFC Mulls Film Distrib Market." *Daily Variety*, September 17, 1997.

———. "Icahn Jumps into Indie Pic Distribution." *Daily Variety*, September 26, 1997.

Rosen, Marjorie. *Popcorn Venus: Women, Movies and the American Dream*. New York: Coward, McCann, and Geoghegan, 1973.

Rosenbaum, Jonathan. *Film: The Front Line*. New York: Arden Press, 1983.

Rosenberg, Jan. *Women's Reflections: The Feminist Film Movement*. Ann Arbor: UMP Research, 1983.

Rothman, Cliff. "Playing Straight with Gays." *Los Angeles Times*, April 19, 1998.

Salamon, Julie. "It's Boomlet Time for Moviedom's Little Guys." *Wall Street Journal*, March 18, 1985.

———. "Film: Independent Dreams." *Wall Street Journal*, February 5, 1986.

Sante, Luc. "The Rise of the Baroque Directors." *Vogue*, September 1992.

Sarris, Andrew. *The American Cinema: Directors and Directions*. New York: Dutton, 1968.

Sayles, John. "How to Stay Independent." *Index on Censorship*, November–December 1995.

Schatz, Thomas. *Hollywood Genres*. Philadelphia: Temple University Press, 1981.

———. *The Genius of the System*. New York: Pantheon, 1988.

Schneider, Wolf. "Barely Bankable." *Los Angeles Weekly*, May 5, 1995.

———. "Fighting Back: Latino Actors Struggle for their Due." *Los Angeles Weekly*, June 23, 1995.

———. "The Milk Train: Where Goes the Indie Film?" *Los Angeles Weekly*, August 7, 1995.

———. "Fest Runner." *Los Angeles Weekly*, November 17, 1995.

———. "Law and Disorder: PBS's Pain, Fox's Gain." *Los Angeles Weekly*, November 24, 1995.

Schrader, Paul. "Notes on Film Noir." *Film Comment*, Spring 1972.

Seger, Linda. *When Women Call the Shots.* New York: Henry Holt, 1998.

Selz, Michael. "Independents Reap Reward at Box Office." *Wall Street Journal*, April 25, 1994.

Setlowe, Richard. "Black Filmmakers." *Daily Variety*, October 8, 1993.

Seymour, Gene. "When Indie Festival Backer Dreams, It's in Vivid Color." *Los Angeles Times*, August 21, 1998.

Silver, Alain, and Elizabeth Ward (eds.). *Film Noir.* Woodstock, New York: Overlook Press, 1979.

Simonds, Cylena. "Serious Reservations." *After Image* 21 (January 1994).

Simpson, Janice C. "Not Just One of the Boyz." *Time*, March 23, 1992.

Sontag, Susan. "The Decay of Cinema." *New York Times* Sunday Magazine, February 25, 1996.

Spines, Christine. "John Sayles: The Lone Star of Independents is Still Marching to His Own Drummer." *Premiere*, July 1996.

Stabiner, Karen. "Tapping the Homosexual Market." *New York Times* Sunday Magazine, May 2, 1982.

Stephens, Chuck. "Gentlemen Prefer Haynes." *Film Comment*, July–August 1995.

Stern, Christopher. "Latin Thesps Blast Biz 'Bias.'" *Daily Variety*, September 24, 1997.

Sterritt, David. "Director Avoids 'Safe' Route with New Movie." *Christian Science Monitor*, July 25, 1995.

Strinati, Dominic. *An Introduction to Theories of Popular Culture.* New York: Routledge, 1995.

Svitil, Torene. "Pop Quiz." *American Film*, August 1990.

Taubin, Amy. "Boys! Boys! Boys!" *Village Voice*, July 18, 1995.

Taylor, Clarke. "Off Hollywood." *American Film*, September 1985.

Taylor, Clarke. "New Films Treat Gays as a Matter of Fact." *Chicago Tribune*, March 12, 1986.

Taylor, Ella. "Call Me Irresponsible: Gregg Araki." *Los Angeles Weekly*, August 21, 1992.

Taylor, Jennifer M. "The Watermelon Woman's Cheryl Dunye." *Filmmaker*, 1996.

Telotte, J. P. *Voices in the Dark: The Narrative Patterns of Film Noir.* Urbana: University of Illinois Press, 1989.

Thompson, Anne. "Back in the Black." *Los Angeles Weekly*, March 15, 1991.

———. "Indies: The New Generation." *Los Angeles Weekly*, February 7, 1992.

———. "Outside Up: Women on the Verge of a Breakthrough." *Los Angeles Weekly*, March 15, 1992.

Thompson, Anne. "Beyond the 'Hood.'" *Los Angeles Weekly*, January 24, 1992.
———. "Low-Wire Act: Indie Marketing Budgets Stretch Thin." *Los Angeles Weekly*, April 24, 1992.
———. "Sophisticated Ladies." *Los Angeles Weekly*, September 24, 1992.
———. "A Me-First Scramble to Find Screen Gems." *New York Times*, July 4, 1993.
Thomson, David. *A Biographical Dictionary of Film*. New York: Knopf, 1994.
Toumarkine, Doris. "Guerrillas," Special Independents Issue, *Hollywood Reporter*, August 1993.
"Twenty-five Most Influential Americans." *Time*, April 21, 1997.
"The Two Hollywoods." *New York Times* Sunday Magazine, Special Issue on Independents, November 16, 1997.
Tuller, David. "Moviemakers Come to Main Street." *New York Times*, April 27, 1986.
Turan, Kenneth. "Two Sides to Myth of Deal-Making at Sundance Festival." *Los Angeles Times*, January 25, 1996.
———. "Deep Skin Racial Lessons." *Los Angeles Times*, October 28, 1998.
———. "Fade to Pitch-Black." *Los Angeles Times*, November 22, 1998.
Tuska, Jon. *Dark Cinema: American Film Noir in Cultural Perspective*. Westport, Conn.: Greenwood, 1984.
Valle, Victor. "Break of Dawn." *Los Angeles Times*, July 5, 1987.
Varney, Ginger. "Robert Young." *Los Angeles Weekly*, October 14, 1983.
Ventura, Michael. "The Vision of El Norte." *Los Angeles Weekly*, April 20, 1994.
Vernet, Marc. "The Filmic Transaction: On the Openings of Film Noirs." *Velvet Light Trap* 20 (1983).
Wallace, Amy. "The Anti-Festival." *Los Angeles Times*, January 16, 1998.
———. "Studios More Aggressively Seek to Capture Latino's Imagination." *Los Angeles Times*, June 28, 1998.
———. "A Studio That Says, 'Roll 'Em.'" *Los Angeles Times*, July 27, 1998.
———. "A Die-Hard Dreamer: Bruce Willis." *Los Angeles Times*, October 19, 1998.
Wallace, Michelle. "I Don't Know Nothin' 'Bout Birthin' No Babies!" *Village Voice*, December 5, 1989.
Walsh, Andrea. *Women's Film and Female Experience, 1940–1950*. New York: Praeger, 1984.
Weiner, Rex. "Legacy Aims to Fill Indie Void." *Variety Weekly*, April 22, 1996.
———. "Indies Translate Well: O'Seas Sales Post Record." *Daily Variety*, January 24, 1997.
Weinstein, Steve. "Shadow Boxing." *Los Angeles Times*, August 29, 1993.
Weiss, Marion. *Martin Scorsese*. Boston: G. K. Hall, 1987.
Welkos, Robert W. "Behind the Lens, Men Still Rule." *Los Angeles Times*, July 17, 1998.

————. "Trying to Write across Color Lines." *Los Angeles Times*, November 18, 1996.

Wiese, Michael. *The Independent Film and Videomakers Guide.* Studio City: M. Wiese Productions, 1990.

Williams, John. "Re-Creating Their Media Image: Two Generations of Black Women Filmmakers." *Black Scholar*, Spring 1995.

Williams, Linda. *Hard Core: Pleasure and the "Frenzy of the Visible."* Berkeley: University of California Press, 1989.

Willman, Chris "Test Screenings for Those Who Answer to a Higher Authority." *Los Angeles Times*, September 15, 1991.

Willis, Holly. "An Interview with Nina Menkes." *Film Quarterly*, Spring 1992.

Winsor, Chris. "Richard Linklater's School Daze: Emperor of the Teenage Wasteland." *Los Angeles Times*, September 20, 1993.

Winters, Laura. "Hal Hartley." *Vogue*, May 1995.

Wong, Lloyd. "Great Expectations." *Afterimage*, October 1992.

Wood, Robin. *Hollywood from Vietnam to Reagan.* New York: Columbia University Press, 1986.

Wright, Will. *Sixguns and Society: A Structural Study of the Western.* Berkeley: University of California Press, 1975.

Yanarella, Ernest J., and Lee Sigelman (eds.). *Political Mythology and Popular Fiction.* Westport, Conn.: Greenwood, 1988.

Zavarzadeh, Mas'ud. "Smithereens." *Film Quarterly*, Winter 1983.

Index